Oil Paintings in Public Ownership in the Arts Council Collection

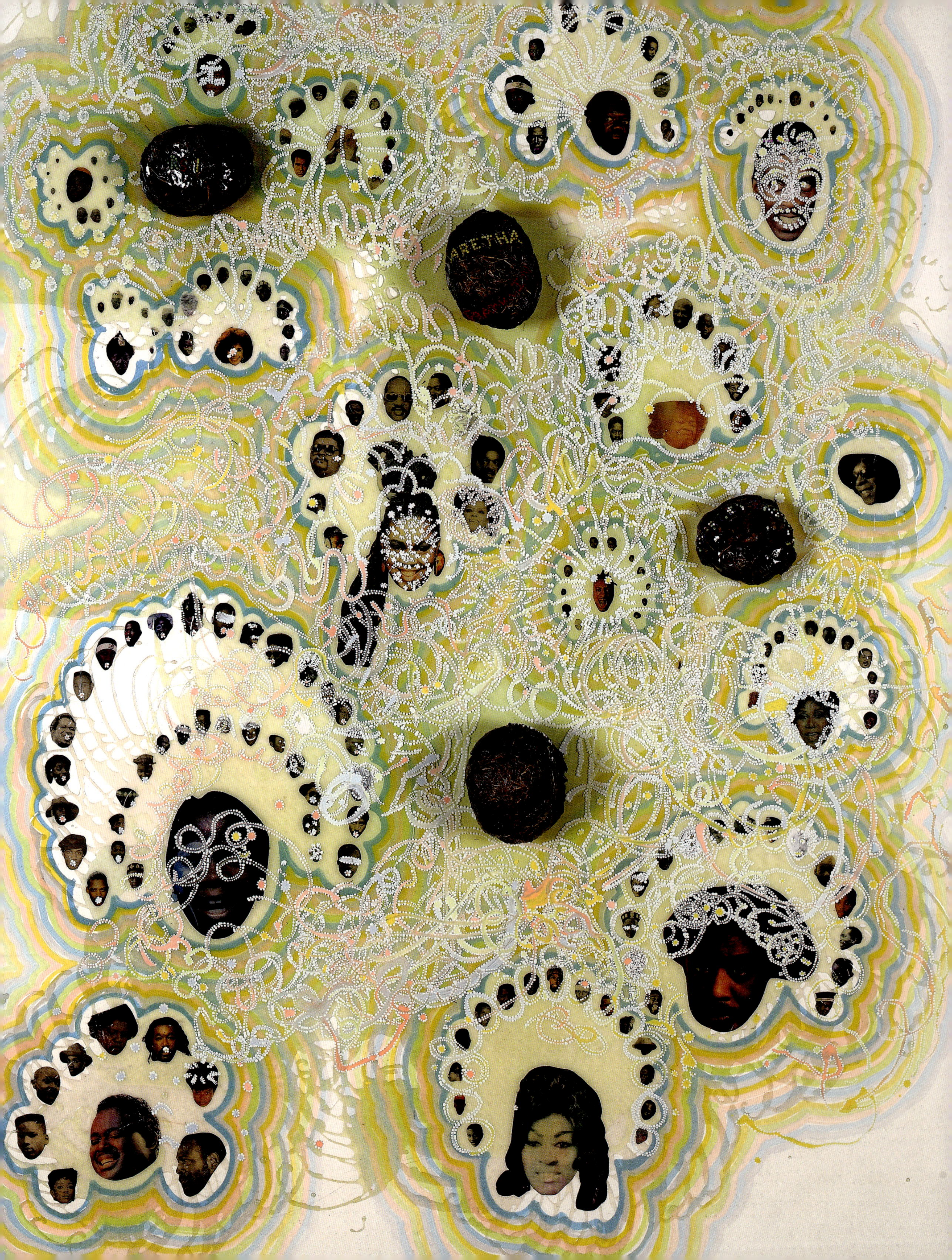
ARETHA

The *Oil Paintings in Public Ownership* series of catalogues is an extraordinary work in progress. Published by The Public Catalogue Foundation, it is the result of the determined efforts of a small team of administrative staff, researchers and photographers spread across the United Kingdom.

Our national collection of oil paintings in public ownership is probably one of the finest anywhere in the world. It is held not just by our museums and galleries but is also to be found in hospitals, universities and other civic buildings throughout the United Kingdom. A large proportion of these paintings are not on display and many have never before been reproduced.

This series of books for the first time allows the public to see an entire photographic record of these works – a collection likely to number some 200,000 in total. In doing so, these volumes provide a unique insight into our nation's artistic and cultural history.

As Patron of The Public Catalogue Foundation, my visits to collections across the country have highlighted to me not only the desire of curators to publicise their paintings, but also the limited resources at their disposal. The Foundation's work goes a long way towards helping to create access to these collections, while at the same time giving the British public the opportunity to see and enjoy *all* the paintings that they own.

I wish The Public Catalogue Foundation every success in its continuing endeavours.

Camilla

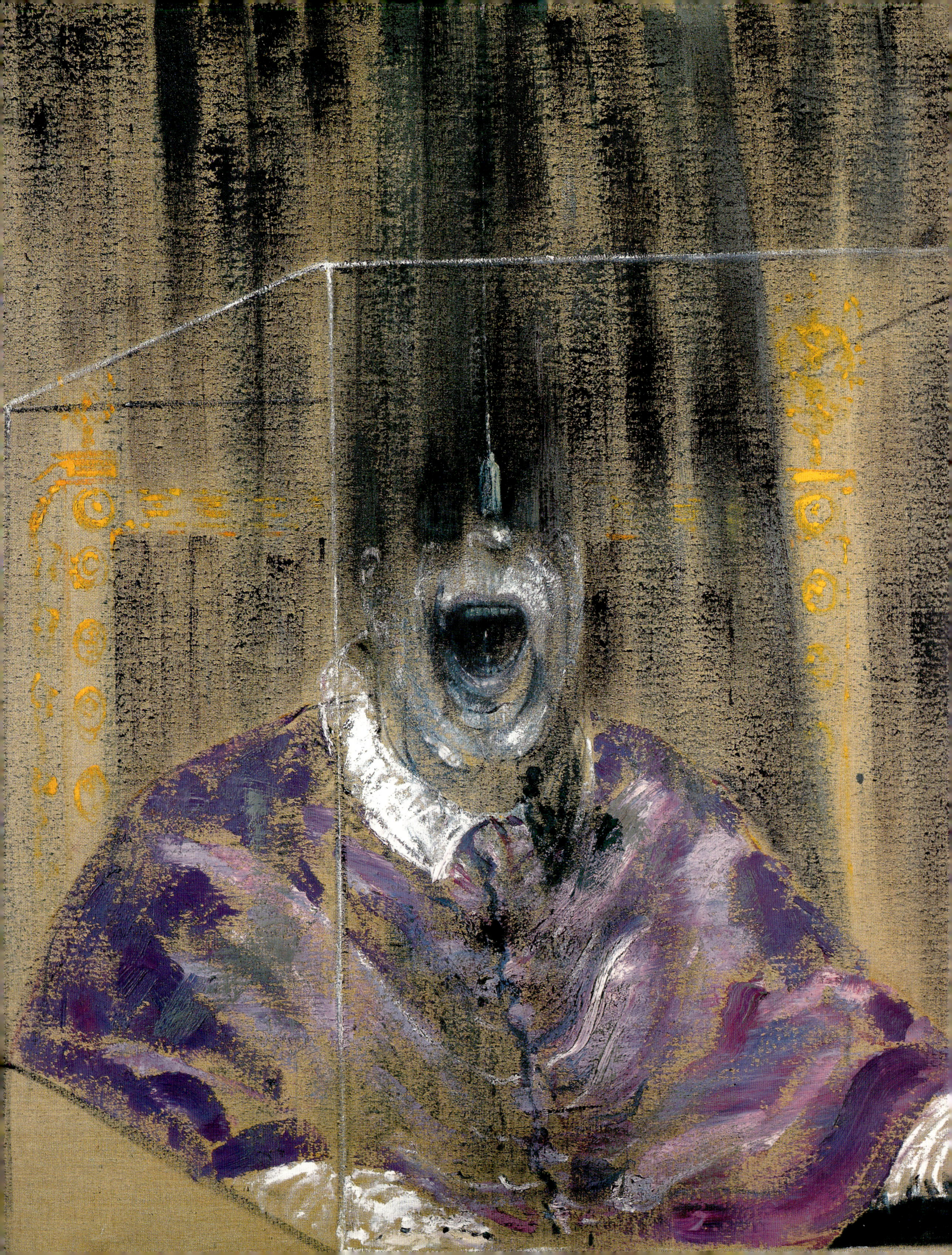

Oil Paintings in Public Ownership in the Arts Council Collection

Coordinators: Katey Goodwin & Natasha Broad

Photographers: Andy Johnson, Anna Arca, Stephen White & Daniel Brown

The Public Catalogue Foundation

Patron HRH The Duchess of Cornwall

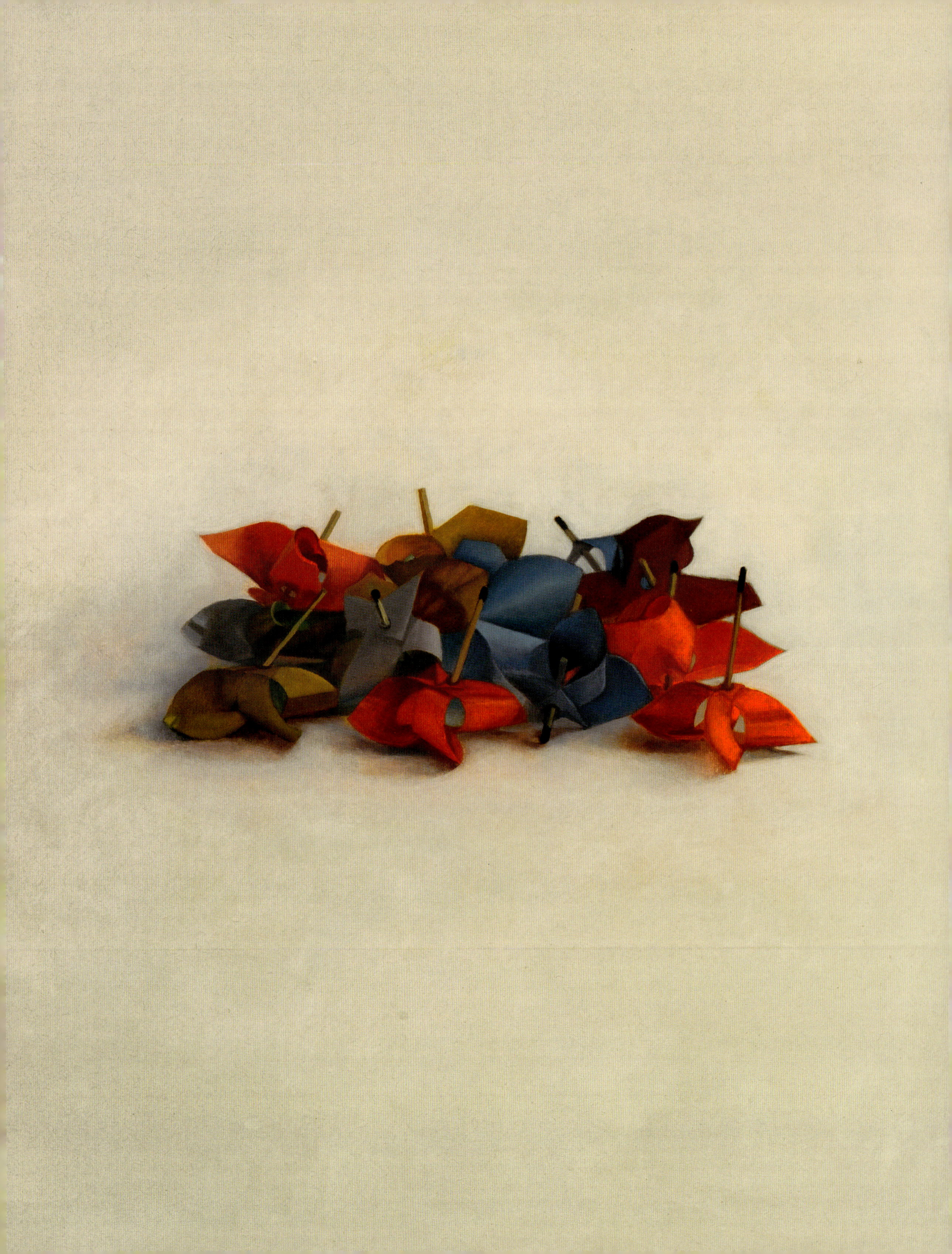

Contents

Facing page: Smith, Sue, b.1925, *Cluster No.3* (detail), 1976–1977, (p. 144)

Image opposite HRH The Duchess of Cornwall's statement: Ofili, Chris, b.1968, *Popcorn Shells* (detail), 1995, (p. 122)
Image opposite title page: Bacon, Francis, 1909–1992, *Head VI* (detail), 1949, (p. 13)

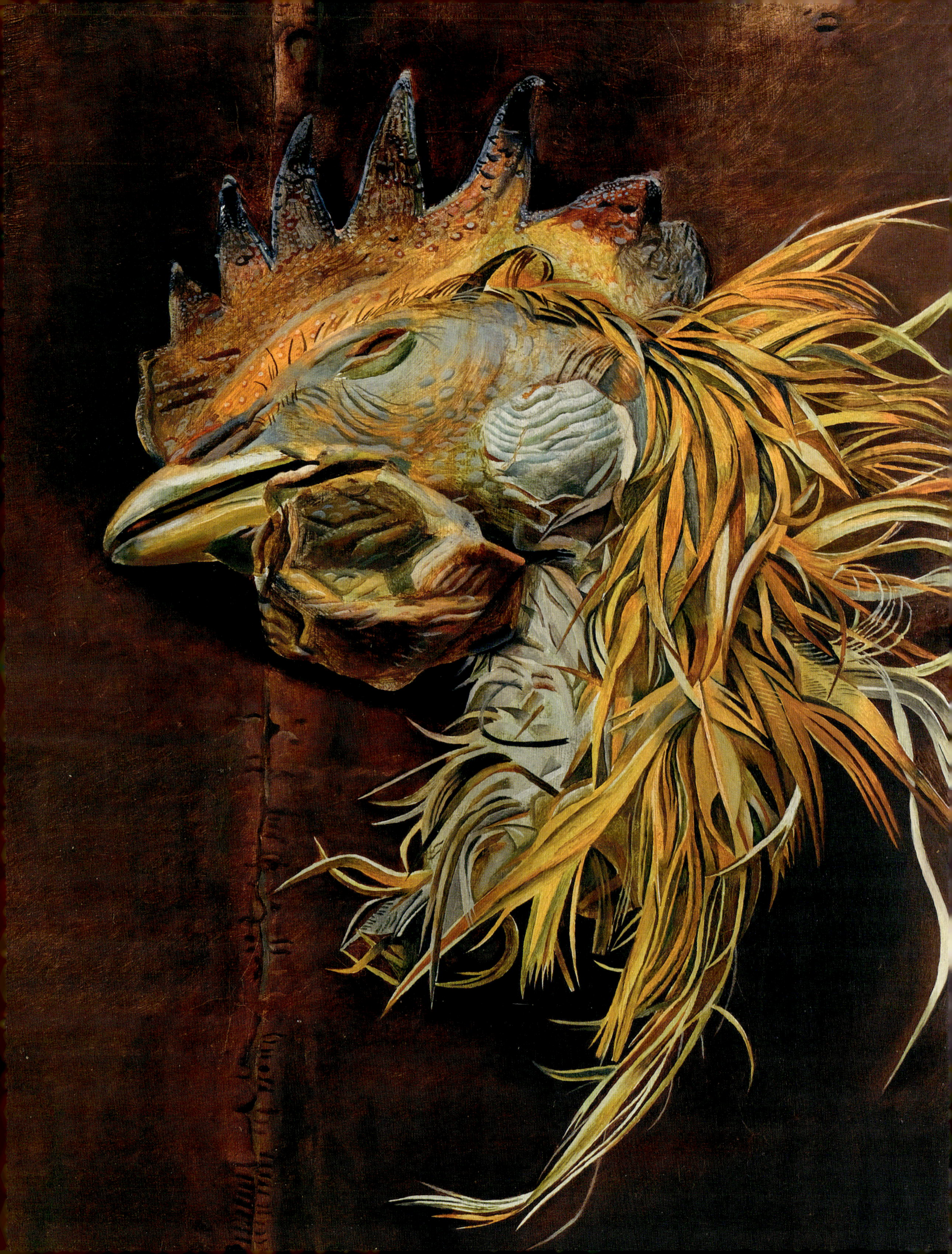

Foreword

Caroline Douglas, in her foreword, reminds us of the origins and purpose of this collection. Looking back over the sixty years that now separate us from its beginnings, we can sense how extraordinary and visionary its birth was. The support of those young artists through the state-funded acquisition of their art, inevitably gave rise to a Collection and that collection, on tour and on loan, not only promoted the artists but, in the bleak early post World War II years, provided colour, inspiration and fun for a population that badly needed it. Those early exhibitions remain vividly in the grateful memories of those who visited them. Equally inevitably though, the Collection grew and joined the also growing collections of the British Council and the Government Art Collection as a Museum without Walls. Each of these is now a major collection in its own right, though each with its own particular purpose.

But to be a Museum without Walls is no longer as exceptional as it once was. With some 90% of all our paintings in store, the whole National Collection of oil paintings might now be defined in the same way. Nearly all our collections now lack walls to a greater or less degree. For some, and for a wide range of reasons, that matters little. For me, it matters a great deal and the Foundation's work is a part remedy. Even so, much of this collection remains imprisoned, with the risk that too much of ourselves is imprisoned with it.

I don't think I will be alone in approaching this collection with scepticism. Is this a state-funded collection of state-approved paintings, a mere survey of Art Establishment taste over a period of years? It could be, and it wouldn't be uninteresting if it were. But as I looked through the catalogue, I understood that this collection had a far wider range and was a great deal more interesting than I had suspected and I am extremely pleased that it now forms part of this series. The real quality of this national treasure store is now available for us all to see and I am most grateful to Caroline Douglas and her team for working so hard and patiently with us to achieve this.

The Foundation's thanks go to all those who made this important volume happen: to the Arts Council team, Jill Constantine, Monika McConnell, Ann Jones and Rachel Arndt; to the coordinators, Katey Goodwin and Natasha Broad and to the photographers, Andy Johnson, Anna Arca, Stephen White and Daniel Brown. To our team in Maiden Lane, especially Daniel Whibley and all the others there who collated and edited the data; and my particular thanks to Sophie Kullmann who has returned as our Consulting Editor at the Printed Cataloguc Division.

Fred Hohler, Founder

Facing page: Freud, Lucian, 1922–2011, *Dead Cock's Head* (detail), 1951, (p. 54)

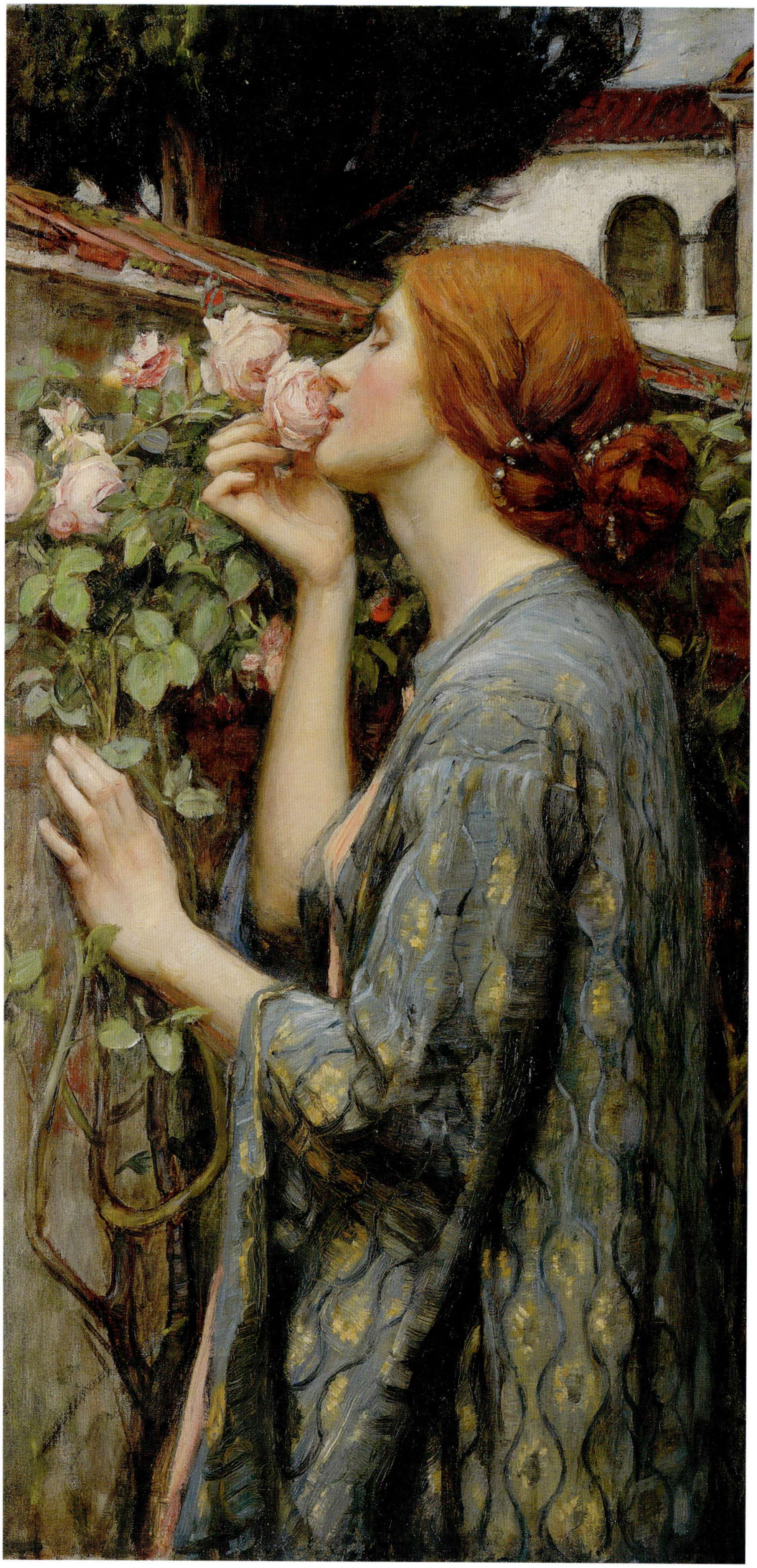

The Public Catalogue Foundation: People Involved

Financial Supporters

The Public Catalogue Foundation would like to express its profound appreciation to the Arts Council England who have made the publication of this catalogue possible.

Catalogue Scope and Organisation

Medium and Support
The principal focus of this series is oil paintings. However, tempera and acrylic are also included as well as mixed media, where oil is the predominant constituent. Paintings on all forms of support (e.g. canvas, panel, etc.) are included as long as the support is portable. The principal exclusions are miniatures, hatchments or other purely heraldic paintings and wall paintings *in situ*.

Public Ownership
Public ownership has been taken to mean any paintings that are directly owned by the public purse, made accessible to the public by means of public subsidy or generally perceived to be in public ownership. The term 'public' refers to both central government and local government. Paintings held by national museums, local authority museums, English Heritage and independent museums, where there is at least some form of public subsidy, are included. Paintings held in civic buildings such as local government offices, town halls, guildhalls, public libraries, universities, hospitals, crematoria, fire stations and police stations are also included.

Geographical Boundaries of Catalogues
The geographical boundary of each county is the 'ceremonial county' boundary. This county definition includes all unitary authorities. Counties that have a particularly large number of paintings are divided between two or more catalogues on a geographical basis.

Criteria for Inclusion
As long as paintings meet the requirements above, all paintings are included irrespective of their condition and perceived quality. However, painting reproductions can only be included with the agreement of the participating collections and, where appropriate, the relevant copyright owner. It is rare that a collection forbids the inclusion of its paintings. Where this is the case and it is possible to obtain a list of paintings, this list is given in the Paintings Without Reproductions section. Where copyright consent is refused, the paintings are also listed in the Paintings Without Reproductions section. All paintings in collections' stacks and stores are included, as well as those on display. Paintings which have been lent to other institutions, whether for short-term exhibition or long-term loan, are listed under the owner collection. In addition, paintings on long-term loan are also included under the borrowing institution when they are likely to remain there for at least another five years from the date of publication of this catalogue. Information relating to owners and borrowers is listed in the Further Information section.

Layout
Paintings are listed in order of artist surname. Where there is more than one painting by the same artist, the paintings are listed chronologically, according to their execution date.

The few paintings that are not accompanied by photographs are listed in the Paintings Without Reproductions section.

There is additional reference material in the Further Information section at the back of the catalogue. This gives the full names of artists, titles and media if it has not been possible to include these in full in the main section. It also provides acquisition credit lines and information about loans in and out, as well as copyright and photographic credits for each painting. Finally, there is an index of artists' surnames.

Key to Painting Information

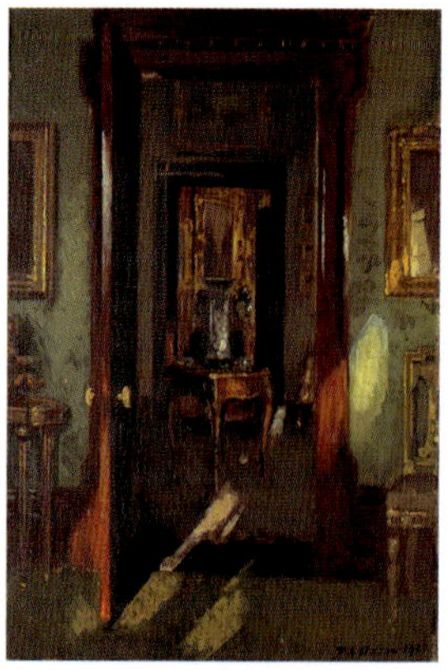

Almost all paintings are reproduced in the catalogue. Where this is not the case they are listed in the Paintings Without Reproductions section. Where paintings are missing or have been stolen, the best possible photograph on record has been reproduced. In some cases this may be black and white. Paintings that have been stolen are highlighted with a red border. Some paintings are shown with conservation tissue attached to parts of the painting surface.

Adam, Patrick William 1854–1929
Interior, Rutland Lodge: Vista through Open Doors 1920
oil on canvas 67.3 x 45.7
LEEAG.PA.1925.0671.LACF ☙

Artist name This is shown with the surname first. Where the artist is listed on the Getty Union List of Artist Names (ULAN), ULAN's preferred presentation of the name is given. In a number of cases the name may not be a firm attribution and this is made clear. Where the artist name is not known, a school may be given instead. Where the school is not known, the painter name is listed as *unknown artist*. If the artist name is too long for the space, as much of the name is given as possible followed by (...). This indicates the full name is given at the rear of the catalogue in the Further Information section.

Painting title A painting title followed by *(?)* indicates that the title is in doubt. Where the alternative title to the painting is considered to be better known than the original, the alternative title is given in parentheses. Where the collection has not given a painting a title, the publisher does so instead and marks this with an asterisk. If the title is too long for the space, as much of the title is given as possible followed by *(...)* and the full title is given in the Further Information section.

Execution date In some cases the precise year of execution may not be known for certain. Instead an approximate date will be given or no date at all.

Artist dates Where known, the years of birth and death of the artist are given. In some cases one or both dates may not be known with certainty, and this is marked. No date indicates that even an approximate date is not known. Where only the period in which the artist was active is known, these dates are given and preceded with the word *active*.

Medium and support Where the precise material used in the support is known, this is given.

Dimensions All measurements refer to the unframed painting and are given in cm with up to one decimal point. In all cases the height is shown before the width. An (E) indicates where a painting has not been measured and its size has been calculated by sight only. If the painting is circular, the single dimension is the diameter. If the painting is oval, the dimensions are height and width.

Collection inventory number In the case of paintings owned by museums, this number will always be the accession number. In all other cases it will be a unique inventory number of the owner institution. (P) indicates that a painting is a private loan. Details can be found in the Further Information section. Accession numbers preceded by 'PCF' indicate that the collection did not have an accession number at the time of catalogue production and therefore the number given has been temporarily allocated by The Public Catalogue Foundation. The ☙ symbol indicates that the reproduction is based on a Bridgeman Art Library transparency (go to www.bridgemanart.com) or that Bridgeman administers the copyright for that artist.

Facing page: Martin, Kenneth, 1905–1984, *Chance, Order, Change 2 (Ultramarine Blue)* (detail), 1976 (p. 105)

THE PAINTINGS

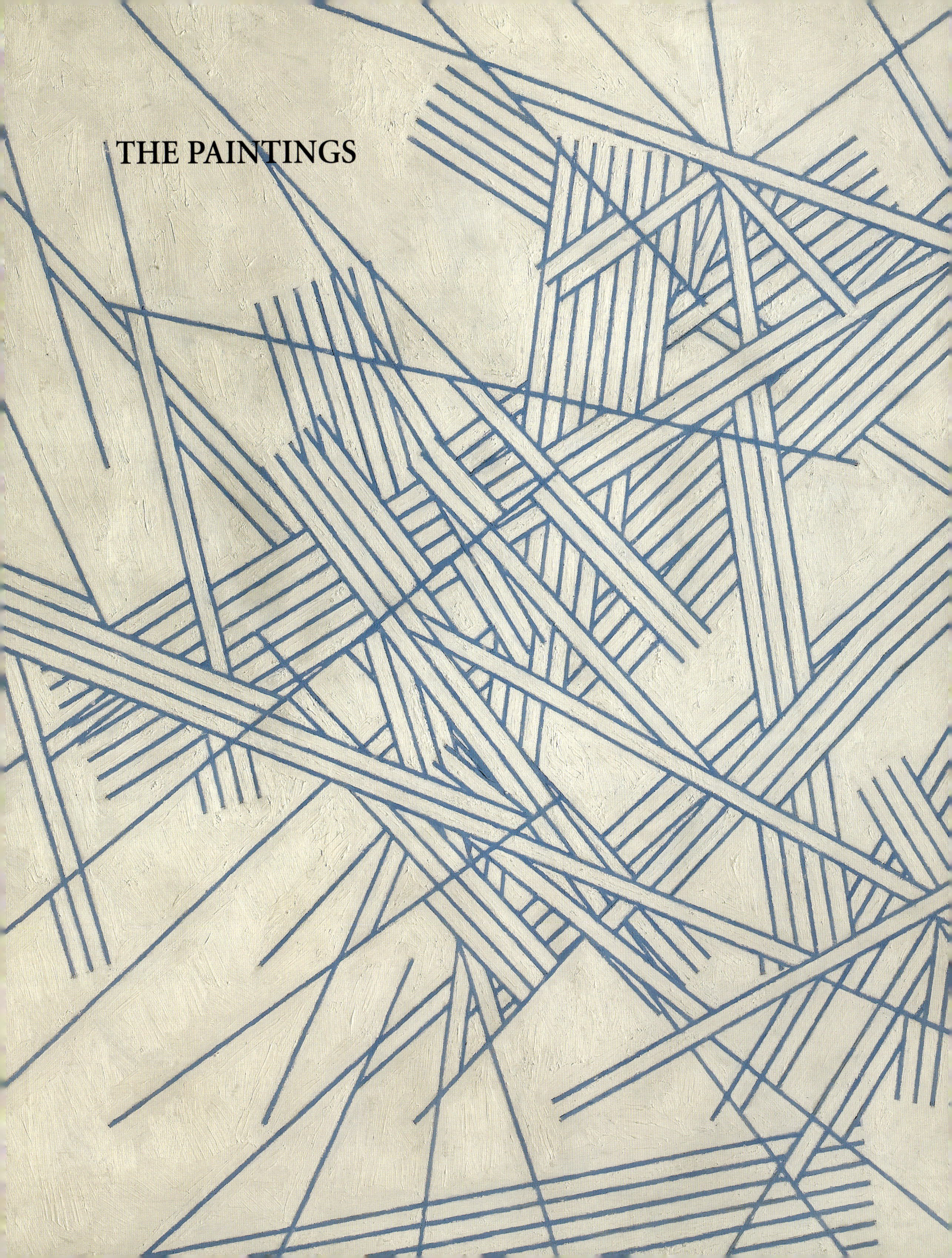

Arts Council Collection

In a variety of respects, the quality that most succinctly characterises the Arts Council Collection is that of youthfulness. Formed in 1946, it is a collection which still encompasses living memory; it is a collection of art that reflects our times and a collection of artworks that have played a material role in forming our sense of self, as a nation. Although this present catalogue focuses exclusively on painting, the Arts Council Collection locates work in that medium within a spectrum of practice in an ever-expanding variety of media.

The Collection was founded in the immediate post-war years, on the altruistic but pragmatic conviction that the best and most appropriate way to support artists in Britain was to buy their work. The Arts Council, and by extension the Arts Council Collection, grew out of an entity that was formed originally in 1939. The Committee for the Encouragement of Music and the Arts was established at the beginning of the Second World War, in order to give financial assistance to societies finding difficulty in maintaining their activities during the war. In 1940 it was formally appointed the Council for the Encouragement of Music and the Arts (CEMA) and began to receive direct funding from the Government.

CEMA became the Arts Council in 1946 and its Visual Arts Department was unusual in that it supported art directly through its own activities rather than indirectly through the funding of others. This was known as direct promotion. The main area in which direct promotion took place was the provision of exhibitions. By itself and in collaboration with others, the Visual Arts Department organised many exhibitions in London and for the regions. The basis for many of these exhibitions was the Arts Council Collection.

In March 1987 a split was made in the Visual Arts Department, between those responsible for putting on exhibitions and looking after the Arts Council Collection, and those staff administering grant-in-aid. It was at this point that the Arts Council Collection began to be administered through the Hayward Gallery and became the responsibility of the South Bank Board, which is where we find ourselves still today.

Sixty years on now from its founding, the Collection has continued to acquire work throughout this time, and at today's date includes more than 7,600 works of art. The acquisitions policy has always been one of supporting young and emerging artists, and as a consequence, fine examples of work from early moments in the career of some of this country's most distinguished artists have been acquired. Where artists have gone on to establish a major reputation here and abroad, the Collection has continued to acquire significant works throughout their career, where funds have allowed. This present catalogue highlights such sustained support by reproducing together paintings by the same artist and demonstrates the depth of collecting in certain areas, as well as the breadth and heterogeneity of the Collection.

Existing collection catalogues, published in four volumes since 1980 have necessarily been unable to do this, reflecting rather the chronological development of the Collection.

The bold, ambitious and experimental approach of successive purchasers for the Collection has also reflected a youthful courageousness and spirit of enquiry. When the sixtieth anniversary exhibition, *How To Improve the World*, was mounted at the Hayward Gallery in 2006, the decision was taken to include on the exhibition labels the date of acquisition, as well as the date of the work. This simple act told an important story, since the two dates were very often the same, and rarely more than a couple of years apart. Rather than waiting for history to validate individual practice, the Collection has seen itself as very much 'in the moment', closely in touch with, or even a part of an evolving scene. Although there are now many more collectors active in Britain than previously, private and public, this swiftly responsive approach to developments in practice and aesthetic debate remains a critical aspect of the Collection's function.

Great collections are built on the passions of individuals, and over the 60 years of its existence, the Arts Council Collection has benefited from the advice of some of the most eminent figures in British art, all of whom agreed to act as purchasers. It would be impossible to overestimate the enormous contribution made in the first decades of its existence by Norbert Lynton, a crucial early champion of abstraction in Britain and for five years from 1970 Director of Exhibitions at the Arts Council and the newly opened Hayward Gallery; Bryan Robertson who purchased for the Collection from 1958, throughout and beyond his inspired directorship of the Whitechapel Art Gallery; Sir Alan Bowness, director of the Tate Gallery from 1980 to 1988, and pre-emininent scholar and critic David Sylvester. The brilliance of the purchases in the first two decades of the Collection – the Bacons, Nicholsons, Hepworths, and Moores, the Pasmores, Frinks, Freuds and Rileys – established a standard for what was to follow.

External members of the Acquisitions Committee now sit for a period of no more than two years; this changing cast of advisors is in itself a way of keeping the Collection close to developments, and has meant that moments of heightened activity, such as happened in the 1990s for example, are responded to. Mel Gooding, Susan Hiller, Adrian Searle and Richard Shone in the early part of that decade spotted the prodigious talents of Peter Doig, Gary Hume and Fiona Rae. The late 90s saw artist and writer David Batchelor, Keith Hartley, Curator at the Scottish National Gallery of Modern Art and curator and writer Sacha Craddock working alongside Isobel Johnstone, then Curator of the Collection, acquiring major works by Chris Ofili, Lisa Milroy and Ross Sinclair. What emerges here is a view of the Collection as a *community* – of artists, writers, curators and academics, brought together not in one building, so much as in a shared activity, and a belief in the *purpose* of the Collection.

As well as assistance in major acquisitions from The Art Fund, The Henry Moore Foundation and the Contemporary Art Society, throughout its history, the Collection has regularly received works as gifts from artists and other benefactors. The Arnolfini Trust gifted a group of works in 2001, and Charles Saatchi 100 works in 1999. Very important works and groups of works have been gifted by artists and their dealers, most notably in recent years Richard Deacon, Keith Coventry, Wolfgang Tillmans and Roger Hiorns.

The Arts Council Collection is a loan collection: it exists to promote the understanding of art through lending work of the highest quality, either in groups, as touring exhibitions, or as single loans to institutions across the UK and worldwide. Alongside the Government Art Collection and the collection of the British Council, it is one of three important national collections, sometimes called a 'museum without walls', having no permanent home of its own.

The three collections perform distinct and complementary functions: the Government Art Collection places work in British Government buildings in the UK and overseas; the British Council exists to promote British culture overseas; the Arts Council Collection is the only one, therefore, which exists to support artists in this country and at the same time to support arts organisations in the promotion of visual arts across the UK. The Collection's sixtieth anniversary exhibition in 2006 took its title from a work by Cerith Wynn Evans: *How to improve the world.* The belief that access to the greatest art of our time can improve our lives is what underpins our activity. Exhibitions of varying sizes, themes and media are curated each year, drawn from the Collection and toured in regional museums and galleries for minimal fees; individual works, and groups of works are loaned throughout this country and the world. Works in the Collection are not only loaned to museums and galleries, but can also be borrowed for display in public buildings in the UK, such as hospitals, charitable trusts, colleges, theatres, housing associations and courtrooms. Via all of these various strands of activity approximately a third of the exhibition is on public display at any one time, and what should not be forgotten is that this is a constantly changing third.

One consequence of being a relatively young collection, and one whose importance should not be overlooked, is the diversity of the artists represented in it. The Arts Council Collection in total comprises almost a third of works by female artists, and for differing reasons over its 60-year history, has always included work by a high proportion of artists not born in this country. Quick to acknowledge the importance of figures such as Barbara Hepworth (the first female artist to be acquired, in 1947), Elisabeth Frink and Bridget Riley in the early years of the Collection, the proportion of female artists increases steadily as one comes up to the present day. Griselda Pollock and Susan Hiller were key figures in the Acquisitions Committees during the 1980s and 1990s respectively, and although today the importance of gender as a part of current debate continues to be contested, and the attitudes of younger women artists towards feminism are changing, it is still necessary to regularly review collecting activity to ensure that a proper balance is achieved.

The Second World War saw an unprecedented movement and displacement of peoples across the world, and many artists found their way to Britain during and immediately after the war years, bringing influences from mainland Europe and beyond that were to prove critical to the development of art. Figures such as Lucian Freud and Gustav Metzger, for example, have had immeasurable influence here. More varied and complex forces continue to bring artists to settle in Britain from the world over and as a result, although the Arts Council Collection is ostensibly a collection of British art, that definition is admirably elastic. Thus in recent years we have purchased work in a variety of media by Serbian-born Breda Beban, Zarina Bhimji, originally from Uganda, Mona Hatoum born in Lebanon, Mark Lewis and Carey Young from Canada and the US respectively. This nicely sums up the profile of Arts Council Collection artists and herein lies the richness of the culture we live with.

The Arts Council Collection is one of the hardest working anywhere, constantly striving to increase its reach by finding new ways to make work accessible to the public. Whether working with young curators still in secondary school, or with postgraduate students, the Collection constantly seeks to find new audiences. Since 2006 the Collection has been online, and the current project with The Public Catalogue Foundation has meant that we are now able to illustrate every painting in the Collection in colour on our website. This is an increasingly powerful resource for public, students and professionals alike, and continues to be developed year on year. We are also pleased to be a part of The Public Catalogue Foundation's own online project Your Paintings with the BBC and to see the Collection properly located within the community of public collections across the country.

Caroline Douglas, Head of the Arts Council Collection

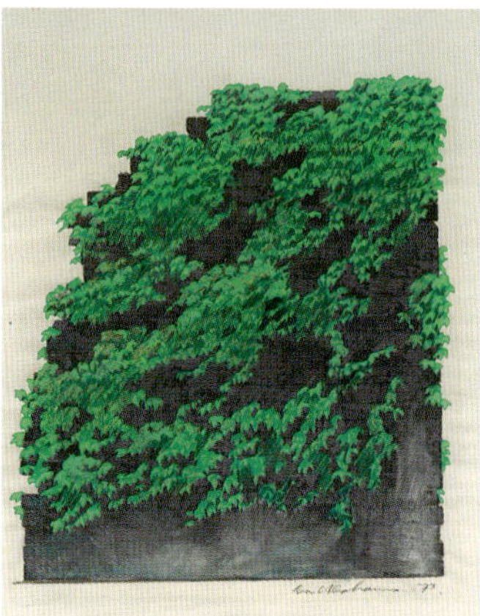

Abrahams, Ivor b.1935
Drawing for Cut-Out Wall 1973
pencil, chalk, acrylic & screen ink ground on paper 63.1 x 53.2
AC 1329

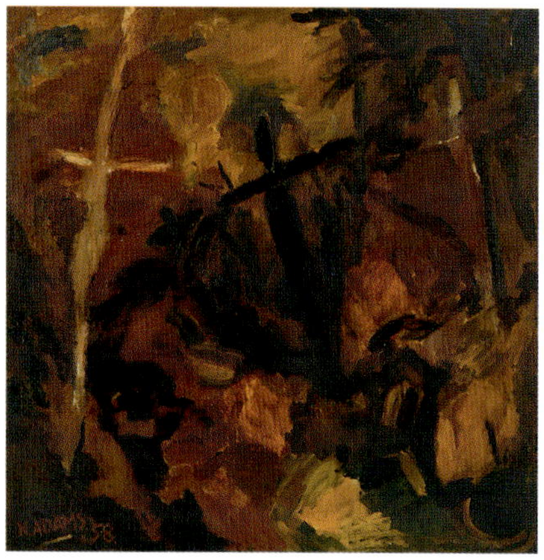

Adams, Norman 1927–2005
The Holy Trees 1958
oil on canvas 136.5 x 137
AC 462

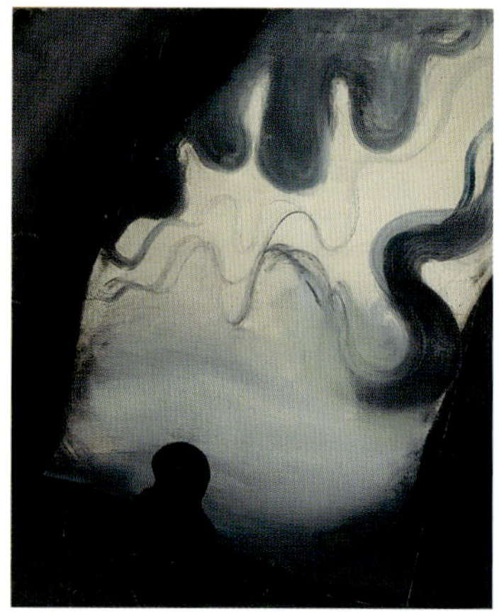

Adams, Norman 1927–2005
The Shore 1965
oil on canvas 151 x 125
ACA 4

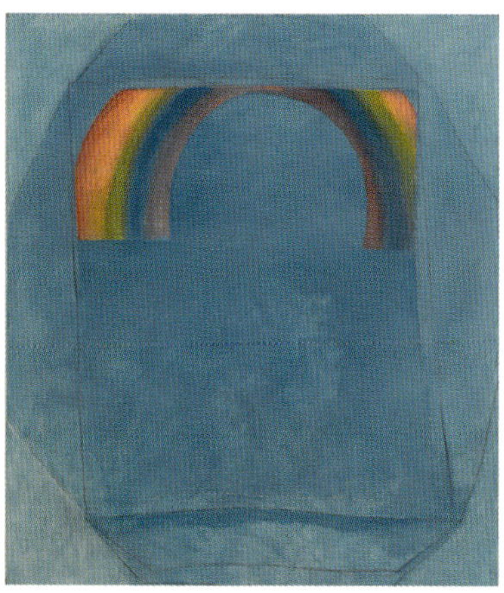

Adams, Norman 1927–2005
Our Mother Who Art in Heaven 1966
oil on canvas 172.7 x 151.8
AC 1063

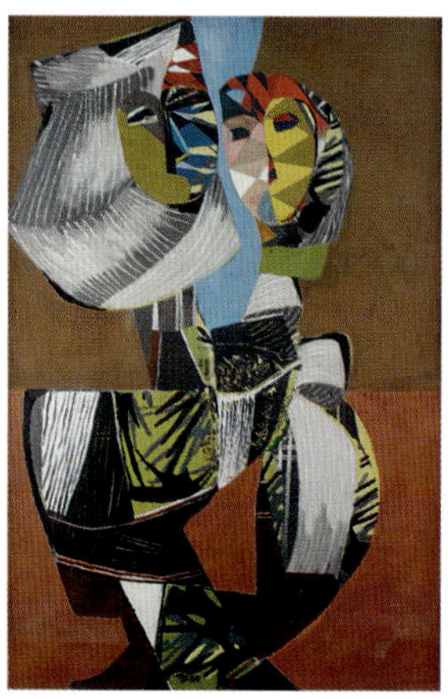

Agar, Eileen 1899–1991
Poet and His Muse 1959
oil on canvas 91.5 x 60.7
AC 492

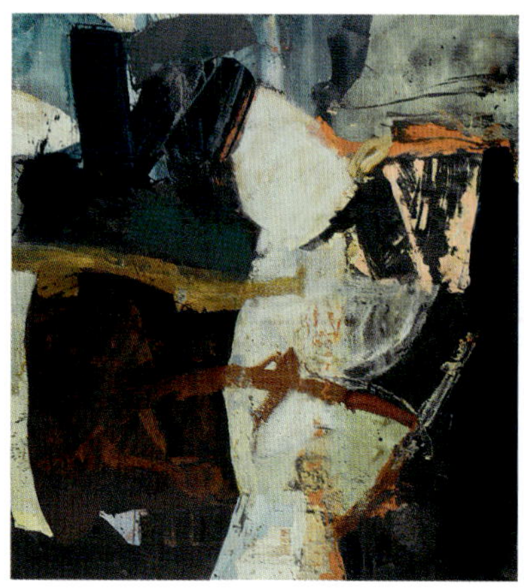

Ainsworth, Mark b.1954
Crag 1978
acrylic on canvas 264.5 x 248
AC 1966

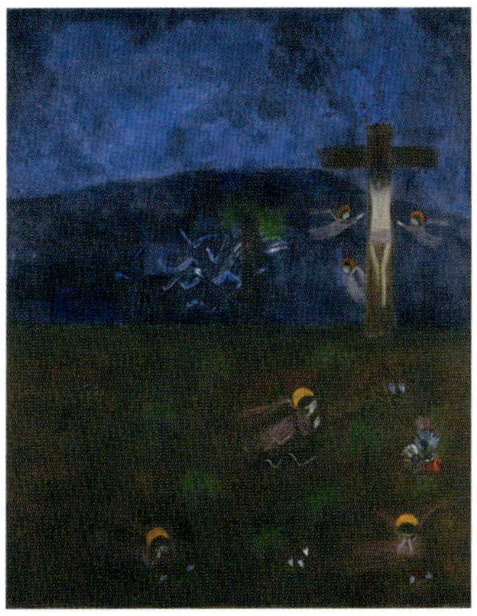

Aitchison, Craigie Ronald John 1926–2009
Crucifixion 1959
oil on canvas 127.3 x 101.6
AC 481

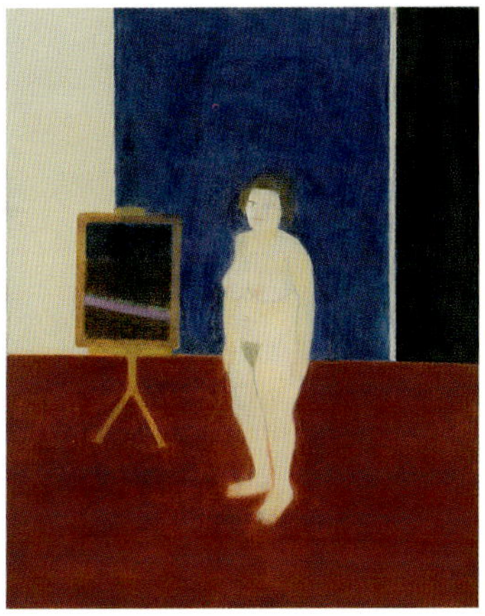

Aitchison, Craigie Ronald John 1926–2009
Female Nude 1965
oil on canvas 196 x 154.4
ACA 3

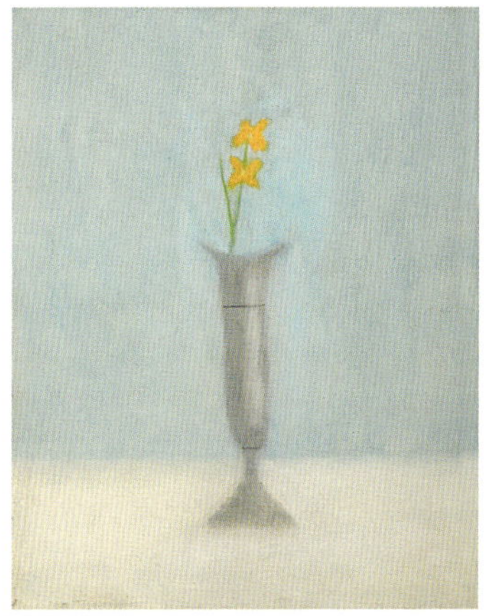

Aitchison, Craigie Ronald John 1926–2009
Grey Vase: Still Life 1965
oil on canvas 29.5 x 25.1
AC 851

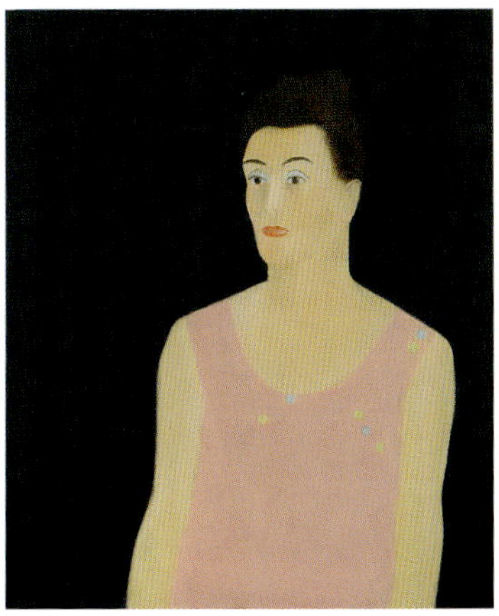

Aitchison, Craigie Ronald John 1926–2009
Daphne Against a Black Background 1968
oil on canvas 75 x 62.3
AC 1019

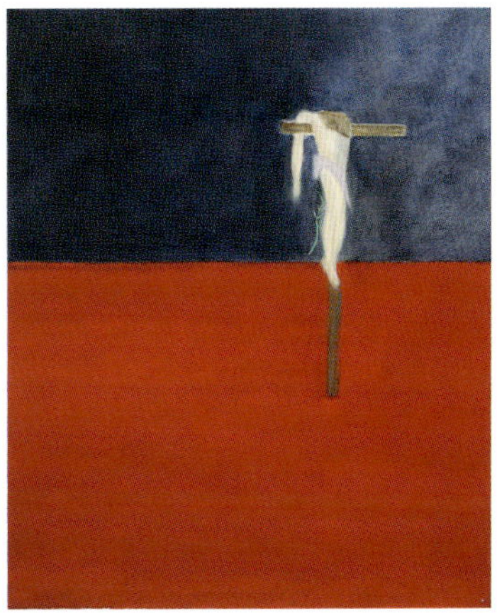

Aitchison, Craigie Ronald John 1926–2009
Crucifixion No.2 1977
oil on canvas 75.9 x 63.4
AC 1815

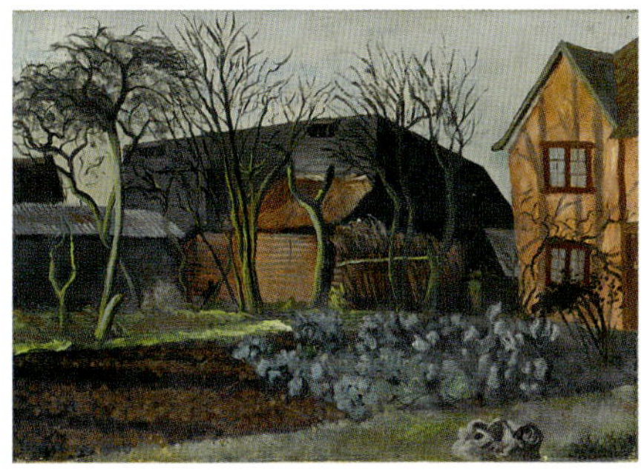

Aldridge, John Arthur Malcolm 1905–1983
The Pink Farm 1940
oil on board 31.4 x 46
AC 59

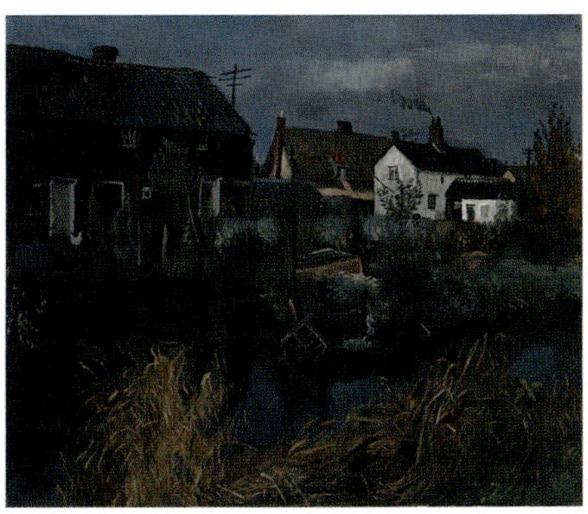

Aldridge, John Arthur Malcolm 1905–1983
Autumn 1946
oil on canvas 50.8 x 61
AC 4

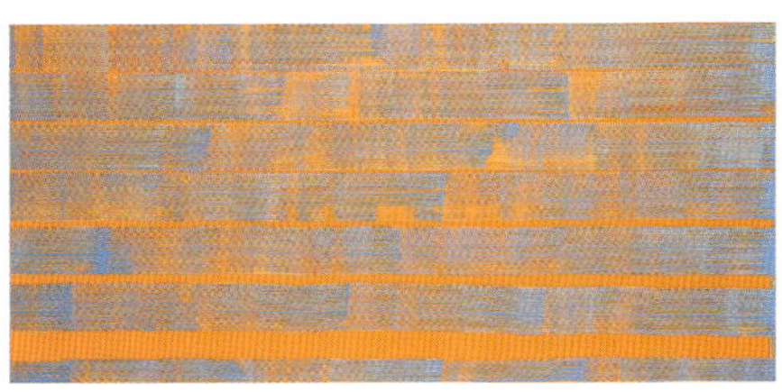

Allen, Tim b.1950
In the Future 1991
acrylic on canvas 152 x 335
ACC12/1992

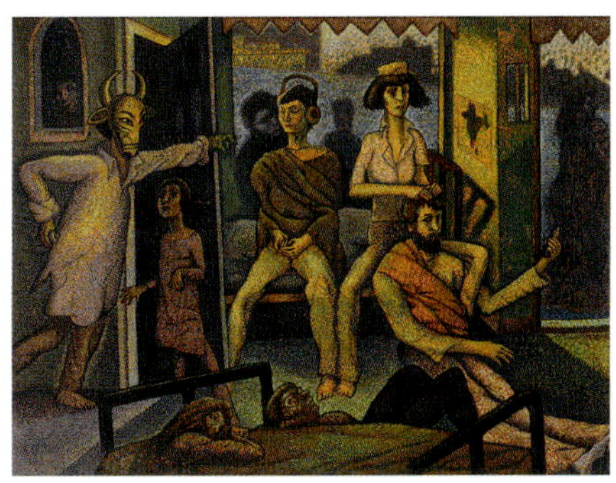

Anderson, Michael b.1952
The Labyrinth 1981
oil & pastel on paper 40 x 54.3
AC 5378

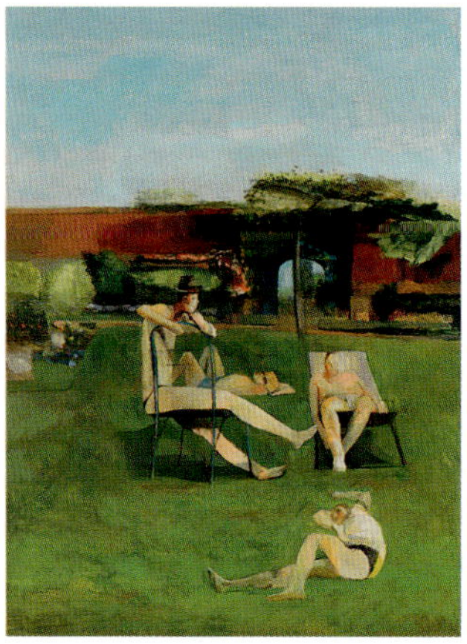

Andrews, Michael 1928–1995
Four People Sunbathing 1955
oil on board 122 x 95.5
AC 380

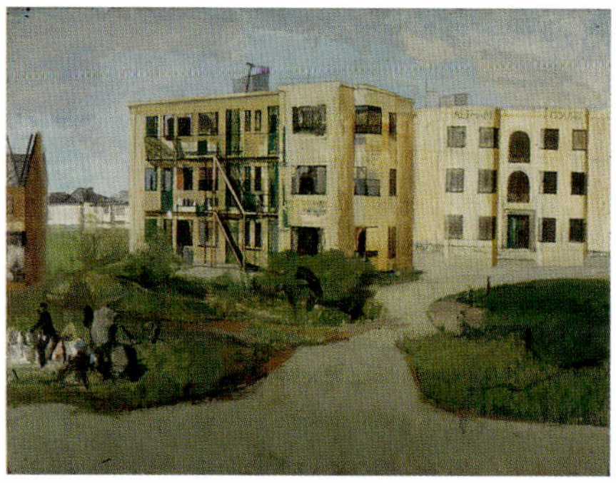

Andrews, Michael 1928–1995
Flats 1959
oil on board 105.4 x 138.4
ACA 1

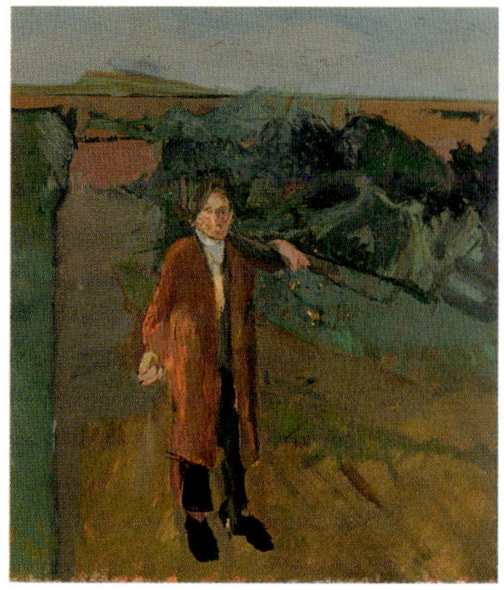

Andrews, Michael 1928–1995
Digswell Man II 1960
oil on board 135.5 x 119.5
ACC1/1963

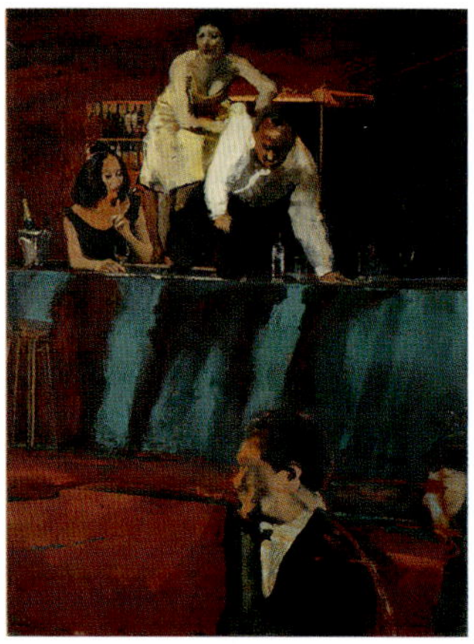

Andrews, Michael 1928–1995
Study for 'All Night Long' 1964
oil on canvas 100 x 74.5
ACC2/1963

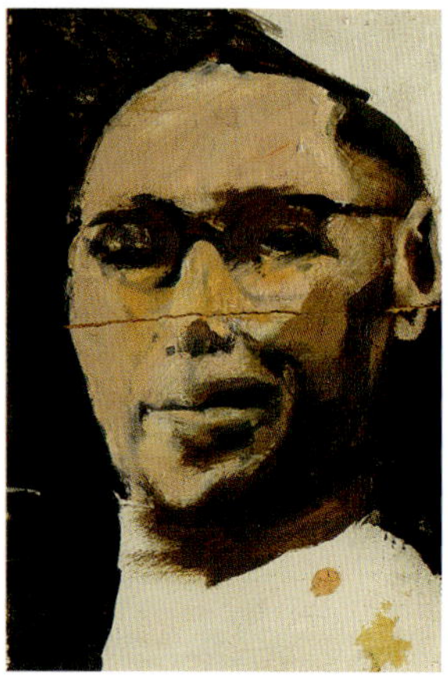

Andrews, Michael 1928–1995
Study of a Head for a Group of Figures No.6 1967
oil on board 22 x 15
AC 1588

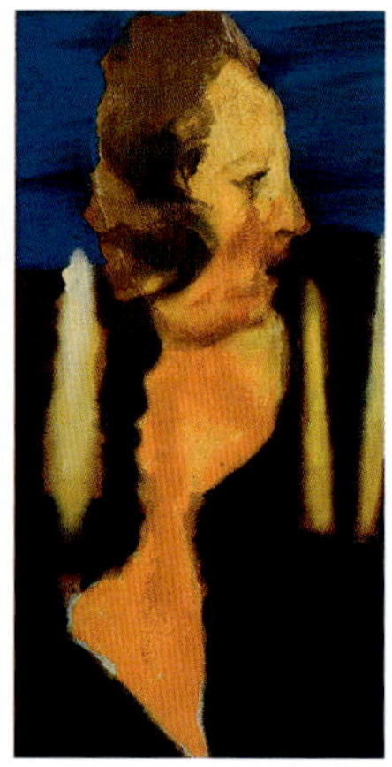

Andrews, Michael 1928–1995
Study of a Head for a Group of Figures No.10 1968
oil on board 31.6 x 16.5
AC 1552

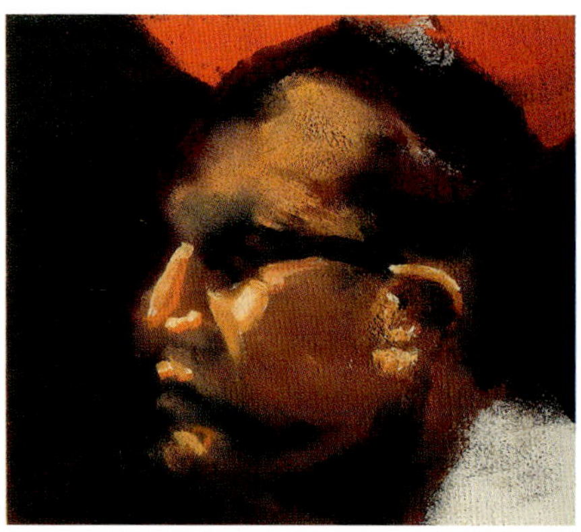

Andrews, Michael 1928–1995
Study of a Head for 'Lights' No.2 1968
oil on board 15 x 17.5
AC 1587

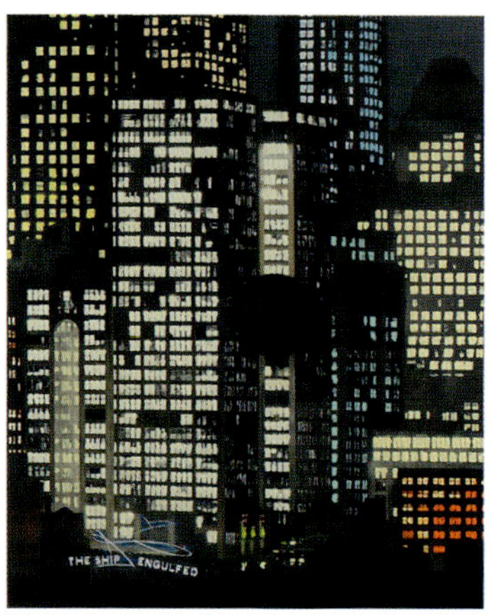

Andrews, Michael 1928–1995
Lights II: The Ship Engulfed 1972
acrylic on canvas 183 x 152.5
AC 1775

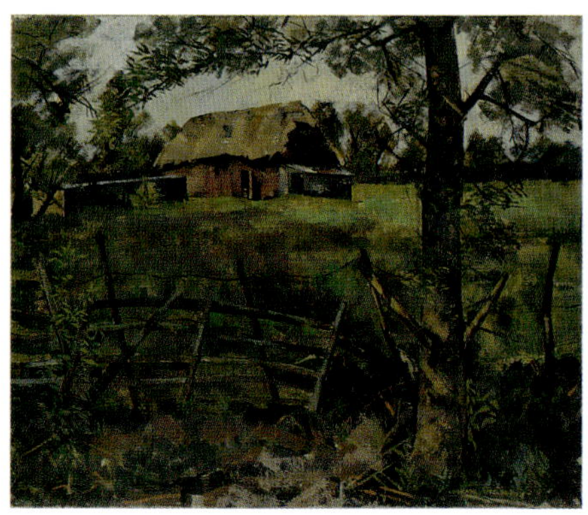

Appelbee, Leonard 1914–2000
Barns in a Field 1940
oil on canvas 50 x 60
AC 60

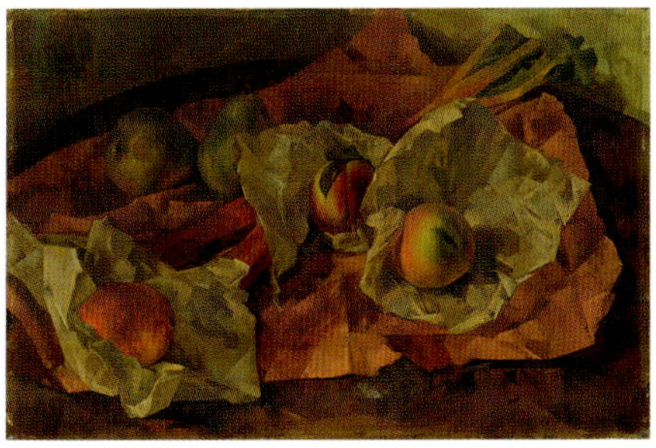

Appelbee, Leonard 1914–2000
Peaches 1947
oil on canvas 31.4 x 49.2
AC 3

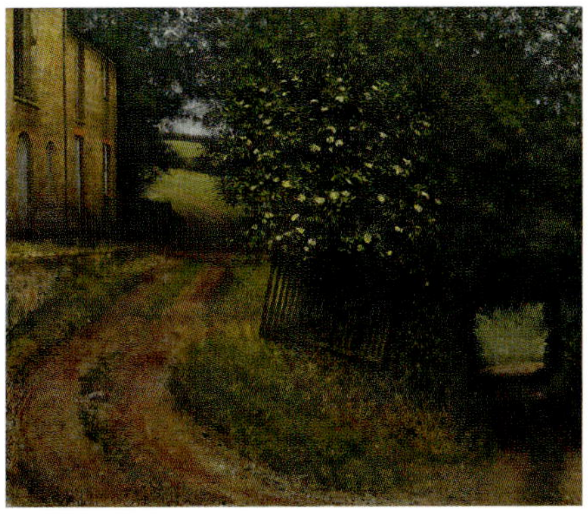

Archer, Peter b.1946
Turning Track 1985
oil on canvas 101.2 x 121.4
AC 5418

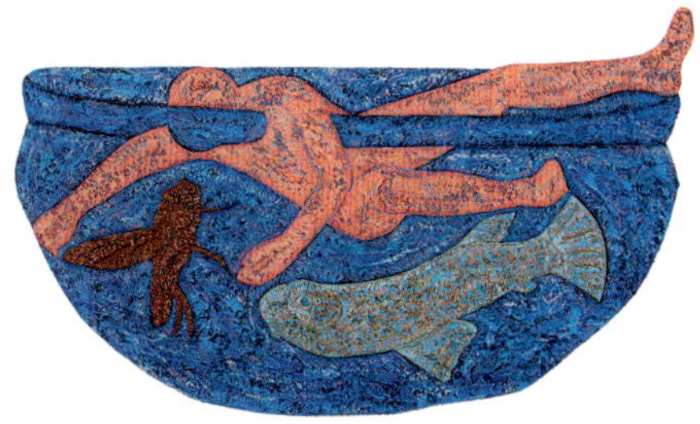

Arif Quadri, Saleem b.1949
Pressed Against Good and Evil 1987–1988
sand & acrylic on muslin-backed paper
81.8 x 134
AC 5560

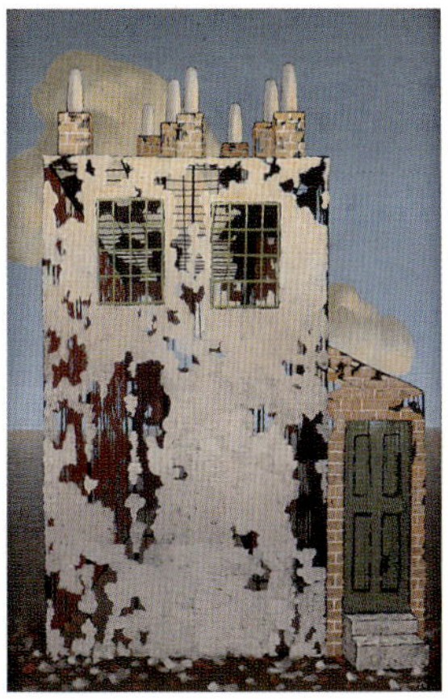

Armstrong, John 1893–1973
The Villa 1940
tempera on board 44.4 x 29.5
AC 61

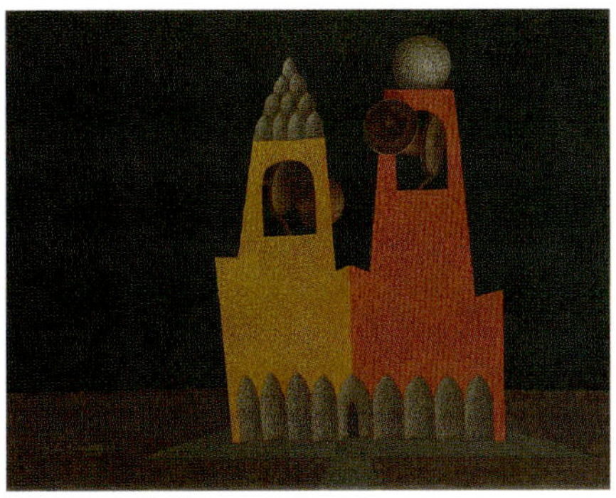

Armstrong, John 1893–1973
Tocsin 1967
oil on canvas 50.5 x 65.5
AC 862

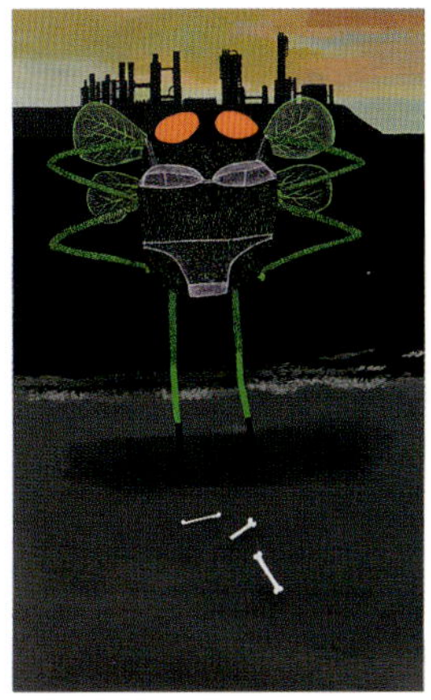

Arnold, Liz 1964–2001
Uncovered 1995
acrylic on canvas 122.5 x 76.2
ACC140/1998

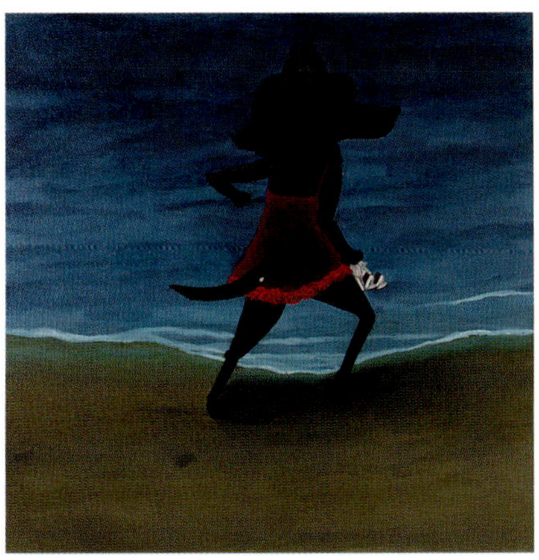

Arnold, Liz 1964–2001
Felicity 1996
acrylic on canvas 73 x 75
ACC141/1998

Arrowsmith, Sue b.1968
Pickett 1996
ink & gesso on board 183 x 183
ACC58/1996

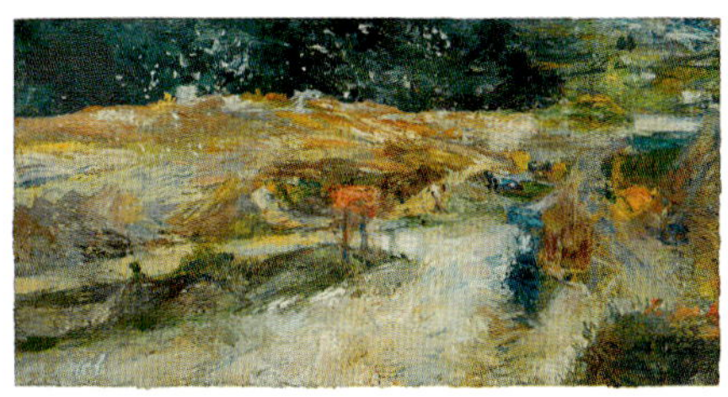

Atkins, Ray b.1937
Cornwall County Council Refuse Tip, Carharrack II 1983
oil on hardboard 127 x 249
AC 5319

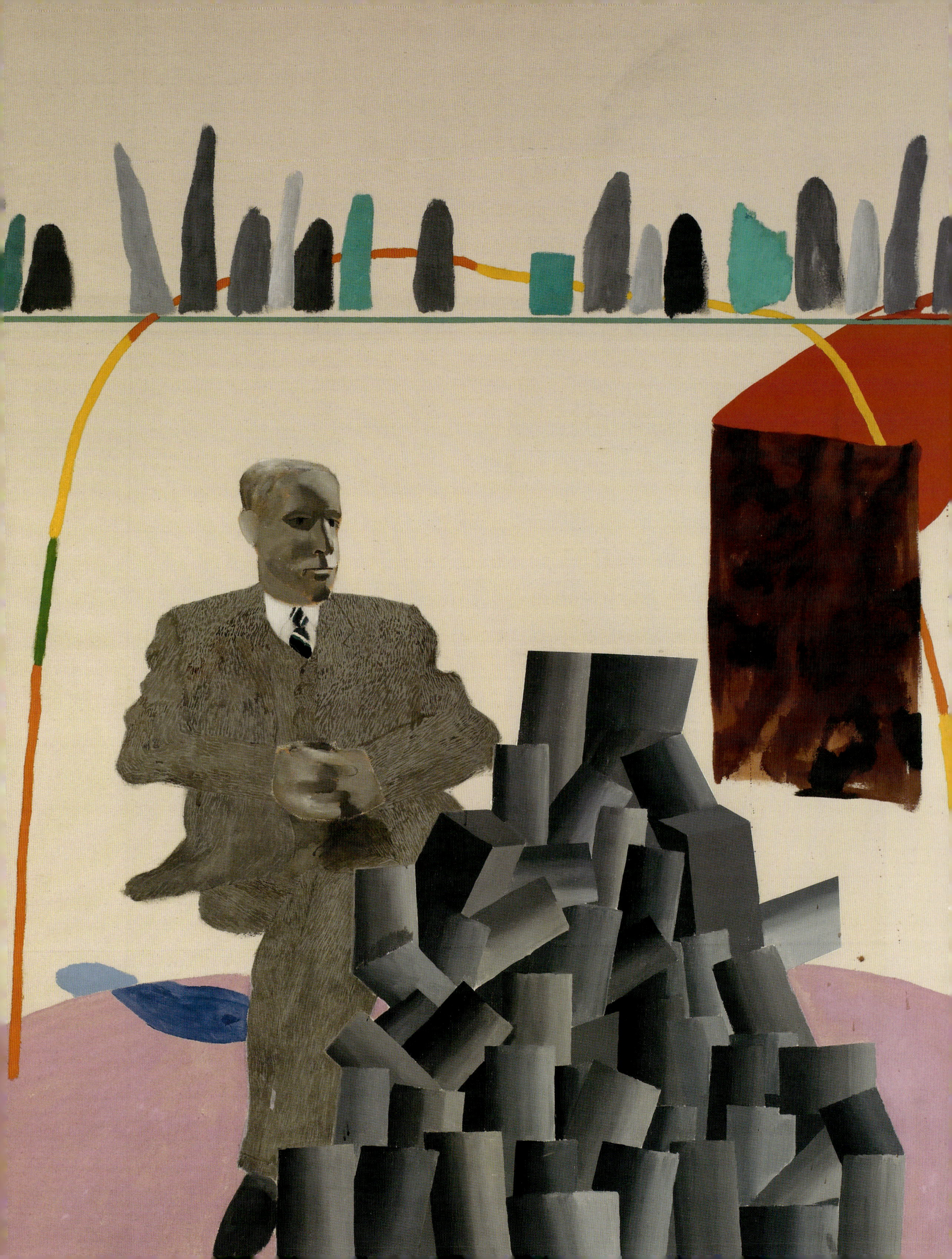

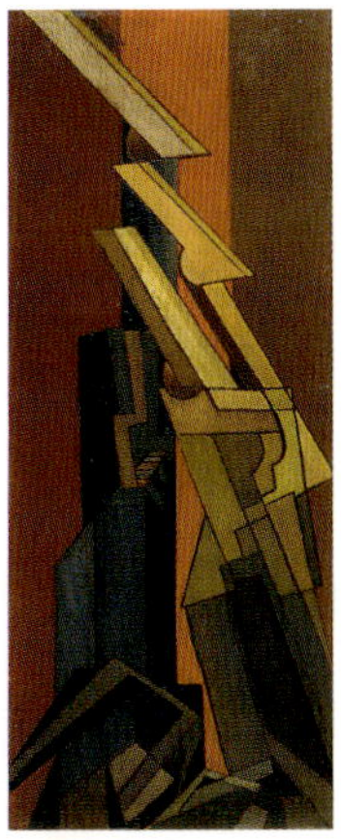

Atkinson, Lawrence 1873–1931
Abstract c.1915–1920
oil on wood 129.5 x 50.8
ACC2/1959

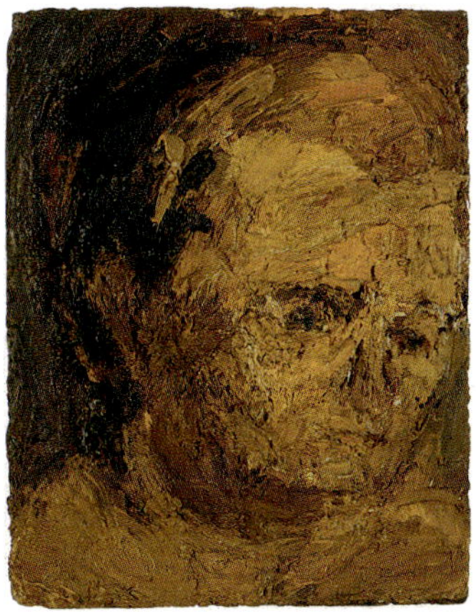

Auerbach, Frank Helmuth b.1931
Head of E. O. W. VIII 1956
oil on board 41 x 32.4
AC 389

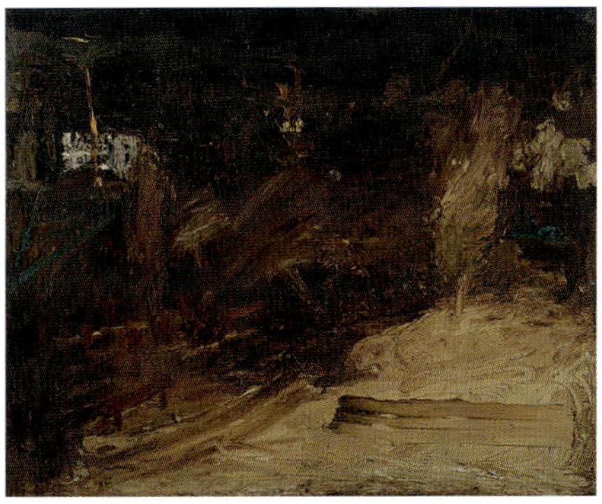

Auerbach, Frank Helmuth b.1931
Primrose Hill 1959
oil on board 121.9 x 151.1
ACC3/1959

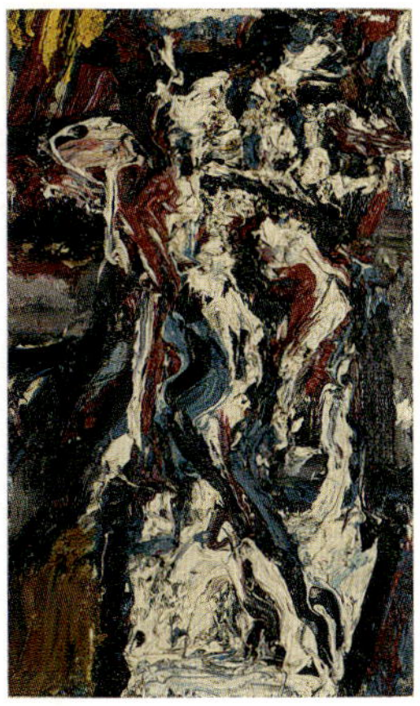

Auerbach, Frank Helmuth b.1931
Jym in the Studio 1963–1964
oil on board 76.2 x 47
AC 850

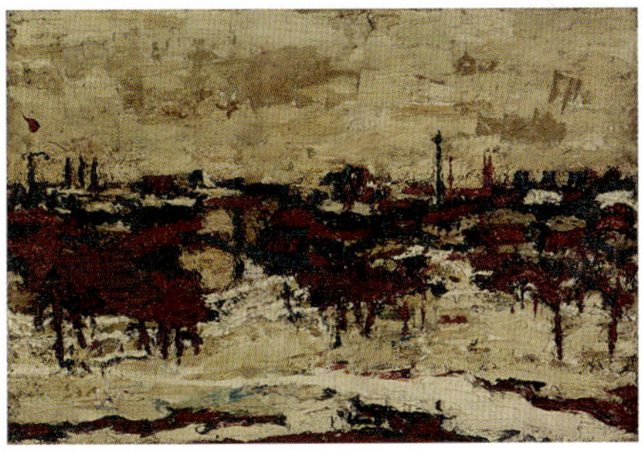

Auerbach, Frank Helmuth b.1931
Primrose Hill, Summer Sunshine 1964
oil on board 102.5 x 152
ACC1/1965

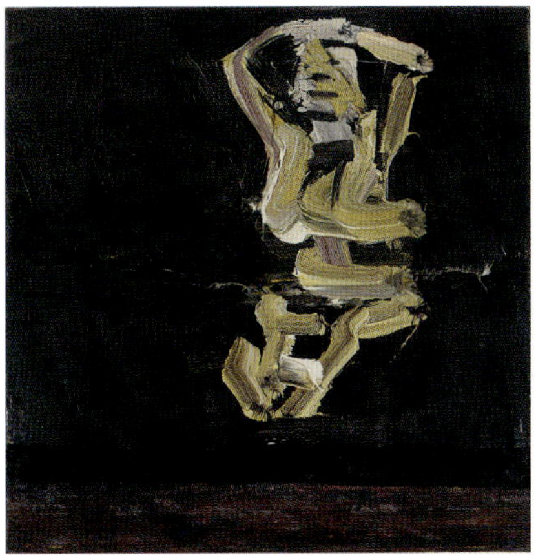

Auerbach, Frank Helmuth b.1931
Seated Figure with Arms Raised 1974
oil on board 51 x 51
ACC3/1975

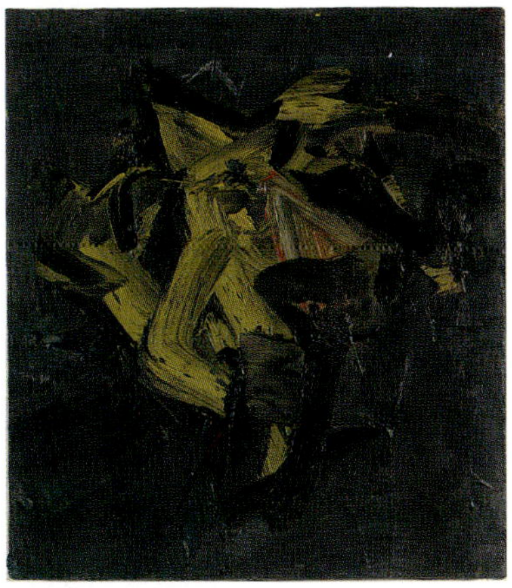

Auerbach, Frank Helmuth b.1931
Reclining Head of J. Y. M. 1974–1975
oil on board 51.5 x 46
AC 1568

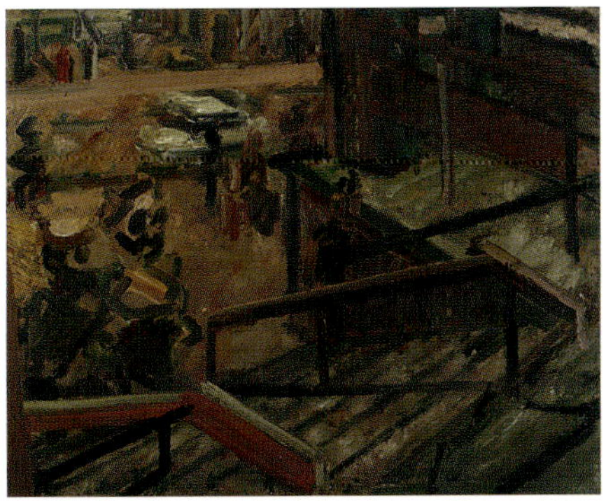

Auerbach, Frank Helmuth b.1931
Euston Steps (study) 1980–1981
oil on board 122.6 x 152.7
AC 4055

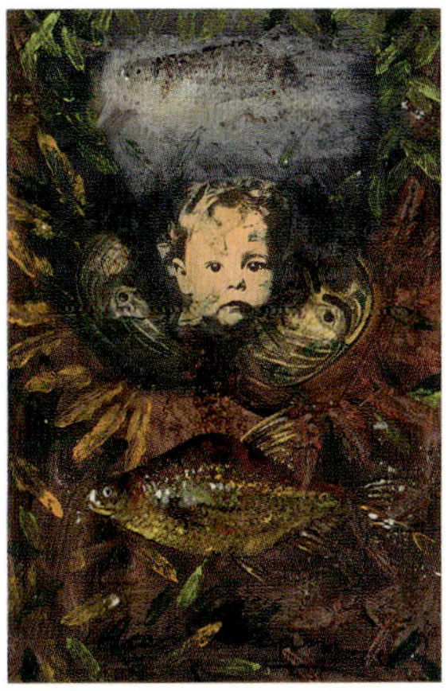

Austen, David b.1960
Mia's Dream 1985
oil, shellac, charcoal & photocopy on canvas
91.5 x 60.6
AC 5386

Facing page: Hockney, David, b.1937, *Portrait Surrounded by Artistic Devices* (detail), 1965, (p. 75)

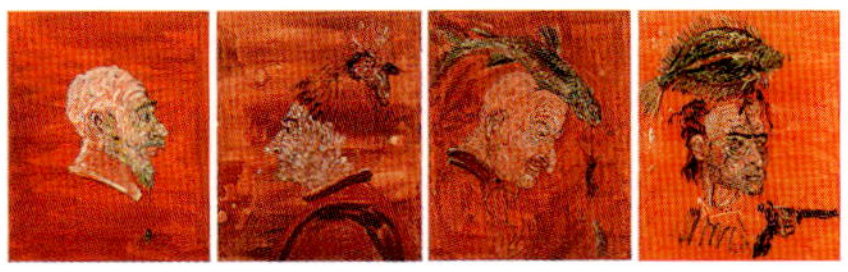

Austen, David b.1960
The King, The Church, The Judge, The Knight 1985
oil on canvas 61 x 51; 61 x 51; 61 x 51; 61 x 51
AC 5385

Austen, David b.1960
Men Kill Sleeping Women 1989
oil on linen 91.4 x 81.3
ACC42/1991

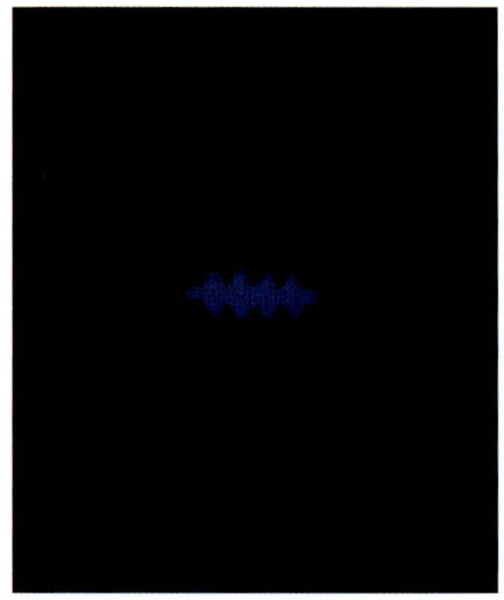

Austen, David b.1960
On the Edge of Night 1991
oil on linen 35.5 x 30.5
ACC43/1991

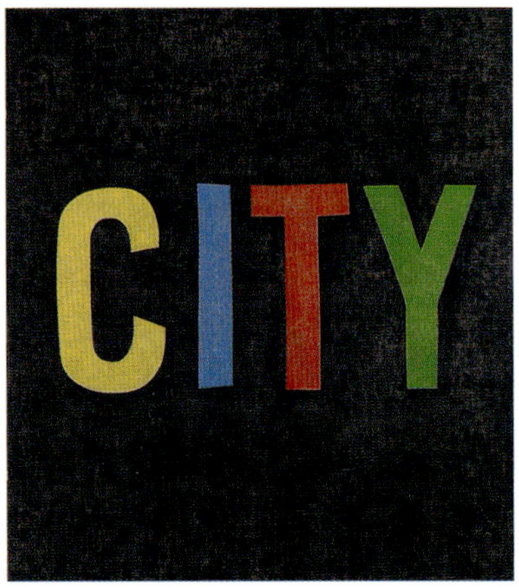

Austen, David b.1960
City 1999
oil on canvas 167.5 x 152
ACC64/1999

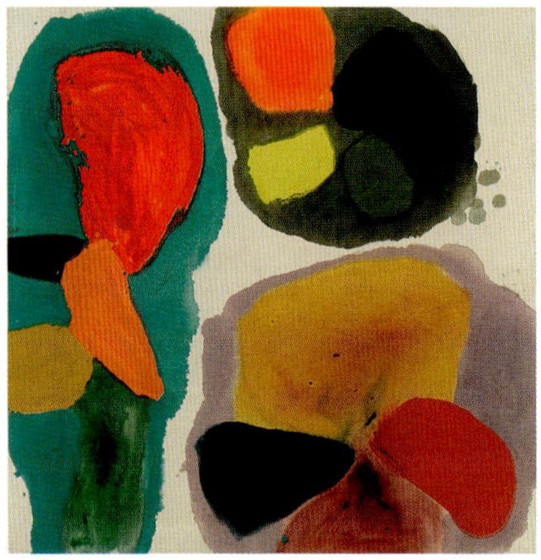

Ayres, Gillian b.1930
Lure 1963
oil on canvas 152.4 x 152.4
AC 705

Ayres, Gillian b.1930
Shiraz 1964
acrylic on canvas 152.4 x 152.4
AC 814

Ayres, Gillian b.1930
Umbria 1966
oil on canvas 152.4 x 152.4
AC 861

Ayres, Gillian b.1930
Untitled 1967
acrylic on canvas 152.4 x 304.8
AC 859

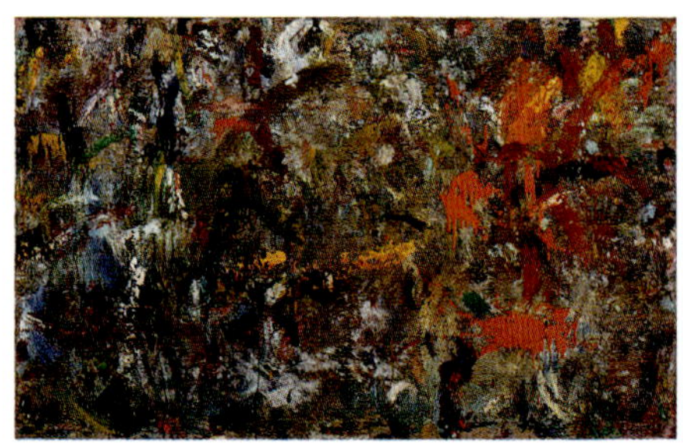

Ayres, Gillian b.1930
Bellona 1976–1978
oil & acrylic on canvas 153.9 x 246
AC 1961

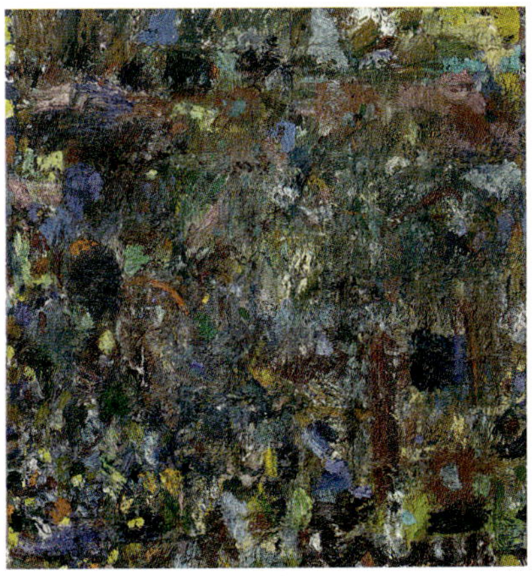

Ayres, Gillian b.1930
Orlando Furioso 1977–1979
oil on canvas 232.9 x 230.5
AC 2086

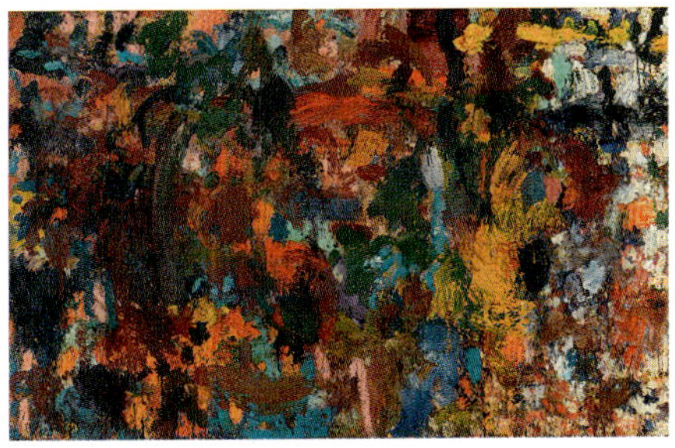

Ayres, Gillian b.1930
Ultima Thule 1978–1980
oil on canvas 225 x 354
AC 4089

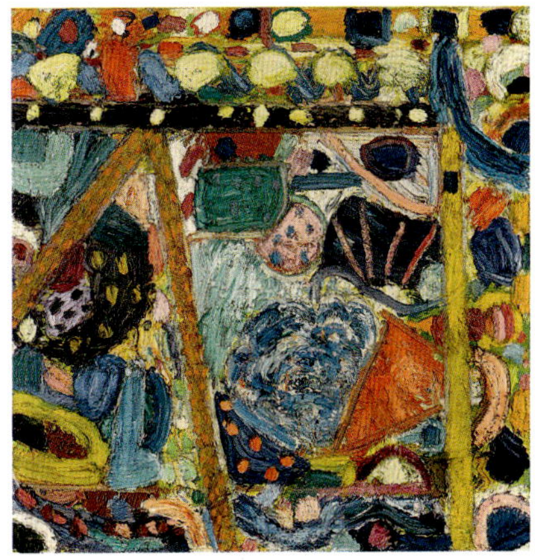

Ayres, Gillian b.1930
Spica 1989–1990
oil on canvas 183 x 183.7
ACC44/1990

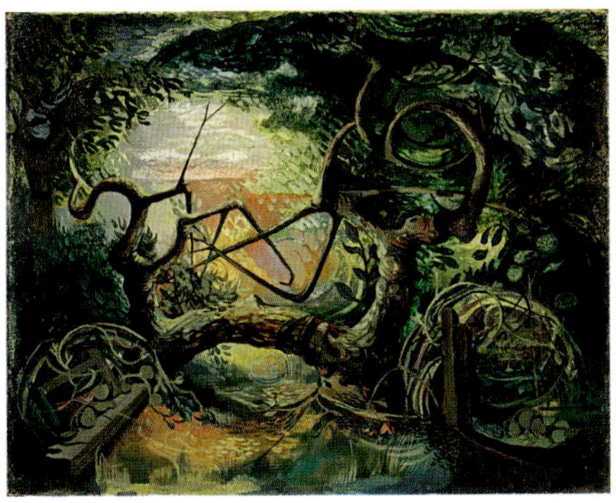

Ayrton, Michael 1921–1975
Entrance to a Wood 1945
oil on canvas 72.4 x 91.4
AC 1

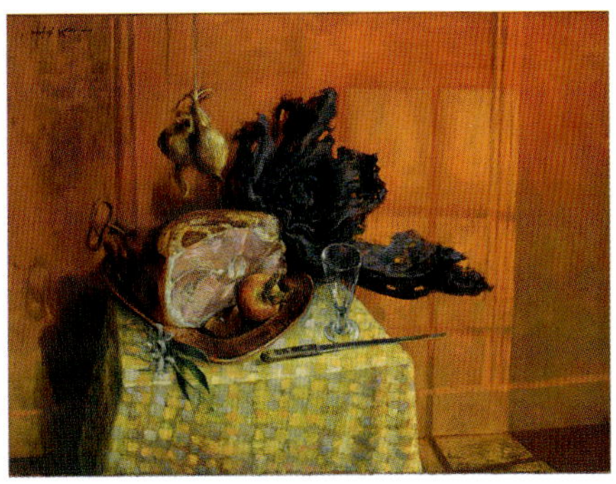

Ayrton, Michael 1921–1975
Still Life at Christmas 1953–1954
oil on canvas 74 x 99
AC 383

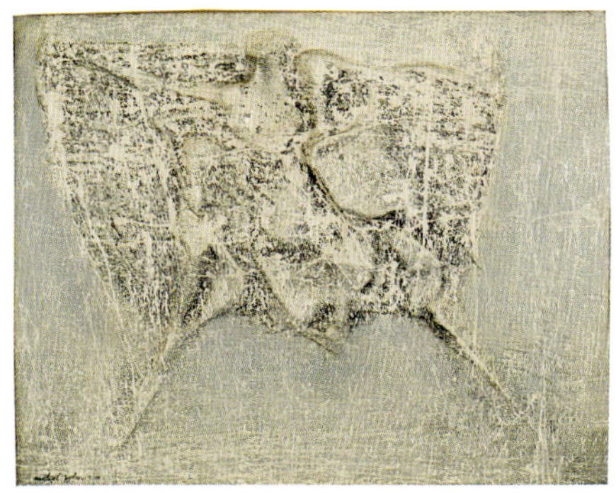

Ayrton, Michael 1921–1975
Icarus in Flight 1960
paint on stucco 40.6 x 50.8
AC 589

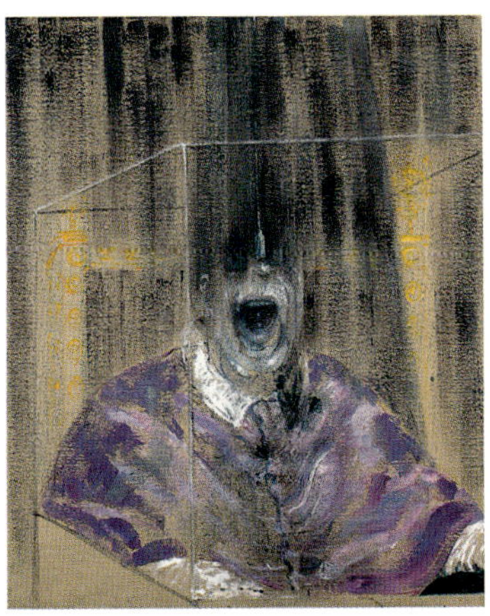

Bacon, Francis 1909–1992
Head VI 1949
oil on canvas 93.2 x 76.5
AC 230

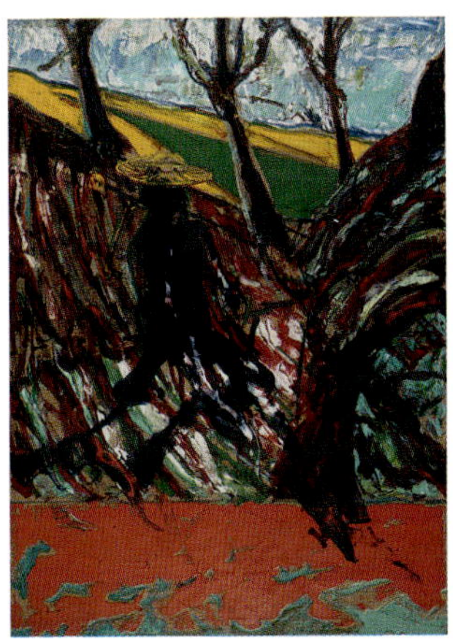

Bacon, Francis 1909–1992
Study for a Portrait of Van Gogh VI 1957
oil on canvas 198.1 x 142.2
AC 424

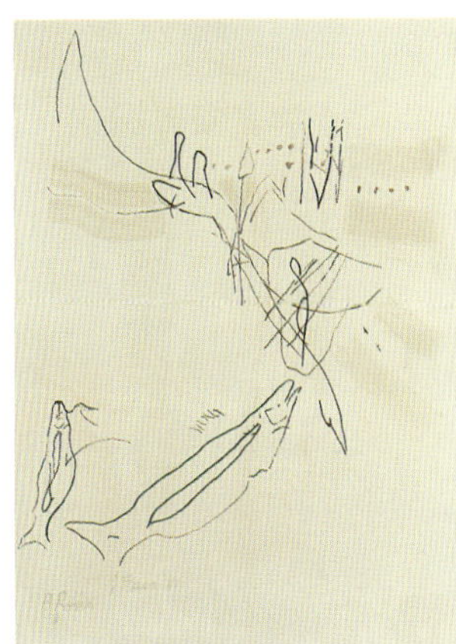

Baer, Jo b.1929 & **Robbins, Bruce** b.1946
Pike 1982
oil on canvas 163.2 x 117.7
AC 5040

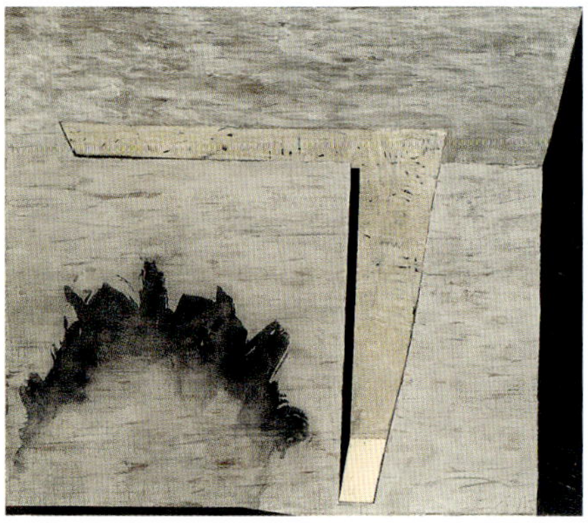

Baker, Chris b.1944
Vent 1982
acrylic & charcoal on canvas 182.5 x 213.2
AC 5206

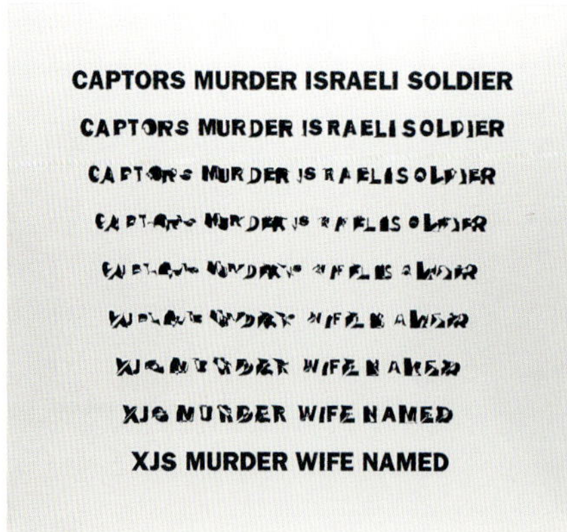

Ball, Alan b.1962
Stress Fracture 1994
acrylic on canvas 157.5 x 175
ACC252/1998

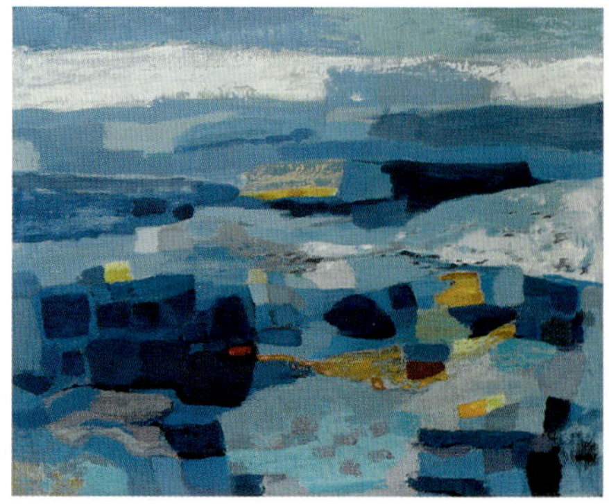

Barclay, Colville 1913–2010
Landscape 1958
oil on board 121.9 x 152.4
AC 496

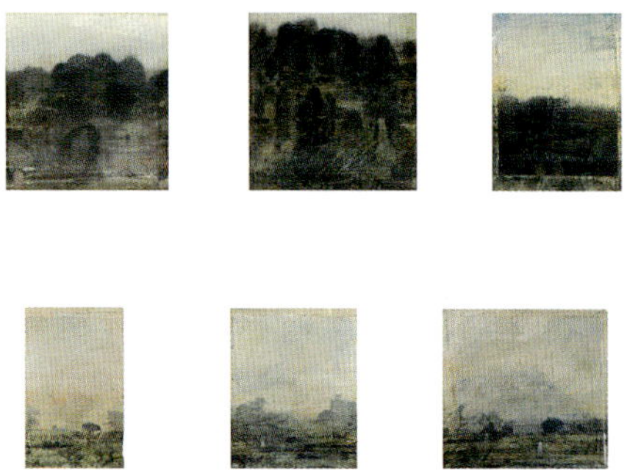

Barker, David Walker b.1947
Six Small Drawings in One Frame 1978
acrylic & watercolour on paper 44.5 x 44.5
AC 5053

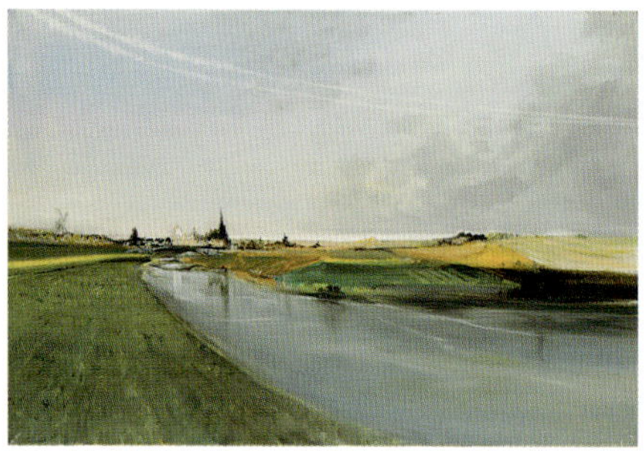

Barker, Kit 1916–1988
Lincolnshire Waterway and Distant Wash
1982
oil on canvas 61.3 x 76.8
AC 5285

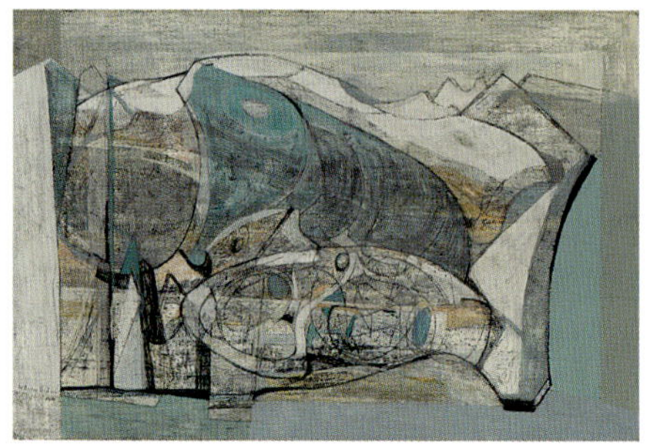

Barns-Graham, Wilhelmina 1912–2004
Grindelwald Glacier 1950
oil on canvas 50 x 76
AC 160

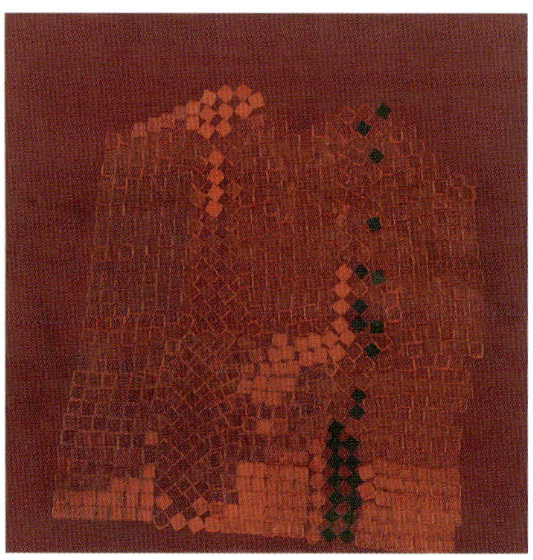

Barns-Graham, Wilhelmina 1912–2004
Purple Painting 1968
oil & acrylic on board 50.8 x 50.8
AC 1152

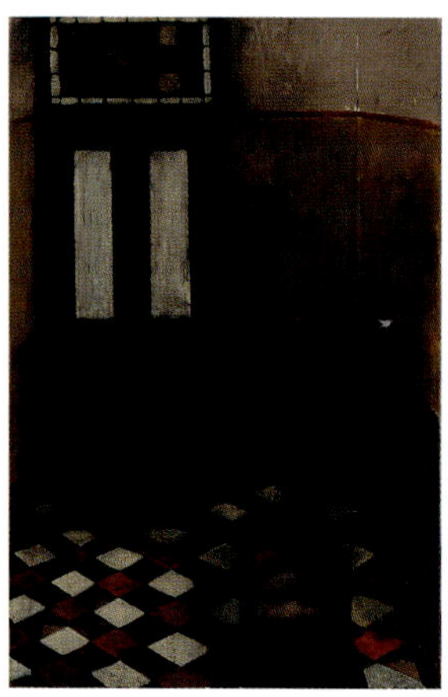

Bassingthwaighte, Lewin 1928–1983
The Front Door 1964
oil on canvas 91.4 x 61
AC 744

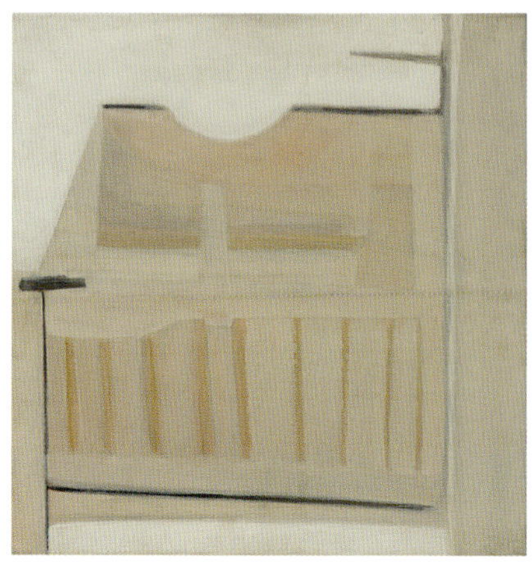

Batty, Joyce 1919–2005
Neilotikos 1964
oil on canvas 55.9 x 55.9
AC 762

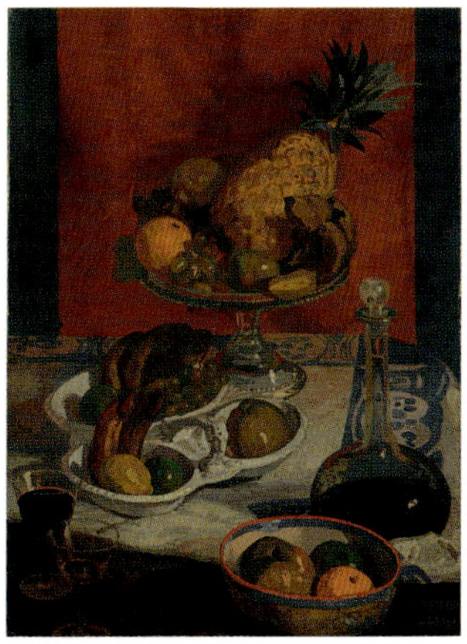

Bayes, Walter 1869–1956
Wine and Fruit 1914–1915
oil on board 78 x 57.5
AC 224

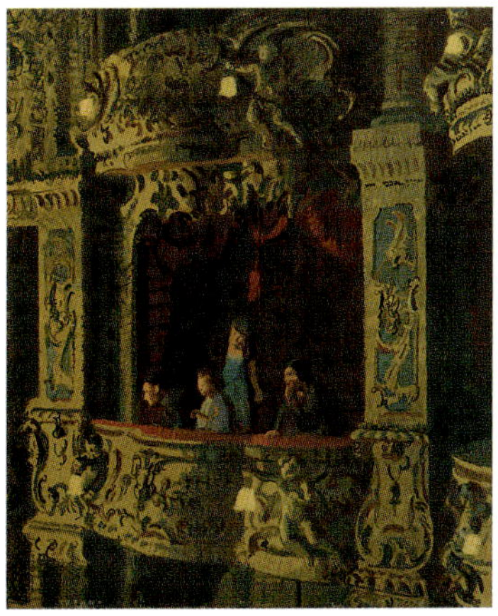

Bayes, Walter 1869–1956
Box at the Lyceum Theatre c.1932
oil on canvas 53.3 x 45.7
AC 84

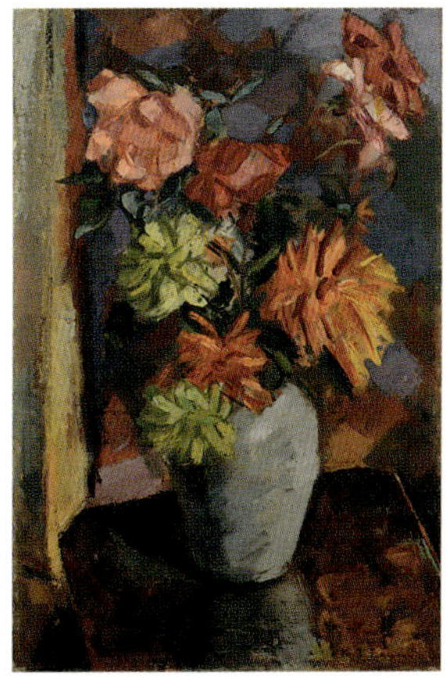

Baynes, Keith 1887–1977
Flowers 1941
oil on canvas 76.5 x 51
AC 62

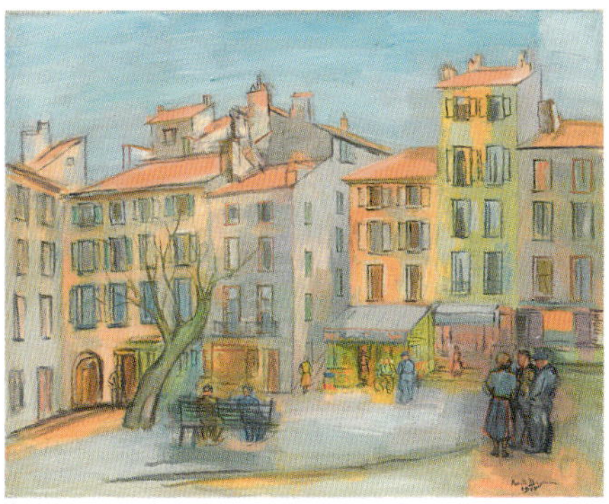

Baynes, Keith 1887–1977
Place des Esplanades, Perpignan, France 1955
oil on board 71.1 x 91.4
AC 379

Beattie, Basil b.1935
Orange No.1 1969
acrylic on canvas 213.4 x 304.8
AC 1103

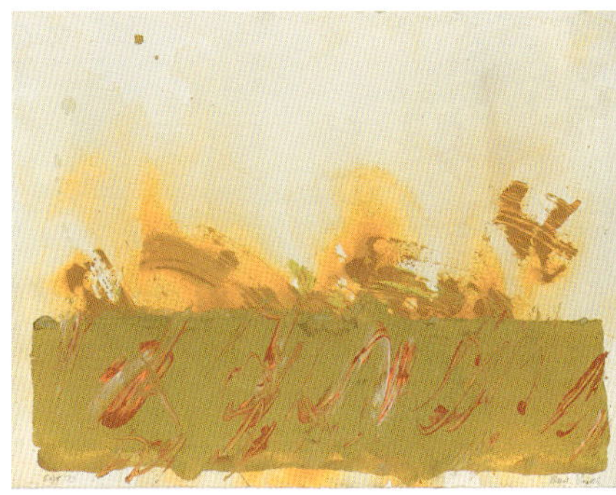

Beattie, Basil b.1935
Cause and Effect IV 1973
acrylic on paper 58.7 x 78.5
AC 1404

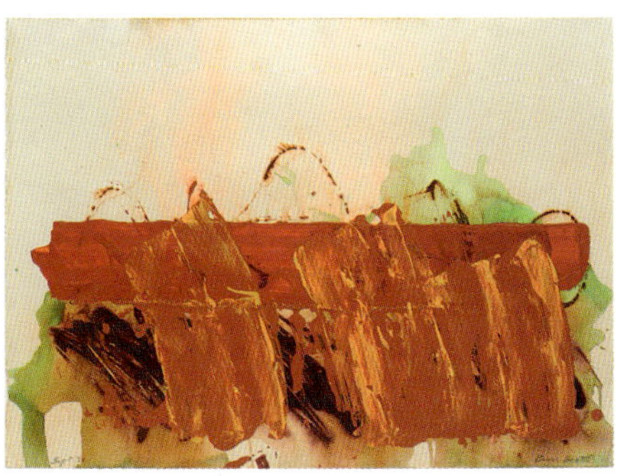

Beattie, Basil b.1935
Cause and Effect V 1973
acrylic on paper 58.4 x 80
AC 1405

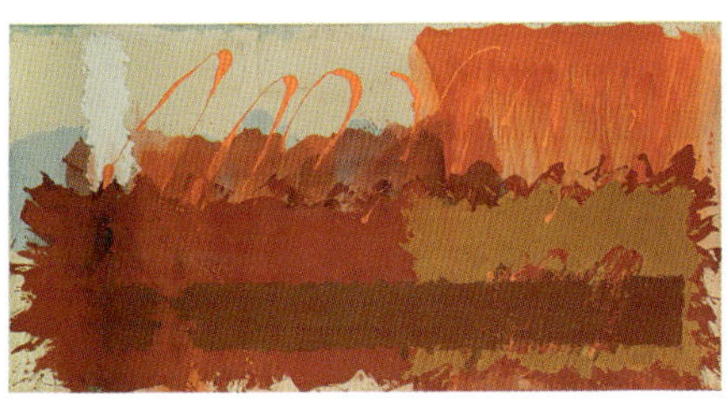

Beattie, Basil b.1935
Reds 1973
acrylic on canvas 215 x 427
AC 0035

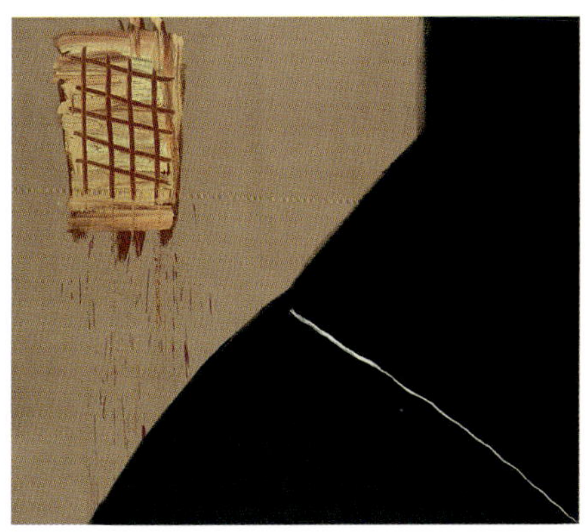

Beattie, Basil b.1935
Imagine If 1993
oil & wax on canvas 259.5 x 304.7
ACC25/1994

Beddington, Sarah b.1964
Forty Nights 1 2001
oil on canvas 25.5 x 34.5
ACC15/2001

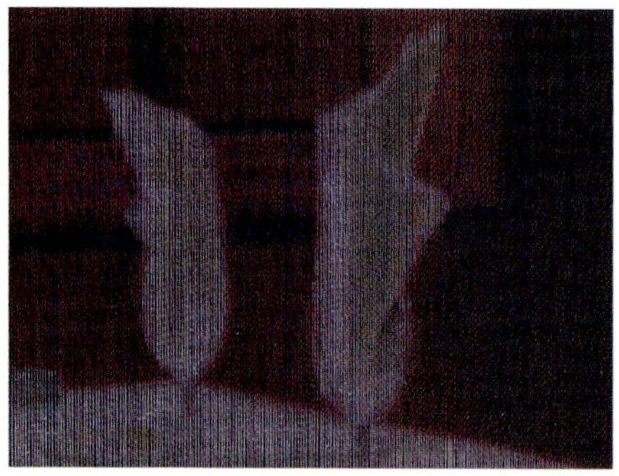

Beddington, Sarah b.1964
Forty Nights 2 2001
oil on canvas 25.5 x 34.5
ACC16/2001

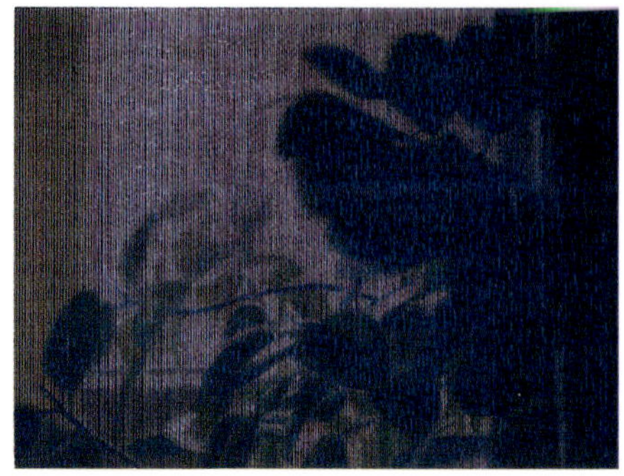

Beddington, Sarah b.1964
Forty Nights 3 2001
oil on canvas 25.5 x 34.5
ACC17/2001

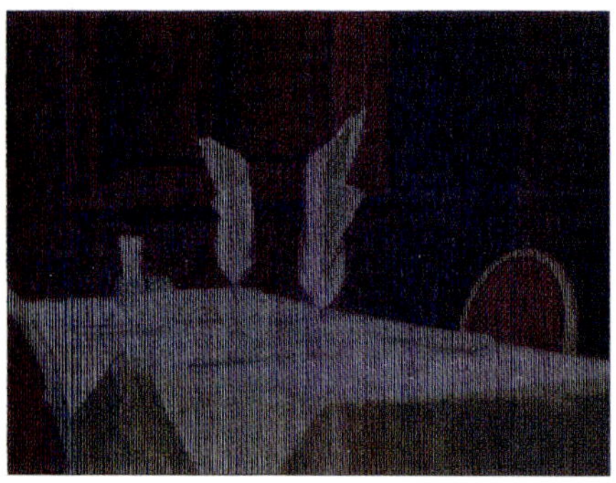

Beddington, Sarah b.1964
Forty Nights 4 2001
oil on canvas 25.5 x 34.5
ACC18/2001

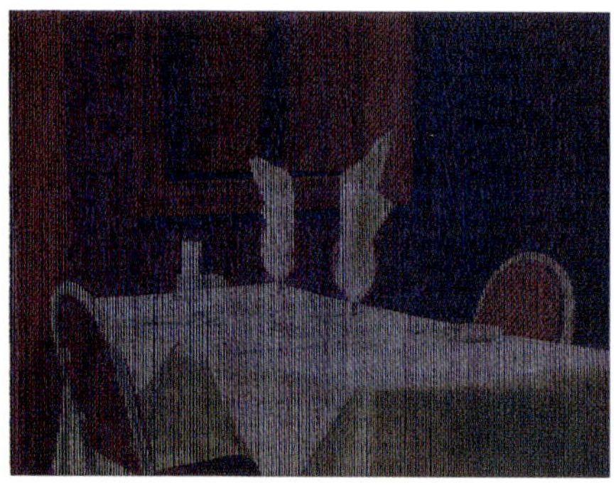

Beddington, Sarah b.1964
Forty Nights 5 2001
oil on canvas 25.5 x 34.5
ACC19/2001

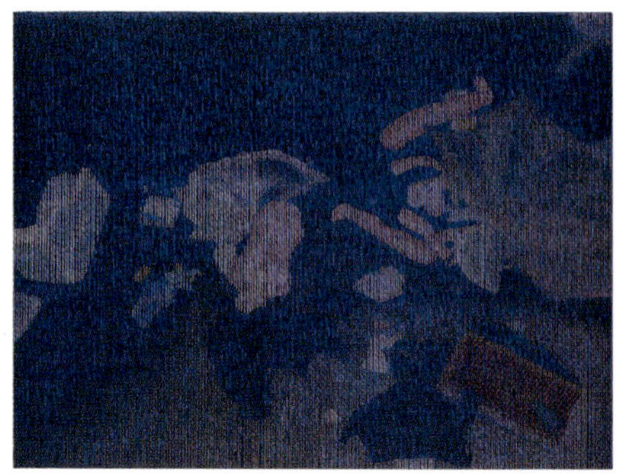

Beddington, Sarah b.1964
Forty Nights 6 2001
oil on canvas 25.5 x 34.5
ACC20/2001

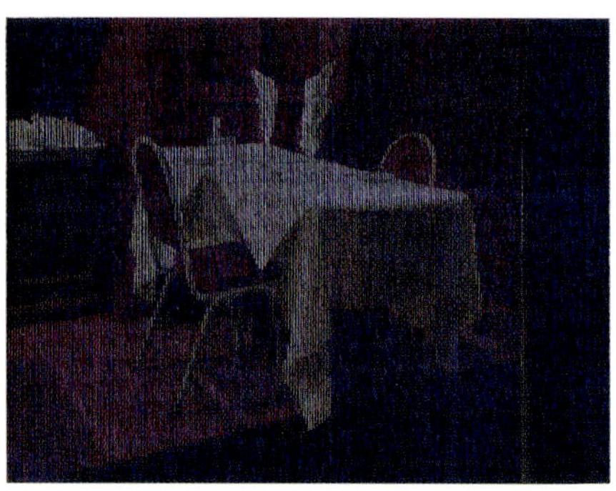

Beddington, Sarah b.1964
Forty Nights 7 2001
oil on canvas 25.5 x 34.5
ACC21/2001

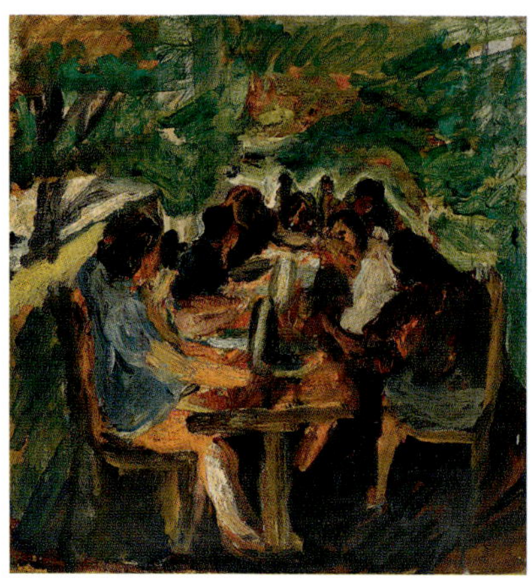

Behrens, Timothy b.1937
A Lunch Party 1961
oil on board 30.5 x 30.5
AC 622

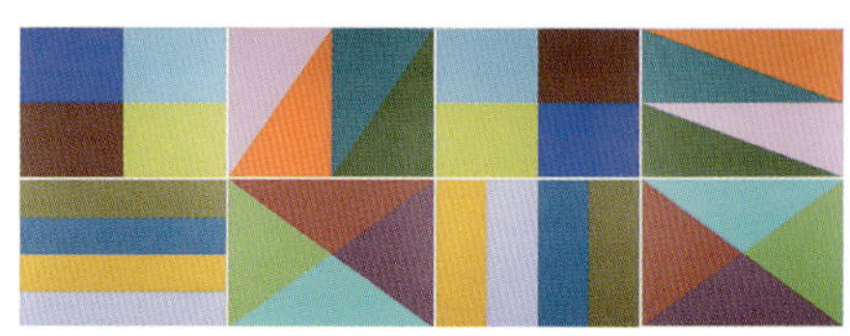

Bell, Richard b.1955
Four Colour Sets Mapped Deictically Presented Twice in Logical Form 1981–1982
oil on canvas 116 x 81.1; 116 x 81.1; 116 x 81.1; 116 x 81.1
AC 5194

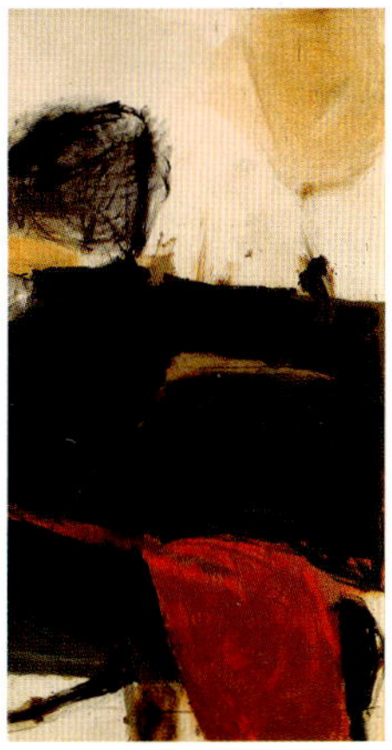

Bell, Trevor b.1930
Yorkshire, January 1960 1960
oil on canvas 167.6 x 91.4
AC 533

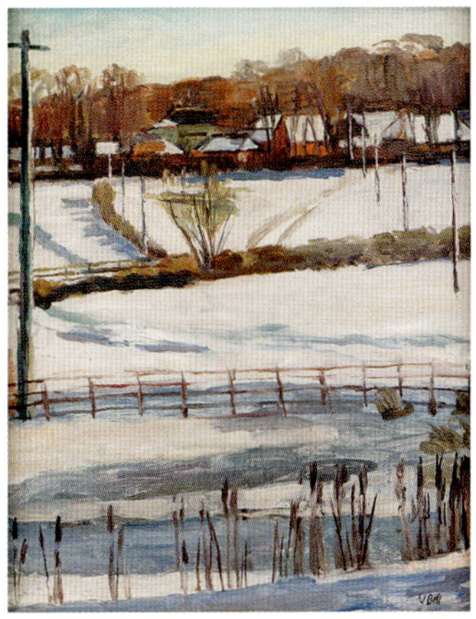

Bell, Vanessa 1879–1961
Snow at Tilton 1941
oil on canvas 36.5 x 29.2
AC 86

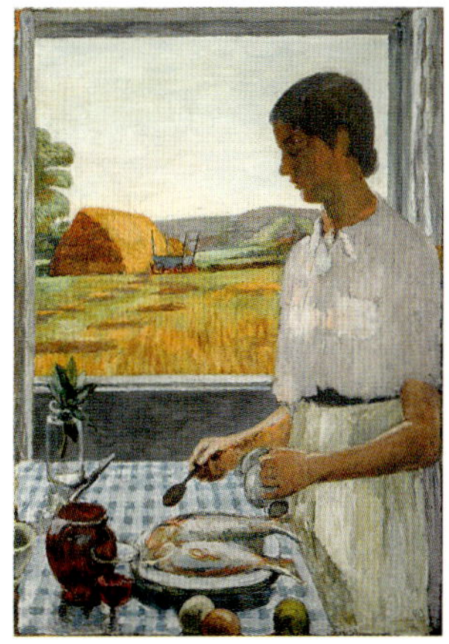

Bell, Vanessa 1879–1961
The Cook 1948
oil on canvas 100.3 x 74.7
AC 138

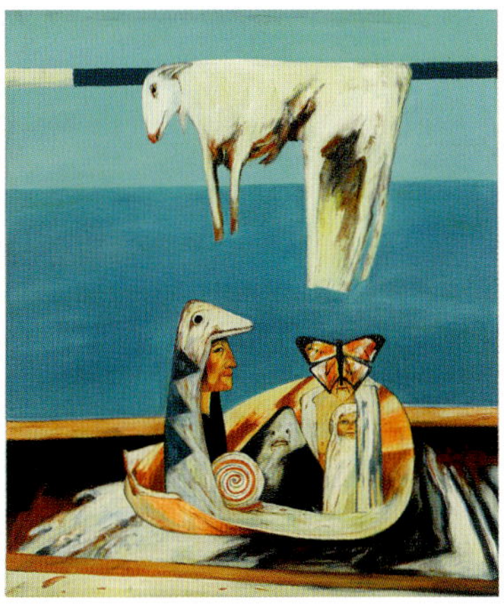

Bellany, John b.1942
The Voyage 1973
oil on canvas 180 x 154.9
AC 1371

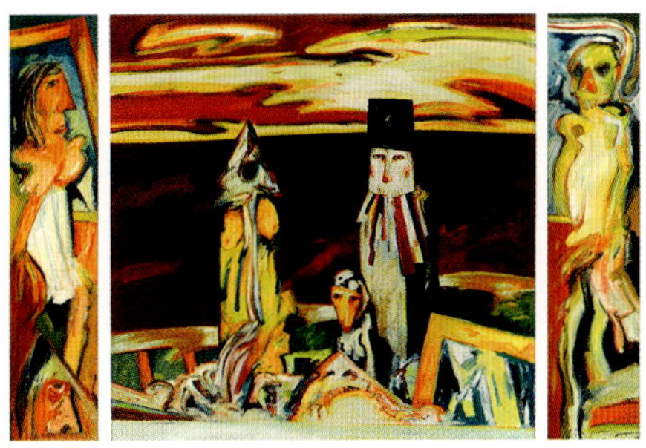

Bellany, John b.1942
The Sea People 1975
oil on canvas 182.9 x 233.7
AC 1866

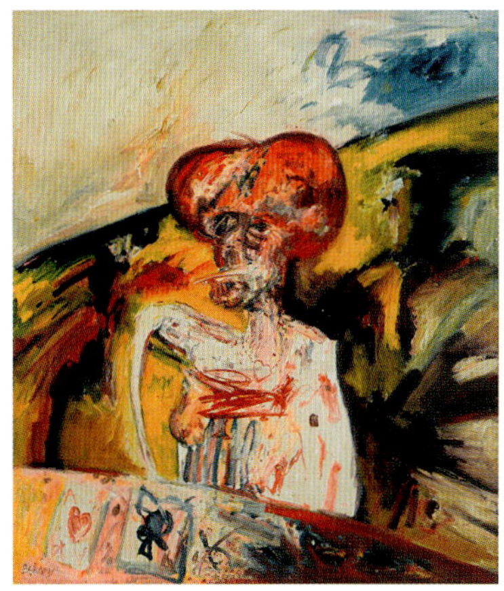

Bellany, John b.1942
The Gambler 1981
oil on canvas 173.4 x 152.9
AC 5288

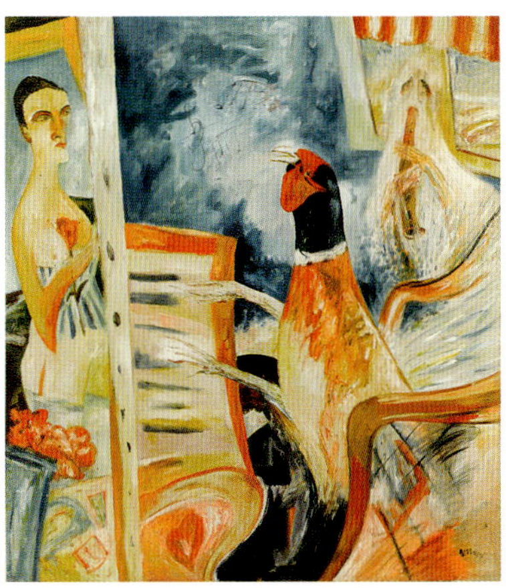

Bellany, John b.1942
The Capercaillie Sings His Lovesong 1985
oil on canvas 173 x 153
AC 5398

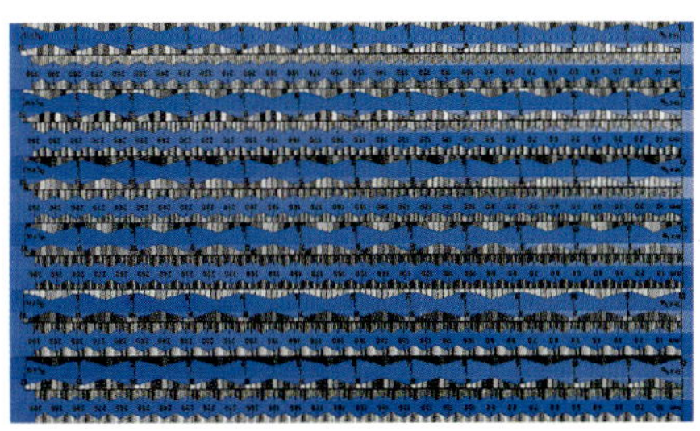

Bellingham, David b.1966
Ruler Painting (blue) 1994
enamel on plastic 18.1 x 31.7
ACC60/1996

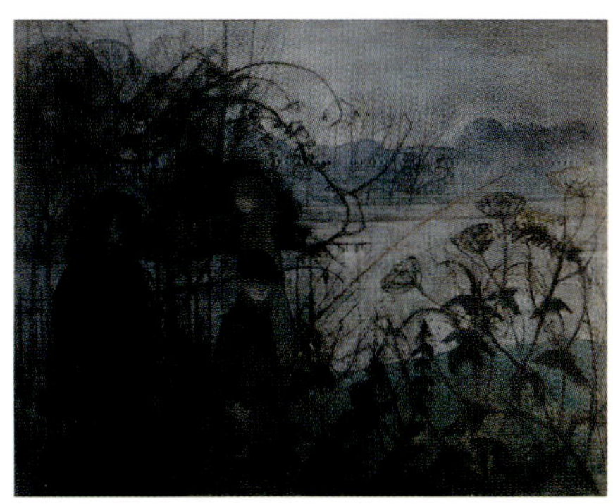

Bellingham-Smith, Elinor 1906–1988
The Island 1951
oil on canvas 142.2 x 182.9
AC 195

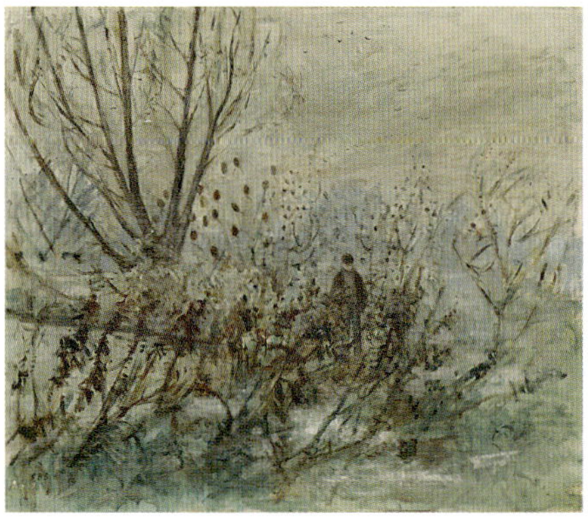

Bellingham-Smith, Elinor 1906–1988
Winter Afternoon 1952
oil on canvas 50.8 x 61
AC 252

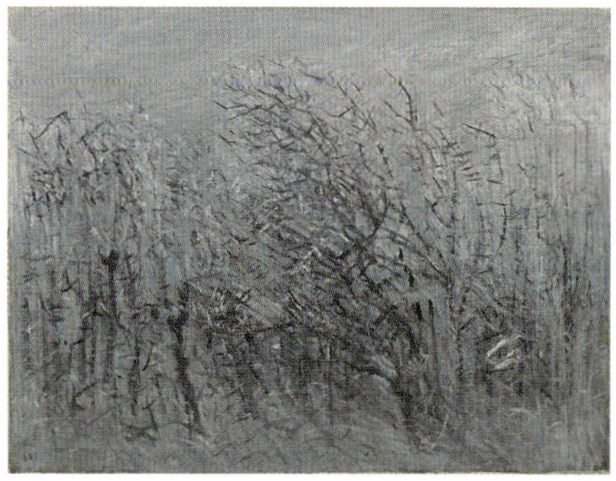

Bellingham-Smith, Elinor 1906–1988
The Fenn, Boxford 1961
oil on canvas 91.4 x 121.9
AC 621

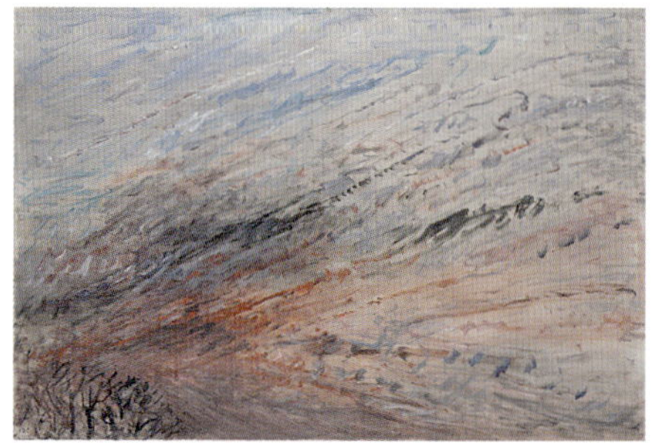

Bellingham-Smith, Elinor 1906–1988
Sunset 1966
oil on canvas 101.6 x 152.4
ACA 35

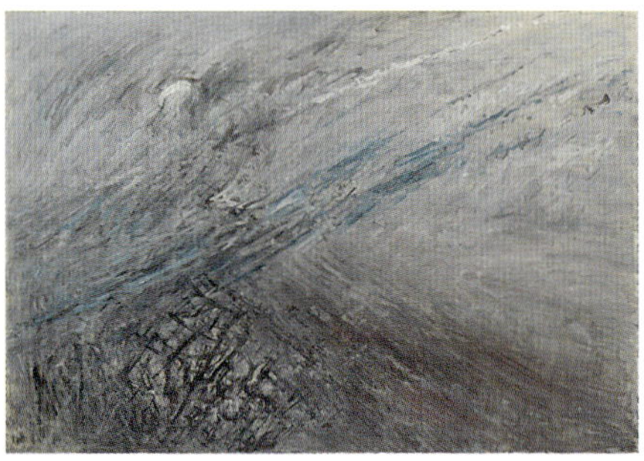

Bellingham-Smith, Elinor 1906–1988
The Sky over Wattisham 1966
oil on canvas 101.6 x 152.4
ACA 34

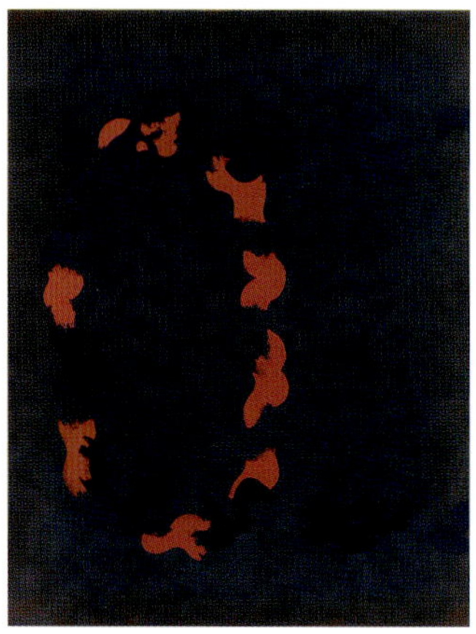

Benjamin, Anthony 1931–2002
On the Edge 1966
oil & PVA on canvas 236 x 184
AC 882

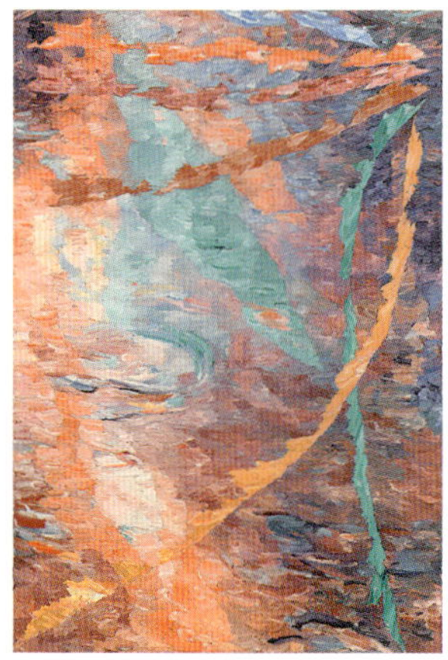

Bennett, Michael b.1948
Crimson Lake 1979
oil on canvas 187.5 x 127.8
AC 2027

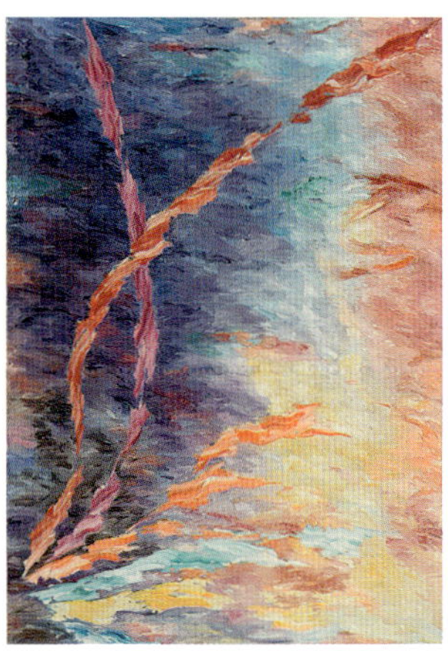

Bennett, Michael b.1948
Midnight Sonata 1979–1980
oil on canvas 183 x 121.7
AC 3054

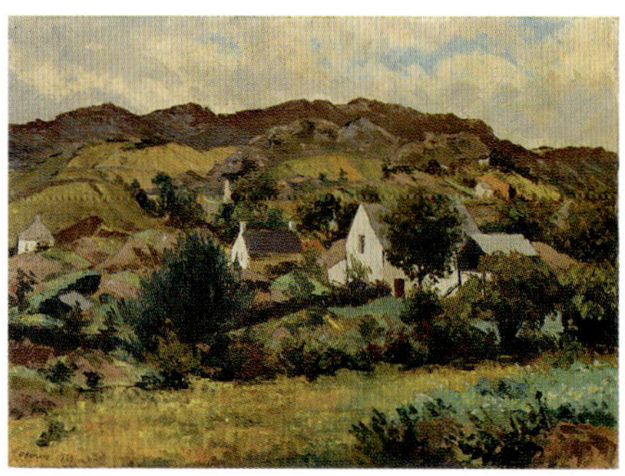

Benois, Nadia 1896–1975
Derrycornerry, Bantry Bay 1935
oil on canvas 50.1 x 70.5
AC 87

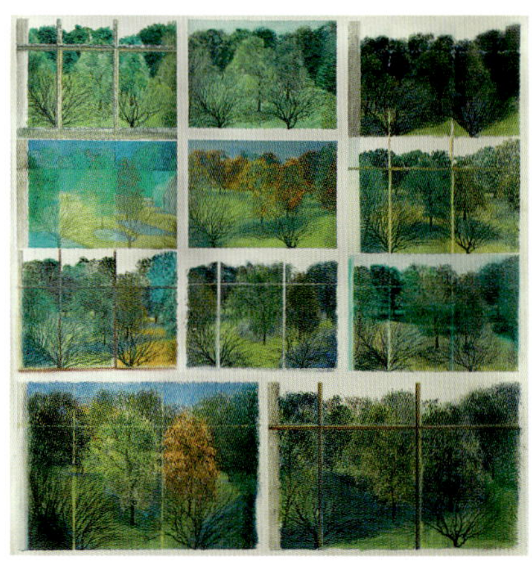

Berg, Adrian 1929–2011
Regent's Park 1967
oil on canvas 116.8 x 116.8
AC 982

Facing page: Doig, Peter, b.1959, *Red Deer* (detail), 1990, (p. 42)

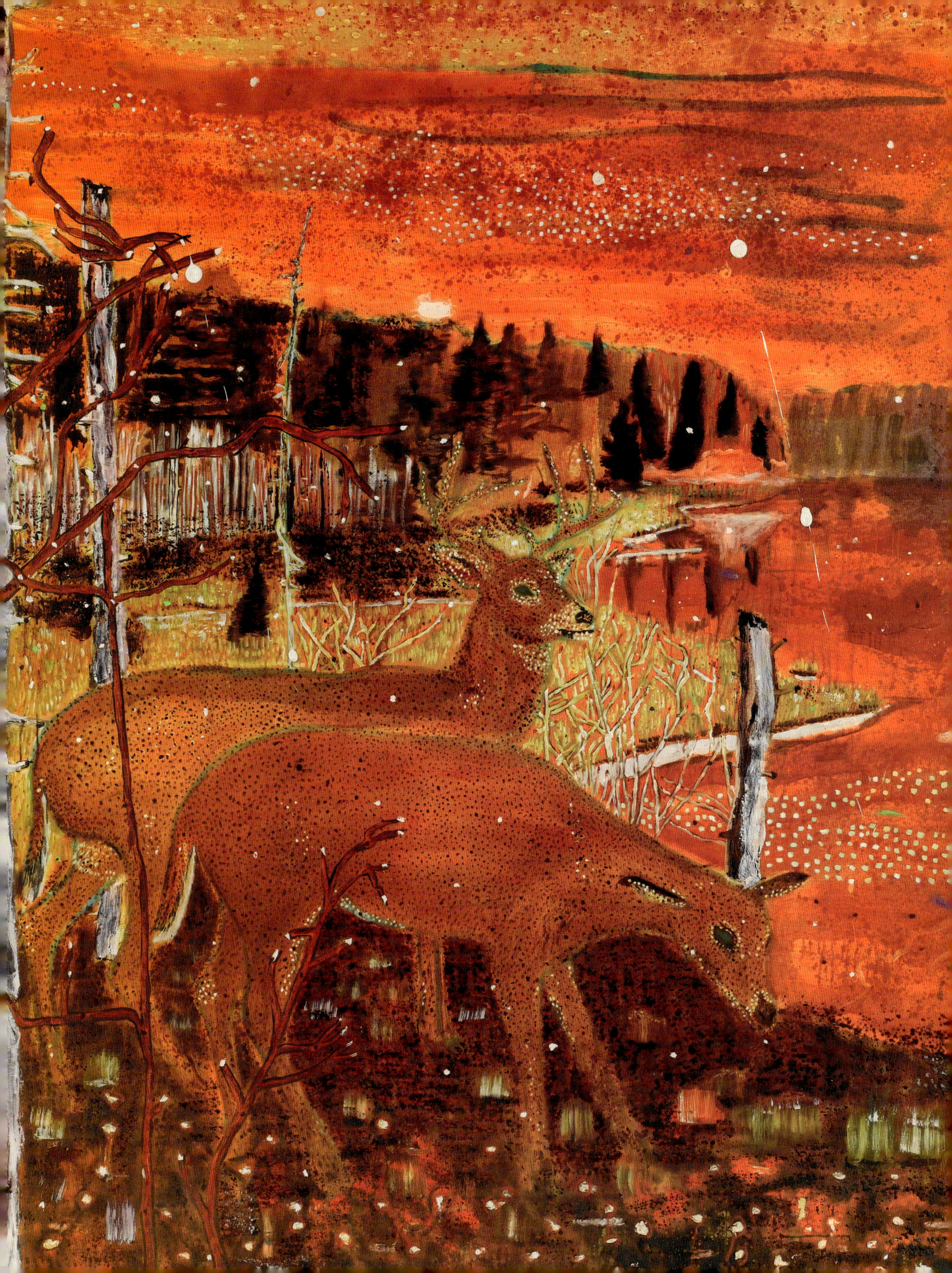

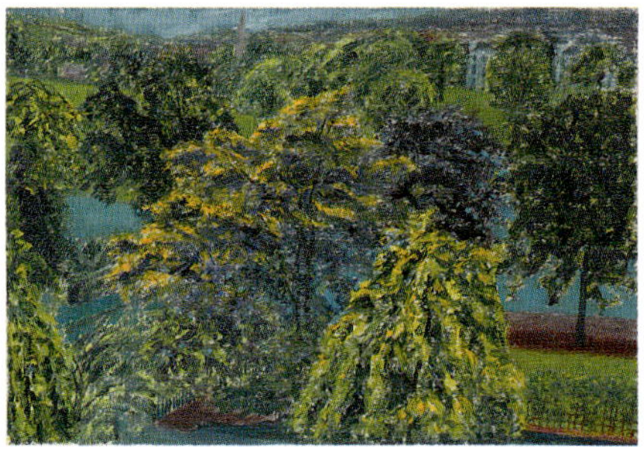

Berg, Adrian 1929–2011
Gloucester Lodge, Regent's Park, Late June 1974 1974
oil on canvas 50.5 x 76
AC 1499

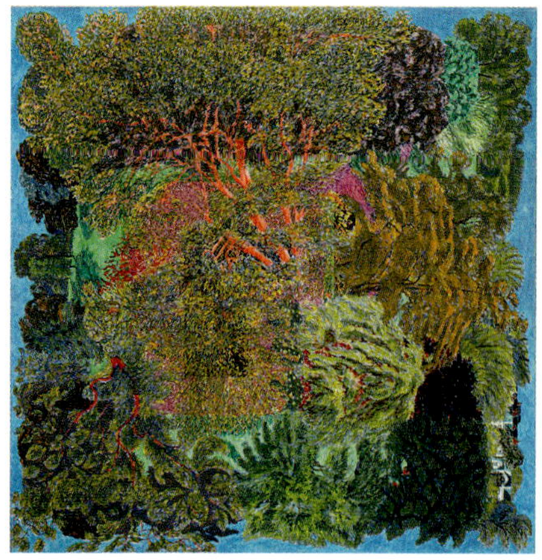

Berg, Adrian 1929–2011
Gloucester Gate, Regent's Park, June 1982 1982
oil on canvas 177.8 x 177.2
AC 5226

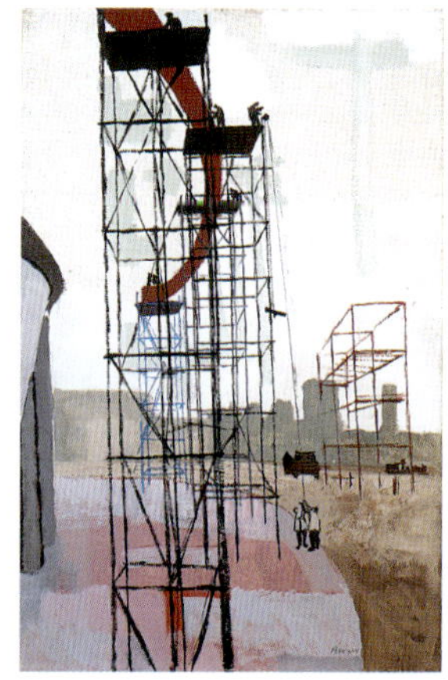

Berger, John b.1926
Scaffolding – Festival of Britain 1950
oil on canvas 76.2 x 50.8
AC 169

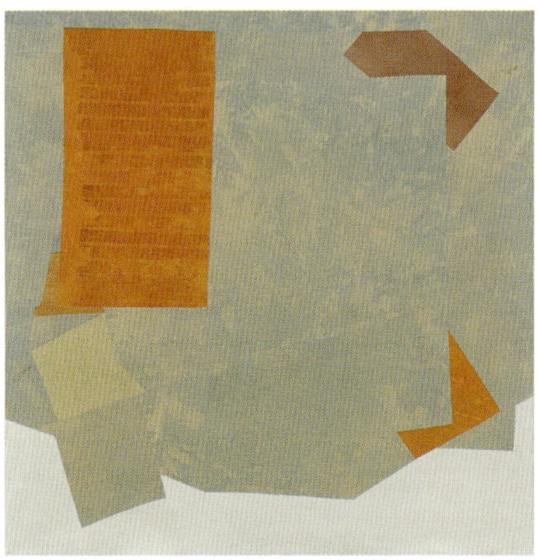

Bergman, Stephenie b.1946
Blind Venetian 1975
paint & dye on canvas 196 x 196
AC 1555

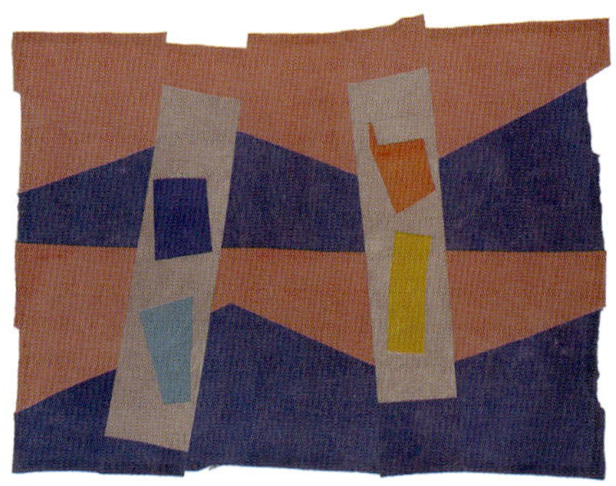

Bergman, Stephenie b.1946
Thunderthighs 1984
acrylic & dye on canvas 217 x 234
AC 5331

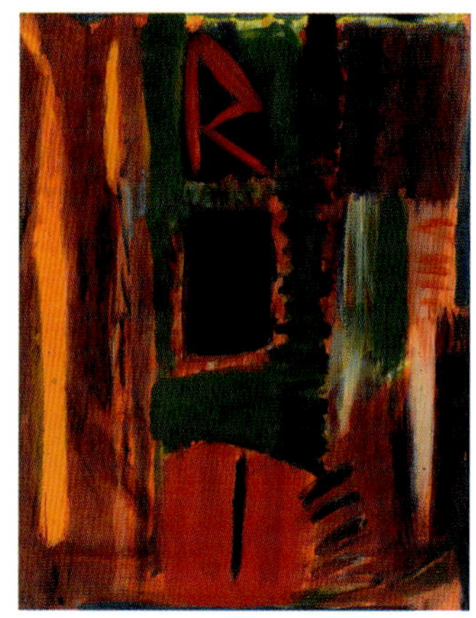

Bevan, Graham 1935–2006
Interior for Figure 1960
oil on canvas 152.4 x 121.9
AC 529

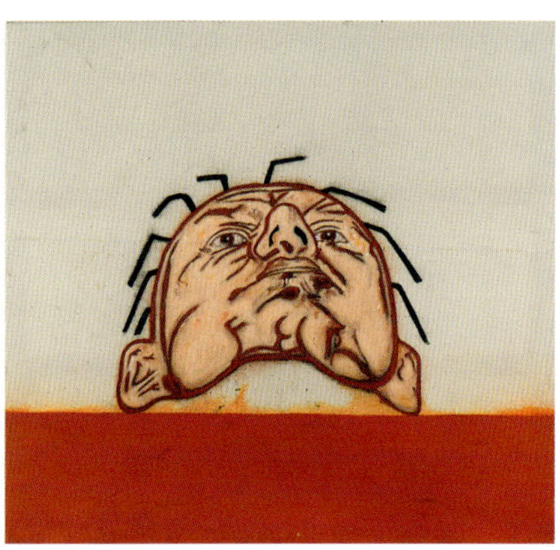

Bevan, Tony b.1951
Head Horizon 1996
acrylic on canvas 157 x 171
ACC10/1996

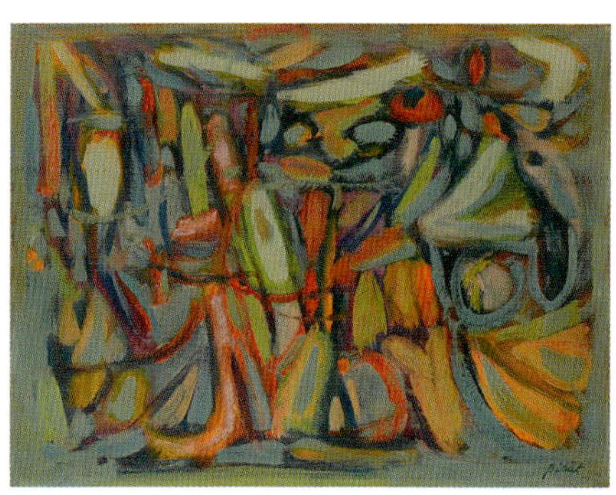

Bicât, André 1909–1996
Fugue 1959
oil on board 45.7 x 60.3
AC 541

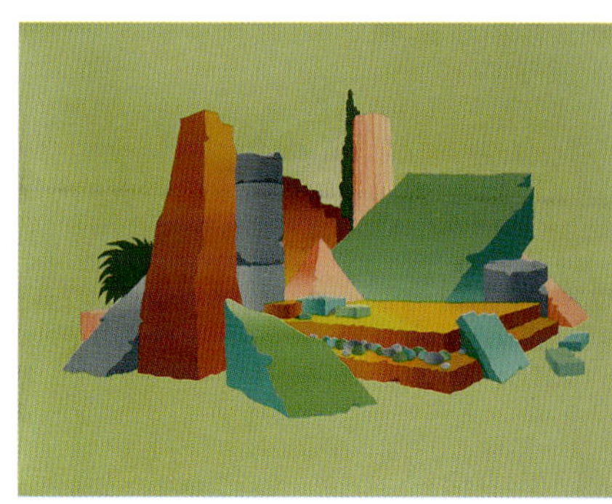

Binder, Douglas b.1941
Ruins 1968
oil on canvas 182.9 x 243.8
AC 1123

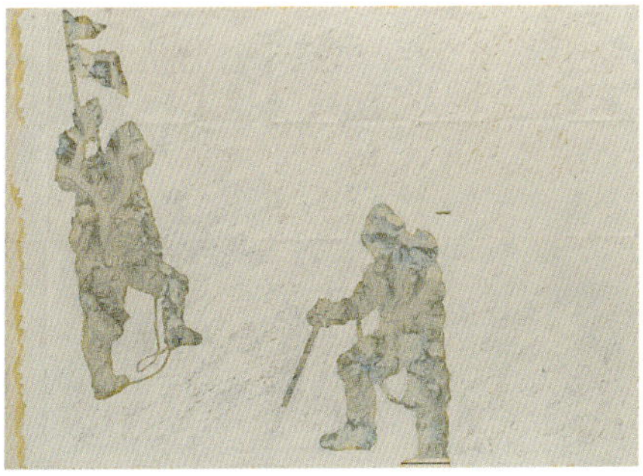

Blacker, Kate b.1955
Khumbu Himal 1981
oil on paper 84.6 x 120
AC 5091

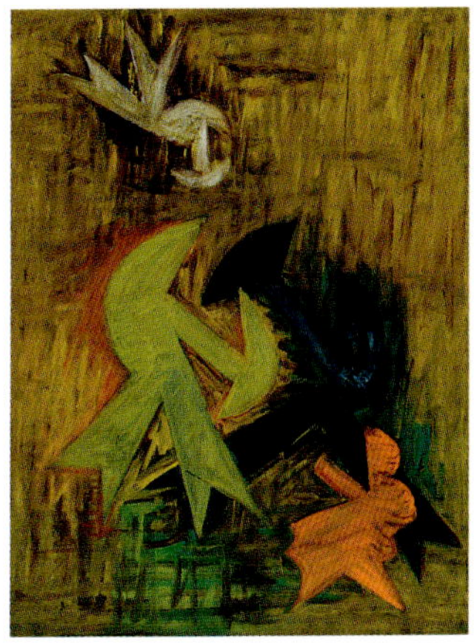

Blacklock, George b.1952
Composition 1979
oil & wax on canvas 96.9 x 73.5
AC 3031

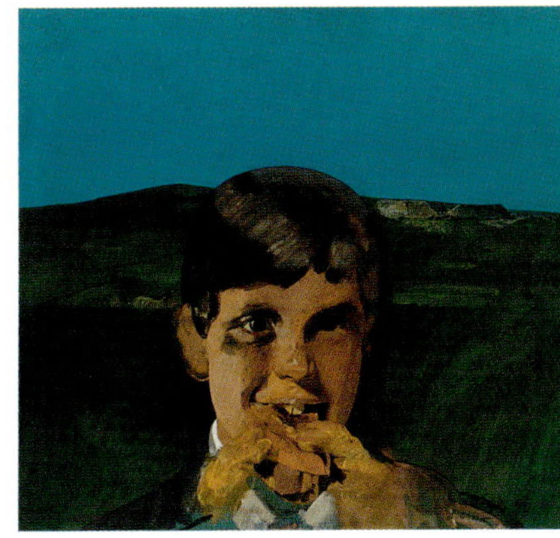

Blake, Peter b.1932
Boy Eating a Hot Dog 1960–1965
acrylic on board 36.5 x 40.7
AC 817

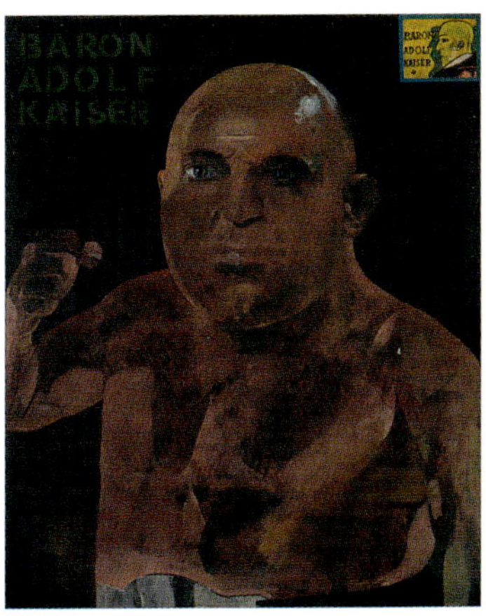

Blake, Peter b.1932
Baron Adolf Kaiser 1961–1963
oil on panel 61 x 51
ACC3/1963

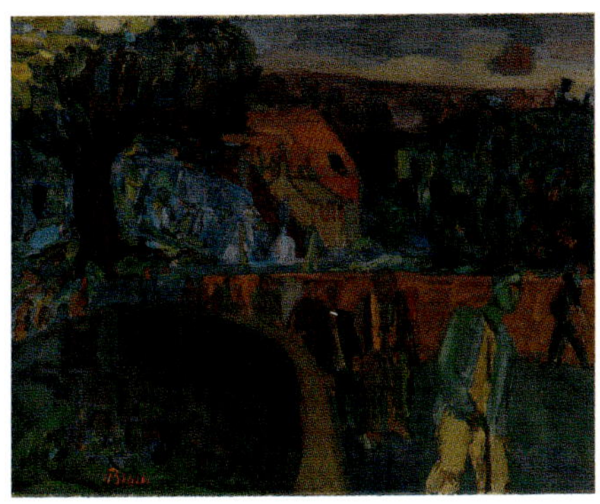

Bloch, Martin 1883–1954
Down from the Welsh Quarries 1948
oil on canvas 71.1 x 90
AC 408

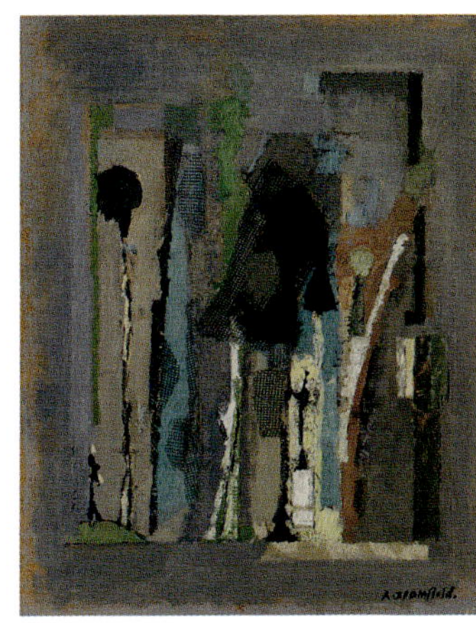

Blomfield, Richard C. b.1930
Strolling Figures, Statue and Trees c.1967
oil, acrylic, net & card collage on board 23.2 x 19
AC 976

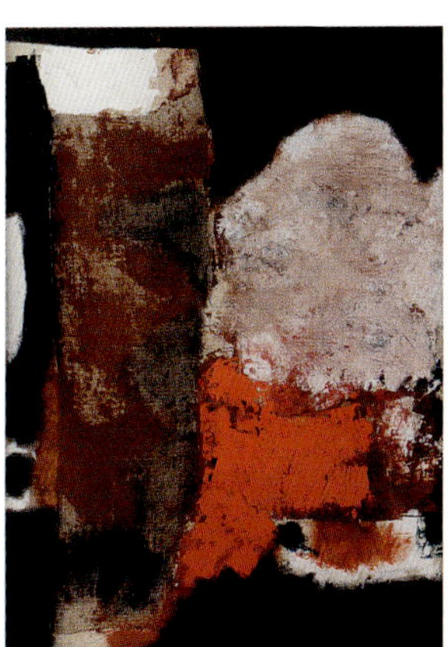

Blow, Sandra 1925–2006
Painting (57) 1957
oil on canvas 121 x 85
AC 447

Blow, Sandra 1925–2006
Painting 1965
oil on canvas 152.4 x 182.9
ACA 5

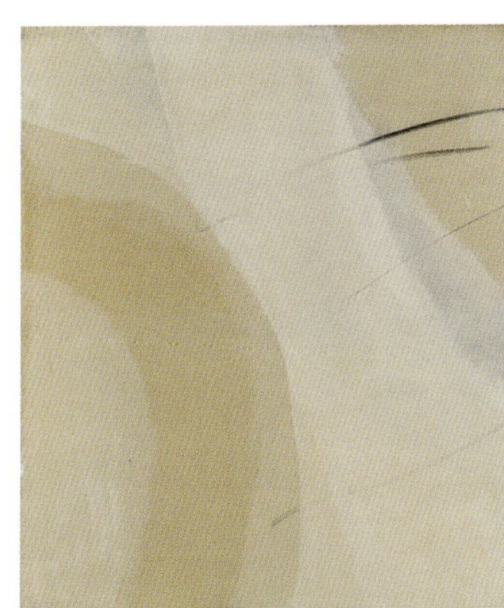

Blow, Sandra 1925–2006
Untitled 1965
oil on canvas 106.7 x 91.4
ACA 24

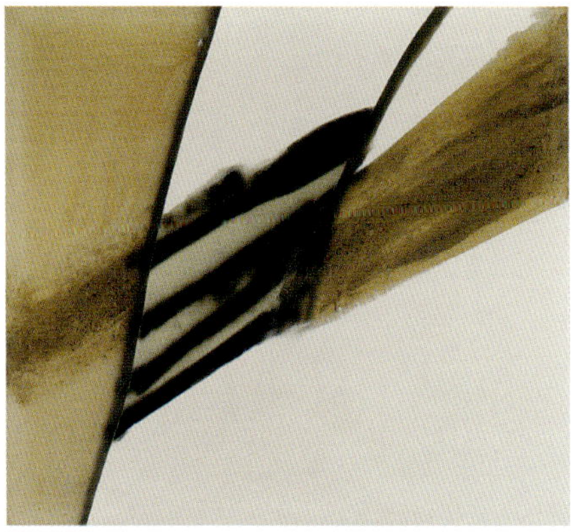

Blow, Sandra 1925–2006
White No.1 1965
oil on canvas 152.4 x 167.6
AC 981

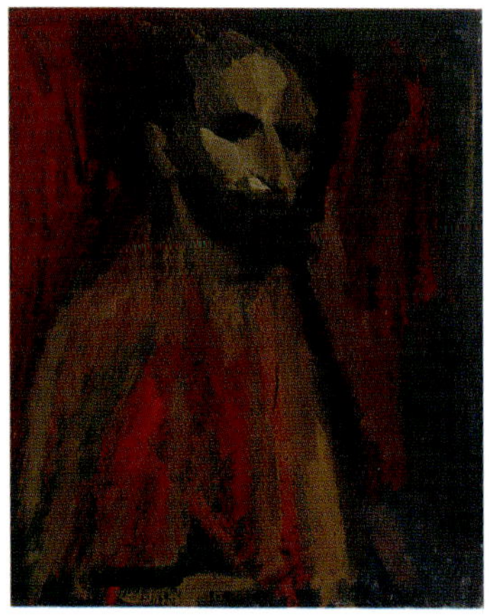

Bomberg, David 1890–1957
Self Portrait (David) 1937
oil on canvas 61 x 50.8
ACC4/1963

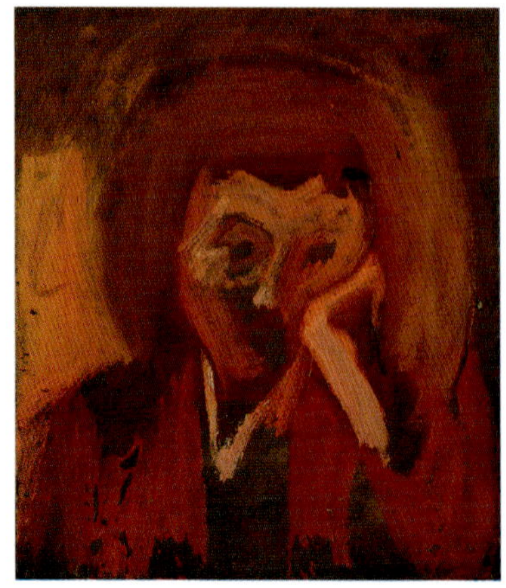

Bomberg, David 1890–1957
Diana 1943
oil on canvas 40.6 x 35.6
AC 667

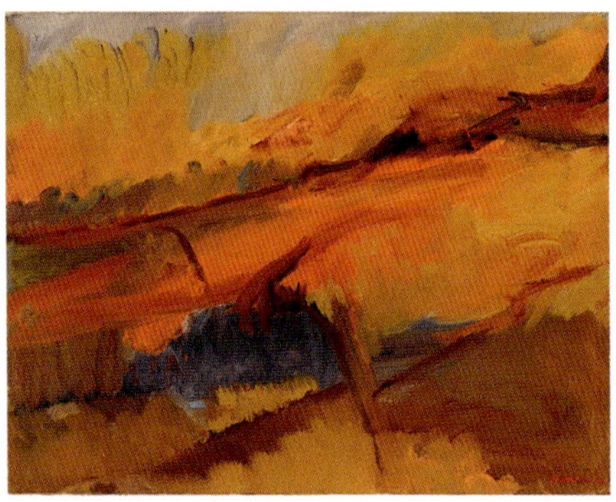

Bomberg, David 1890–1957
Trendrine, Cornwall 1947
oil on canvas 81.3 x 106.7
AC 446

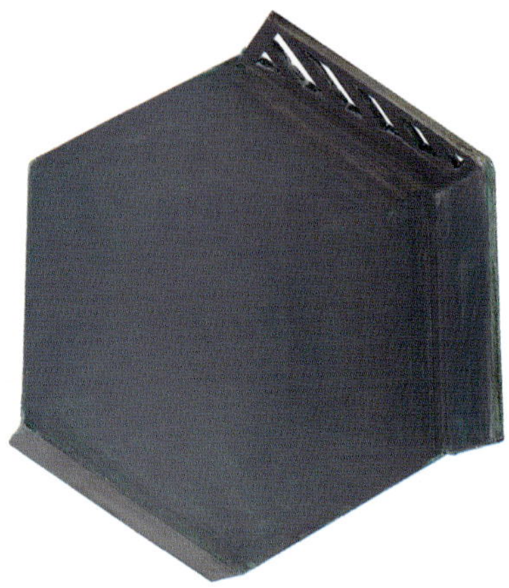

Bonvin, Susan b.1948
Adrift 1991
oil on canvas & wood 66 x 62
ACC75/1991

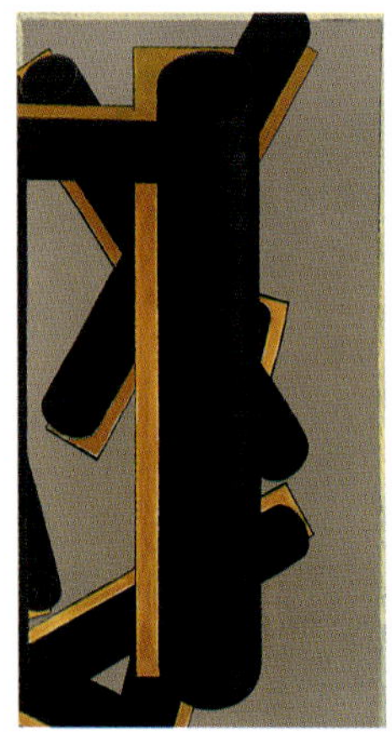

Boston, Allan b.1951
Untitled 1981–1982
oil, acrylic & paper collage on canvas
208.2 x 109.3
AC 5193

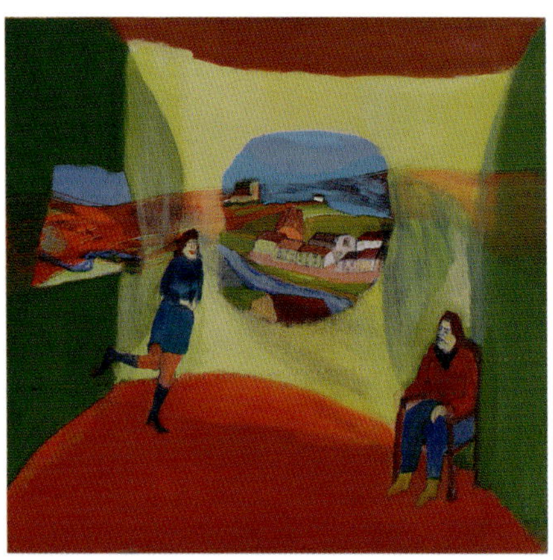

Bourne, Bob b.1931
Lover's Leap 1972
oil on canvas 77.5 x 81.3
AC 3019

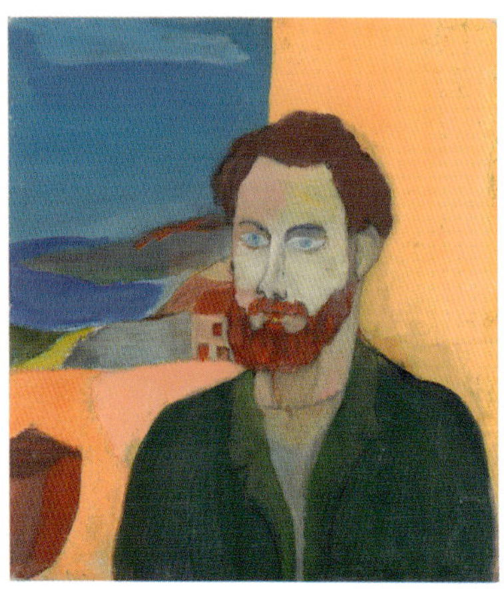

Bourne, Bob b.1931
Self Portrait 1977
oil on canvas 72.5 x 70.5
AC 3018

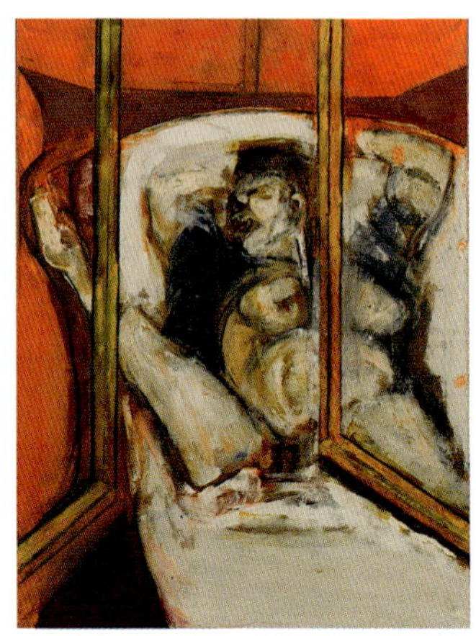

Bowling, Frank b.1936
Birthday 1962
oil on canvas 121.9 x 91.4
AC 658

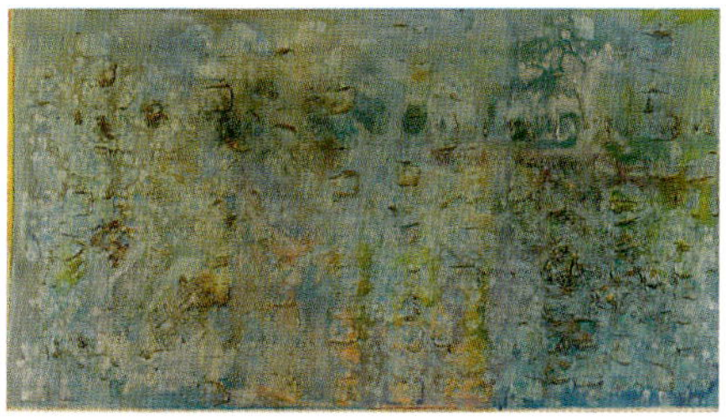

Bowling, Frank b.1936
Great Thames IV 1988–1989
acrylic on canvas 181 x 321
ACC8/1990

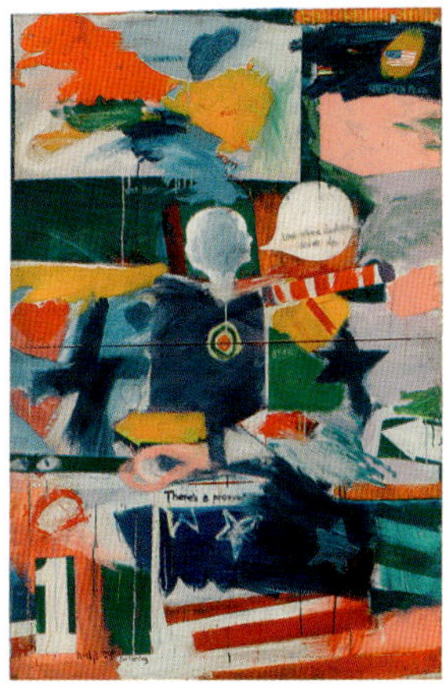

Bowstead, John b.1940
The Language of Love 1962
oil on board 183.2 x 122
AC 636

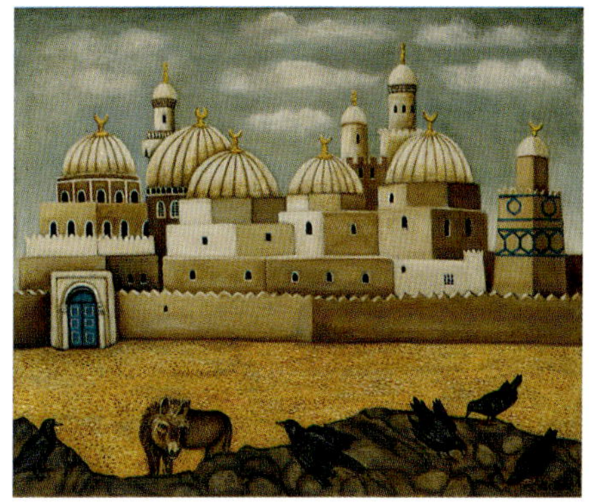

Box, Eden 1919–1988
Holy City 1968
oil on canvas 50.6 x 61.1
AC 5131

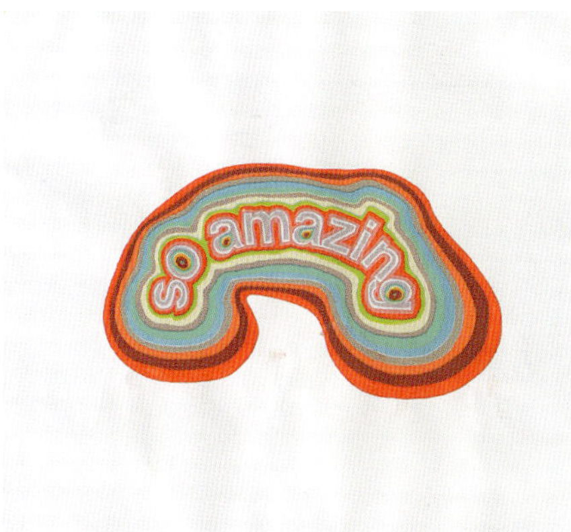

Boyce, Sonia b.1962
So Amazing 2001–2002
acrylic on paper 51.8 x 51.8
ACC14/2002

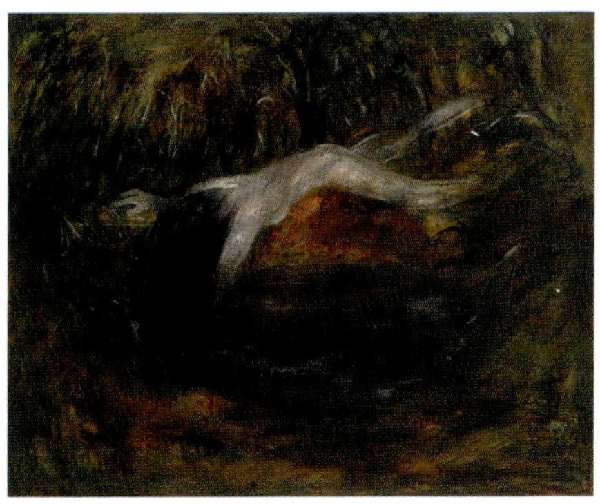

Boyd, Arthur 1920–1999
Nude Floating over a Dark Pond II 1962
oil on board 121.9 x 152.4
AC 637

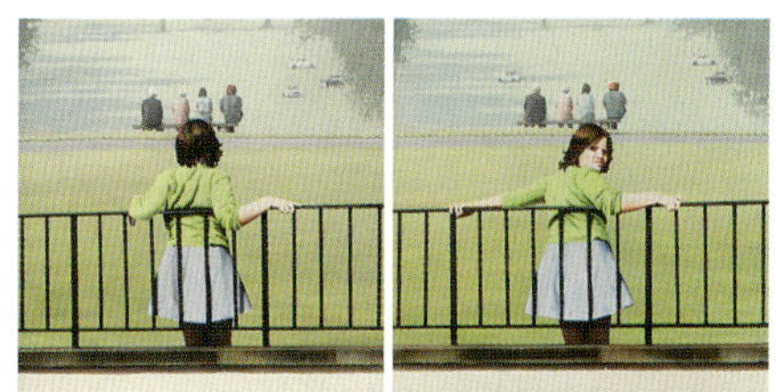

Boyd, Fionnuala b.1944 & **Evans, Leslie** b.1945
Views 1 and 2 1973
acrylic on canvas 91.5 x 91.5; 91.5 x 91.5
AC 1620

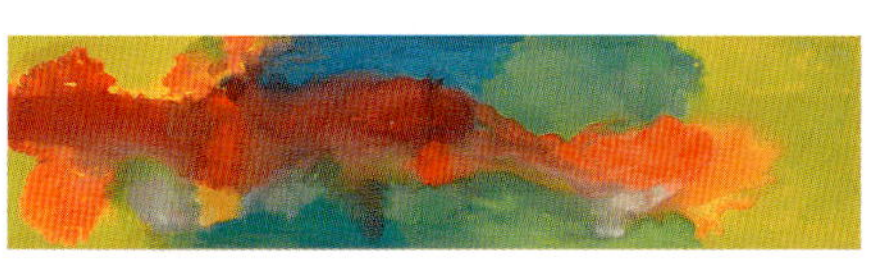

Branch, Winston b.1947
First Light 'For Polly' 1979
acrylic on canvas 87.5 x 364
AC 3080

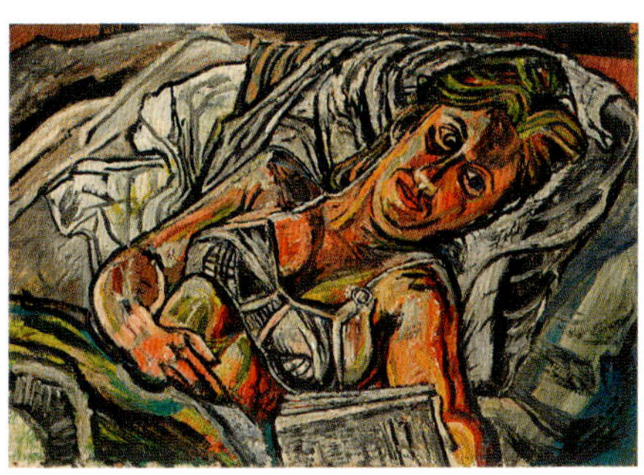

Bratby, John Randall 1928–1992
Jean Reading 1953
oil on hardboard 53.3 x 78.5
AC 329

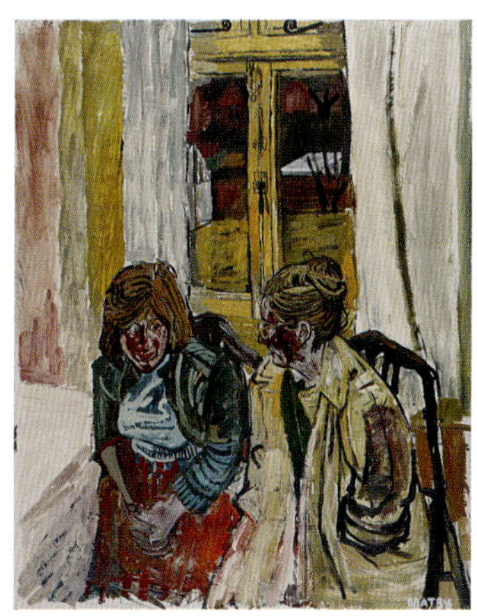

Bratby, John Randall 1928–1992
Jean and Susan 1956
oil on board 122 x 97.5
AC 416

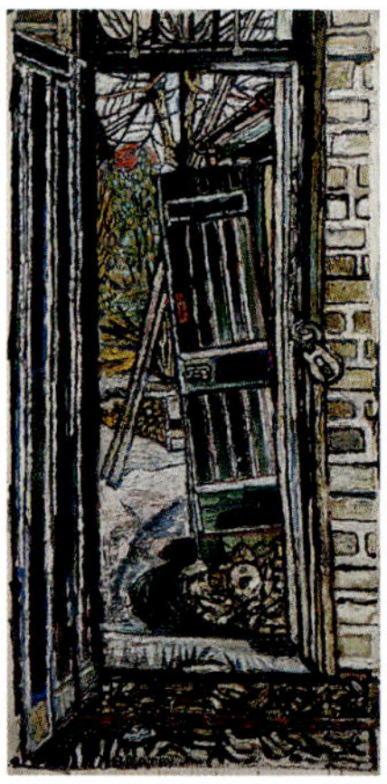

Bratby, John Randall 1928–1992
Coach House Door 1959
oil on board 121.9 x 61
AC 507

Breakwell, Ian 1943–2005
Gathering Storm 1985
oil on canvas 193 x 162.5
AC 5456

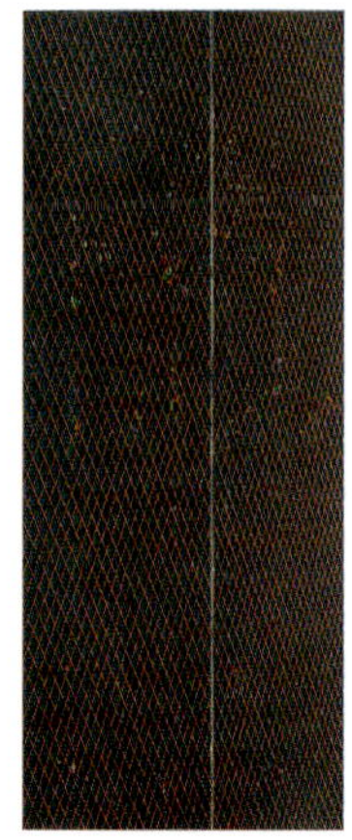

Brick, Michael b.1946
Sous-Bois III 1978
acrylic on canvas 280 x 114
AC 1965

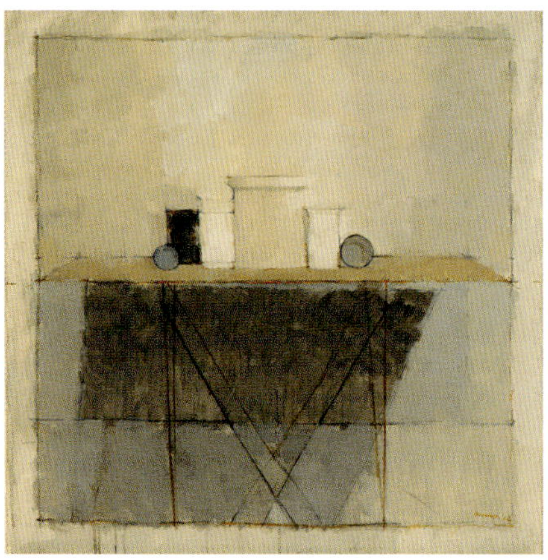

Brooker, William 1918–1983
Ikaria 1963
oil on canvas 101.6 x 101.6
AC 983

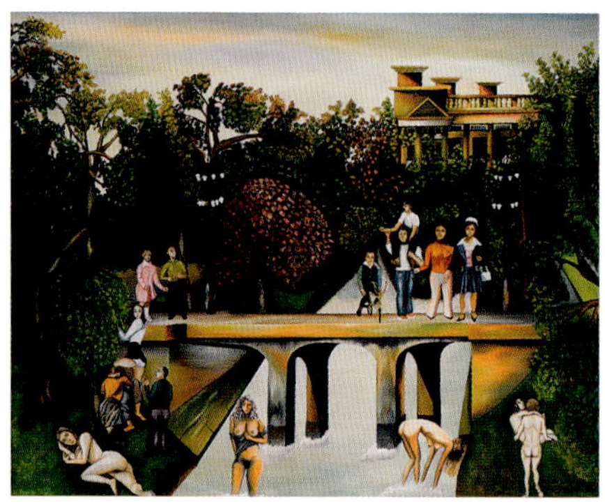

Brown, Cleveland b.1943
St James's Park 1978
oil on canvas 101.5 x 127.5
AC 1951

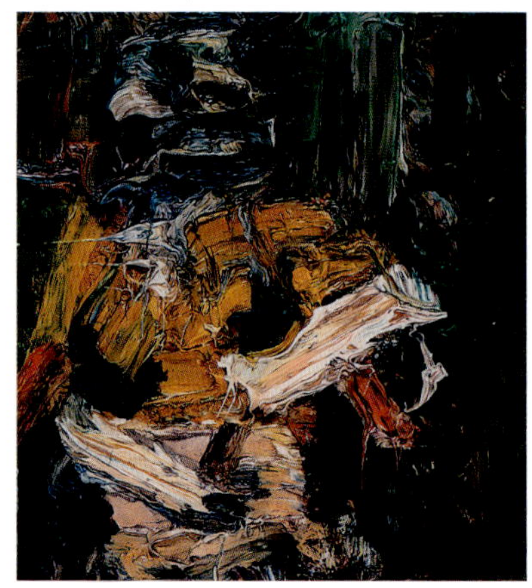

Brown, Glenn b.1966
Decline and Fall 1995
oil & canvas on board 58.4 x 54.6
ACC9/1995

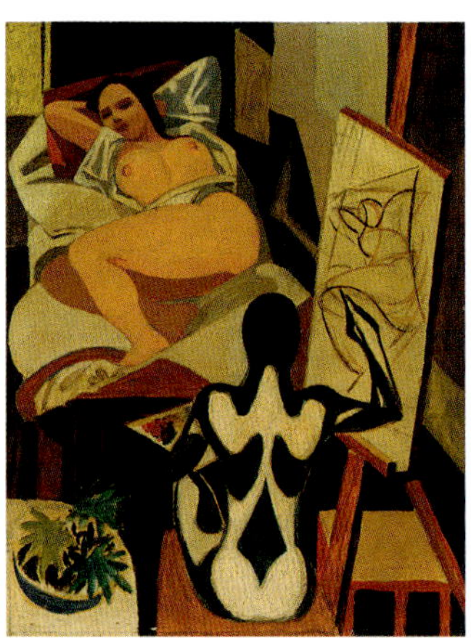

Buckland Wright, John 1897–1954
Interior 1941
oil on paper 17.9 x 14
AC 344

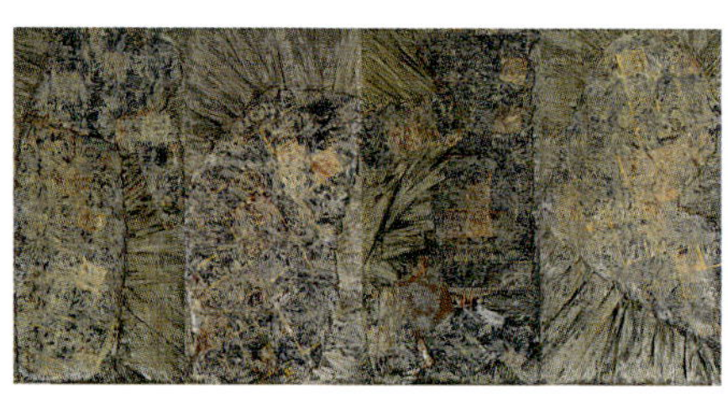

Buckley, Stephen b.1944
Rannoch 1971
acrylic & fibreglass on canvas 110 x 213.4
AC 1167

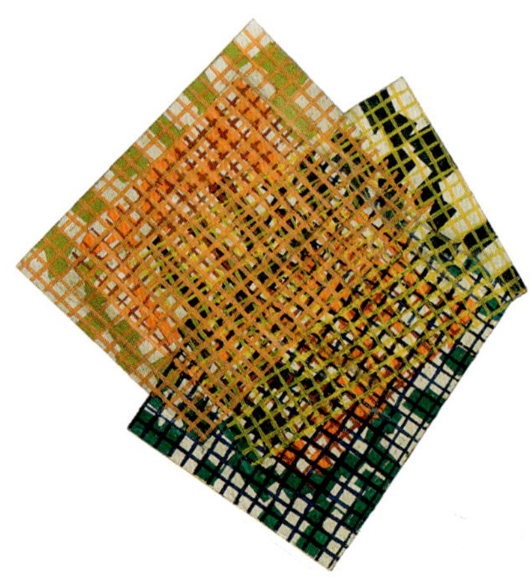

Buckley, Stephen b.1944
Head of a Young Girl No.2 1974
oil & acrylic on canvas 200 x 190
AC 1548

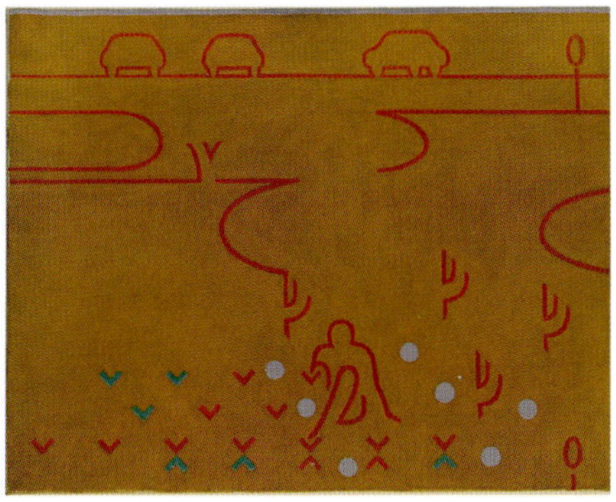

Buhler, Michael 1940–2009
Figure and Cars 1965
oil on canvas 71.1 x 91.5
AC 844

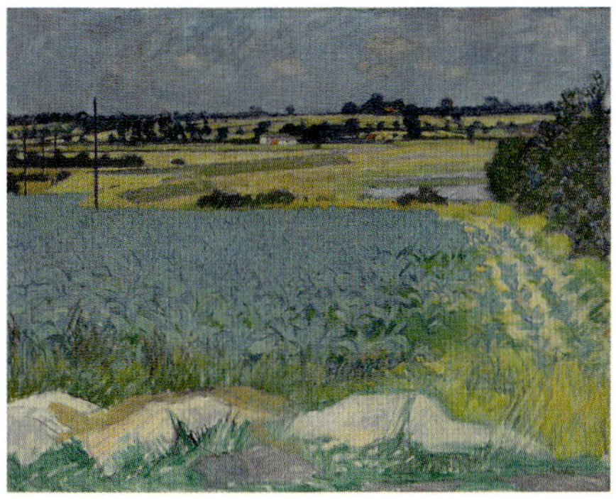

Buhler, Robert A. 1916–1989
Kale Field, Beaumont Quay 1950
oil on canvas 70 x 90.5
AC 159

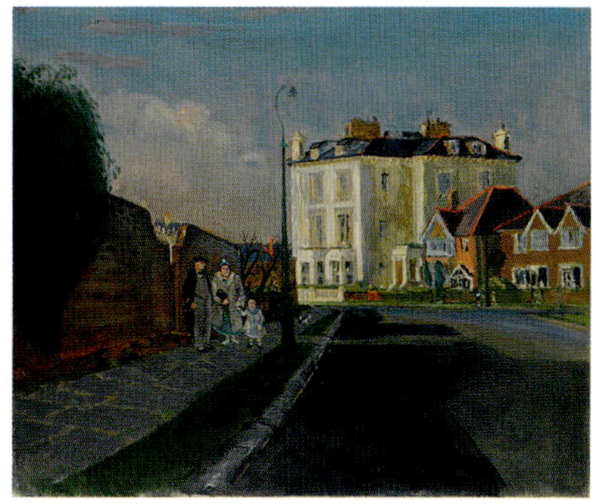

Burn, Rodney Joseph 1899–1984
White House, Chiswick 1961
oil on canvas 66 x 81.3
AC 563

Callery, Simon b.1960
Borough and Trinity 1993
oil & oil pastel on canvas 259.5 x 366
ACC150/1998

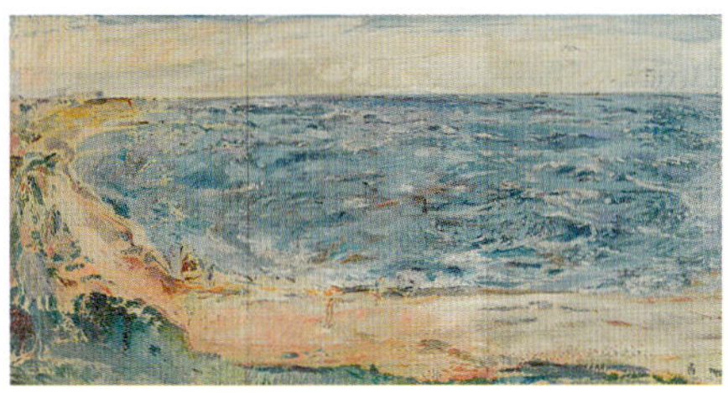

Camp, Jeffery b.1923
Blue Sea 1959
oil on board 101.5 x 195
AC 490

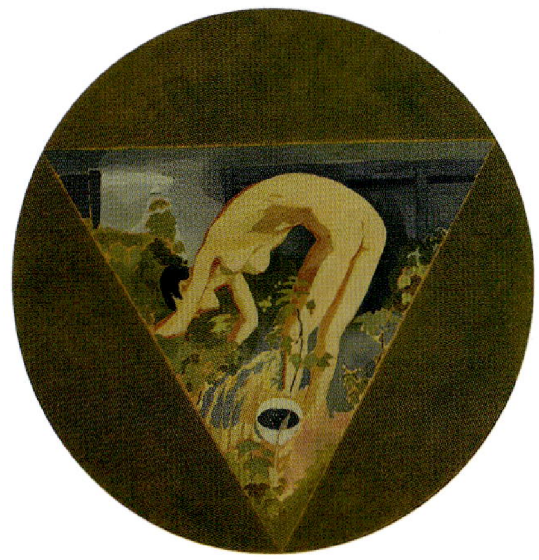

Camp, Jeffery b.1923
Laetitia Picking Blackcurrants 1967
oil & alkyd resin on board 61
AC 956

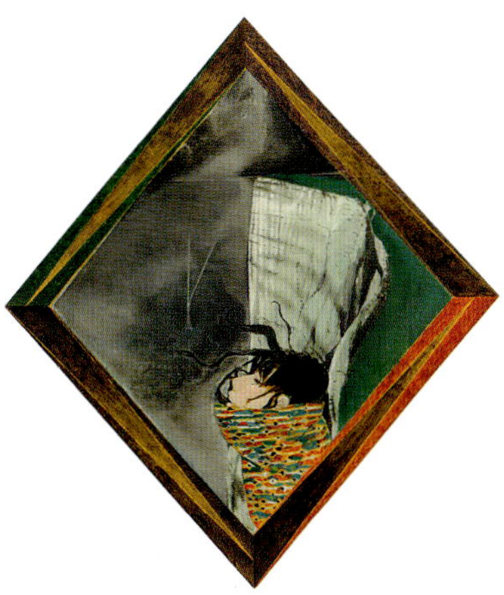

Camp, Jeffery b.1923
Beachy Head: Lighthouse by Night 1969
oil & alkyd resin on board 135.9 x 121
AC 1272

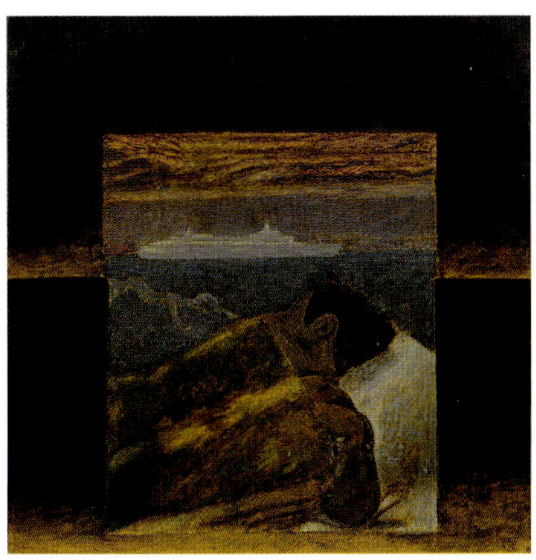

Camp, Jeffery b.1923
Sleeper with Passing Liner 1975
oil on board 50.8 x 51.1
AC 1909

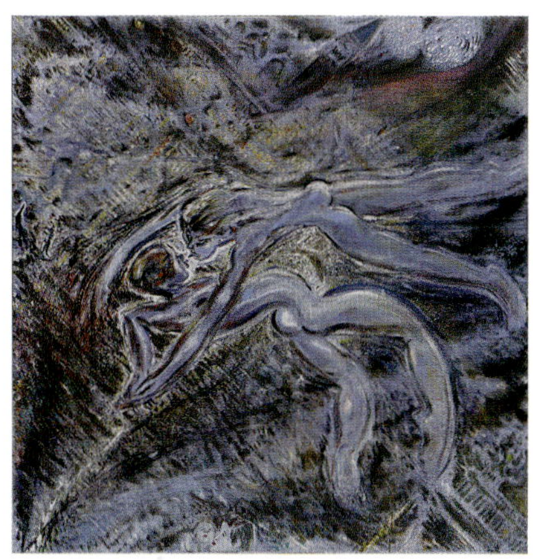

Camp, Jeffery b.1923
Venice 1986
oil on canvas 215.5 x 215.5
AC 5419

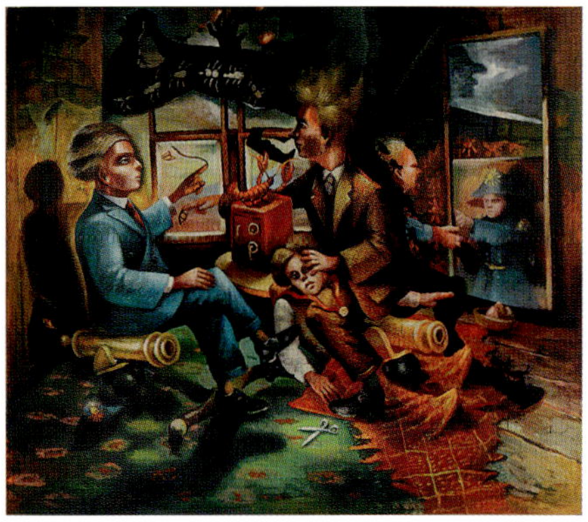

Campbell, Steven 1953–2007
Napoleonic Silhouettist Cutting the Progress of the War 1986–1987
oil on canvas 240 x 281
AC 5468

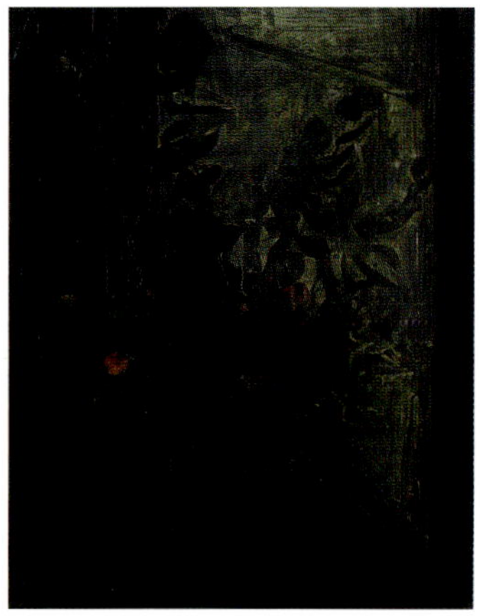

Carnegie, Gillian b.1971
Mono 2005
oil on board 73.3 x 58.7
ACC2/2005

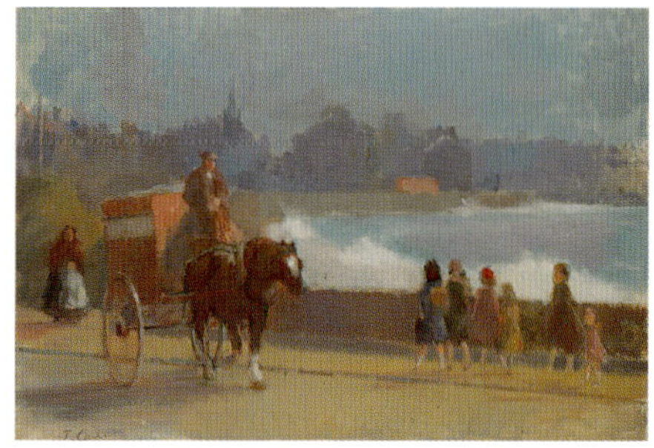

Carr, Thomas James 1909–1999
High Tide
oil on canvas 50.5 x 75.9
AC 88

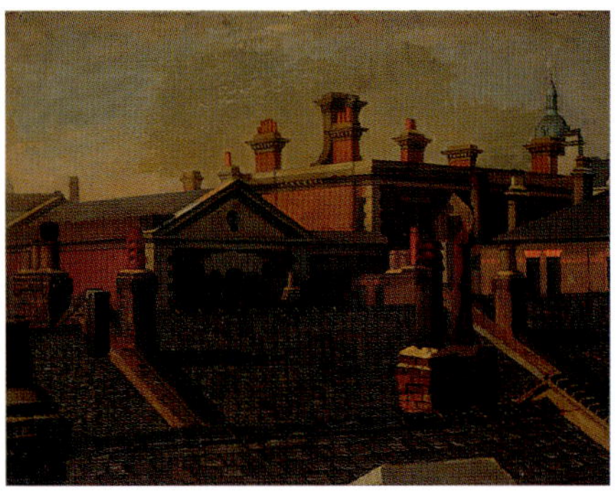

Carter, Bernard Arthur Ruston (Sam) 1909–2006
Roofs at Swiss Cottage 1952
oil on canvas 38.1 x 50.8
AC 769

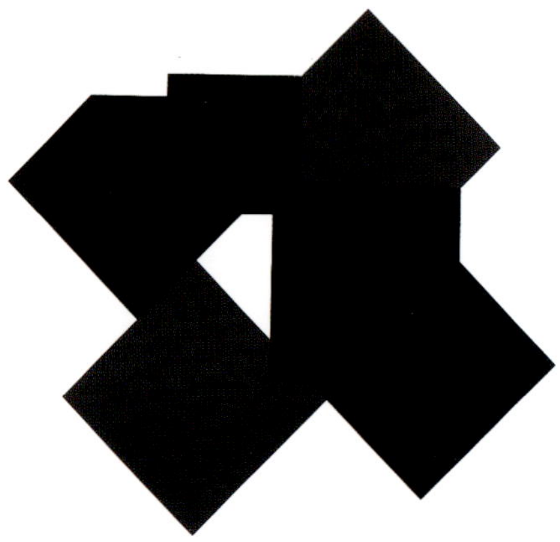

Carter, John b.1942
Squares I 1977–1978
oil on wood 103.4 x 111
AC 2006

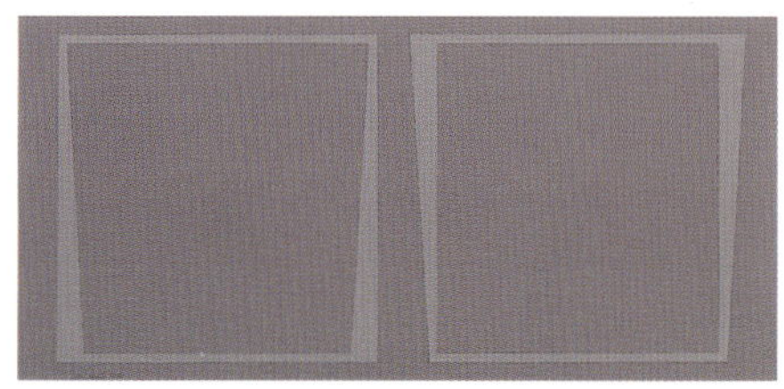

Carter, John b.1942
Two Frames: Greys 1980
acrylic on paper 25.7 x 55
AC 5245

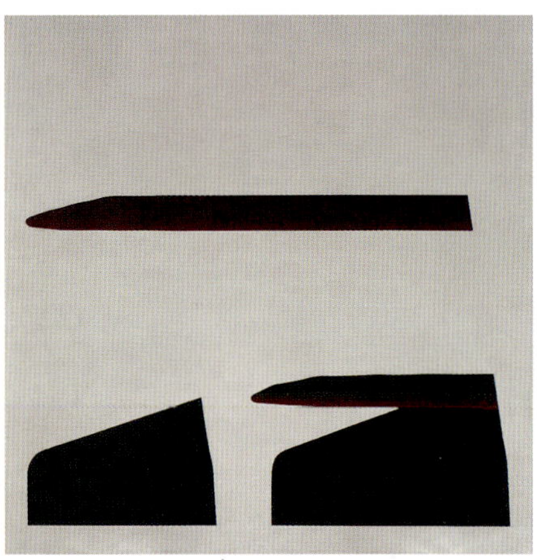

Cartwright, Peter b.1939
Three 1967
oil on canvas 142.2 x 144.8
AC 926

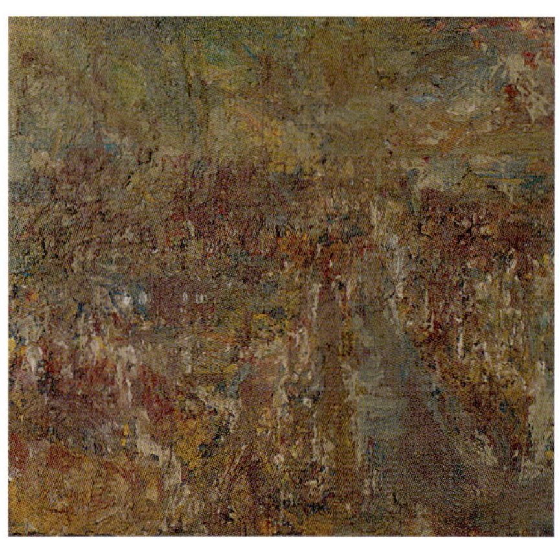

Caughlin, Ian b.1948
View from a Roof, Rostrevor Road, Fulham 1976–1978
oil on canvas 111.8 x 127
AC 1983

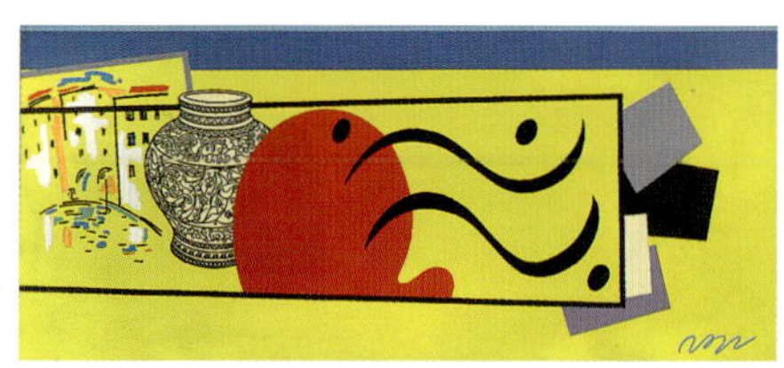

Caulfield, Patrick 1936–2005
Artist's Studio 1964
oil on board 91.4 x 281.4
AC 774

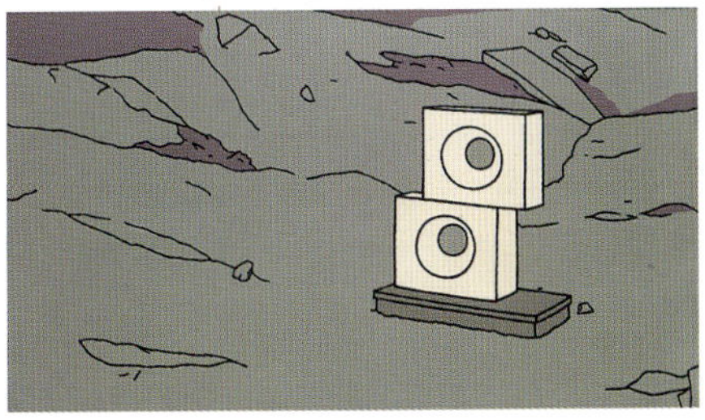

Caulfield, Patrick 1936–2005
Sculpture in a Landscape 1966
oil on board 121.9 x 213.3
AC 889

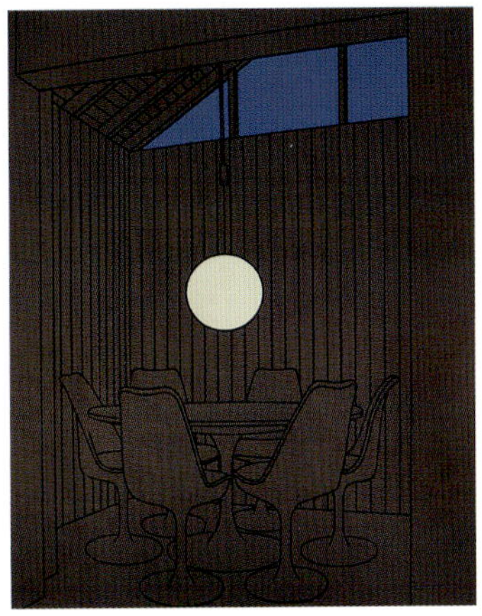

Caulfield, Patrick 1936–2005
Dining Recess 1972
oil on canvas 274.5 x 213.5
AC 1431

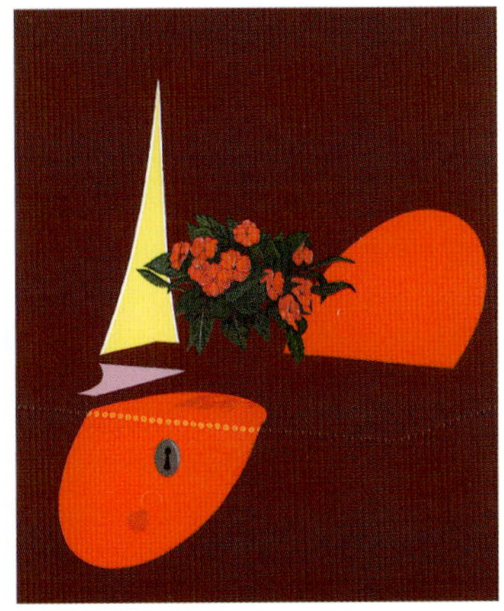

Caulfield, Patrick 1936–2005
Registry Office 1997
acrylic on canvas 92.1 x 76.8
ACC52/1997

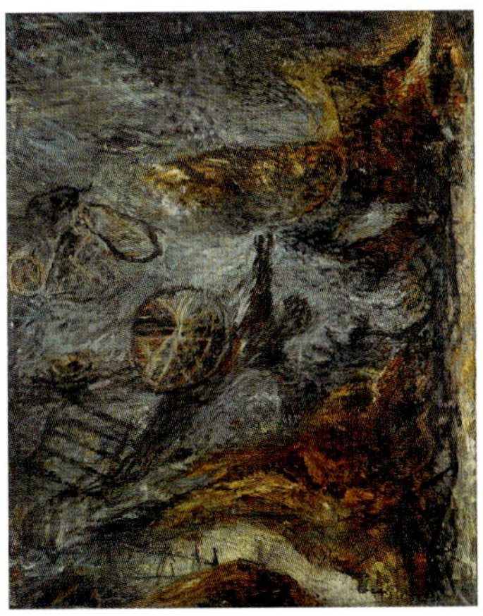

Chalkley, Brian b.1948
Stratford Landscape 1986
oil on canvas 298.6 x 236.8
AC 5482

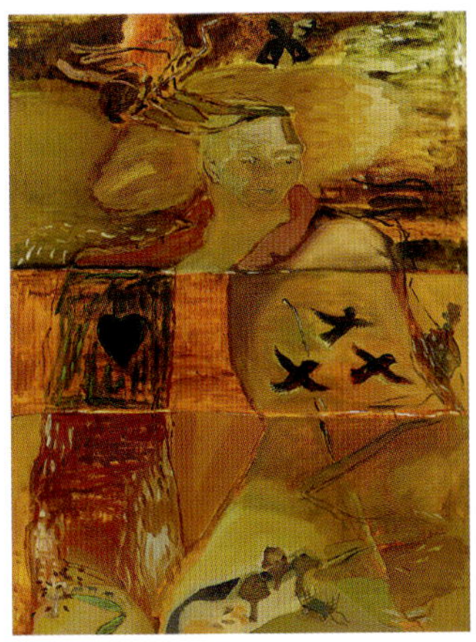

Chambers, Stephen b.1960
Sicily 1986
oil on canvas 243.7 x 187.7
AC 5435

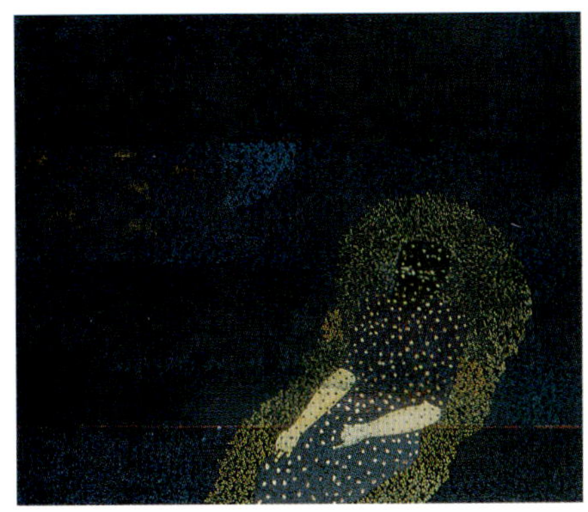

Chambers, Stephen b.1960
This is a Woman You Know Well 1993–1995
oil on canvas 152.5 x 183
ACC12/1996

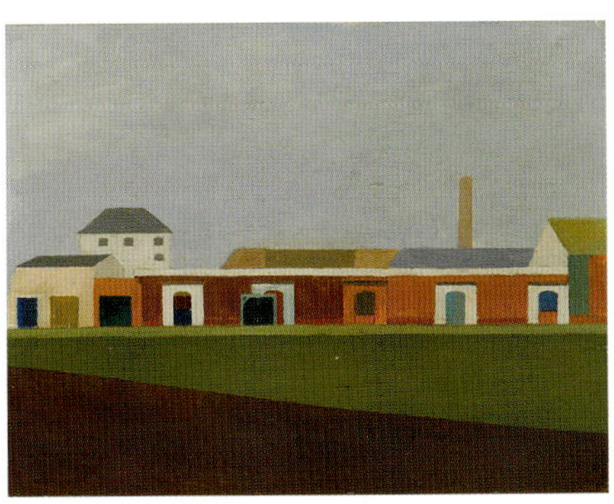

Chaplin, Stephen b.1934
Painting 1967: 1 1967–1968
oil on hardboard 40.5 x 53.5
AC 1157

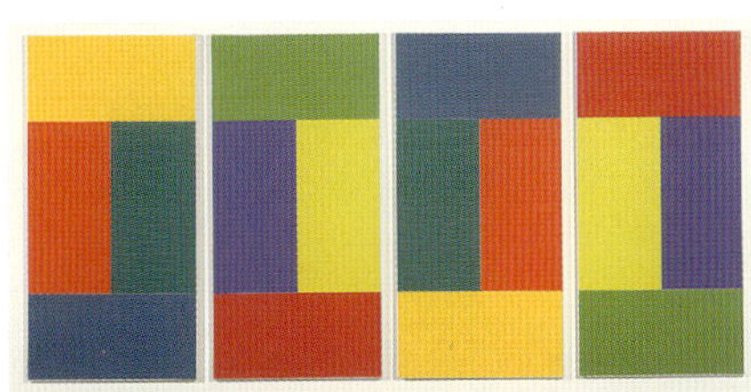

Charlett, Nicole b.1957
4 Colour Elements, 2 Directions 1981–1982
oil on cotton duck 122.5 x 61.7; 122.5 x 61.7; 122.5 x 61.7; 122.5 x 61.7
AC 5195a-d

Charlton, Alan b.1948
Channel, 1972 1972
acrylic on canvas 269 x 142
AC 1265

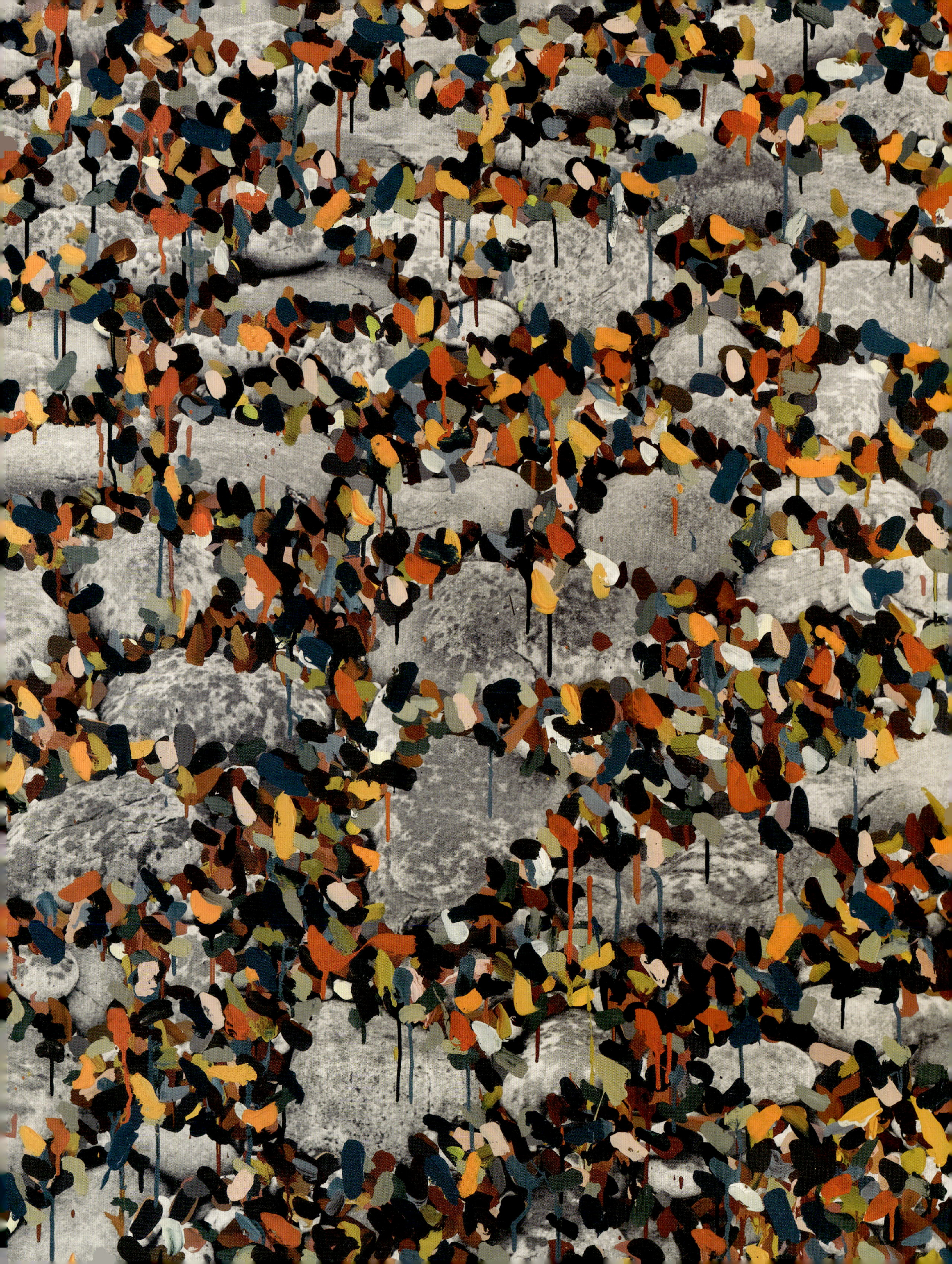

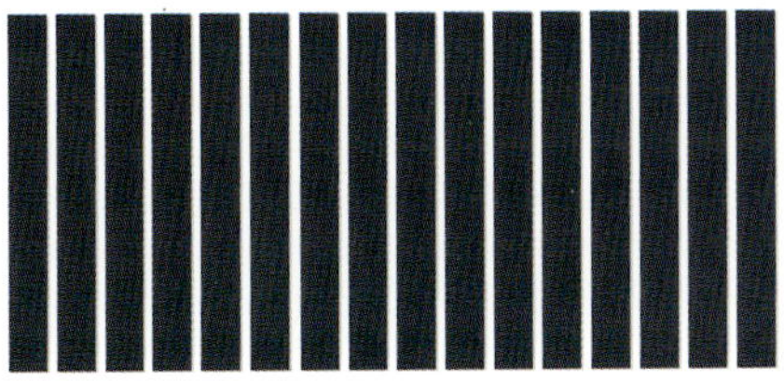

Charlton, Alan b.1948
Sixteen Part Line Painting 1985
acrylic & emulsion on cotton duck
211.5 x 427.5
AC 5401

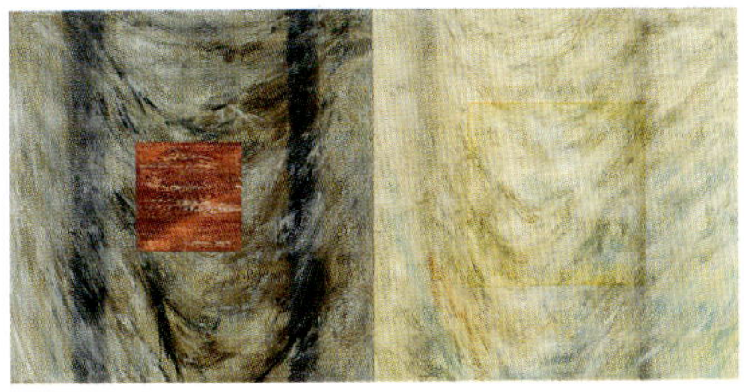

Chevska, Maria b.1948
Convulsive Cloak 1989–1990
oil & encaustic on linen on canvas
169.7 x 335.6
ACC4/1990

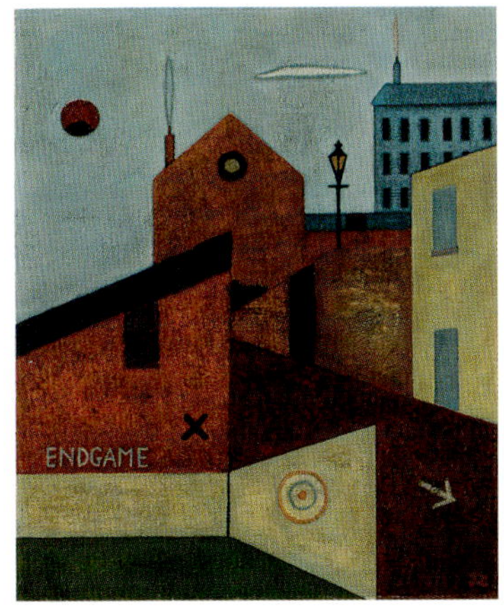

Christopherson, John 1921–1996
Endgame 1973
oil on board 59.1 x 49.5
AC 2014

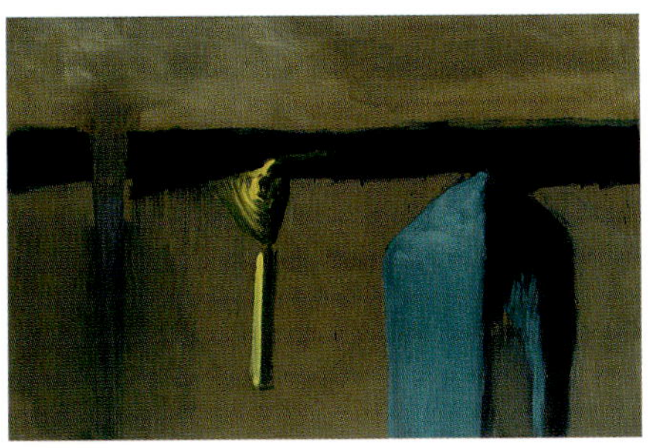

Christophorou, Christopher b.1957
Remnants 1987
oil on canvas 167 x 259
AC 5555

Chubb, Shirley b.1959
Change 1991
acrylic, PVA & paper on canvas 112.5 x 112
ACC45/1991

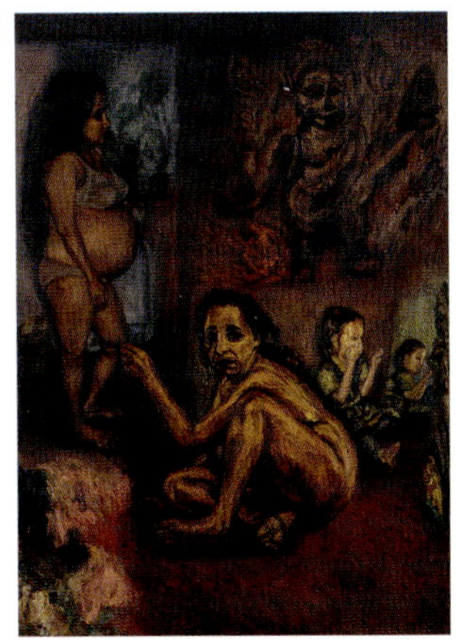

Chuhan, J. b.1955
Self Portrait 1995
oil on canvas 210 x 150
ACC40/1995

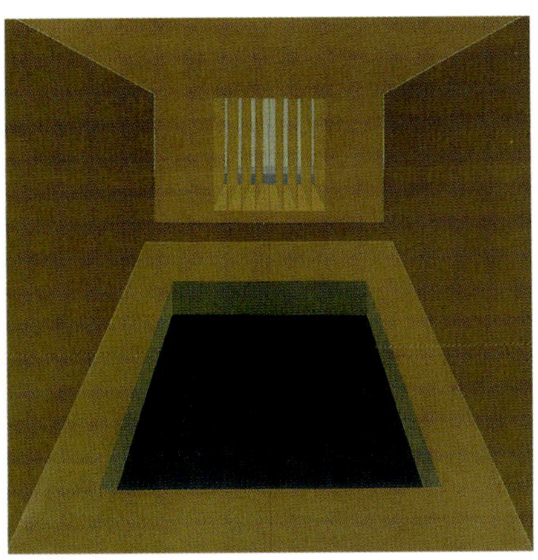

Cina, Colin b.1943
Running Deep 1967
acrylic on canvas 213.4 x 213.4
AC 923

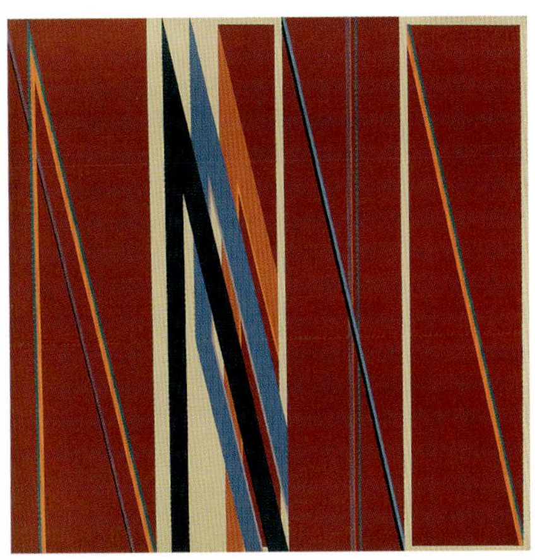

Cina, Colin b.1943
MH/8 1970
acrylic on canvas 274.3 x 274.3
AC 1154

Cina, Colin b.1943
Untitled Drawing V 1974
acrylic, gouache, watercolour & pencil on paper 24.9 x 34.2
AC 1409

Facing page: McKeever, Ian, b.1946, *Islands 8a 1981* (detail), 1981, (p. 107)

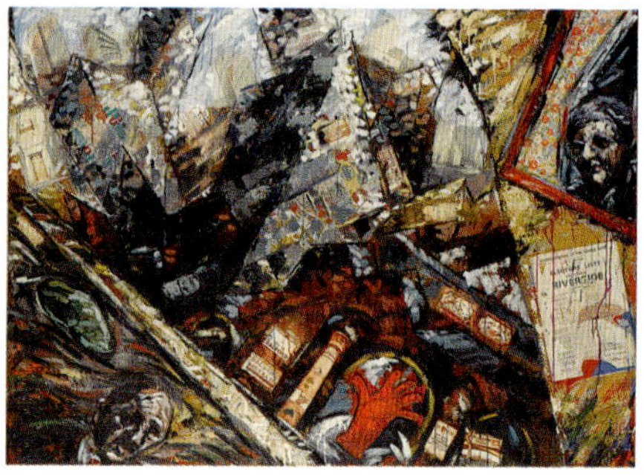

Clarke, Pete b.1951
Municipal Modernism: The Cloth Cap and the Red Glove 1986
oil & collage on canvas 152.7 x 214
AC 5479

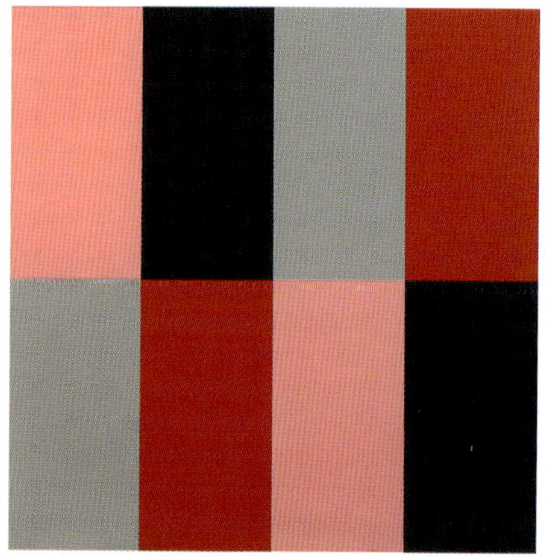

Clarke, Trevor b.1949
Rotated Variations in Relation to a Constant, Series 2, T. C. O. Variations III B4 1980
oil on canvas 150.6 x 150.3
AC 5184

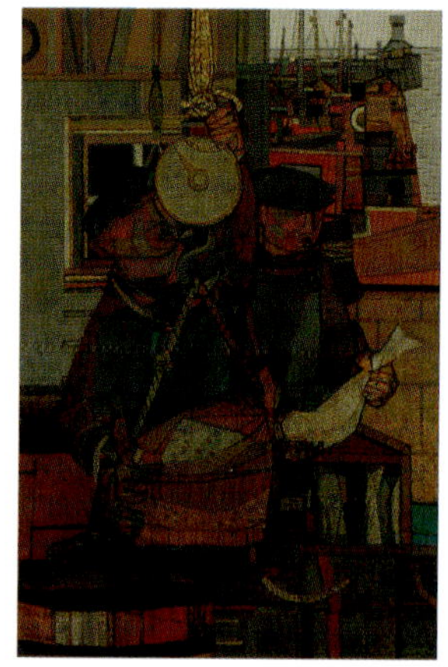

Clough, Prunella 1919–1999
Lowestoft Harbour 1951
oil on canvas 162.6 x 106.7
AC 186

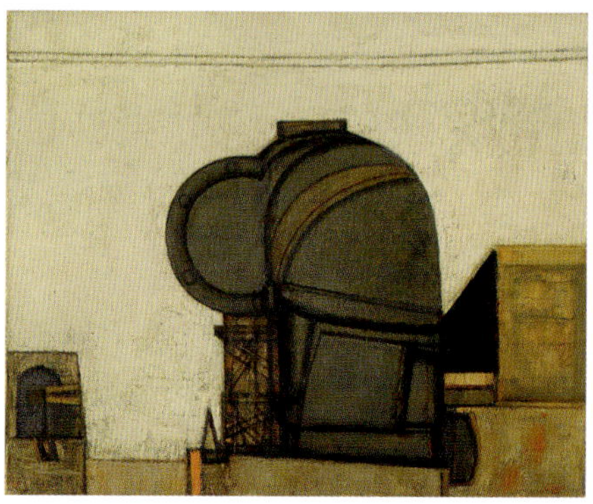

Clough, Prunella 1919–1999
Industrial Plant II 1954
oil on canvas 70 x 87.2
AC 453

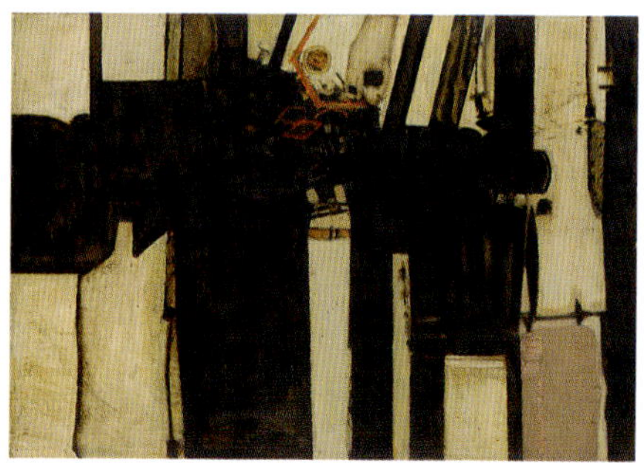

Clough, Prunella 1919–1999
Industrial Interior V 1960
oil on board 83 x 122
AC 538

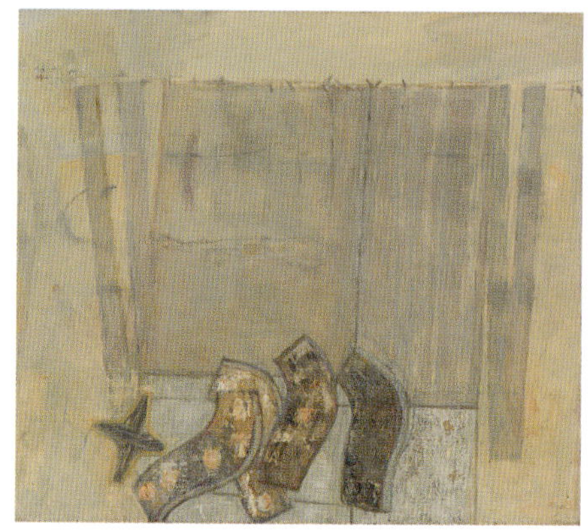

Clough, Prunella 1919–1999
Landscape with Sections 1962
oil on canvas 76 x 86.5
AC 758

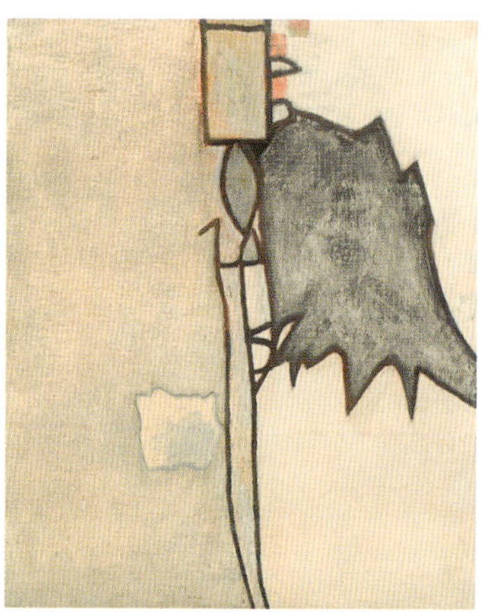

Clough, Prunella 1919–1999
Garden Hedge 1965
oil on canvas 76 x 64
ACA 40

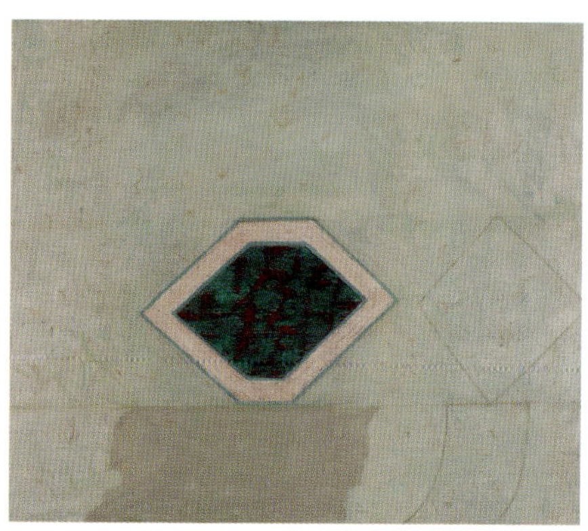

Clough, Prunella 1919–1999
Untitled 1965
oil on canvas 72.2 x 85
AC 951

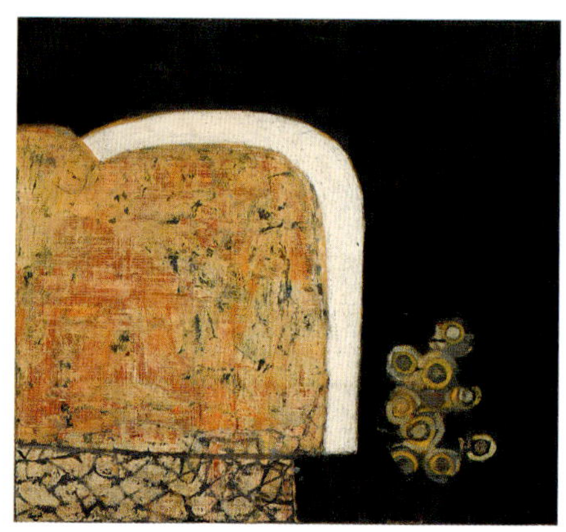

Clough, Prunella 1919–1999
Edge 1966
oil on canvas 101.6 x 106.7
ACA 39

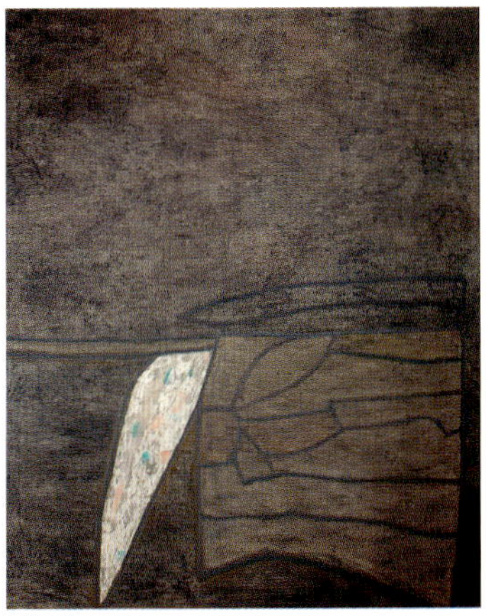

Clough, Prunella 1919–1999
South-West Nocturne 1970
oil on canvas 142 x 116.5
AC 1133

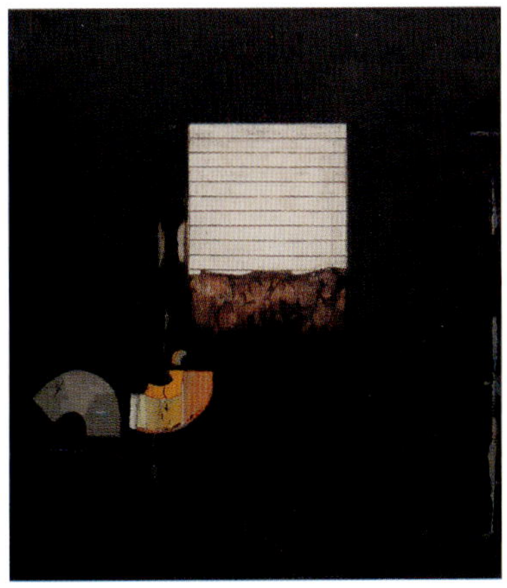

Clough, Prunella 1919–1999
Waterford Yard 1970
oil on canvas 146.5 x 111
AC 1134

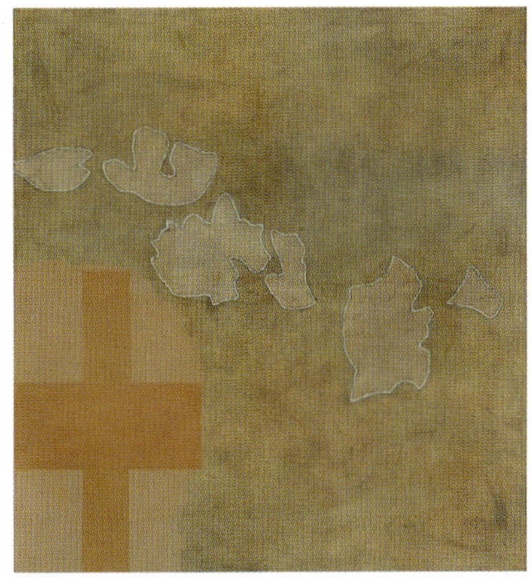

Clough, Prunella 1919–1999
Inside and Outside 1970–1975
oil on canvas 152.4 x 142.2
AC 1609

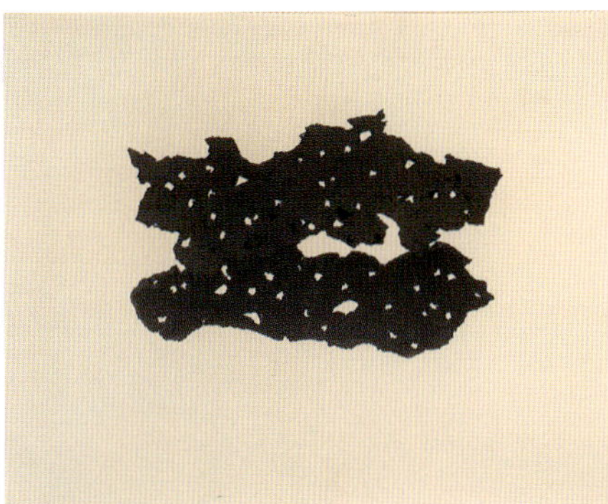

Clough, Prunella 1919–1999
Study for 'Perforated Fragment' 1985
acrylic on paper 51.4 x 55.3
AC 5405

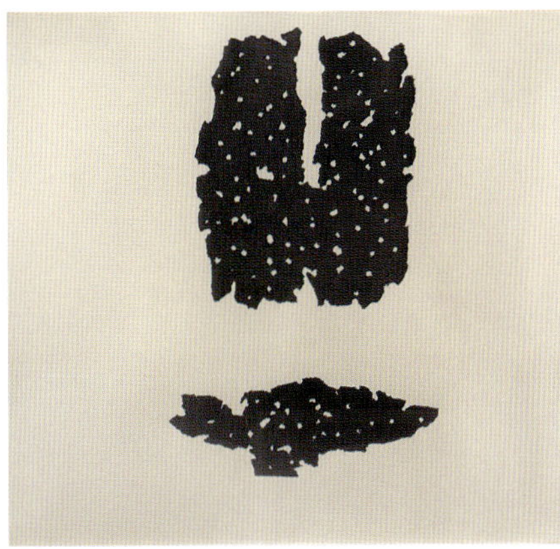

Clough, Prunella 1919–1999
Study for 'Perforated Fragment' 1985
acrylic on paper 33.6 x 43.3
AC 5478

Clough, Prunella 1919–1999
Perforated Fragment 1985
oil on canvas 149.9 x 123.2
AC 5404

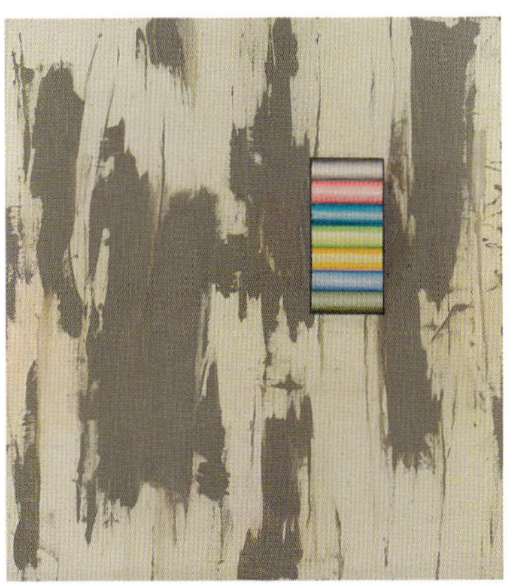

Clough, Prunella 1919–1999
Samples 1997
oil on canvas 131.5 x 119.6
ACC27/1998

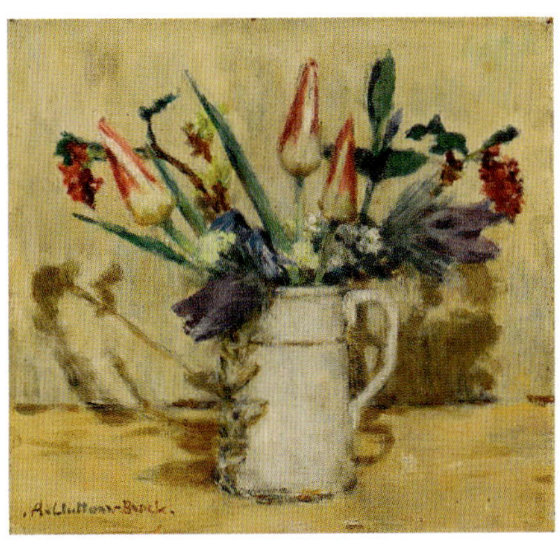

Clutton-Brock, Alan Francis 1904–1976
Early Tulips 1953
oil on canvas 22.9 x 26
AC 295

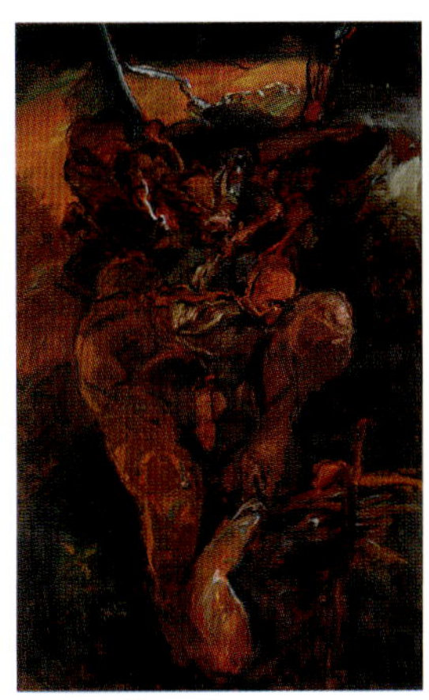

Cockrill, Maurice b.1936
Night 1983
oil on canvas 245 x 153
AC 5369

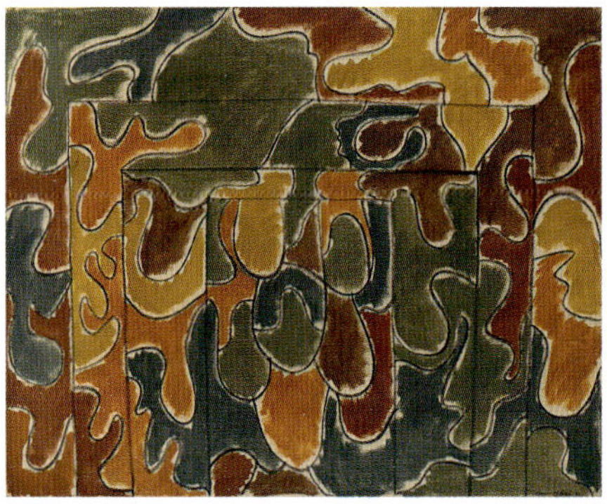

Cohen, Bernard b.1933
Petersburg 1962
oil on canvas 102 x 126
AC 605

Cohen, Bernard b.1933
Glow 1965
acrylic on canvas 213.4 x 274.3
AC 816

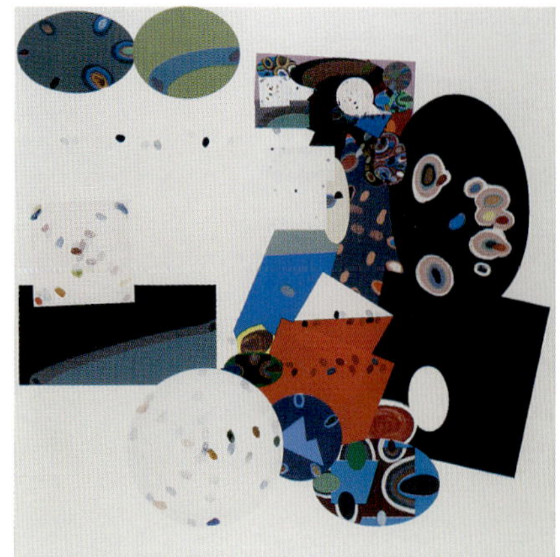

Cohen, Bernard b.1933
Mask 1975–1976
acrylic on linen 91.4 x 91.4
AC 1592

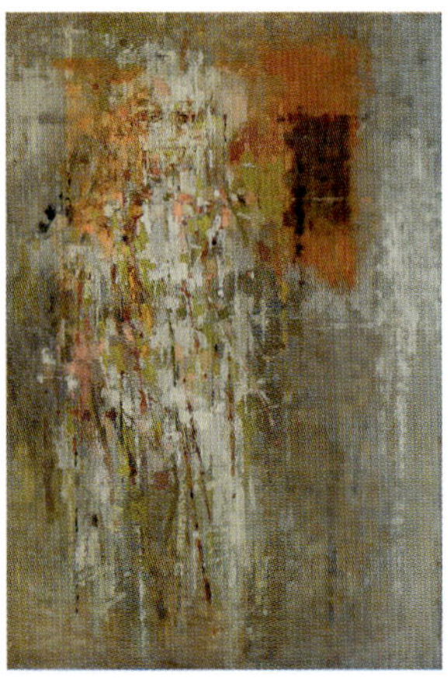

Cohen, Harold b.1928
Standing Figure 1954
oil on board 106.3 x 77.8
AC 354

Cohen, Harold b.1928
Beta Orionis 1961
oil on canvas 152 x 136.5
AC 583

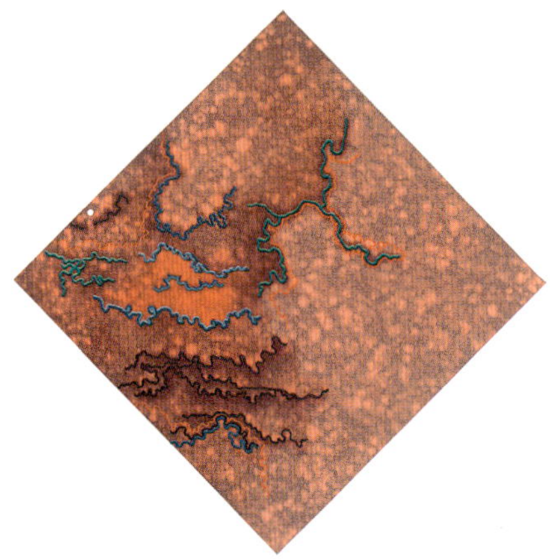

Cohen, Harold b.1928
Untitled 1965
oil on canvas 99 x 99
AC 825

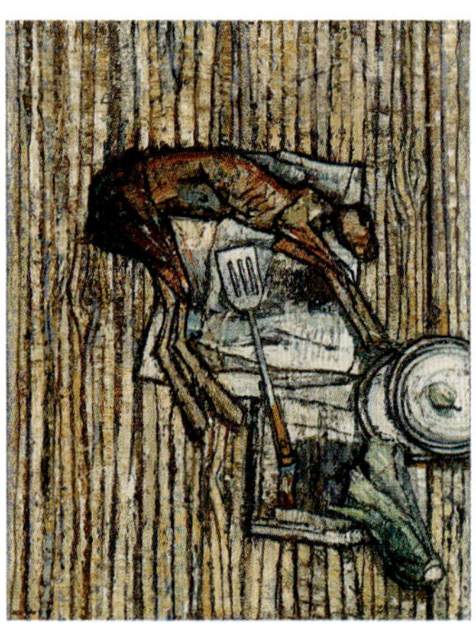

Coker, Peter 1926–2004
Dead Hare on Table 1955
oil on canvas 126.5 x 101.2
AC 391

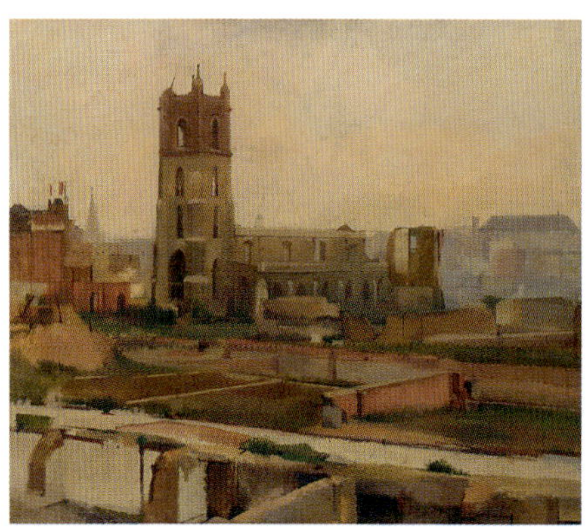

Coldstream, William Menzies 1908–1987
Cripplegate c.1946
oil on canvas 78.7 x 91.4
AC 134

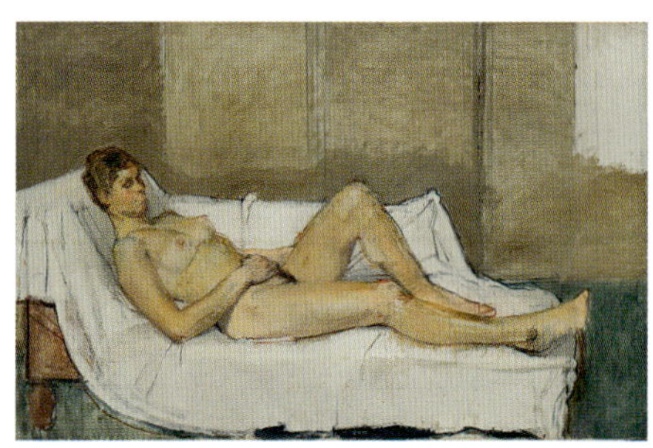

Coldstream, William Menzies 1908–1987
Reclining Nude 1953–1954
oil on canvas 87 x 134.5
ACC5/1958

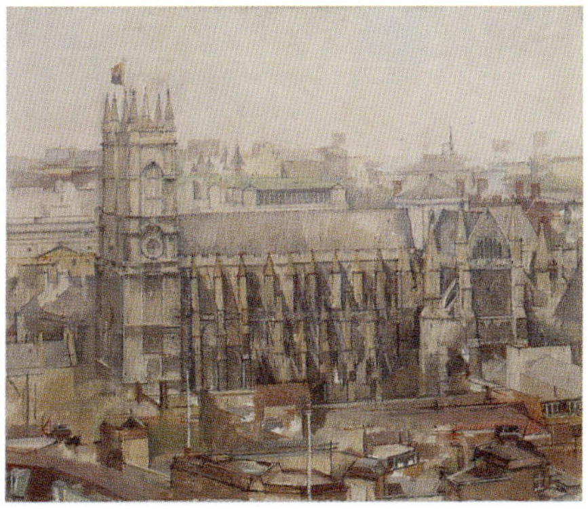

Coldstream, William Menzies 1908–1987
Westminster Abbey 1973–1974
oil on canvas 50.8 x 61
AC 1616

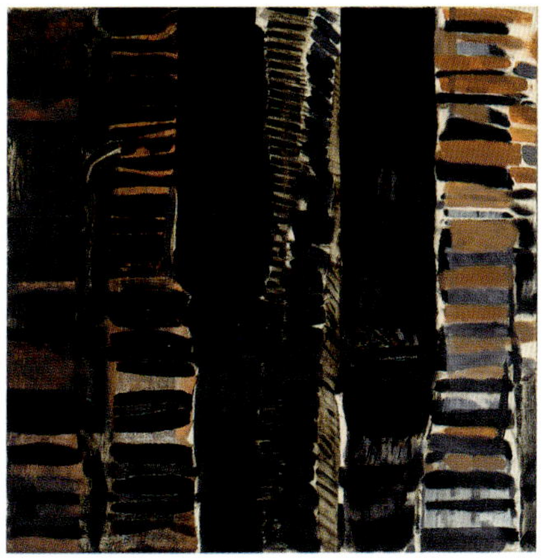

Collinge, Robert Anthony b.1934
Grey and Brown III 1965
oil on canvas 152.4 x 152.4
AC 784

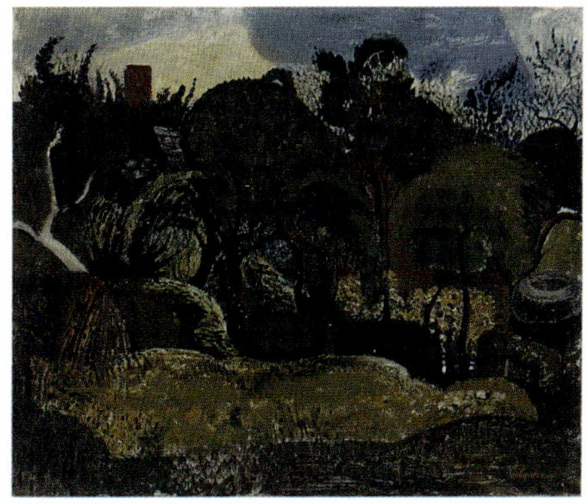

Colquhoun, Robert 1914–1962
Church Lench 1942
oil on canvas 50.8 x 60.5
AC 63

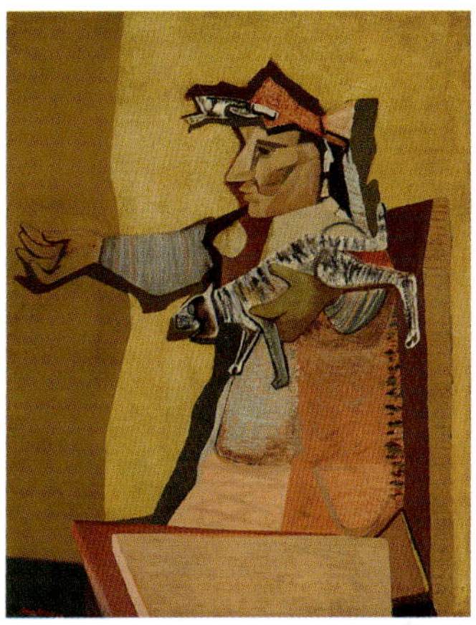

Colquhoun, Robert 1914–1962
Seated Woman and Cat 1946
oil on canvas 97 x 76
AC 6

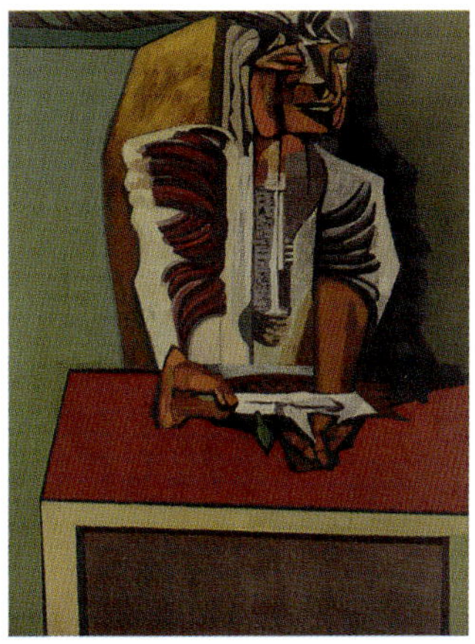

Colquhoun, Robert 1914–1962
The Gardener 1953
oil on canvas 101.6 x 78.7
AC 452

Constable, Martin b.1961
Untitled 1992
oil on MDF 54 x 46
ACC3/1992

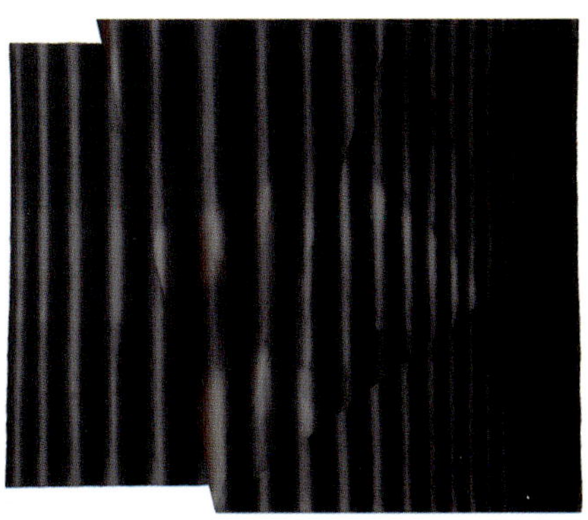

Cook, Barrie b.1929
Coleshill 1970
acrylic on canvas 243 x 300
AC 1136

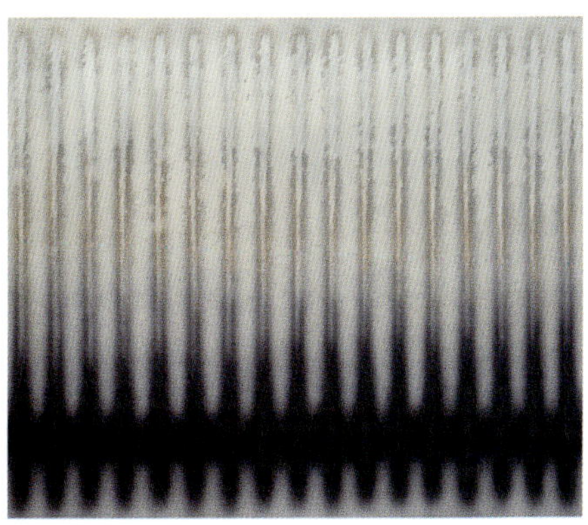

Cook, Barrie b.1929
Continuum 1976–1978
acrylic & chalk on canvas 169.3 x 203
AC 4087

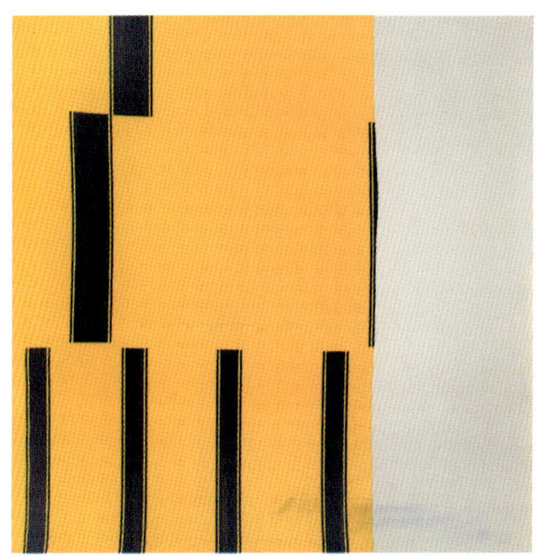

Cook, Ben b.1967
Aerial View of the Harbour, Marseilles (from the 'Found Paintings' series) 1998
printed acrylic fabric 145 x 145
ACC125/1998

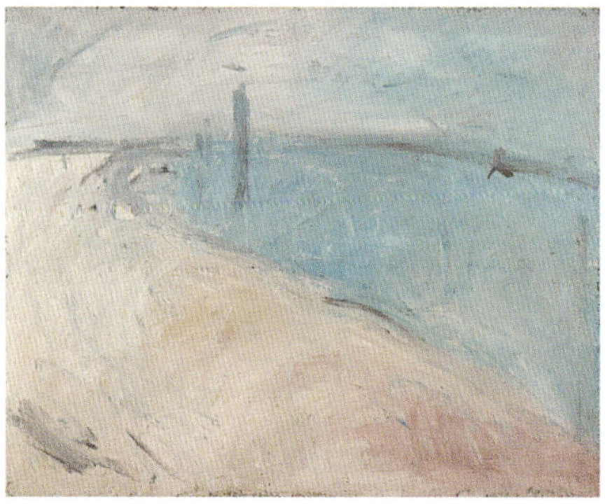

Cook, Richard Vernon Francis b.1947
Summer Morning, Lelant 2000
oil on marine plywood 122 x 152
ACC28/2000

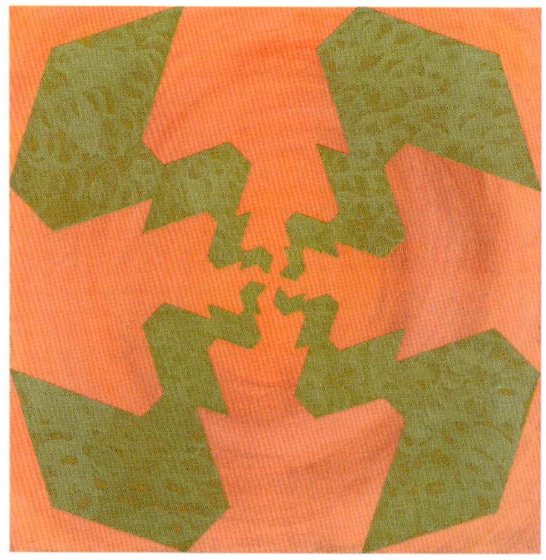

Cook, Roger b.1940
Untitled R.11 1964
PVA on canvas 182.9 x 182.9
AC 752

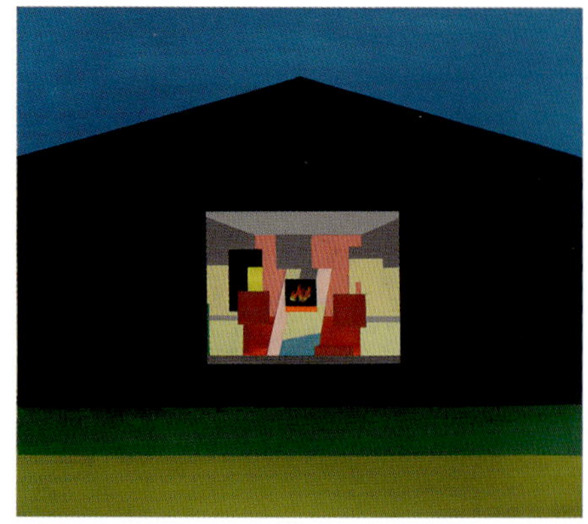

Coombs, Daniel b.1971
Night Bungalow I 1995
acrylic on canvas 213.3 x 243.8
ACC155/1998

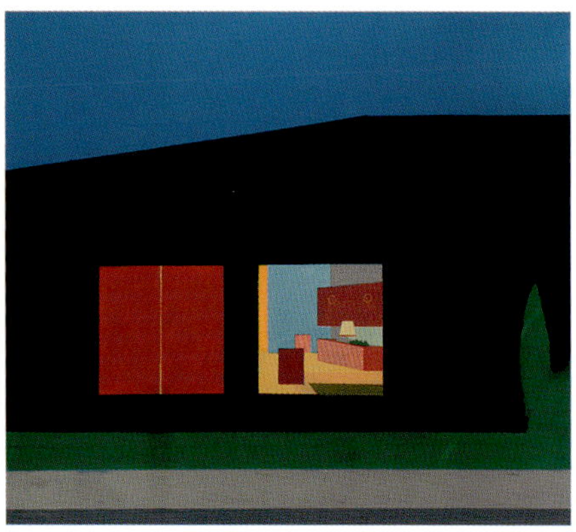

Coombs, Daniel b.1971
Night Bungalow II 1996
acrylic on canvas 213.3 x 243.8
ACC156/1998

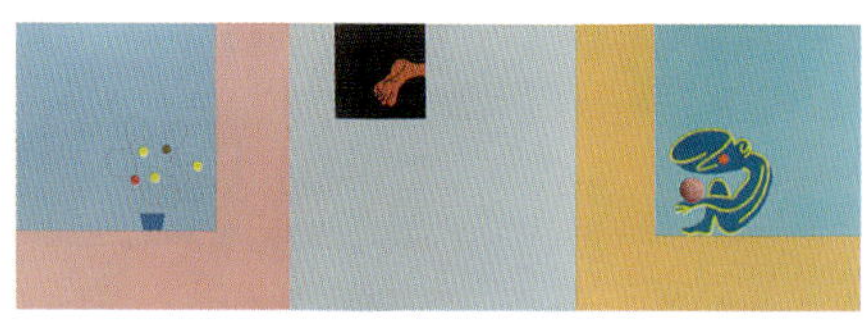

Coombs, Daniel b.1971
The Creation of the World 1995
acrylic on canvas 210 x 210; 210 x 210; 210 x 210
ACC154/1998

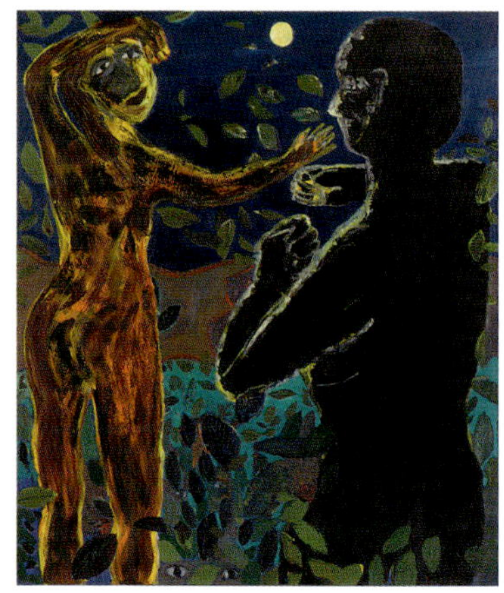

Cooper, Eileen b.1953
Going Ape 1983
oil on canvas 167.8 x 143.8
AC 5266

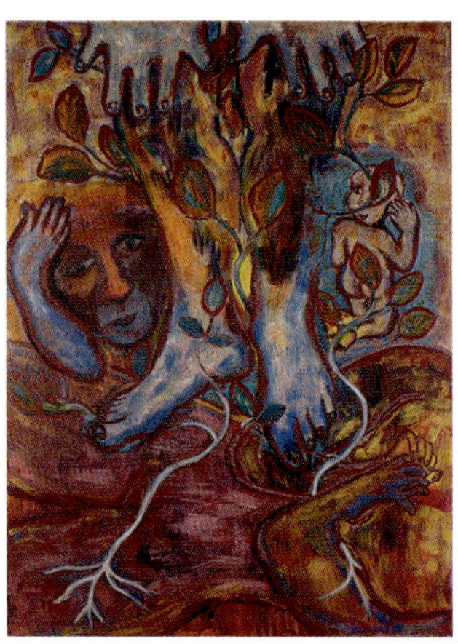

Cooper, Eileen b.1953
Putting Down Roots 1985
oil on canvas 243.3 x 182.8
AC 5375

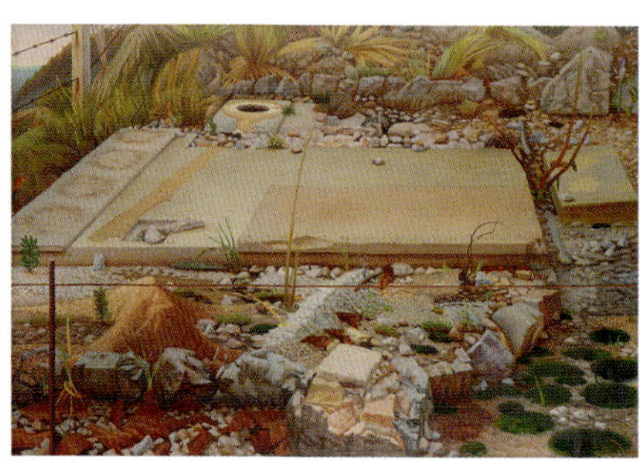

Cooper, Julian b.1947
Piece of Ground near Vence 1976
oil on canvas 122.3 x 183.2
AC 2042

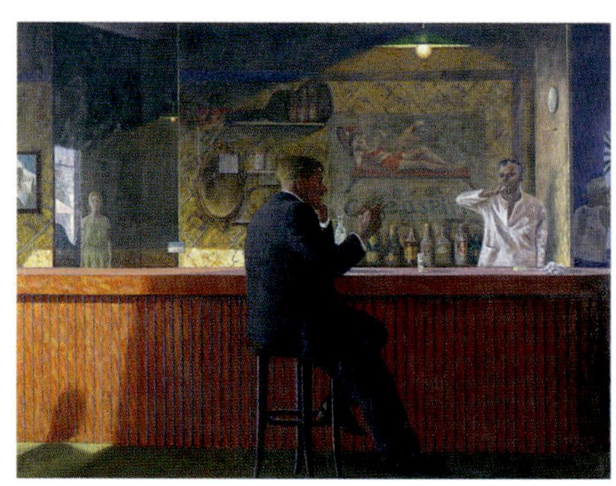

Cooper, Julian b.1947
Bella Vista Hotel (Under the Volcano) 1981–1983
oil on canvas 137.2 x 182.3
AC 5257

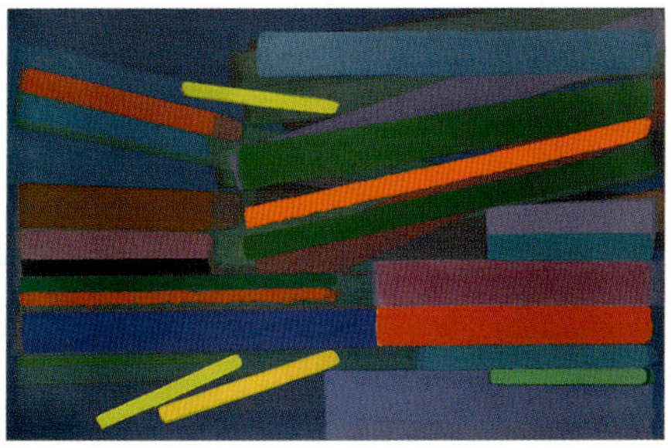

Copnall, John 1928–2007
Diagonals No.1 1976
acrylic on canvas 226 x 355
AC 1792

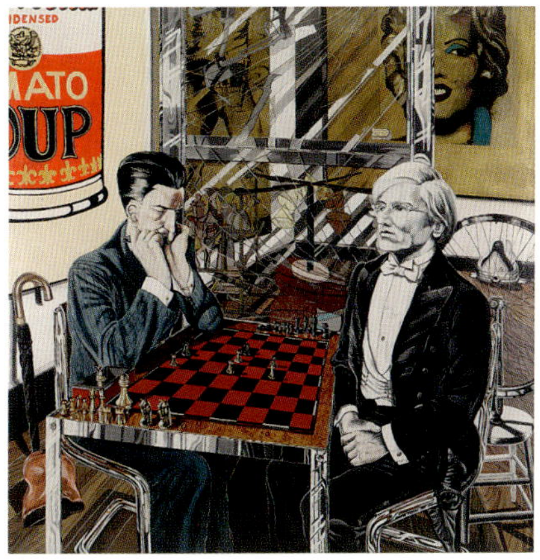

Core, Philip 1951–1989
The Chance Meeting on an Operating Table of a Sewing Machine and an Umbrella: Andy Warhol and Marcel Duchamp 1978
oil, acrylic & gouache on board 152.4 x 152.4
AC 1981

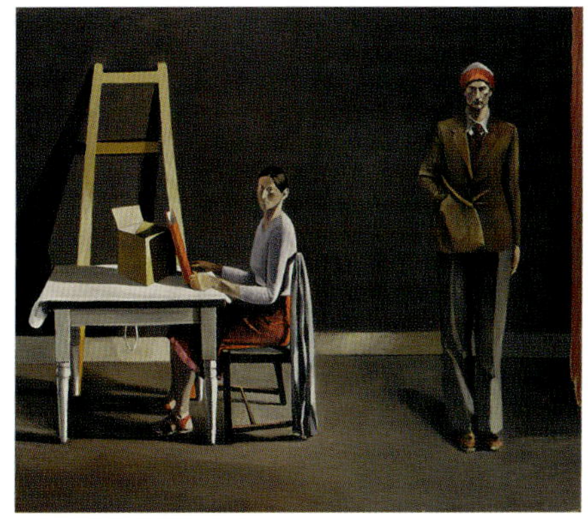

Couch, Christopher b.1946
Saturday 1979–1980
oil on canvas 228.2 x 264.5
AC 3072

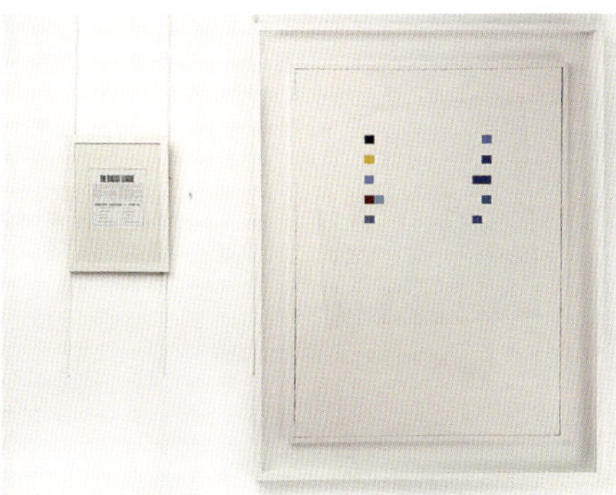

Coventry, Keith b.1958
White Suprematist Painting 1993
oil & ink on canvas, wood & paper 125 x 97
ACC14/1992

Coventry, Keith b.1958
White Abstract (Ullein Reviesky, the Last Deb) 1994
oil on canvas, wood, linen, gesso & glass 74.9 x 59.7
ACC157/1998

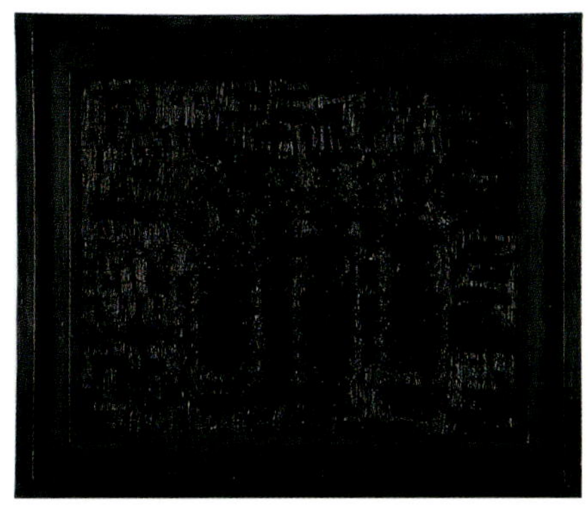

Coventry, Keith b.1958
Black Crack Pipes 1999
oil on canvas, wood, gesso & glass 36 x 43.5
ACC20/2008

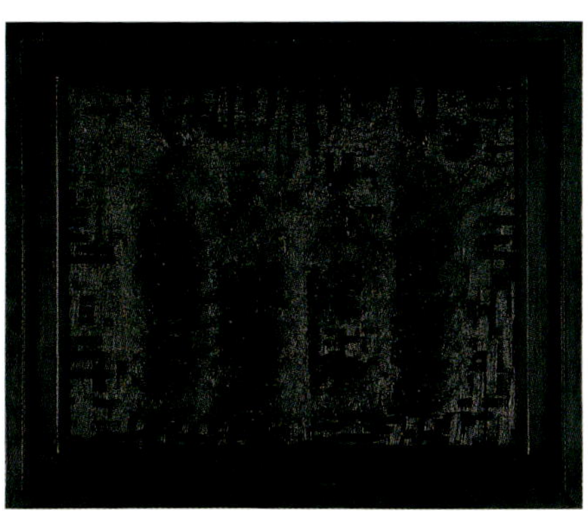

Coventry, Keith b.1958
Crack Pipes 1999
oil on canvas, wood, gesso & glass 36 x 43.5
ACC22/2008

Coventry, Keith b.1958
Crack Pipes 3 1999
oil on canvas, wood, gesso & glass 36 x 43.5
ACC21/2008

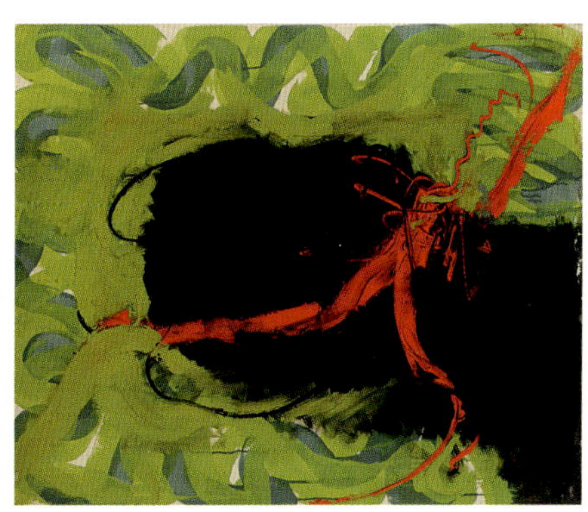

Coviello, Peter b.1930
Hanuman 1964–1967
oil & acrylic on canvas 101.6 x 127
AC 920

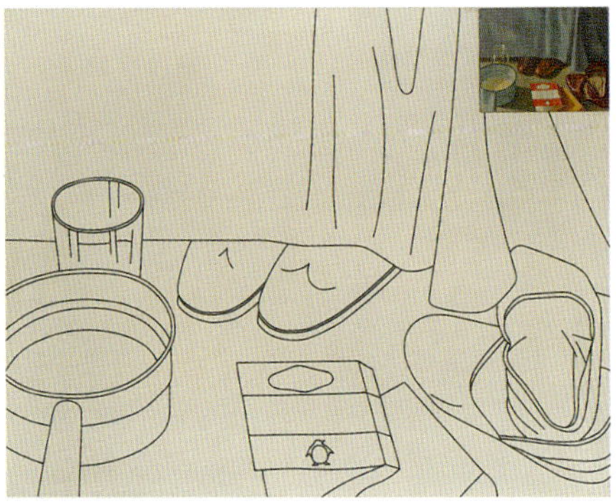

Craig-Martin, Michael b.1941
Painting and Picturing 1978
oil & tape on canvas 165.9 x 214
AC 2013

Craig-Martin, Michael b.1941
History Painting 1995
acrylic on canvas 183 x 366
ACC25/1995

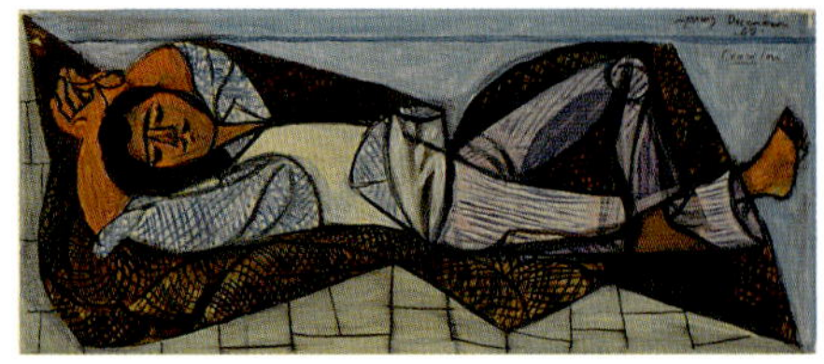

Craxton, John 1922–2009
Study for 'Sleeping Fisherman' 1948
oil on paper 23.5 x 56.5
AC 167

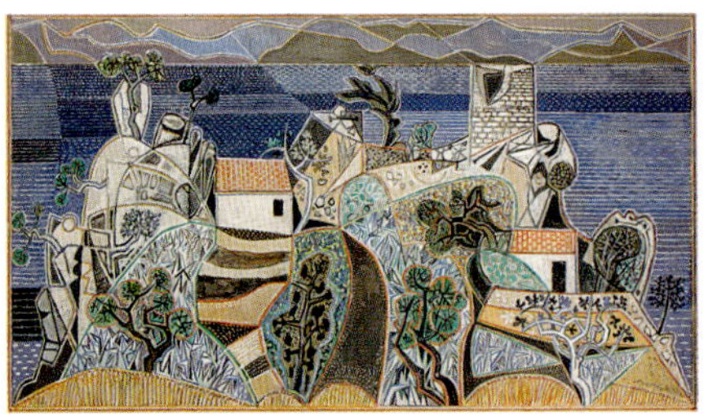

Craxton, John 1922–2009
Landscape, Hydra 1960–1961
filler & tempera on board 66.7 x 120.7
AC 566

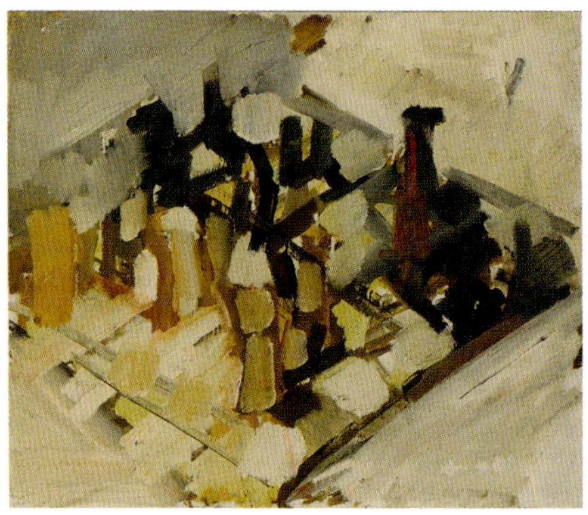

Creffield, Dennis b.1931
Chessmen 1965
oil on board 63.5 x 76.2
AC 849

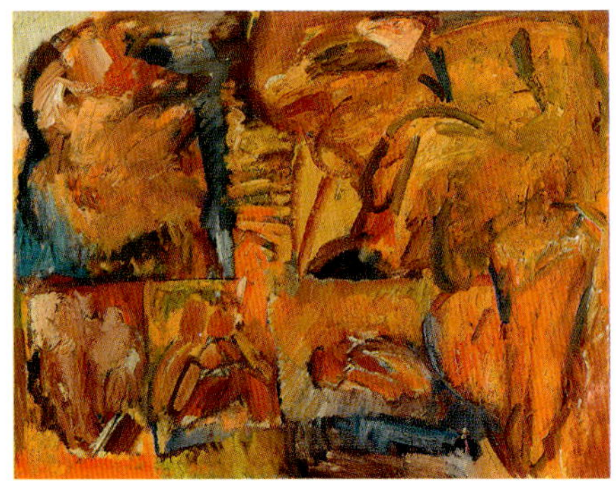

Creffield, Dennis b.1931
The Resource of Loneliness 1977
oil on canvas 121.9 x 152.4
AC 1852

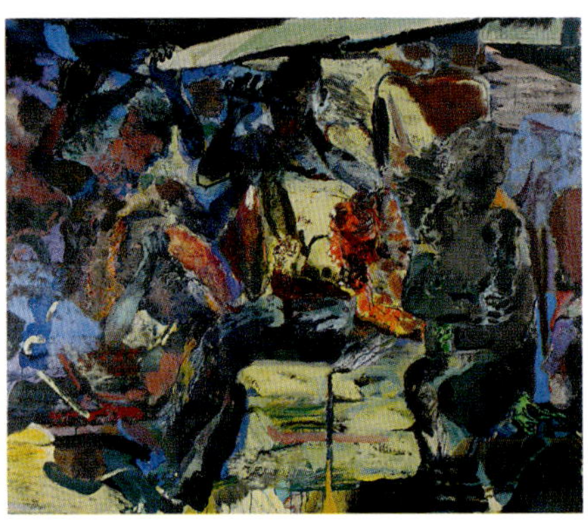

Crone, David b.1937
Summer Music 1989
oil on canvas 152 x 183
ACC12/1990

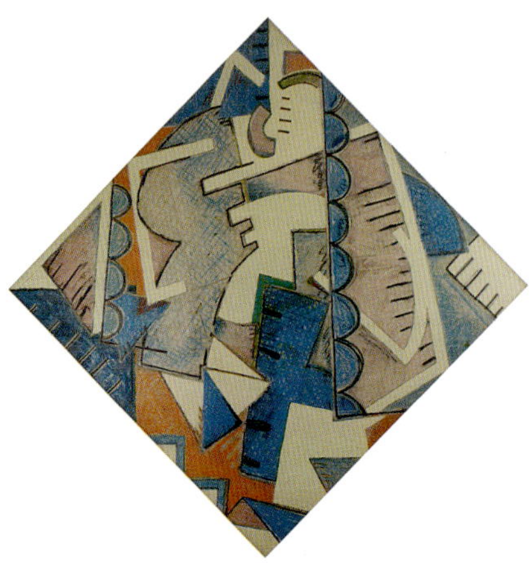

Crowley, Graham b.1950
Tug 1975
chalk, acrylic & charcoal on canvas 201 x 201
AC 1677

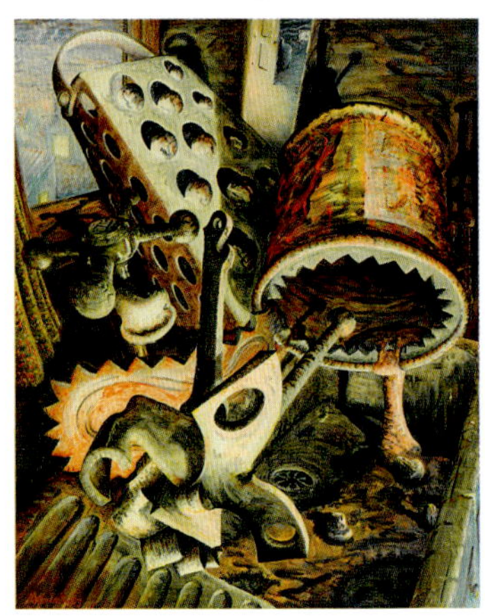

Crowley, Graham b.1950
Spider with Mushroom Soup 1982–1983
oil on canvas 152.4 x 121.9
AC 5225

Facing page: Cumming, Diana, b.1929, *The Flood* (detail), 1954, (p. 39)

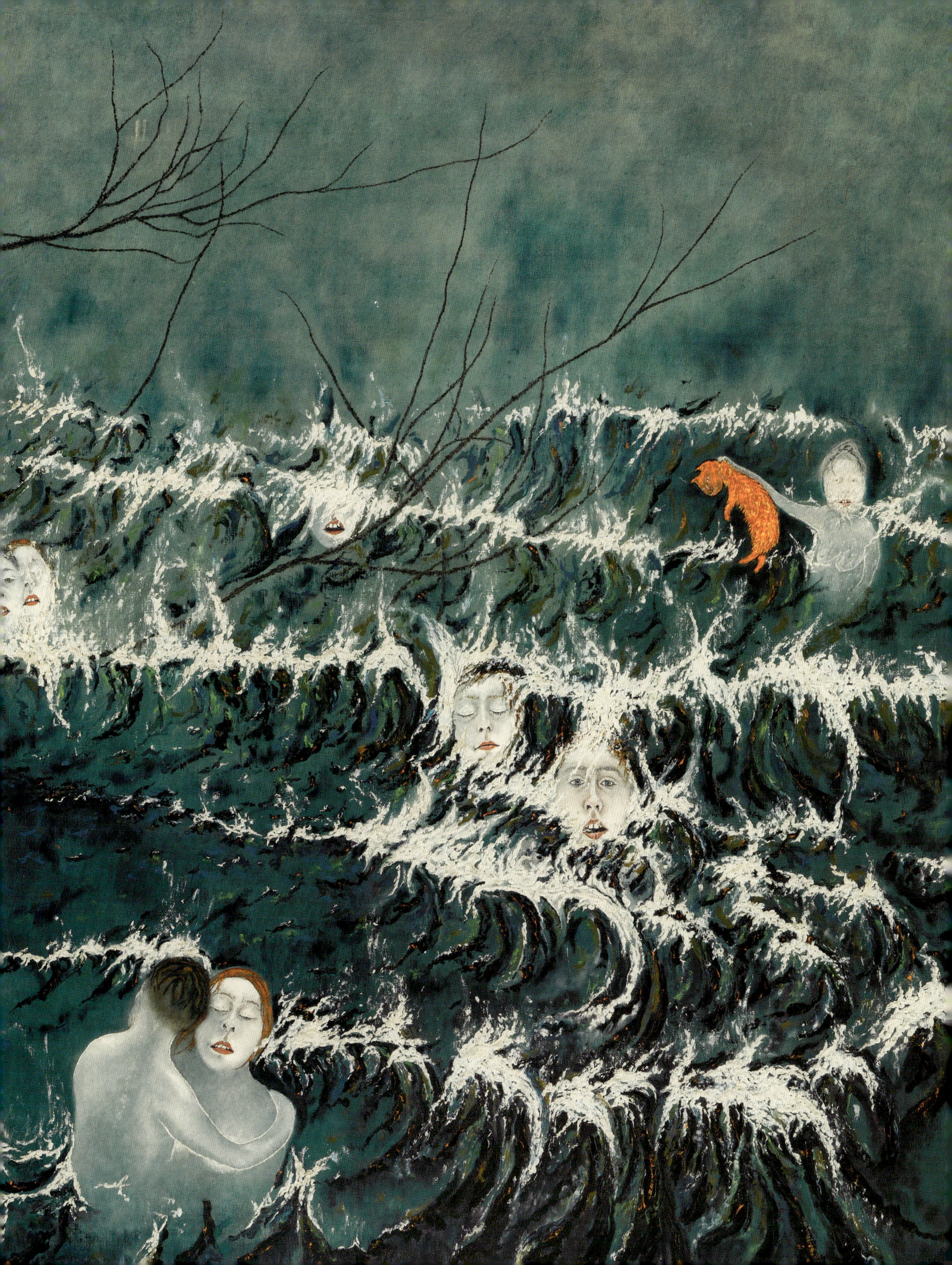

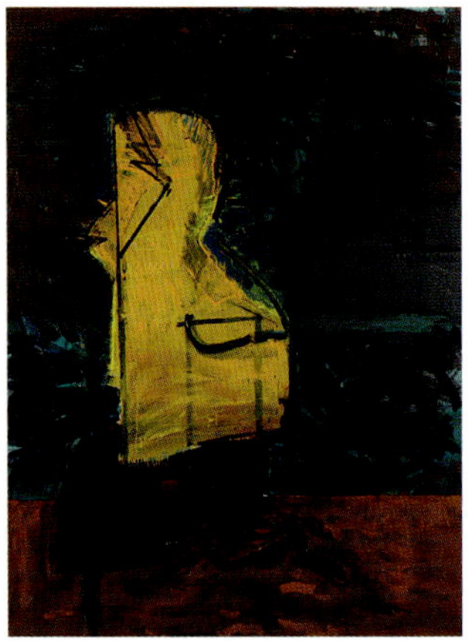

Crowther, Michael b.1946
Salvo II 1981
acrylic on canvas 244.2 x 183.8
AC 4085

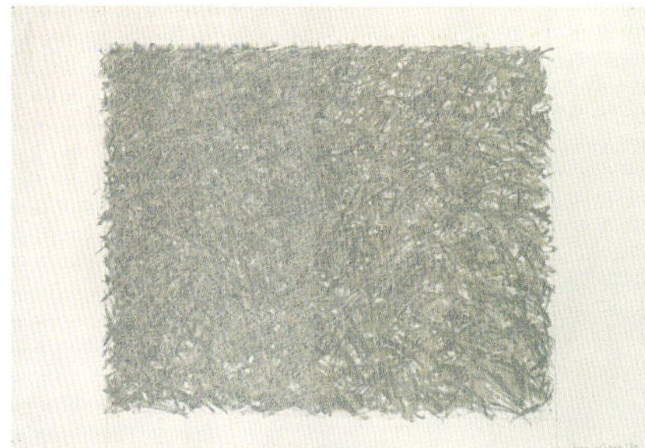

Croxon, Jeanne b.1932
Untitled (Green) 1979
oil on paper 50.9 x 76.7
AC 2077

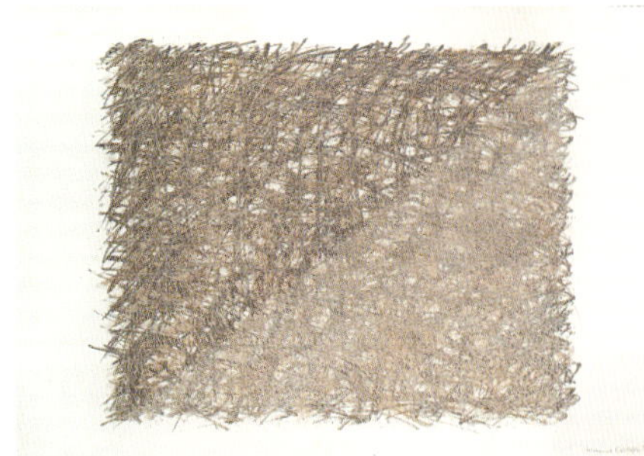

Croxon, Jeanne b.1932
Untitled (Pink) 1979
oil on paper 50.6 x 76.2
AC 2076

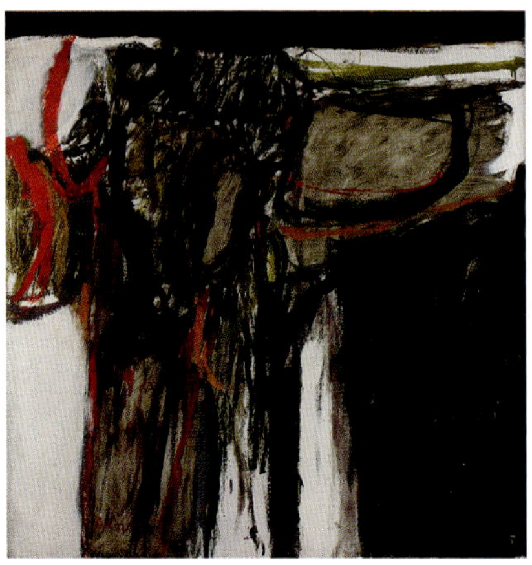

Crozier, William 1930–2011
Landscape, Wivenhoe 1960
oil on board 121.9 x 121.9
AC 531

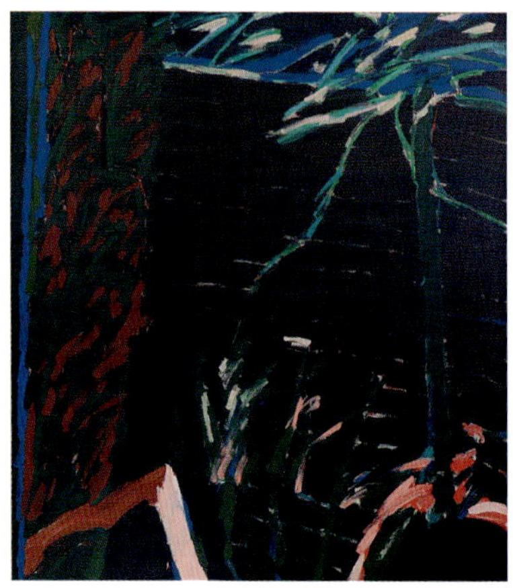

Crozier, William 1930–2011
North London Garden 1980
oil on canvas 172.7 x 157.5
AC 4010

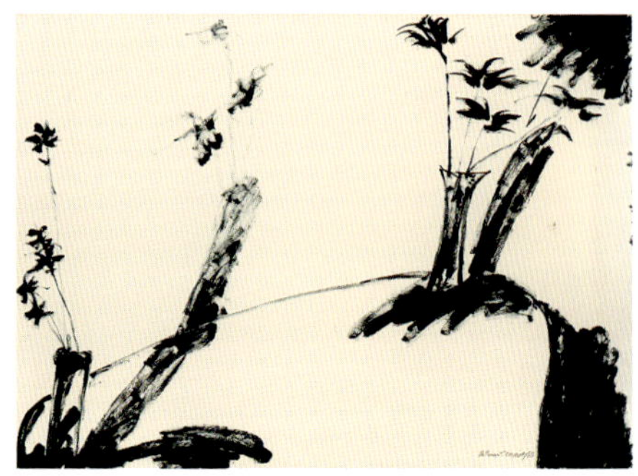

Crozier, William 1930–2011
Still Life 1980
oil on paper 75 x 105
AC 3093

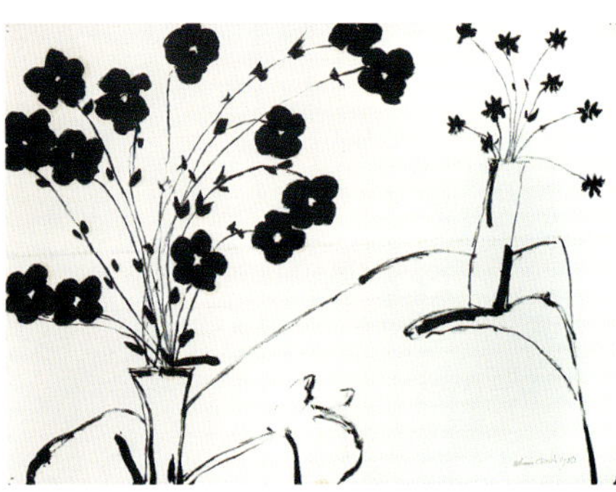

Crozier, William 1930–2011
Still Life 1980
oil on paper 75 x 105
AC 3094

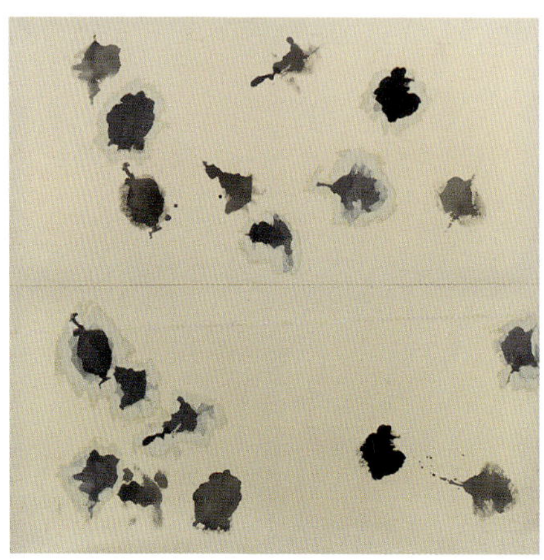

Crumplin, Colin b.1946
Coincidence VII 1980
acrylic & oil on cotton duck 135.5 x 136.7
AC 4005

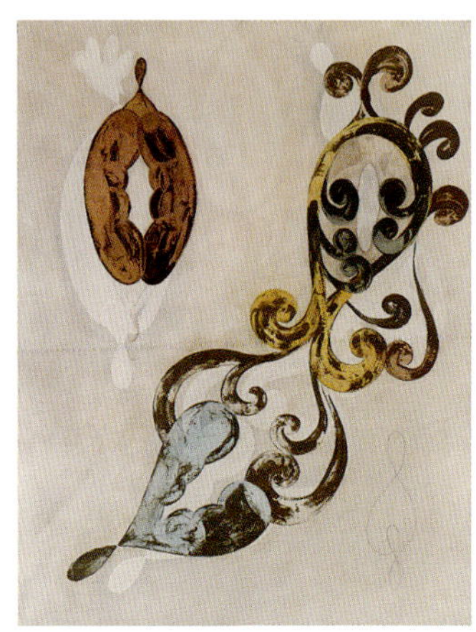

Cuddihy, Mikey b.1952
Iron Gates of Life: Strength and Sweetness
1991
acrylic & graphite on canvas 236.5 x 178.2
ACC41/1991

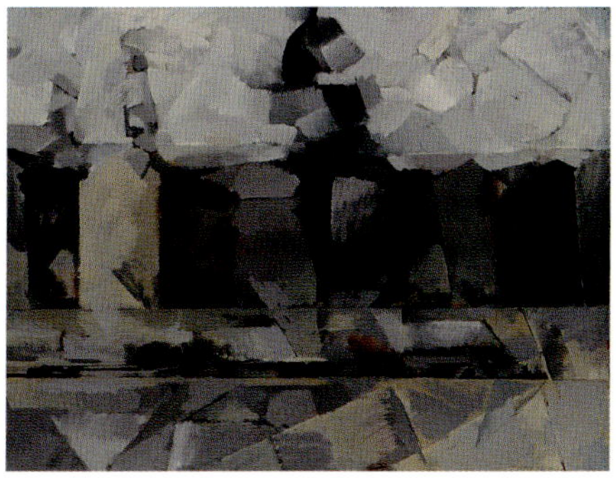

Culbert, Bill b.1935
St Paul's 1961
oil on board 73.7 x 99
ACC6/1961

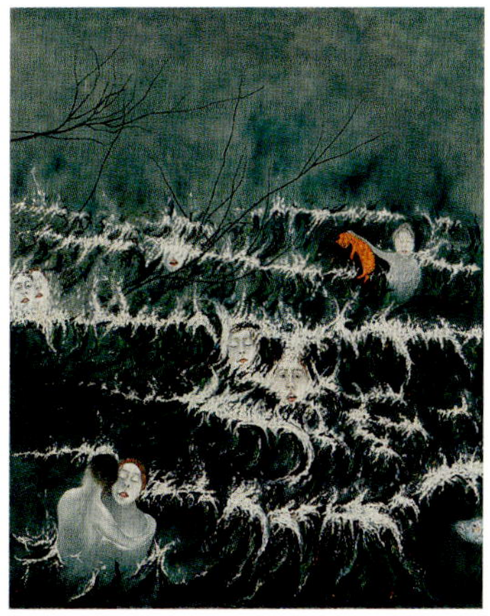

Cumming, Diana b.1929
The Flood 1954
oil on canvas 127 x 101.6
AC 323

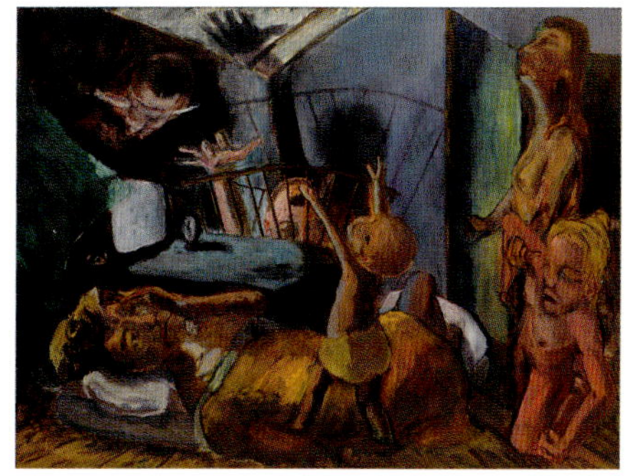

Dalwood, Dexter b.1960
The Room 1984–1985
oil on canvas 113 x 153.3
AC 5383

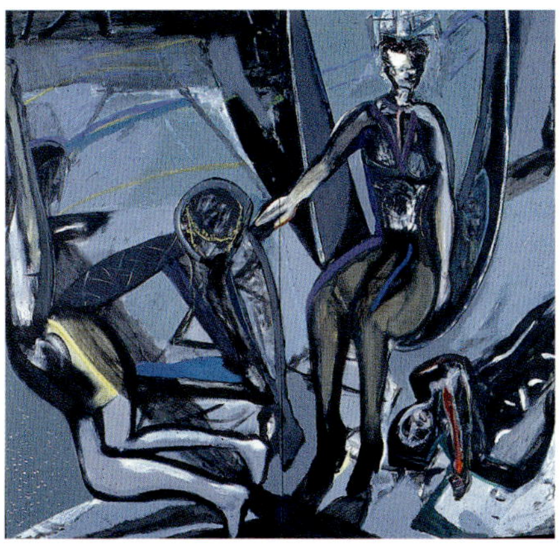

Darach, Peter b.1940
The Swing 1984
oil on board 226 x 224
AC 5390

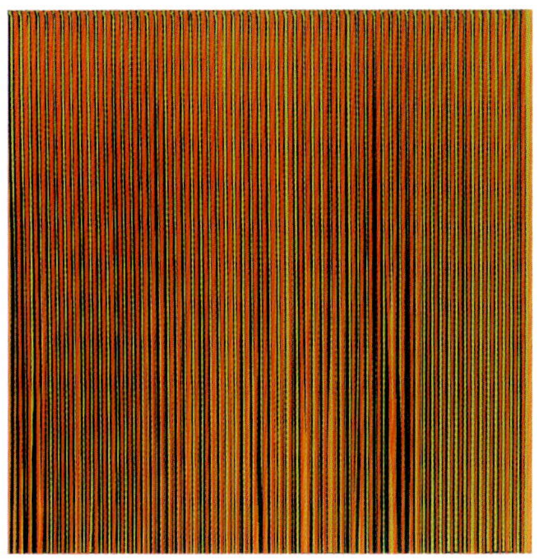

Davenport, Ian b.1966
Poured Lines: Light Orange, Blue, Yellow, Dark Green and Orange 1995
emulsion on canvas 213.4 x 213.4
ACC38/1995

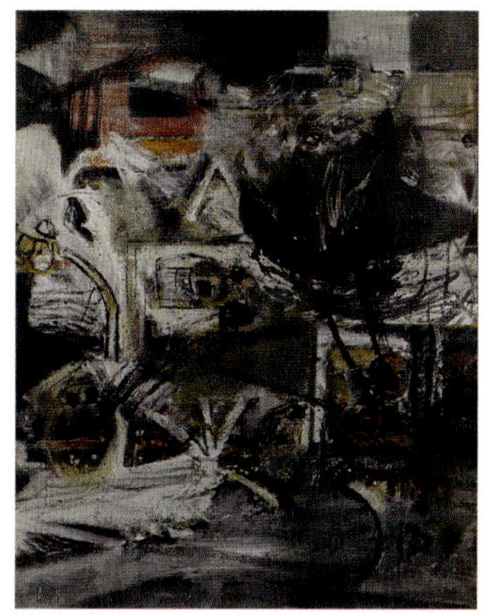

Davie, Alan b.1920
Ghost Creation 1951
oil on board 152.4 x 121.9
AC 463

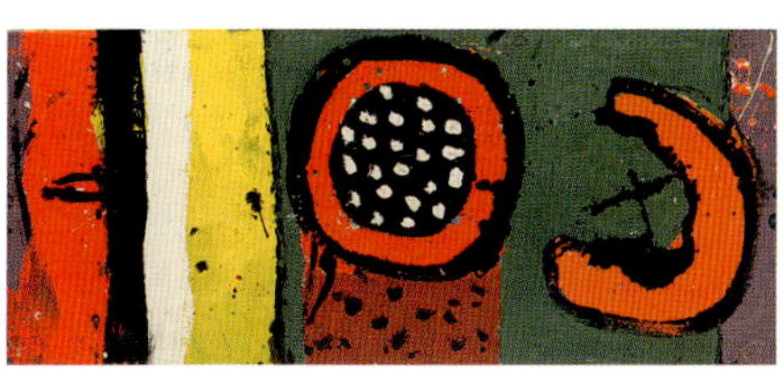

Davie, Alan b.1920
Target 1959
resin & oil on paper 38.1 x 91.4
AC 520

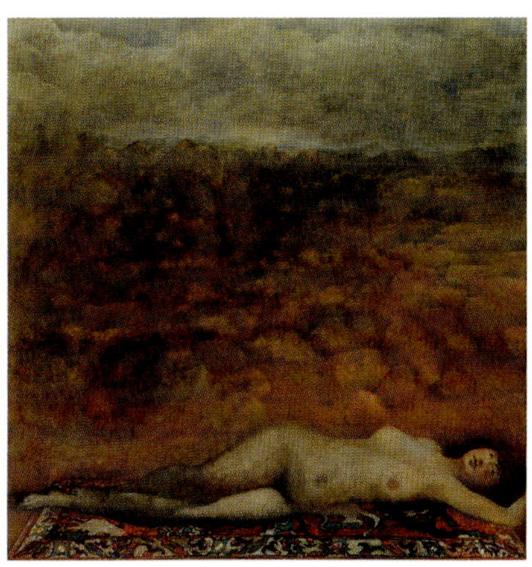

Davies, Ivor b.1935
At the Photographer's 1983
oil on cotton duck 152.2 x 152
AC 5295

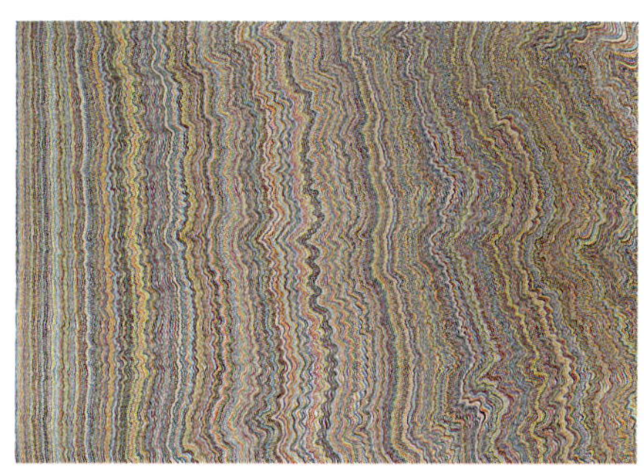

Davies, Peter b.1970
Striped Painting 1997
acrylic on canvas 228.6 x 330.2
ACC73/1997

Davis, Peter b.1972
Untitled 3mm Blue – November 1995 1995
gloss paint & satinwood on canvas
99.6 x 208.8
ACC159/1998

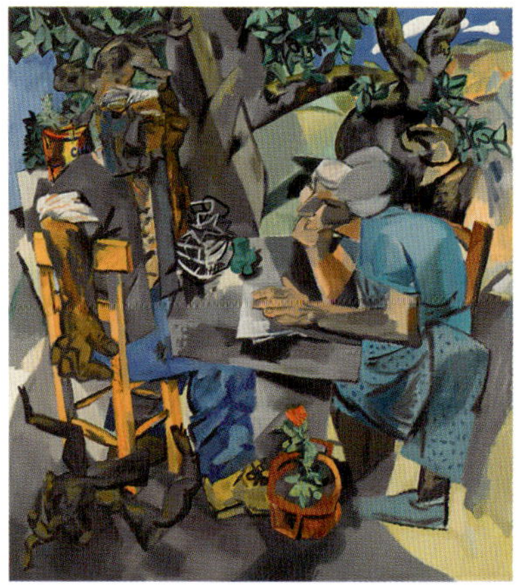

de Francia, Peter 1921–2012
Monsieur et Madame Beylac 1974
oil on canvas 170 x 152
AC 1833

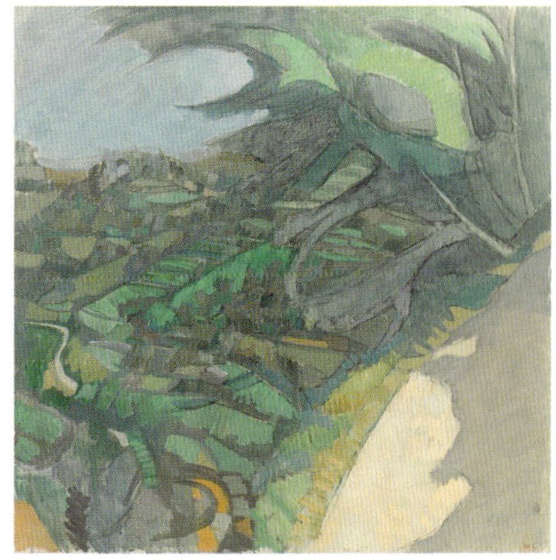

de Grey, Roger 1918–1995
Contre-jour II 1966
oil on canvas 101.6 x 101.6
AC 864

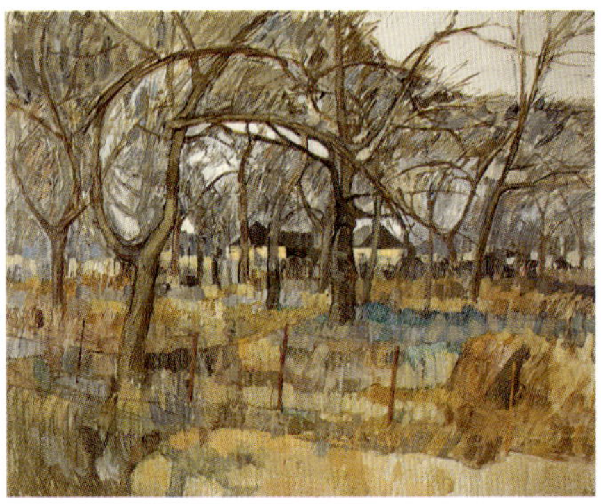

de Grey, Roger 1918–1995
Orchard, Meopham 1966
oil on canvas 121.9 x 152.4
AC 884

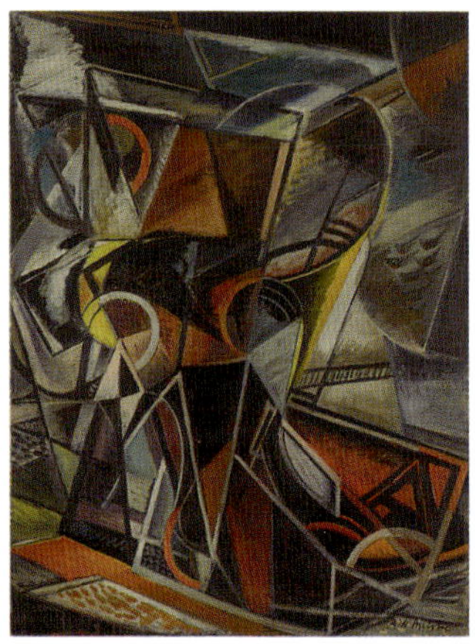

de Maistre, Leroy Leveson Laurent Joseph
1894–1968
Third Station of the Cross 1948
oil on canvas 78.7 x 61
AC 470

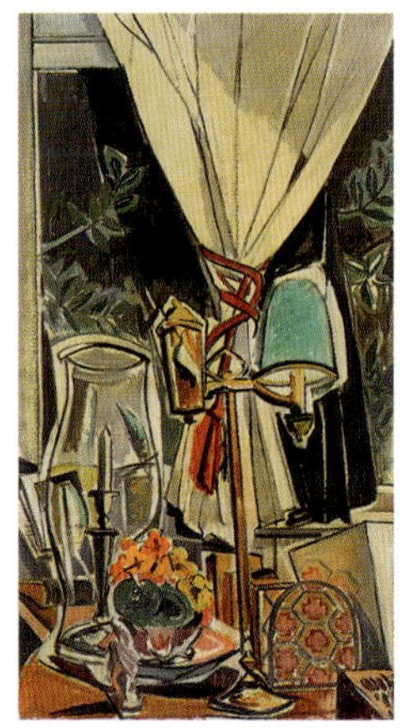

de Maistre, Leroy Leveson Laurent Joseph
1894–1968
The Green Shade 1949
oil on canvas 96.5 x 50
AC 158

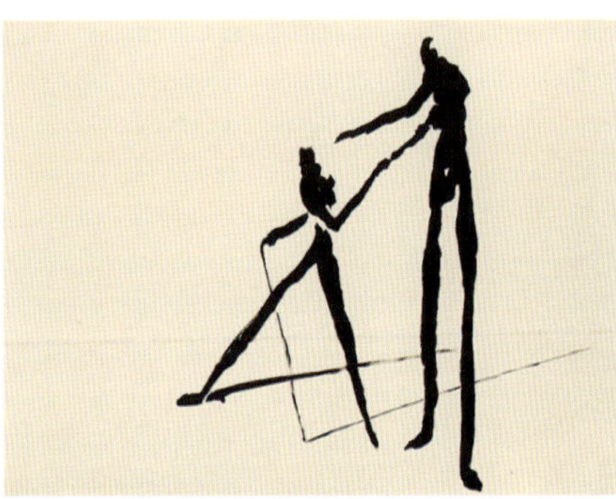

de Thame, Gerard b.1958
Tall and Old 1983
acrylic on paper 55.8 x 75.7
AC 5273

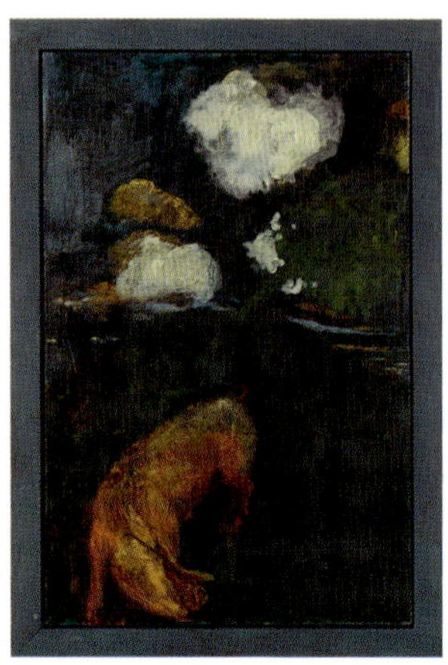

Delargy, Diarmuid b.1958
Breda 1990
oil on canvas 183.4 x 121.3
ACC2/1991

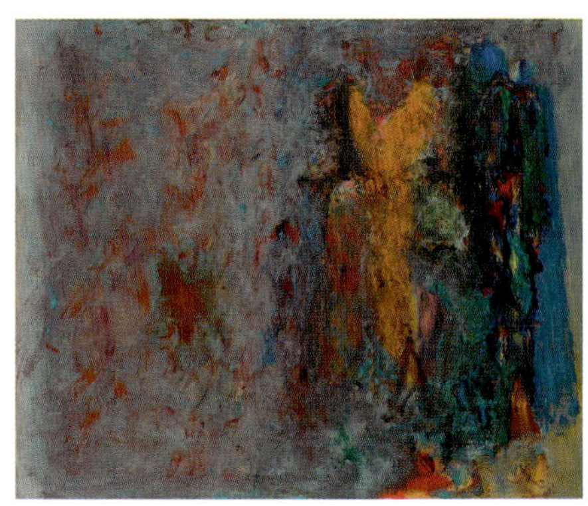

Dellow, Jeffrey b.1949
Marsyas 1982
acrylic on canvas 161.9 x 194.6
AC 5064

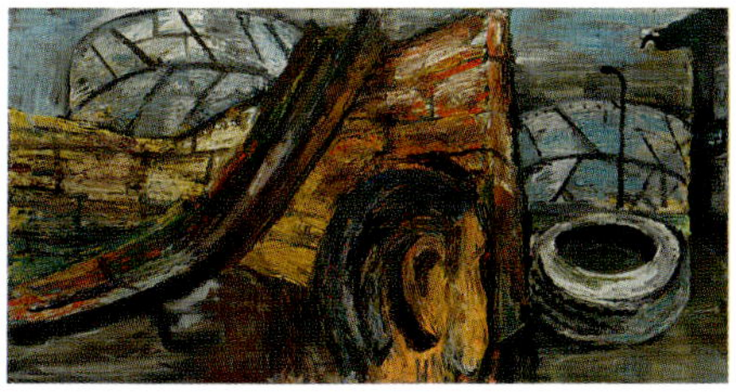

Dennis, Jeffrey b.1958
Echo 1981
oil on canvas 133.2 x 269.8
AC 5055

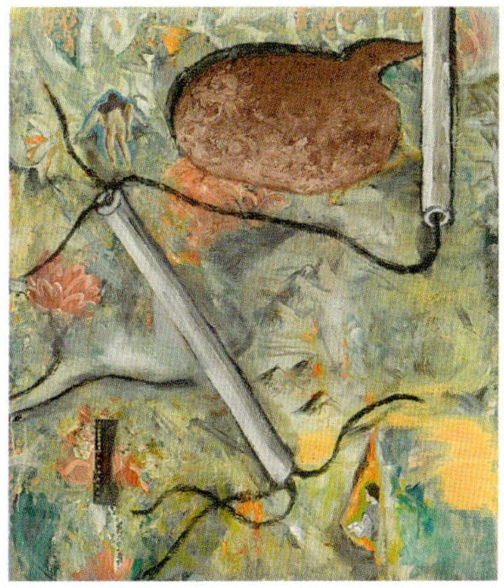

Dennis, Jeffrey b.1958
A Spy in the House of Frank 1985
oil on canvas 114.3 x 99
ACC160/1998

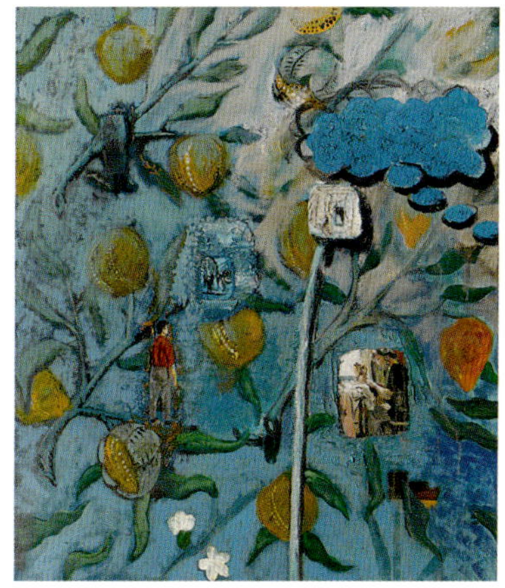

Dennis, Jeffrey b.1958
Strange Fruit 1985
oil on canvas 86.4 x 74.4
ACC161/1998

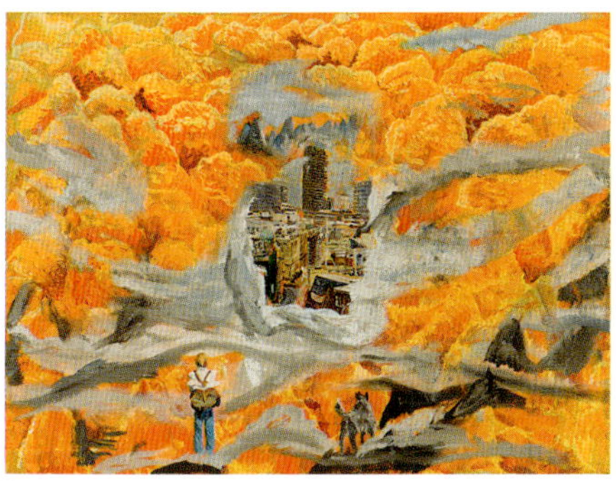

Dennis, Jeffrey b.1958
The Lost City 1985
oil on canvas 53.4 x 71
ACC162/1998

Denny, Robyn b.1930
Bland 1963
oil on canvas 213.4 x 182.9
AC 723

Denny, Robyn b.1930
Over Reach 1965–1966
oil on canvas 243.5 x 198.1
AC 887

Denny, Robyn b.1930
Gently 1966
oil on canvas 243.8 x 198.1
AC 992

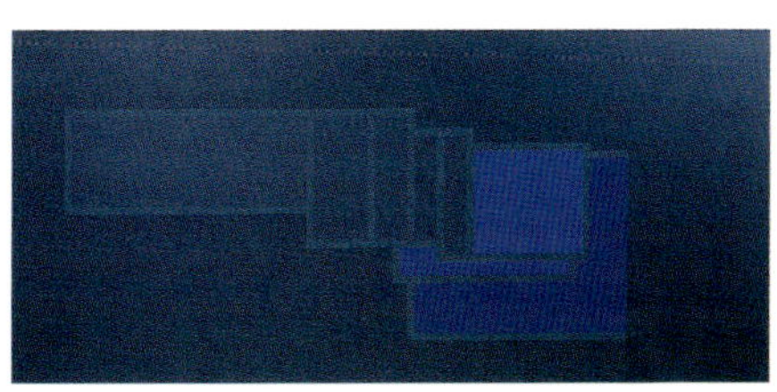

Denny, Robyn b.1930
Landscape Painting No.5 1978–1981
oil & canvas on board 112 x 208.3
AC 5006

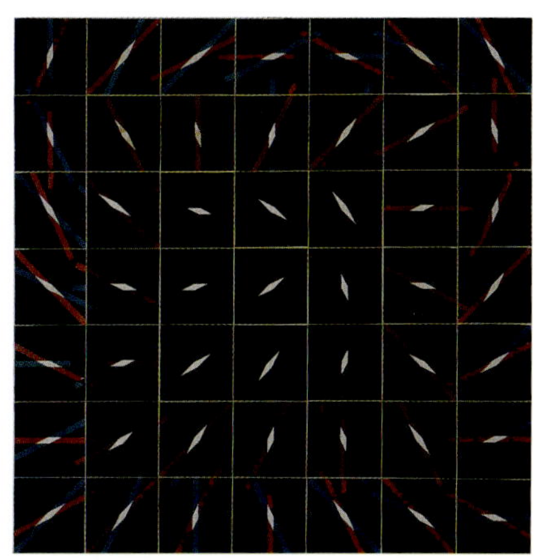

Derges, Susan b.1955
Spiral Construction 1977
acrylic & paper on board 303.9 x 304.2
AC 2043

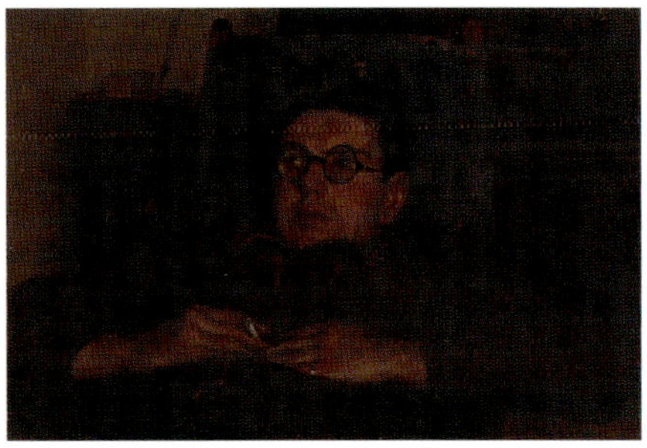

Devas, Anthony 1911–1958
Six O'Clock News 1940
oil on canvas 50.8 x 76
AC 89

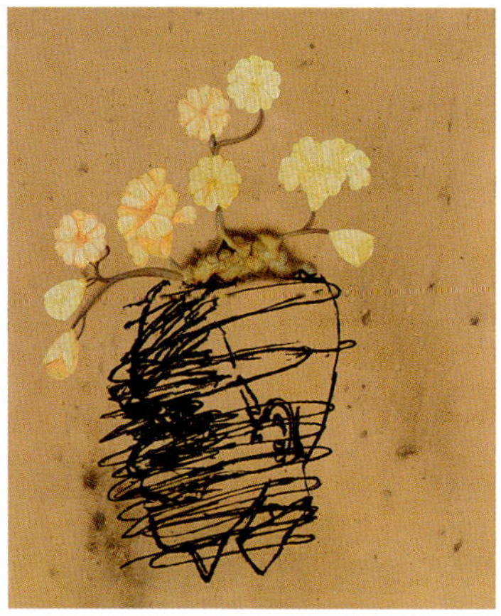

Dickinson, Rod b.1965
Egg Bag 1991
oil, dust, silicon & latex on canvas
213.5 x 183
ACC163/1998

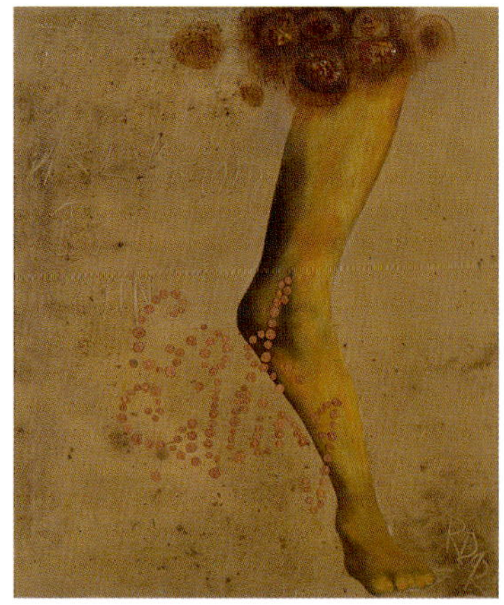

Dickinson, Rod b.1965
Venereal Daze 1992
oil, dust, silicon & latex on canvas
213.5 x 183
ACC164/1998

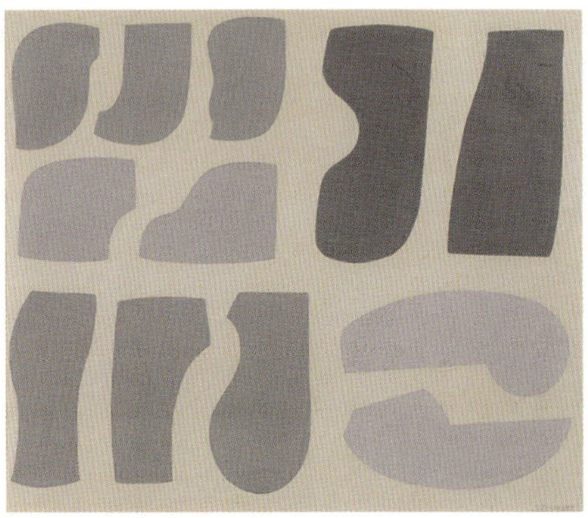

Dismorr, Jessica 1885–1939
Related Forms c.1936–1939
collage & tempera on board 39.9 x 46.8
AC 806

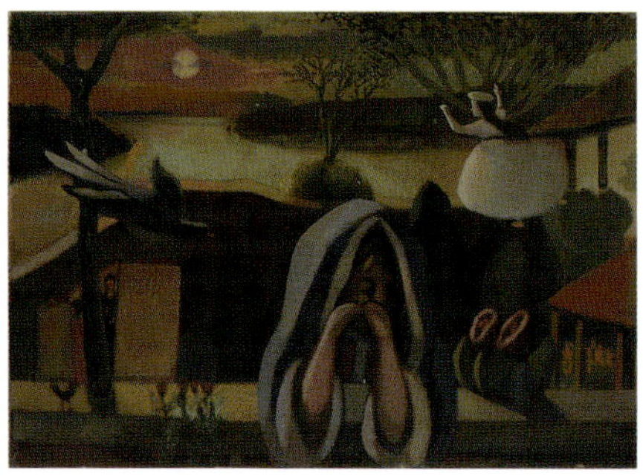

Dodgson, John Arthur 1890–1969
Death of a Child 1946
oil on canvas 63.5 x 88.9
AC 494

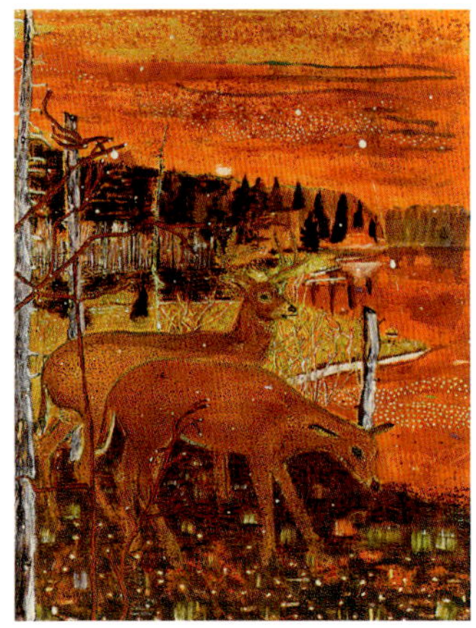

Doig, Peter b.1959
Red Deer 1990
oil on canvas 237.5 x 182.6
ACC86/1991

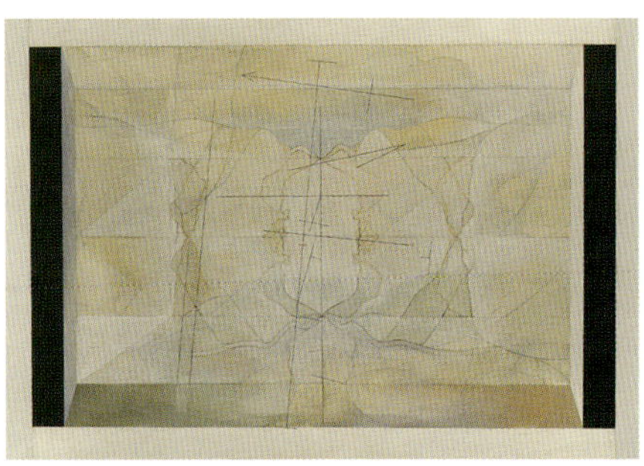

Donagh, Rita b.1939
'Taking the trouble to sound it' 1970
oil & coloured pencil on board 91.4 x 121.9
AC 1256

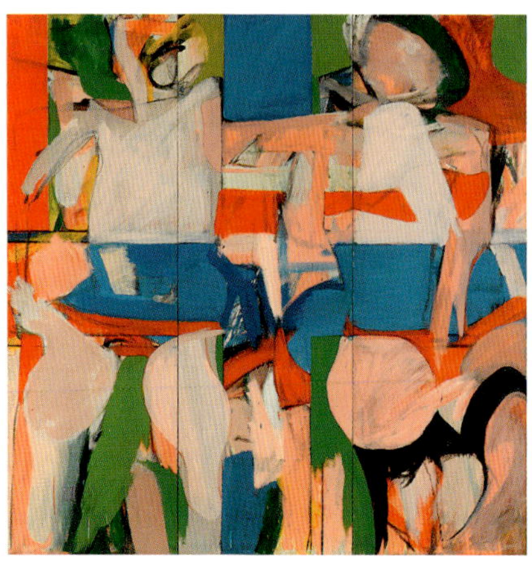

Donaldson, Antony b.1939
'Starr-Queen' – for Jenny Davis 1962
oil & pencil on board 186 x 189
AC 628

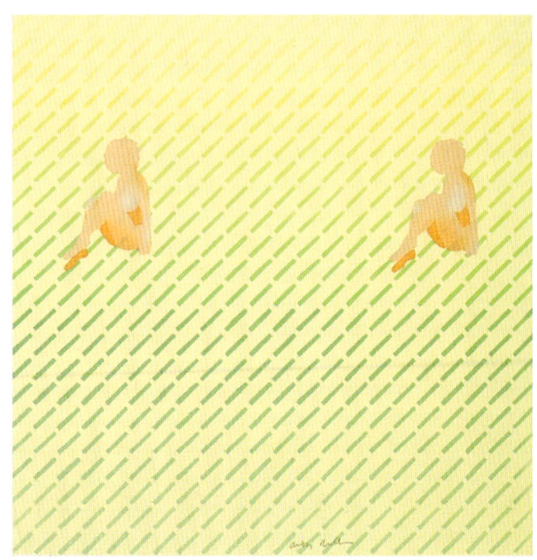

Donaldson, Antony b.1939
Untitled 'I' 1967
acrylic on paper 55.9 x 55.9
AC 988

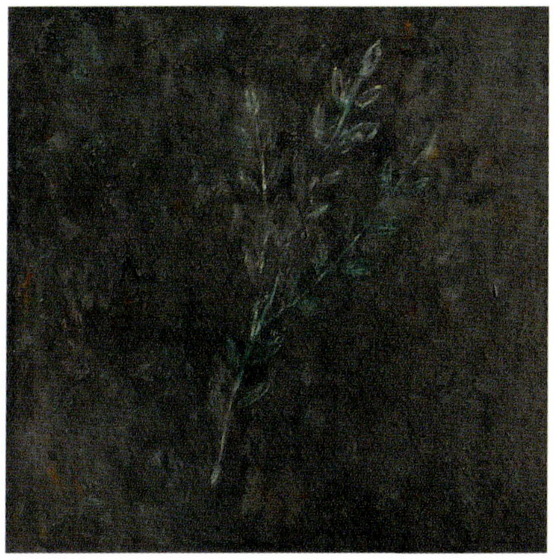

Donnelly, Micky b.1952
Olive 1990
oil & pumice powder on canvas 56.5 x 56.5
ACC73/1991

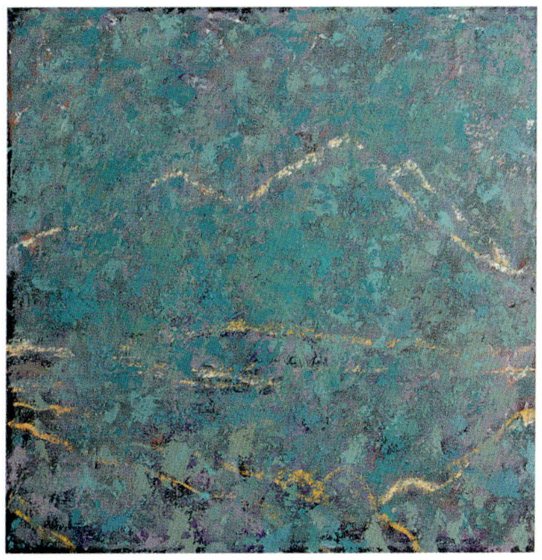

Donnelly, Micky b.1952
Landscape Painting No.5 (after Paul Henry) 1991
oil & pumice powder on canvas 56.5 x 56.5
ACC72/1991

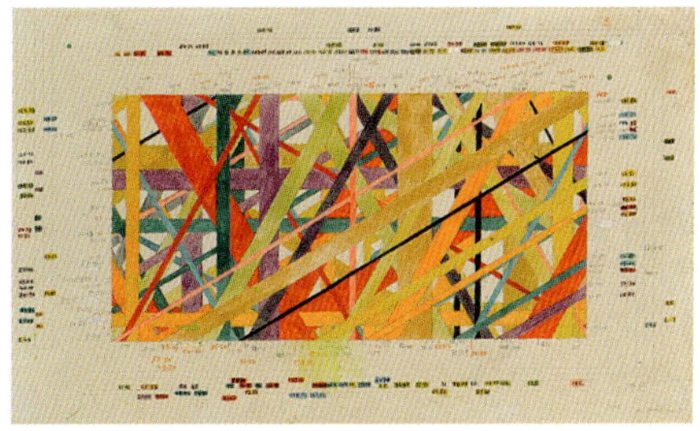

Dower, Natalie b.1931
Working Drawing, Double Square 1980 1980
pencil, ink & acrylic on paper 36.4 x 61.8
AC 5117

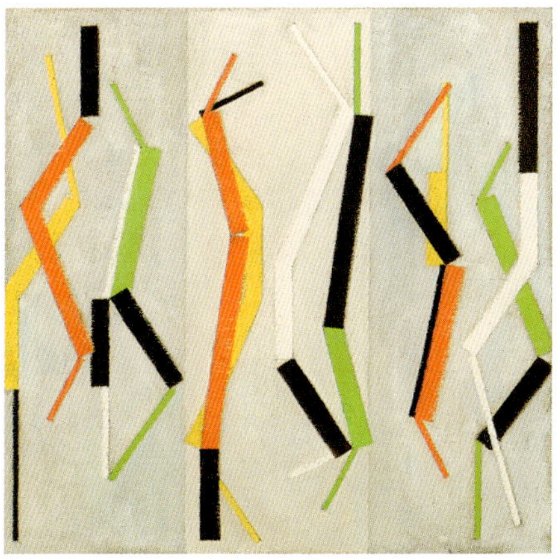

Dower, Natalie b.1931
Sortie 2001
oil & canvas on board 36.1 x 36.1
ACC6/2001

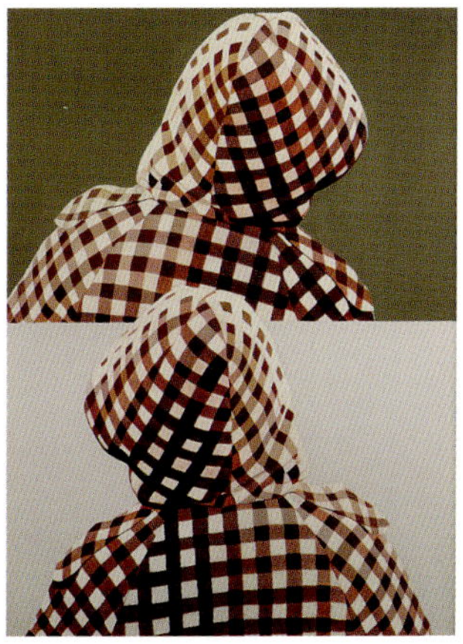

Dragicevic, Milena b.1965
Opet 2002
oil on linen 108.5 x 79
ACC4/2002

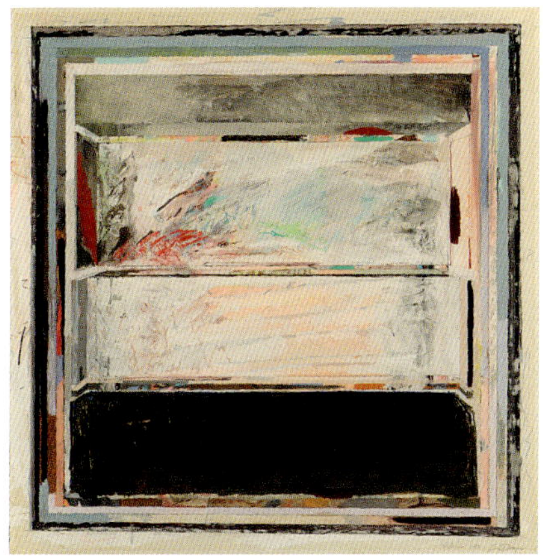

Draper, Kenneth b.1944
Enclosures 1980
oil crayon & paint on paper 79.2 x 79.2
AC 4033

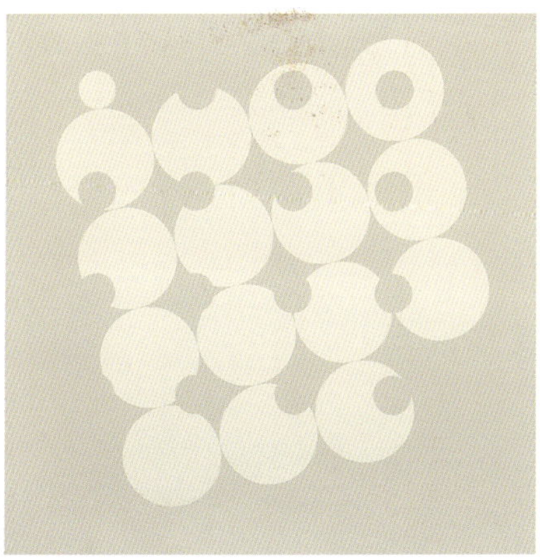

Drever, Timothy b.1935
Negatron 1967
oil on canvas 91.4 x 91.4
AC 952

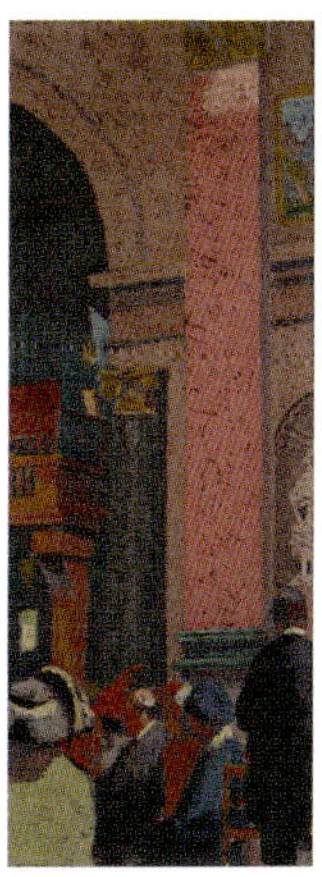

Drummond, Malcolm 1880–1945
Brompton Oratory c.1912
oil on canvas 53.3 x 20.3
AC 324

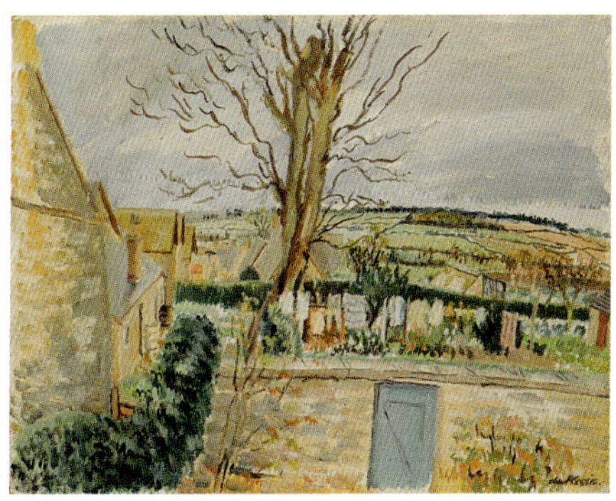

Du Plessis, Enslin 1894–1978
Cotswold Landscape 1942
oil on canvas 31.8 x 47
AC 92

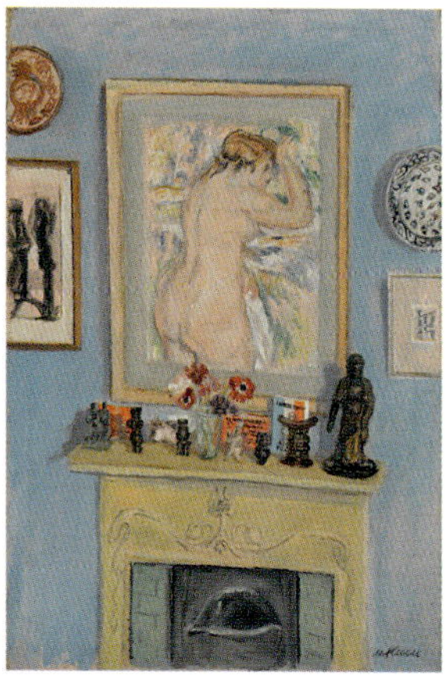

Du Plessis, Enslin 1894–1978
The Mantelpiece 1948
oil on canvas 74.9 x 49.5
AC 503

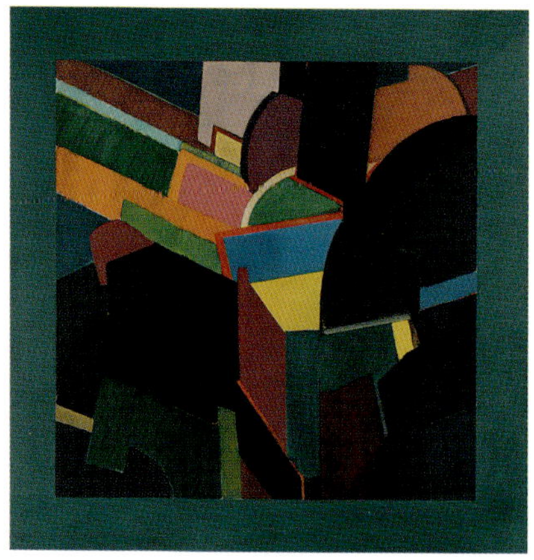

Dubsky, Mario 1939–1985
Svodebka 1969
oil on canvas 213.4 x 213.4
AC 1096

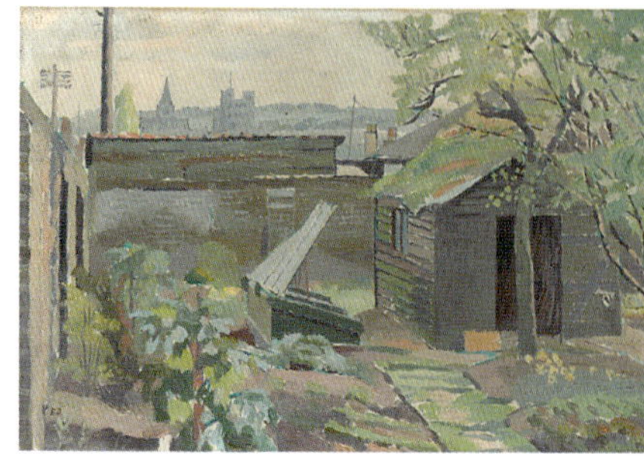

Dunbar, Evelyn Mary 1906–1960
Rochester from Strood 1938
oil on canvas 20.3 x 30.5
AC 90

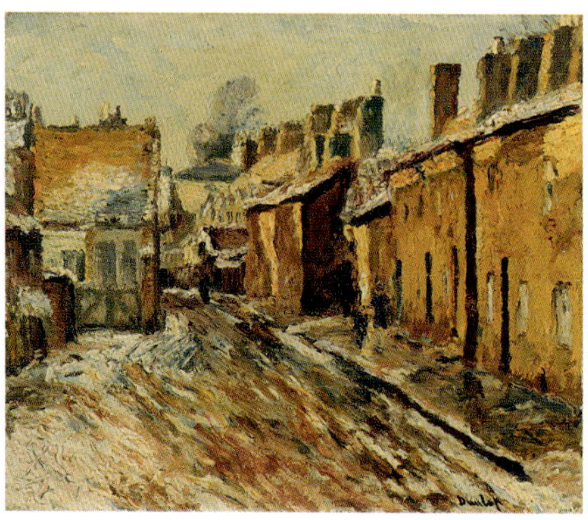

Dunlop, Ronald Ossory 1894–1973
Snow at Stratford-on-Avon 1940
oil on canvas 50.8 x 61
AC 91

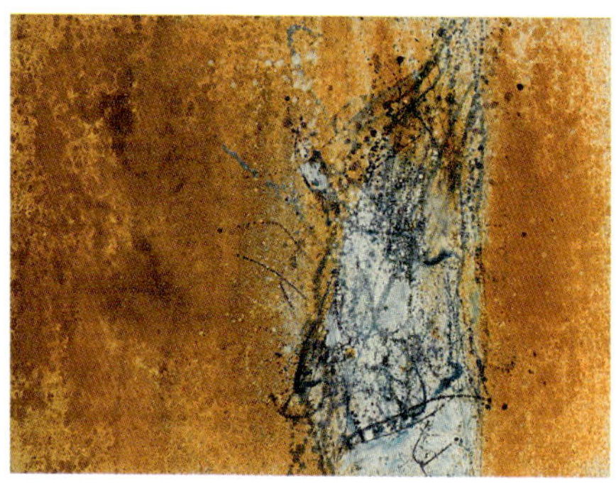

Dunn, Anne b.1929
Watercourse 1964
oil on canvas 73.7 x 100.2
AC 760

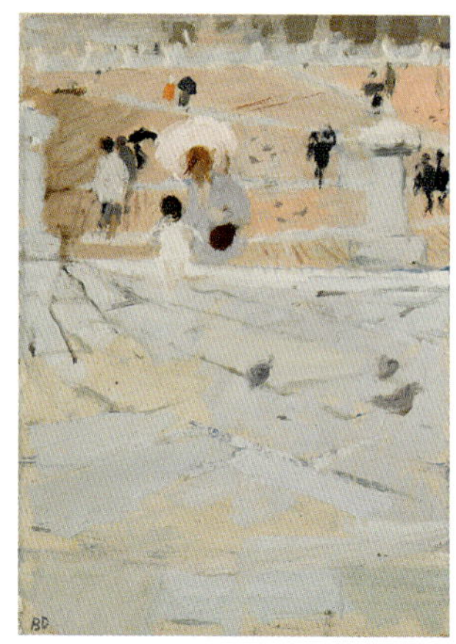

Dunstan, Bernard b.1920
The Campo, Siena 1965
oil on board 25.5 x 18
AC 890

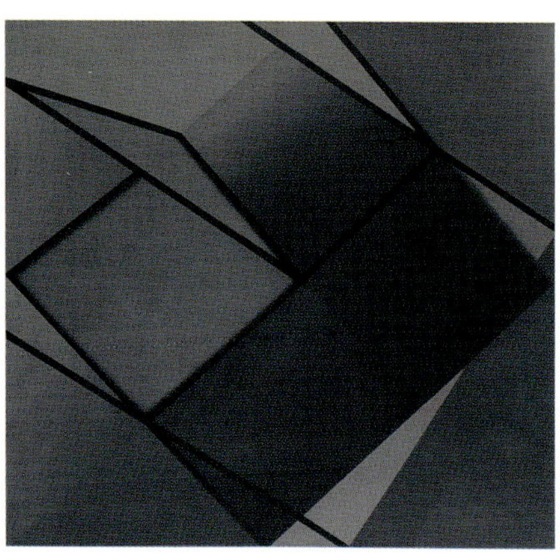

Durrant, Jennifer b.1942
Slide 1967
oil on canvas 182.9 x 198.1
AC 927

Durrant, Jennifer b.1942
Birthday I 1974
acrylic on paper 100 x 74.9
AC 1410

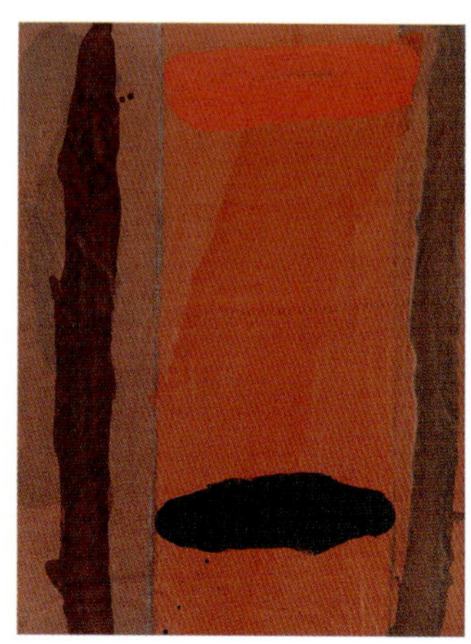

Durrant, Jennifer b.1942
Lone 1974
acrylic on paper 100 x 74.9
AC 1412

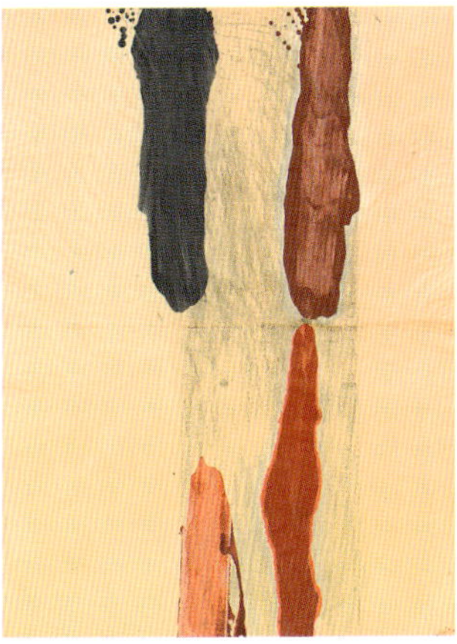

Durrant, Jennifer b.1942
Scar Series Number Eleven, June 1974 1974
acrylic on paper 100 x 74.9
AC 1411

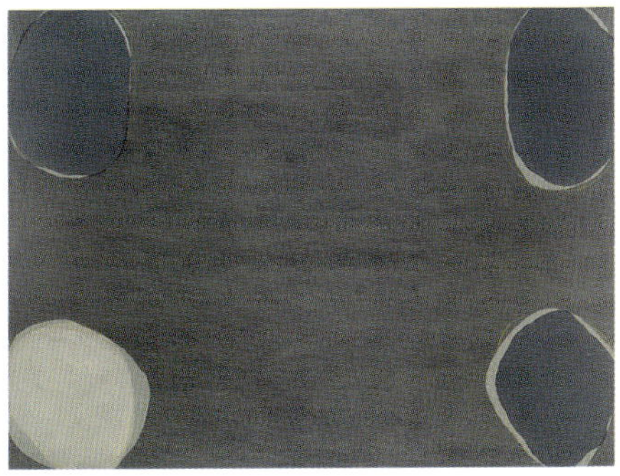

Durrant, Jennifer b.1942
Jean Blue Painting 1975
acrylic on cotton duck 269 x 343
AC 1628

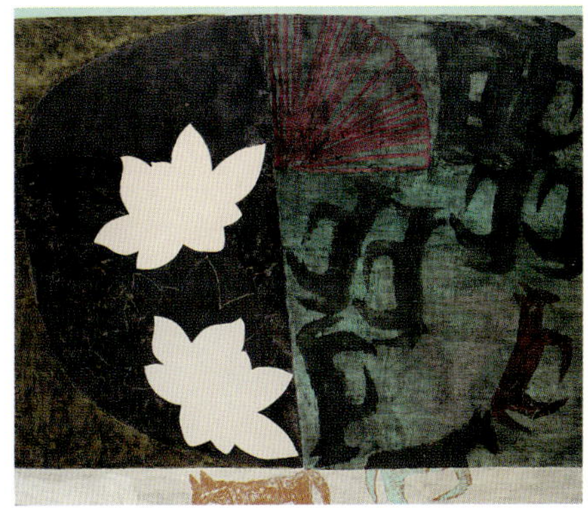

Durrant, Jennifer b.1942
Early On 1981
acrylic on canvas 259 x 306.3
ACC8/1982

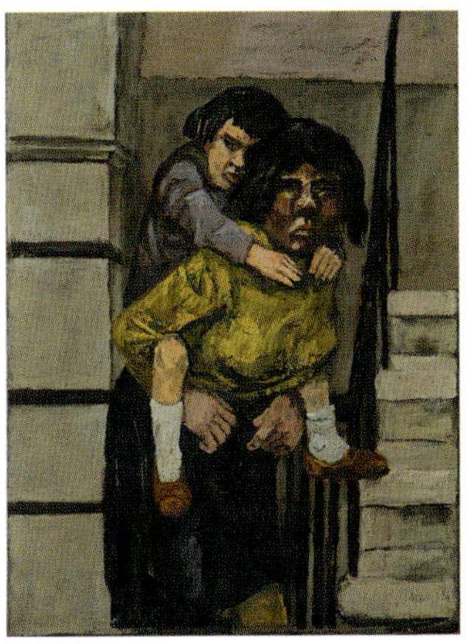

Duxbury, Leslie 1921–2001
Tenement Dwellers
oil on canvas 114.3 x 83.8
AC 407

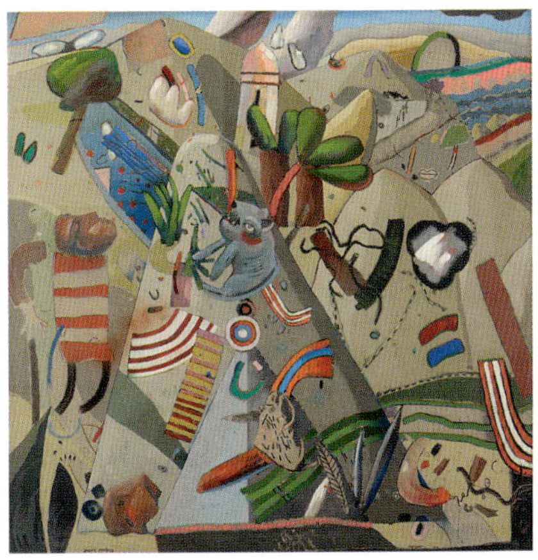

Dyer, Alan b.1944
Desert Painting No.3 1979
oil on canvas 120.5 x 120.5
AC 2090

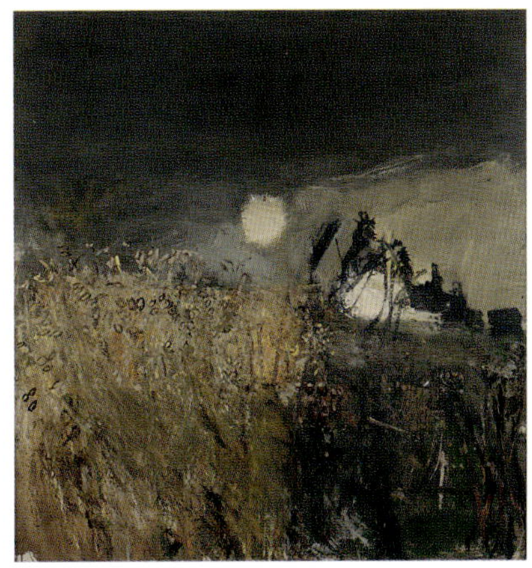

Eardley, Joan Kathleen Harding 1921–1963
A Field of Oats 1962
oil on board 100.2 x 96.7
AC 689

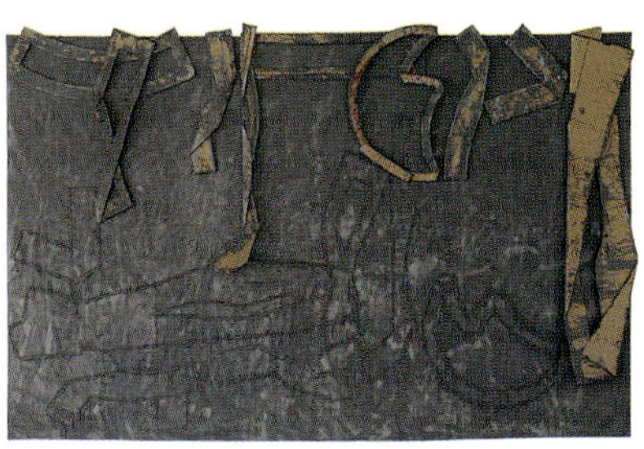

Easydorchik, Edwin b.1949
Girone della Mano – One Criminal Passion
1978
acrylic, cement & card on canvas 250.5 x 392
AC 2087

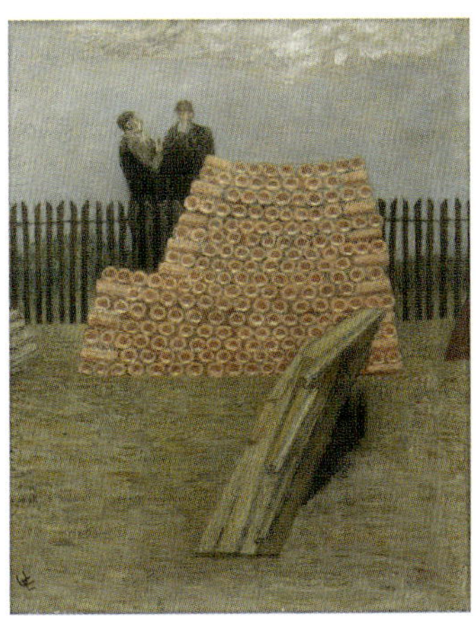

Edgcumbe, Ursula 1900–1985
Drainpipes c.1950
oil on canvas 40.8 x 30
AC 5045

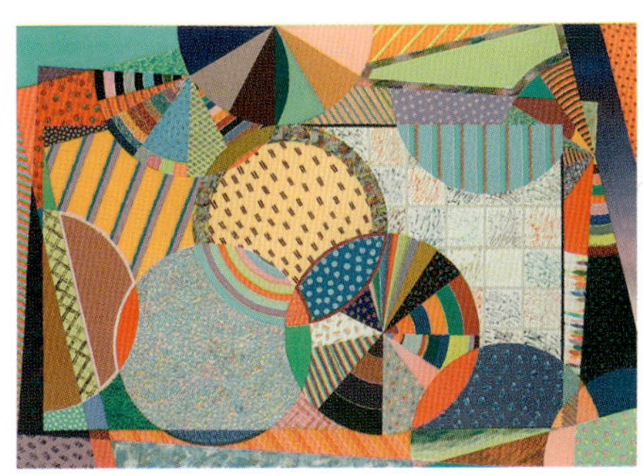

Edmond, Terry b.1947
Sekela Khuluma 1980
acrylic on canvas 167 x 243.5
AC 5102

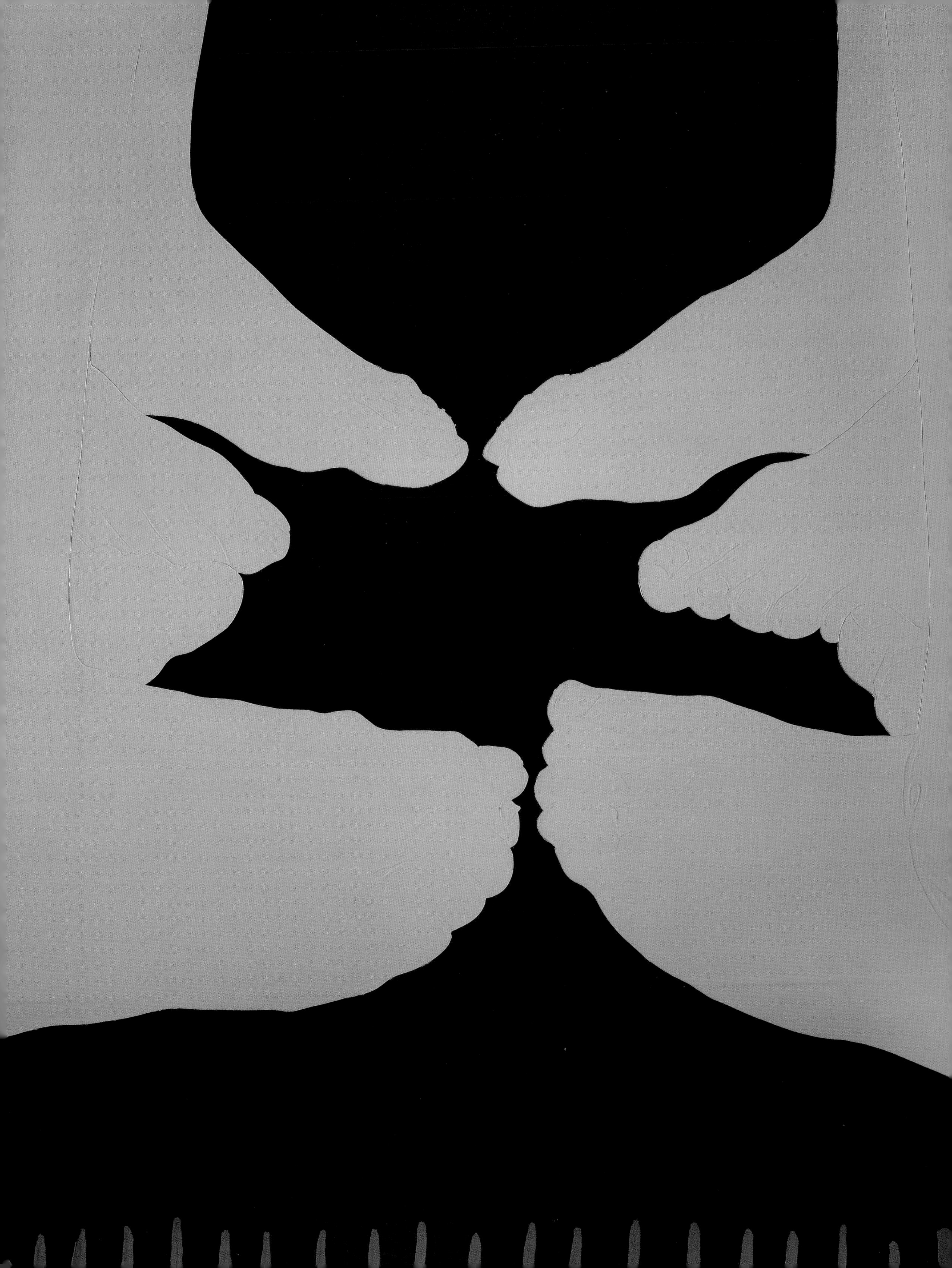

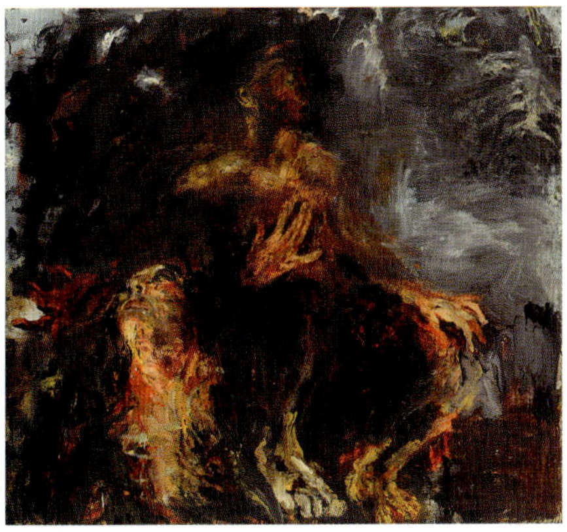

Edmondson, Simon b.1955
Second Night 1984
oil on canvas 162 x 179.7
AC 5343

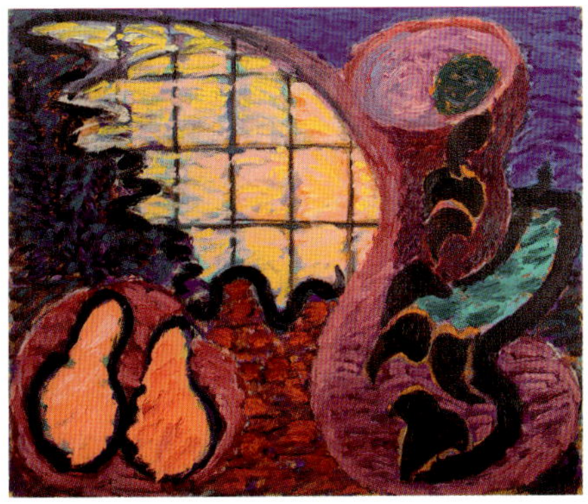

Edwards, John 1938–2009
Interiors 1983
oil on cotton duck 137 x 167.7
AC 5327

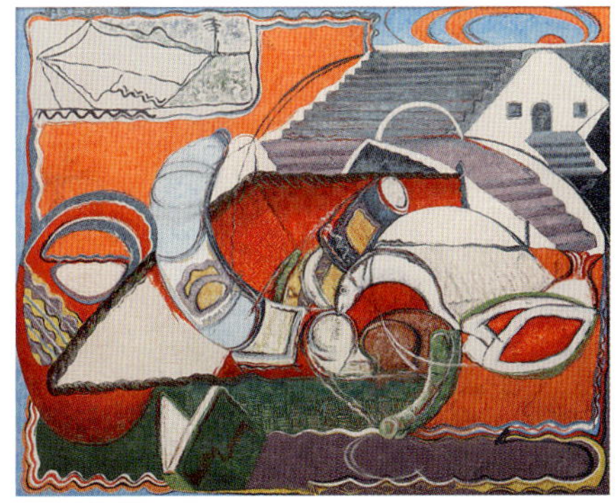

Egonu, Uzo 1928–1996
A New Lease of Life 1988
oil on canvas 99.8 x 124.5
AC 5548

Elliott, Ashley b.1974
A100-100 (Uniform White, Red, Ultramarine Blue) 1996
oil on canvas 104.8 x 104.5
ACC45/1996

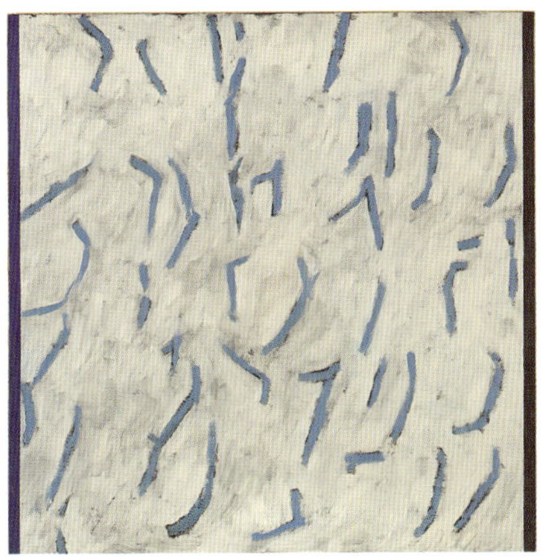

Elliott, John b.1953
Phaeax 1980
oil on canvas 71 x 70.9
AC 4067

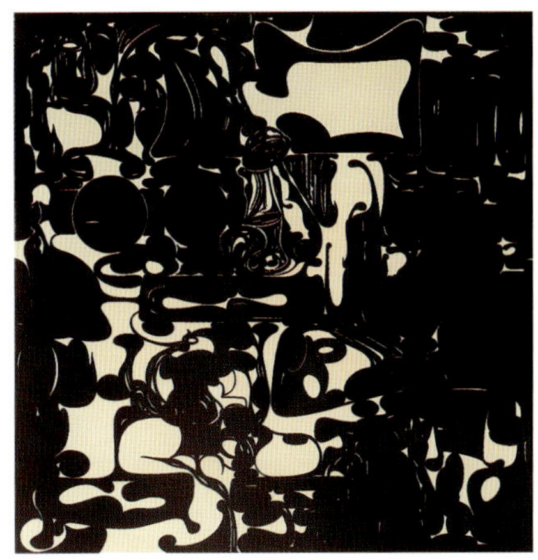

Ellis, Peter b.1951
Blank Firing 1997
oil on canvas 152 x 152
ACC61/1997

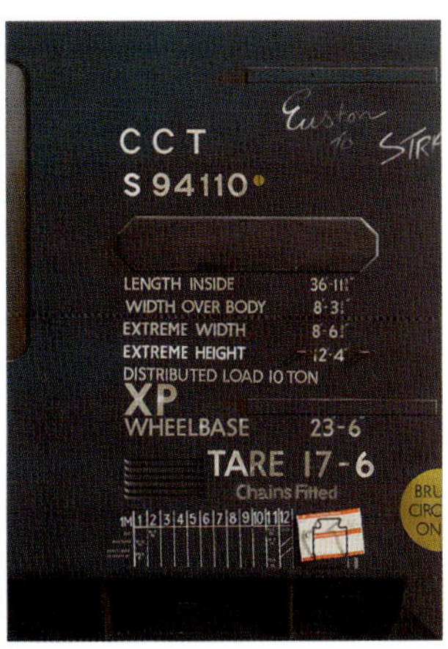

English, Michael 1941–2009
Man Machine Side of British Rail Parcels Van 1979
acrylic & gouache on card 106.5 x 76
AC 3062

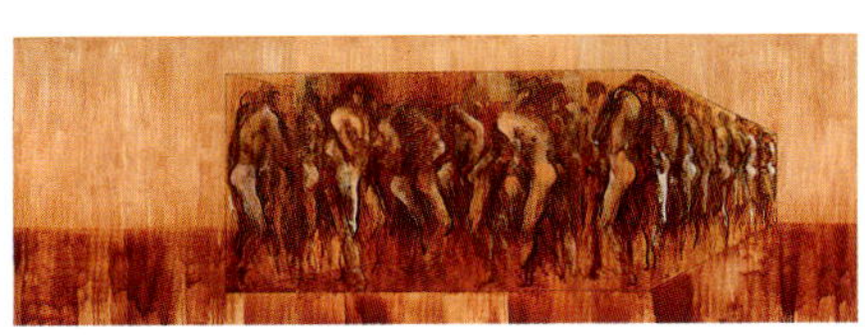

English, Simon b.1959
Box II (Large) 1993
oil on canvas 200 x 600
ACC165/1998

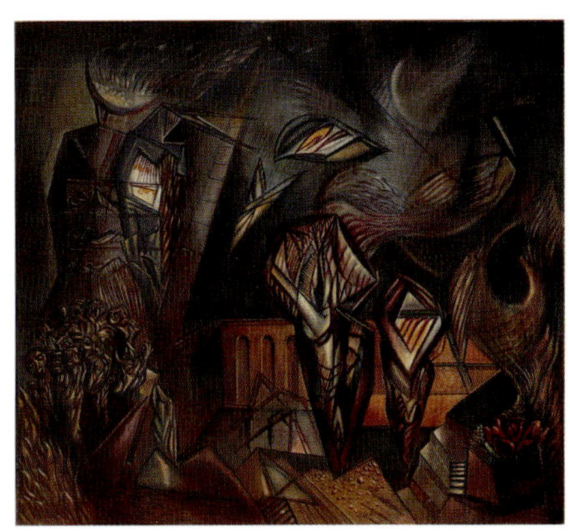

Evans, Merlyn Oliver 1910–1973
Nocturnal Drama (Fantasy) 1944
oil on canvas 70 x 80
AC 651

Facing page: Hume, Gary, b.1962, *Four Feet in the Garden* (detail), 1995, (p. 80)

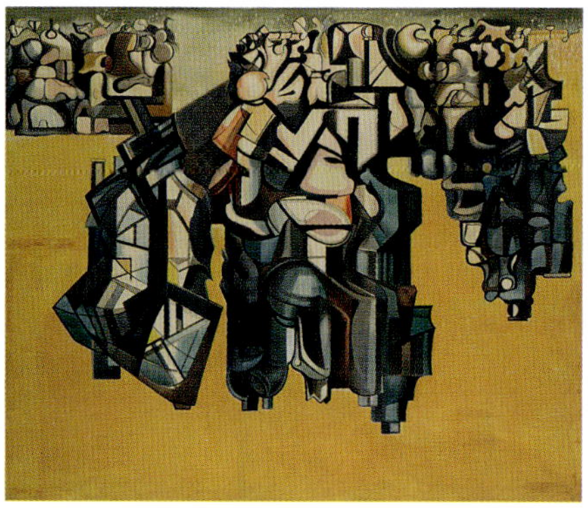

Evans, Merlyn Oliver 1910–1973
Metropolitan Crowd Forming a Procession 1953–1954
tempera on canvas 304.8 x 365.8
AC 1110

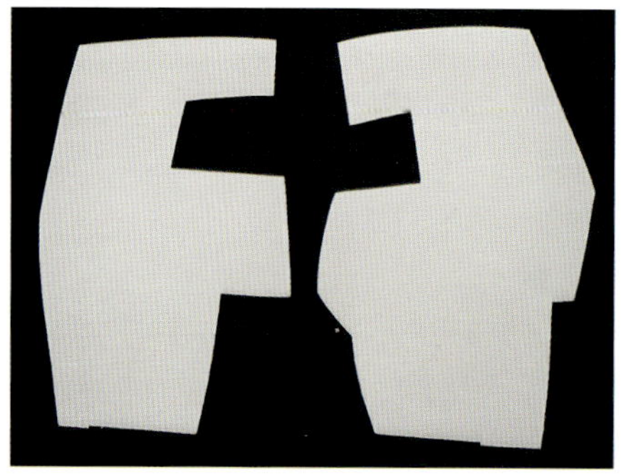

Evans, Merlyn Oliver 1910–1973
Relief 1963
oil on board 61 x 81.3
AC 706

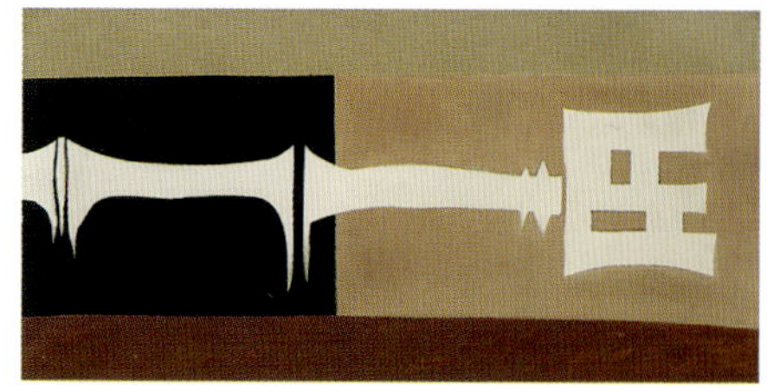

Evans, Merlyn Oliver 1910–1973
Composition 1965
oil on canvas 84.5 x 171.5
AC 864/ACA 25

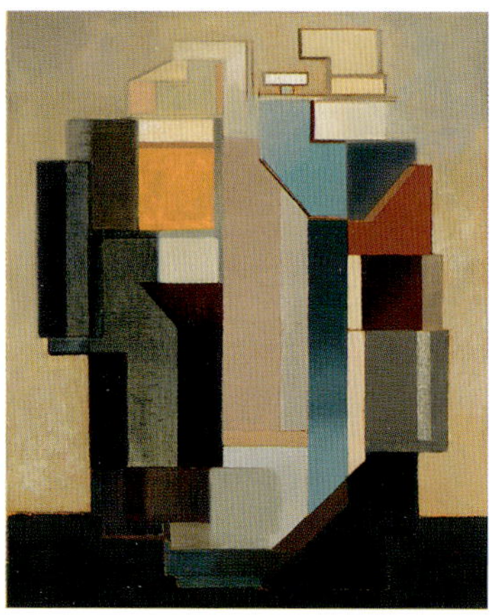

Evans, Merlyn Oliver 1910–1973
Building – Morning
oil on canvas 61 x 50.8
AC 263

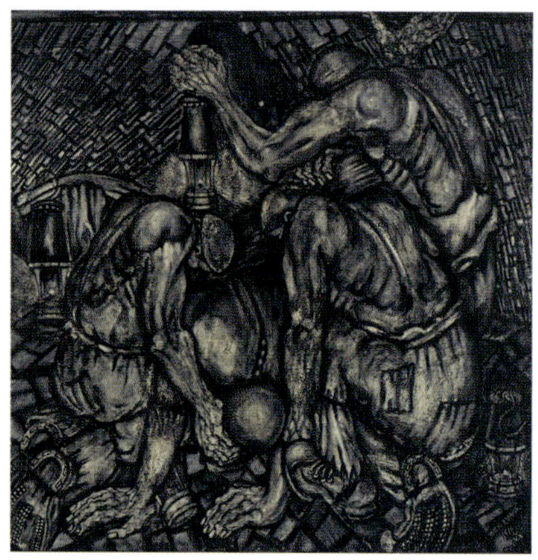

Evans, Nicholas 1907–2004
Collapse of the Roof 1978
oil on board 121.9 x 121.9
AC 1927

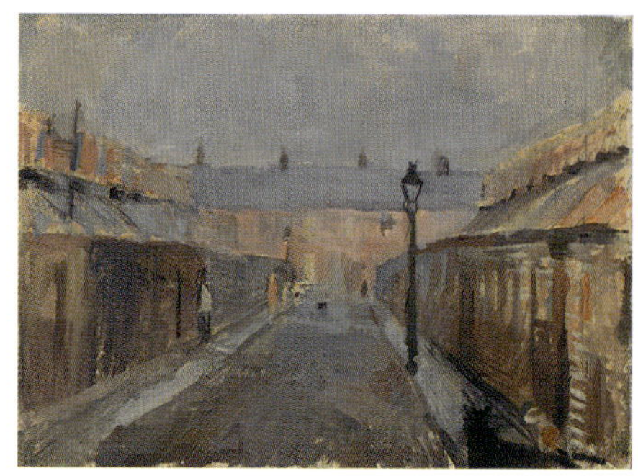

Eyton, Anthony John Plowden b.1923
Newcastle c.1955
oil on paper 21 x 30
AC 358

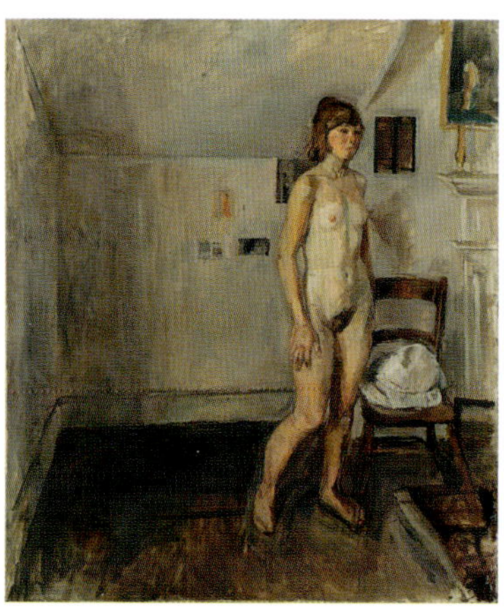

Eyton, Anthony John Plowden b.1923
Standing Nude 1958
oil on canvas 148.5 x 130
AC 601

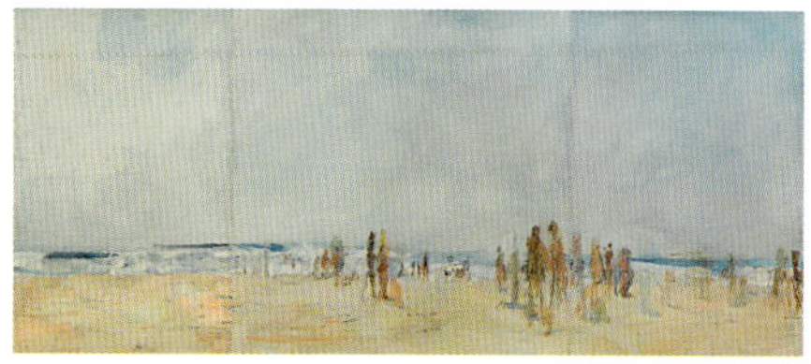

Eyton, Anthony John Plowden b.1923
Bathers 1973–1975
oil on canvas 188 x 420
AC 1619

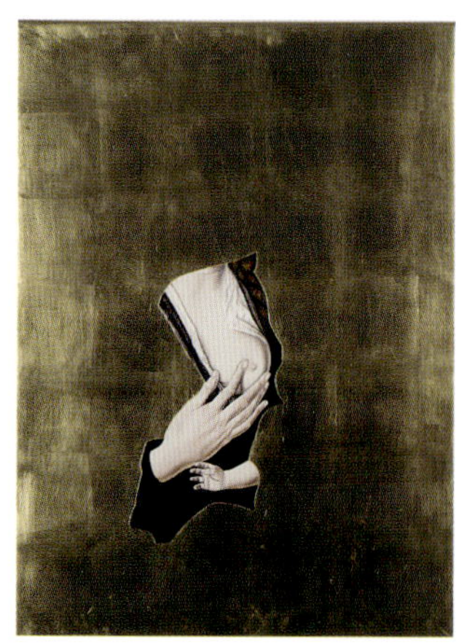

Fairnington, Mark b.1957
The Greek Madonna 1993
oil & gold leaf on panel 60 x 44
ACC167/1998

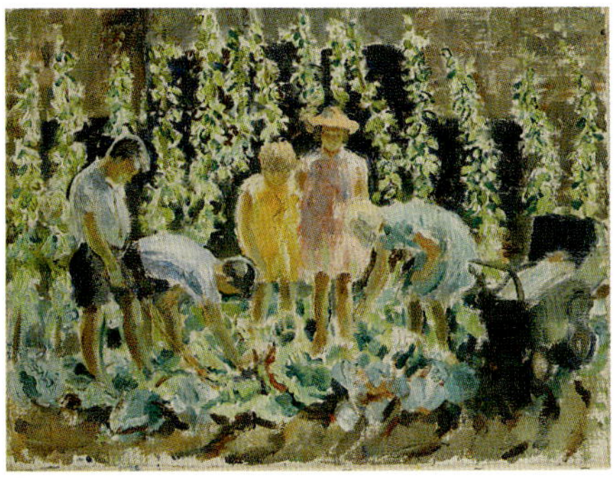

Faithfull, Leila 1896–1994
Evacuees 1941
oil on canvas 30.2 x 40.3
AC 64

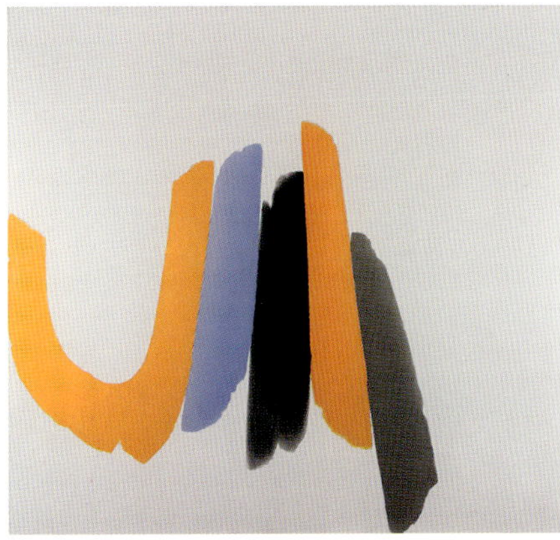

Farmer, Bernard 1919–2002
Pelagic II 1967
acrylic on canvas 163.5 x 179.7
AC 961

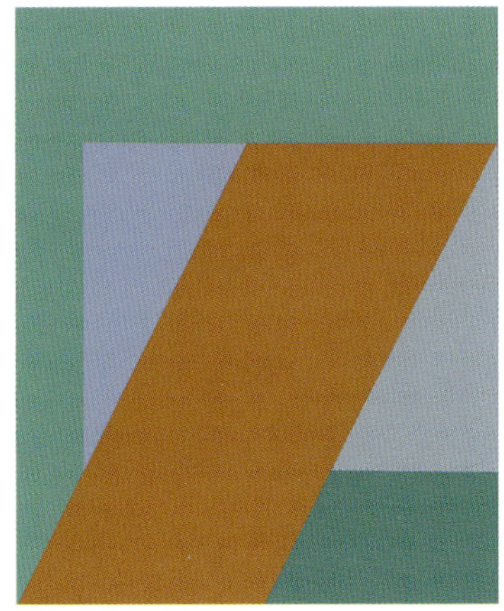

Farmer, Bernard 1919–2002
Helios II 1982
acrylic on canvas 170 x 139.2
AC 5077

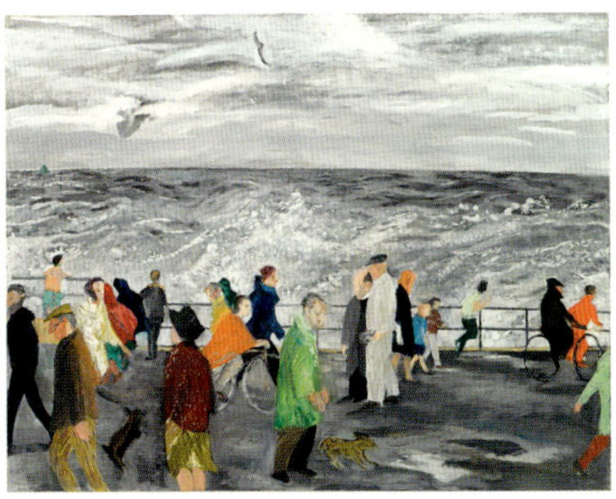

Farrell, Anthony b.1945
Winter, Leigh Beach 1984–1985
oil on canvas 117 x 152
AC 5434

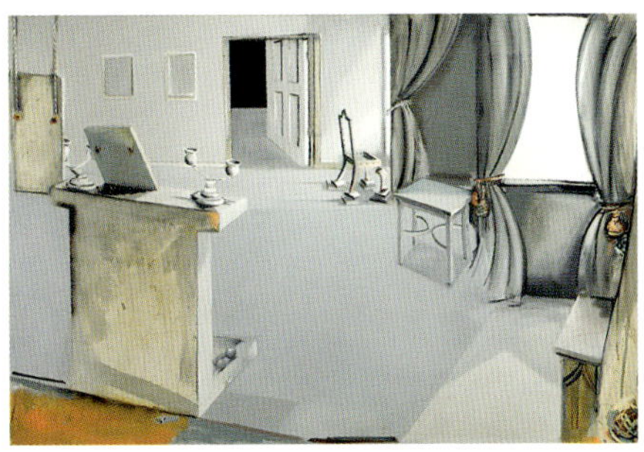

Farthing, Stephen b.1950
Mrs G's Chair 1982
encaustic on canvas 165 x 269
AC 5167

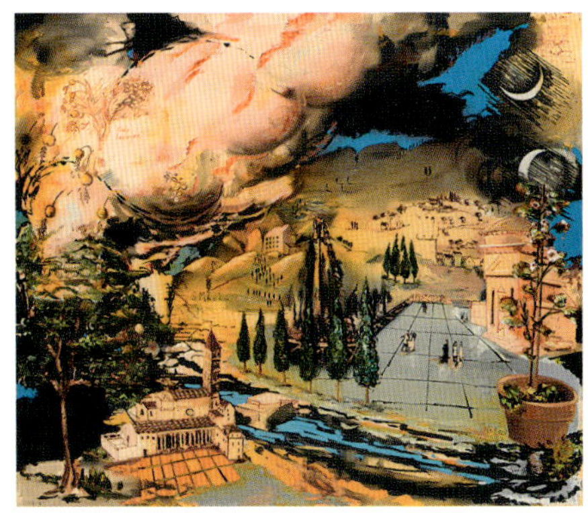

Farthing, Stephen b.1950
Florence 1989
oil on canvas 173 x 207
ACC54/1989

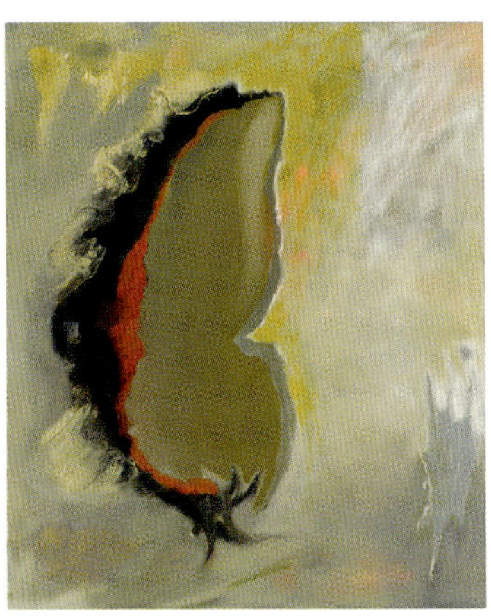

Feeney, Jacinta b.1954
This Brief Transit 1989
oil on canvas 182.1 x 160
ACC36/1991

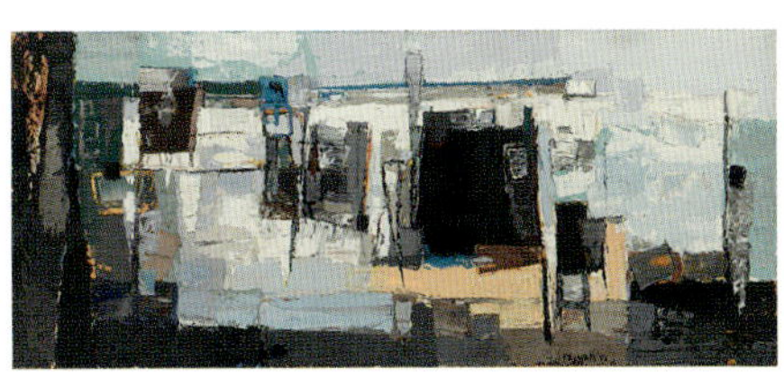

Feiler, Paul b.1918
Large Welsh Bay 1952
oil on board 52 x 122
AC 259

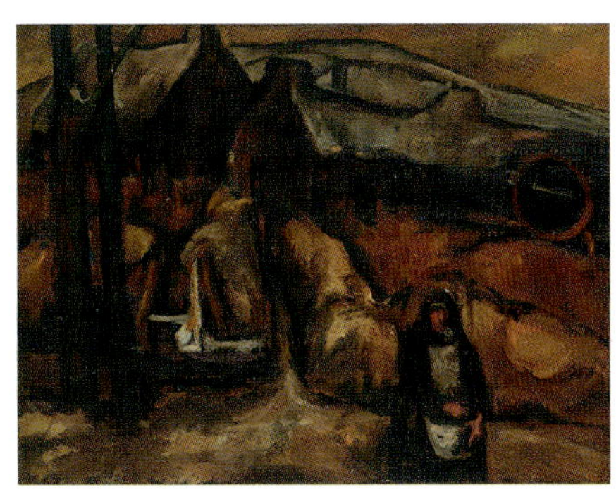

Fell, Sheila Mary 1931–1979
Woman in the Snow 1955
oil on canvas 76.2 x 101.6
ACA 42

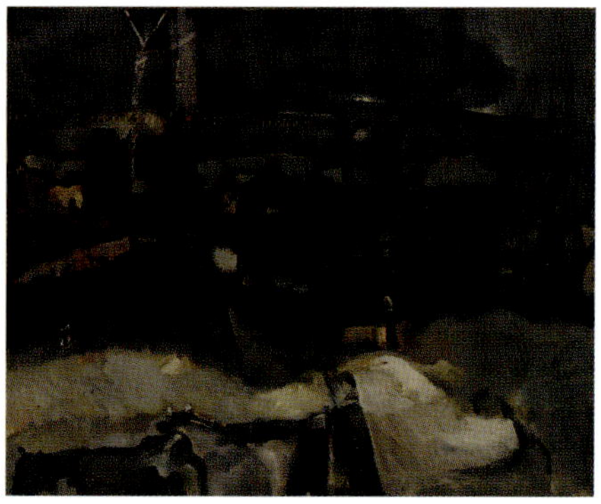

Fell, Sheila Mary 1931–1979
Snowscape with Clouds 1958
oil on canvas 101.6 x 126.6
AC 455

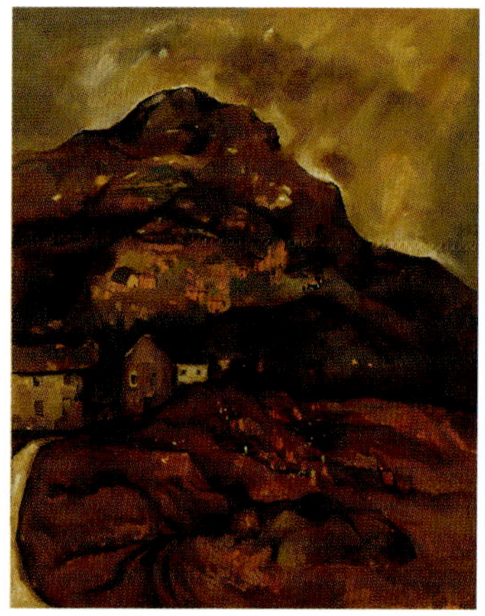

Fell, Sheila Mary 1931–1979
Potato Pickers I 1960
oil on canvas 127.6 x 101.6
ACC2/1960

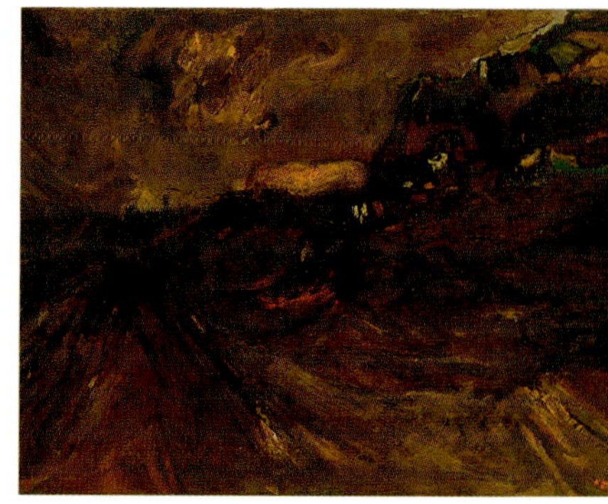

Fell, Sheila Mary 1931–1979
Silage Heap and Cows, Drumburgh 1964
oil on canvas 70 x 90
ACA 41

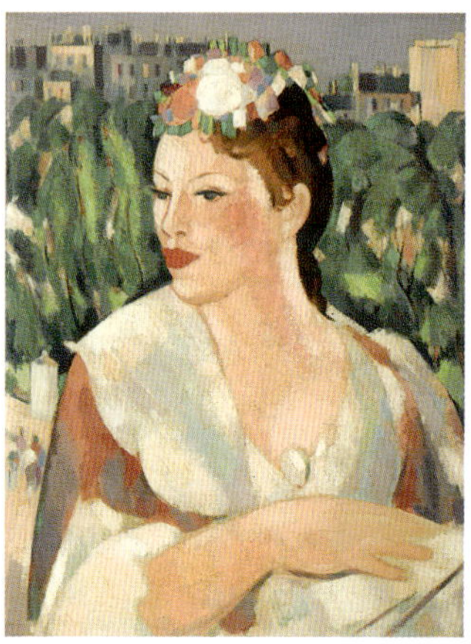

Fergusson, John Duncan 1874–1961
'Hillhead', Eileen 1941
oil on canvas 65 x 53
AC 502

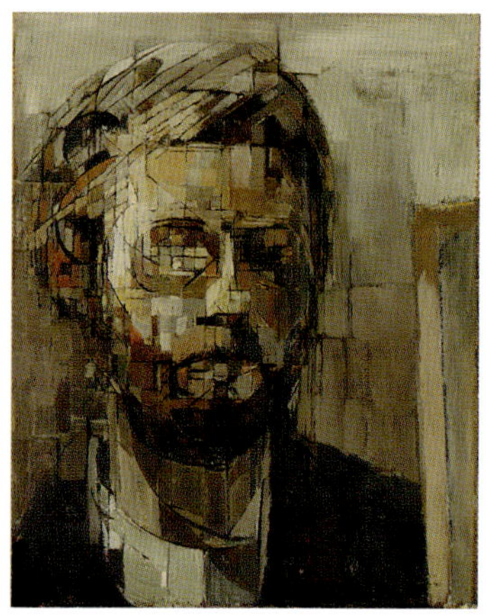

Fergusson, John Duncan 1874–1961
Self Portrait 1955
oil on canvas 50.5 x 40
AC 400

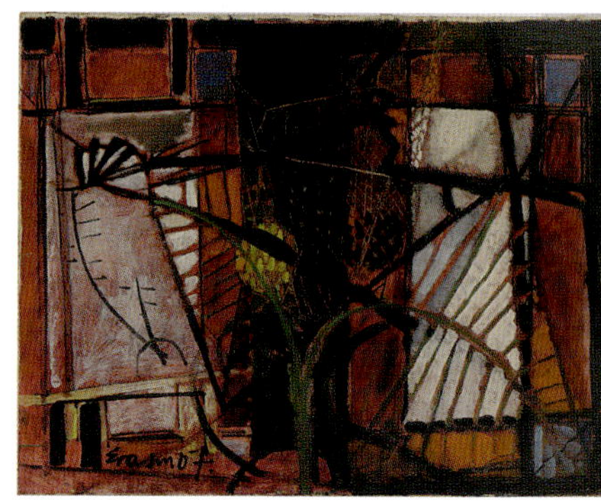

Fernández, Erasmo b.1924
Untitled (Abstract: Fish and Nets)
oil on board 71.4 x 91.8
AC 655

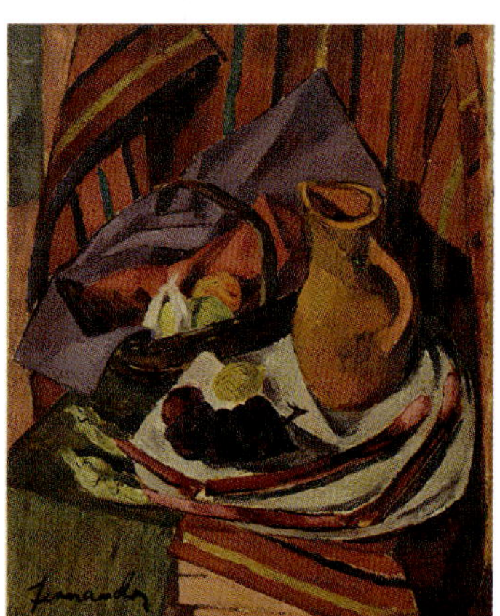

Fernández, Erasmo b.1924
Untitled Still Life (Jug, Basket and Fruit)
oil on canvas 79 x 64.5
AC 654

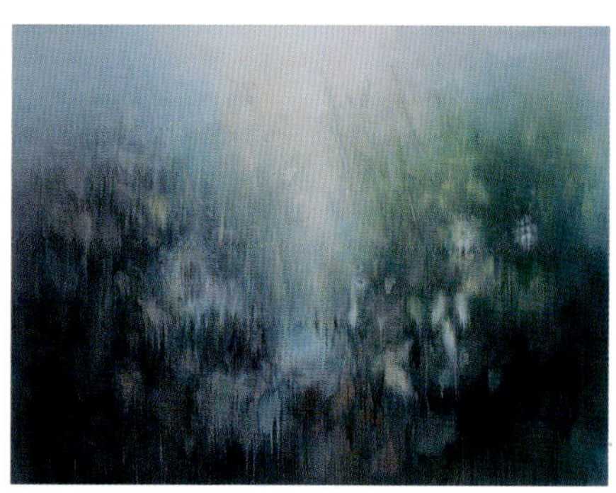

Ferris, Dee b.1973
Ideal Homes (this is the beginning of forever)
2005
oil on canvas 170 x 230
ACC1/2005

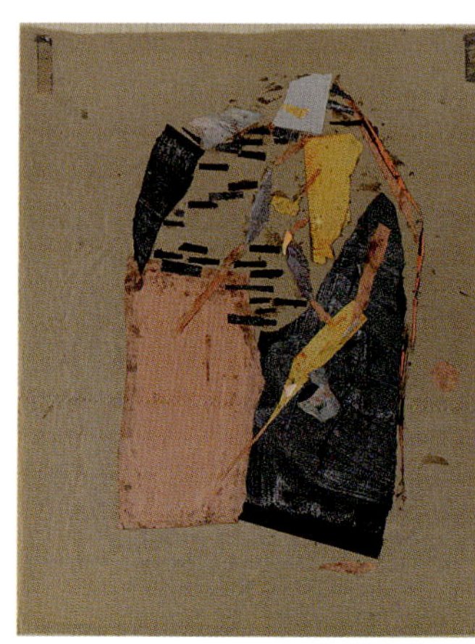

Few, Elsie Evelyn 1909–1980
The Iron Maiden 1968
paper, lacquer & paint on canvas 79.5 x 63.3
AC 1997

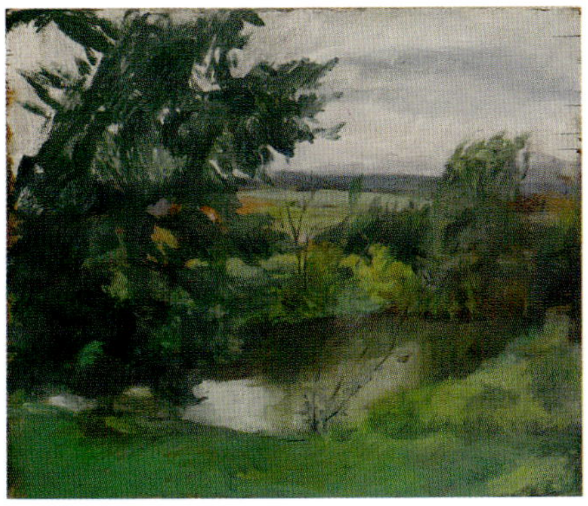

Few, Elsie Evelyn 1909–1980
The Pond at Hawkshall
oil on board 19.5 x 24
AC 343

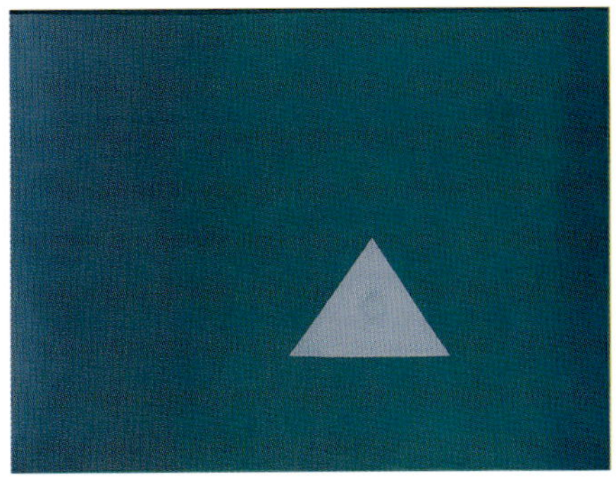

Fielding, Brian 1933–1987
Mandala 39 1966
acrylic on canvas 152.4 x 203.2
AC 928

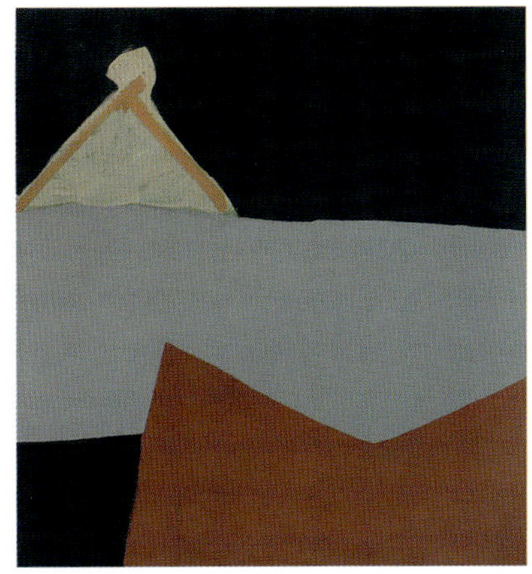

Fielding, Brian 1933–1987
Painting No.323 1974
acrylic on canvas 207 x 195
AC 1504

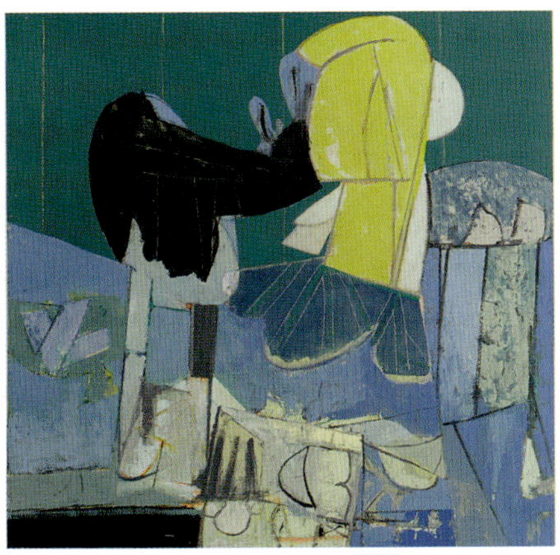

Fielding, Brian 1933–1987
Milk Bar 1986
oil on canvas 191 x 203
AC 5490

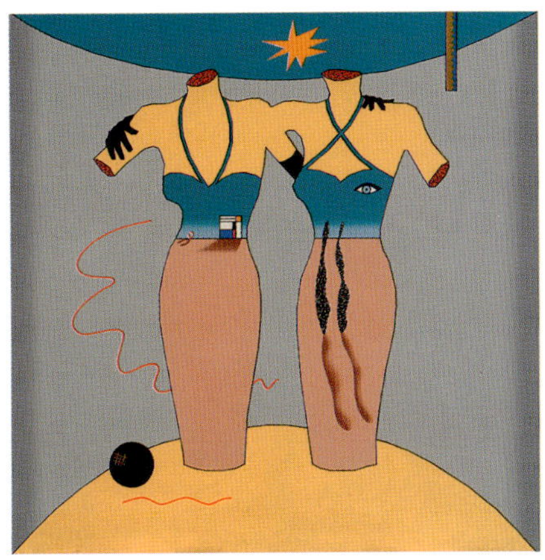

Fields, Duggie b.1945
Stumped 1976
acrylic on canvas 182.8 x 182.5
AC 2024

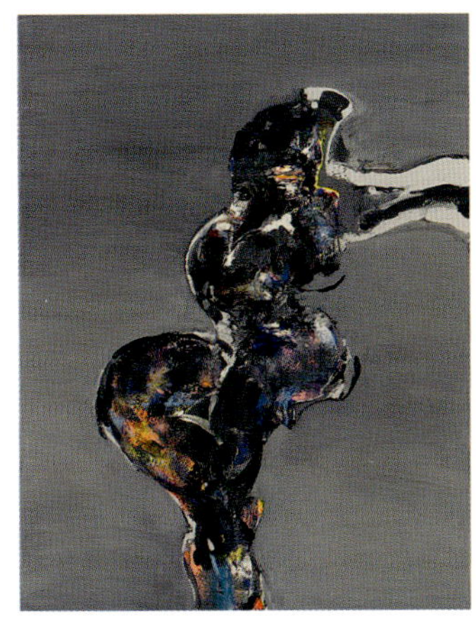

Finer, Stephen b.1949
Seated Nude 1979
oil on canvas 124.5 x 96.9
AC 5228

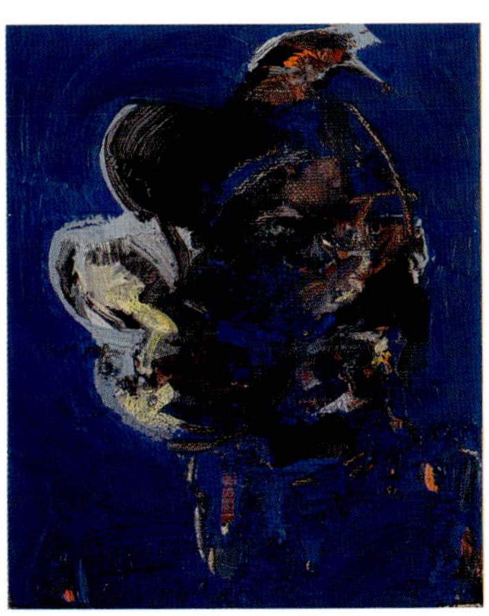

Finer, Stephen b.1949
Sandra Fisher 1979
oil on canvas 30.2 x 25.2
AC 2071

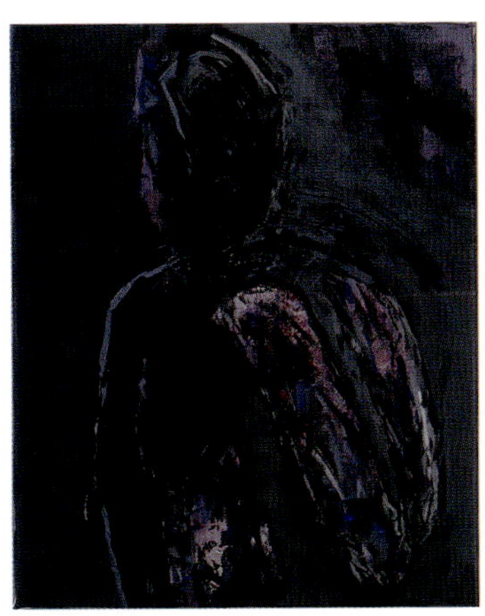

Finer, Stephen b.1949
Woman Handling Her Left Breast 1986
oil on canvas 56 x 46
AC 5428

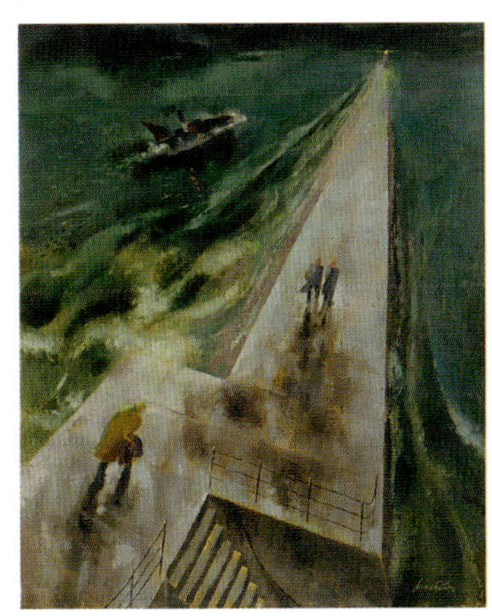

Fitton, James 1899–1982
The Breakwater
oil on canvas 76.8 x 63.5
AC 65

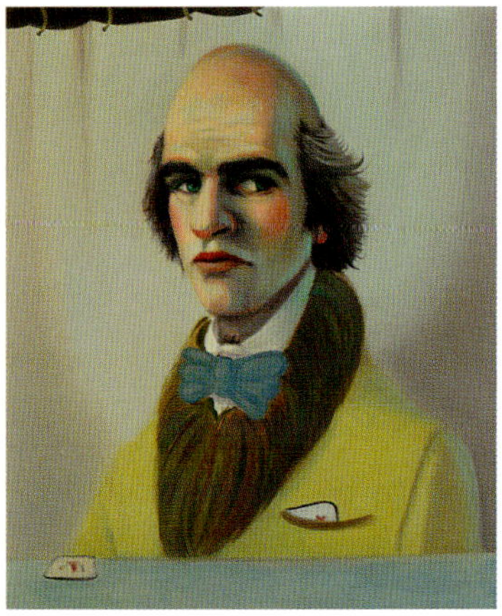

Flannigan, Moyna b.1963
The Last Minister 2002
oil on canvas 65 x 55
ACC54/2002

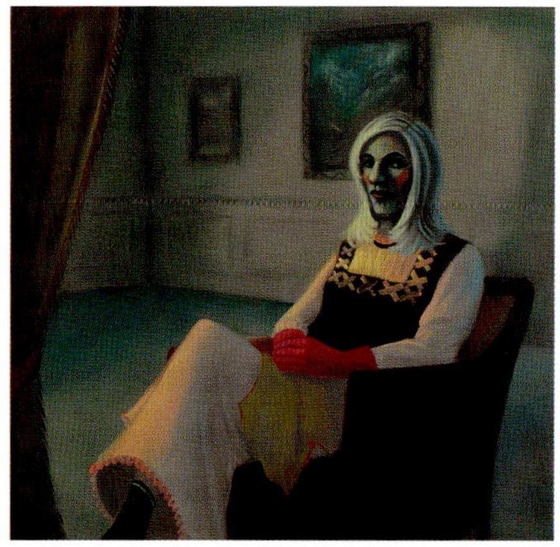

Flannigan, Moyna b.1963
Toujours la même chose 2002
oil on canvas 150 x 160
ACC55/2002

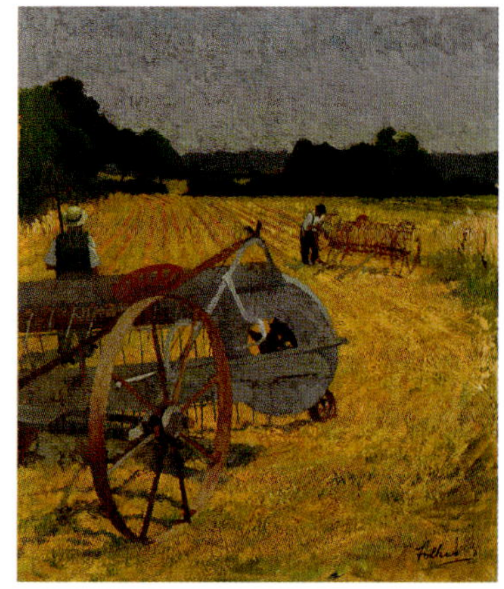

Folkes, Peter L. b.1923
The Hayfield
oil on canvas 34.3 x 29.2
AC 254

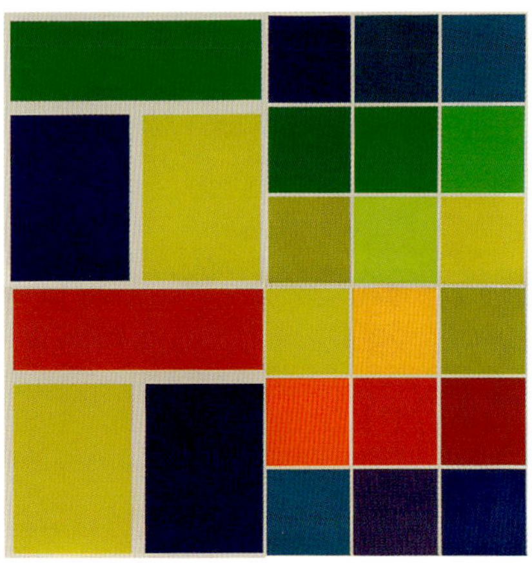

Forbes, Richard b.1953
Two Lexical Groups for L1, Two Morphemic Groups for L1 1982
oil on canvas 124 x 124
AC 5165

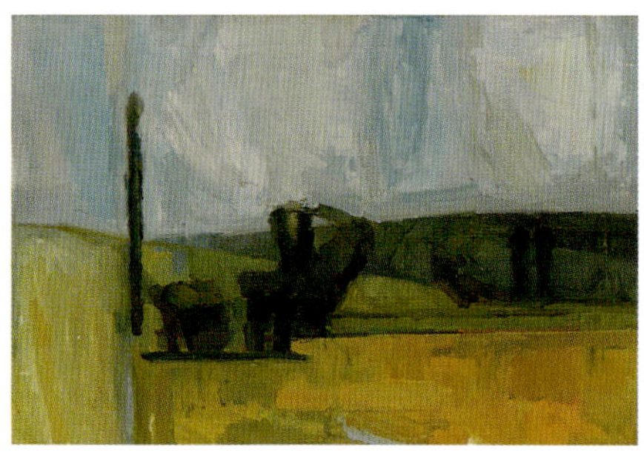

Forge, Andrew 1923–2002
Landscape, Ericeira 1959
oil on canvas 60 x 90.5
AC 565

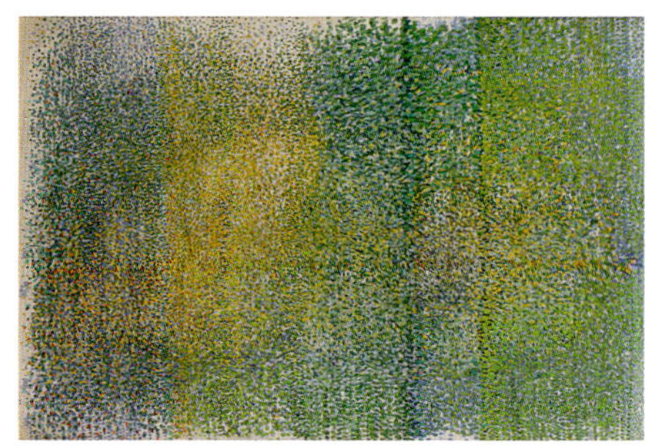

Forge, Andrew 1923–2002
Summertime c.1964
oil on canvas 102.9 x 152.4
AC 893

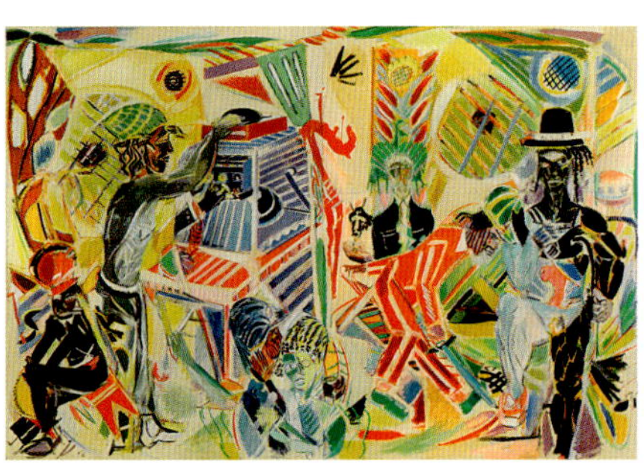

Forrester, Denzil b.1956
Witchdoctor 1983
oil on canvas 274 x 396
AC 5251

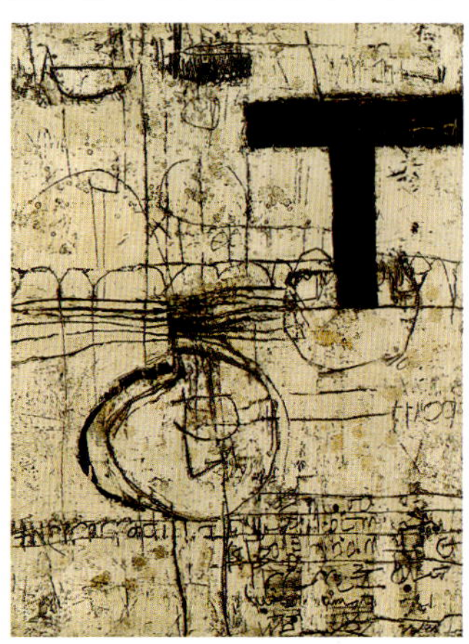

Forrester, John 1922–2002
Two of a Kind 1962
oil on canvas 116 x 89
AC 632

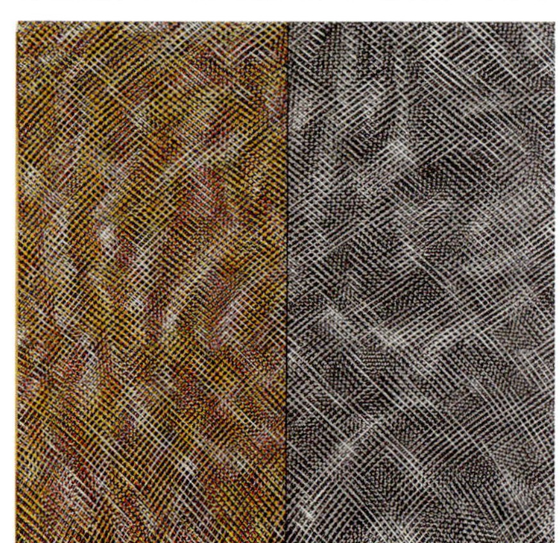

Forster, Noel 1932–2007
Two Units, One in Grey 1975
acrylic on linen 305 x 305
AC 1818

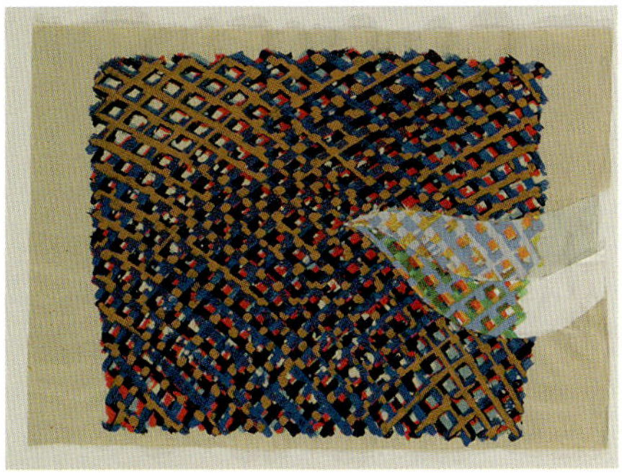

Forster, Noel 1932–2007
Untitled 1982
acrylic on paper 42.7 x 61
AC 5085

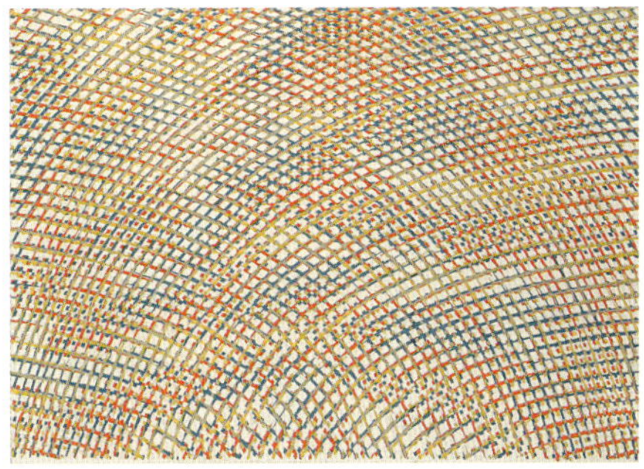

Forster, Noel 1932–2007
Untitled 1990–1991
oil on linen 152.5 x 213.5
ACC60/1997

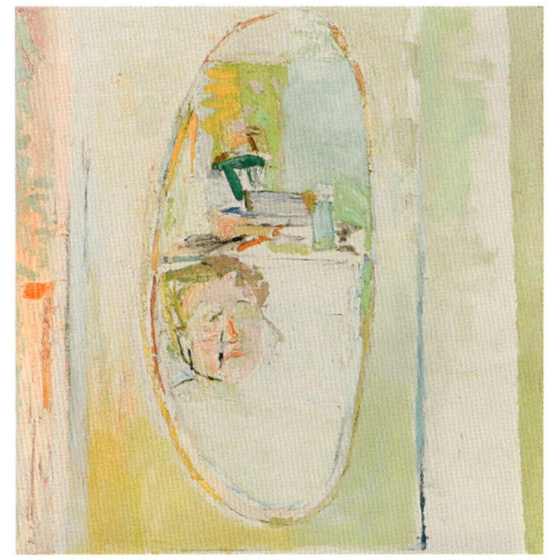

Foster, Dilys
Pink Head 1977
oil on canvas 94.3 x 94.5
AC 1910

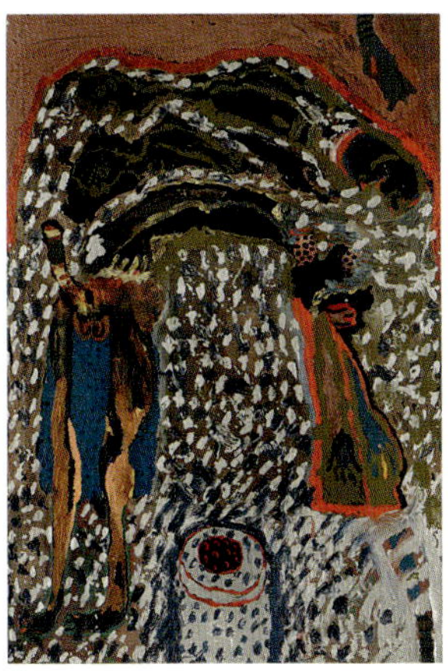

Foster, Graham b.1950
Untitled 1976–1979
oil, acrylic & industrial paint on board 243.6 x 167.5
AC 4043

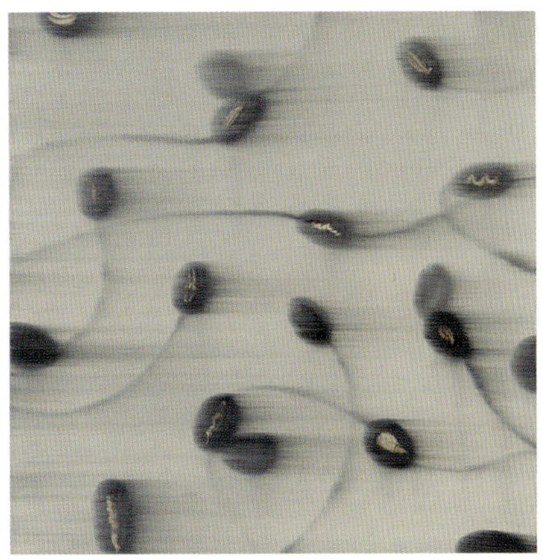

Francis, Mark b.1962
Positive 1992
oil on canvas 76 x 76
ACC172/1998

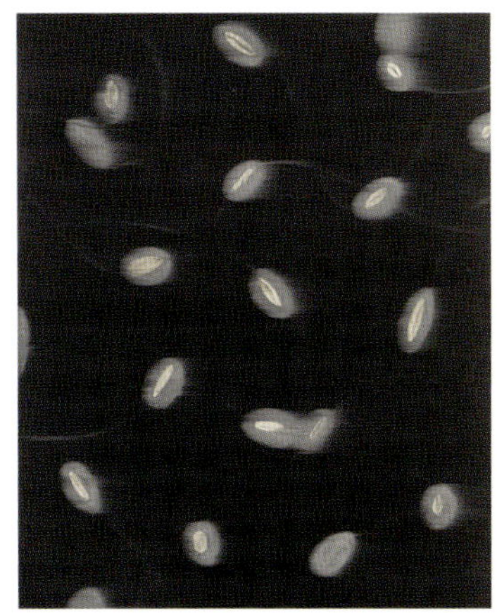

Francis, Mark b.1962
Untitled (Negative 2) 1992
oil on canvas 107 x 91.5
ACC173/1998

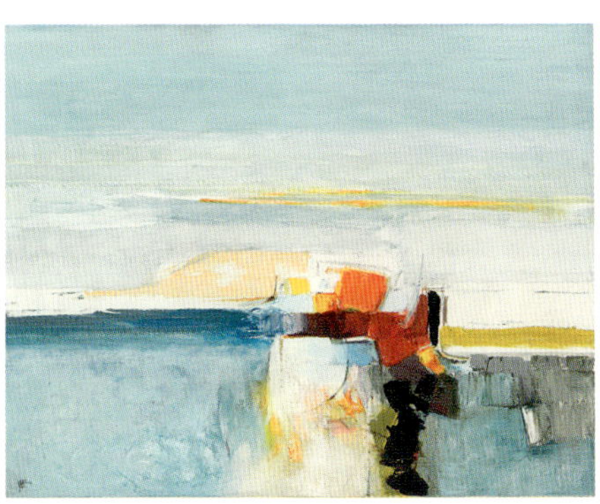

Fraser, Donald Hamilton 1929–2009
Beachscape II 1955
oil on canvas 70.5 x 90.5
AC 376

Fraser, Donald Hamilton 1929–2009
Mont Saint-Geneviève 1965
oil on canvas 122 x 91
AC 818

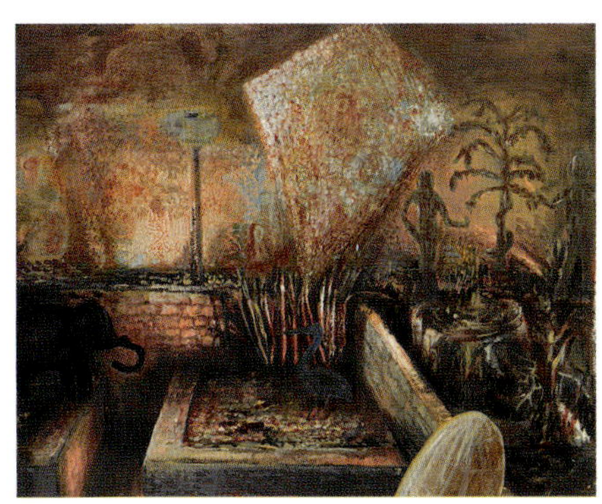

Fredman, Nick b.1955
In My Back Yard 1986
acrylic on paper 39 x 50
ACC6/1986

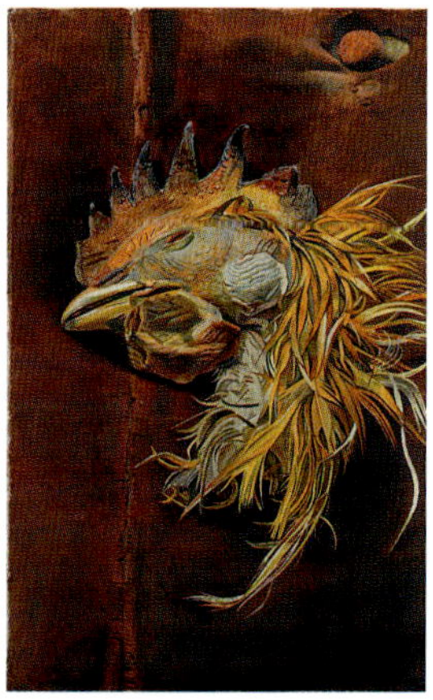

Freud, Lucian 1922–2011
Dead Cock's Head 1951
oil on canvas 20.3 x 12.7
AC 243

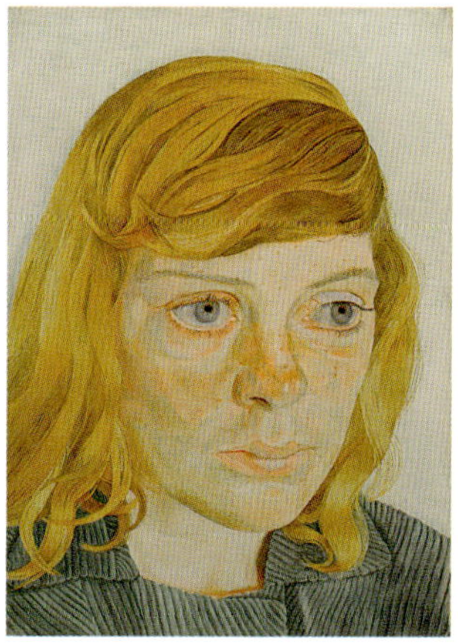

Freud, Lucian 1922–2011
Girl in a Green Dress 1954
tempera on board 32.5 x 23.6
AC 363

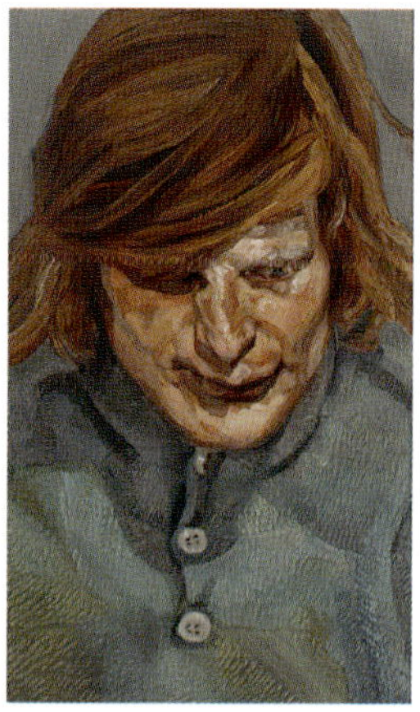

Freud, Lucian 1922–2011
Small Head 1973–1974 & 1981
oil on canvas 26.3 x 15.7
ACC2/1981

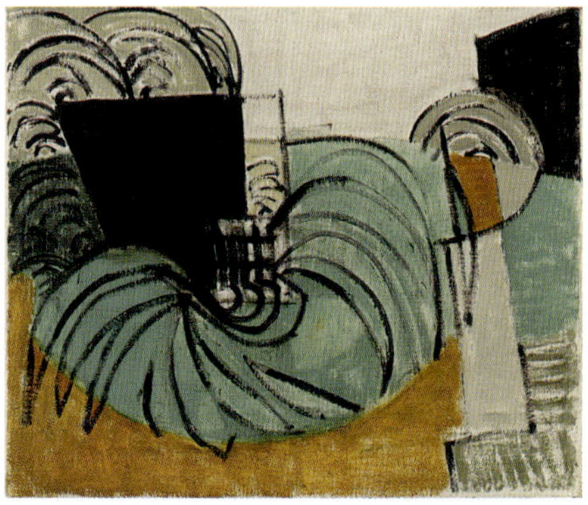

Frost, Terry 1915–2003
Movement, Green and Black 1952
oil on canvas 50.5 x 61
AC 251

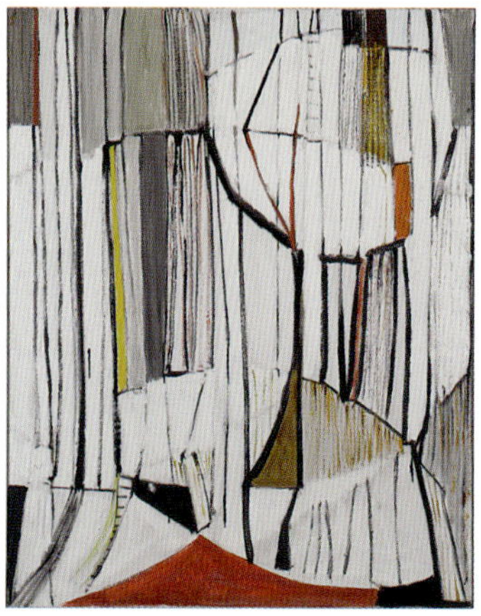

Frost, Terry 1915–2003
Red, Black, White (1955) 1955
oil & collage on canvas 124.5 x 101.2
AC 393

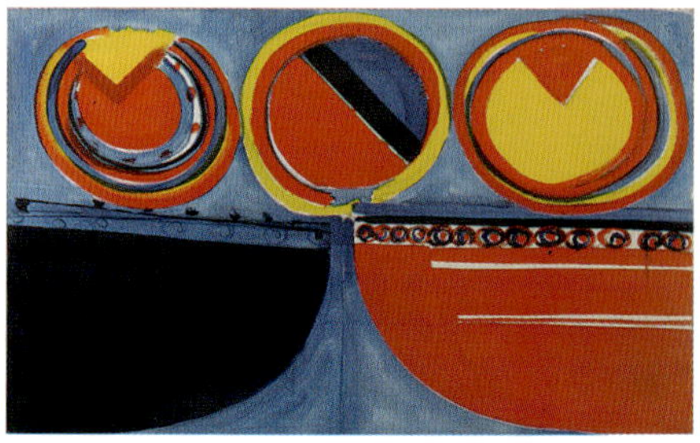

Frost, Terry 1915–2003
Red, Yellow and Blue 1962
oil on canvas 92.7 x 145.4
AC 708

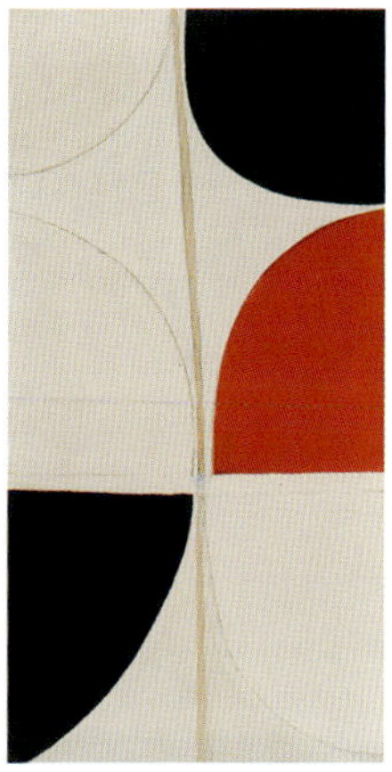

Frost, Terry 1915–2003
Red, Black, White (1965) 1965
oil & collage on canvas 121.6 x 63.7
ACA 43

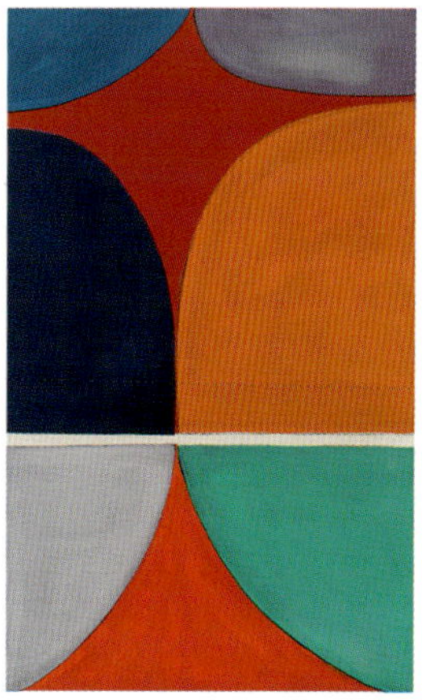

Frost, Terry 1915–2003
Ginger and Purple 'Chirpy' 1966
oil on canvas 144.8 x 91.4
ACA 44

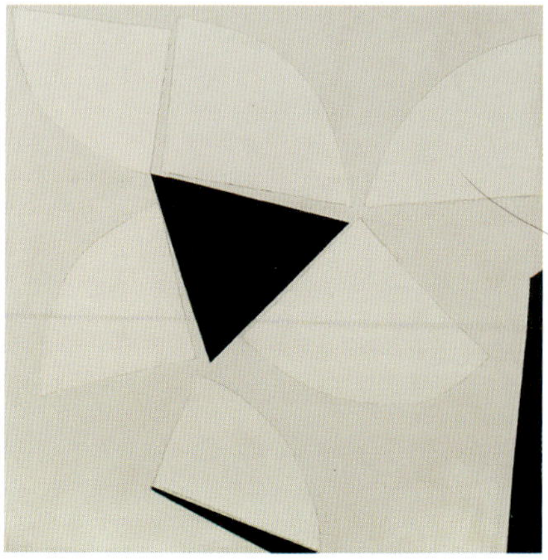

Frost, Terry 1915–2003
Black and White Sept. 78 1978
acrylic & collage on canvas 180.3 x 180.3
AC 3005

Facing page: Aitchison, Craigie Ronald John, b.1926, *Crucifixion* (detail), 1959, (p. 7)

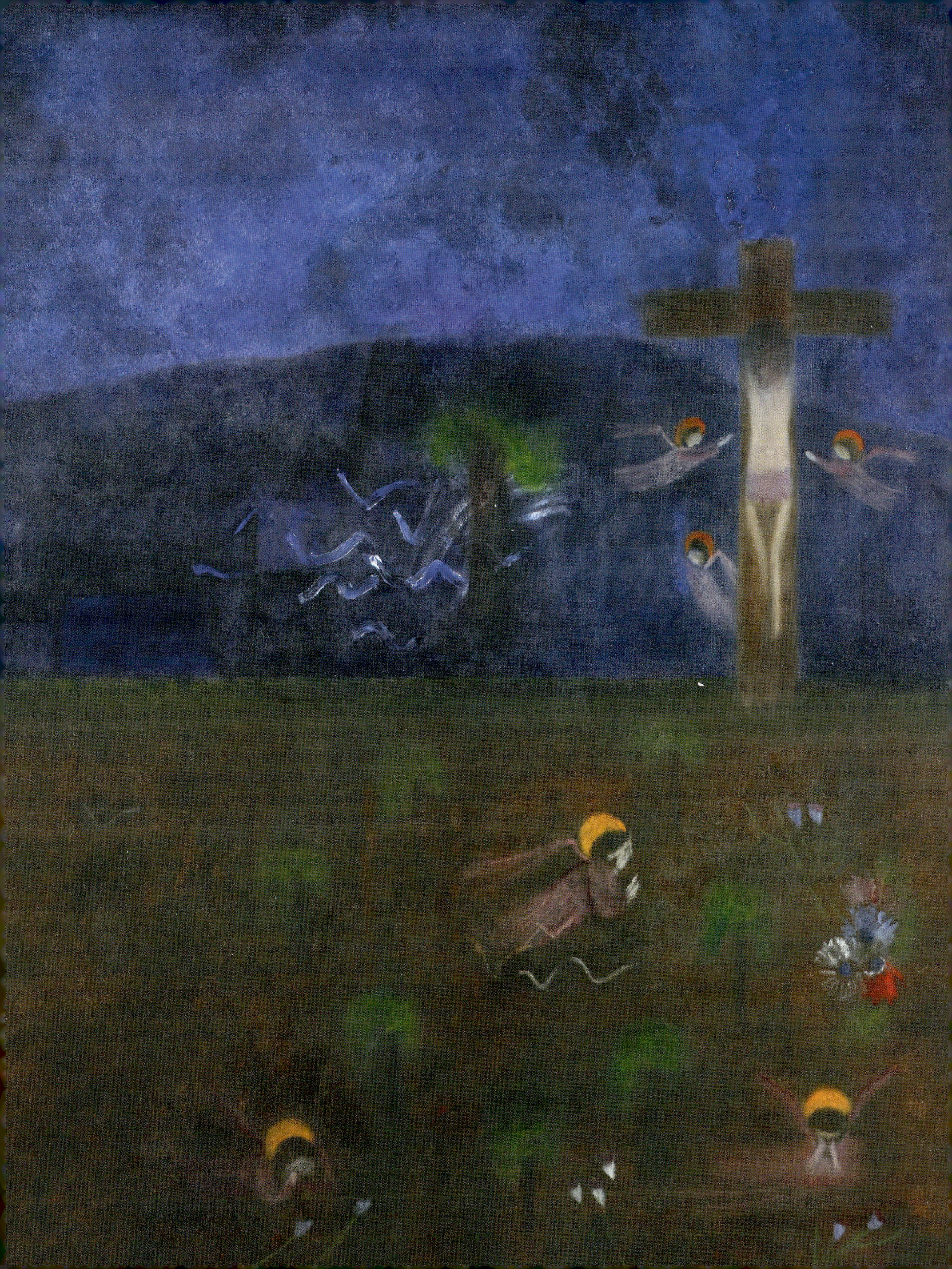

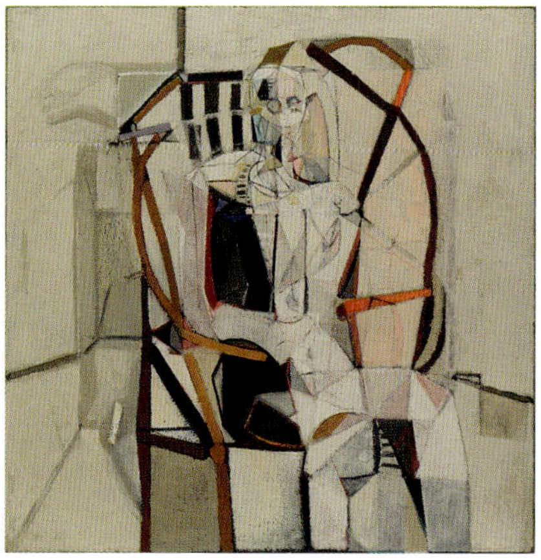

Froy, Martin b.1926
Seated Girl 1952
oil on board 121 x 121
AC 244

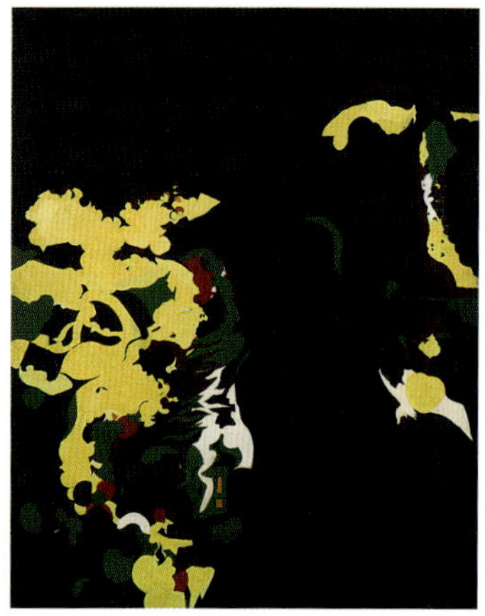

Froy, Martin b.1926
Landscape with Figures 1963–1966
acrylic on board 152 x 122
AC 916

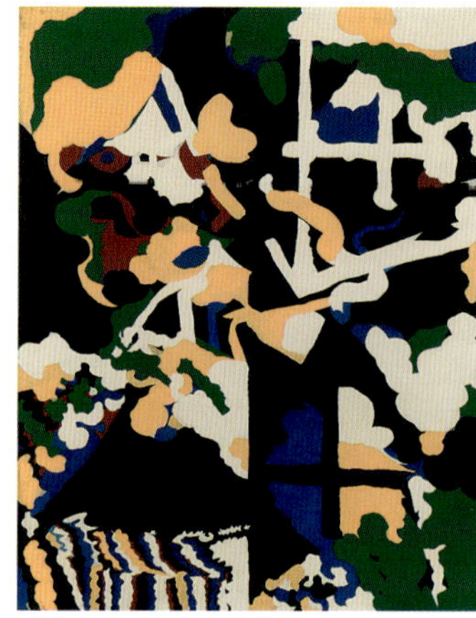

Froy, Martin b.1926
Colham 1968
acrylic on canvas 152 x 121.3
AC 978

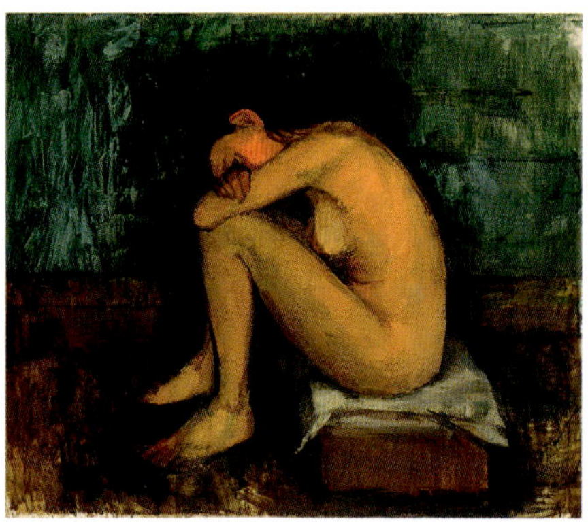

Fry, Anthony b.1927
Nude 1954
oil on canvas 76.2 x 91.8
AC 342

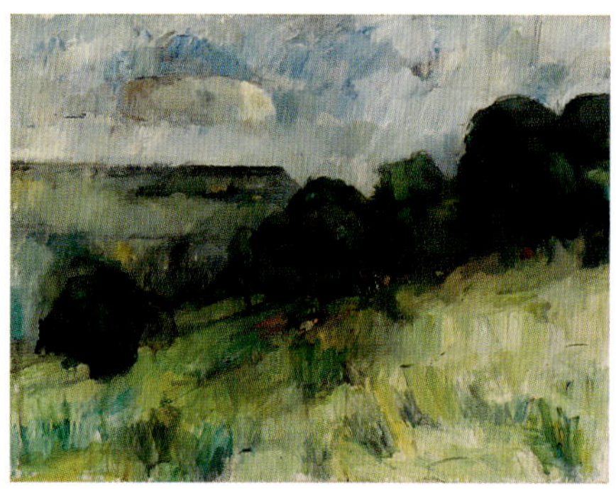

Fry, Anthony b.1927
Landscape 1955
oil on canvas 74 x 99
AC 386

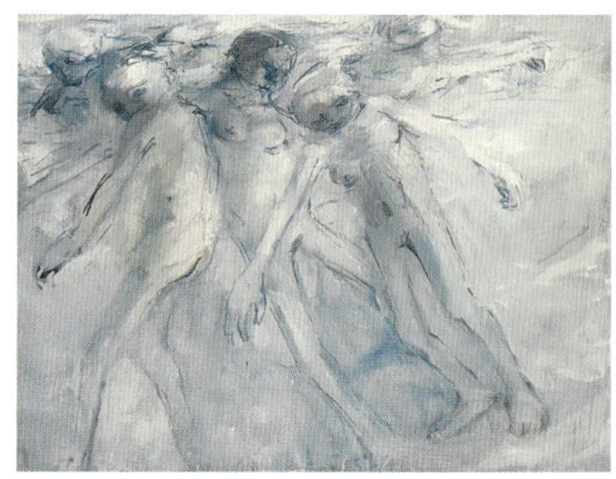

Fry, Anthony b.1927
Dance White 1960
oil on canvas 91.4 x 121.9
AC 553

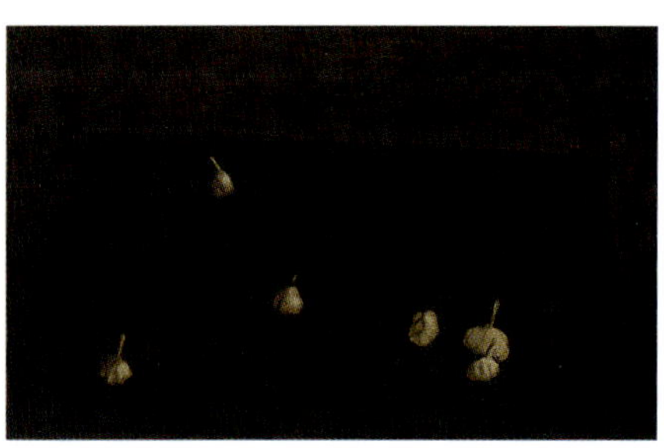

Fussell, Michael 1927–1974
Garlic c.1956
oil on canvas 75.5 x 127
AC 414

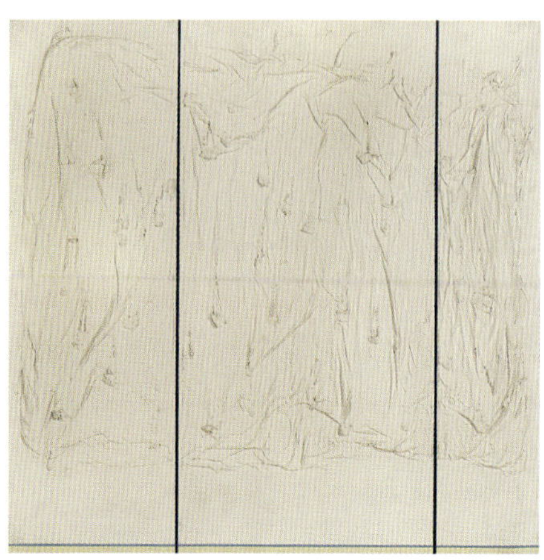

Fussell, Michael 1927–1974
Sharp Division 1961
oil & collage on canvas 86 x 86
AC 603

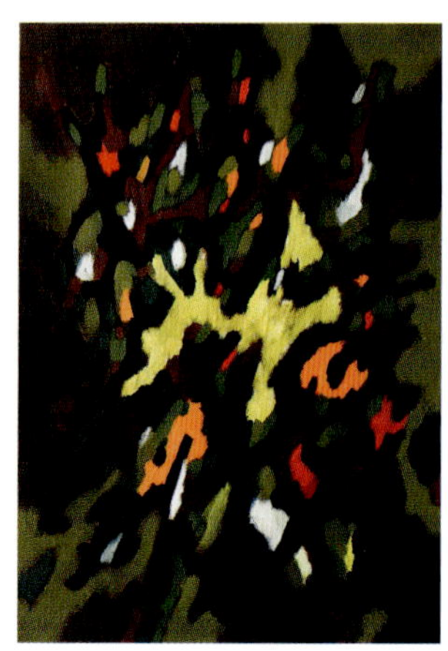

Gear, William 1915–1997
Christmas Tree 1950
oil on canvas 99 x 71.5
AC 187

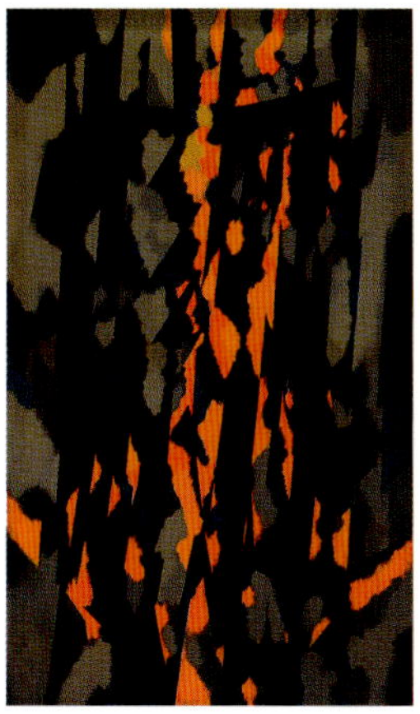

Gear, William 1915–1997
Black Armature with Yellow 1965
oil on canvas 152.4 x 91.4
AC 892

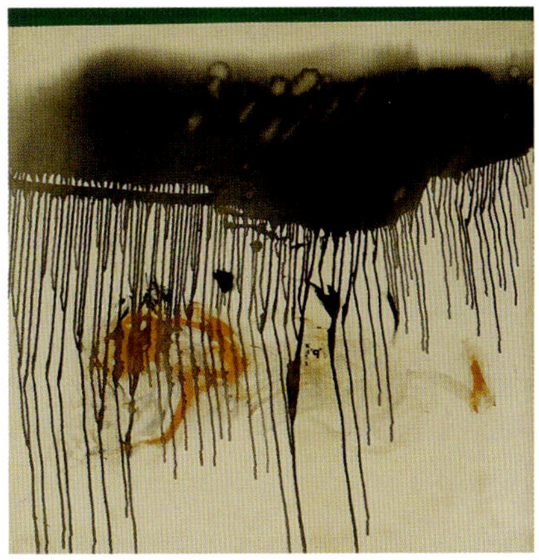

Geoffrey, Iqbal b.1939
In Search of the Ideal Landscape 1965
oil on canvas 121.9 x 121.9
AC 885

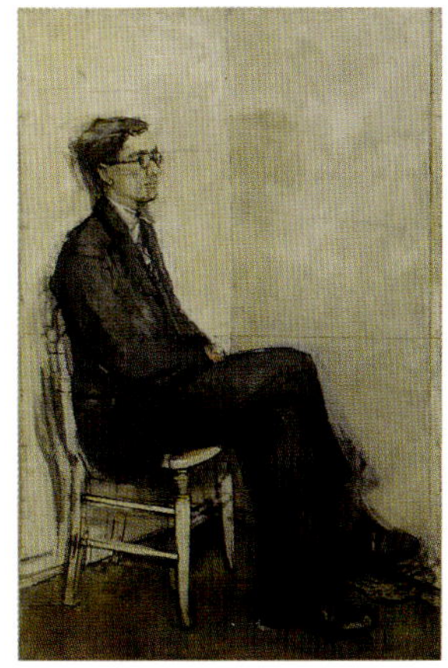

George, Patrick b.1923
Nicholas Browne 1952–1957
oil on canvas 183 x 123.5
AC 449

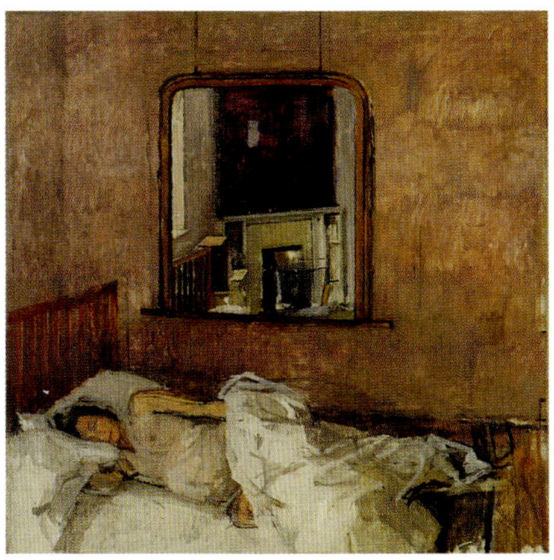

George, Patrick b.1923
June in Bed 1955
oil on canvas 121.9 x 121.9
AC 402

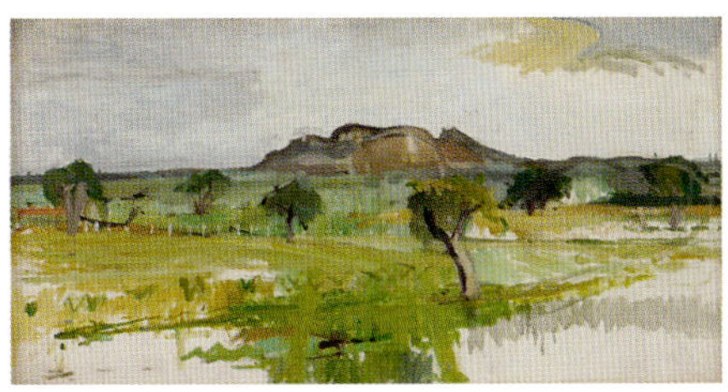

George, Patrick b.1923
Nigerian Landscape: View of Kuffena 1959
oil on board 60.7 x 121.8
ACA 26

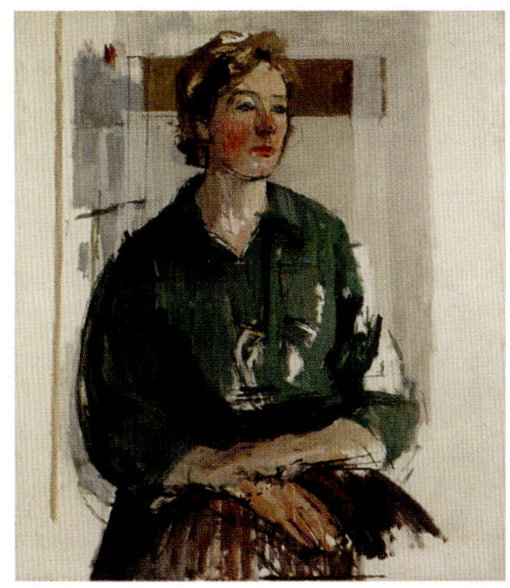

George, Patrick b.1923
Joanna Drew (1929–2003) 1960–1961
oil on canvas 102 x 92
ACC16/1992

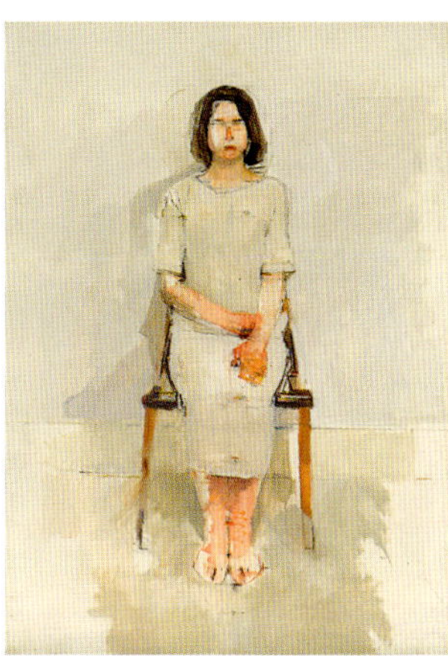

George, Patrick b.1923
Seated Girl 1964
oil on canvas 125.5 x 90
ACA 9

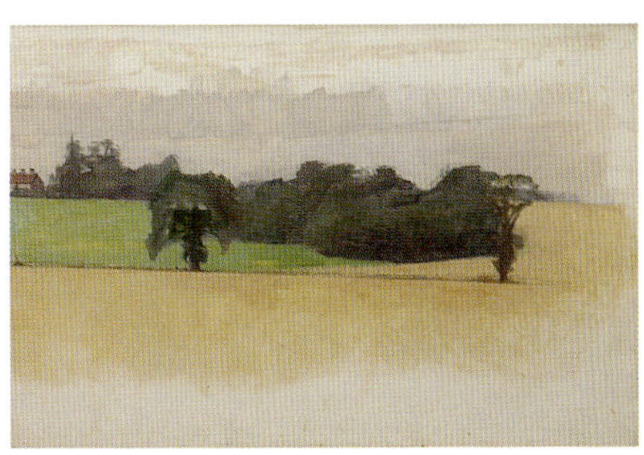

George, Patrick b.1923
View Towards Henny Church from Little Hickbush 1972
oil on canvas 90 x 134.5
AC 3082

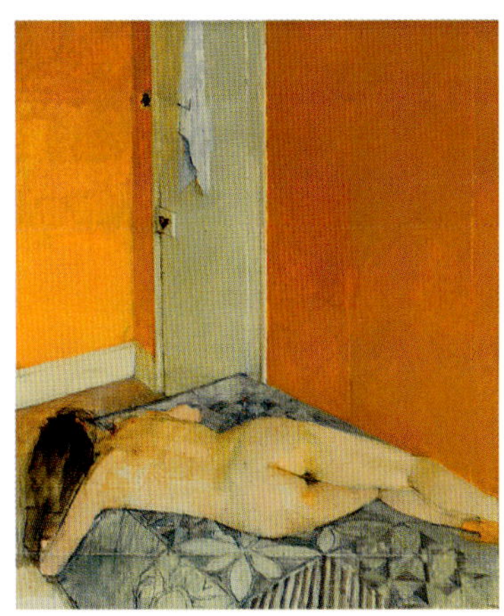

George, Patrick b.1923
Interior: Nude on a Bed 1976
oil on canvas 106.5 x 91
AC 1617

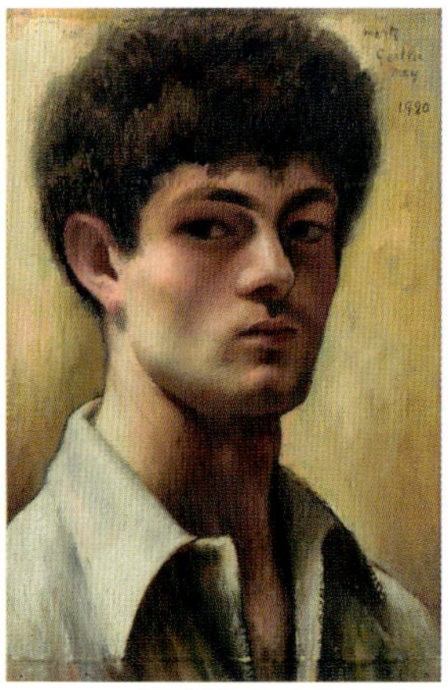

Gertler, Mark 1891–1939
Self Portrait 1920
oil on canvas 42.5 x 29.2
AC 331

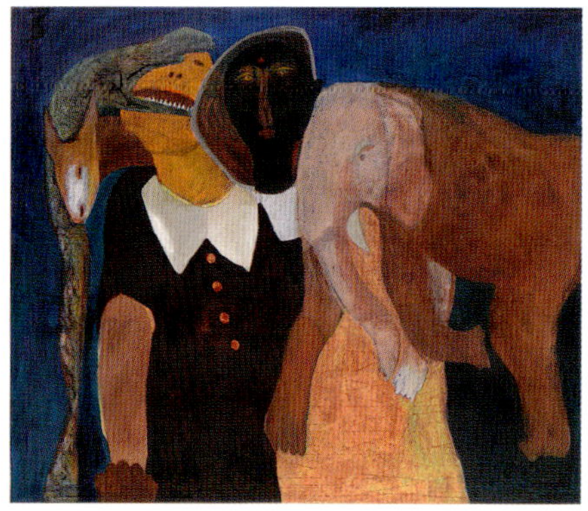

Ghosh, Amal b.1933
Allegory III 1987
acrylic on canvas 127 x 153
ACC28/1989

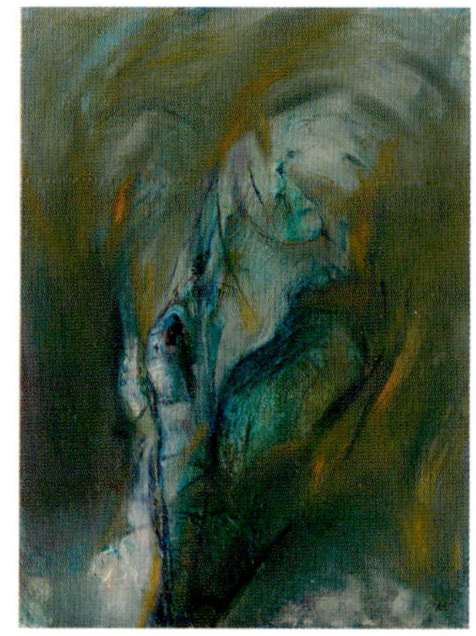

Gibbs, Evelyn 1905–1991
Cliff Projection 1965
oil on canvas 101.6 x 76.2
AC 1113

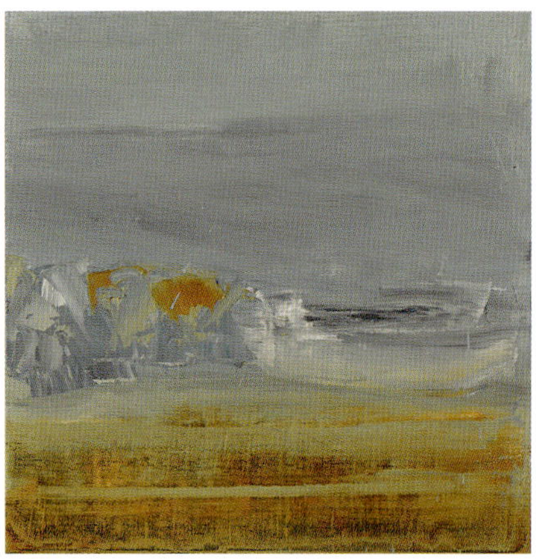

Gilbert, Dick 1935–2008
Approaching Wave 1965
oil on canvas 61 x 61
AC 800

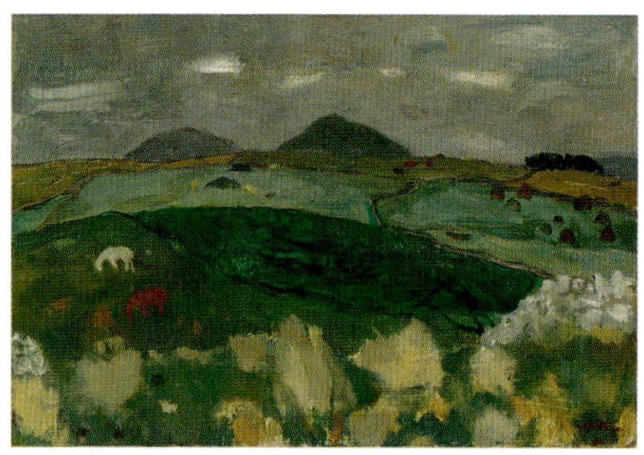

Gillies, William George 1898–1973
Eildon 1949
oil on canvas 31.8 x 47
AC 211

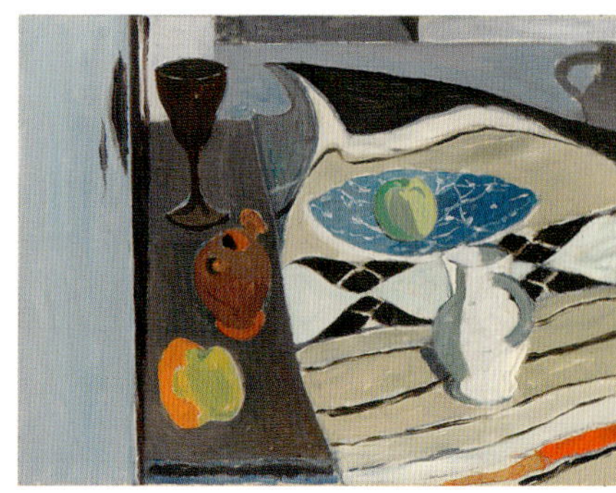

Gillies, William George 1898–1973
Still Life
oil on canvas 58.4 x 78.7
AC 355

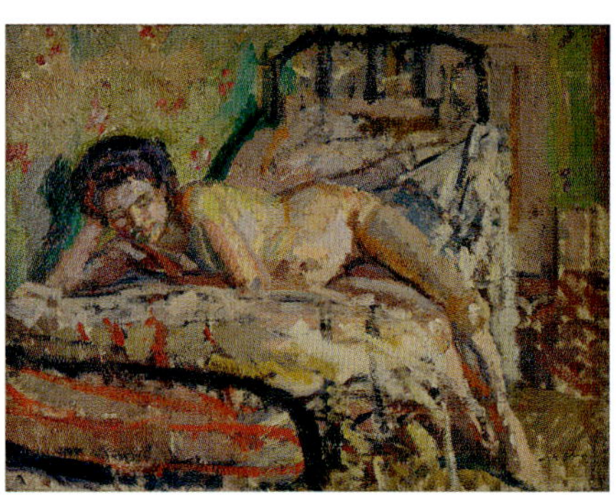

Gilman, Harold 1876–1919
The Model 1911
oil on canvas 45.7 x 61
ACC4/1958

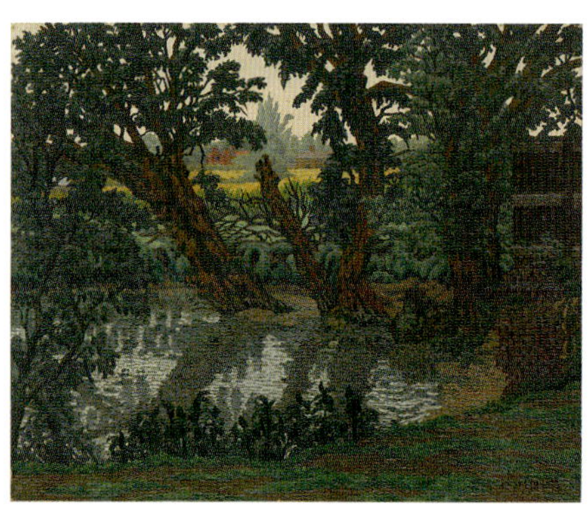

Ginner, Charles 1878–1952
The Rib, Standon, 1939 1939
oil on canvas 43.2 x 53.3
AC 66

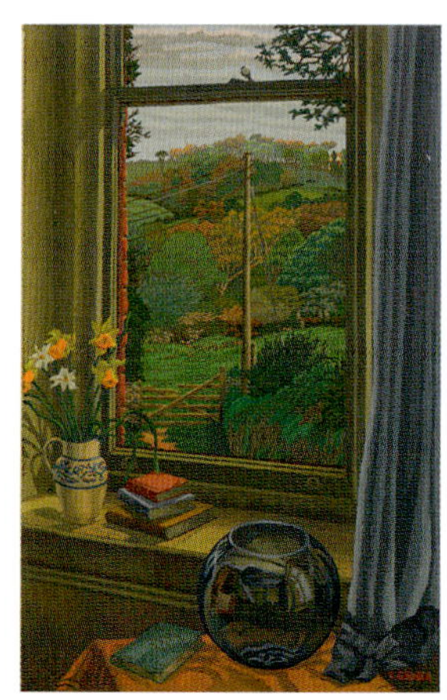

Ginner, Charles 1878–1952
Spring Day at Boscastle 1943
oil on canvas 83.8 x 53.3
AC 139

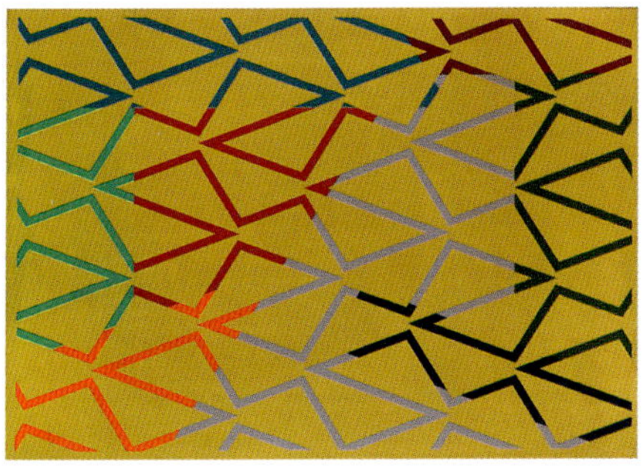

Ginsborg, Michael b.1943
Untitled 1969
acrylic on canvas 208 x 304.8
AC 1097

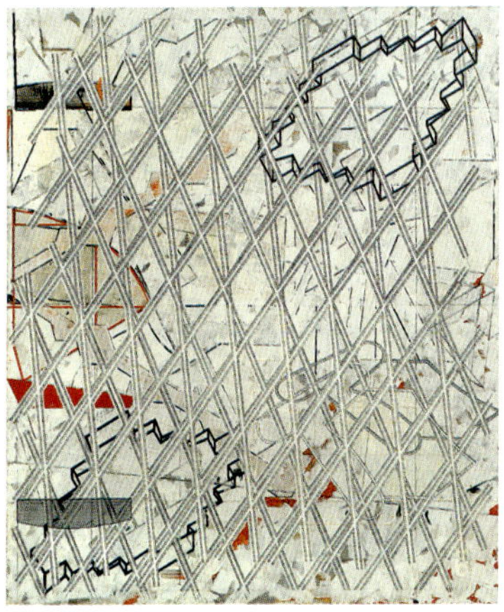

Ginsborg, Michael b.1943
Echoes 1974–1976
acrylic on cotton duck 193.4 x 162.8
AC 1730

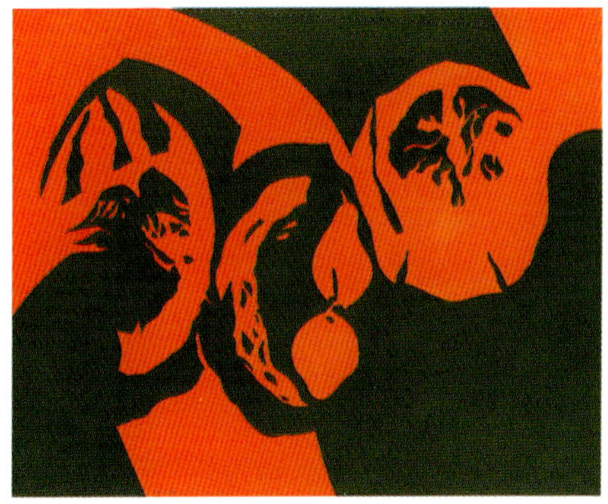

Gladwell, Rodney 1928–1979
Pumpkin and Pears 1970
oil on canvas 114 x 137
AC 1141

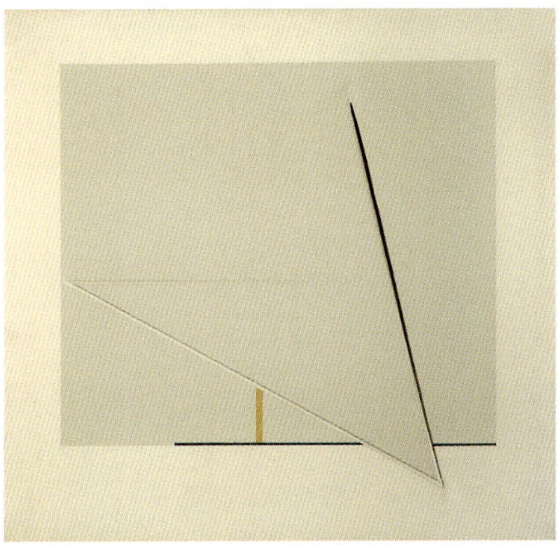

Goede, Jules de 1937–2007
SS7 No.1 1977
oil on canvas 72.7 x 84.2
AC 1834

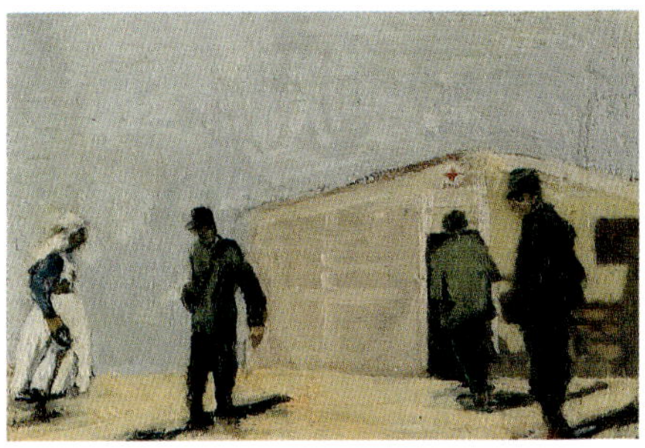

Golden, Pamela b.1959
Mrs Watson, Signor Treci and Traldi at the Hospital (from the 'Mrs Watson Pours the Coffee' series) 1995
oil & encaustic on paper 4.6 x 7
ACC43/1996

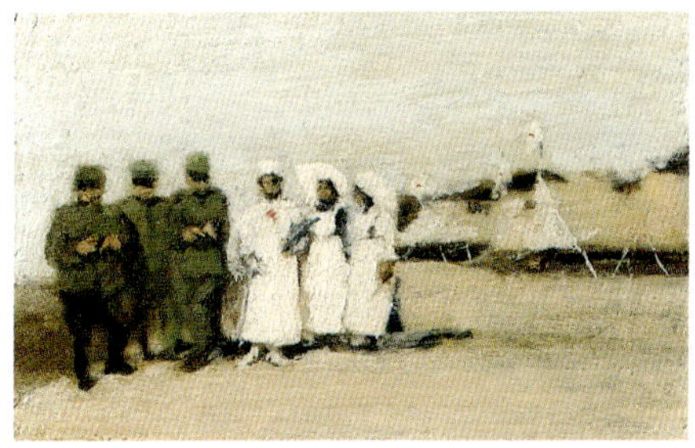

Golden, Pamela b.1959
Three Men, Three Women (from the 'Mrs Watson Pours the Coffee' series) 1995
oil & encaustic on paper 4.4 x 7
ACC44/1996

Golding, John b.1929
Phaestos – Green 1965–1966
acrylic on canvas 188 x 142.2
AC 857

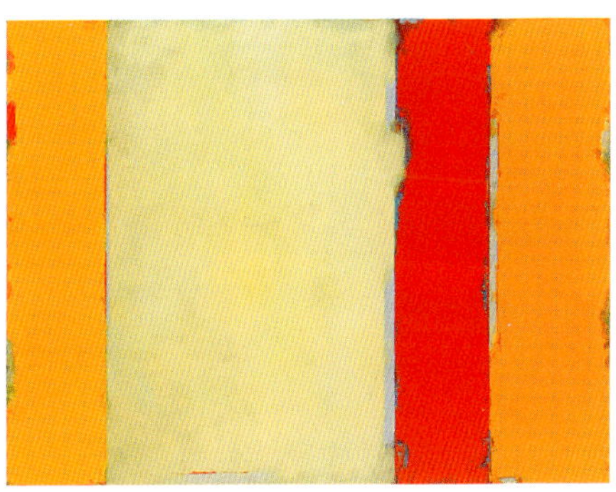

Golding, John b.1929
D (C. S.) VI 1975
acrylic on canvas 182.9 x 243.8
AC 1531

Gordon, Douglas b.1966
Painting No.19: Mark Rothko/Betty Parsons 1992
acrylic on canvas 100 x 66
ACC98/1991

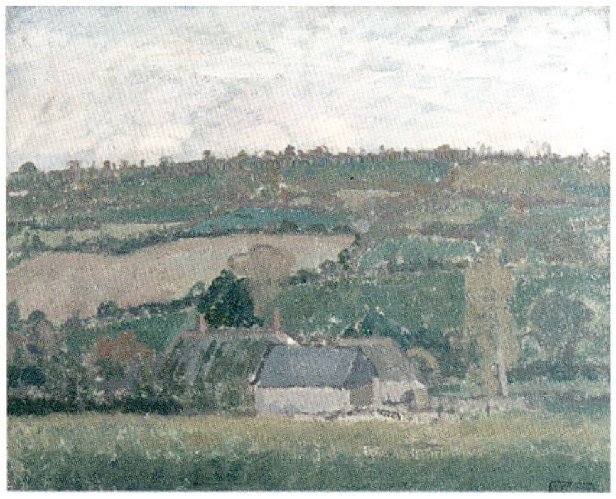

Gore, Spencer 1878–1914
Landscape, Somerset 1909
oil on canvas 40.6 x 50.8
AC 606

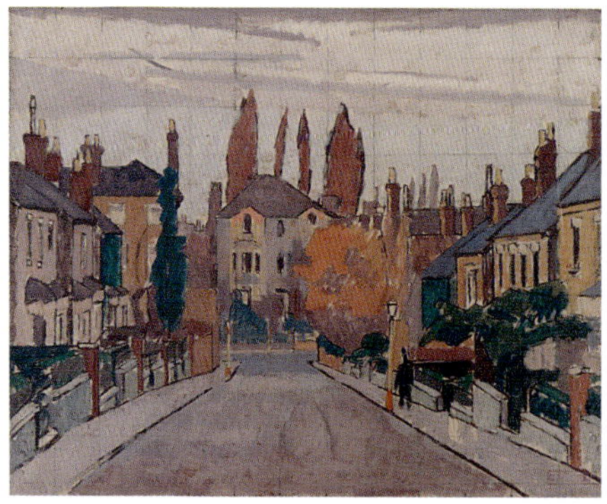

Gore, Spencer 1878–1914
Chisholm Road, Richmond 1913
oil on canvas 40.6 x 50.8
ACC3/1955

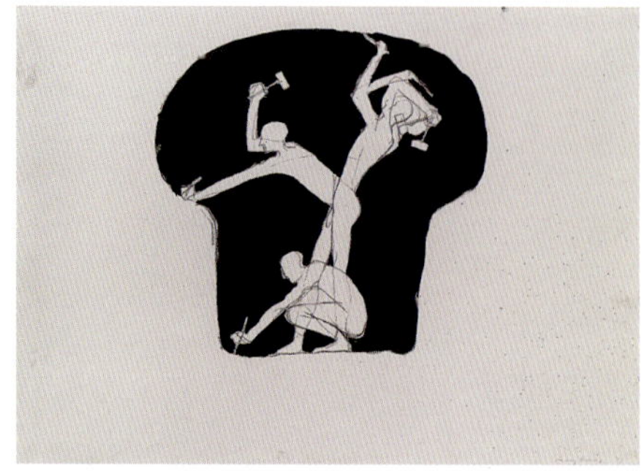

Gormley, Antony b.1950
Art 1981
charcoal & oil on paper 57.7 x 82.1
AC 5096

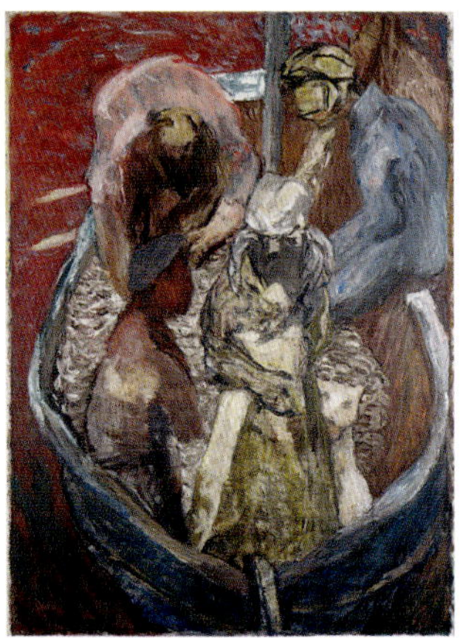

Gotlib, Henryk 1890–1966
The Boat 1960
oil on canvas 135.9 x 101.6
AC 559

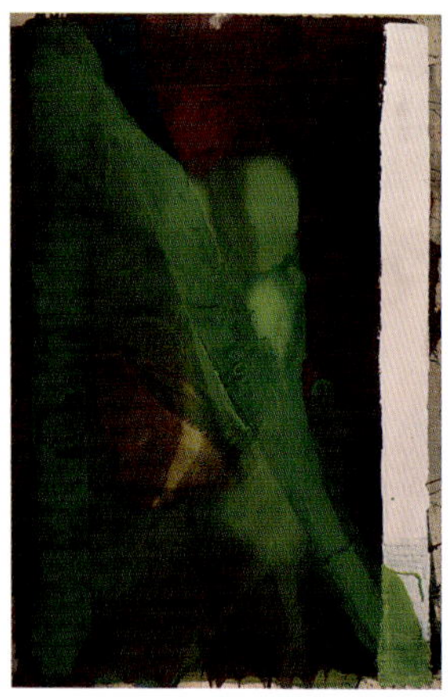

Gouk, Alan b.1939
Painting No.7 1969
oil on canvas 254 x 200.7
AC 1084

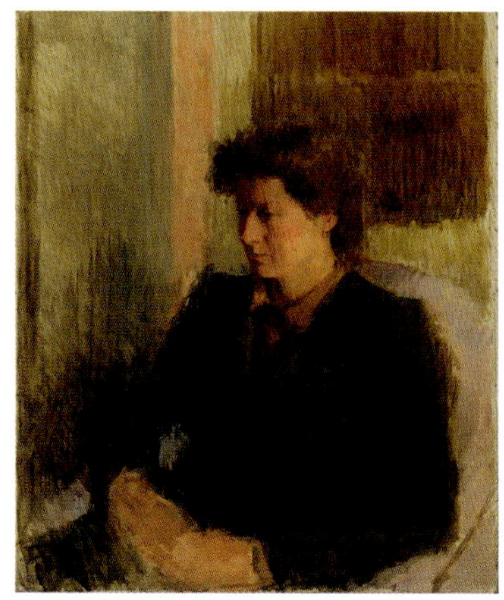

Gowing, Lawrence 1918–1991
Julia Strachey (1901–1979) 1940
oil on canvas 75 x 62
AC 94

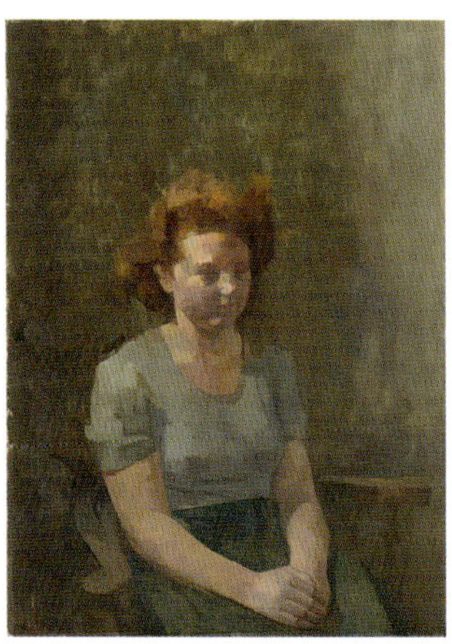

Gowing, Lawrence 1918–1991
Miss Baker 1947
oil on canvas 75 x 54.6
AC 8

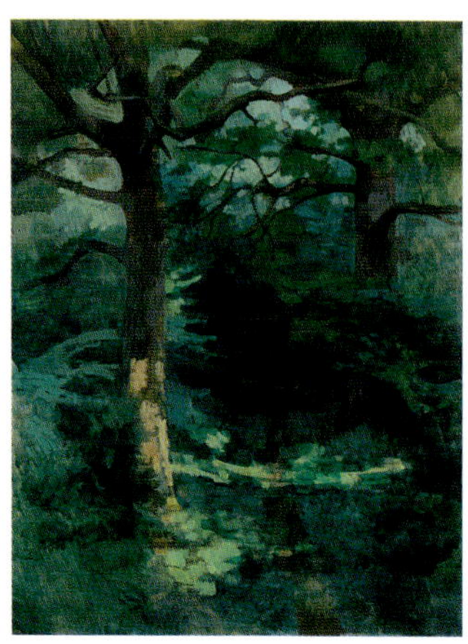

Gowing, Lawrence 1918–1991
Cherry Copse at Stock Close, near Aldbourne 1951
oil on canvas 90.5 x 69.5
AC 245

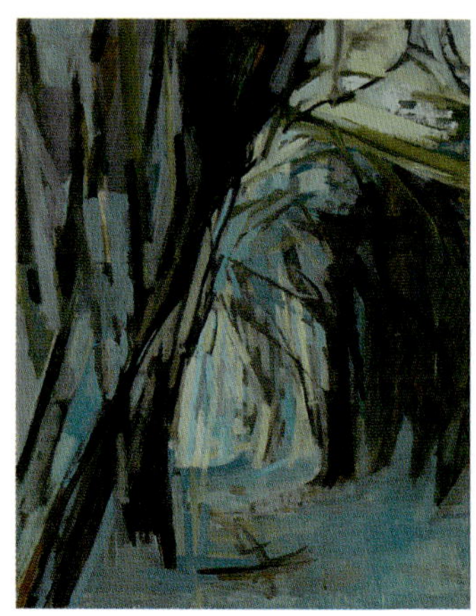

Gowing, Lawrence 1918–1991
Gifford's Copse 1961
oil on canvas 80 x 63.5
AC 617

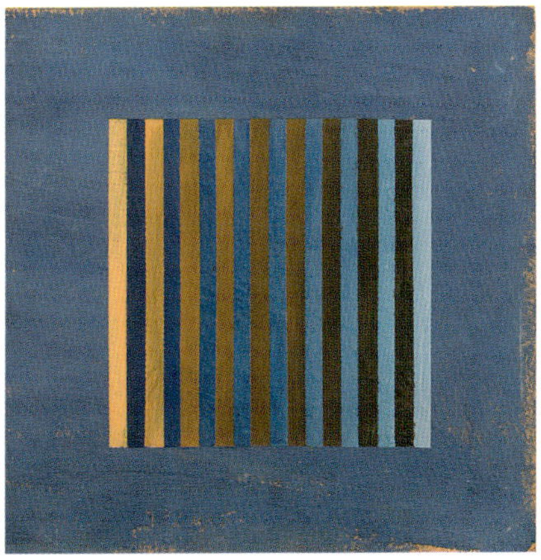

Gowing, Lawrence 1918–1991
Wood: Yellow and Blue II 1964
acrylic on board 50.8 x 50.8
AC 767

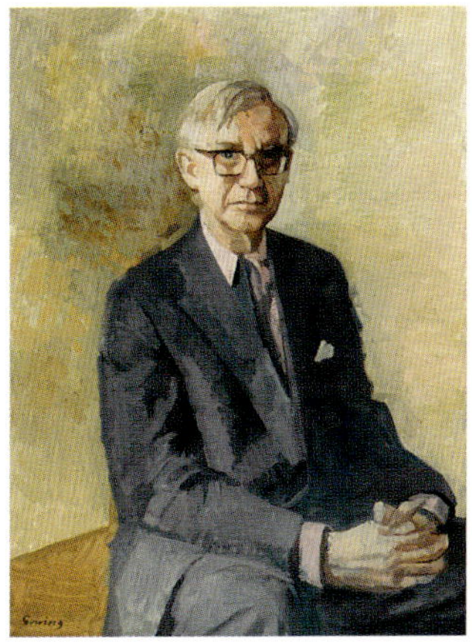

Gowing, Lawrence 1918–1991
Sir William Rees-Mogg (b.1928) 1986
oil on canvas 100.5 x 74.7
AC 5437

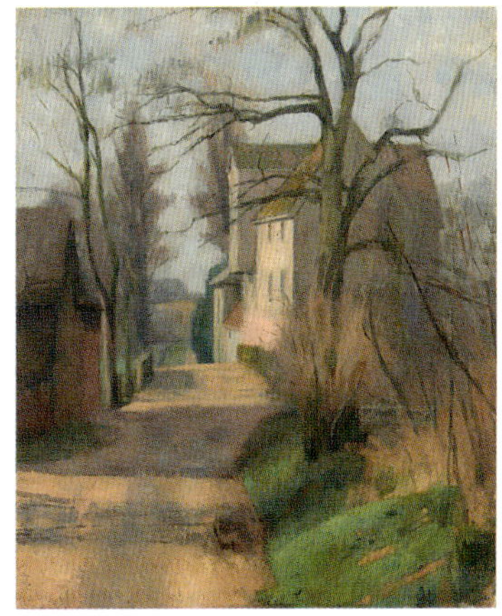

Graham Bell, Frank 1910–1943
Baylham Mill 1940
oil on canvas 59.7 x 49.5
AC 85

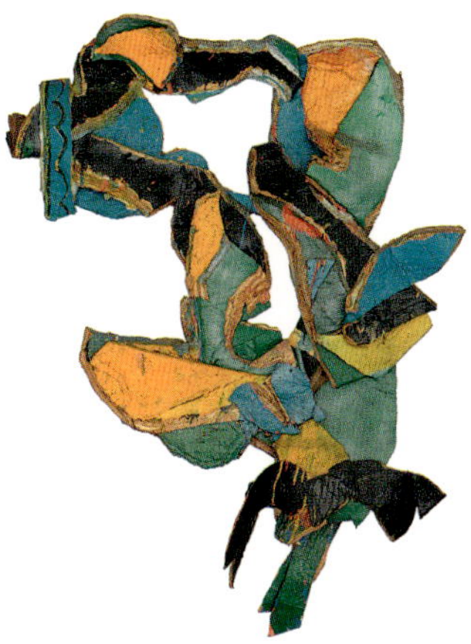

Grandjean, Lee b.1949
Dancer 1975
acrylic, paper & wood 170.5 x 148
AC 1606

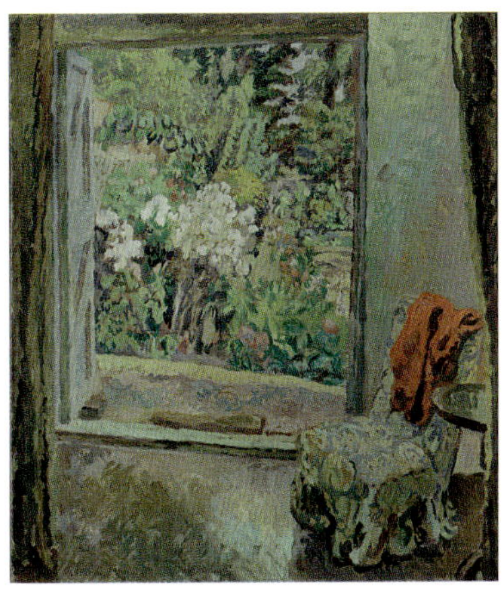

Grant, Duncan 1885–1978
The Doorway 1929
oil on canvas 88 x 77.5
AC 212

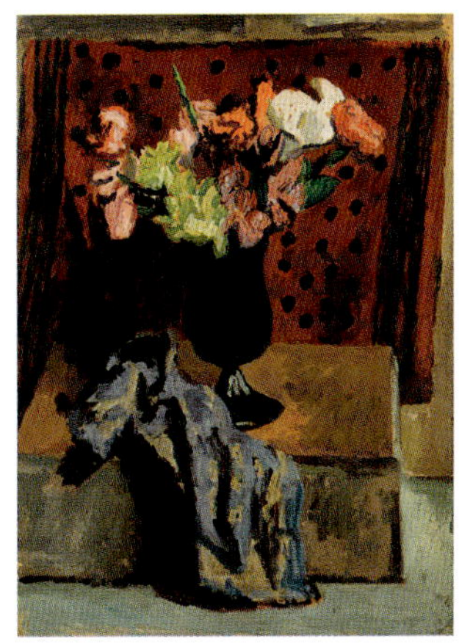

Grant, Duncan 1885–1978
Artificial Flowers 1934
oil on canvas 76.2 x 55.9
AC 192

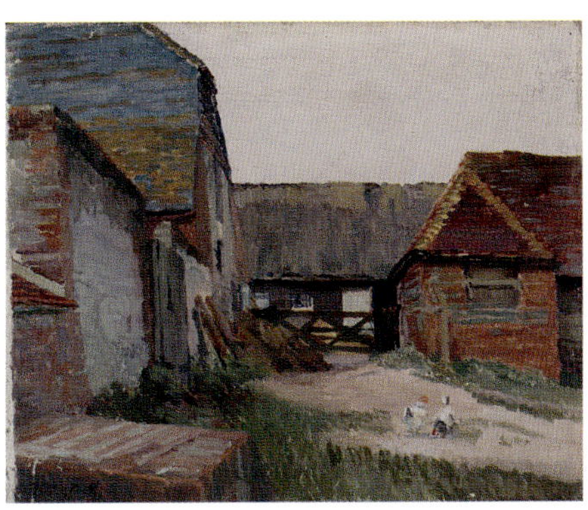

Grant, Duncan 1885–1978
Cow Stalls 1942
oil on canvas 43 x 53
AC 95

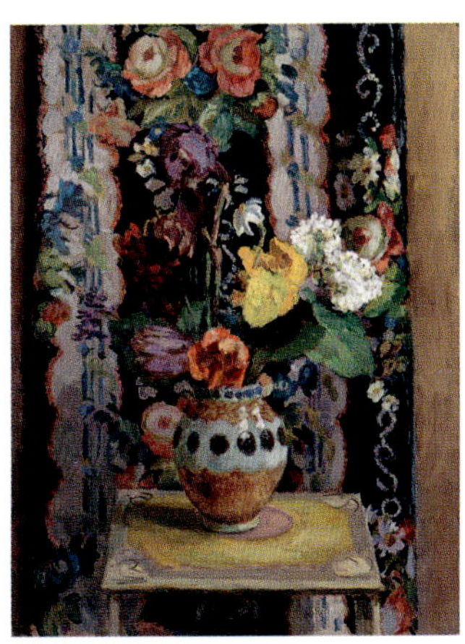

Grant, Duncan 1885–1978
Flowers Against Chintz 1956
oil on board 75.6 x 54.9
AC 429

Grant, Keith b.1930
Skroven from Svolvær 1978
acrylic, watercolour & ink on paper 33 x 48.3
AC 2044

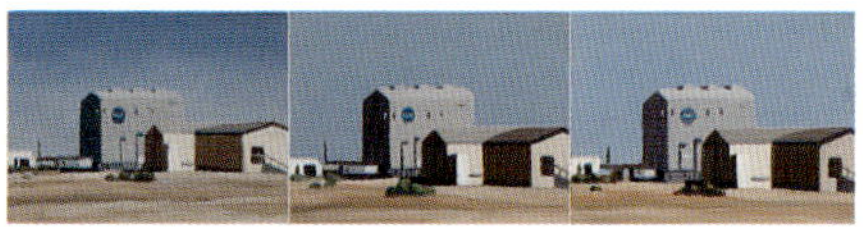

Grassie, Andrew b.1966
Edward Airforce Base 1, 2, 3 1998
oil on board 20.5 x 28.5; 20.5 x 28.5; 20.5 x 28.5
ACC61/1999

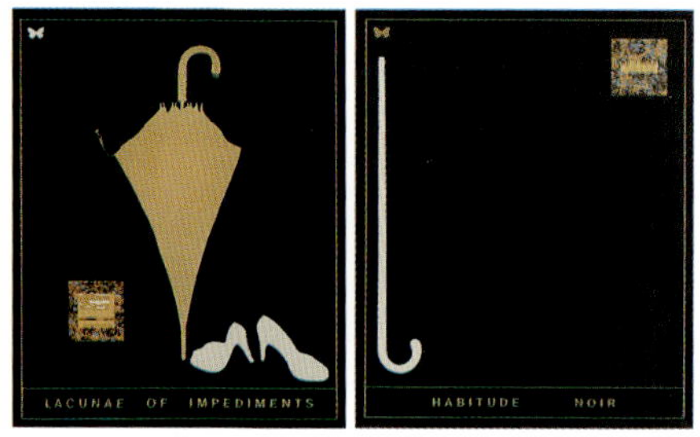

Grayson, Roy b.1936
The Blind Poet in Pursuit of the Muse of Fashion 1983
oil & collage on canvas 134 x 258
AC 5345

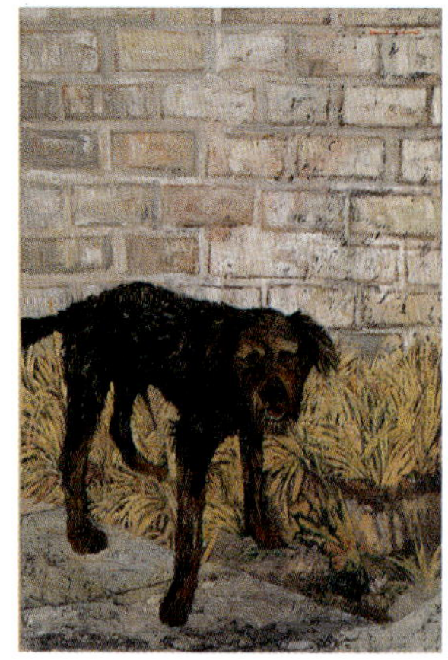

Greaves, Derrick b.1927
Dog 1955
oil on canvas 118.1 x 78.7
AC 367

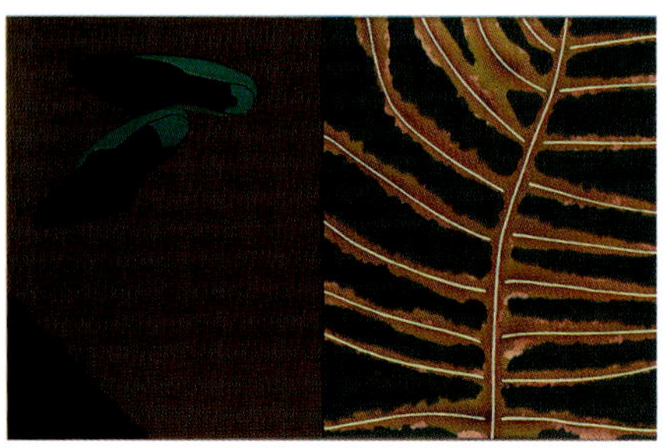

Greaves, Derrick b.1927
A Pair of Green Shoes c.1967
oil on canvas 70.5 x 114.5
ACA 46

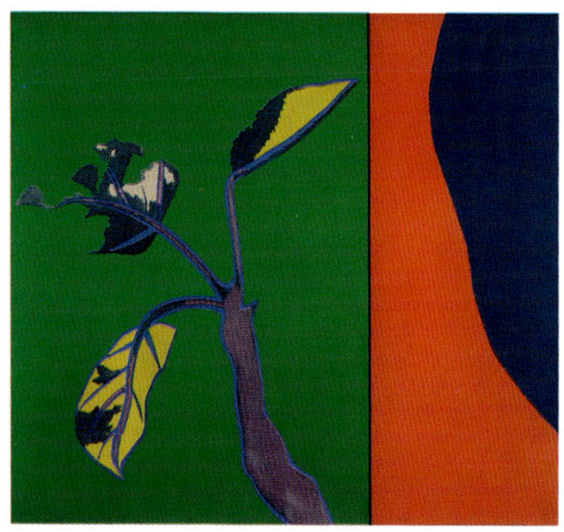

Greaves, Derrick b.1927
Three Leaves (Second Day of Spring) c.1967
oil on canvas 102.9 x 115.6
ACA 45

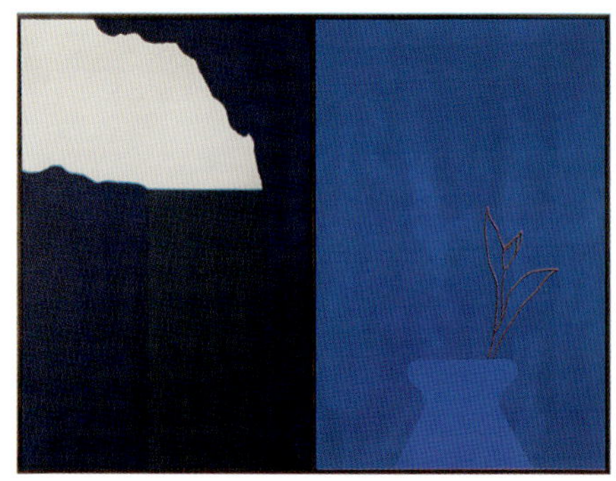

Greaves, Derrick b.1927
Chimney and Iris 1968–1969
oil & acrylic on canvas 139.7 x 185.7
AC 1092

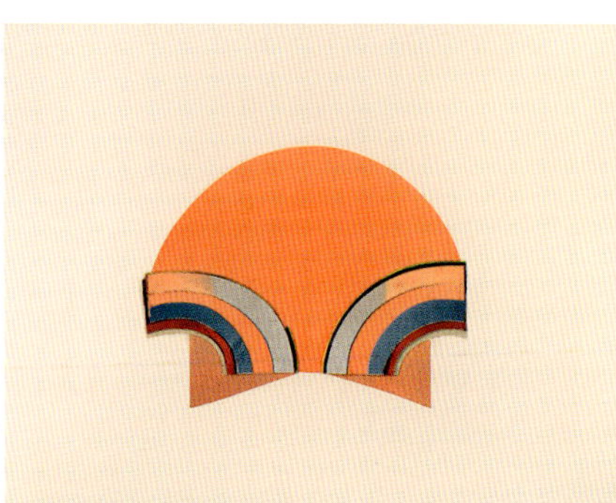

Green, Alan 1932–2003
Sugar Ice 1968
oil, acrylic & paper collage on card 50.5 x 63.2
AC 972

Green, Alan 1932–2003
Exit 1974
acrylic on canvas 175 x 259
AC 1498

Green, Alan 1932–2003
Red over Crimson 1980
oil on canvas 130.2 x 130.5
AC 4060

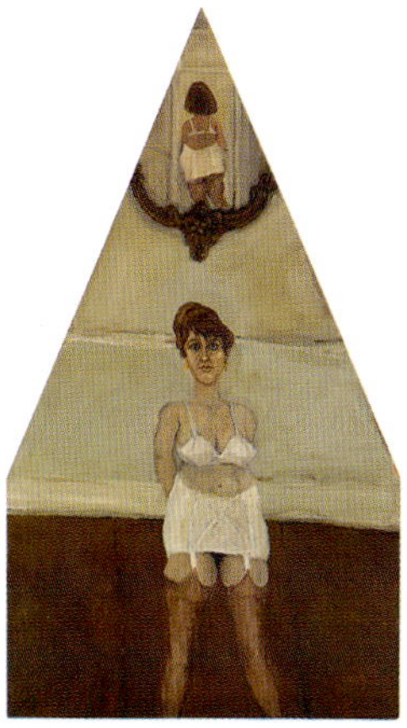

Green, Anthony b.1939
Mary in Her Bra and Corset 1965
oil on board 106 x 60.2
AC 828

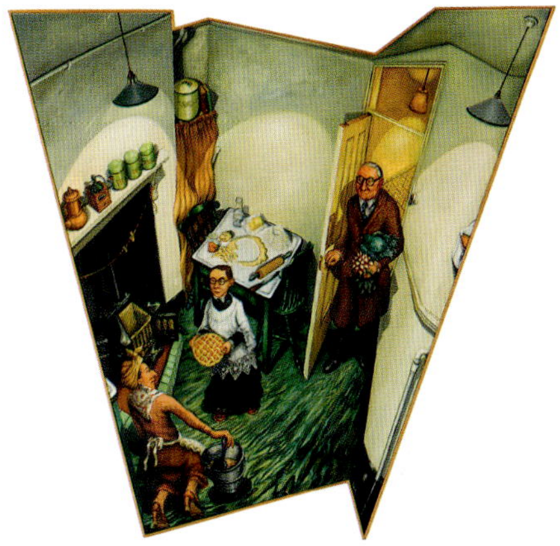

Green, Anthony b.1939
Victory in Europe/The Greens 1945 1981
oil on board 176 x 185
AC 4094

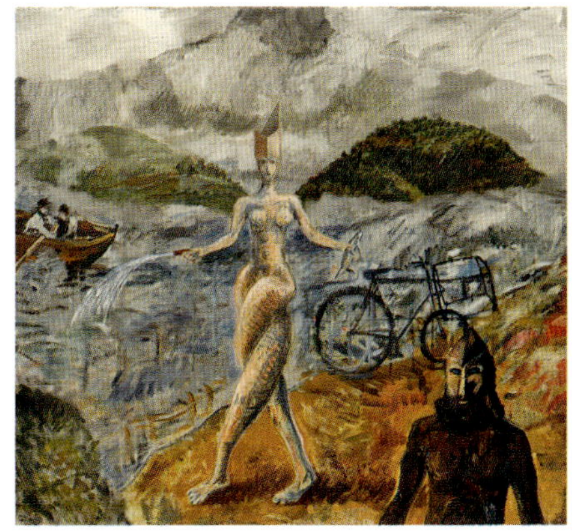

Green, Paul Henry b.1951
Graig Yr Hesg 1983
oil on canvas 68.7 x 76.3
AC 5504

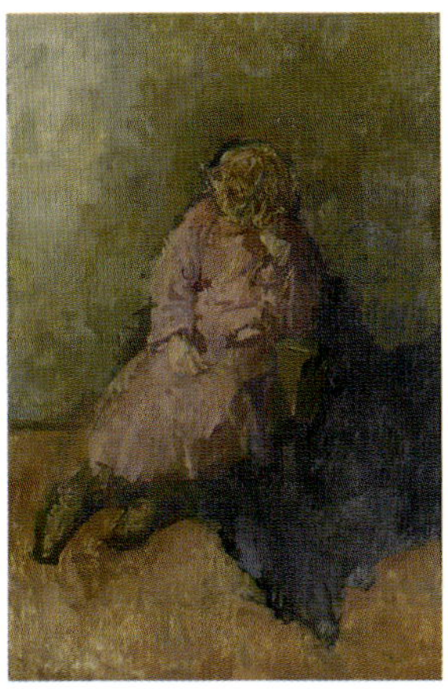

Greenham, Peter 1909–1992
Study 1981
oil on canvas 76 x 50.9
AC 4057

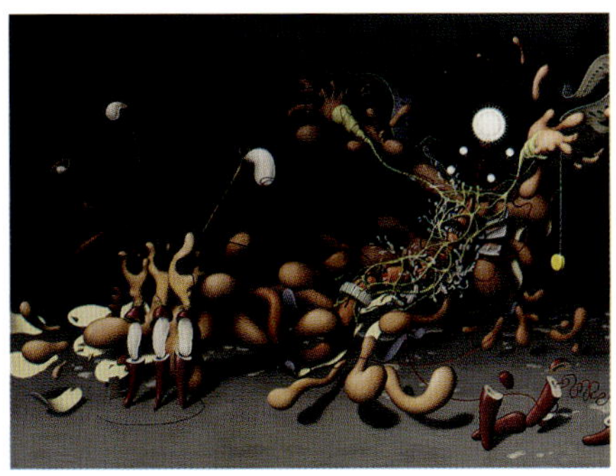

Greenwood, John b.1959
Enjoy Yourself 1991
oil on canvas 138 x 183
ACC177/1998

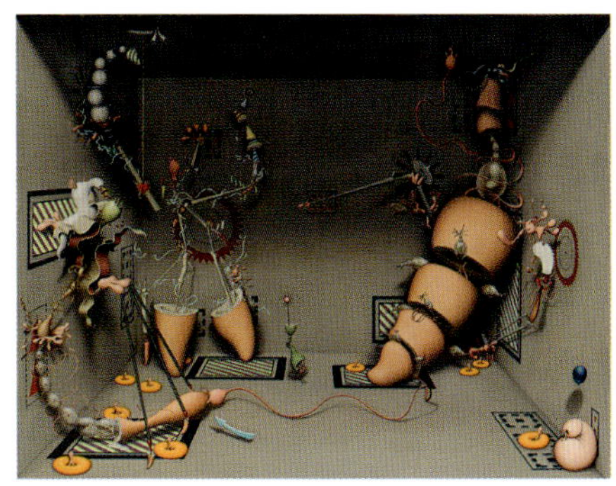

Greenwood, John b.1959
How Many Doughnuts Have You Collected? 1992
oil on canvas 138 x 183
ACC176/1998

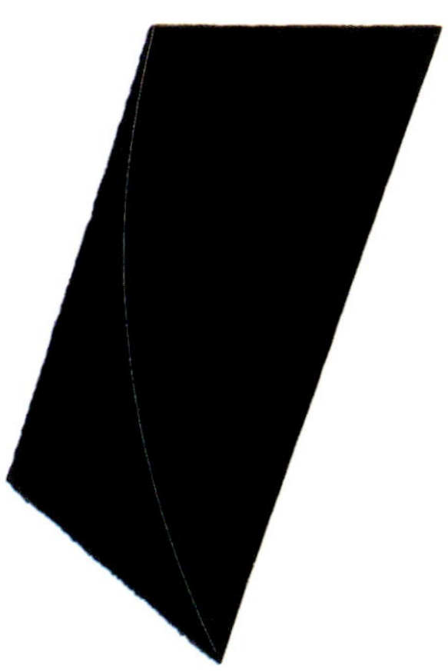

Groom, Jon b.1953
Untitled II 1979
acrylic on canvas 161 x 65.3
AC 3001

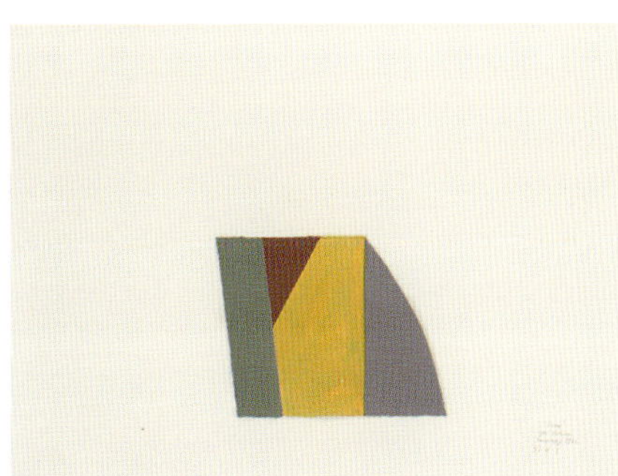

Groom, Jon b.1953
Clay 1981
oil on paper 58 x 77.2
AC 5095

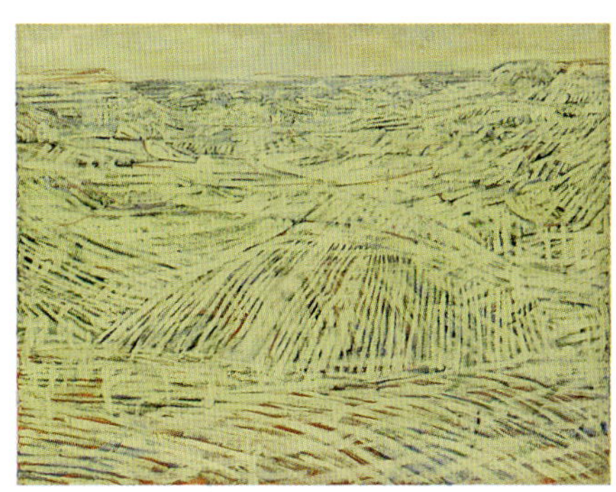

Gross, Anthony 1905–1984
Yellow Valley 1957
oil on canvas 96.5 x 130
AC 425

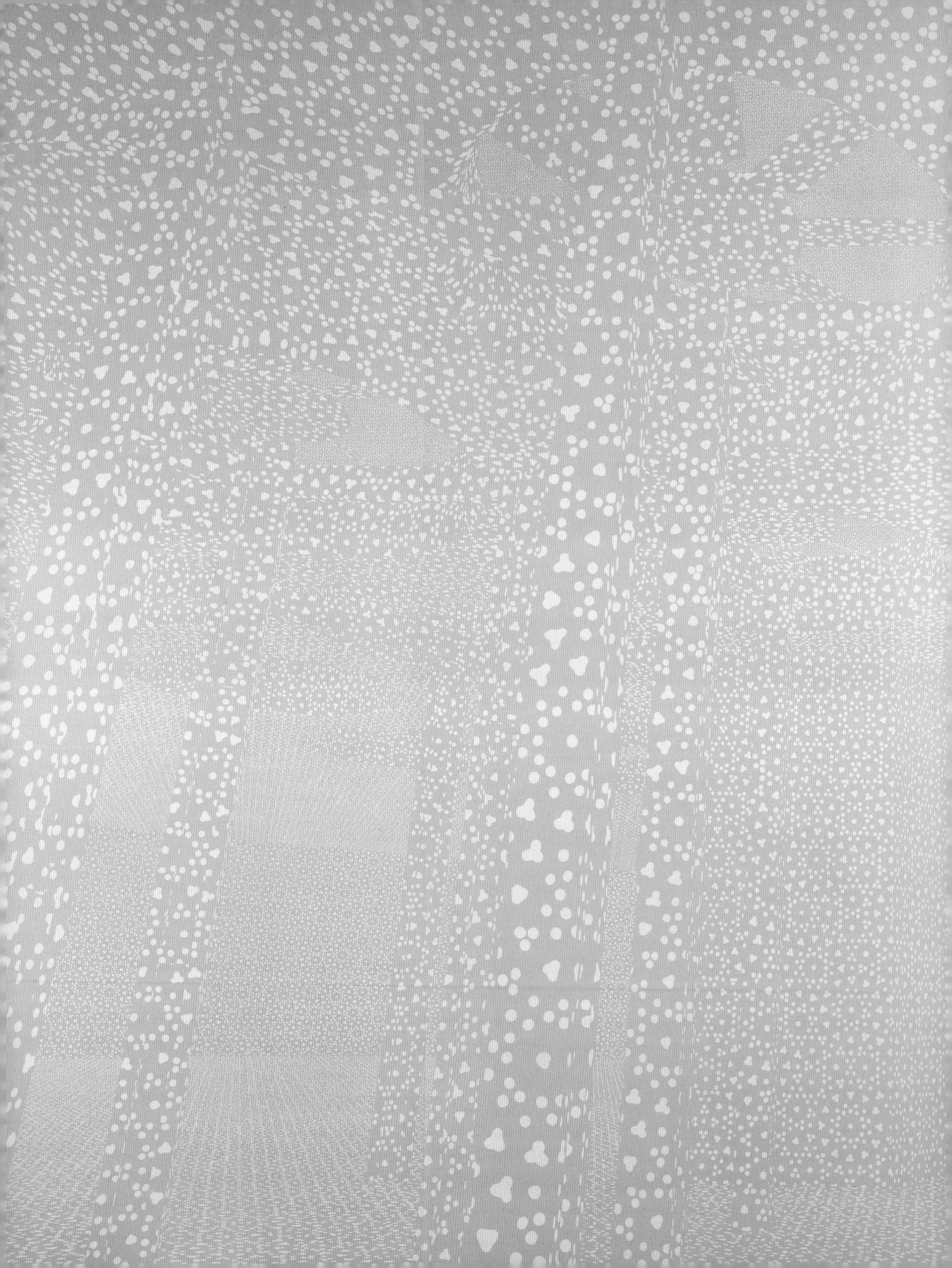

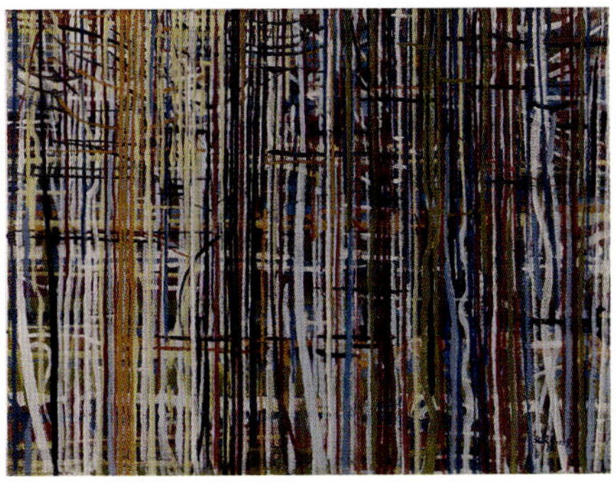

Gross, Anthony 1905–1984
Saplings 1961
oil on canvas 45.1 x 60
AC 619

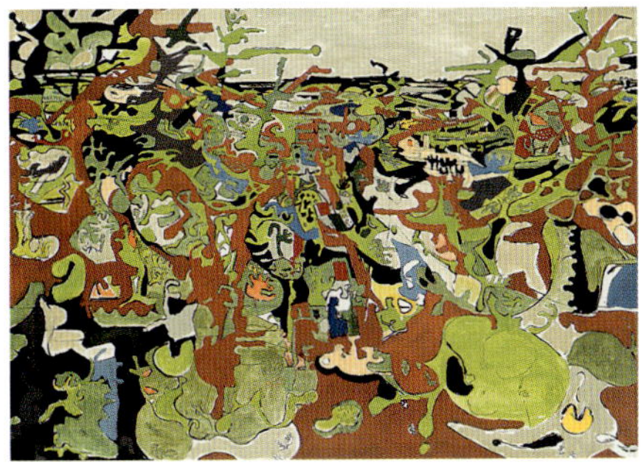

Gross, Anthony 1905–1984
Landscape with Stones 1966
oil on canvas 128 x 184
ACA 47

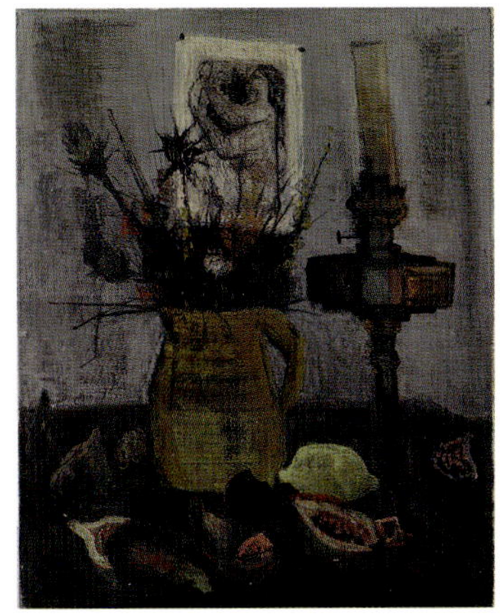

Guerrier, Barrero
Untitled (Still Life: Lamp, Jug of Thistles)
oil on canvas 72.4 x 60.3
AC 653

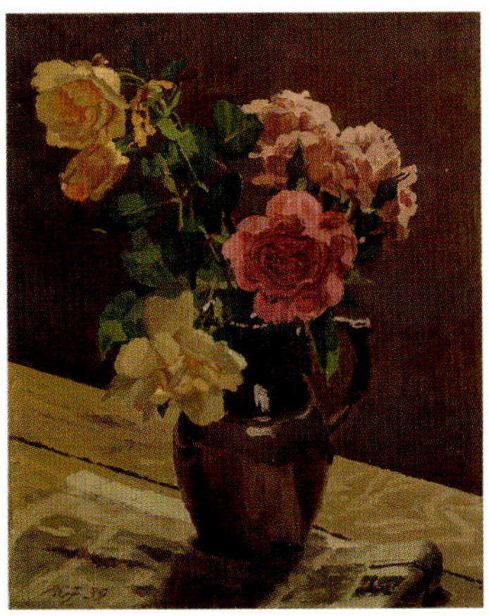

Gwynne-Jones, Allan 1892–1982
Roses 1939
oil on canvas 52.7 x 42.5
PR 225

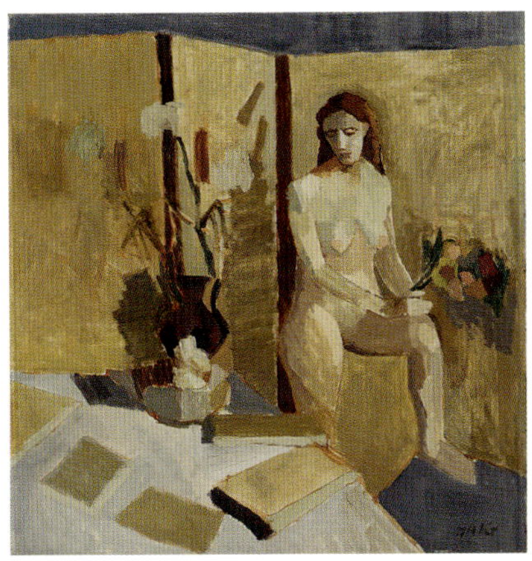

Haig, George Douglas 1918–2009
Red-Haired Nude c.1954
oil on canvas 68.6 x 67.3
AC 360

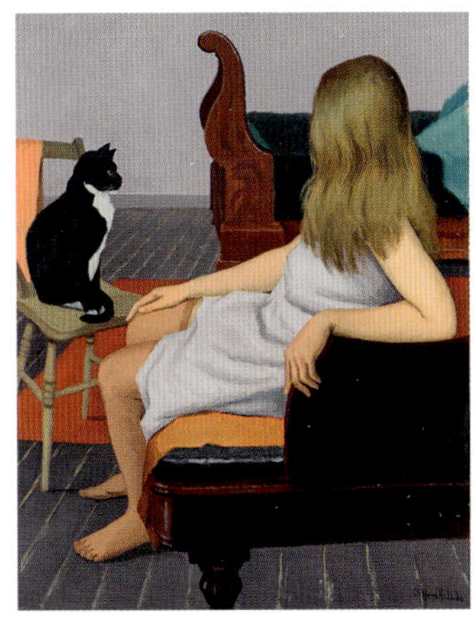

Hall, Clifford 1904–1973
The Girl with a Cat 1969
acrylic on board 91.4 x 71.1
AC 1105

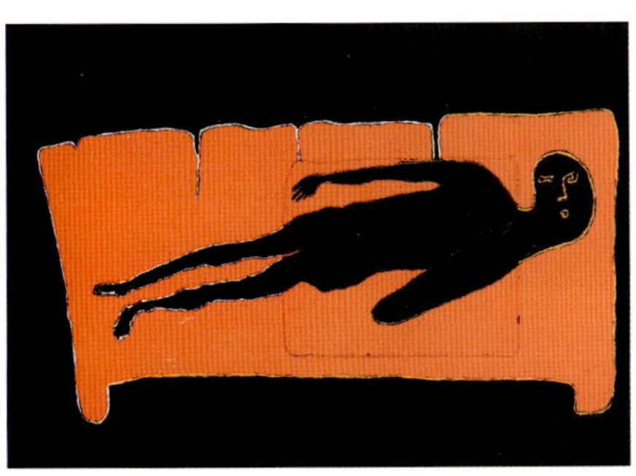

Hall, Colin b.1952
Man on a Couch 1976
ink & emulsion on etching plate on board
29.3 x 42.2
AC 3050

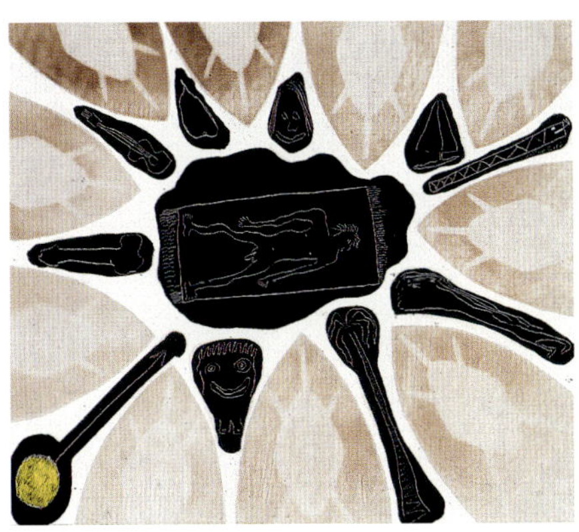

Hall, Colin b.1952
Sunbather 1978
cotton, gesso, oil & acrylic 43.7 x 37.8
AC 3049

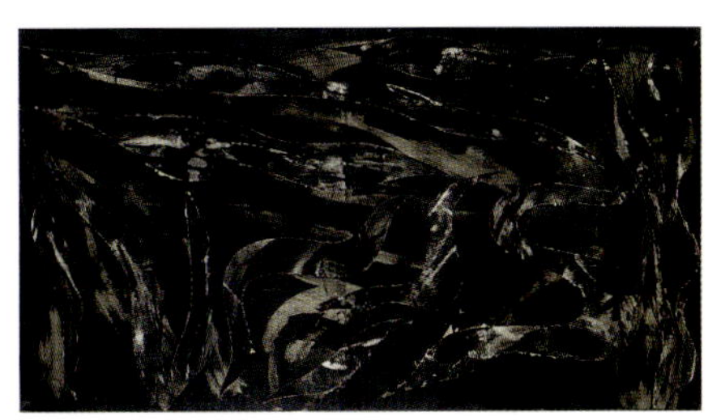

Halliday, Trevor b.1939
Tardibigge 1971
acrylic on canvas 216.5 x 429.9
AC 1166

Facing page: Ziegler, Toby, b.1972, *Je t'adore, baby*, (detail), 2003–2004, (p. 172)

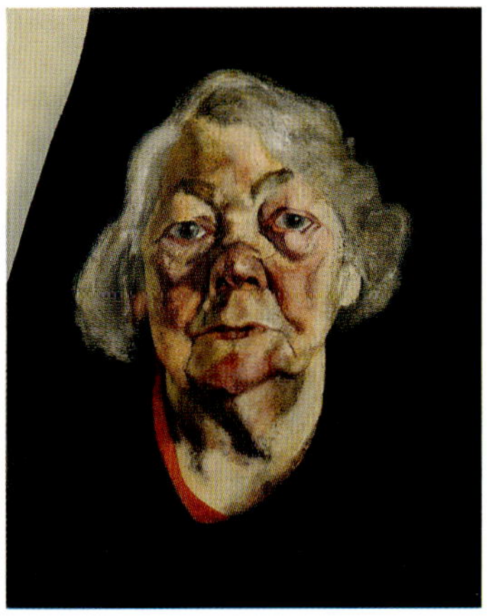

Hambling, Maggi b.1945
Frances Rose (3) 1973
oil on canvas 53 x 42.9
AC 1778

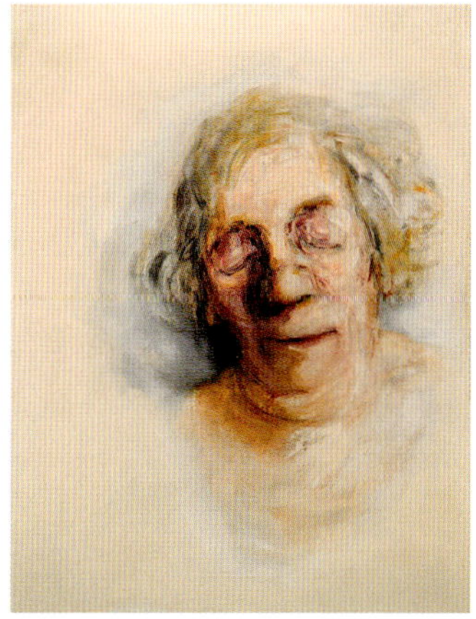

Hambling, Maggi b.1945
Frances Rose (4) 1975
oil on canvas 57.9 x 52.9
AC 1779

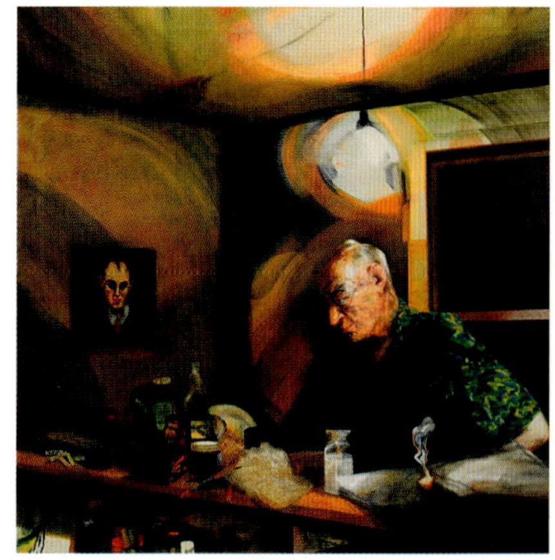

Hambling, Maggi b.1945
Lett, Evening 1977–1978
oil on canvas 141.9 x 140.4
AC 2060

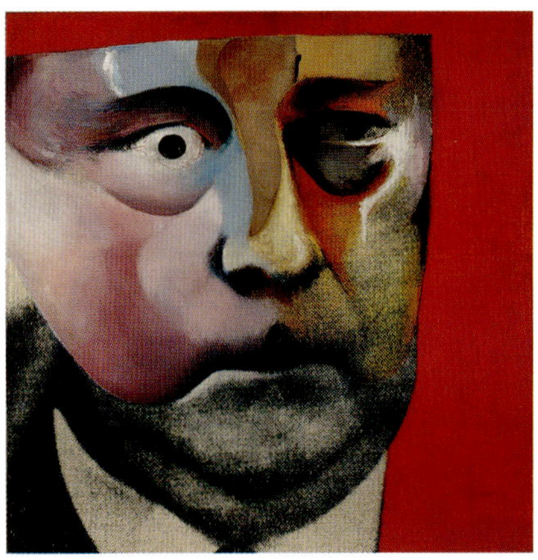

Hamilton, Richard 1922–2011
Hugh Gaitskell as a Famous Monster of Filmland 1964
oil & photomontage on panel 61 x 61
AC 724

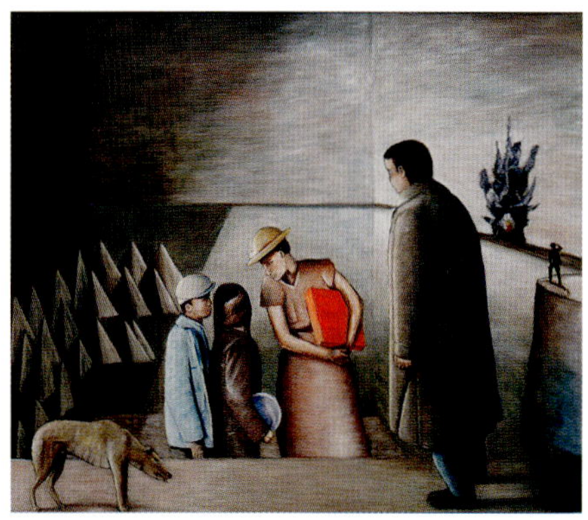

Hampson, Derek b.1952
From Cairo to the Gulf of Mexico 1982
oil on canvas 118 x 140
AC 5392

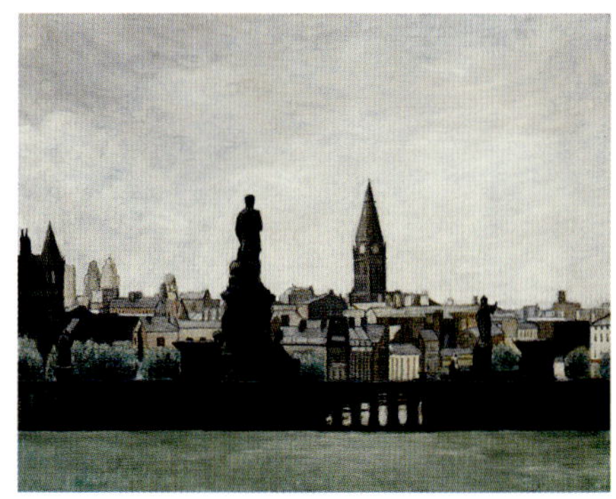

Hampson, Derek b.1952
Liverpool '64 1983
oil on canvas 50.8 x 64.5
AC 5393

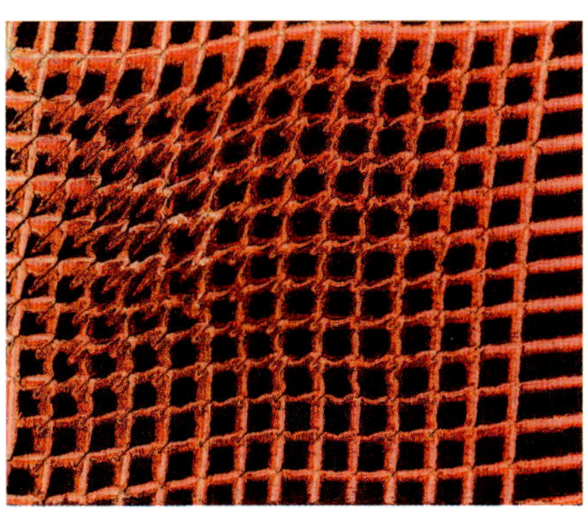

Harding, Alexis b.1973
Untitled (study) 1995
oil & gloss on canvas 61 x 76.2
ACC24/1995

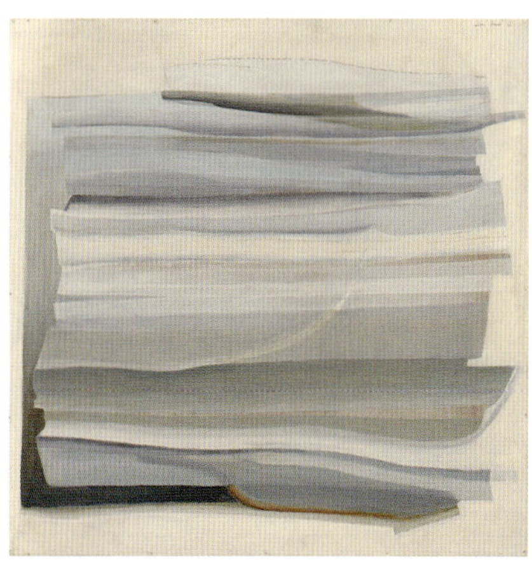

Harris, Jane b.1937
Sea 1962
oil & pencil on board 91 x 91.5
AC 668

Harris, Jane b.1956
Aureole 1992–1994
oil on canvas 137 x 213
ACC111/1995

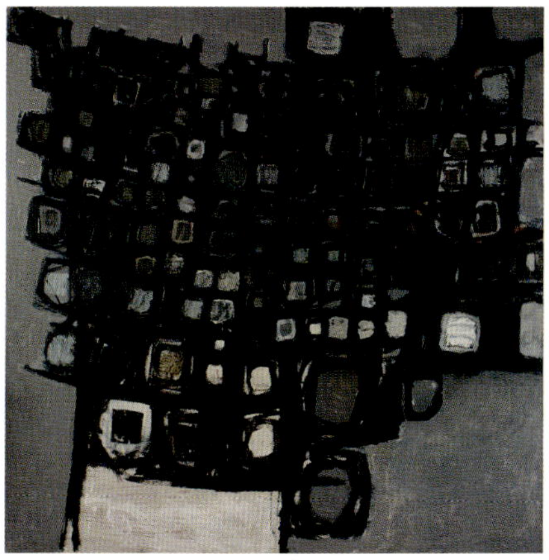

Harris, Jeffrey b.1932
Black, Grey and White 1959
oil on board 122 x 122
AC 547

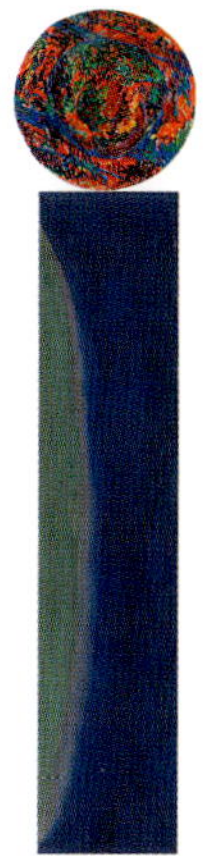

Harrison, Jon b.1961
Hors-d'oeuvre 1987
oil on canvas 138 x 29
AC 5494

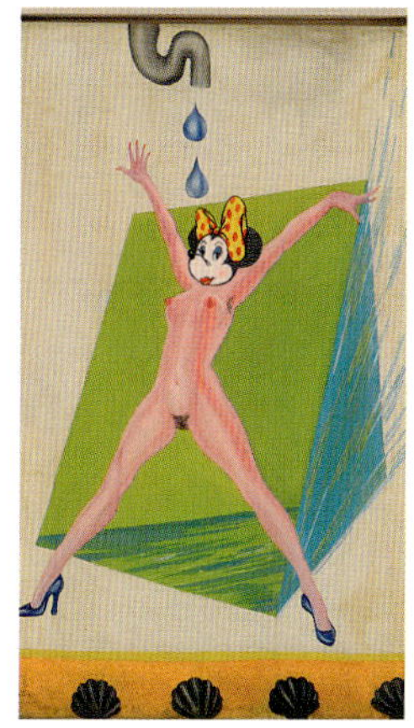

Harrison, Margaret b.1940
Women of the World Unite, You have Nothing to Lose but Cheese Cake 1969
acrylic on canvas 88 x 53
ACC2/2008

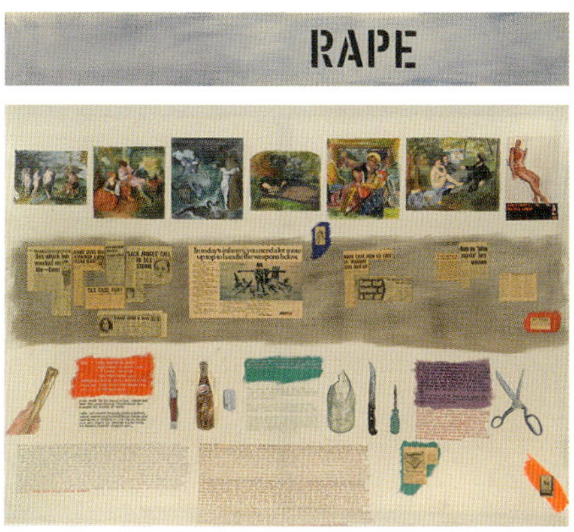

Harrison, Margaret b.1940
Rape 1978
acrylic & collage on canvas 223.7 x 244
AC 1946

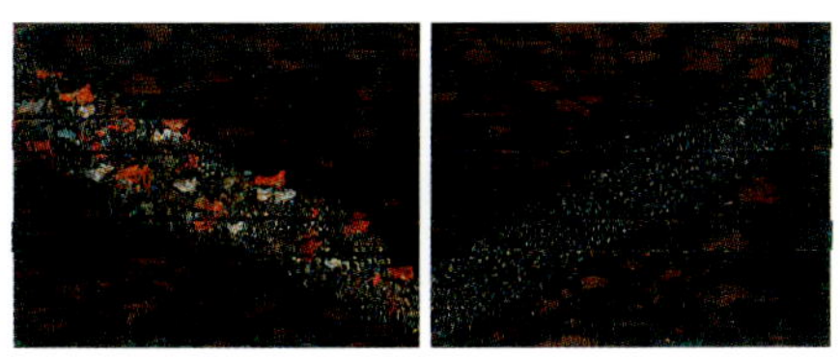

Harvey, William b.1957
Mirror 1987
acrylic, canvas & wood 168 x 214; 168 x 214
AC 5513

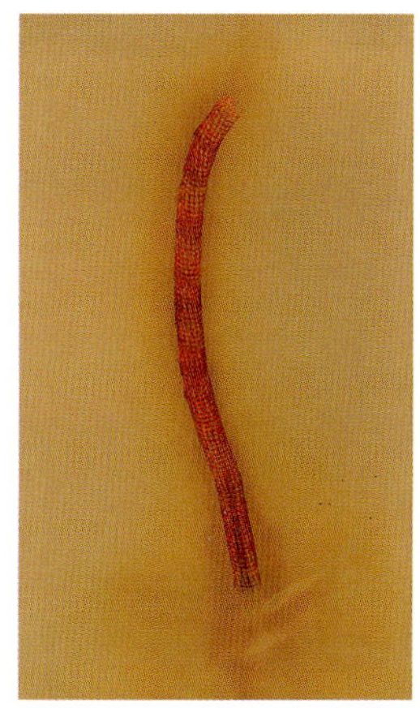

Haselden, Ron b.1944
Mexican Desert 1979
paint, ink & lacquer on paper 151.9 x 90.7
AC 3028

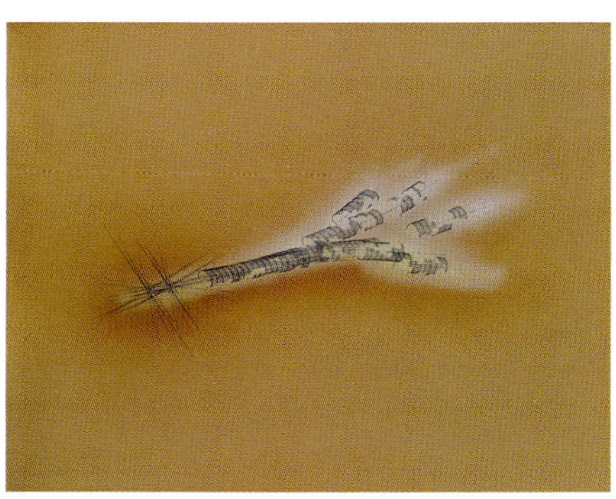

Haselden, Ron b.1944
Plant 1979
paint, ink & lacquer on paper 88.1 x 116.4
AC 3027

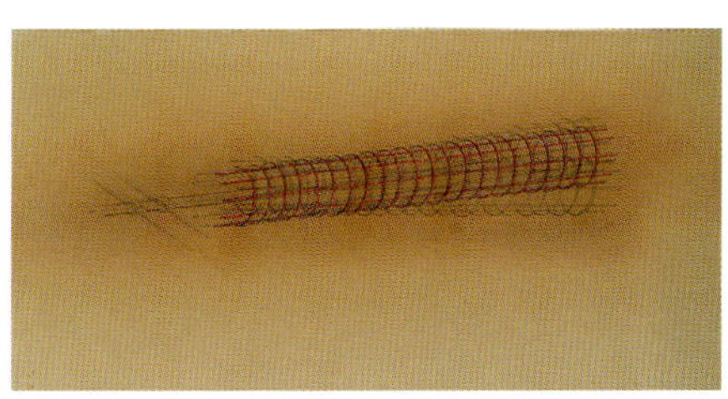

Haselden, Ron b.1944
Red Engine 1979
paint, ink, lacquer & pencil on paper
44.8 x 90.8
AC 3029

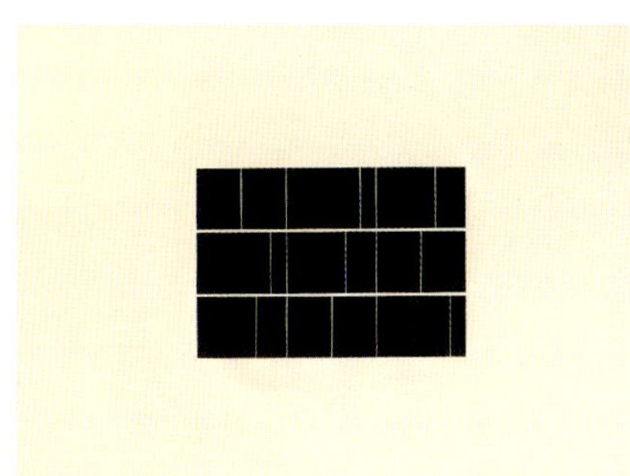

Hatt, Christine b.1954
Painting No.5iii 1982
acrylic on paper 47.4 x 65.4
AC 5191

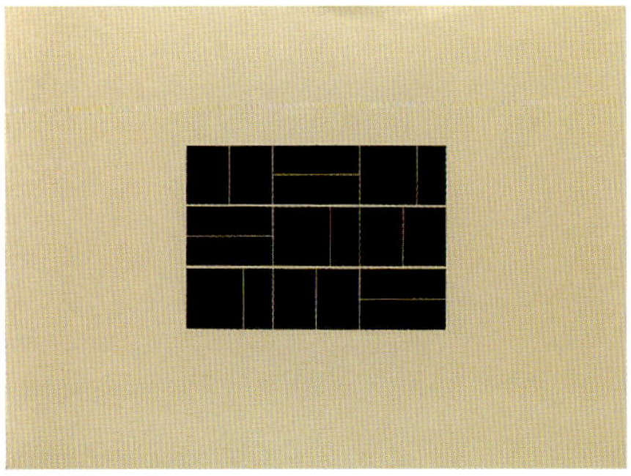

Hatt, Christine b.1954
Painting No.6iii 1982
acrylic on paper 47.3 x 65.5
AC 5192

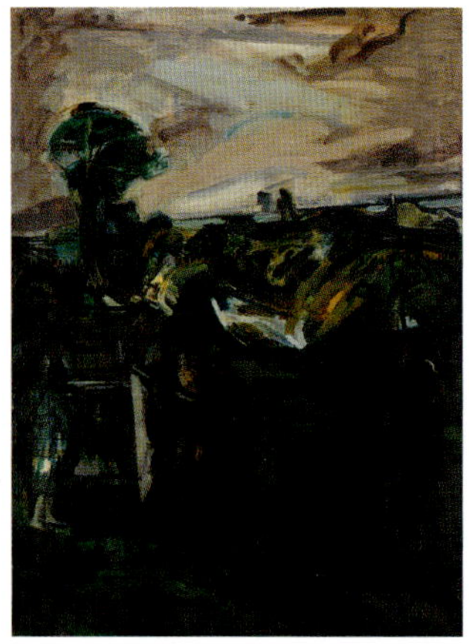

Haugas, Maret
Dark Landscape c.1960
oil on canvas 121.9 x 91.1
AC 542

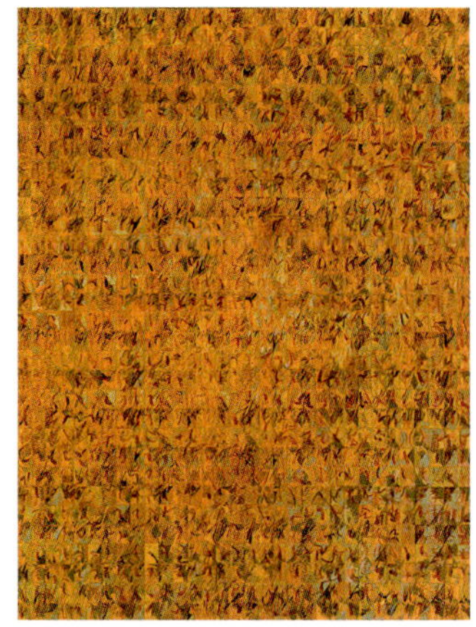

Haughton, David 1924–1991
Yellow Grid 1967–1972
oil on canvas 122 x 91.5
AC 1546

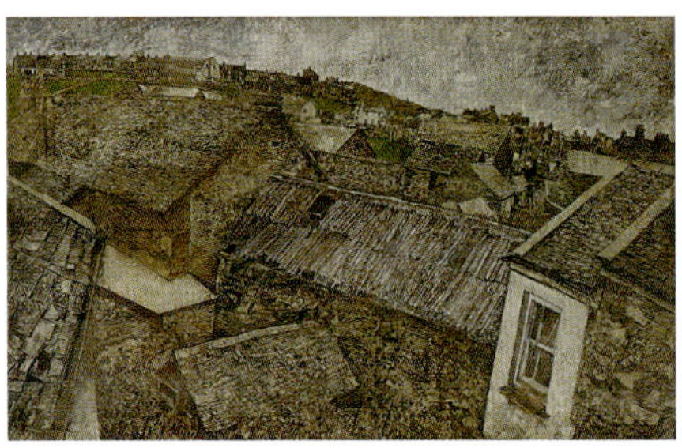

Haughton, David 1924–1991
Rooftops St Just 1978
oil on canvas 111.5 x 182.8
AC 5300

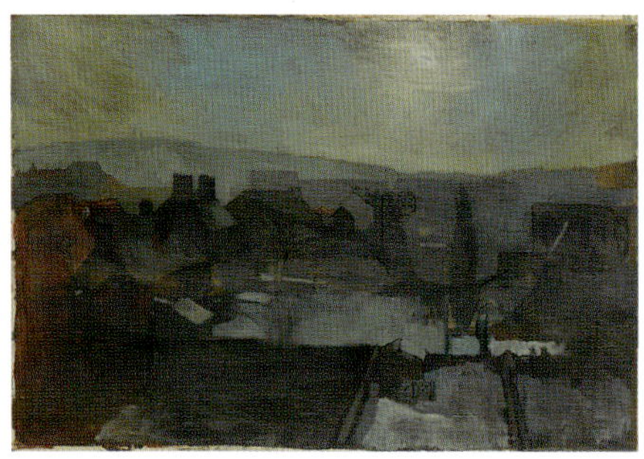

Hayes, Colin Graham Frederick 1919–2003
Oxford Roofs, January 1947 1947
oil on canvas 50.8 x 78.7
AC 135

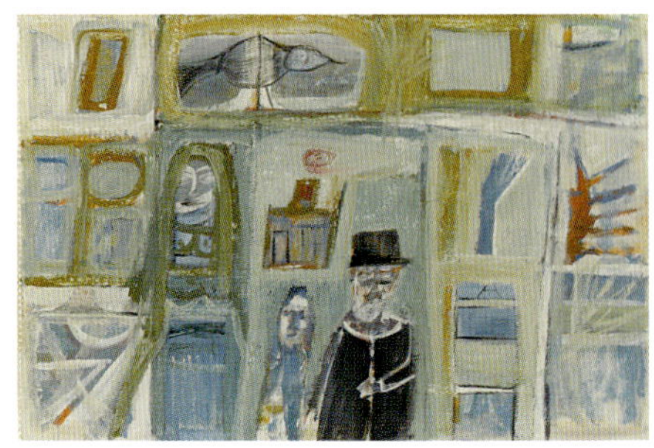

Hayman, Patrick 1915–1988
King Lear and Cordelia 1962
tempera on paper 29.4 x 44
AC 750

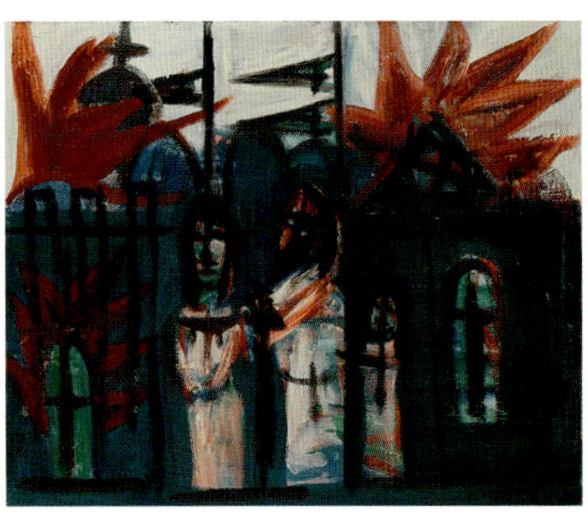

Hayman, Patrick 1915–1988
The Fall of Byzantium 1965
oil on board 40 x 50
AC 942

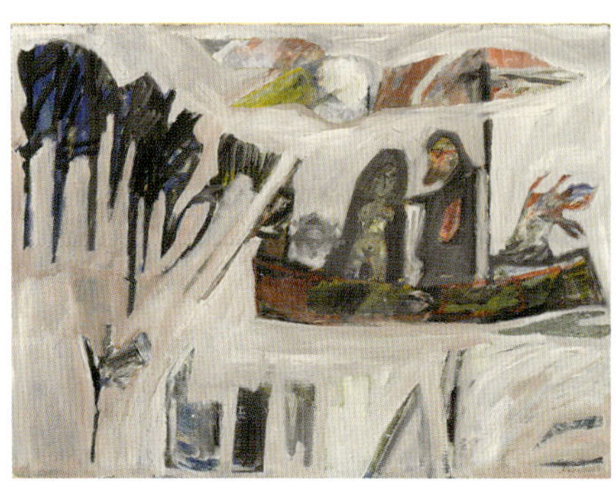

Hayman, Patrick 1915–1988
Night-Sea Crossing 1967
oil on card 40.6 x 55.9
AC 941

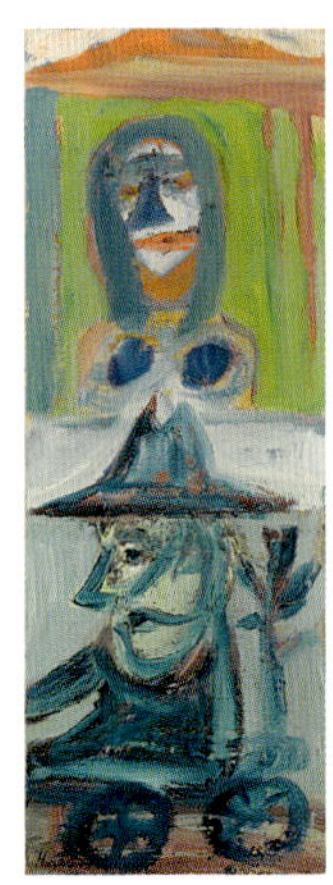

Hayman, Patrick 1915–1988
Lady with a Friend on Wheels 1982
oil on card 35.8 x 13.2
AC 5376

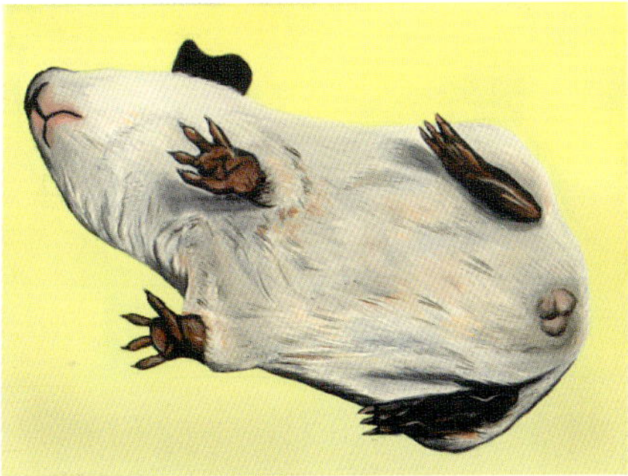

Hays, Dan b.1966
Guinea Pig 1995
oil on canvas 16 x 22
ACC39/1995

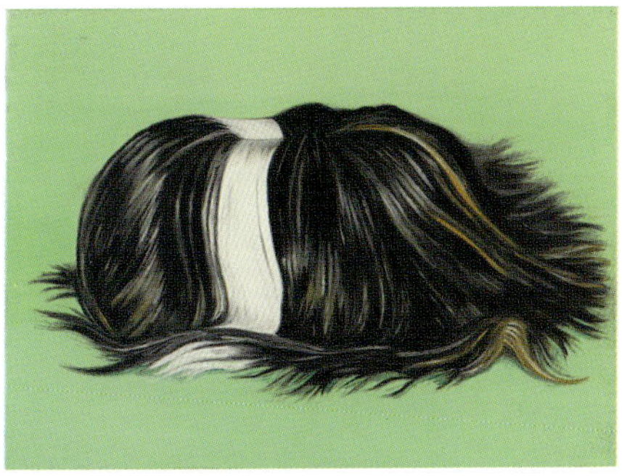

Hays, Dan b.1966
Guinea Pig 1995
oil on canvas 16 x 22
ACC91/1995

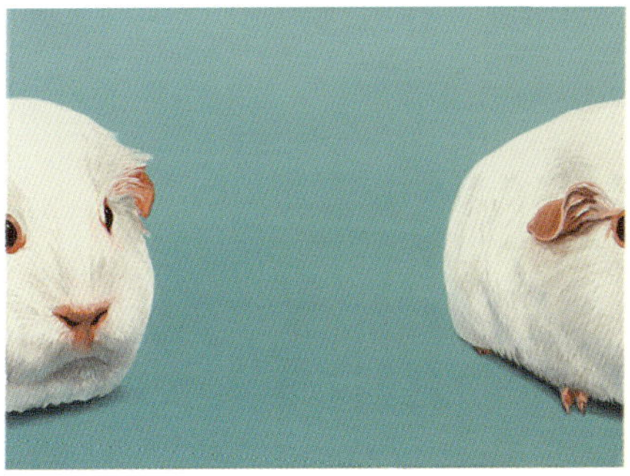

Hays, Dan b.1966
Guinea Pig 1995
oil on canvas 16 x 22
ACC92/1995

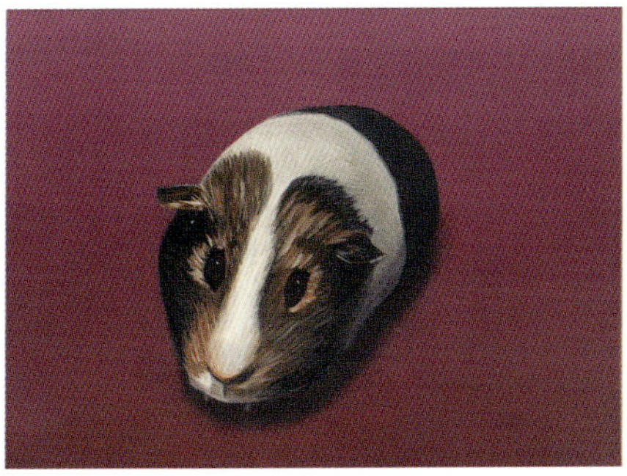

Hays, Dan b.1966
Guinea Pig 1995
oil on canvas 16 x 22
ACC93/1995

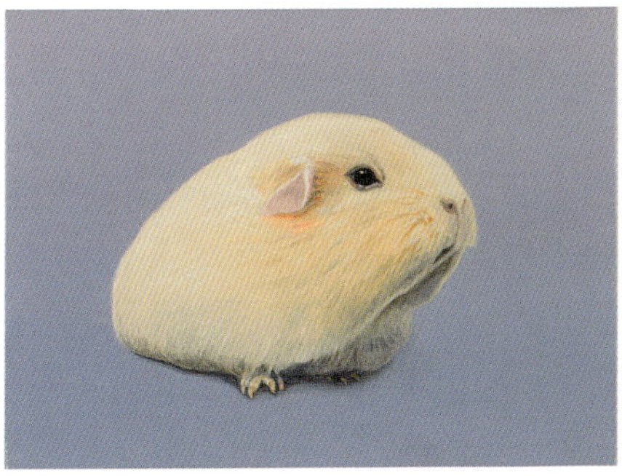

Hays, Dan b.1966
Guinea Pig 1995
oil on canvas 16 x 22
ACC94/1995

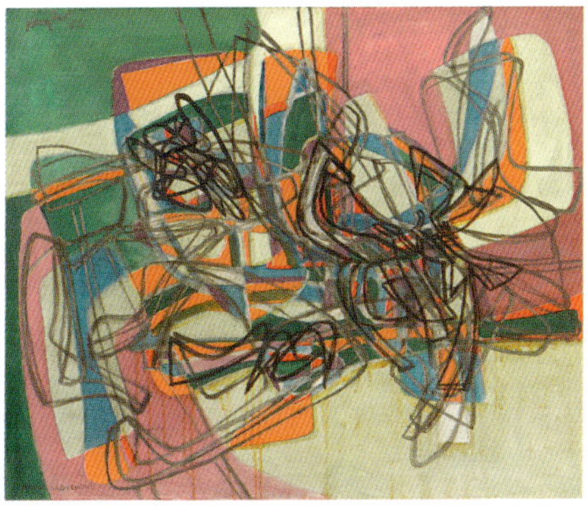

Hayter, Stanley William 1901–1988
Island Labyrinth 1956
oil on canvas 81.3 x 100.1
AC 406

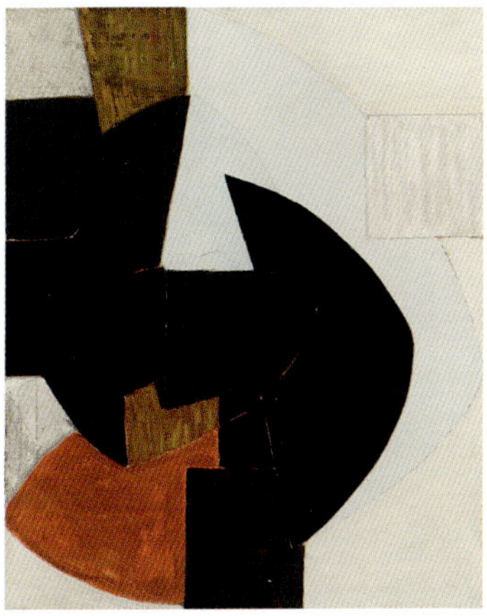

Heath, Adrian 1920–1992
Curved Form, Black and White 1954
oil on canvas 75.5 x 63.5
AC 353

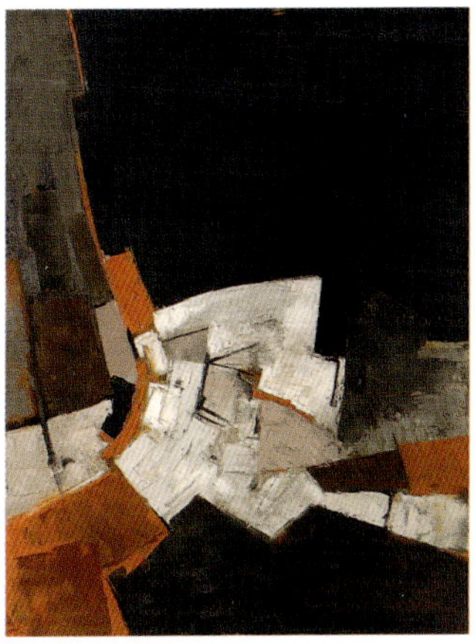

Heath, Adrian 1920–1992
Composition, Black and Grey 1958
oil on canvas 120.7 x 90.8
AC 486

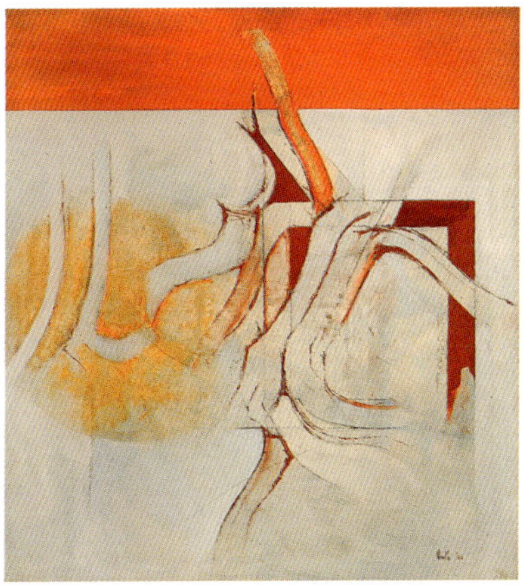

Heath, Adrian 1920–1992
Debdou 1966
oil on canvas 128.3 x 123.2
AC 852

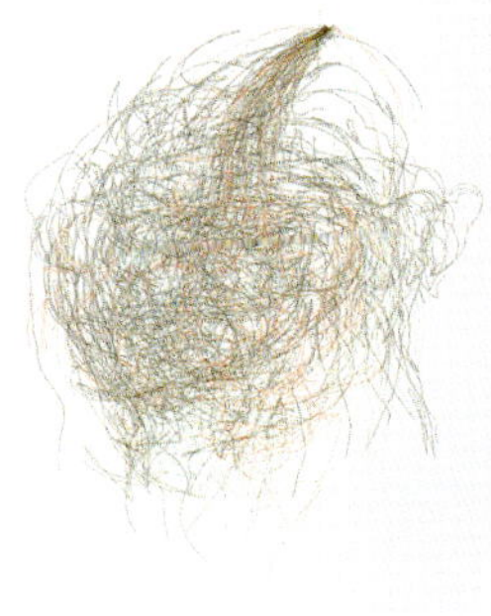

Heath, Claude b.1964
Tender Ground No.1 1996
chalk, oil & acrylic on canvas 383.5 x 317.5
ACC181/1998

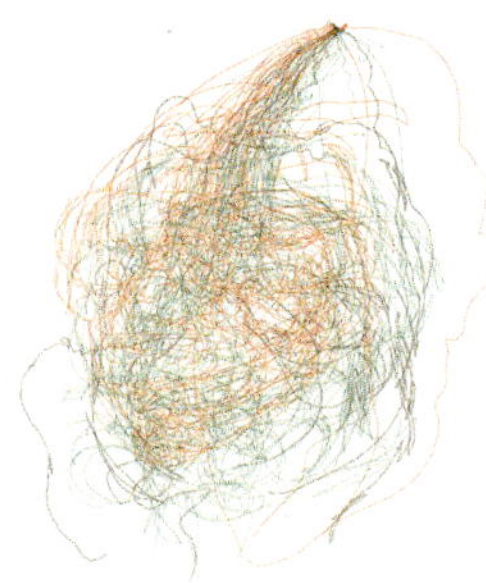

Heath, Claude b.1964
Tender Ground No.2 1996
chalk, oil & acrylic on canvas 383.5 x 317.5
ACC182/1998

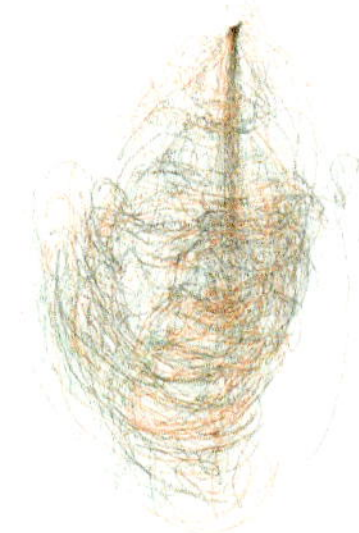

Heath, Claude b.1964
Tender Ground No.3 1996
chalk, oil & acrylic on canvas 383.5 x 317.5
ACC183/1998

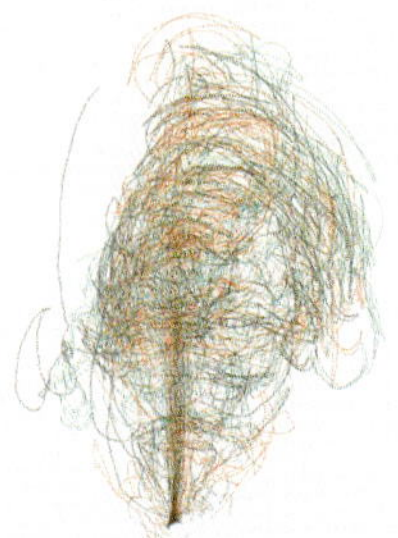

Heath, Claude b.1964
Tender Ground No.4 1996
chalk, oil & acrylic on canvas 383 x 317.5
ACC184/1998

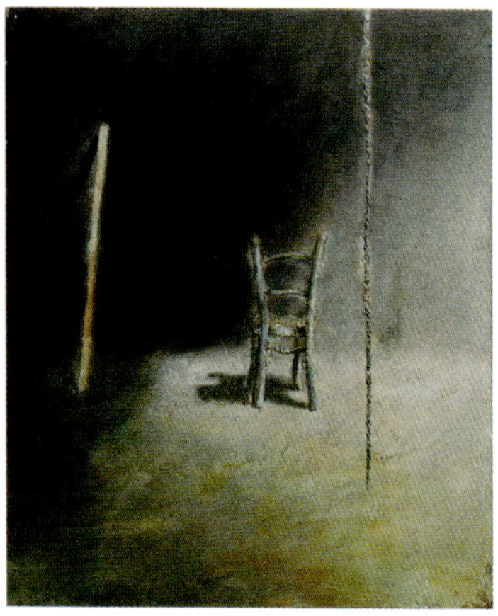

Heindorff, Michael b.1949
I.1 1978
tempera on canvas 152 x 127
AC 1945

Hempton, Paul b.1946
Marker V – Hill, Rod and Stone 1976–1977
oil on canvas 181.5 x 242
AC 2026

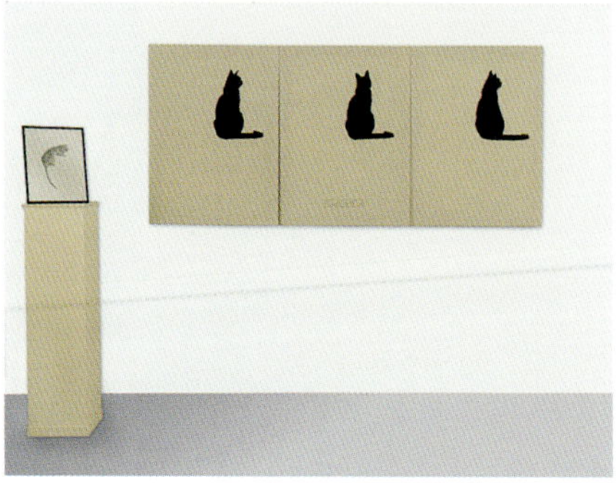

Hemsworth, Gerard b.1945
Scenario 1980
acrylic, canvas & pencil on paper, glass & wood 200 x 300
AC 5007

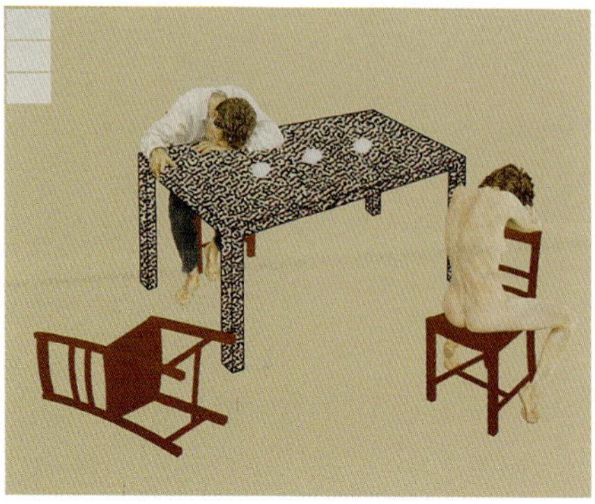

Hemsworth, Gerard b.1945
Table Manners 1983
acrylic on canvas 243.8 x 305
AC 5344

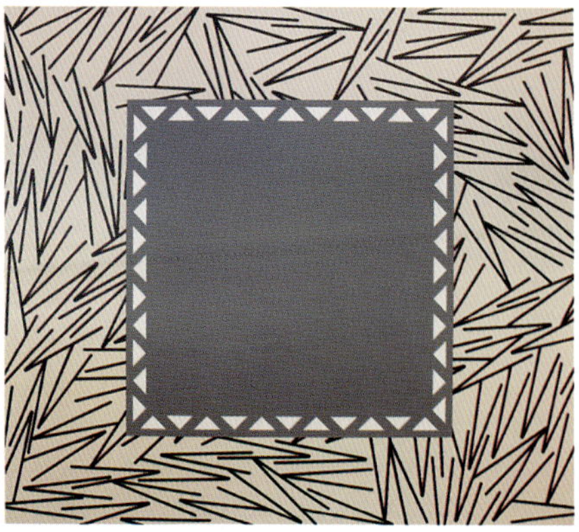

Hemsworth, Gerard b.1945
Kiss My Arse 1994
acrylic on canvas 214 x 244
ACC95/1995

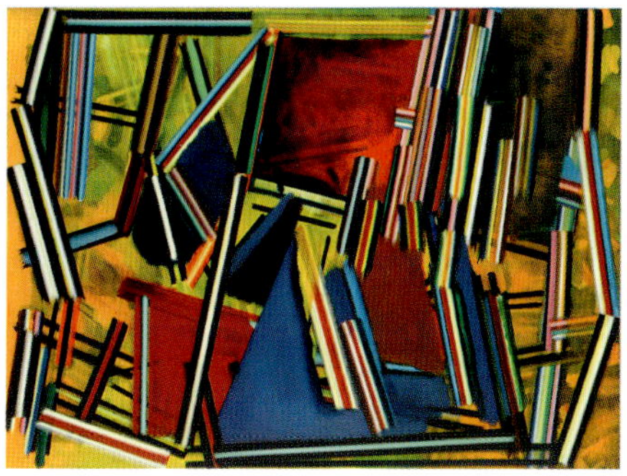

Henderson, William b.1941
Gjalla 1979
acrylic on canvas 167.5 x 228.5
AC 1987

Henri, Adrian 1932–2000
Edge of a Wood, Early Summer 1978
acrylic on canvas 182.2 x 121.9; 182.2 x 121.9
AC 1949

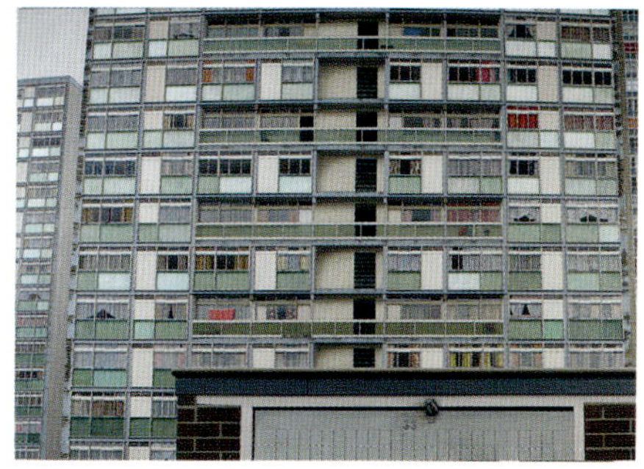

Hepher, David b.1935
Arrangement in Turquoise and Cream
1979–1981
oil on canvas 193 x 275
AC 5010

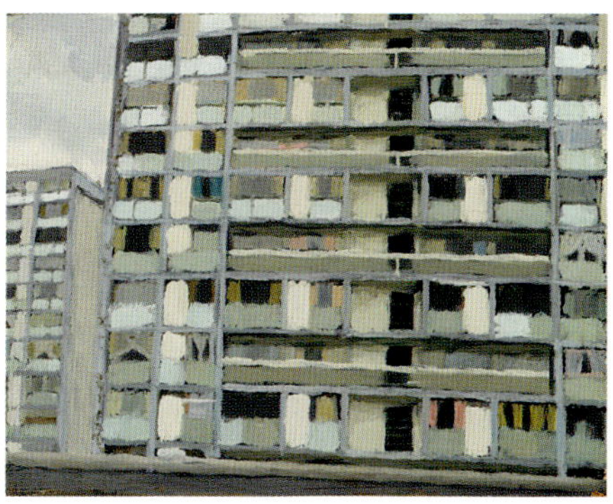

Hepher, David b.1935
Study for 'Arrangement in Turquoise and Cream' 1981
oil on board 30.5 x 39.4
AC 5011

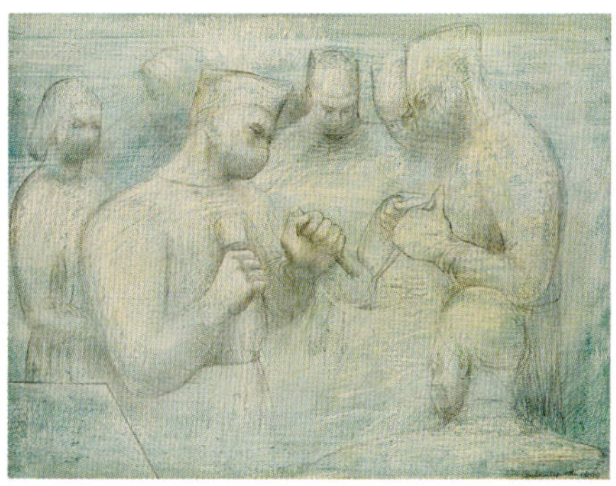

Hepworth, Barbara 1903–1975
Reconstruction 1947
oil & pencil on board 34.3 x 46.4
ACC1/1947

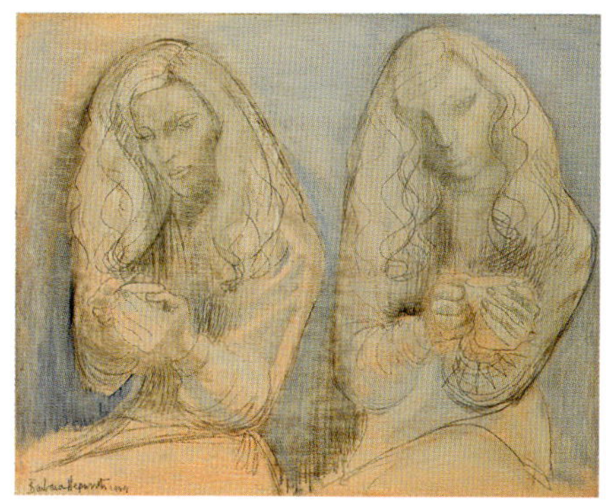

Hepworth, Barbara 1903–1975
Two Girls with Teacups 1949
oil & pencil on board 33.3 x 42.1
AC 157

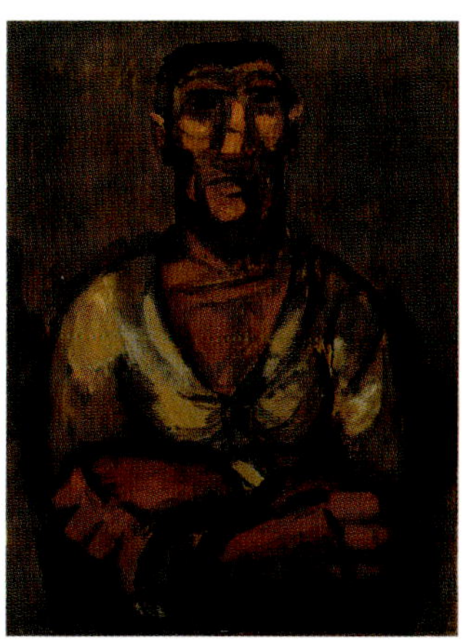

Herman, Josef 1911–2000
The Welsh Miner 1948
oil on board 78 x 58
AC 142

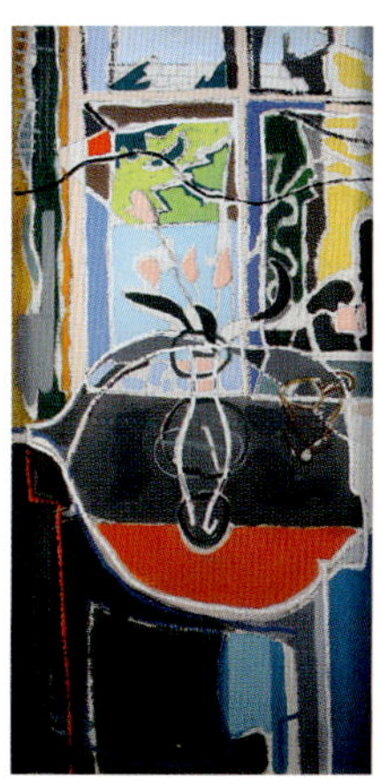

Heron, Patrick 1920–1999
The Round Table: 1950 1950
oil on canvas 91.4 x 45.7
AC 161

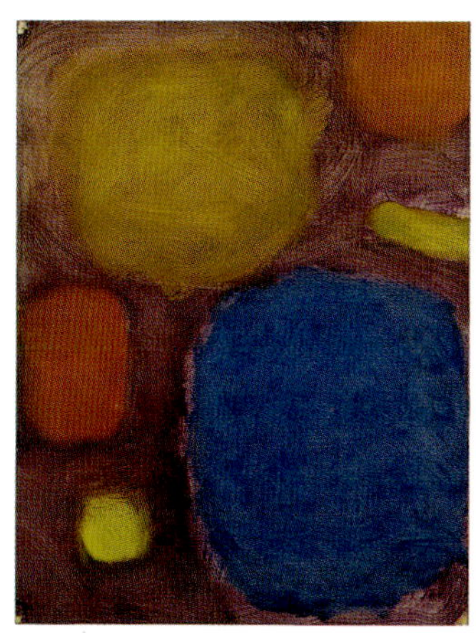

Heron, Patrick 1920–1999
Ultramarine, Cinnamon and Dull Yellow: August 1960 1960
oil on paper 44.2 x 34.2
AC 550

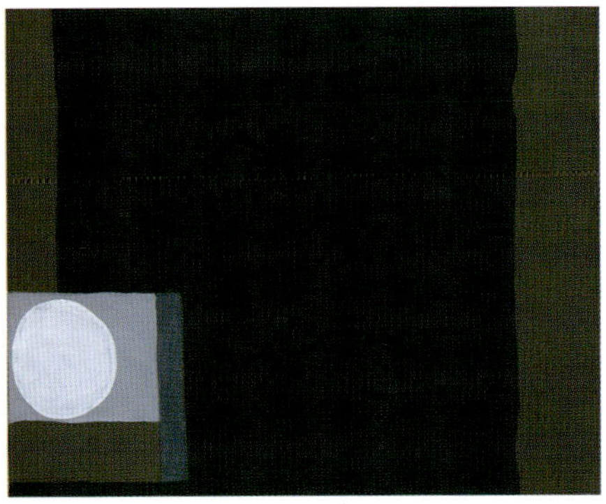

Heron, Patrick 1920–1999
Green Painting with White Disc: 1964 1964
oil on canvas 122 x 152.3
AC 761

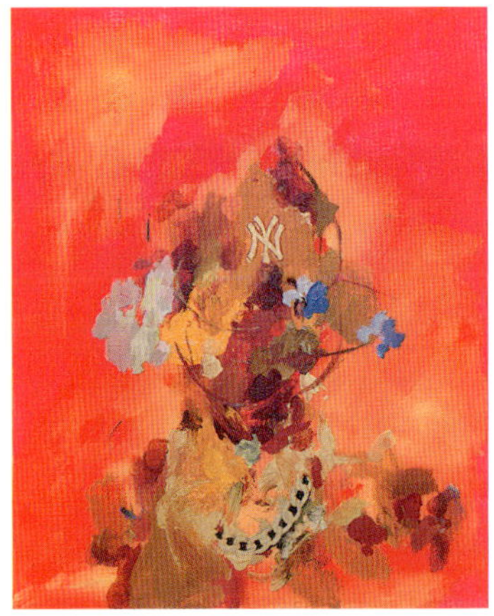

Hetherington, Iain b.1978
Composite Picture 3 (Diversified Cultural Worker) 2008
acrylic on canvas 55.9 x 45.7
ACC6/2009

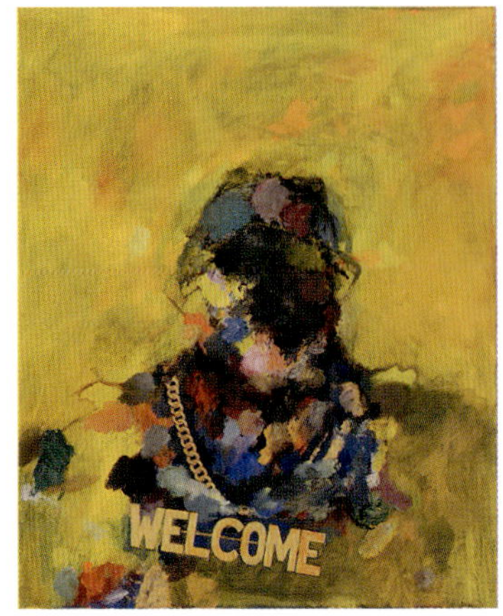

Hetherington, Iain b.1978
Diversified Cultural Worker 3 2008
oil on canvas 56 x 46
ACC4/2009

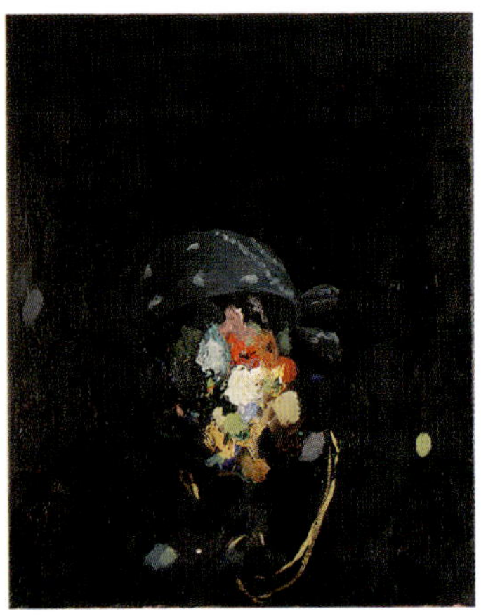

Hetherington, Iain b.1978
Diversified Cultural Worker 4 2008
oil & swarovski crystals on canvas 56 x 46
ACC5/2009

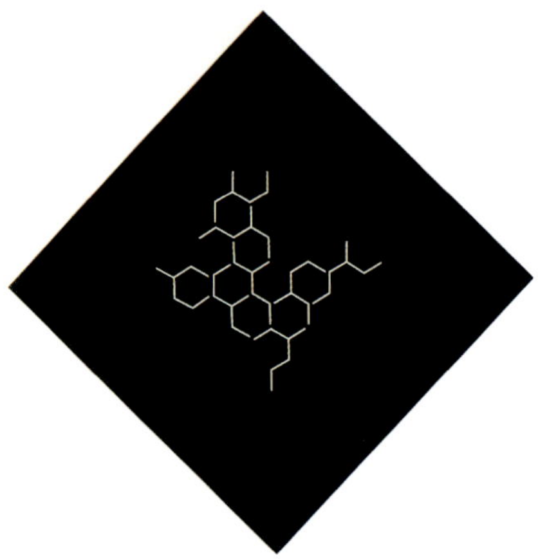

Hill, Anthony b.1930
Parity Study No.2 First Version 1970–1974
paint on perspex 175.7 x 170.7
AC 1738

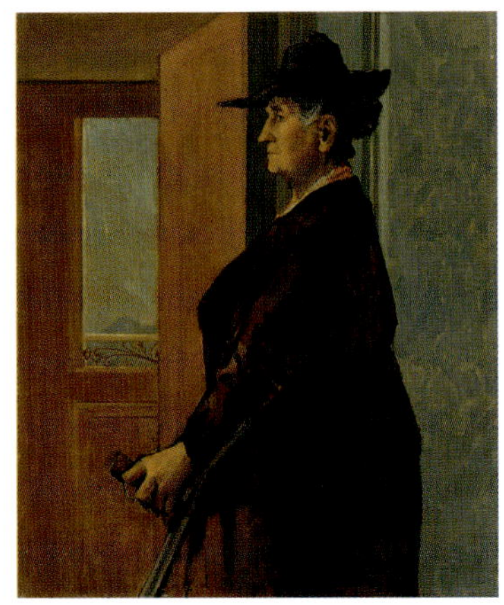

Hill, Derek 1916–2000
Mrs Aubrey Waterfield c.1948
oil on canvas 66 x 55.9
AC 166

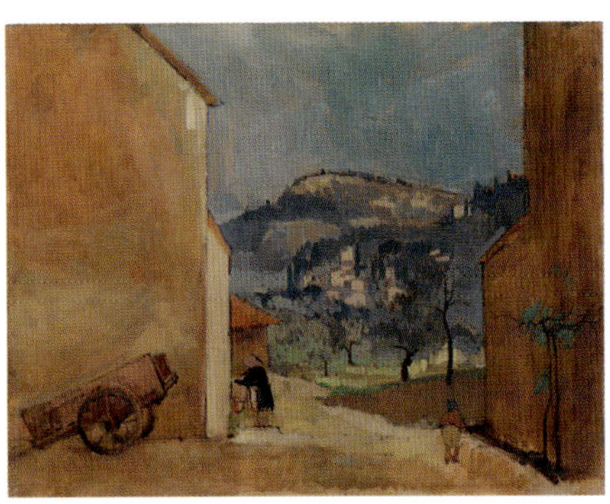

Hill, Derek 1916–2000
Corbignano c.1951
oil on canvas 58.4 x 71.1
AC 191

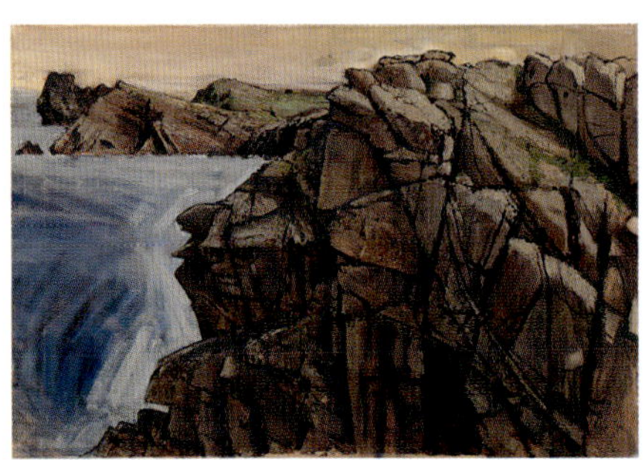

Hill, Derek 1916–2000
Cliff Face, Tory Island 1958
oil on canvas 61 x 91.4
AC 478

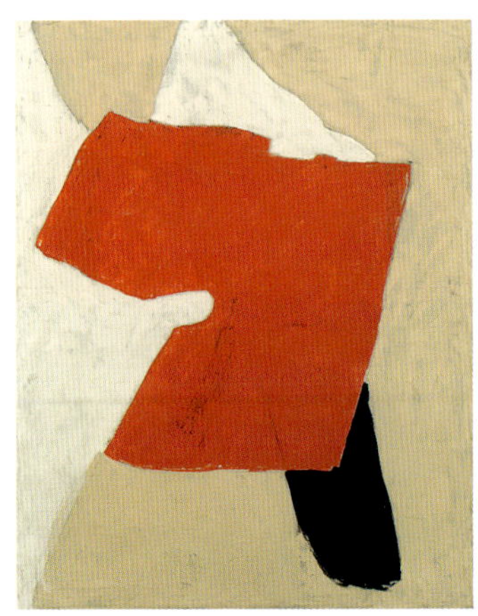

Hilton, Roger 1911–1975
February – March 1954 1954
oil on canvas 127 x 101.6
AC 445

Facing page: MacKinnon, Hugh, b.1925, *Girl's Head* (detail), 1953, (p. 103)

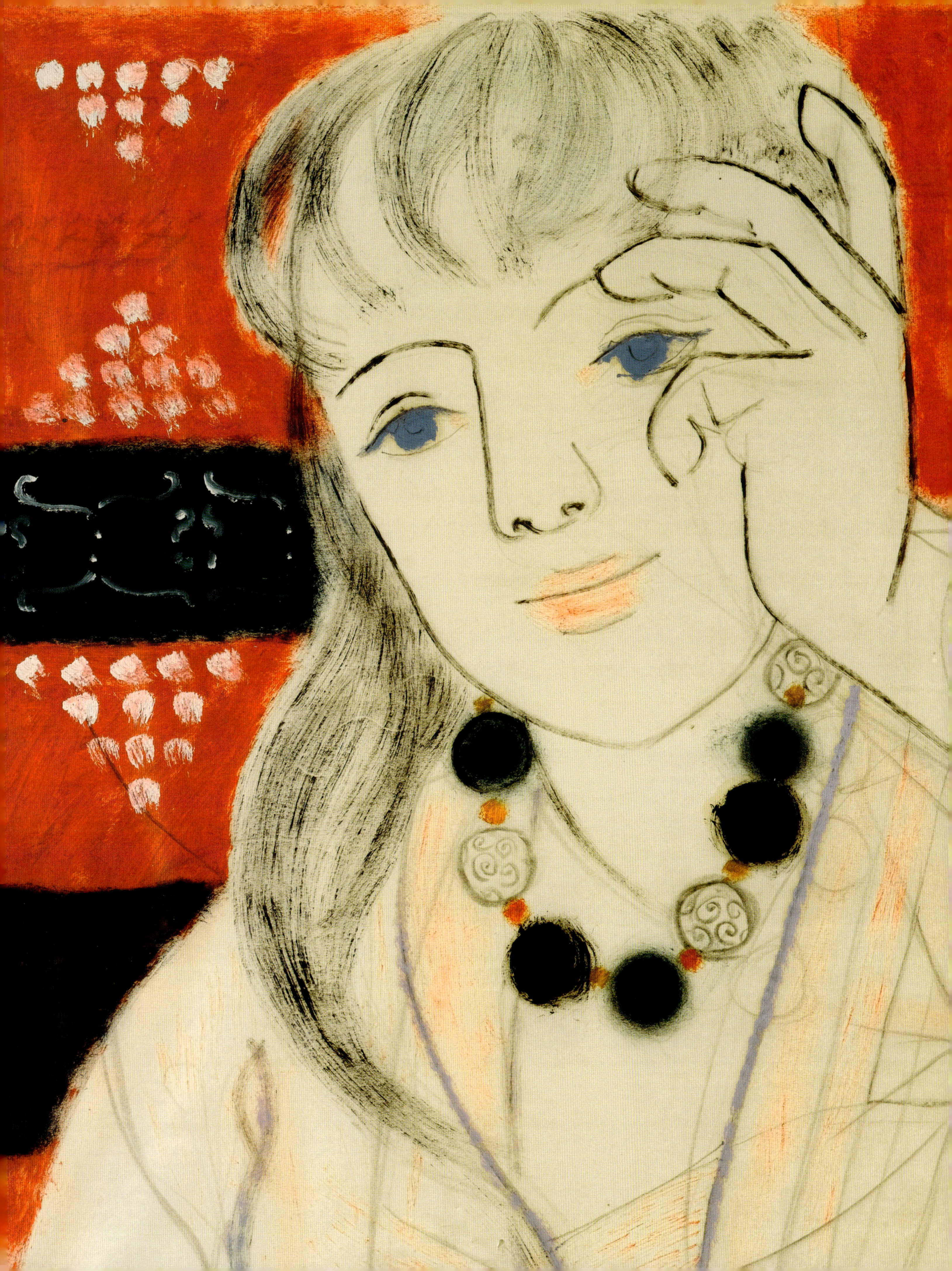

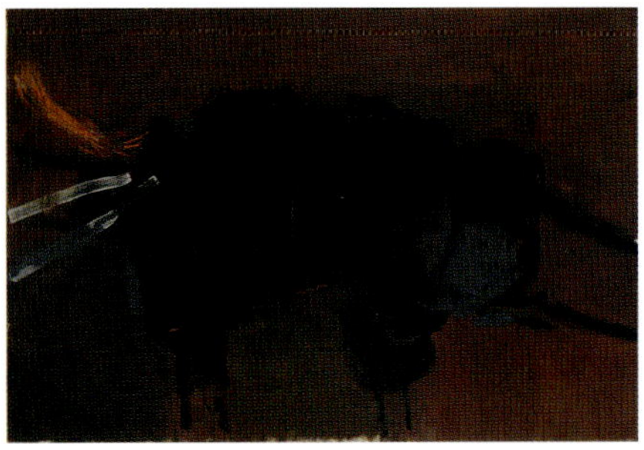

Hilton, Roger 1911–1975
Dark Continent 1958
oil on canvas 101.6 x 152.4
AC 527

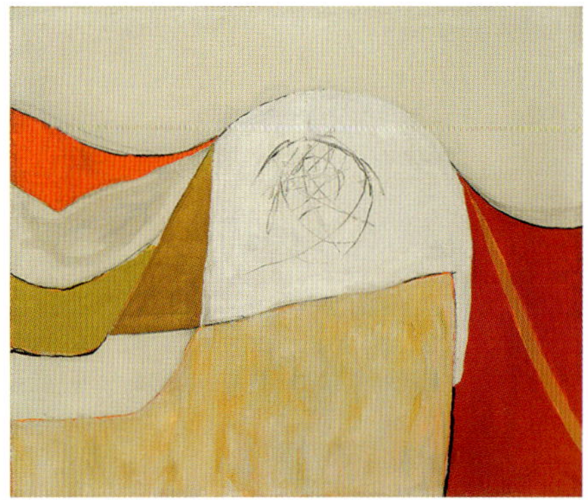

Hilton, Roger 1911–1975
January 1964, Red 1964
oil on canvas 126.9 x 152.4
AC 1384

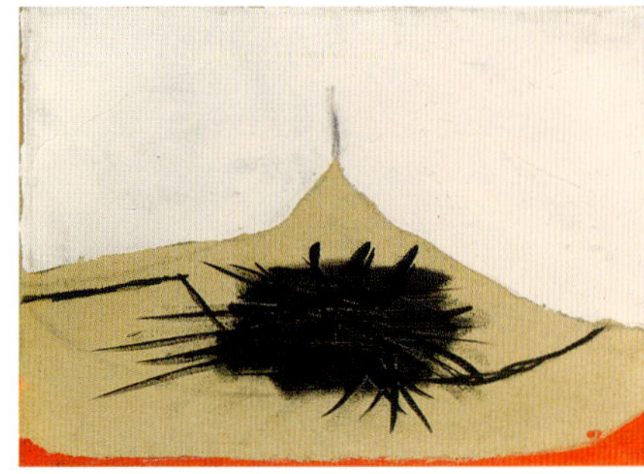

Hilton, Roger 1911–1975
Shell 1968
oil on canvas 25 x 35.5
AC 958

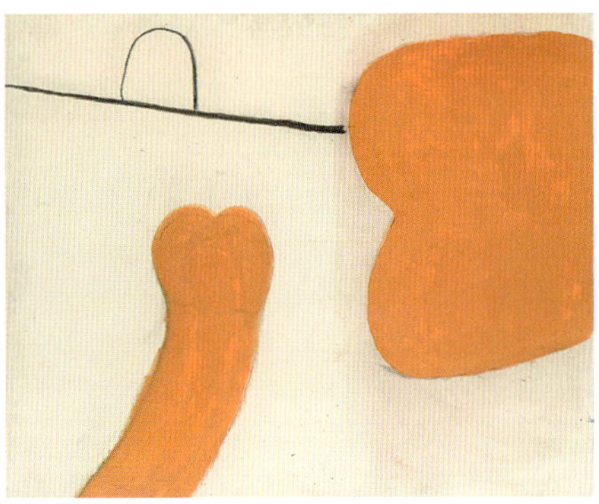

Hilton, Roger 1911–1975
Untitled 1972
oil on canvas 101.2 x 126.5
AC 1757

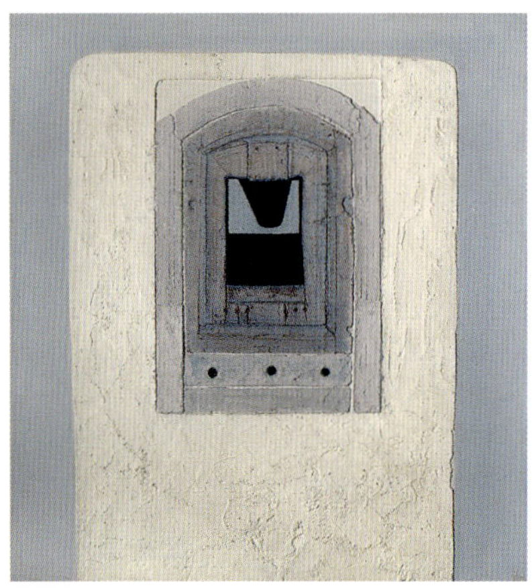

Hirst, Derek 1930–2006
Perdido 1962
oil on canvas 101.6 x 91.4
AC 620

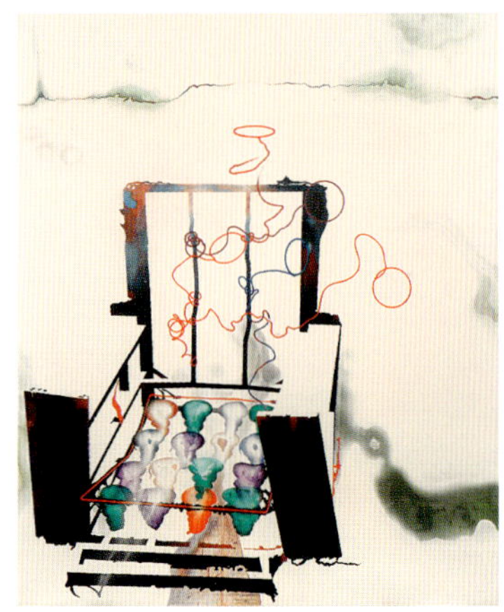

Hirst, Derek 1930–2006
Second Visit: Second Variation 1966–1967
acrylic on canvas 183 x 152.5
AC 3000

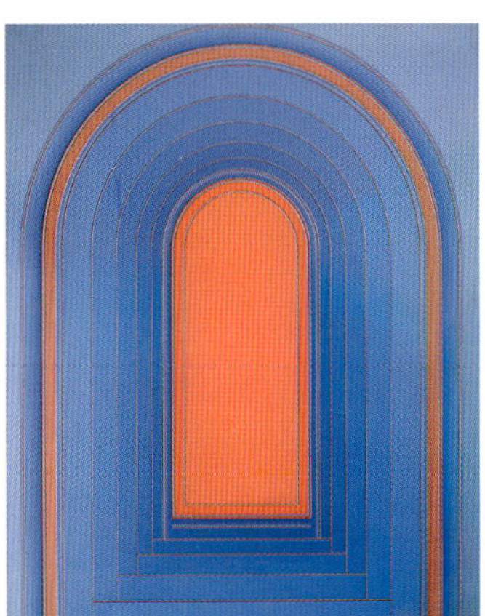

Hirst, Derek 1930–2006
Odeon: Red/Blue 1970–1973
acrylic on board 152.4 x 121.9
AC 1380

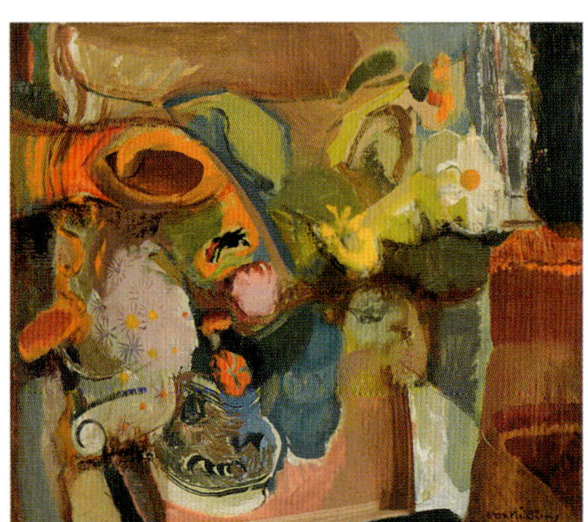

Hitchens, Ivon 1893–1979
Flowers 1941
oil on canvas 63.5 x 73.7
AC 67

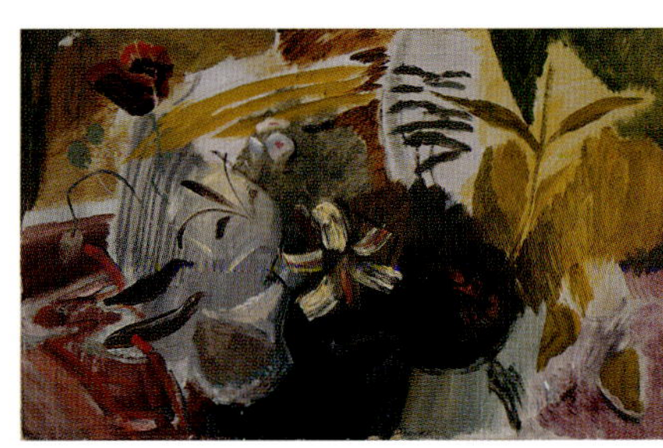

Hitchens, Ivon 1893–1979
Lilies and Purple Poppy 1948
oil on canvas 66 x 83.8
AC 143

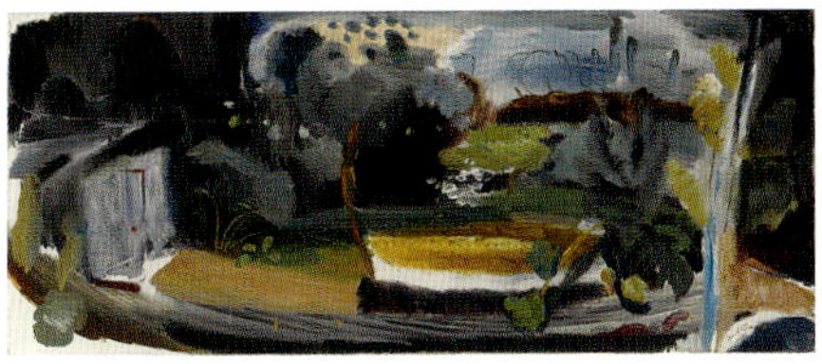

Hitchens, Ivon 1893–1979
Garden Cove 1948–1950
oil on canvas 44 x 108
AC 265

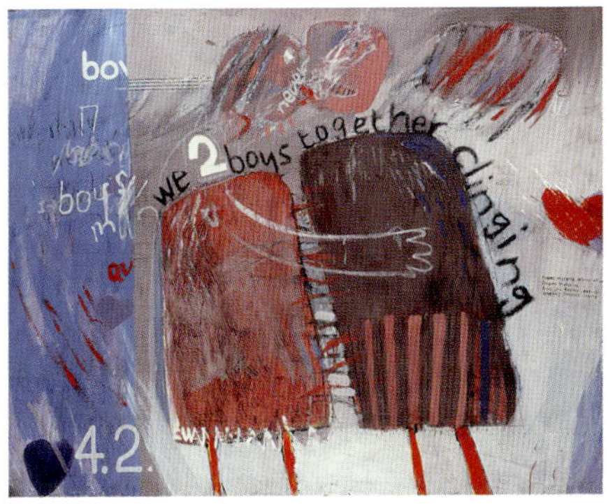

Hockney, David b.1937
We Two Boys Together Clinging 1961
oil on board 121.9 x 152.4
ACC5/1961

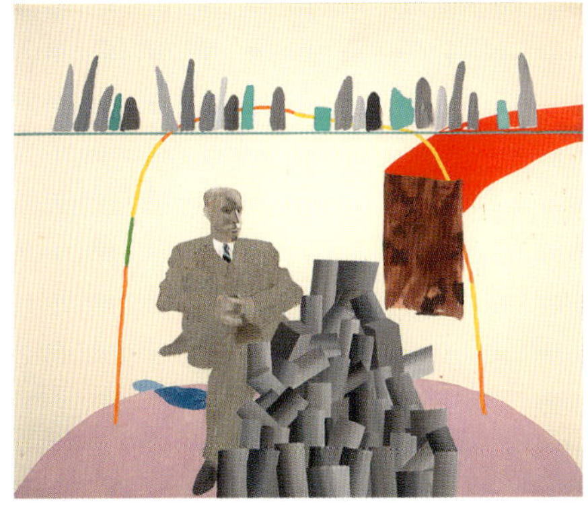

Hockney, David b.1937
Portrait Surrounded by Artistic Devices 1965
acrylic on canvas 152.4 x 182.9
AC 823

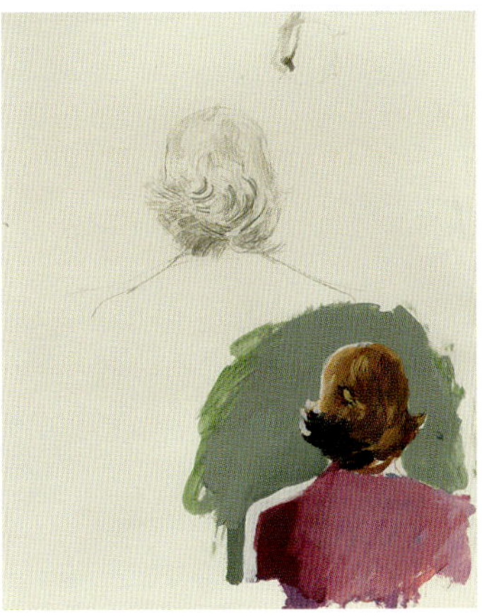

Hockney, David b.1937
Study for 'Sur la Terrasse' 1971
oil, watercolour & pencil on paper
43.1 x 35.2
AC 1216 h

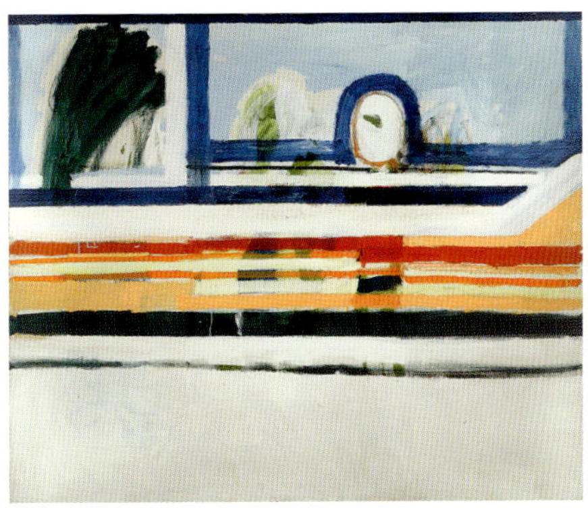

Hodgkin, Howard b.1932
Luxembourg Gardens 1960–1962
oil on canvas 106.7 x 126.4
AC 665

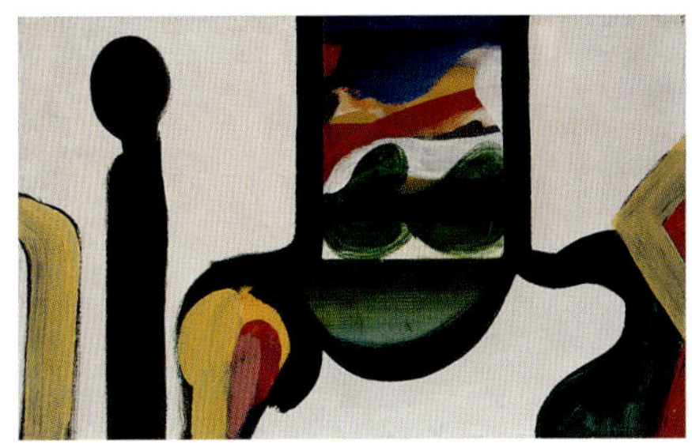

Hodgkin, Howard b.1932
Widcombe Crescent 1966
oil on canvas 40.6 x 66
ACA 50

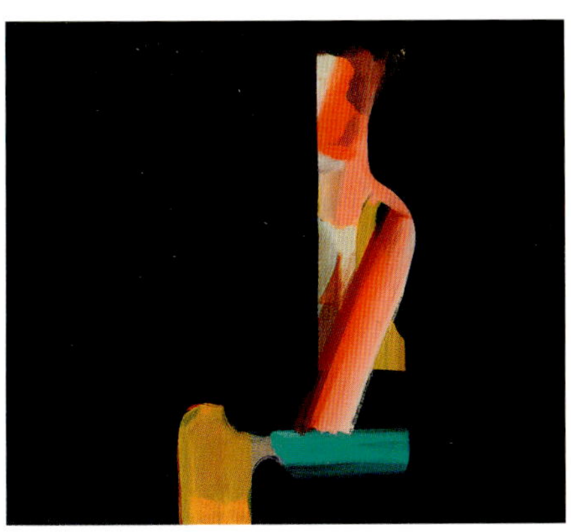

Hodgkin, Howard b.1932
Mrs K 1966–1967
oil on canvas 86.4 x 99
ACA 49

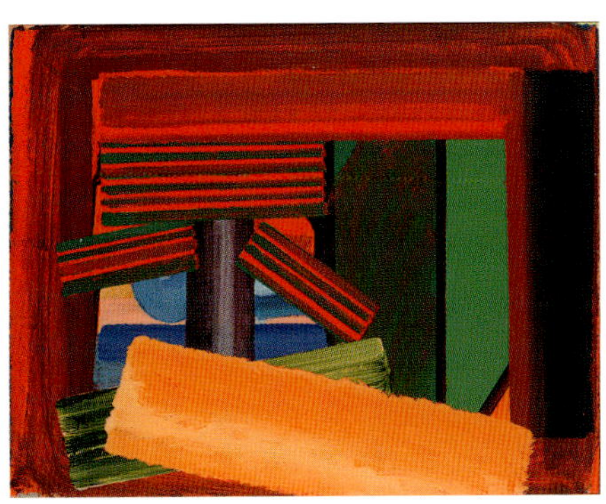

Hodgkin, Howard b.1932
Foy Nissen's Bombay 1975–1977
oil on wood 71.1 x 91.6
ACC1/1977

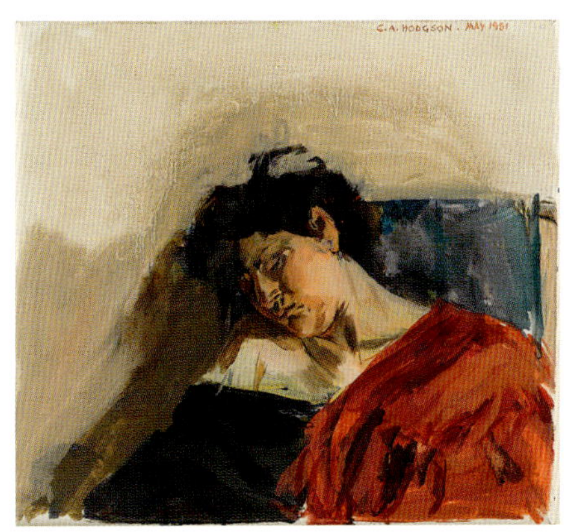

Hodgson, Clive b.1953
Angela Asleep 1981
oil on canvas 45.3 x 50.6
AC 5026

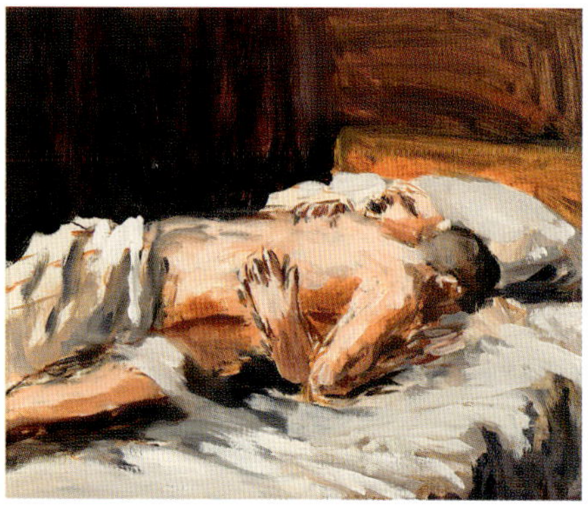

Hodgson, Clive b.1953
Intimate Scene 1982
oil on board 25.1 x 30.4
AC 5027

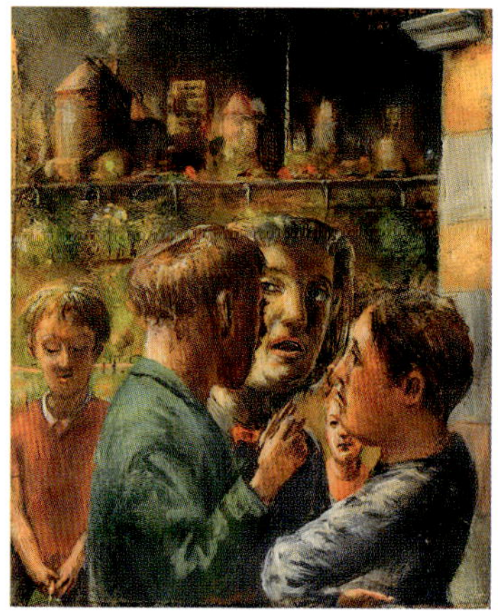

Hodgson, Clive b.1953
A Little Conversation 1987
oil on board 13.2 x 11.4
AC 5486

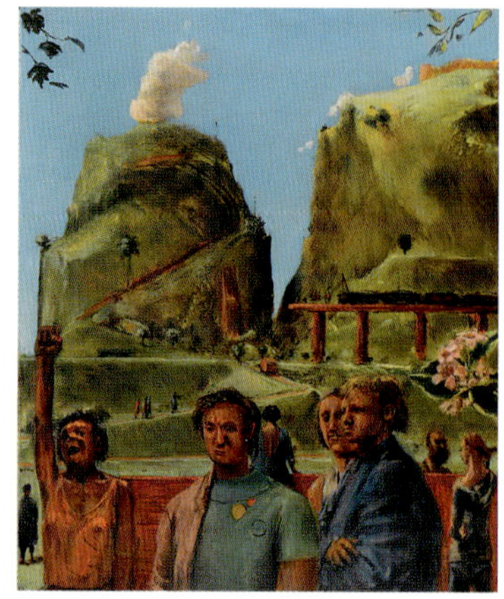

Hodgson, Clive b.1953
Blossom and blue sky 1987
oil on board 36.3 x 30.4
AC 5487

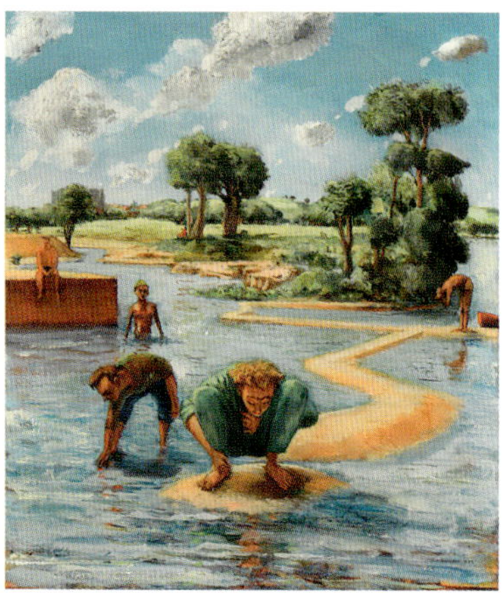

Hodgson, Clive b.1953
People and Water 1987
oil on canvas 40.6 x 36
AC 5485

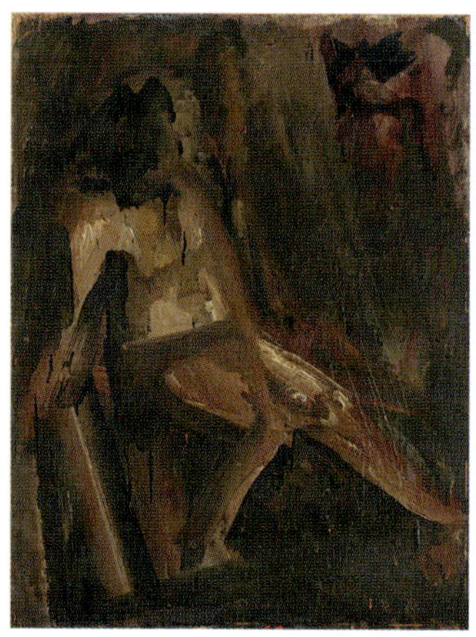

Holden, Cliff b.1919
Seated Figure 1950
oil on board 73.7 x 55.9
AC 895

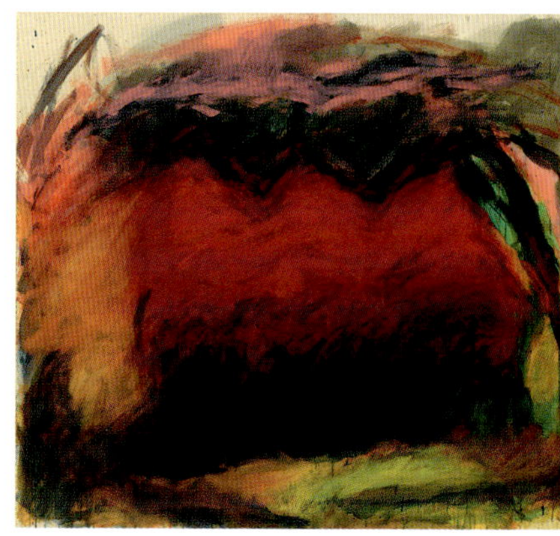

Hopkins, Clyde D. F. b.1946
Untitled/Sturm 1979
acrylic on canvas 169 x 184.5
AC 3033

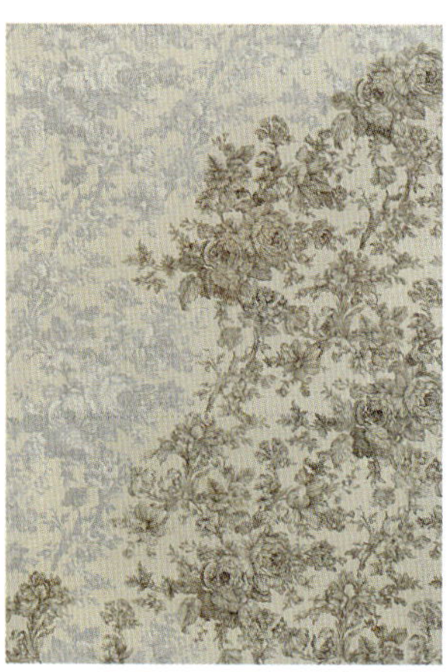

Hopkins, Louise b.1965
Aurora 13 1995–1996
oil on reverse of furnishing fabric 183 x 130
ACC186/1998

Horsfield, Nicholas 1917–2005
Le Pollet Noir, Dieppe 1959
oil on canvas 71.1 x 90.8
AC 511

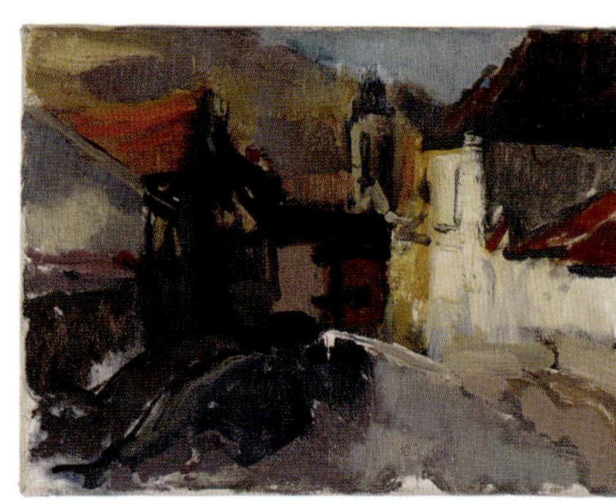

Horsfield, Nicholas 1917–2005
Vétheuil Street Scene 1959
oil on canvas 22.9 x 30.5
AC 638

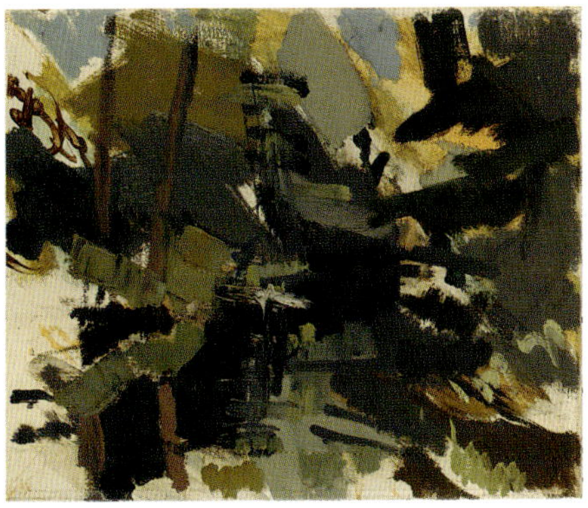

Horsfield, Nicholas 1917–2005
'River Epte' (Oil) 1973
oil on canvas 36 x 43.2
AC 1959

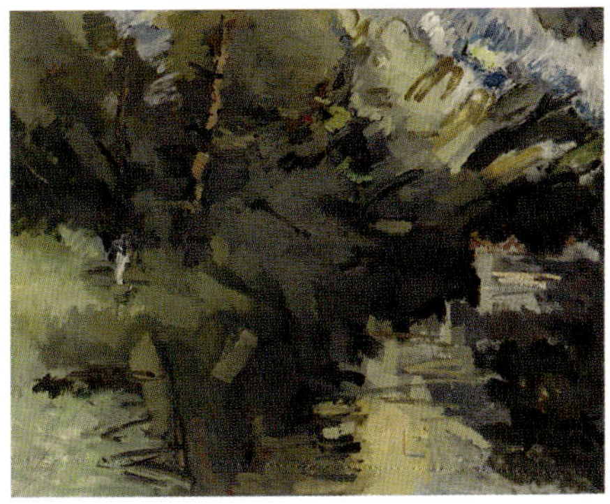

Horsfield, Nicholas 1917–2005
'River Epte' (2) (Oil) 1974
oil on canvas 101.7 x 127
AC 1958

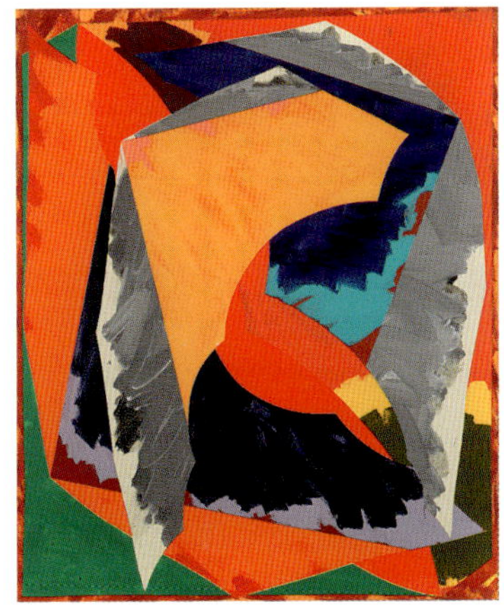

Horsley, Michael Leonard b.1941
Untitled 77–78 1977–1978
acrylic on canvas 211 x 180
AC 3022

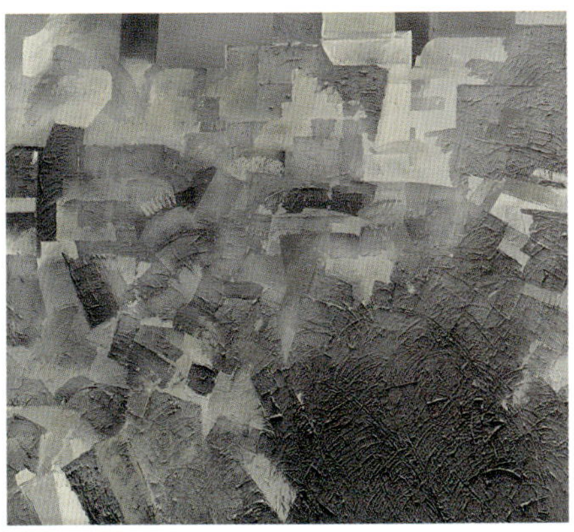

Hosking, Knighton Stephen b.1944
Earth Band 1974–1975
acrylic on canvas 243.8 x 274.3
AC 1538

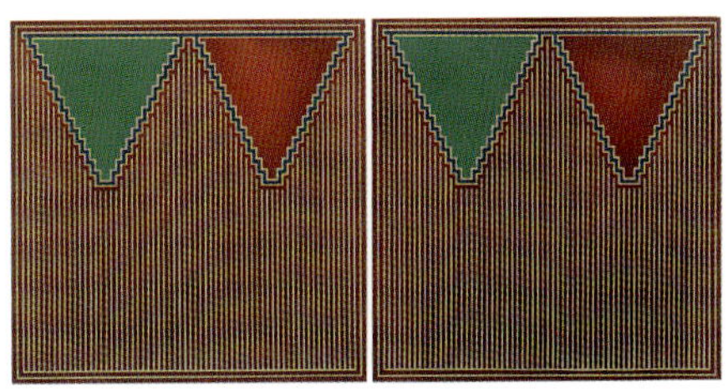

House, Gordon 1932–2004
Double Green Dropped Initial 1968–1969
acrylic on canvas 152.4 x 304.8
AC 1279

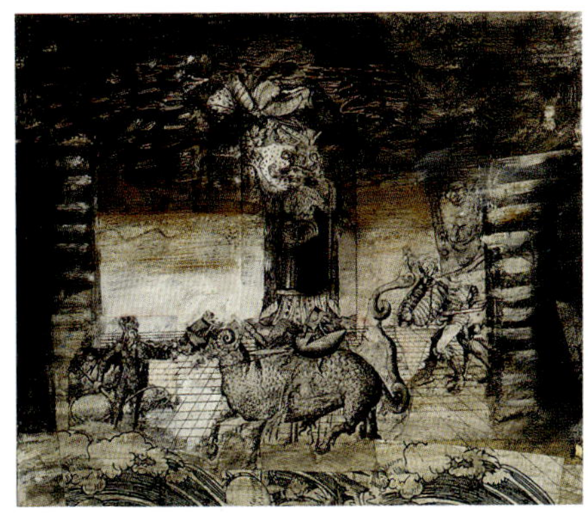

Howard, Ian b.1952
Summa Theologiae 1987
acrylic & collage on card 38 x 46
AC 5534

Howlin, John b.1941
Brandenburg 1970
acrylic on canvas 198.1 x 241.3
AC 1139

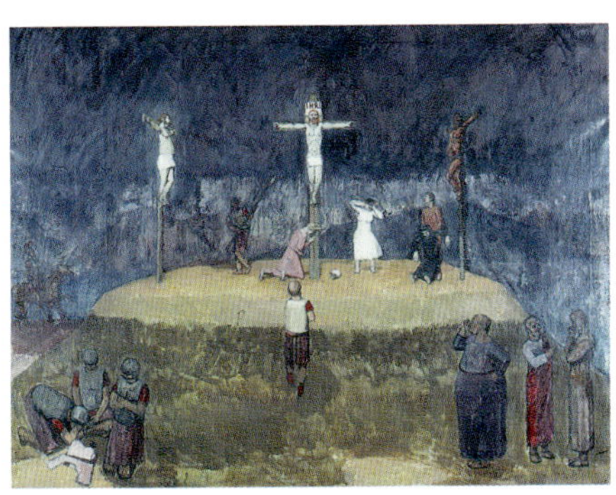

Hoyland, Francis b.1930
Crucifixion 1956
oil on canvas 95.3 x 127
AC 598

Hoyland, John 1934–2011
19.12.66 1966
oil on canvas 182.9 x 304.8
AC 891

Hoyland, John 1934–2011
20.5.68 1968
acrylic on canvas 198.1 x 367
AC 1070

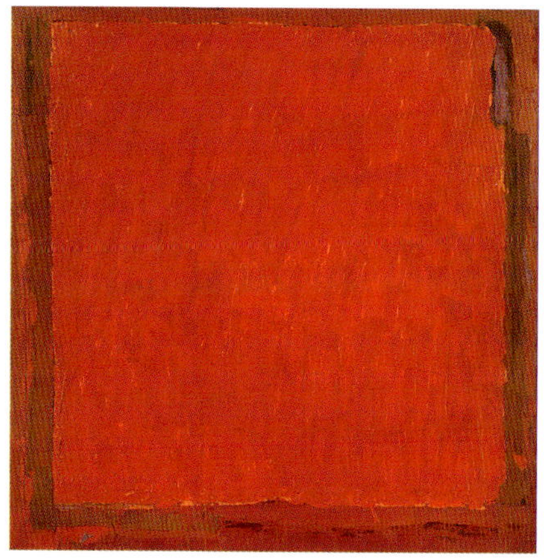

Hoyland, John 1934–2011
Red Over Yellow, 18.9.73 1973
acrylic on canvas 244.5 x 248
AC 1432

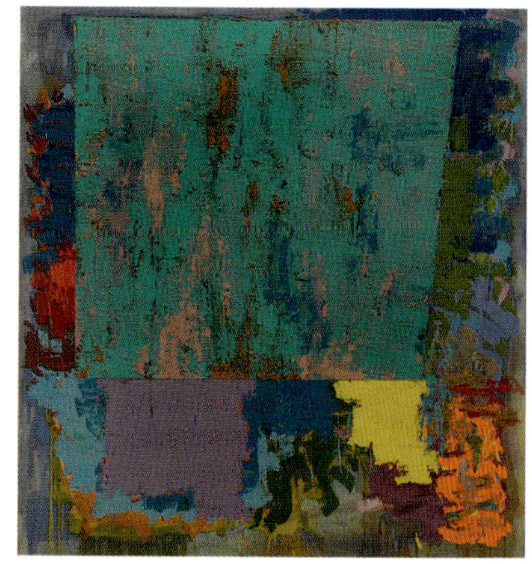

Hoyland, John 1934–2011
Wotan 1977
acrylic on canvas 243.8 x 228.6
AC 1863

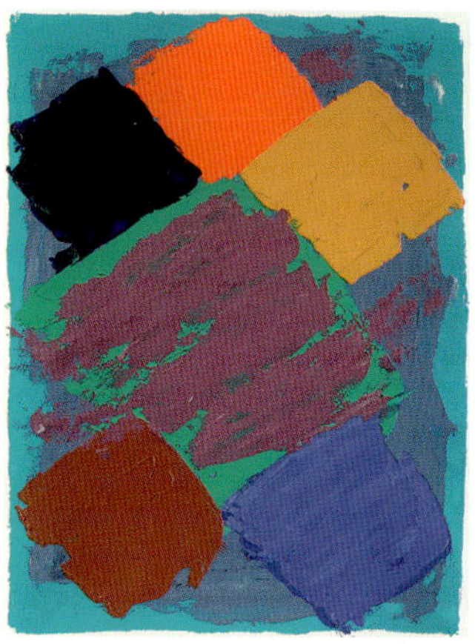

Hoyland, John 1934–2011
Untitled Drawing (Blue) 1980
acrylic on paper 77.2 x 57
AC 4064

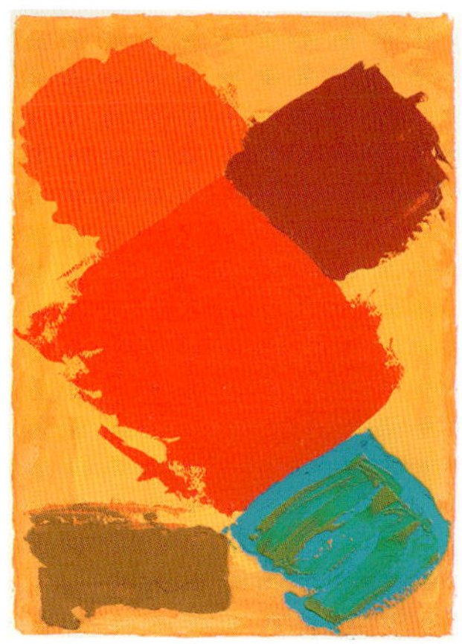

Hoyland, John 1934–2011
Untitled Drawing (Yellow) 1980
acrylic on paper 77.2 x 57
AC 4063

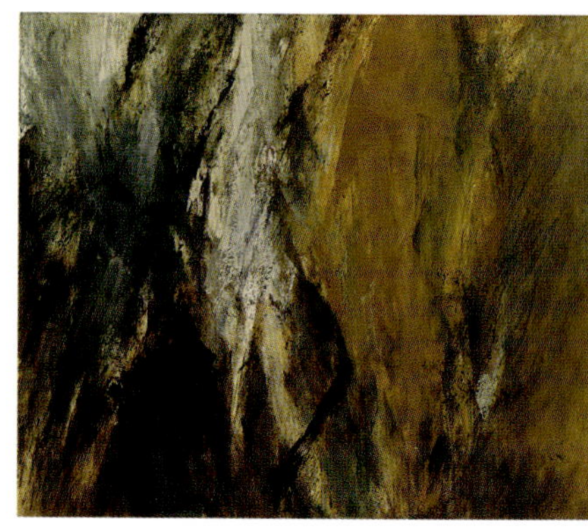

Hubbard, John b.1931
Wood with Filtered Light 1965
oil on canvas 172.7 x 203.2
AC 815

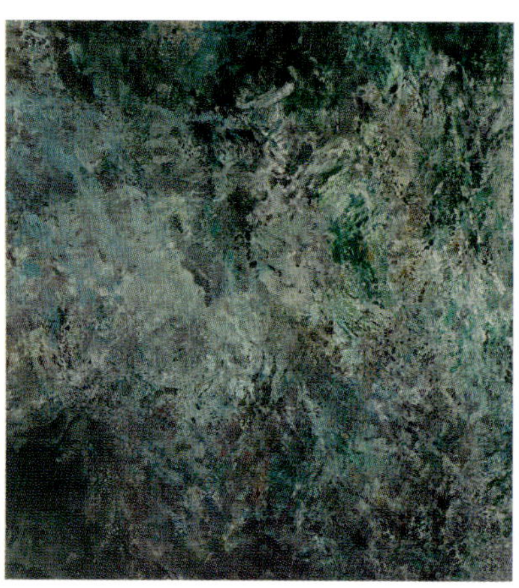

Hubbard, John b.1931
In the High Atlas 1970
oil on canvas 182.9 x 172.7
AC 1128

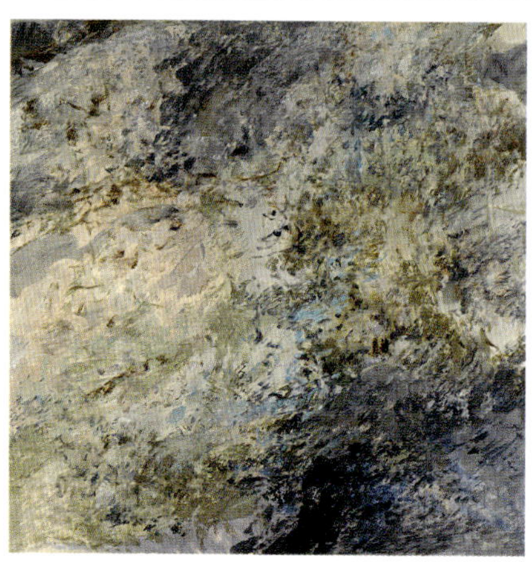

Hubbard, John b.1931
Quarry 1975
oil on paper 115 x 115
AC 1575

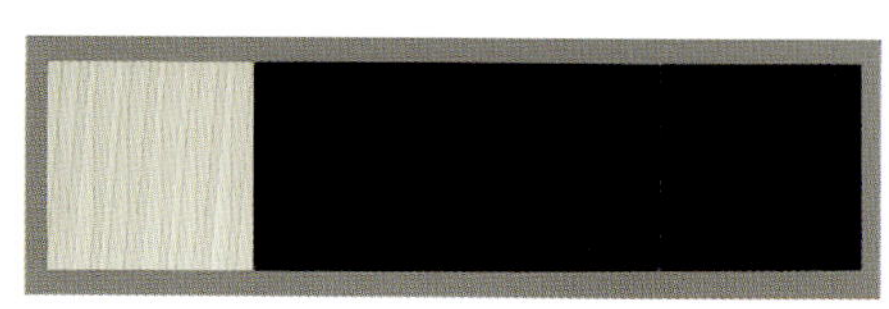

Hughes, Malcolm Edward 1920–1997
Three Unit Relief/Painting 1973
PVA & oil on wood 58.6 x 243.8
AC 1596

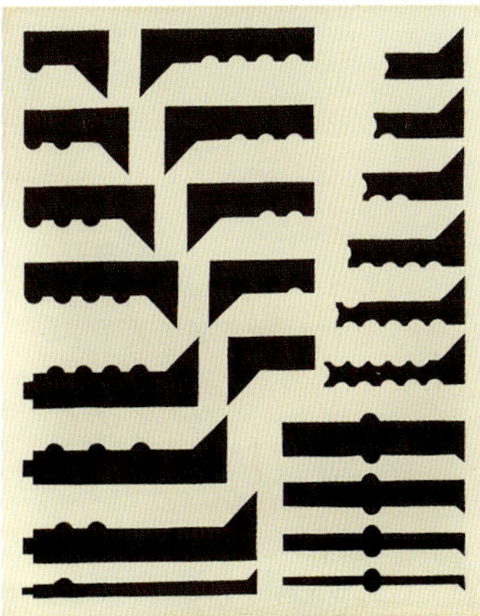

Hughes, Patrick 1939–2004
The Differentiation of Nothing 1962
enamel on board 90 x 74
AC 634

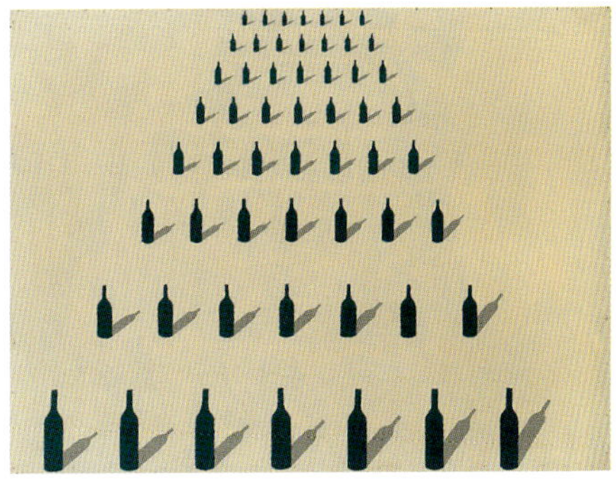

Hughes, Patrick 1939–2004
The Revolting Bottle 1965
enamel on board 91.5 x 122
AC 824

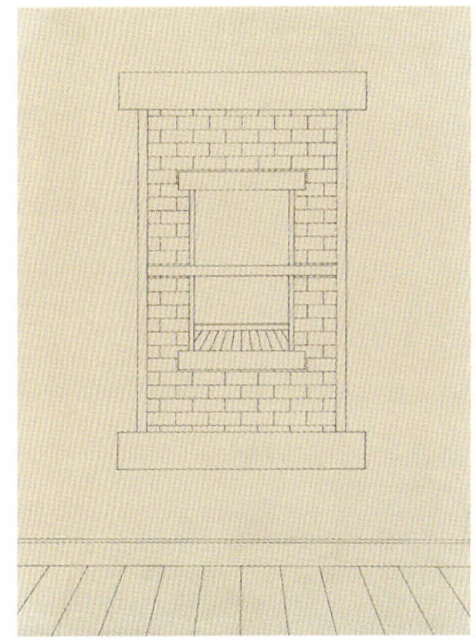

Hughes, Patrick 1939–2004
Next Door 1971
gloss paint & ink on board 121.3 x 90.8
AC 1176

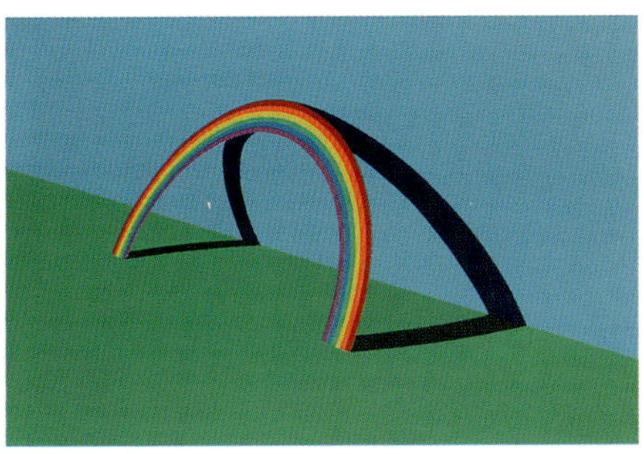

Hughes, Patrick 1939–2004
Leaning on a Landscape 1978
gloss paint on board 121.9 x 182.5
AC 1894

Hugonin, James b.1950
White Drawing, Light Grey Intervals V 1977
acrylic & pencil on paper 56.6 x 46.6
AC 1875

Hugonin, James b.1950
White Drawing, Light Grey Intervals VIII 1977
acrylic & pencil on paper 56.2 x 45.9
AC 1876

Hugonin, James b.1950
Untitled 1988–1989
oil & wax on plywood 170.2 x 152.4
ACC23/1989

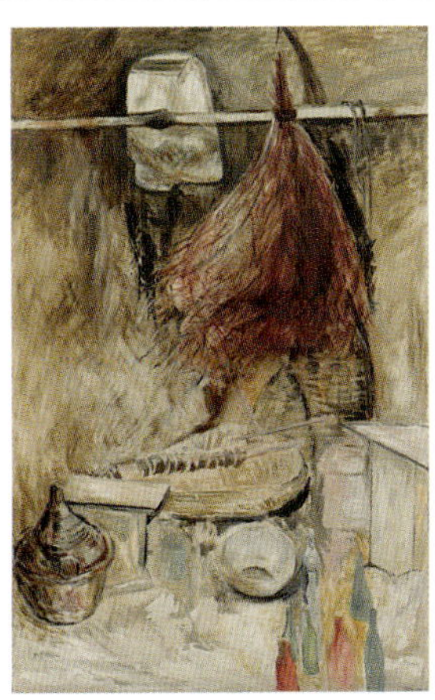

Hulbert, Thelma 1913–1995
The Cellar, Ischia 1958
oil on canvas 148 x 95.3
AC 480

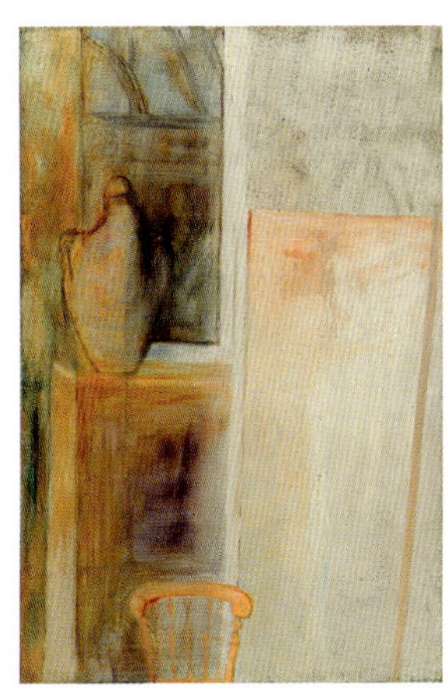

Hulbert, Thelma 1913–1995
The Studio I 1961
oil on board 152.4 x 101.6
AC 1114

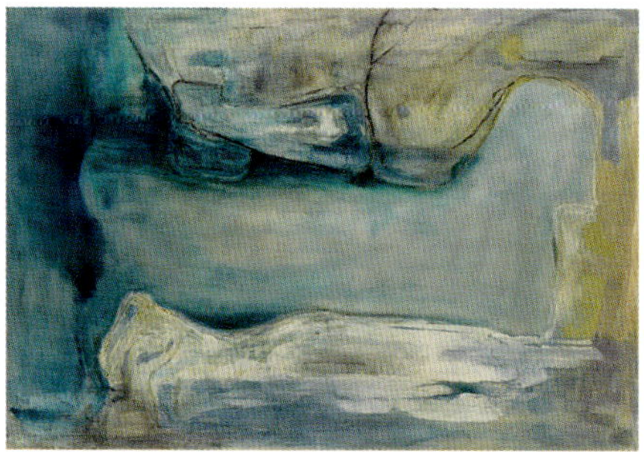

Hulbert, Thelma 1913–1995
Rocks under Water 1962–1965
oil on canvas 127 x 186.7
AC 1111

Hume, Gary b.1962
Moonbeam Rising 1994
gloss paint, eggshell & satin paint on board
244.4 x 122.5
ACC21/1994

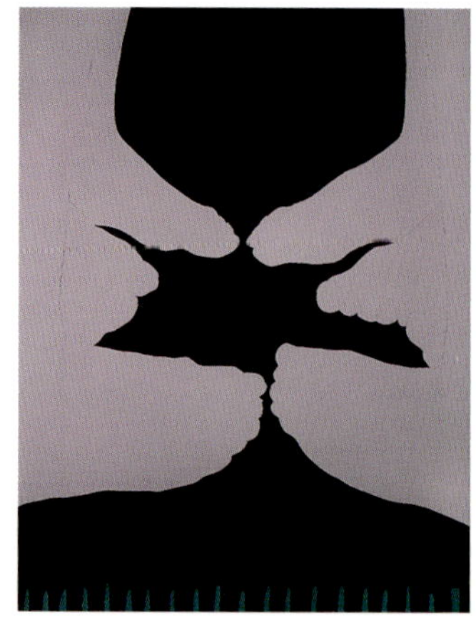

Hume, Gary b.1962
Four Feet in the Garden 1995
gloss paint on aluminium 221 x 170.9
ACC3/1995

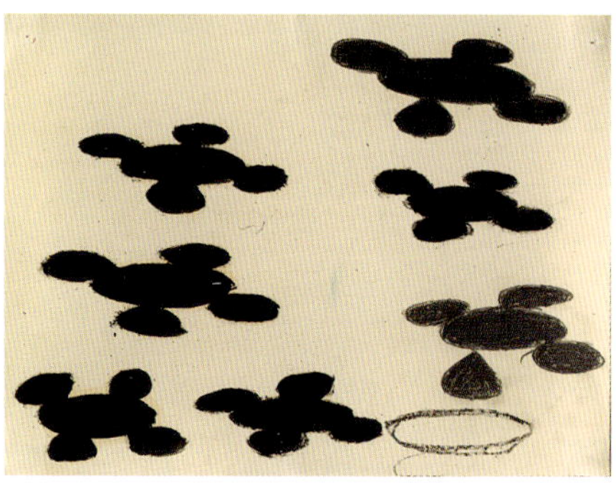

Huxley, Paul b.1938
Drawing Related to 'Untitled No.28' (1963)
1963
oil & graphite on paper 27.9 x 38.1
AC 1218

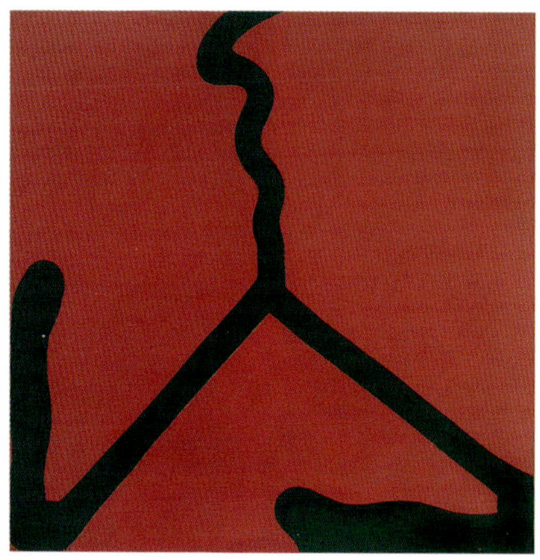

Huxley, Paul b.1938
Untitled No.32 1964
acrylic on canvas 172.7 x 172.7
AC 785

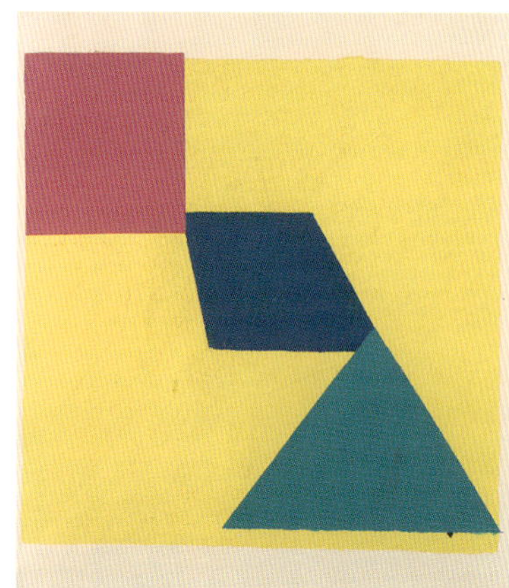

Huxley, Paul b.1938
Untitled No.57 1966
acrylic on paper 69.2 x 57.8
AC 987

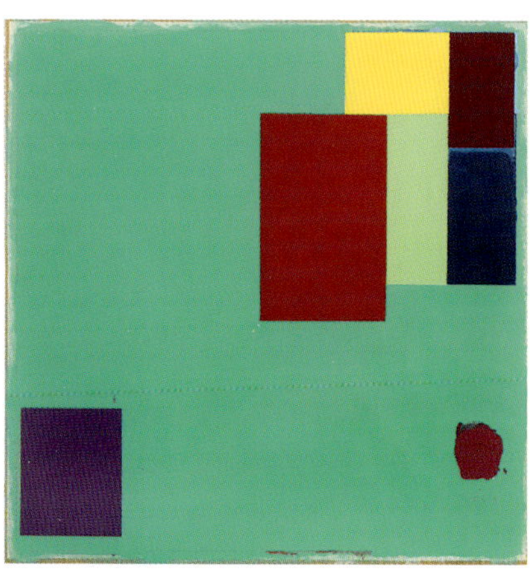

Huxley, Paul b.1938
Untitled No.146 1974
acrylic on paper 128.3 x 127.2
AC 1429

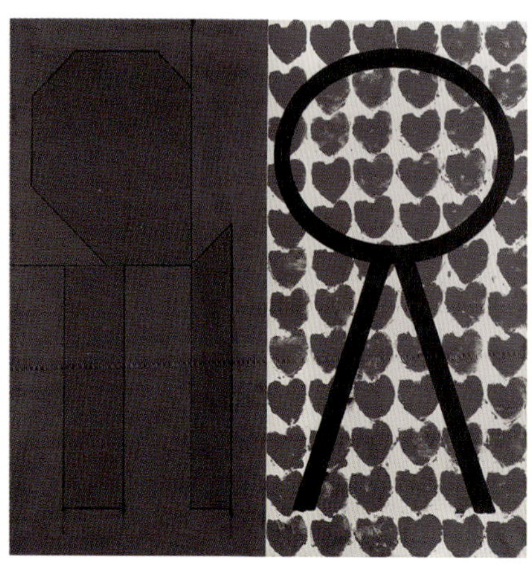

Huxley, Paul b.1938
Neither Dead nor Alive 1978
acrylic on canvas 203.1 x 203.1
AC 1928

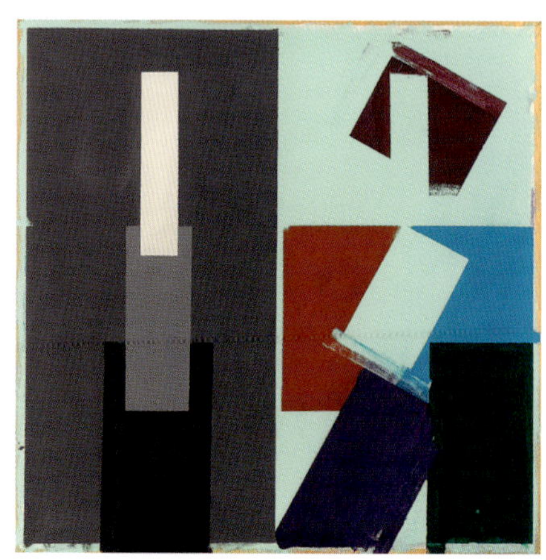

Huxley, Paul b.1938
Herald 1982–1983
acrylic on paper 113.5 x 113
AC 5299

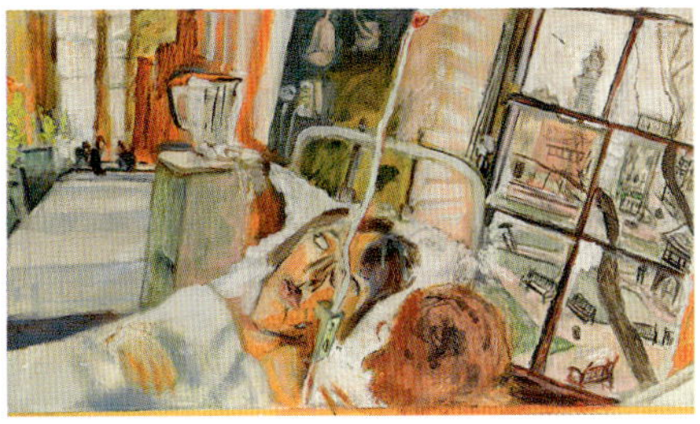

Hyman, Timothy b.1946
Judith in Hospital 1986
oil on paper 30 x 53
AC 5563

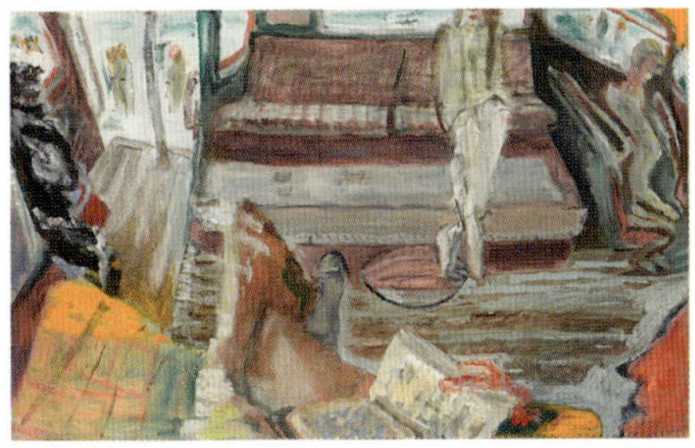

Hyman, Timothy b.1946
Reading on the Bus 1986–1987
oil on paper 44.4 x 73.7
AC 5564

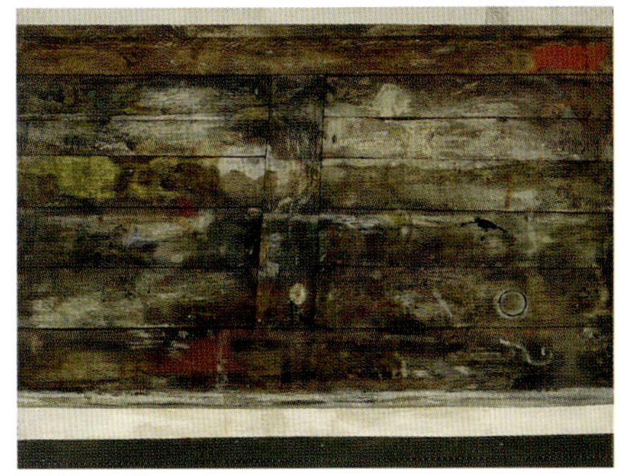

Ingham, Bryan 1936–1997
Table Top 1961
oil on hardboard 91.4 x 121.9
AC 756

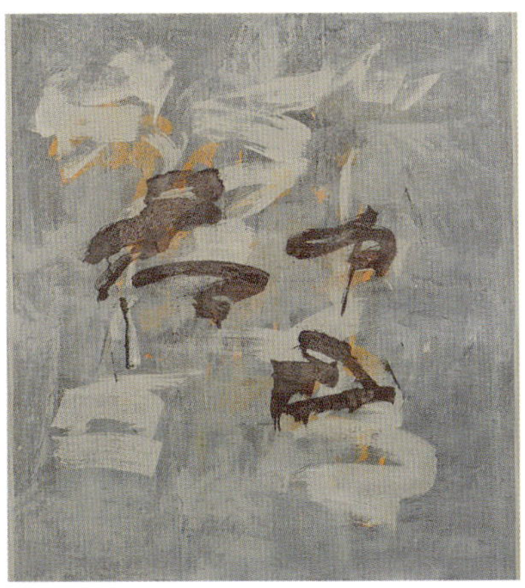

Ingham, Gillian b.1951
Grey Spirit 1978
acrylic on canvas 188 x 169.5
AC 1999

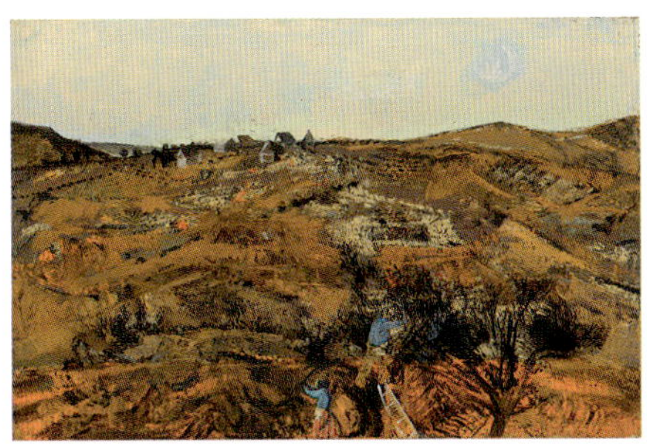

Inlander, Henry 1925–1983
Italian Landscape 1955
oil on canvas 65.4 x 100.3
AC 361

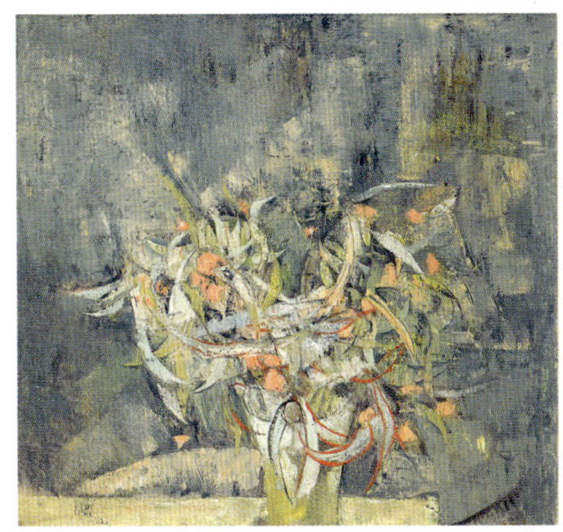

Inlander, Henry 1925–1983
Eucalyptus 3 1956
oil on canvas 69.7 x 70.2
AC 415

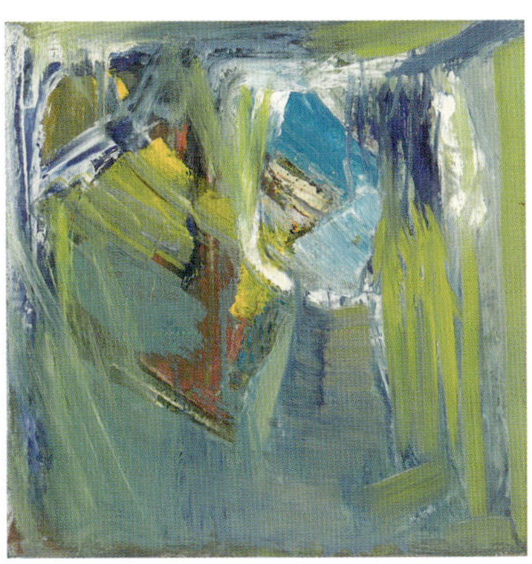

Inlander, Henry 1925–1983
Water Reflection 1961
oil on canvas 49.5 x 49.5
AC 567

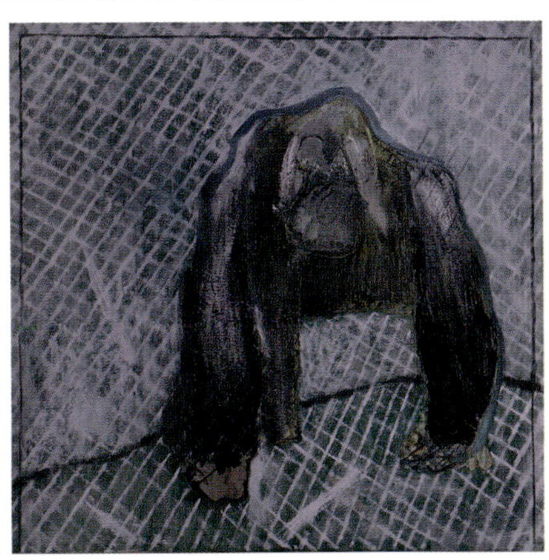

Inlander, Henry 1925–1983
Orang-Outang II 1966
oil on canvas 89 x 101.5
ACA 68

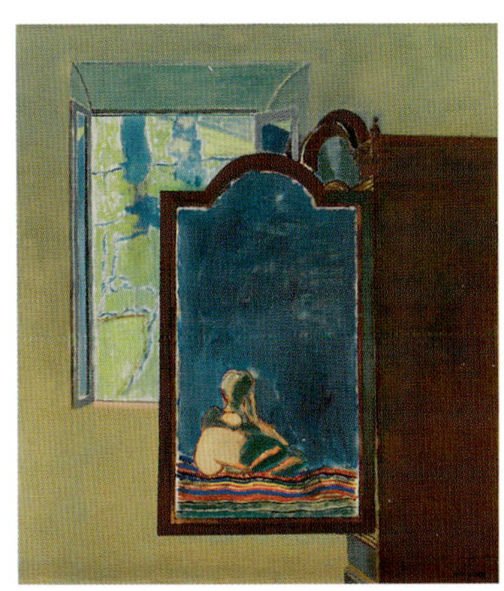

Inlander, Henry 1925–1983
Open Window (Mirror Image) 1968
oil on canvas 93.5 x 85
AC 993

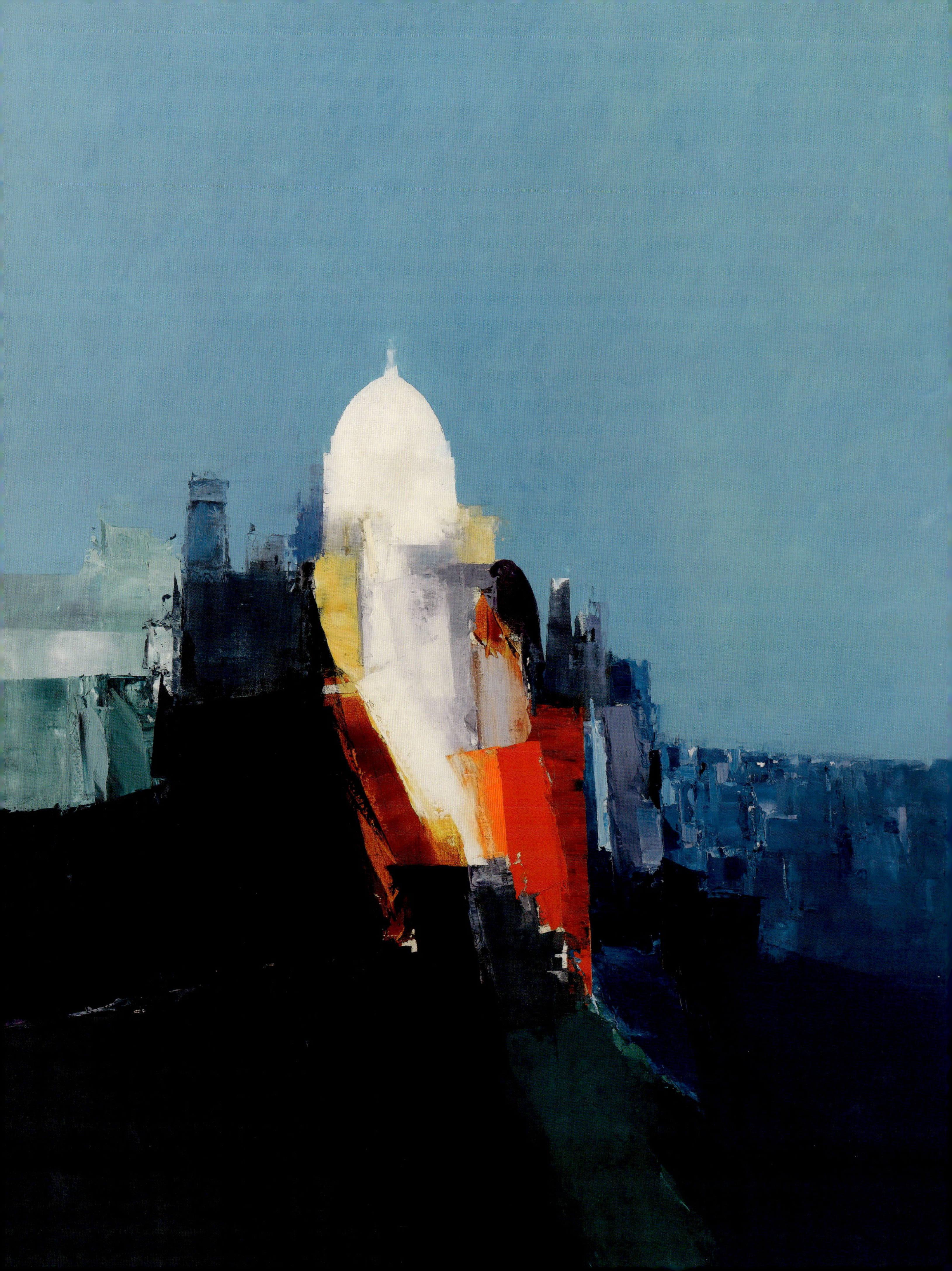

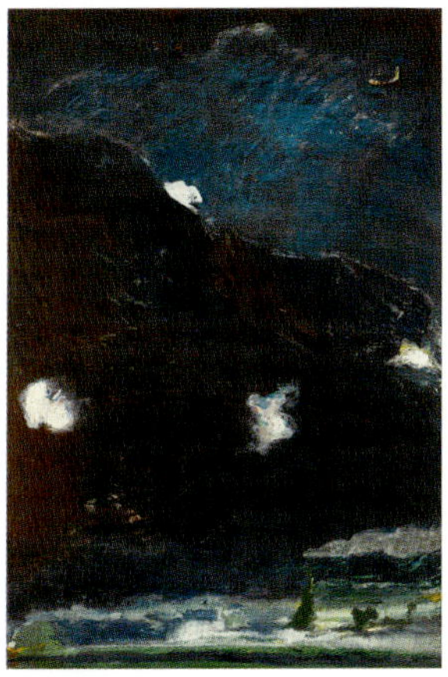

Inlander, Henry 1925–1983
Night Landscape 1976
oil on canvas 213.3 x 147.3
AC 1905

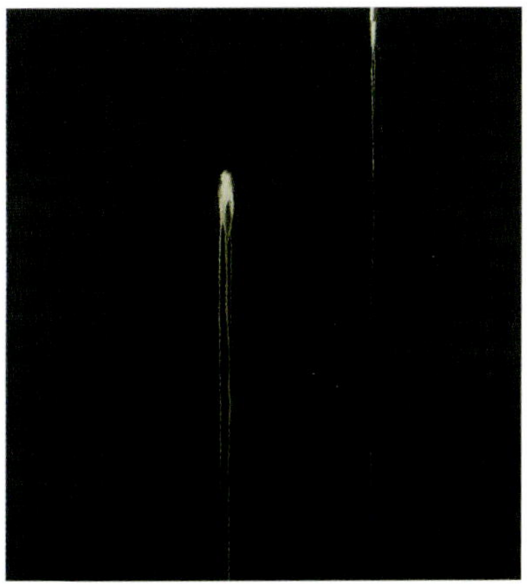

Innes, Callum b.1962
Two Identified Forms 1991
oil on canvas 164.7 x 149.7
ACC84/1991

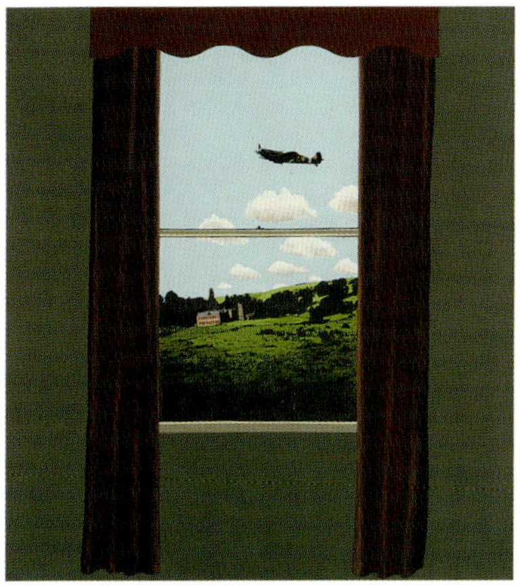

Inshaw, David b.1943
Window 1968
acrylic & oil on canvas 182.9 x 168.3
AC 1140

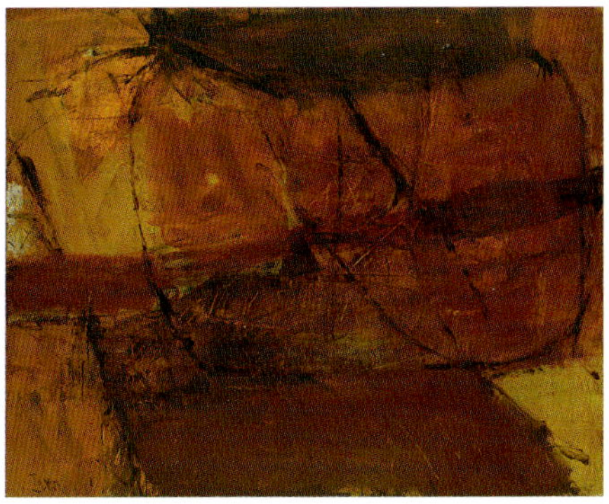

Irvin, Albert b.1922
Evening c.1961
oil on board 122 x 152.4
AC 587

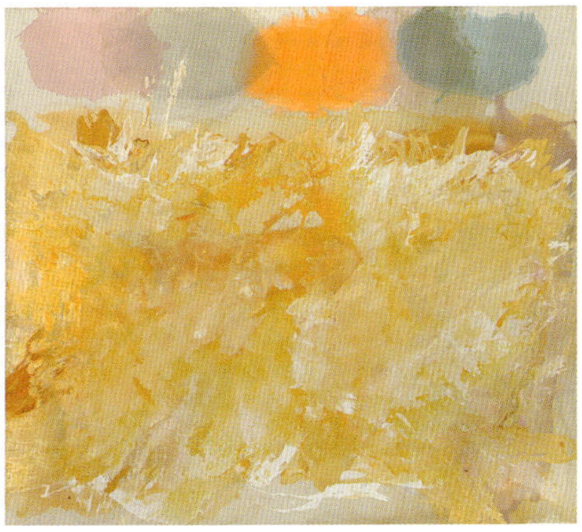

Irvin, Albert b.1922
Musbury 1975
acrylic on cotton duck 178 x 204
AC 1554

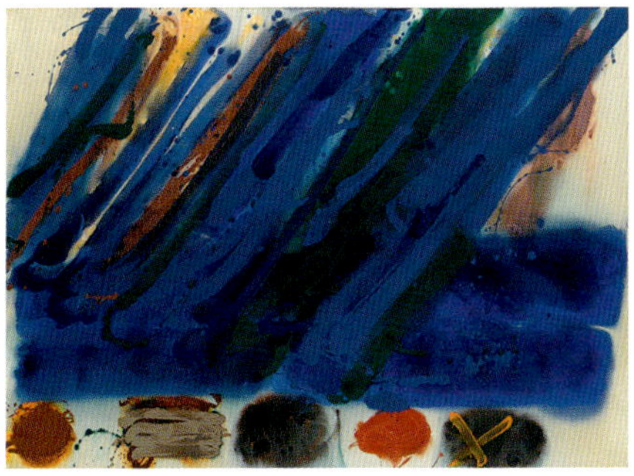

Irvin, Albert b.1922
Admiral 1981
acrylic on canvas 214 x 305
AC 4099

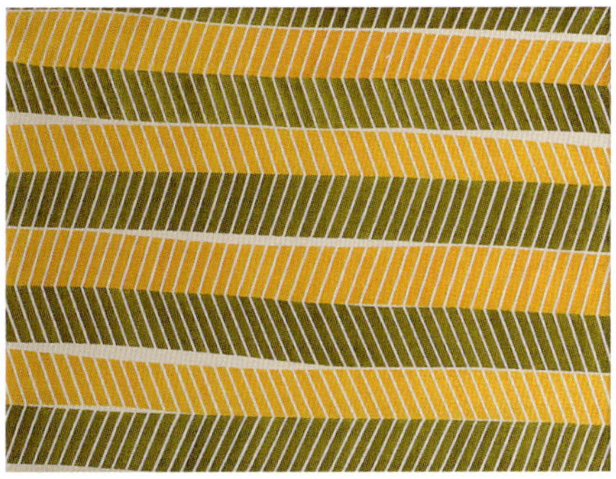

Irwin, Gwyther 1931–2008
Medium Straight 1963
oil on canvas 91.4 x 121.9
AC 707

Jacklin, Bill b.1943
Erebus 1971
acrylic on canvas 214 x 213.5
AC 1215

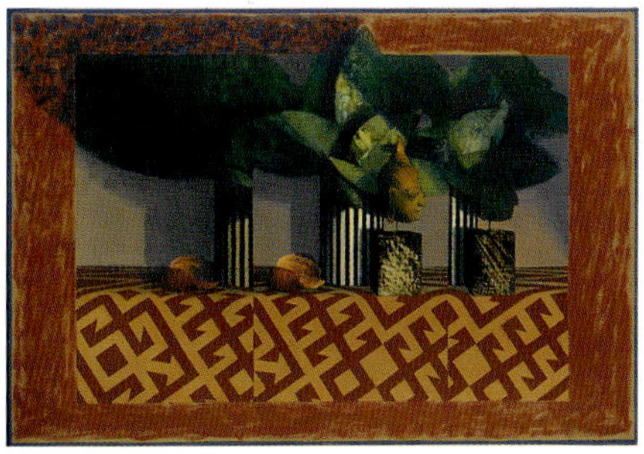

Jacklin, Bill b.1943
Double Buddha 1976–1977
oil & wax on canvas & wood 80.2 x 111.7
AC 1828

Facing page: Fraser, Donald Hamilton, b.1929, *Mont Saint-Geneviève, Paris* (detail), 1965, (p. 53)

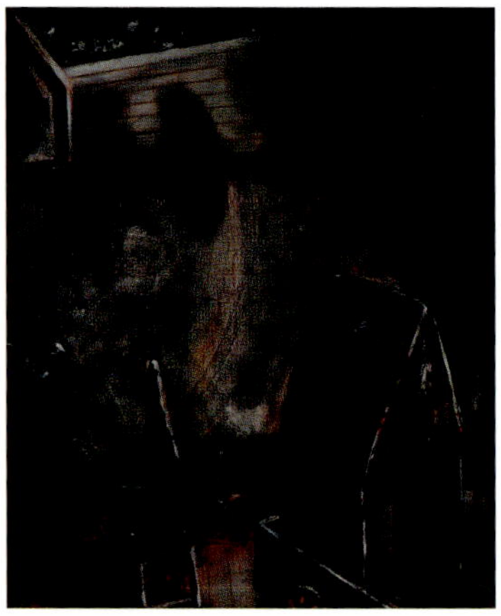

Jackowski, Andrzej b.1947
The Tower of Copernicus 1980
oil on canvas 136.6 x 117
AC 4061

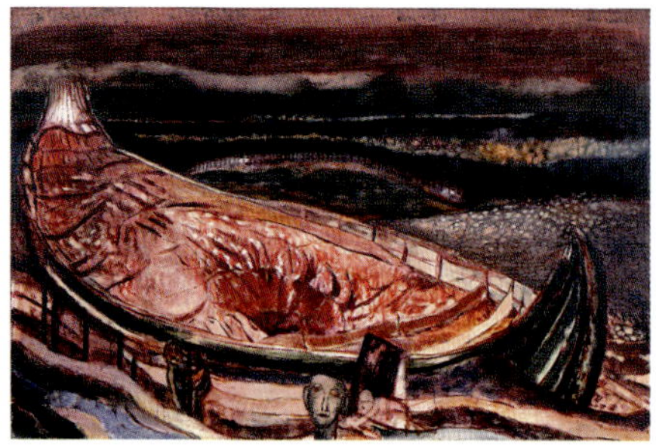

Jackowski, Andrzej b.1947
Settlement 1986
oil on canvas 154 x 235
AC 5439

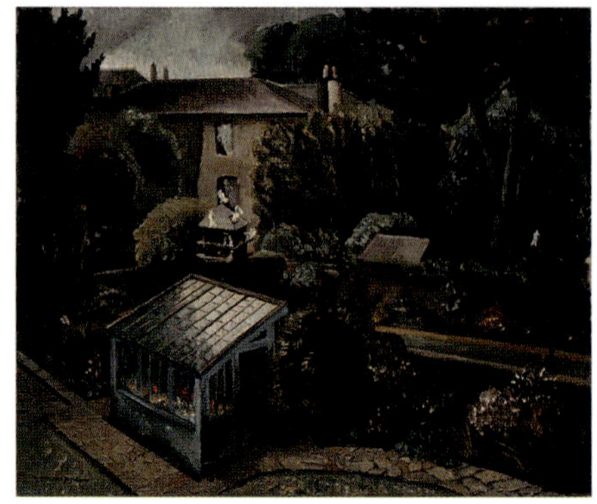

Jamieson, Robert Kirkland 1881–1950
London Garden 1937
oil on canvas 64.1 x 77.5
AC 69

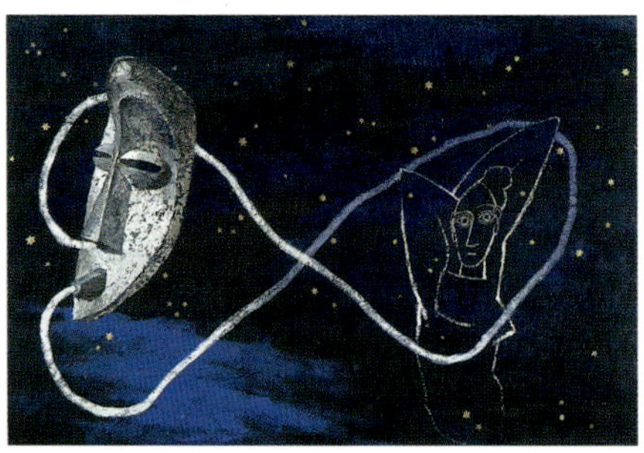

Jantjes, Gavin b.1948
Untitled 1989
sand, tissue paper & acrylic on canvas
200 x 300
ACC29/1990

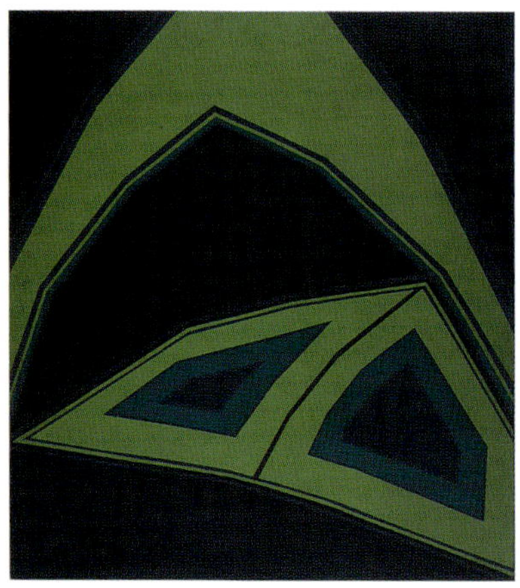

Jaray, Tess b.1937
St Stephen's Way 1964
oil on canvas 182.9 x 167.6
AC 803

Jaray, Tess b.1937
Mistral 1969
oil on canvas 221 x 259
AC 1072

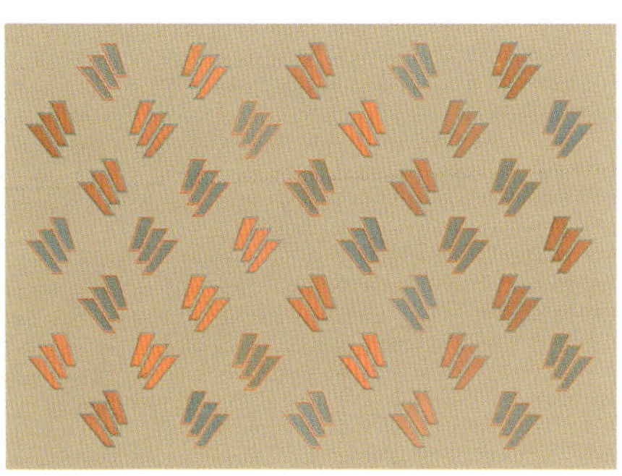

Jaray, Tess b.1937
Follies 1977
acrylic on cotton duck 198 x 278
AC 1884

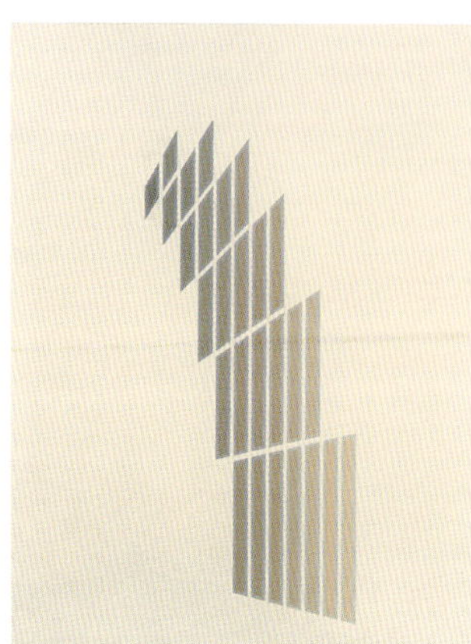

Jaray, Tess b.1937
Always Now 1981
acrylic on cotton duck 220.7 x 167.6
AC 5063

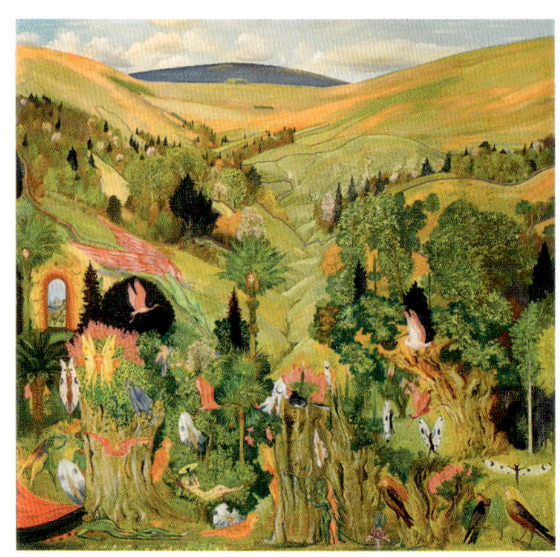

Jardine, George Wallace 1920–2002
The Coming of Spring 1979
oil on board 90 x 90
AC 1995

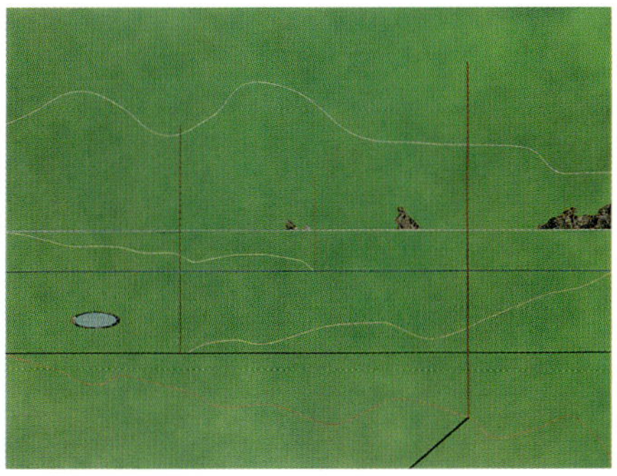

Jarman, Derek 1942–1994
Landscape with a Blue Pool 1967
oil on canvas 151.8 x 202.6
AC 980

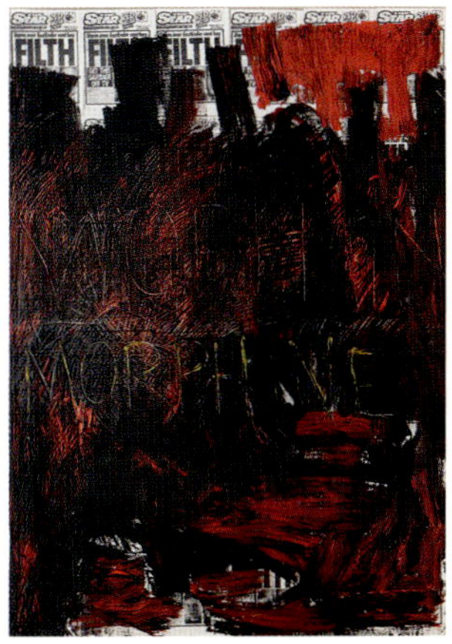

Jarman, Derek 1942–1994
Morphine 1992
oil on photocopy on canvas 251.5 x 179
ACC11/1992

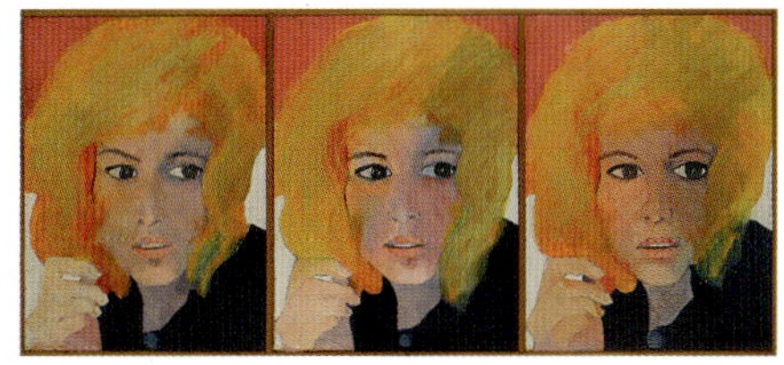

Jeffs, Roger b.1942
Vittis 1963
oil on board 104.1 x 238.8
AC 663

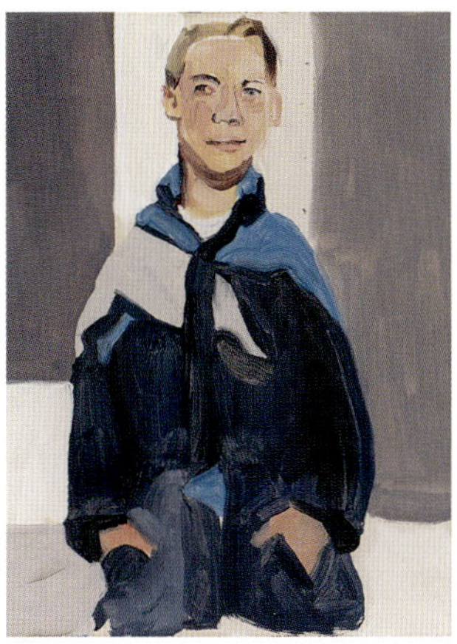

Joffe, Chantal b.1969
Untitled (No.1) 1995–1996
oil & gesso on board 28 x 21.5
ACC189/1998

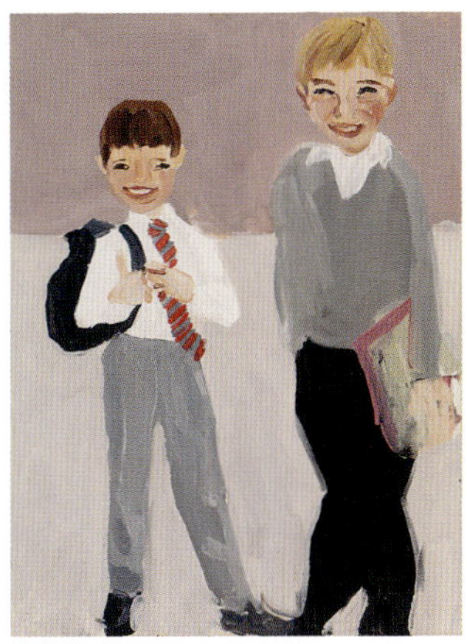

Joffe, Chantal b.1969
Untitled (No.2) 1995–1996
oil on gesso on board 28 x 21.5
ACC190/1998

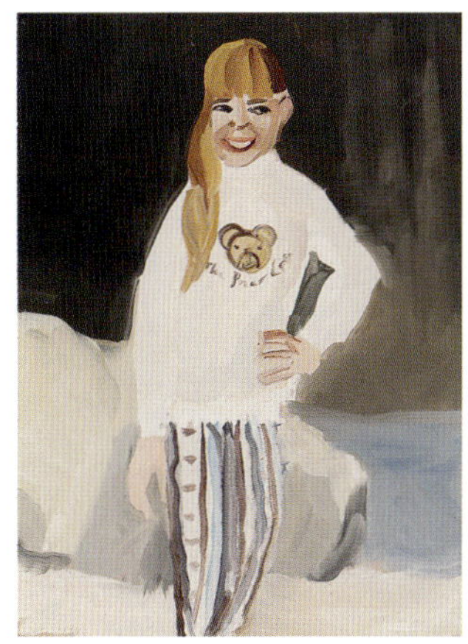

Joffe, Chantal b.1969
Untitled (No.3) 1995–1996
oil on gesso on board 28 x 21.5
ACC191/1998

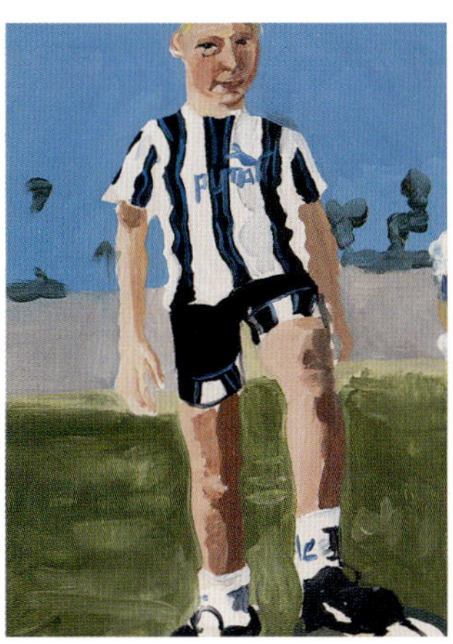

Joffe, Chantal b.1969
Untitled (No.4) 1995–1996
oil on gesso on board 28 x 21.5
ACC192/1998

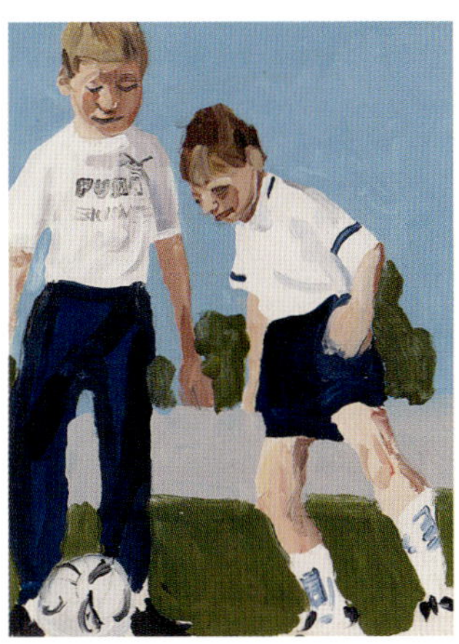

Joffe, Chantal b.1969
Untitled (No.5) 1995–1996
oil on gesso on board 28 x 21.5
ACC193/1998

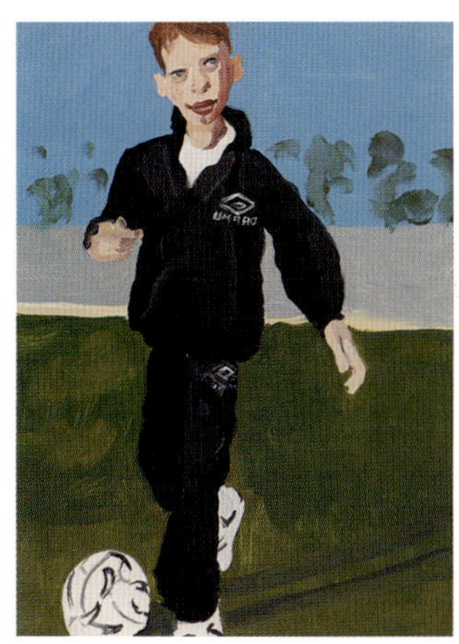

Joffe, Chantal b.1969
Untitled (No.6) 1995–1996
oil on gesso on board 28 x 21.5
ACC194/1998

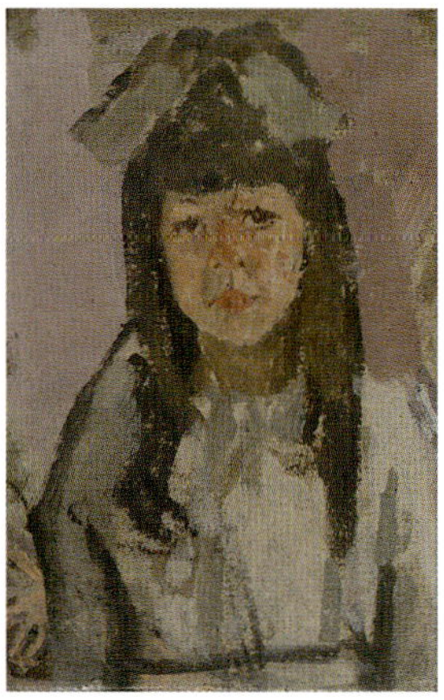

John, Gwen 1876–1939
Bust of a Girl with a Bow Before a Pink Background c.1915–1920
oil on canvas 23 x 13.7
AC 418

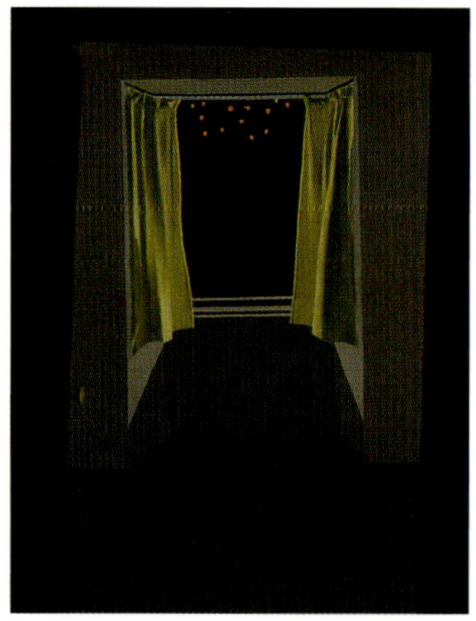

Johnstone, John 1937–2001
Entering an Innocent Room 1970
oil on canvas 125.5 x 100
AC 1156

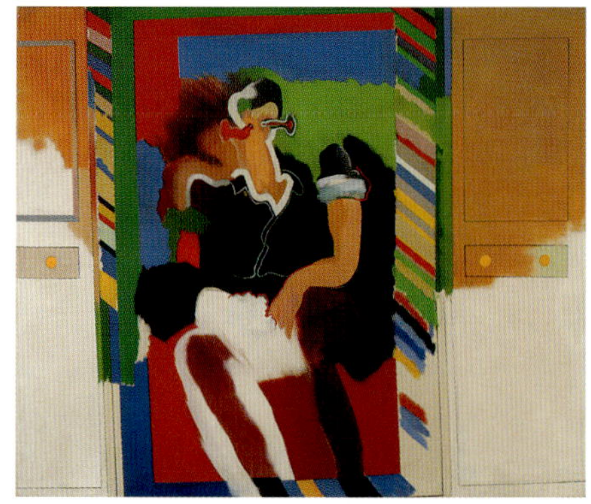

Jones, Allen b.1937
Reflected Man 1963
oil on canvas 152.4 x 182.9
AC 720

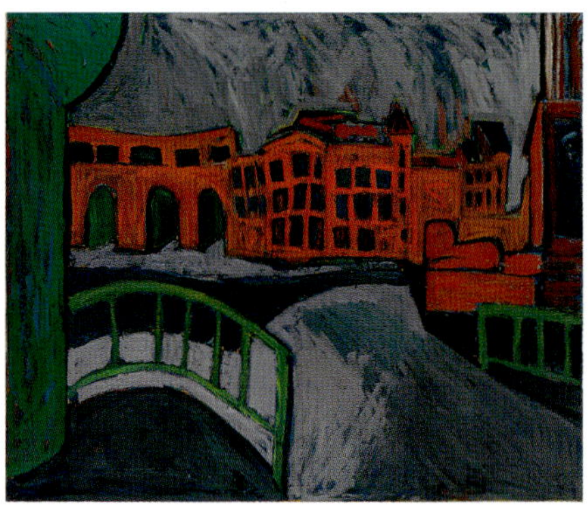

Jones, Lucy b.1955
Admiralty Arch 1985
oil on canvas 175 x 213.4
AC 5423

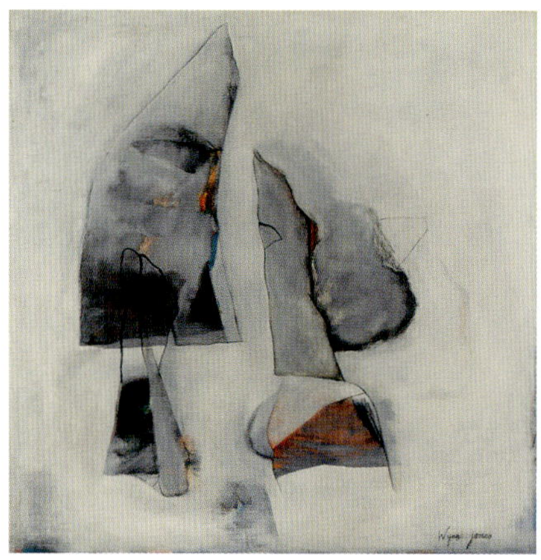

Jones, Wynn b.1939
Getting Ready 1977–1978
acrylic & charcoal on canvas 127 x 127
AC 1952

Jones, Zebedee b.1970
Blue/Green 1993
oil & wax on canvas 101 x 66.5
ACC23/1994

Image removed due to copyright restrictions

Jonzen, Basil 1913–1967
Still Life (Dead Birds and Lemons) 1936
oil on canvas 76.8 x 64.1
AC 70

Joseph, Peter b.1929
Untitled 1967
acrylic on canvas 152.4 x 268
AC 929

Joseph, Peter b.1929
Yellow Painting 1969
acrylic on canvas 228.6 x 259
AC 1065

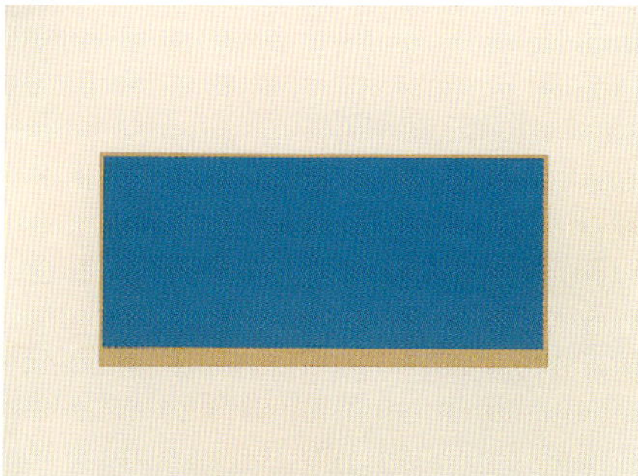

Joseph, Peter b.1929
Drawing 1971 (Untitled, Blue/Green) 1971
acrylic & collage on paper 24.1 x 52.5
AC 1168

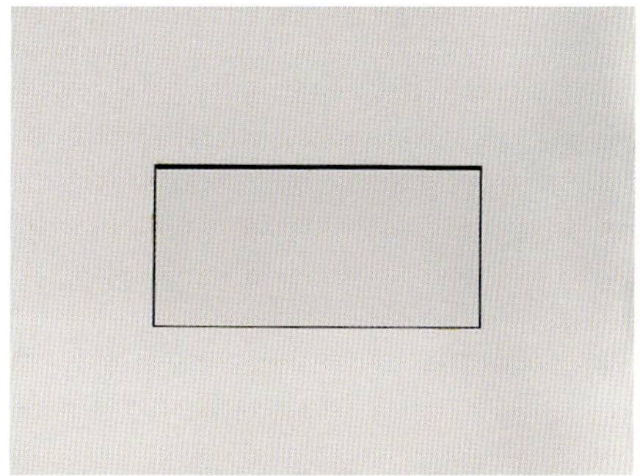

Joseph, Peter b.1929
Drawing 1971 (Untitled, Cream/Black) 1971
acrylic & collage on paper 18.7 x 39.2
AC 1169

Joseph, Peter b.1929
Dark Ochre with Black Border 1973
acrylic on canvas 152.4 x 127
AC 1273

Joseph, Peter b.1929
Brown Colour with Grey/Black Border 1979
acrylic on canvas 120.7 x 152.3
AC 4042

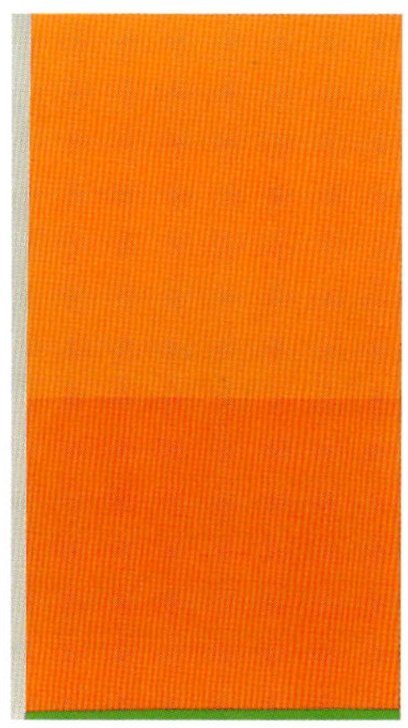

Joseph, Peter b.1929
Bright Orange with Green 1988
acrylic on canvas 151 x 137
ACC8/1992

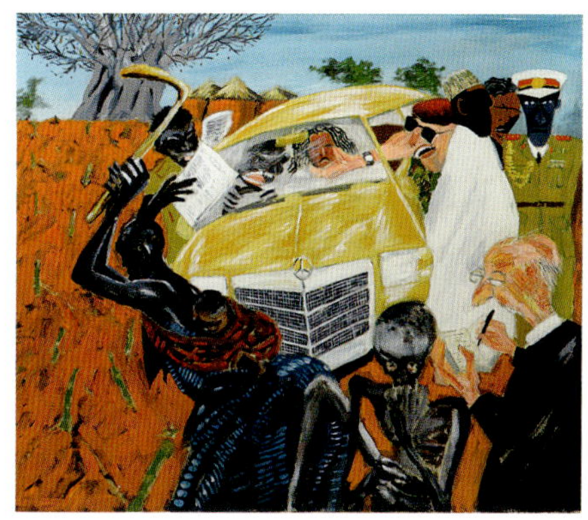

Joseph, Tam b.1947
Monkey dey Chop, Baboon dey Cry 1984
acrylic on canvas 155 x 225
AC 5553

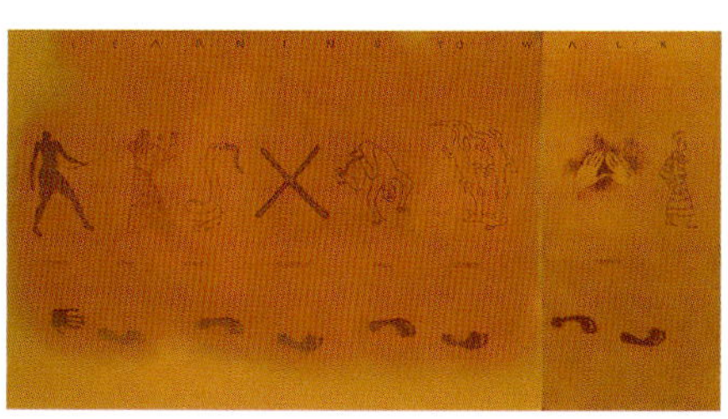

Joseph, Tam b.1947
Learning to Walk 1988
sand, acrylic & pigment on canvas 201 x 386
AC 5554

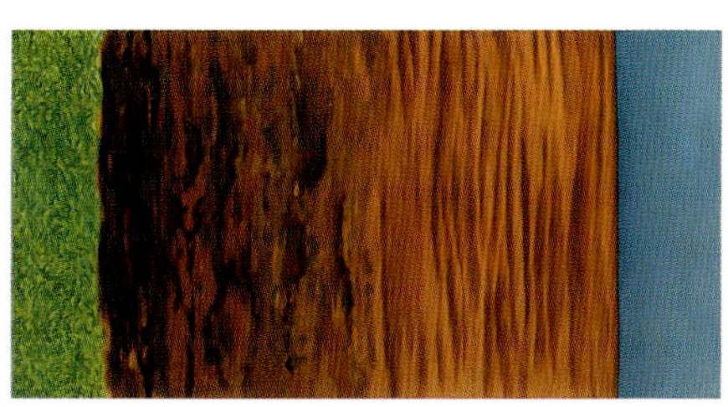

Joy, Clair b.1958
Untitled 1986
oil on canvas 157.5 x 315
AC 5460

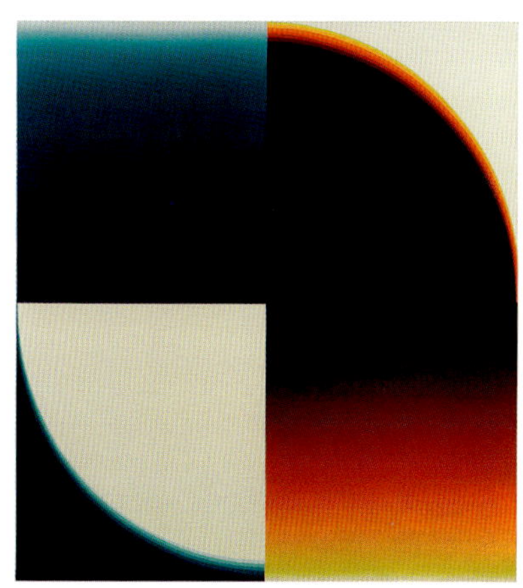

Kalkhof, Peter b.1933
Centrepoint Colour and Space Series 1975
acrylic on canvas 198 x 183
AC 1622

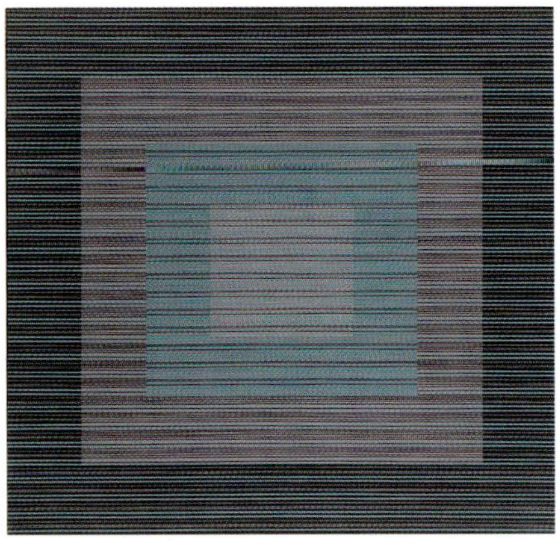

Kent, Sarah b.1941
Orthian 1 c.1966
acrylic on canvas 167.6 x 183
AC 930

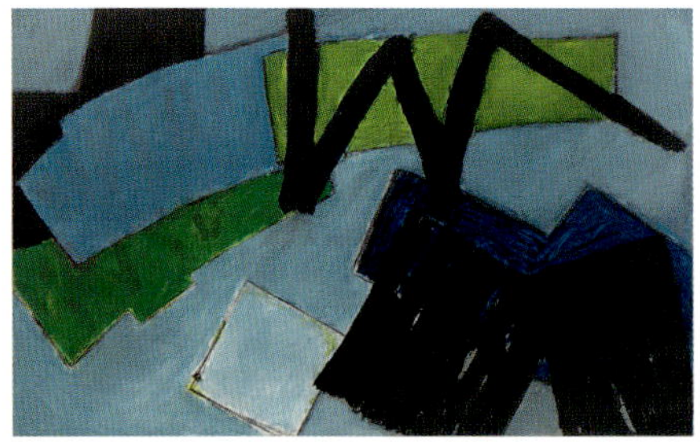

Kerma, Ingrid b.1942
Brutum fulmen 1976
acrylic on canvas 152.4 x 304.8
AC 1676

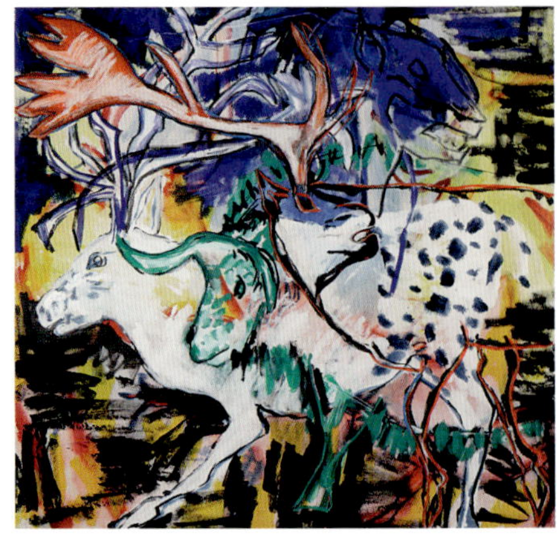

Kerma, Ingrid b.1942
The Fugitives 1983
oil on canvas 163 x 172.3
AC 5304

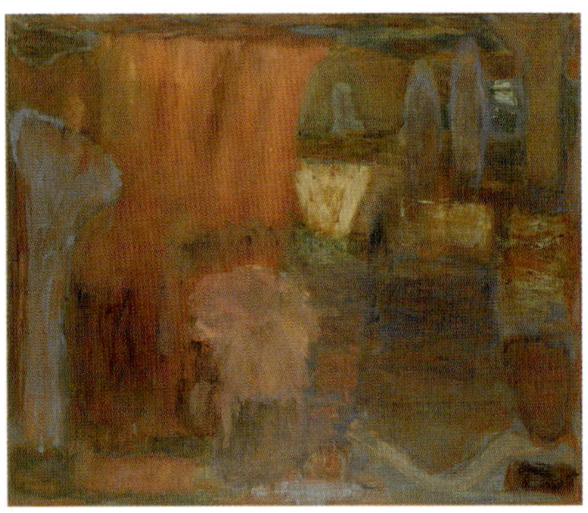

Kerr, Bernadette b.1958
Red Curtain 1988
oil on canvas 147.5 x 178
AC 5572

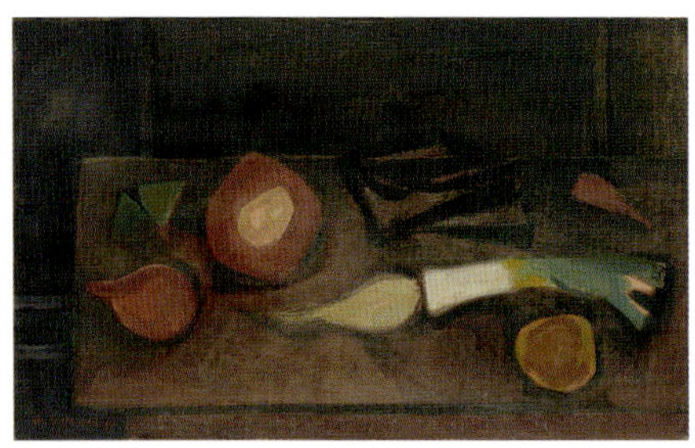

Kestelman, Morris 1905–1998
Still Life with Vegetables 1958
oil on canvas 45.7 x 76.2
AC 569

Kevill Davies, Benita b.1954
Two Bushes 1986
oil on board 21.6 x 20.1
AC 5457

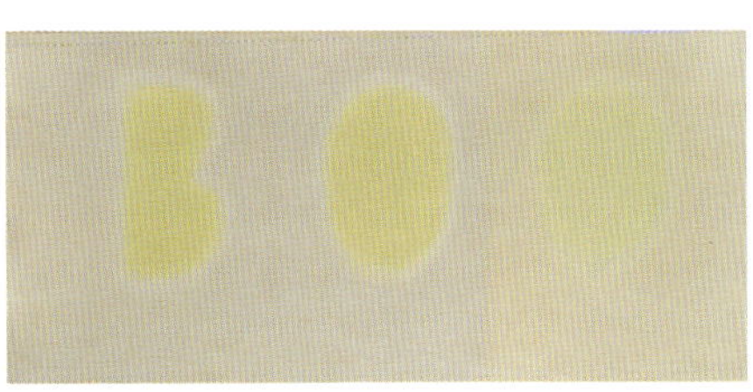

Key, Joan b.1948
BOO (II) 1994
oil on canvas 137 x 305
ACC5/1996

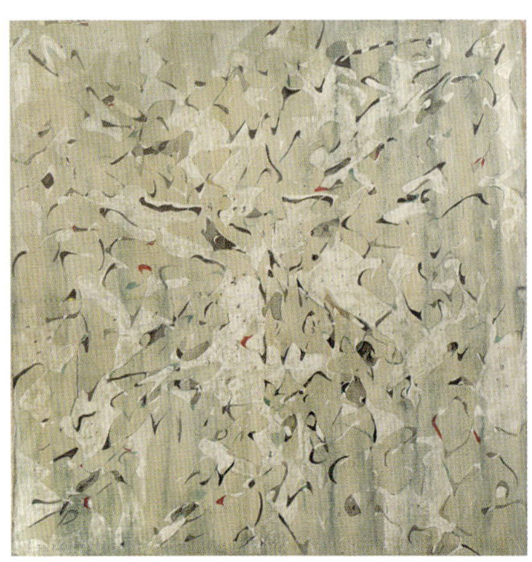

Khanna, Balraj b.1940
Splash 1970
oil on canvas 181.3 x 181.5
AC 1915

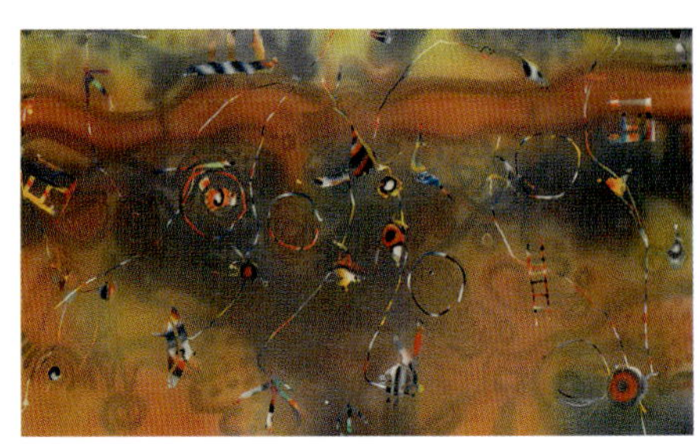

Khanna, Balraj b.1940
Coming from Rajasthan 1984
acrylic on canvas 168 x 304
ACC28/1990

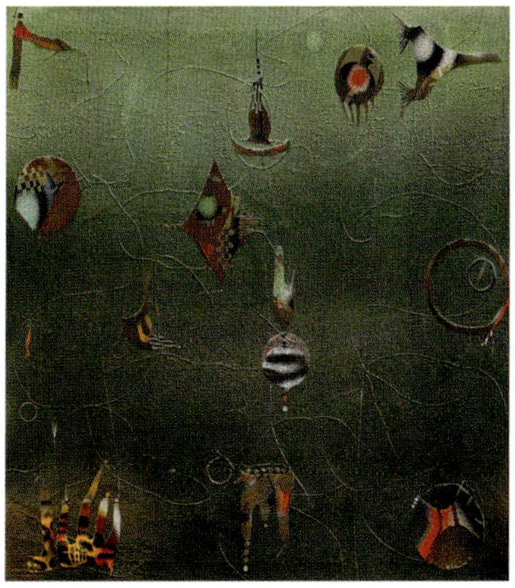

Khanna, Balraj b.1940
Apple Green (detail) 1991
acrylic on canvas 114 x 114
ACC38/1991

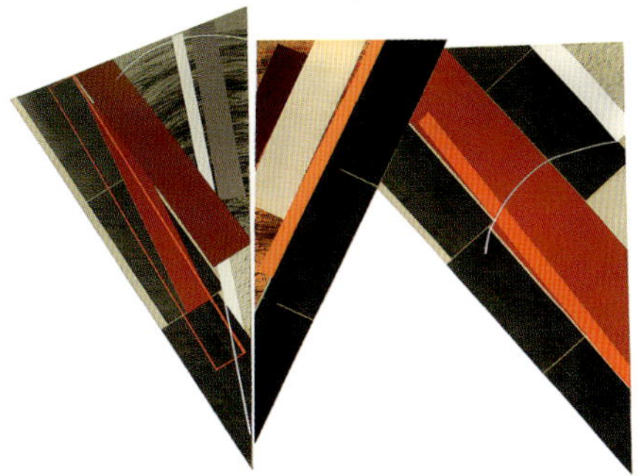

Kidd, Richard 1952–2008
Soul Patter 1976
acrylic & graphite on canvas 270 x 330
AC 1715

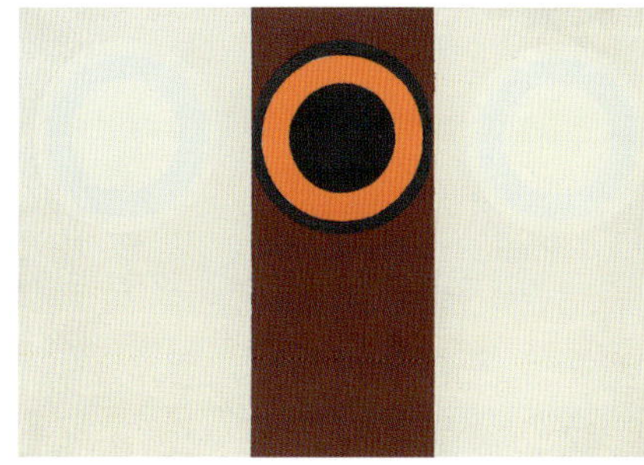

Kidner, Michael 1917–2009
Mars, Violet and White 1961
oil on canvas 80.5 x 121
AC 623

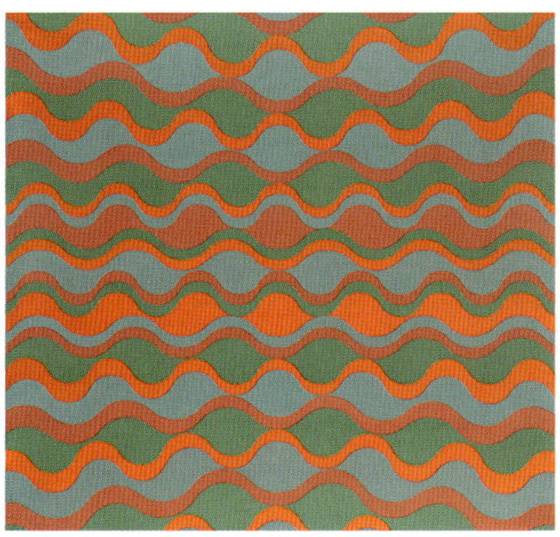

Kidner, Michael 1917–2009
Orange, Blue, Pink and Green No.2 1965
oil on canvas 168.9 x 182.9
AC 912

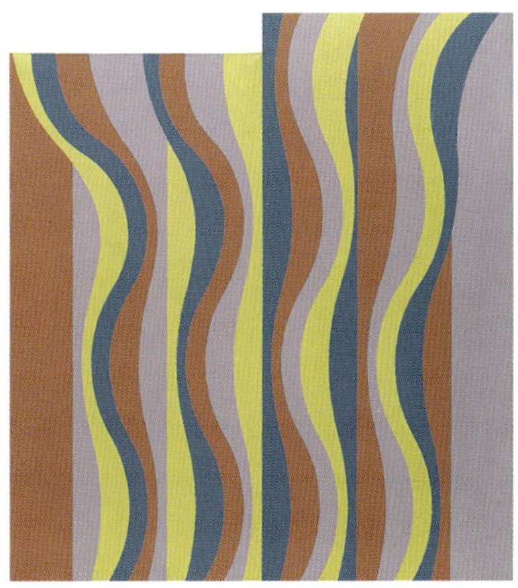

Kidner, Michael 1917–2009
Yellow, Violet, Light Red and Blue 1967
oil on canvas 179.1 x 162.6
ACC15/1968

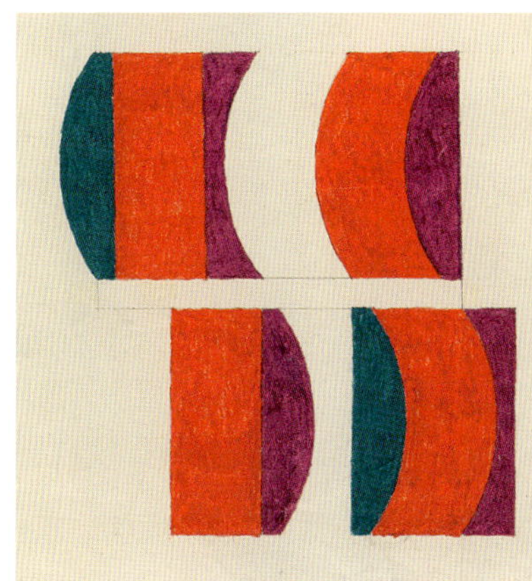

Kidner, Michael 1917–2009
Red, Green, Violet and White 1968
tempera on paper 39.7 x 38.4
AC 973

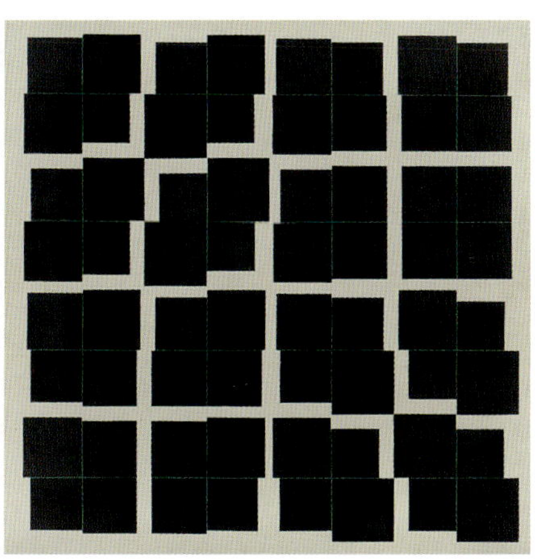

Kidner, Michael 1917–2009
Analysis of a Wave Pattern 1973
acrylic on canvas 91.5 x 91.5
AC 1751

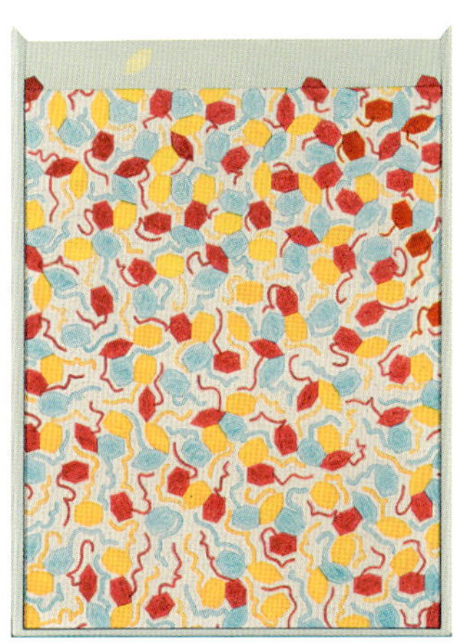

Kidner, Michael 1917–2009
Mosquito Larvae II 2001
acrylic on board 140 x 102
ACC5/2003

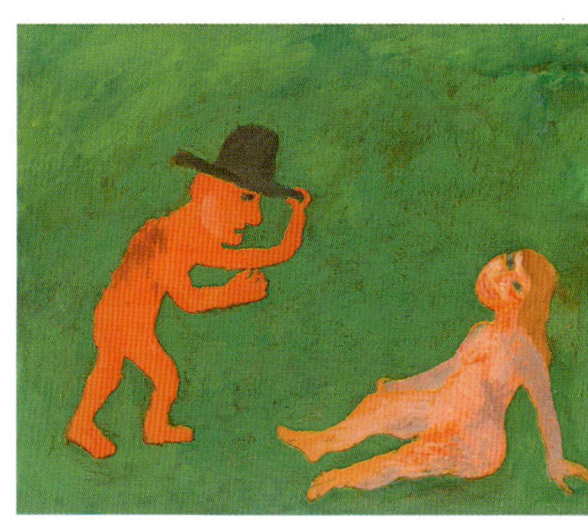

Kiff, Ken 1935–2001
Man Greeting Woman 1965–1966
oil, tempera & gesso on board 122 x 152
AC 984

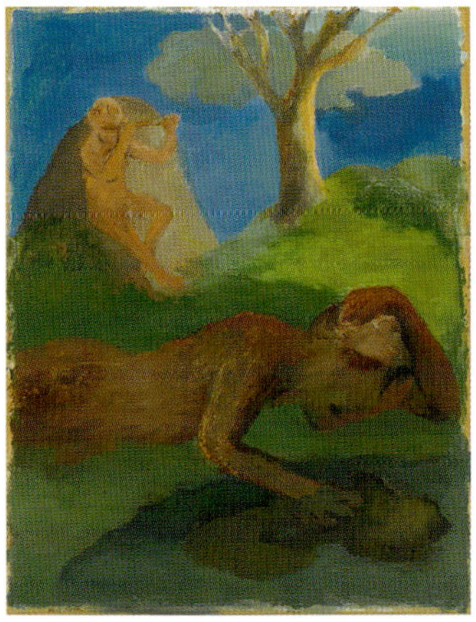

Kiff, Ken 1935–2001
Echo and Narcissus, Sequence 81 1977
acrylic on paper 66.3 x 52.3
AC 5297

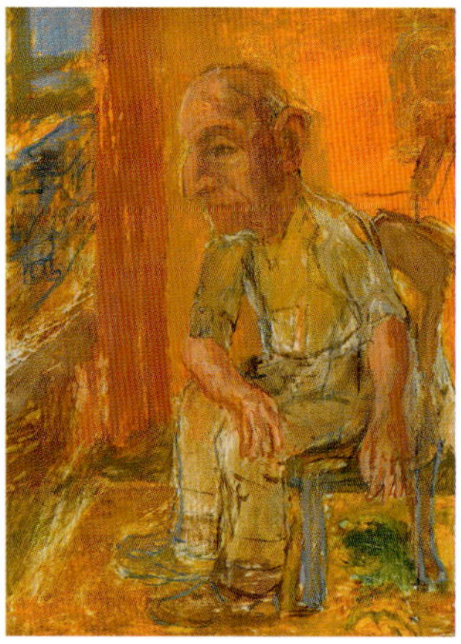

Kiff, Ken 1935–2001
Portrait from Memory 1980–1985, reworked 1988
oil, acrylic & pastel on board 122.2 x 90.7
AC 5420

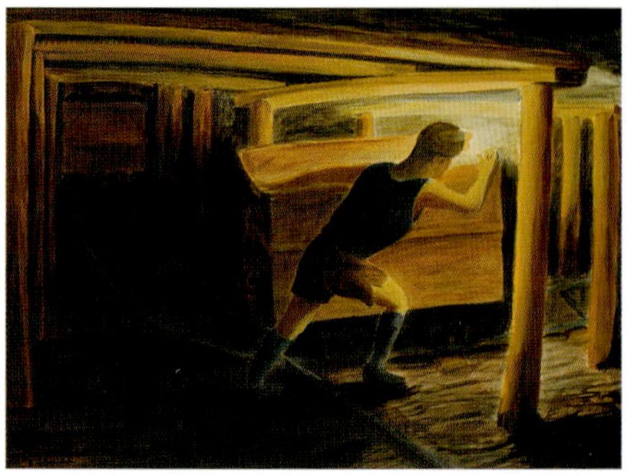

Kilbourn, Oliver 1904–1993
Changing the Chummin, Giving the Final Twist before Rounding the Turn 1976
acrylic on paper 54.1 x 74.4
AC 1859

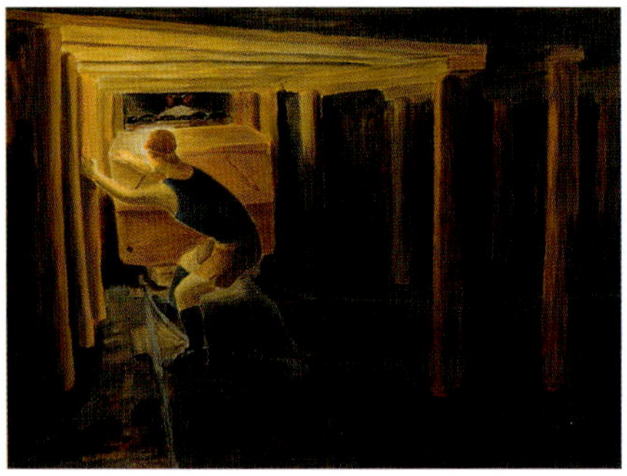

Kilbourn, Oliver 1904–1993
Shoving the Chummin in by Hand and Changing the Points 1976
acrylic on paper 54.2 x 76.6
AC 1860

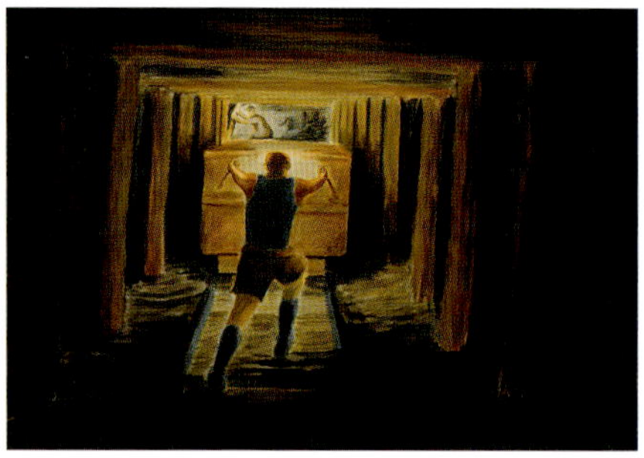

Kilbourn, Oliver 1904–1993
Shoving the Chummin in from Behind after Rounding the Turn 1976
acrylic on paper 50.4 x 76
AC 1858

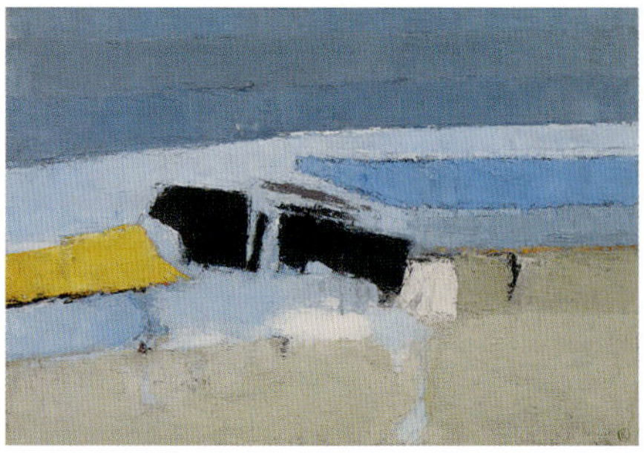

Kinley, Peter 1926–1988
Seascape 1954
oil on canvas 76 x 122
AC 349

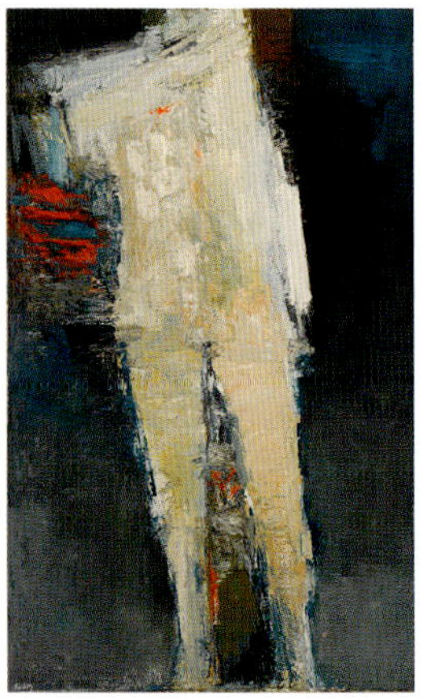

Kinley, Peter 1926–1988
Standing Figure No.1 1956
oil on canvas 144.5 x 90
AC 423

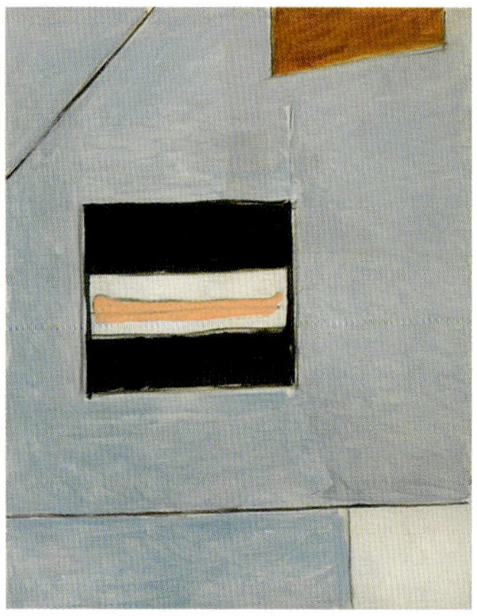

Kinley, Peter 1926–1988
Interior 1967
oil on canvas 75 x 60
ACA 69

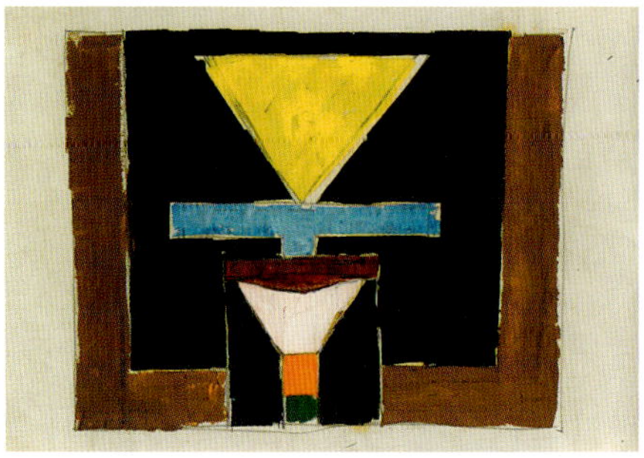

Kinley, Peter 1926–1988
Still Life 1967
oil on paper 61 x 76.2
ACA 70

Facing page: Martin, Michael, b.1955, *Young Miner* (detail), 1979–1980, (p. 105)

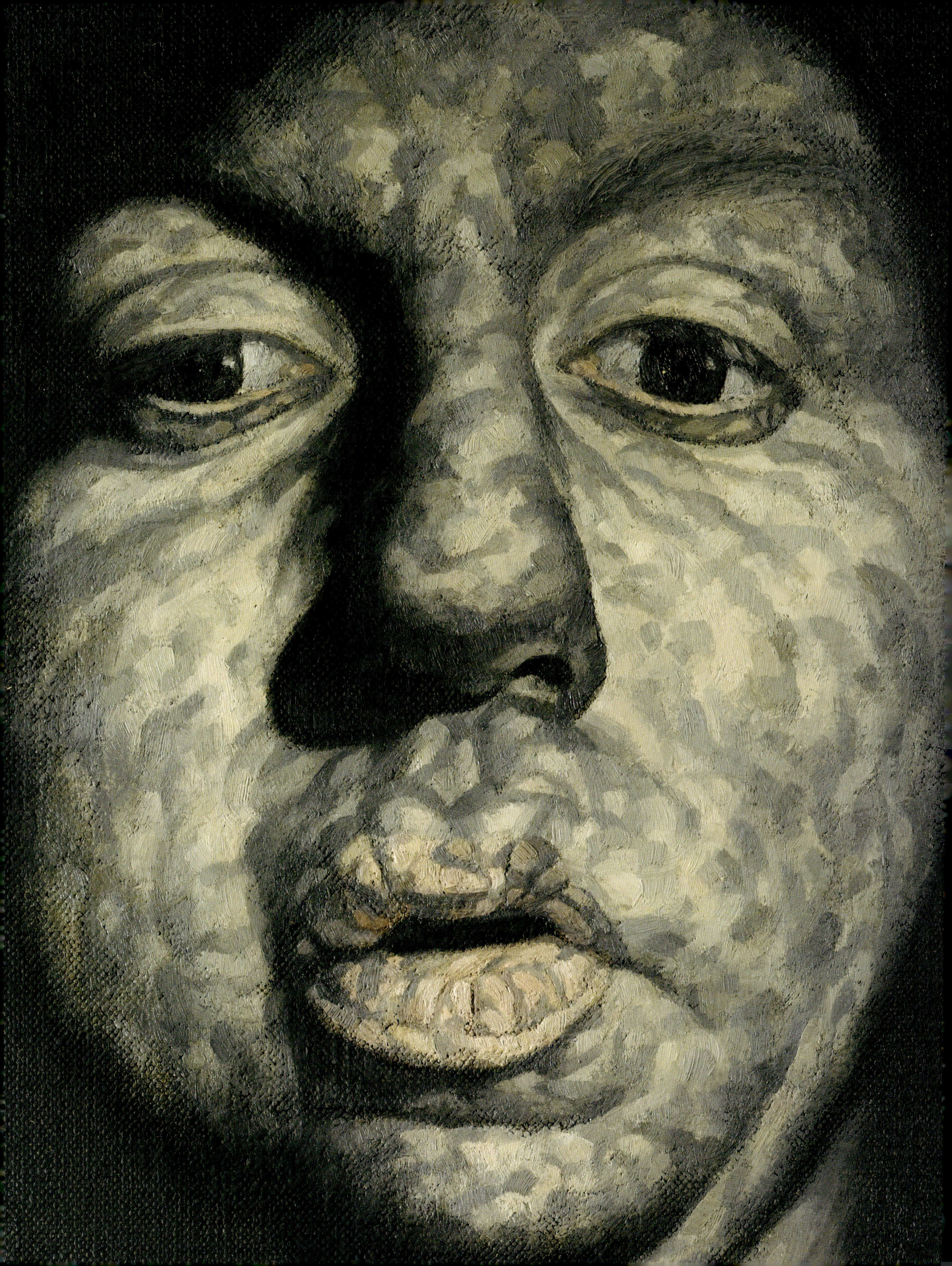

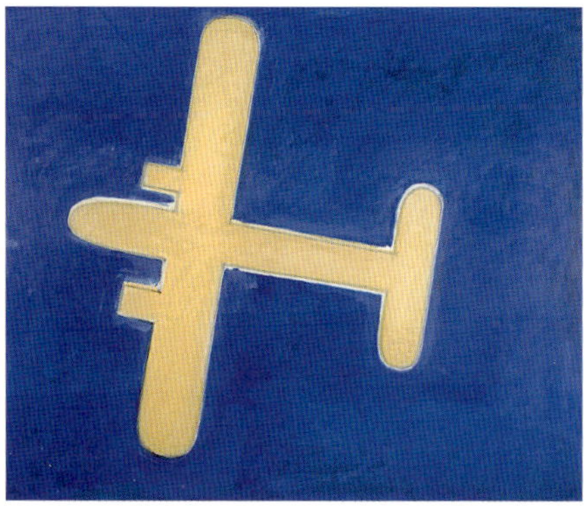

Kinley, Peter 1926–1988
Aeroplane 1977–1983
oil on canvas 154.3 x 188
AC 5289

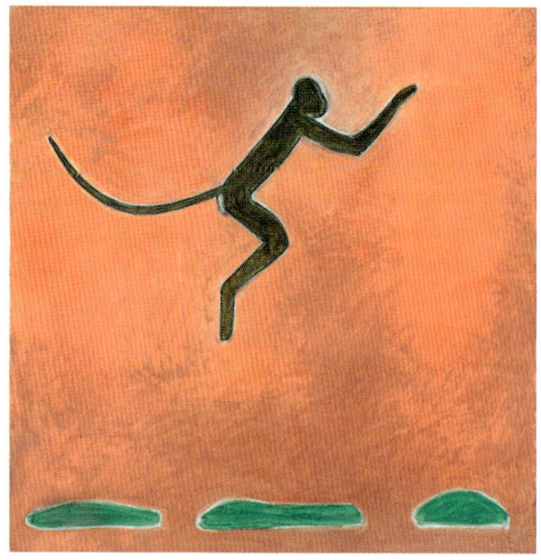

Kinley, Peter 1926–1988
Red Monkey 1978
oil on canvas 172.4 x 182
AC 3039

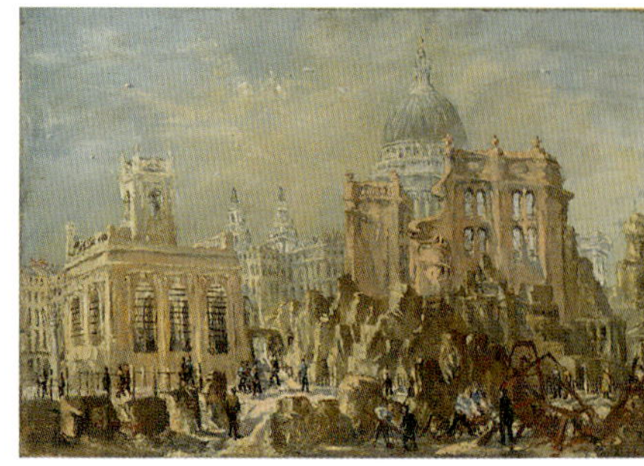

Kirk, Eve 1900–1969
Demolition near St Paul's 1942
oil on canvas 51.4 x 74.3
AC 72

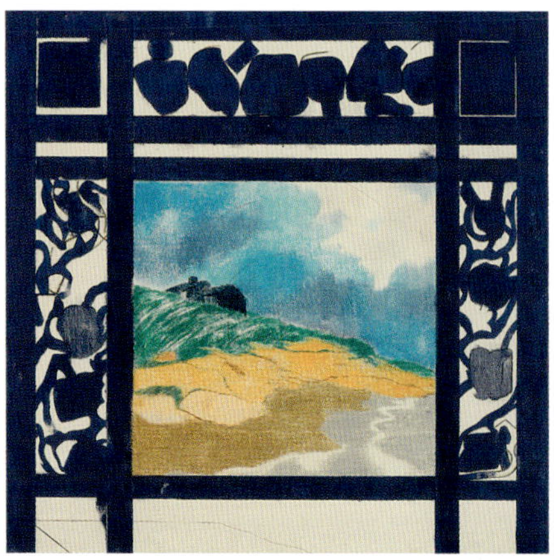

Kitaj, R. B. 1932–2007
Screenplay 1967
oil on canvas 78.7 x 78.7
AC 915

Kite, Roger b.1947
Diagonal I 1976
acrylic on canvas 154 x 152.3
AC 1832

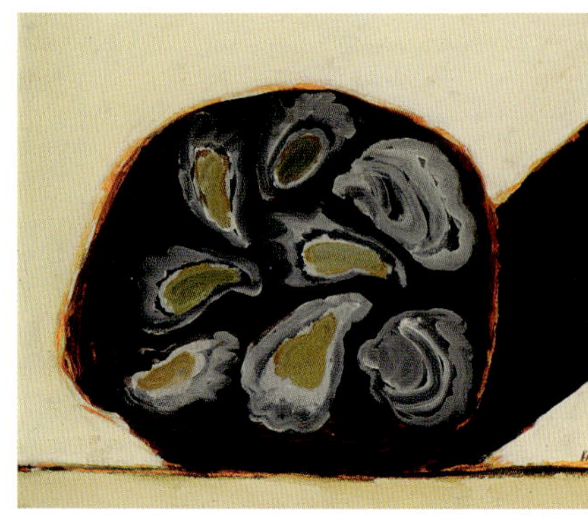

Knox, Jack b.1936
Oysters in a Basket 1979
PVA on board 49.4 x 59.1
AC 2066

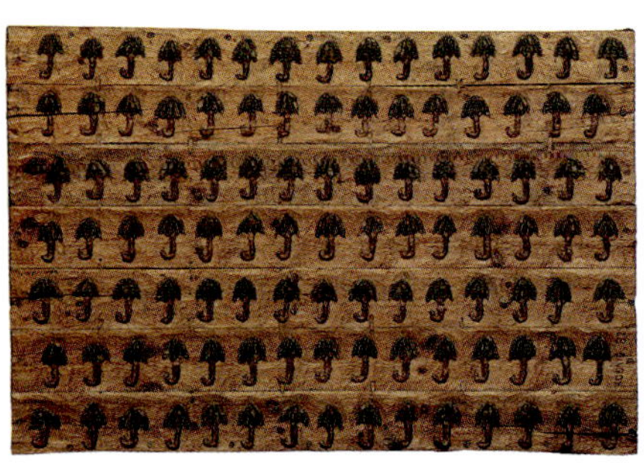

Koenig, Robert b.1951
Rustic Umbrellas 1982
paint on wood 70 x 105.3
AC 5224

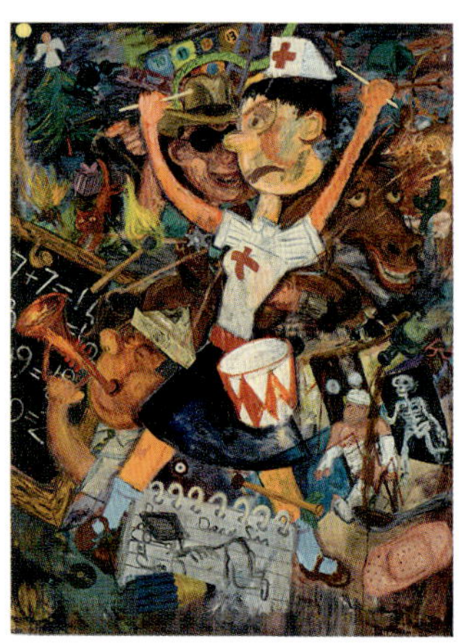

Kondracki, Henry b.1953
Gifts 1985
oil & collage on paper 244 x 184
AC 5449

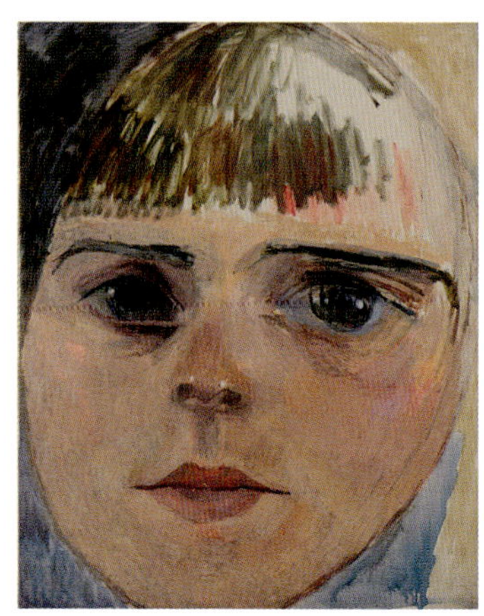

Koppel, Heinz 1919–1980
Head 1954
oil on canvas 76.2 x 61
AC 460

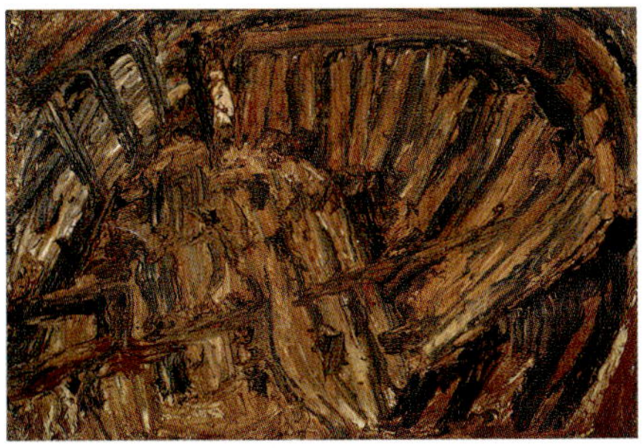

Kossoff, Leon b.1926
Building Site, Victoria Street 1961
oil on board 122.5 x 184.8
ACC5/1962

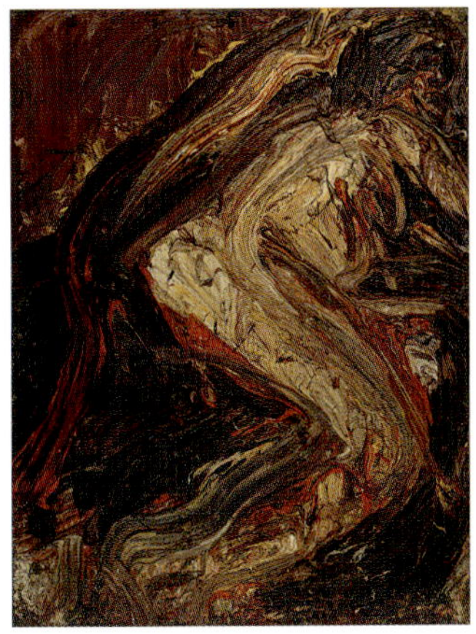

Kossoff, Leon b.1926
Seated Nude 1963
oil on board 156 x 120
ACA 13

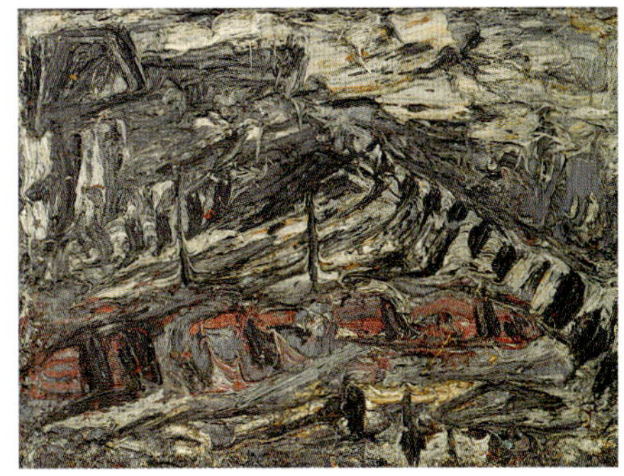

Kossoff, Leon b.1926
York Way Railway Bridge from Caledonian Road, Stormy Day 1967
oil on board 121.9 x 167.6
AC 860

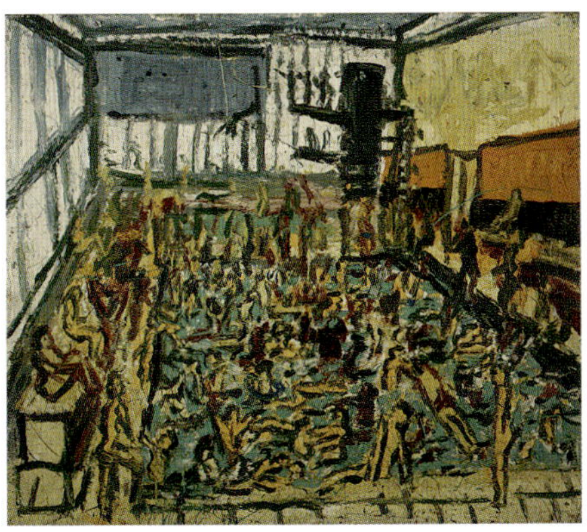

Kossoff, Leon b.1926
Children's Swimming Pool, Autumn 1972
1972
oil on board 182.9 x 213.4
ACC7/1978

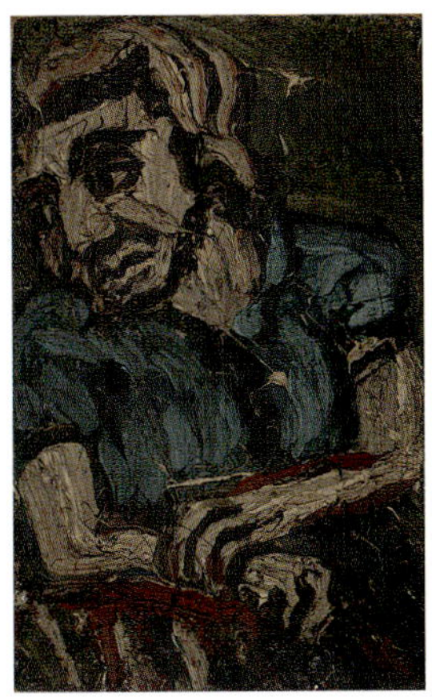

Kossoff, Leon b.1926
George Thompson 1975
oil on board 123 x 78
AC 1513

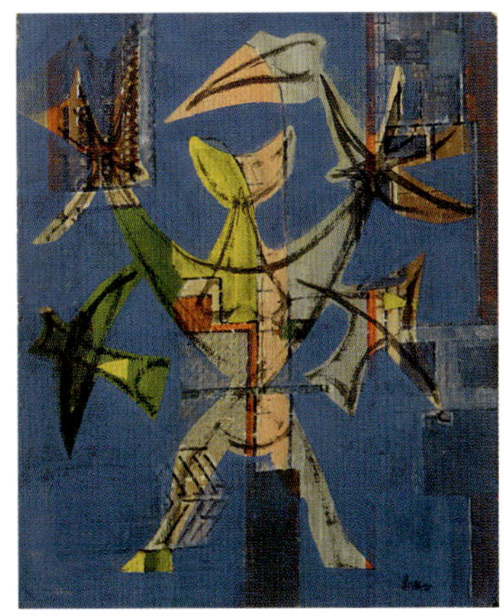

Lake, John Gascoyne 1903–1975
Feeding Birds c.1958
oil on board 76.2 x 63.5
AC 704

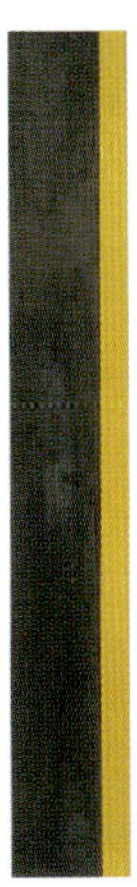

Lalić, Maria b.1952
Lead Fall – Chrome Yellow 1991
oil, linen, lead & wood 210 x 30
ACC71/1991

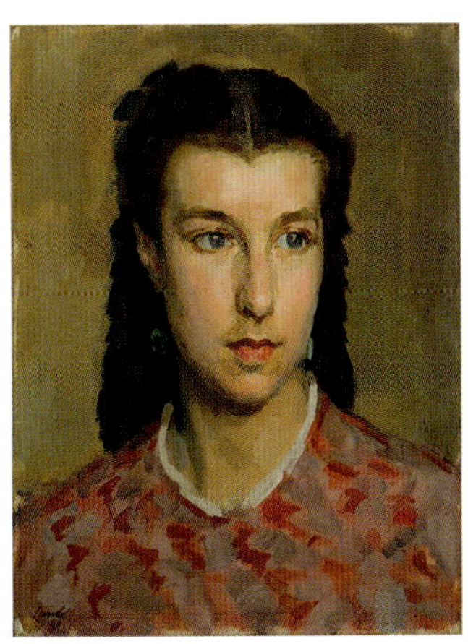

Lamb, Henry 1883–1960
Manon 1946
oil on canvas 40 x 29.8
AC 17

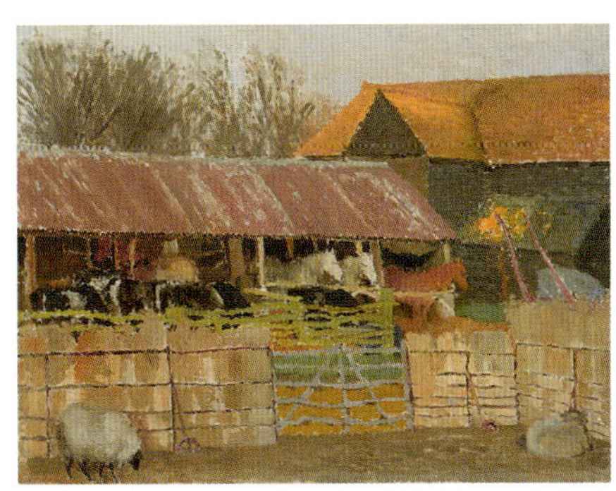

Lamb, Lynton Harold 1907–1977
Sandon Place 1949
oil on canvas 50.8 x 68.6
AC 152

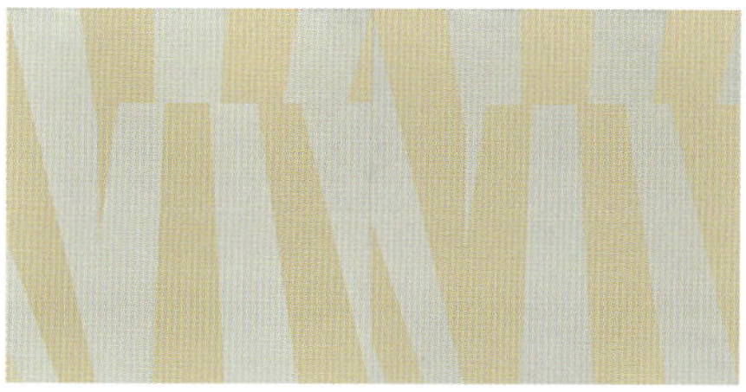

Lancaster, Mark b.1938
First Spread 1966
acrylic on canvas 152.4 x 152.4; 152.4 x 152.4
AC 870

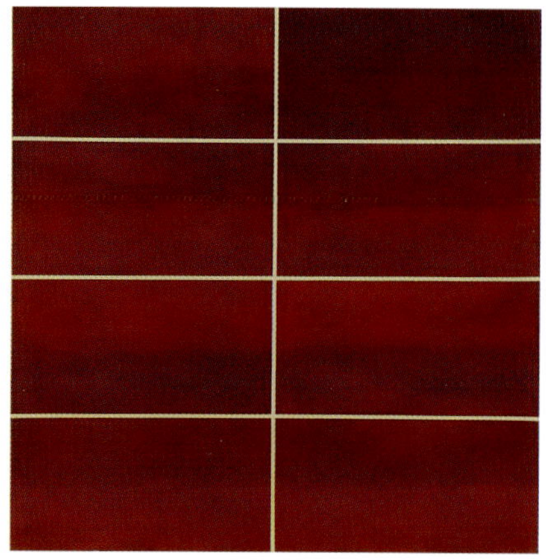

Lancaster, Mark b.1938
Cambridge Violet 1968
acrylic on canvas 172.7 x 172.7
AC 986

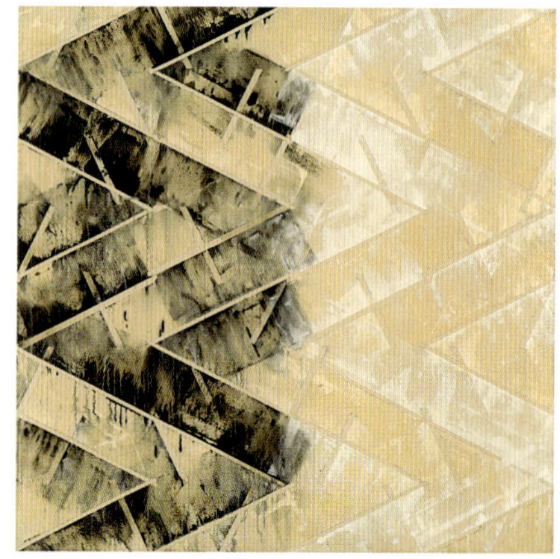

Lancaster, Mark b.1938
Henry VI Black and White 1971
acrylic on canvas 172.7 x 172.7
ACC31/1974

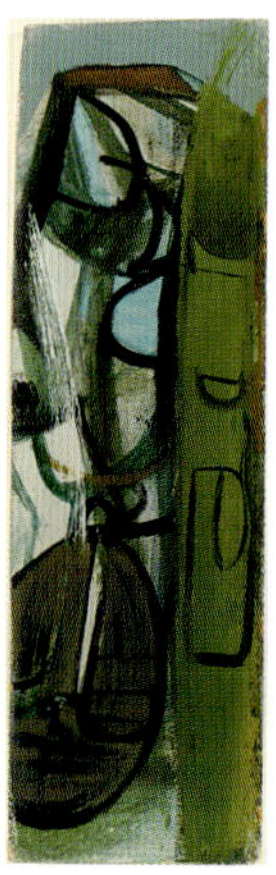

Lanyon, Peter 1918–1964
Bicyclist in Penwith 1952
oil on chipboard 50.8 x 15.2
AC 240

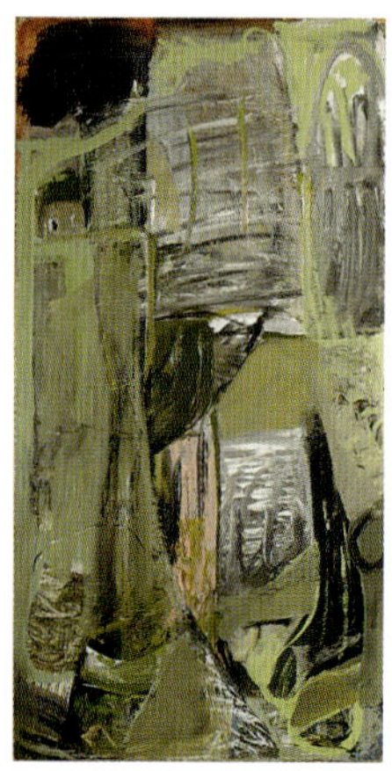

Lanyon, Peter 1918–1964
Moor Cliffe, Kynance 1953
oil on board 129.5 x 68.6
AC 307

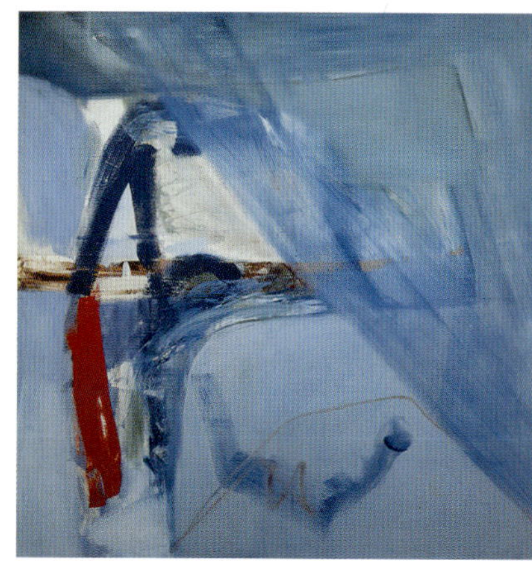

Lanyon, Peter 1918–1964
Soaring Flight 1960
oil on canvas 152.4 x 152.4
ACC1/1960

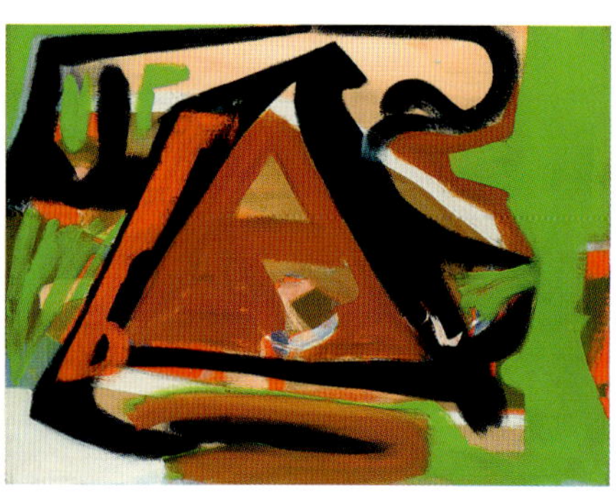

Lanyon, Peter 1918–1964
Mexico 1963
oil on canvas 90.8 x 119.4
AC 977

Law, Bob 1934–2004
Bordeaux Black Blue Black 1977
acrylic on cotton duck 152.5 x 160
AC 2002

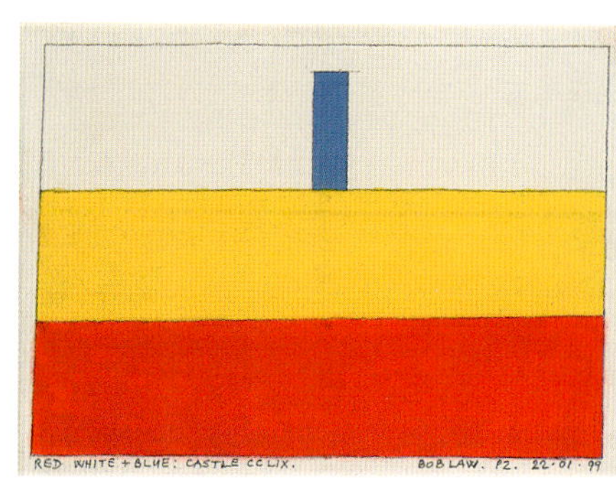

Law, Bob 1934–2004
Red, White + Blue Castle CCLIX PZ 22.01.99
1999
oil & pencil on linen 26 x 36
ACC29/1999

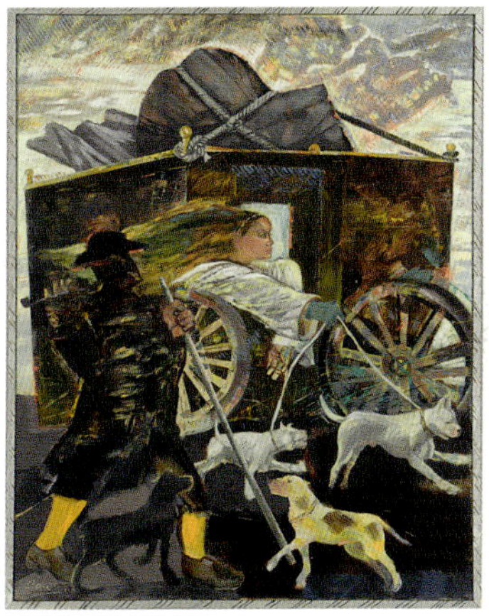

Lawson, Sonia b.1934
Exercising Dogs on Watling Street 1979–1980
oil on canvas 152.5 x 122
AC 3081

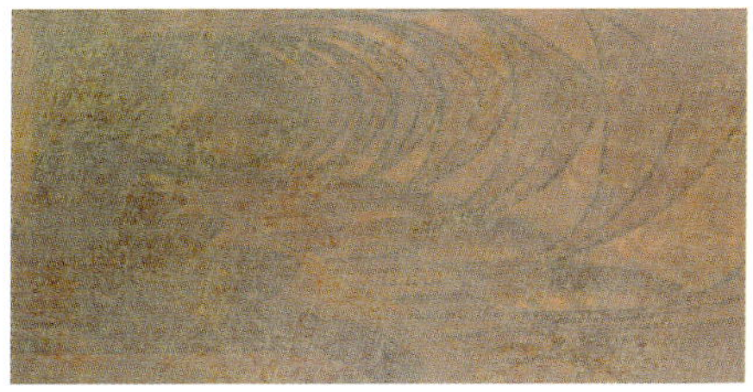

Lawson, Thomas b.1951
Christminster 1984
oil on canvas 183.5 x 366.6
ACC43/1990

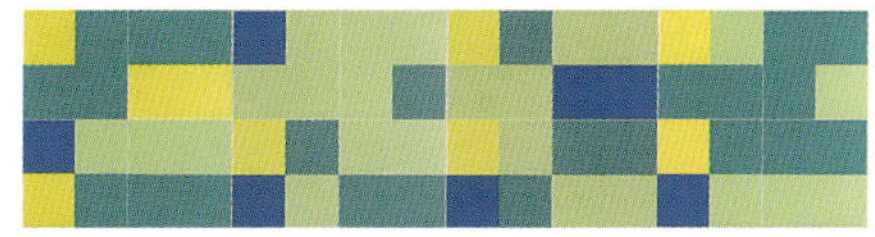

Lawtey, Brian b.1945
Summation Series sy.B.Op. III (A.I.B + Y = O) Set 1.0. 1982
oil on canvas 91.5 x 91.5; 91.5 x 91.5; 91.5 x 91.5; 91.5 x 91.5
AC 5205

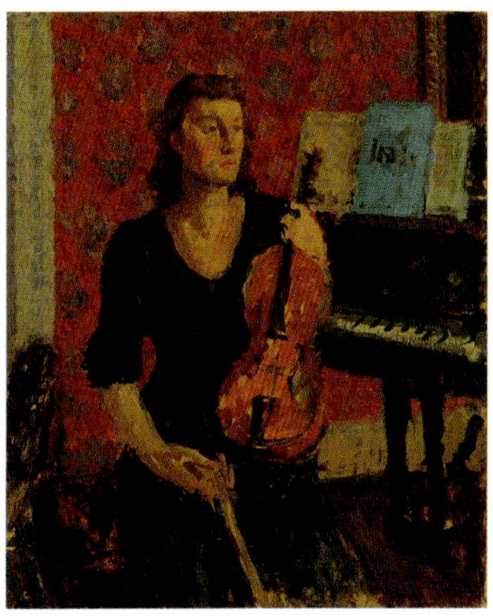

Le Bas, Edward 1904–1966
Girl with Violin c.1940
oil on card 64.5 x 54
AC 97

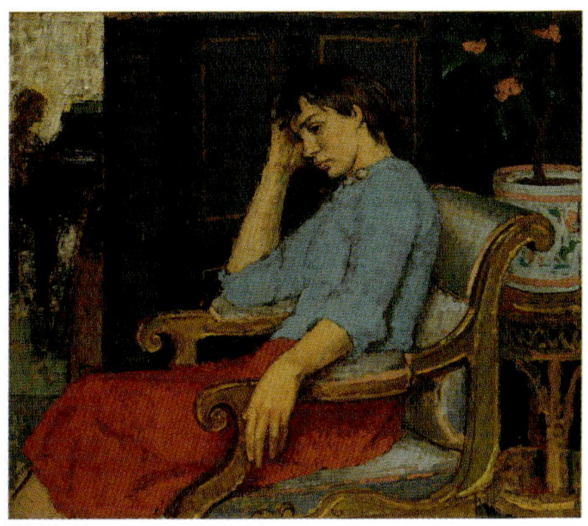

Le Bas, Edward 1904–1966
Angelica Garnett (b.1918) 1950
oil on card 70.5 x 82.5
AC 304

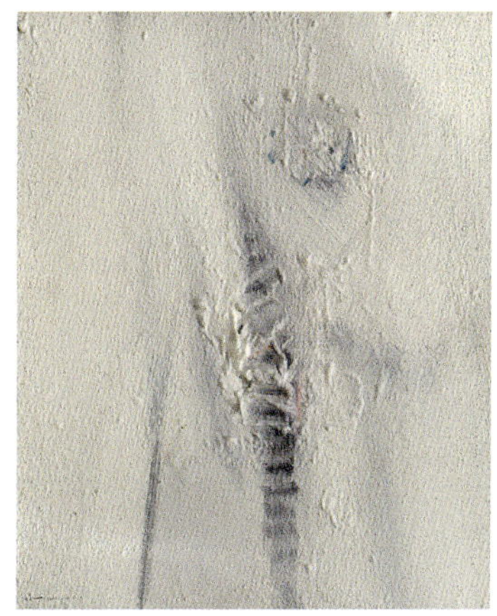

le Brocquy, Louis b.1916
Head 1959
oil on canvas 33 x 25.4
AC 510

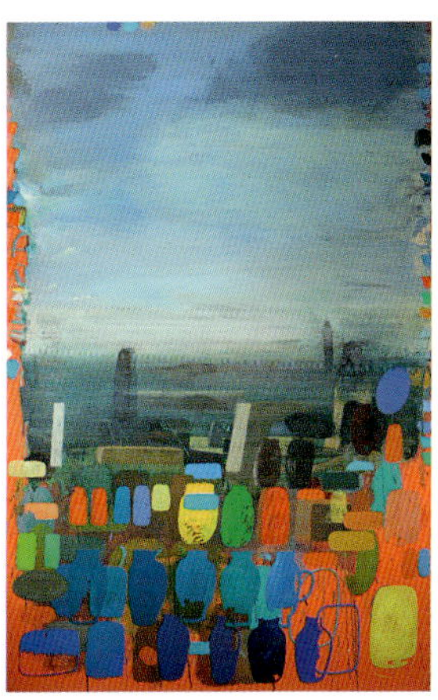

Le Brun, Christopher b.1951
Painting on a Red Ground 1979
oil on canvas 259 x 167.6
AC 3021

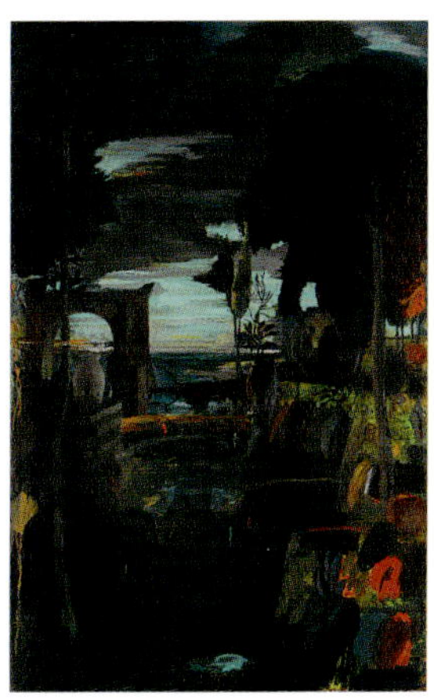

Le Brun, Christopher b.1951
Painting on a Dark Ground 1980
oil on canvas 267.2 x 167.9
AC 3020

Leapman, David b.1959
Past Behaviour 1990
acrylic on canvas 117.8 x 180.2
ACC6/1990

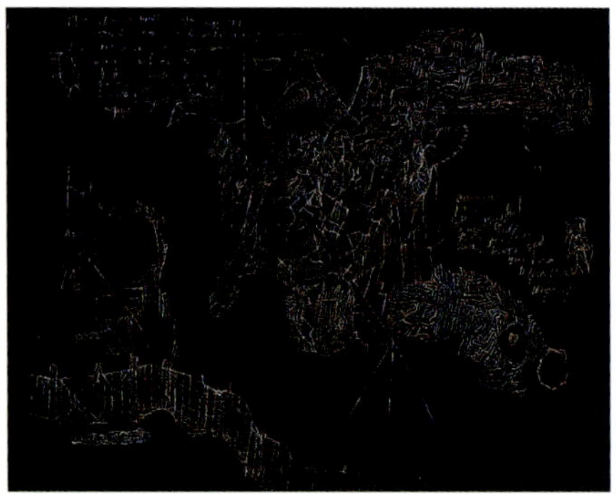

Leapman, David b.1959
Pilot Schemer 1992
acrylic & interference acrylic on canvas
166 x 216
ACC205/1998

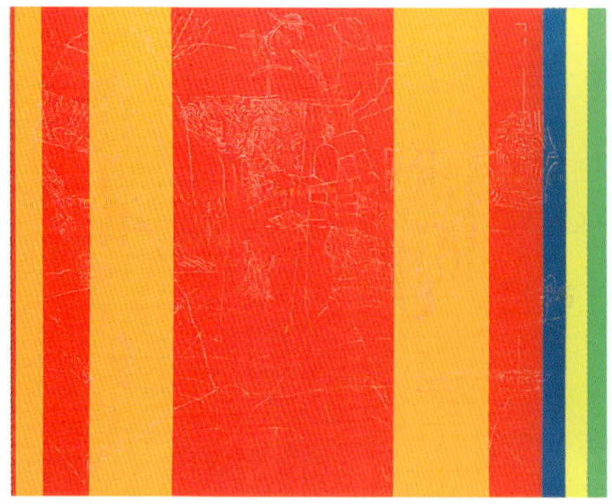

Leapman, David b.1959
Slowburn Escort 1992
day-glo acrylic & interference acrylic on canvas 171 x 215
ACC204/1998

Leapman, Edwina b.1931
Untitled '77 No.6 1977
acrylic on canvas 166.6 x 182.5
AC 1799

Leapman, Edwina b.1931
Untitled No.5 1978
acrylic on canvas 167.2 x 182.4
AC 3006

Leapman, Edwina b.1931
Tall, Very Dark Blue 1991
acrylic on canvas 218.5 x 163.1
ACC70/1991

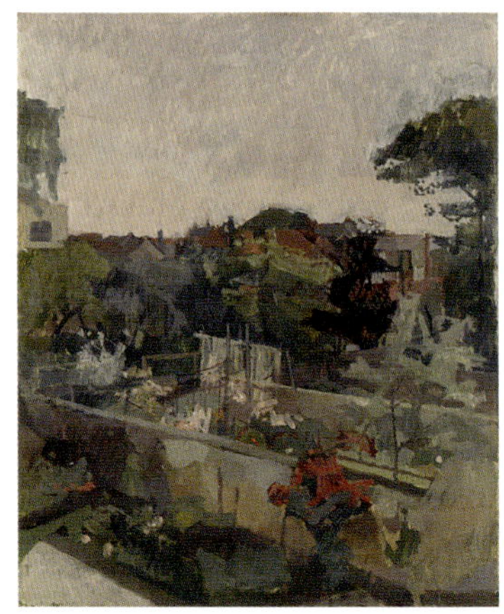

Lee, Dick 1923–2001
Summer 1958
oil on board 76.2 x 63.5
AC 472

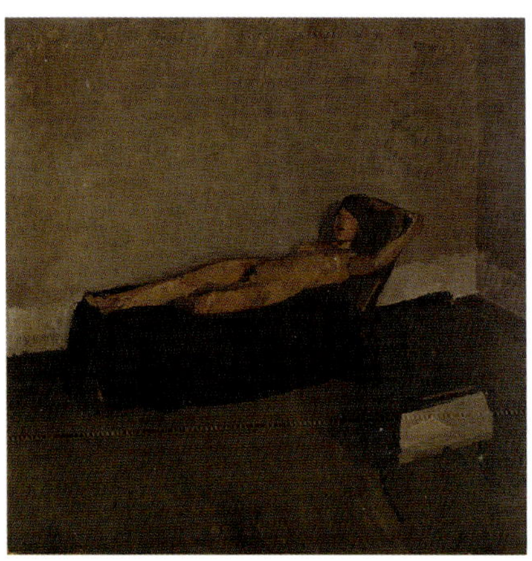

Lee, Dick 1923–2001
Laetitia c.1965
oil on plywood 91.4 x 91.4
AC 771

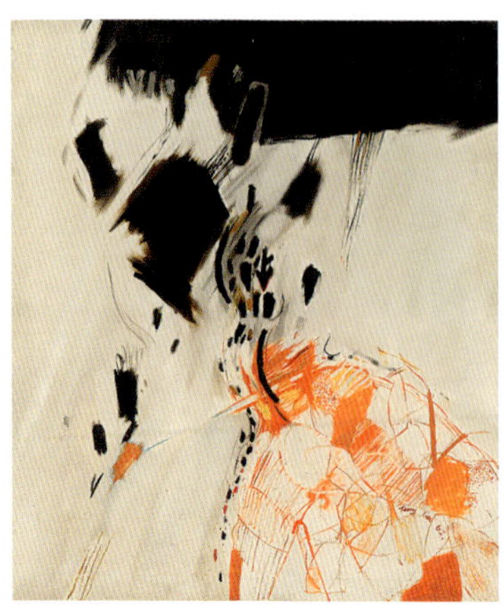

Lee, Terry b.1932
The Spider's Debris 1962
oil on canvas 122 x 107
AC 697

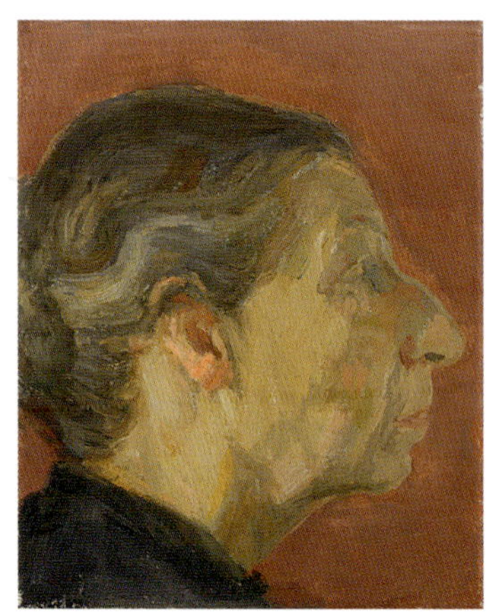

Lessore, Helen 1907–1994
Self Portrait II 1966
oil on canvas 28 x 23
AC 967

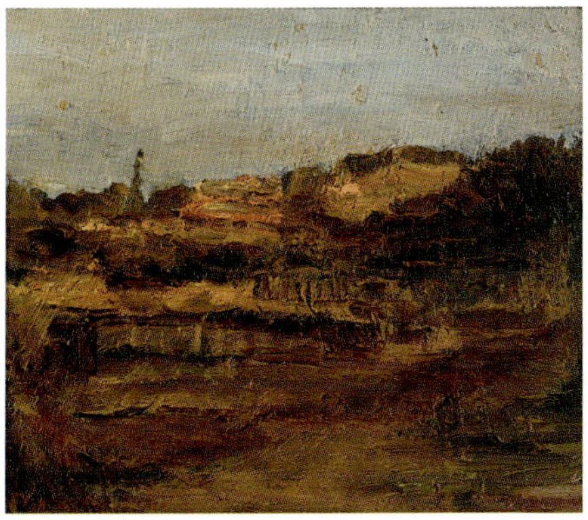

Lessore, John b.1939
La Gardie 1964
oil on board 17.5 x 21.8
AC 768

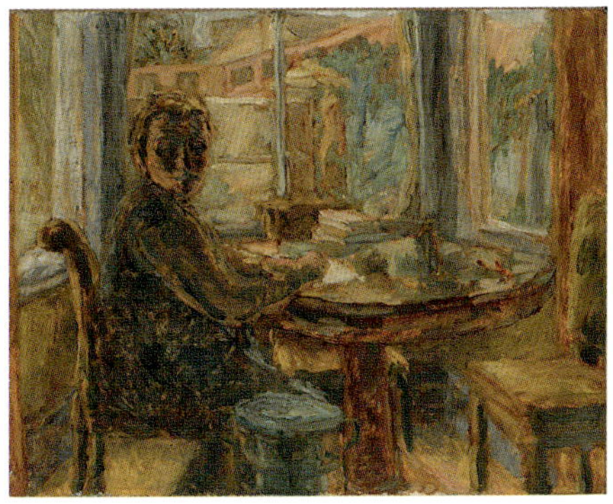

Lessore, John b.1939
Writing a Letter 1966
oil on board 61.5 x 78.5
AC 940

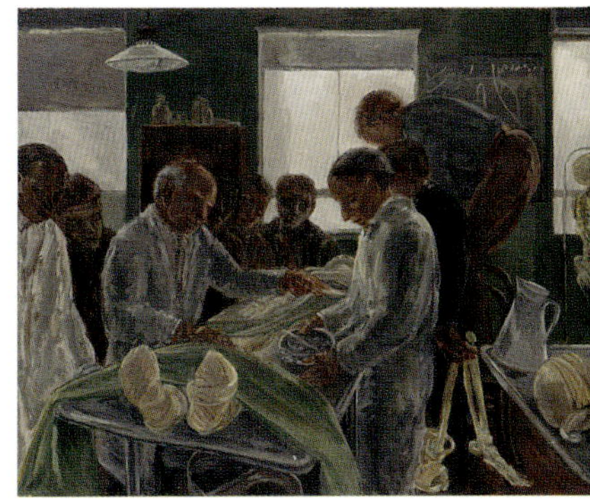

Lessore, John b.1939
The Articulation of the Knee 1982–1984
oil on board 121.3 x 155.6
AC 5451

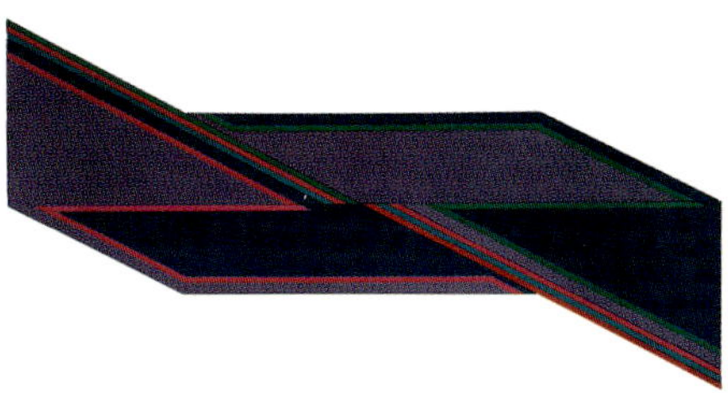

Leverett, David b.1938
Centre Point Shift 1970
acrylic on canvas 125 x 245
AC 1115

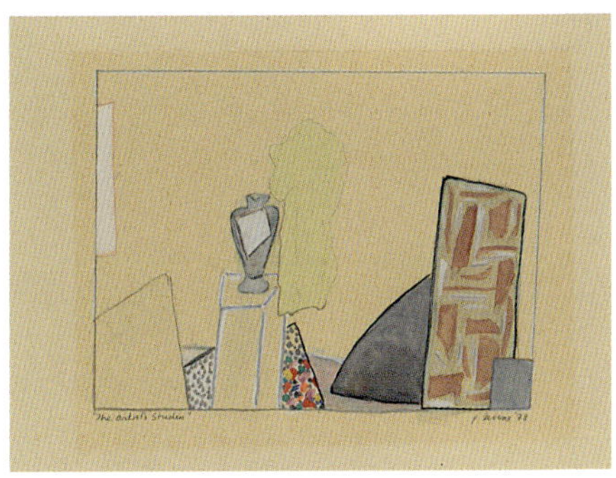

Levine, Paula b.1948
The Artist's Studio 1978
watercolour, poster paint & pencil on paper
24.9 x 34.1
AC 1964

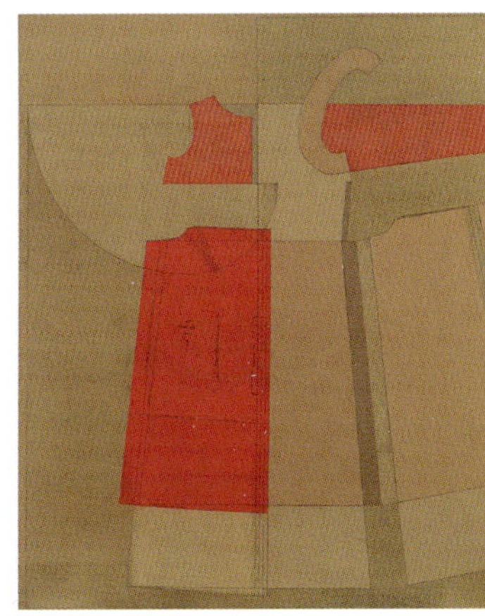

Lewis, Greg b.1950
'Red Dress' 1977
acrylic, pencil & paper collage on canvas
183 x 152.5
AC 1790

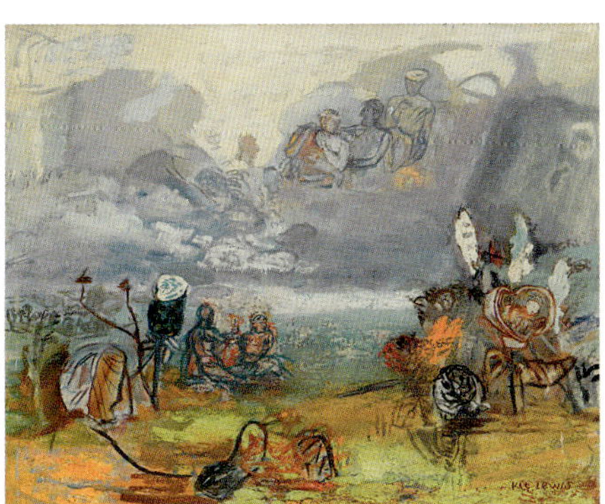

Lewis, Kit 1911–1998
Amphytrion 1951
oil on canvas 61 x 71.1
AC 185

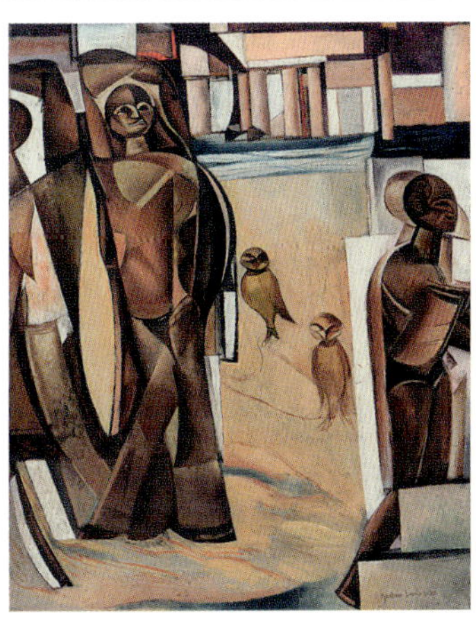

Lewis, Wyndham 1882–1957
Inca with Birds 1933
oil on canvas 67.3 x 54.6
ACC4/1959

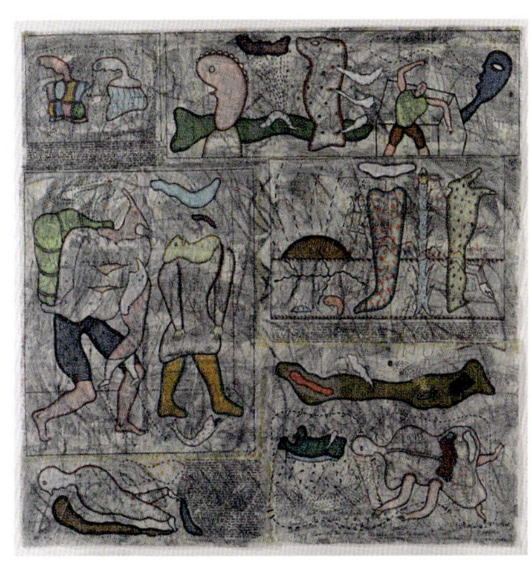

Lewty, Simon b.1941
The Return 1984
ink, crayon & acrylic on paper 196 x 206
ACC6/1984

Lin, Richard b.1933
Painting Relief 1961 1961
perspex & oil on canvas 101 x 101
AC 722

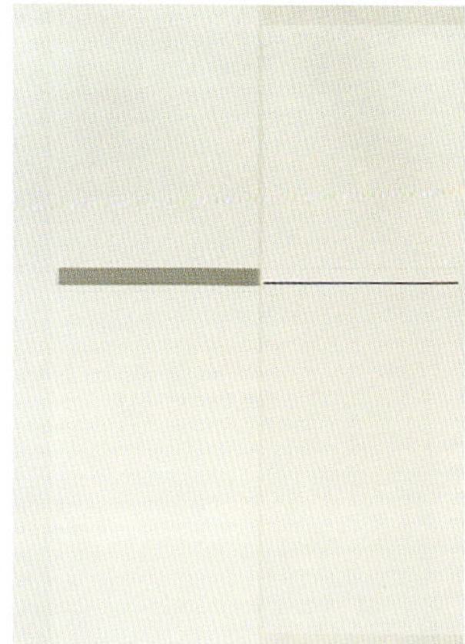

Lin, Richard b.1933
Painting Relief 1965 1965
aluminium & oil on canvas 142 x 101.5
AC 914

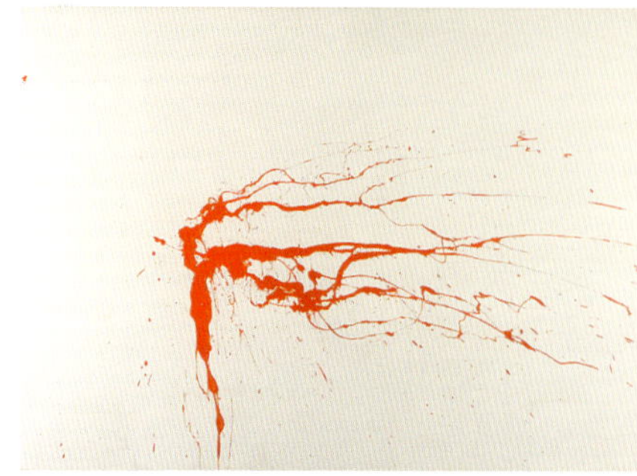

Linke, Simon b.1958
Untitled 1993
oil on canvas 94 x 107
ACC3/1994

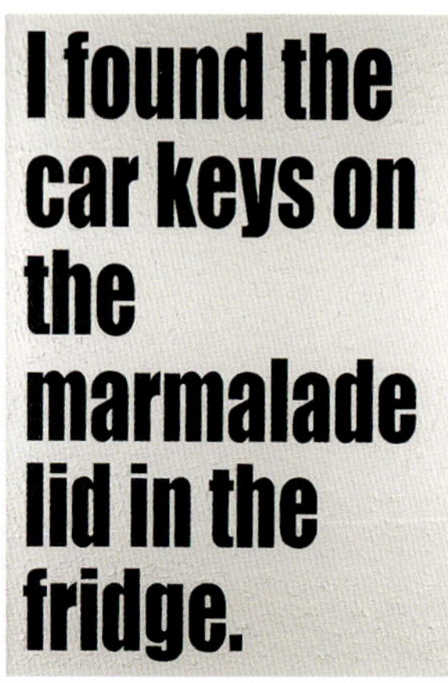

Linke, Simon b.1958
Lost 1996
oil on canvas 126.9 x 89.6
ACC50/1996

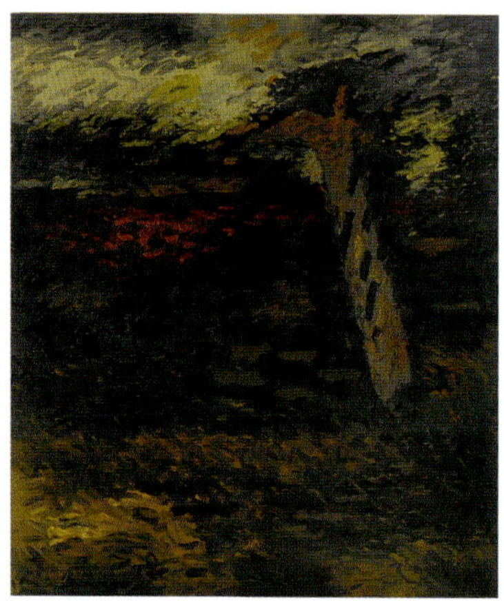

Linley, David b.1954
Tree/Dark Rain/Red Pool 1986–1987
oil on canvas 240.1 x 207.2
AC 5463

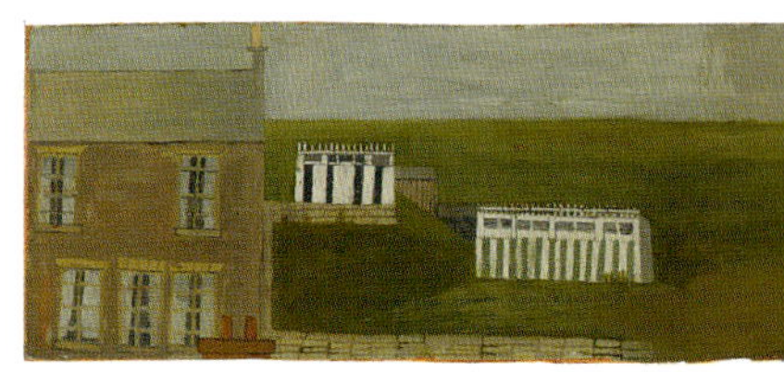

Lloyd, Pamela b.1932
Pigeon Lofts, Whitby
oil on board 12 x 30
AC 404

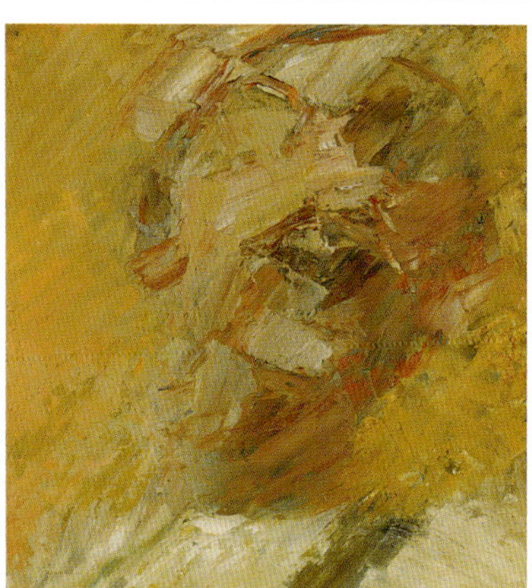

Lloyd-Jones, Peter 1940–2001
Laughter (9 conditions) 1979–1980
oil on paper on card 24.8 x 22.7
ACC3/1980

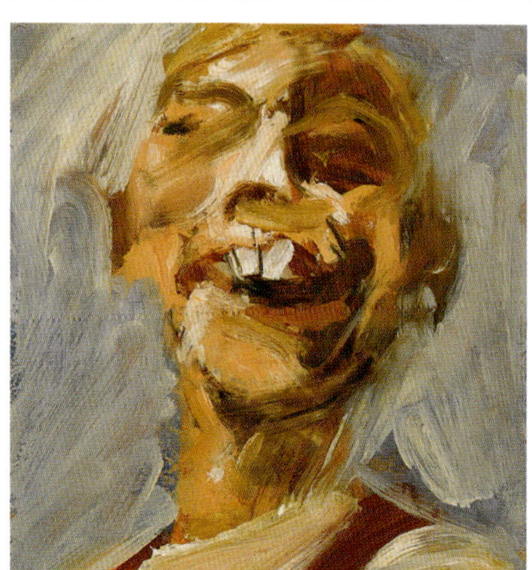

Lloyd-Jones, Peter 1940–2001
Laughter (9 conditions) 1979–1980
oil on paper on card 24.8 x 23.4
ACC4/1980

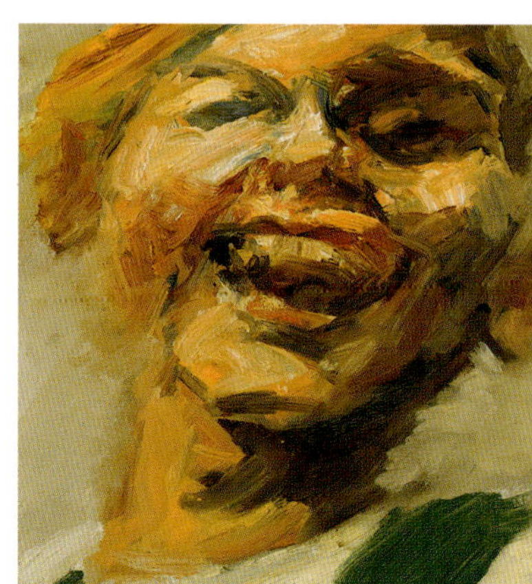

Lloyd-Jones, Peter 1940–2001
Laughter (9 conditions) 1979–1980
oil on paper on card 24.8 x 23.4
ACC5/1980

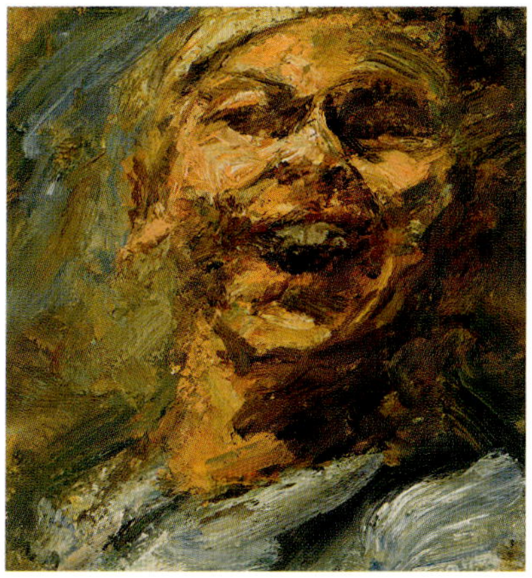

Lloyd-Jones, Peter 1940–2001
Laughter (9 conditions) 1979–1980
oil on paper on card 24.9 x 22.9
ACC6/1980

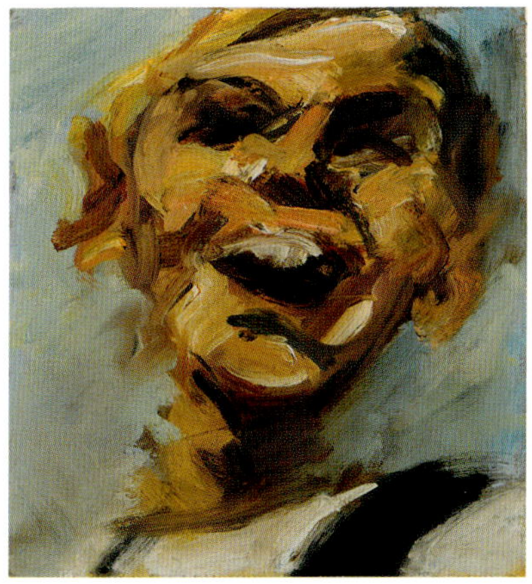

Lloyd-Jones, Peter 1940–2001
Laughter (9 conditions) 1979–1980
oil on paper on card 24.4 x 23.2
ACC7/1980

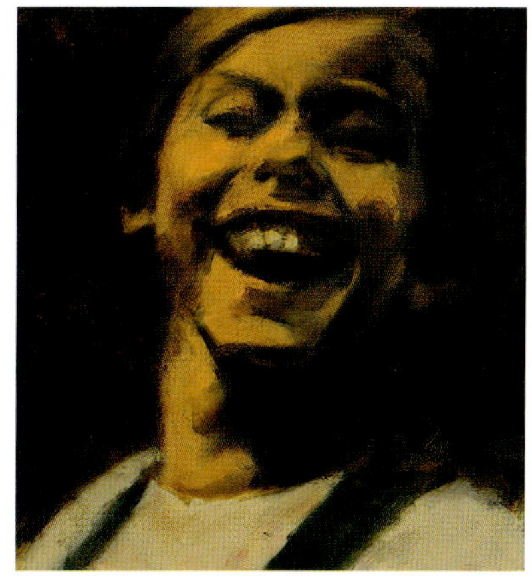

Lloyd-Jones, Peter 1940–2001
Laughter (9 conditions) 1979–1980
oil on paper on card 24.5 x 23.2
ACC8/1980

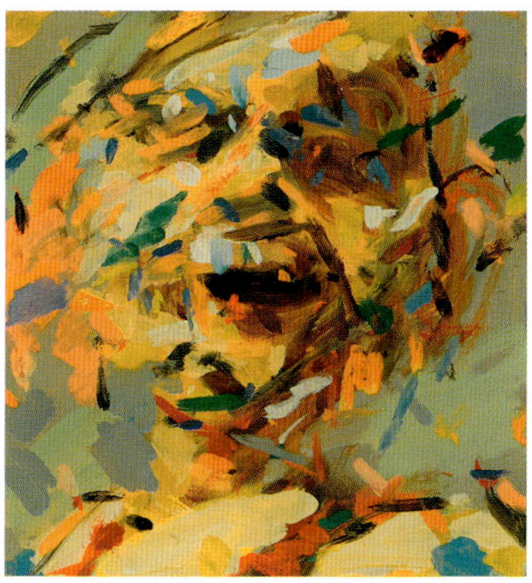

Lloyd-Jones, Peter 1940–2001
Laughter (9 conditions) 1979–1980
oil on paper on card 24.2 x 23.2
ACC9/1980

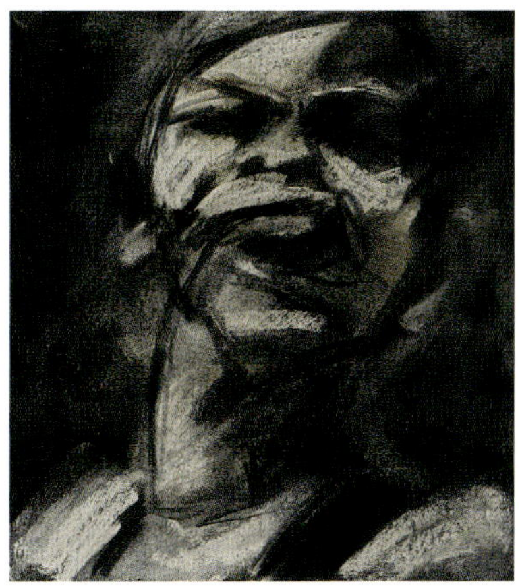

Lloyd-Jones, Peter 1940–2001
Laughter (9 conditions) 1979–1980
oil on paper on card 24.8 x 22.8
ACC10/1980

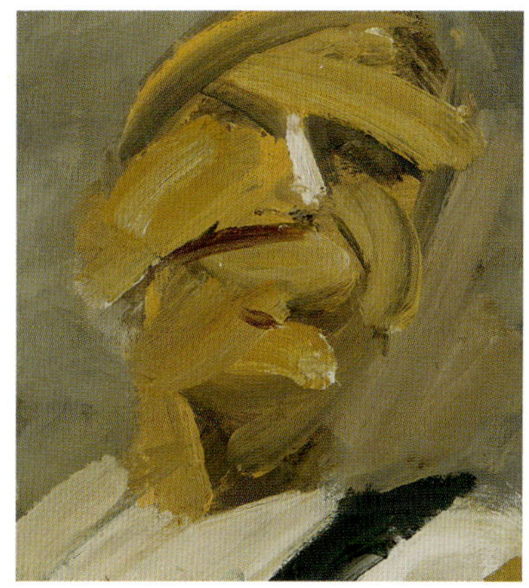

Lloyd-Jones, Peter 1940–2001
Laughter (9 conditions) 1979–1980
oil on paper on card 24.5 x 22.5
ACC11/1980

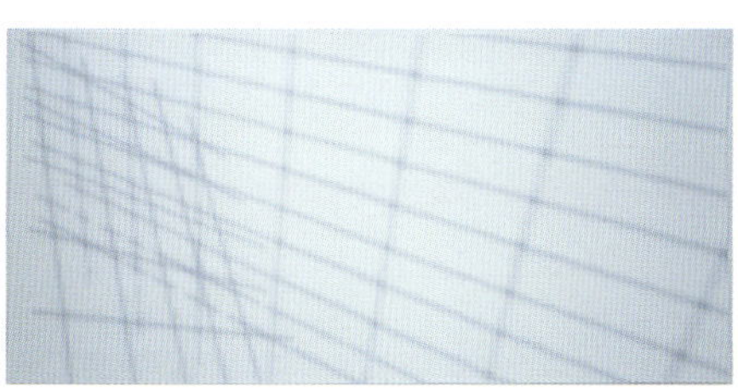

Lochore, Brad b.1960
Shadow No.52 1994
oil on canvas 290 x 610
ACC206/1998

Loker, John b.1938
Dorset Horizon I Series 2 1973
pencil & acrylic on paper 40.6 x 76.2
AC 1326

Loker, John b.1938
Dorset Horizon II Series 2 1973
pencil & acrylic on paper 40.6 x 76.2
AC 1327

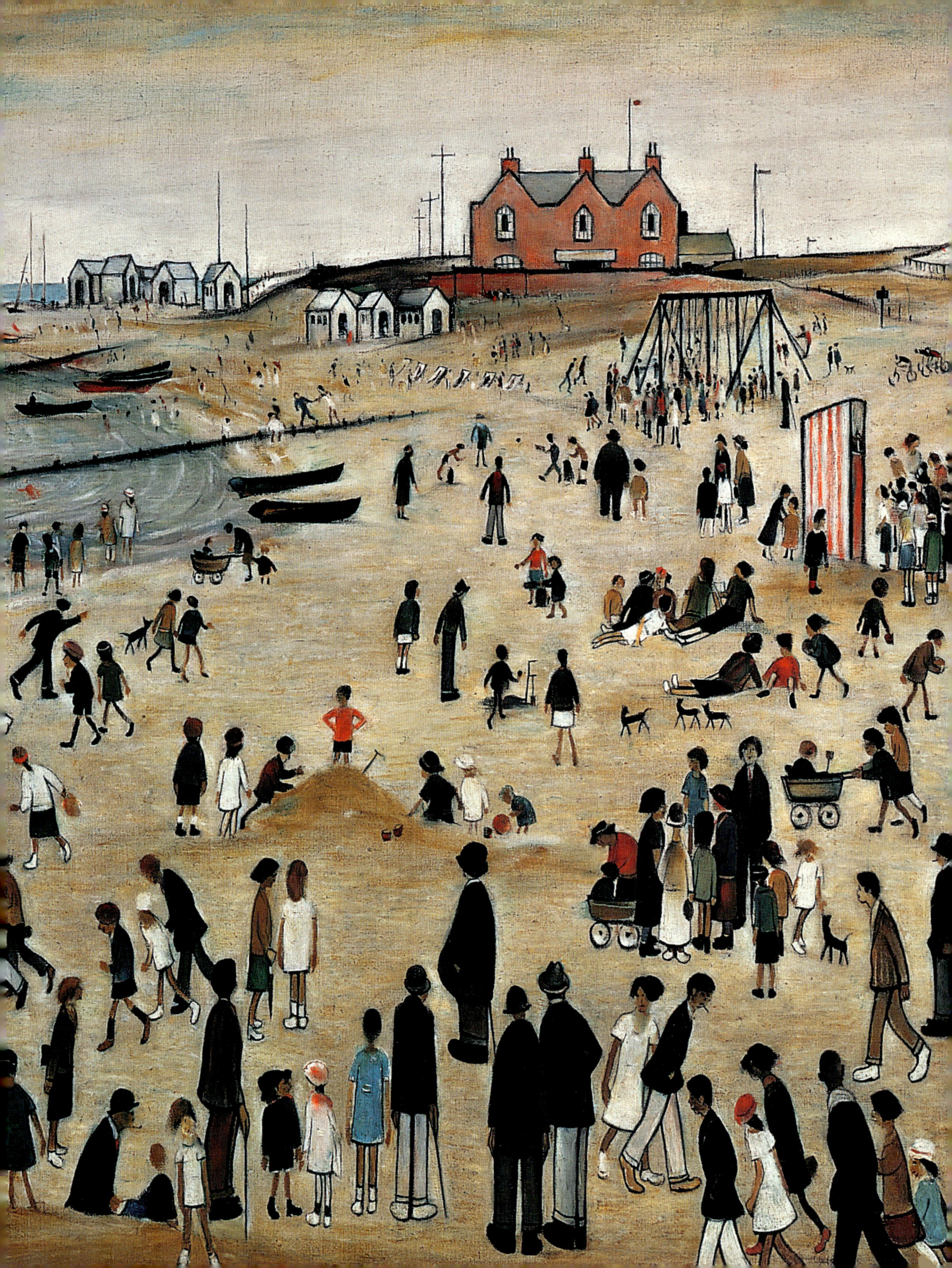

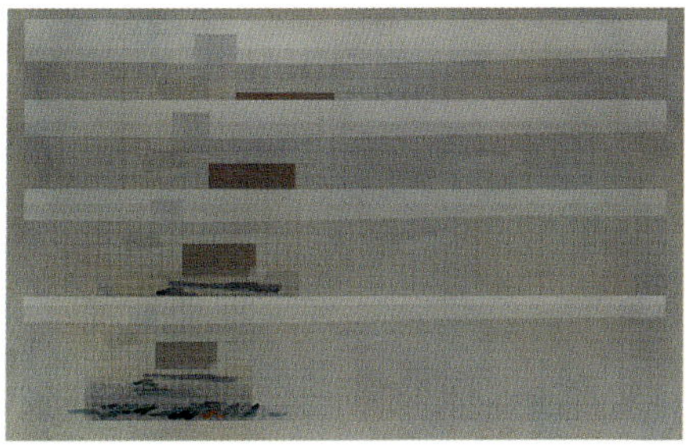

Loker, John b.1938
Four Extracts II 1976
acrylic & pencil on canvas 150 x 244
AC 1627

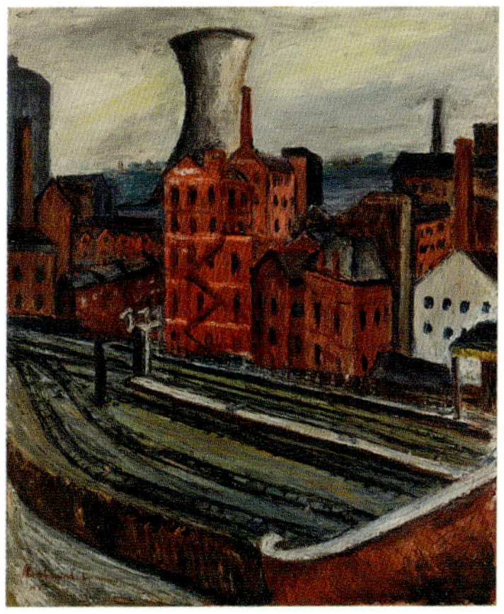

Lowndes, Alan 1921–1978
Stockport 1953
oil on canvas 76.2 x 63.5
ACA 57

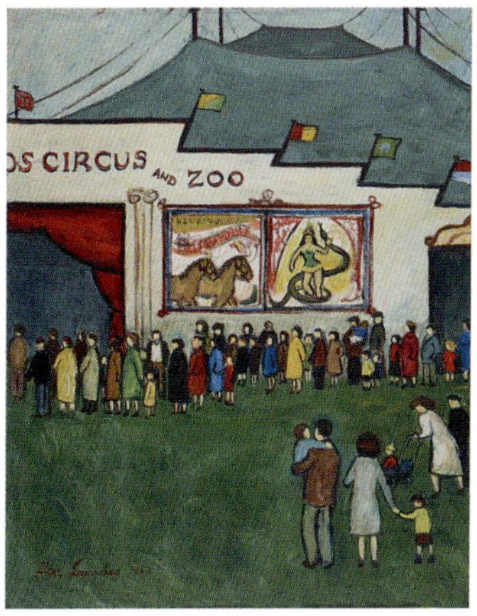

Lowndes, Alan 1921–1978
Entering the Circus (1) 1963
oil on canvas 99 x 81.3
ACA 58

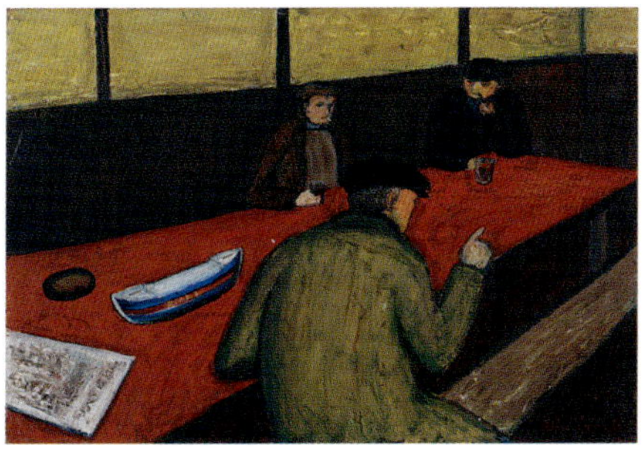

Lowndes, Alan 1921–1978
Telling the Tale 1964
oil on board 54.6 x 81.3
ACA 59

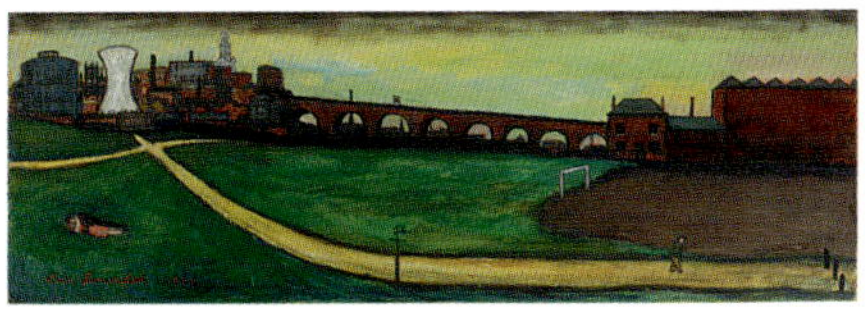

Lowndes, Alan 1921–1978
The Park: Panorama of Stockport 1964
oil on canvas 61 x 183
AC 820

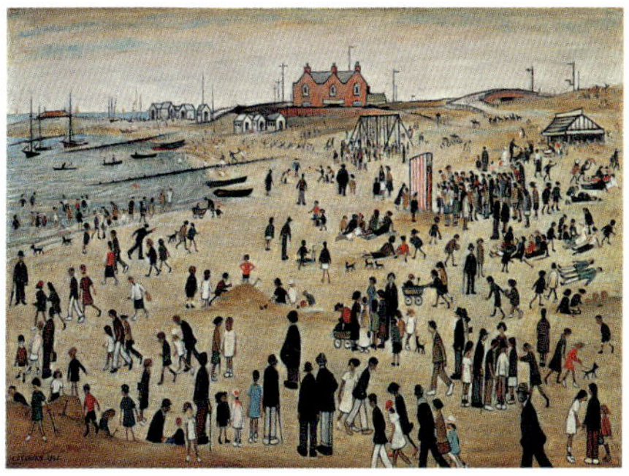

Lowry, Laurence Stephen 1887–1976
July, the Seaside 1943
oil on canvas 66.7 x 92.7
ACC1/1943

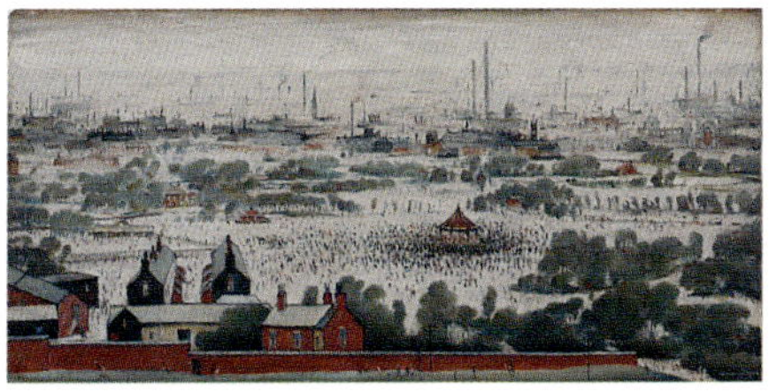

Lowry, Laurence Stephen 1887–1976
The Park 1946
oil on canvas 38 x 80
ACC2/1951

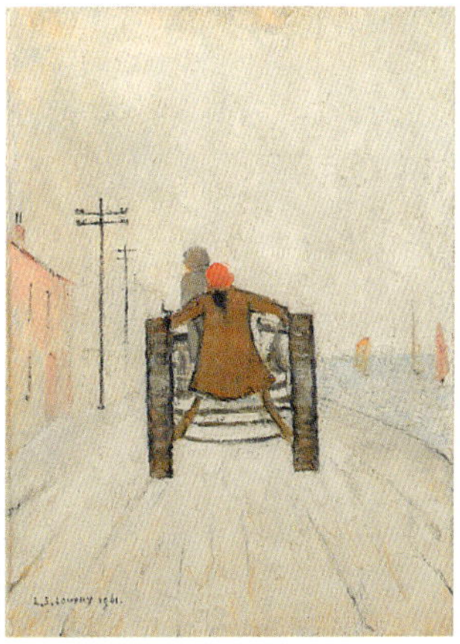

Lowry, Laurence Stephen 1887–1976
Woman Riding on a Tractor 1961
oil on canvas 35.5 x 25.3
AC 5263

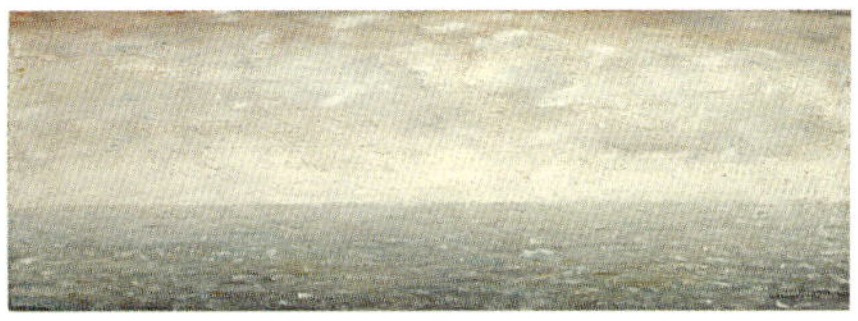

Lowry, Laurence Stephen 1887–1976
Seascape 1965
oil on panel 26.7 x 77.8
AC 906

Facing page: Lowry, Laurence Stephen, 1887–1976, *July, the Seaside* (detail), 1943, (p. 101)

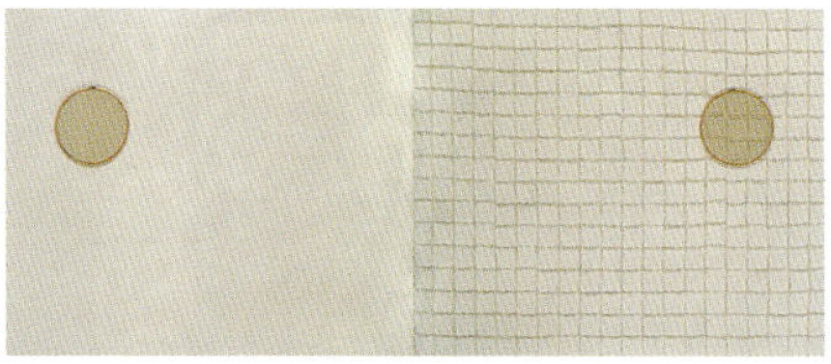

Lydiat, Anne b.1947
The Craft of Art/The Art of Craft 1986
canvas, wood primer & embroidery hoop
147 x 178
AC 5496

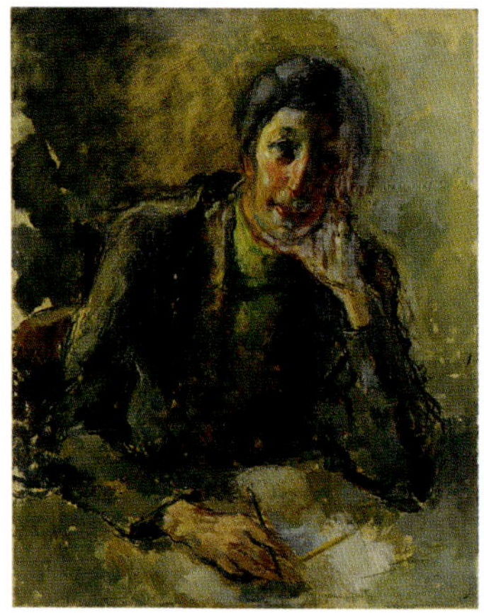

Lyon, Robert 1894–1978
K. F. M. Prescott, Author 1941
oil on canvas 76.8 x 61.6
AC 73

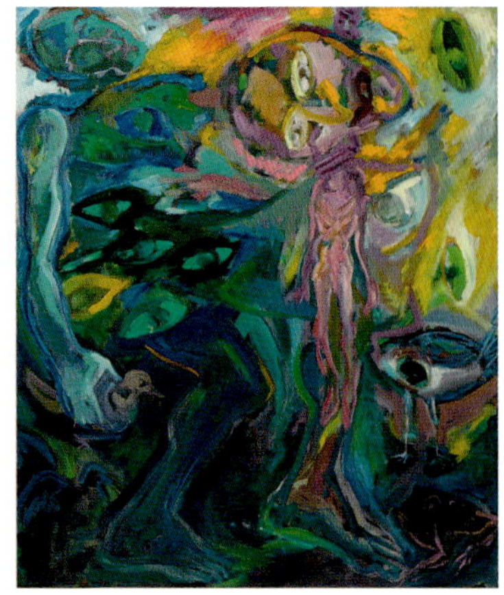

Lyons, John C. M. b.1933
Victim of Papa Bois 1990–1992
oil on canvas 146.6 x 127
ACC46/1995

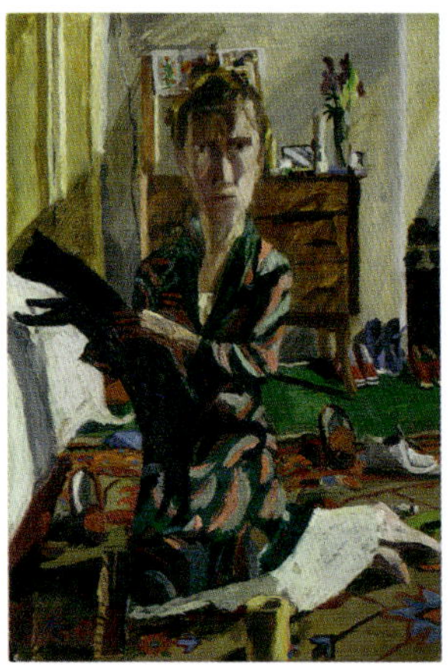

Mabbutt, Mary b.1951
Study for 'Self Portrait with Poussin' 1980
oil on board 27.6 x 20
AC 4023

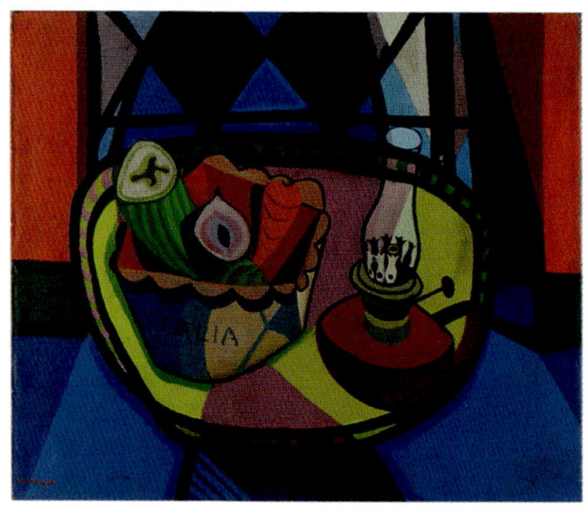

MacBryde, Robert 1913–1966
Table in a Red Room 1950
oil on canvas 65 x 76.5
AC 165

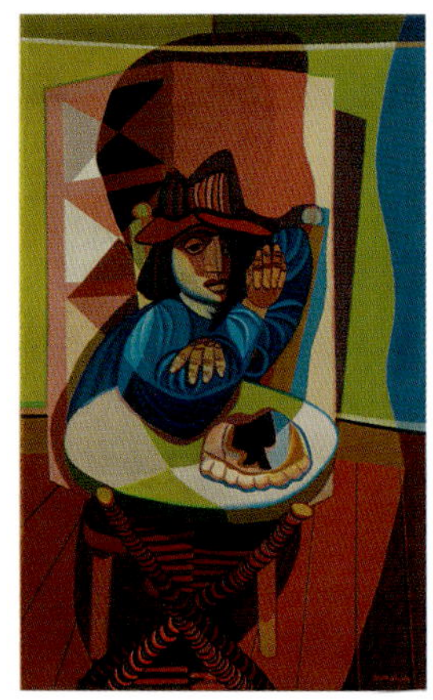

MacBryde, Robert 1913–1966
Figure and Still Life 1951
oil on canvas 172.7 x 101.6
ACC4/1951

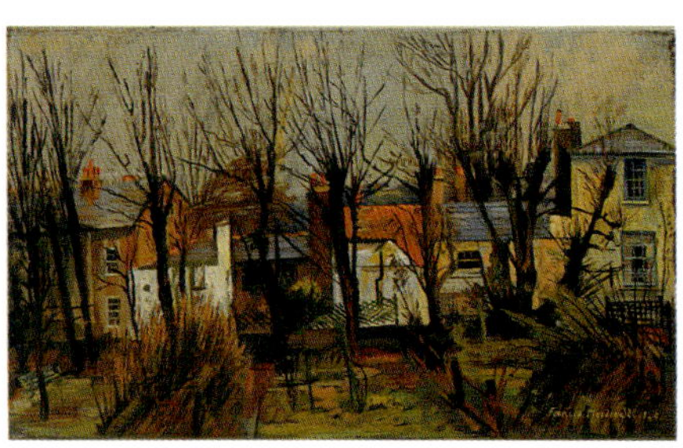

Macdonald, Frances 1914–2002
Backs of Houses, Keats Grove, Hampstead
1940
oil on canvas 33 x 55.9
AC 74

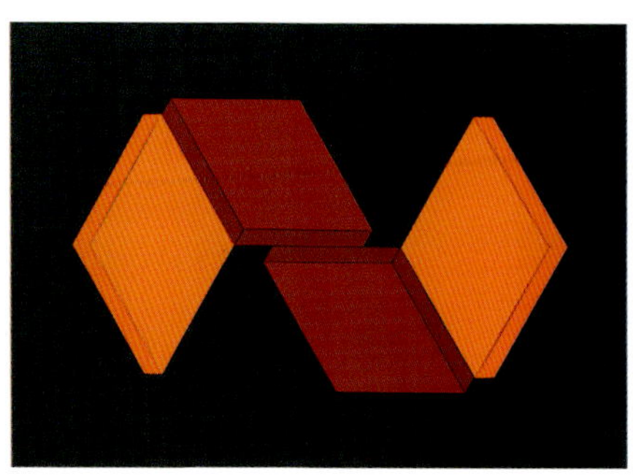

Machin, Geoffrey b.1937
Untitled 1969
emulsion on canvas 150.5 x 210.8
AC 1264

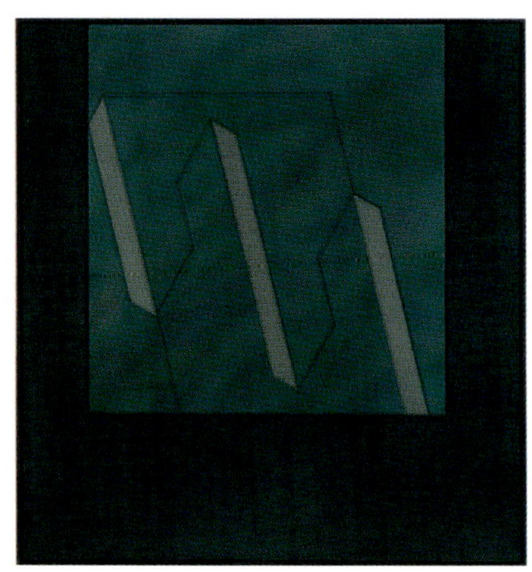

Machin, Geoffrey b.1937
Italic Towers 1972
acrylic on canvas 218 x 210
AC 1263

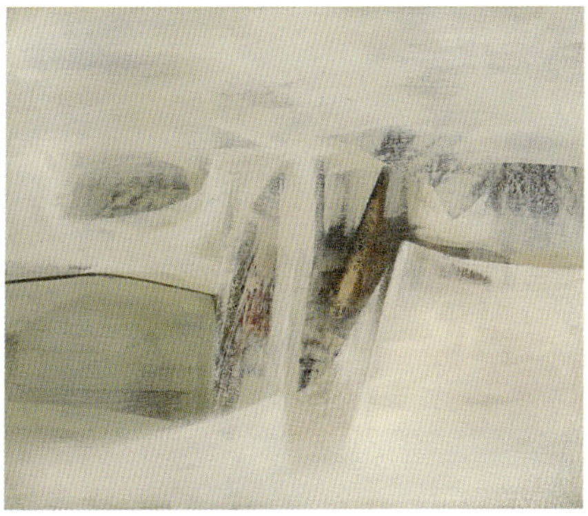

MacKenzie, Alexander 1923–2001
White Painting 1960
oil on board 45.7 x 55.9
AC 561

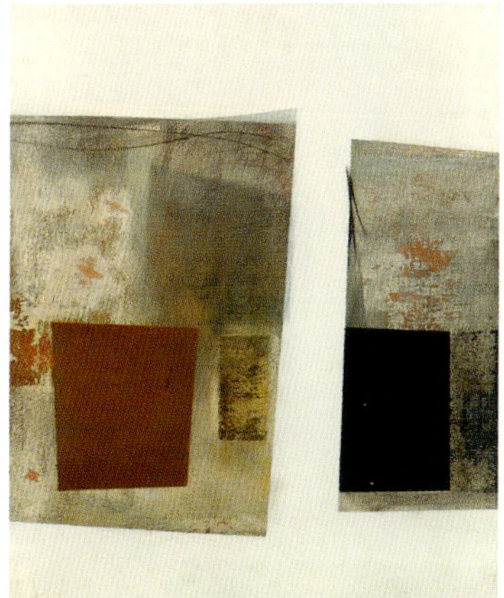

MacKenzie, Alexander 1923–2001
Granite, Brown, Black on White 1963
oil on board 73.7 x 61
AC 688

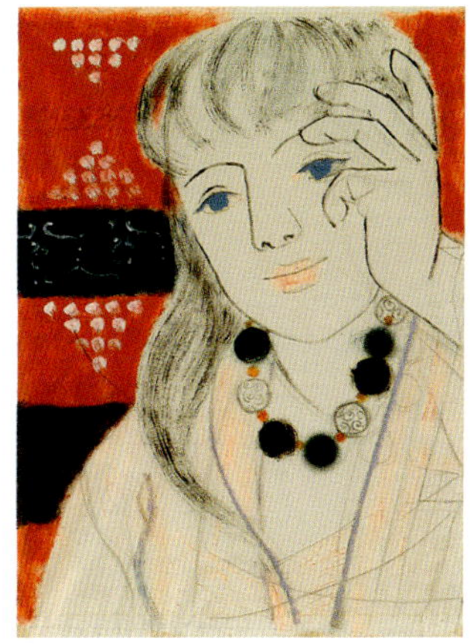

MacKinnon, Hugh b.1925
Girl's Head 1953
oil on paper 53.5 x 42
AC 350

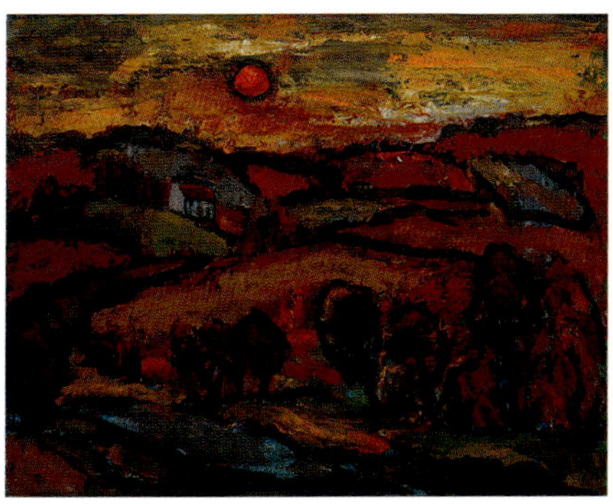

MacTaggart, William 1903–1981
Winter Sunset, the Red Soil 1956
oil on canvas 69.9 x 90.2
AC 437

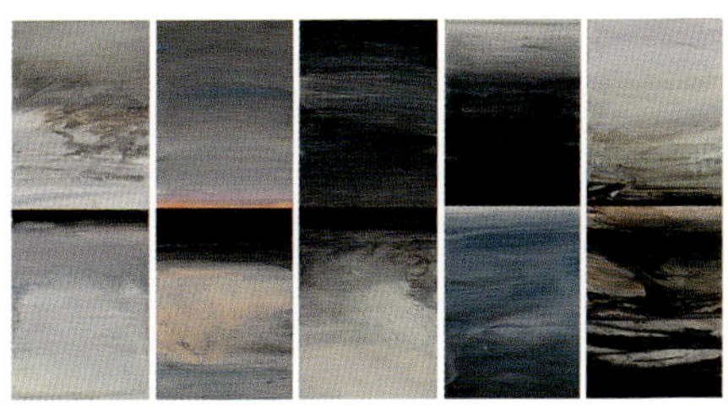

Madden, Anne b.1932
Atlantic Suite 1977–1978
oil on paper 61.6 x 116
AC 1885-9

Magill, Elizabeth b.1959
Without 2002
oil on canvas 91 x 122
ACC56/2002

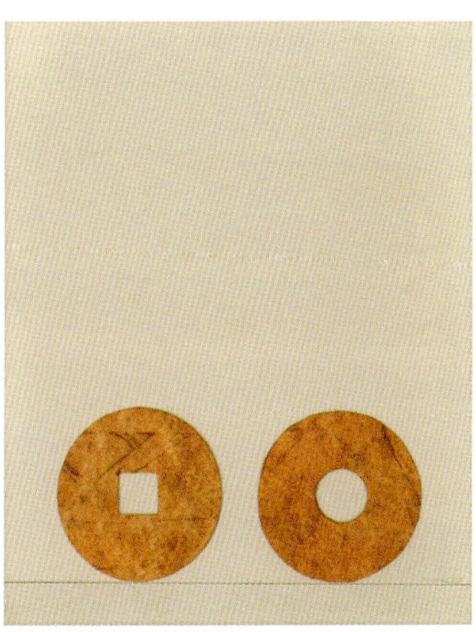

Mak, Kum-Siew b.1940
Singapore I 1967
tempera & acrylic on paper on card
55.9 x 45.7
AC 1073

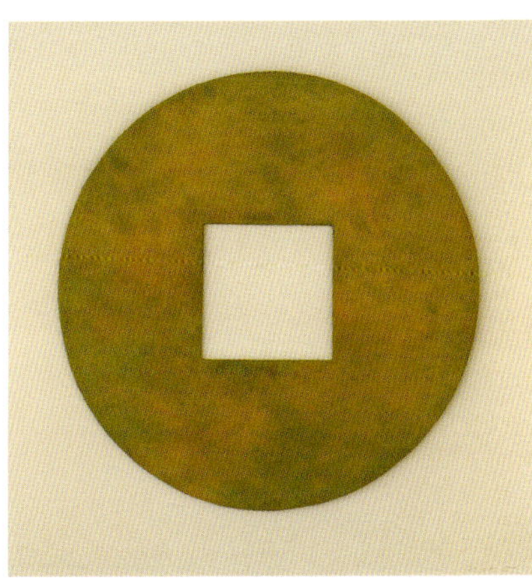

Mak, Kum-Siew b.1940
Singapore II 1967
tempera & acrylic on paper on card 61 x 58.4
AC 1074

Mak, Kum-Siew b.1940
Buddhist Television I 1975–1976
acrylic on cotton duck 239 x 239
AC 1731

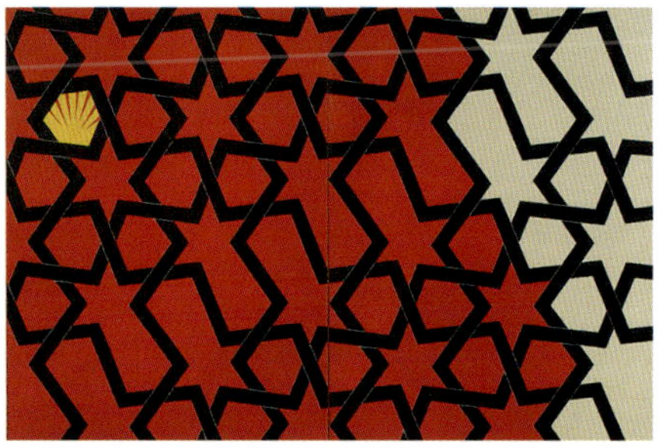

Makhoul, Bashir b.1963
Zigzag 1992
acrylic on canvas 230 x 175; 230 x 175
ACC22/1994

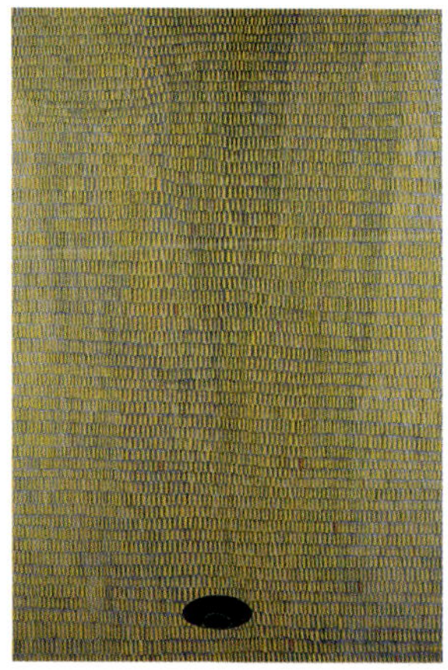

Malinowski, Antoni b.1955
Not titled 1990
acrylic on canvas 244 x 167.5
ACC5/1990

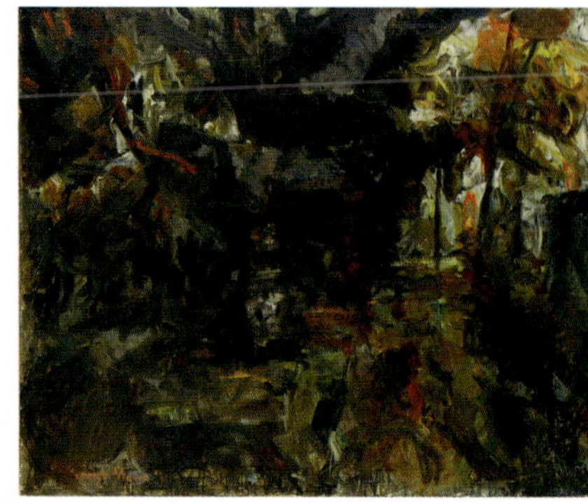

Mann, Sargy b.1937
River Box, Evening Sun 1981
oil on wood 122 x 151.8
AC 5388

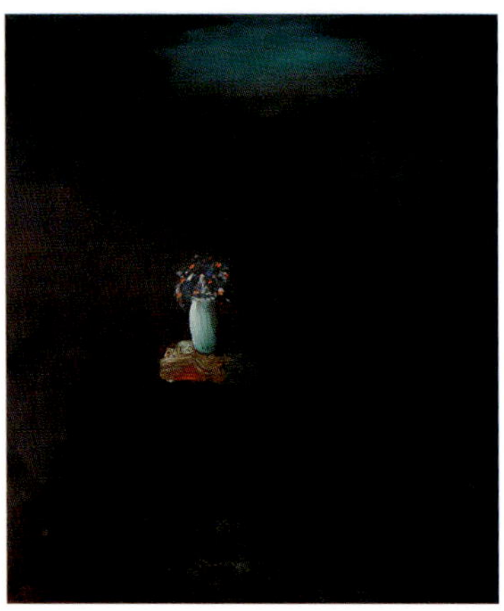

Mansfield, Andrew b.1953
Nature morte 1985
oil on canvas 195.7 x 167.7
AC 5384

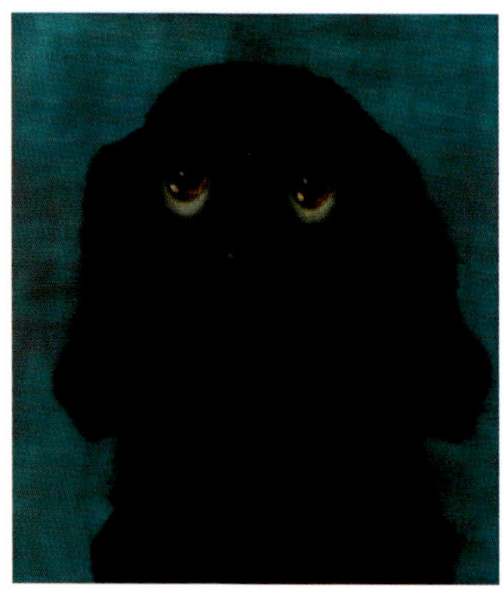

Mansfield, Andrew b.1953
Untitled No.130 1995
oil on canvas 152.9 x 137.7
ACC45/1995

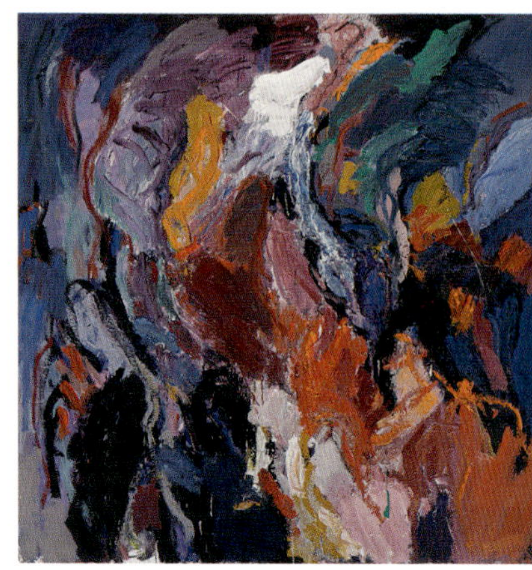

Marks, Gerald b.1921
Untitled 1982–1983
acrylic on canvas 182.9 x 182.9
AC 5323

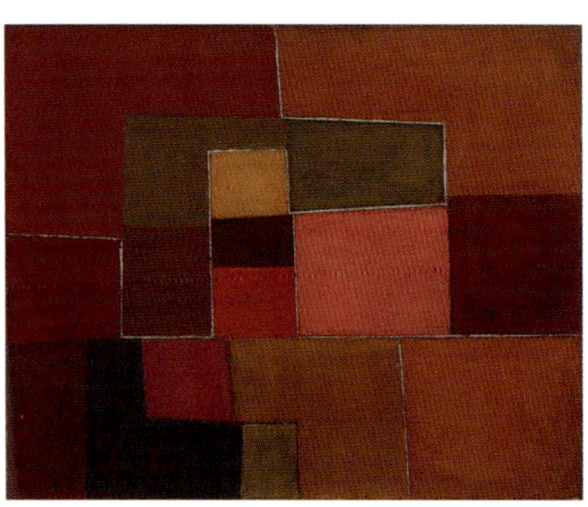

Martin, Kenneth 1905–1984
Abstract, Orange and Red 1956
oil on canvas 40.6 x 50.8
AC 479

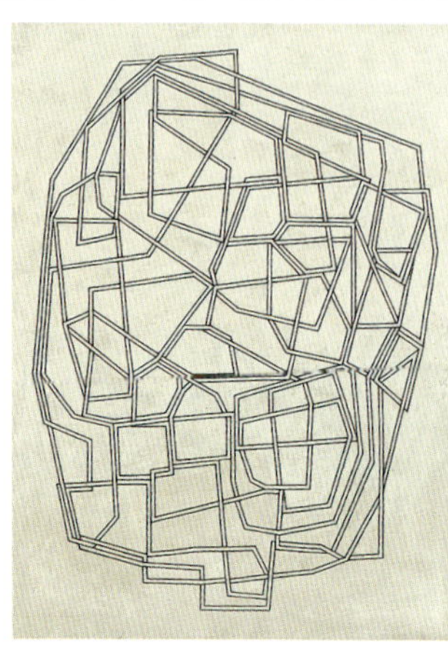

Martin, Kenneth 1905–1984
Endless Configuration 1964
oil on board 160.7 x 122.9
AC 742

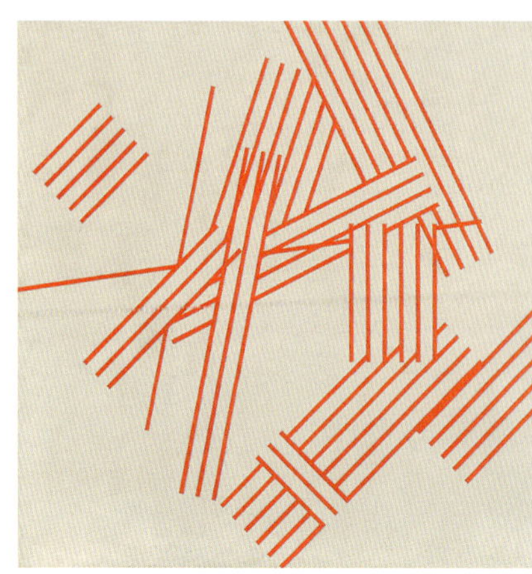

Martin, Kenneth 1905–1984
Chance and Order 5 (Red) 1970
oil on canvas 121.9 x 121.9
ACC5/1971

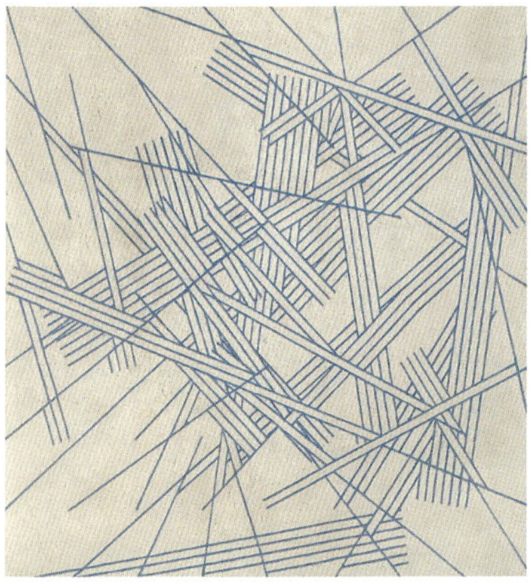

Martin, Kenneth 1905–1984
Chance, Order, Change 2 (Ultramarine Blue)
1976
oil on canvas 91.4 x 91.4
AC 1742

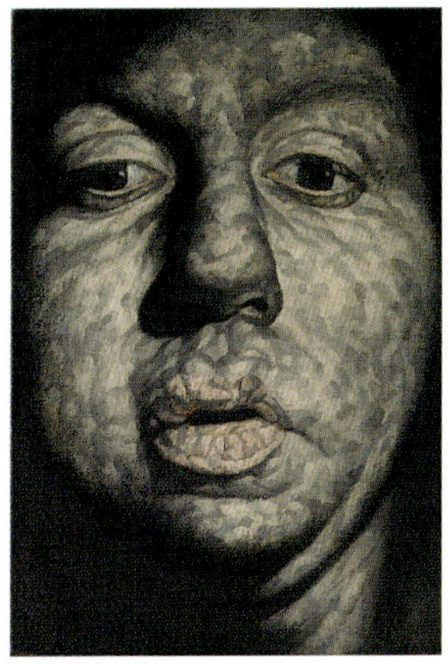

Martin, Michael b.1955
Young Miner 1979–1980
oil on canvas 20.8 x 14.5
AC 4013

Masoero, Jeanne b.1937
At an Instant 1971
oil & acrylic on canvas 109.2 x 101.6
AC 1182

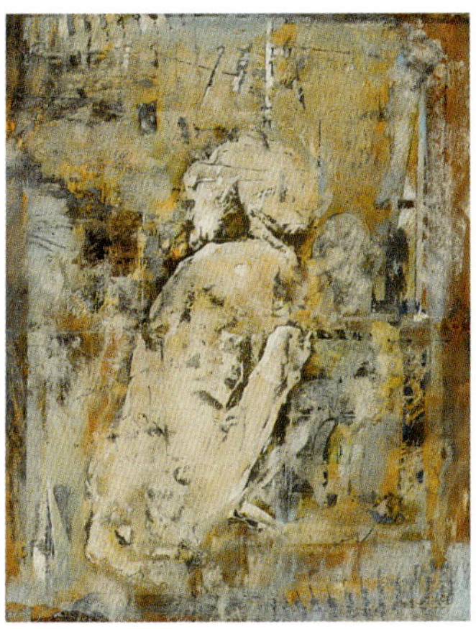

Mason, Robert b.1946
From Tougourt 1978
acrylic & paper on board 87 x 68.5
AC 1973

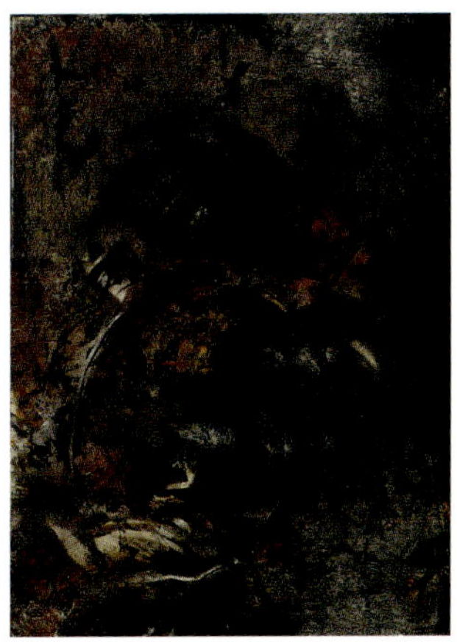

Mason, Robert b.1946
From the Oulad III 1979–1980
acrylic, rhoplex, charcoal & paper on board
109.5 x 80
AC 3085

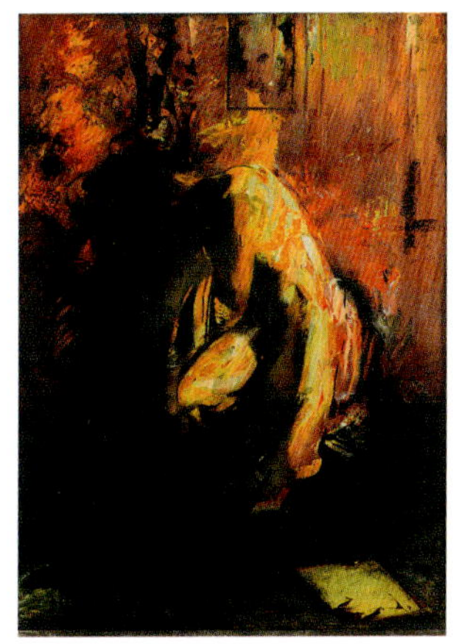

Mason, Robert b.1946
The Bowl (of Shadows) 1984
acrylic, charcoal & pastel on board
106 x 76.5
AC 5366

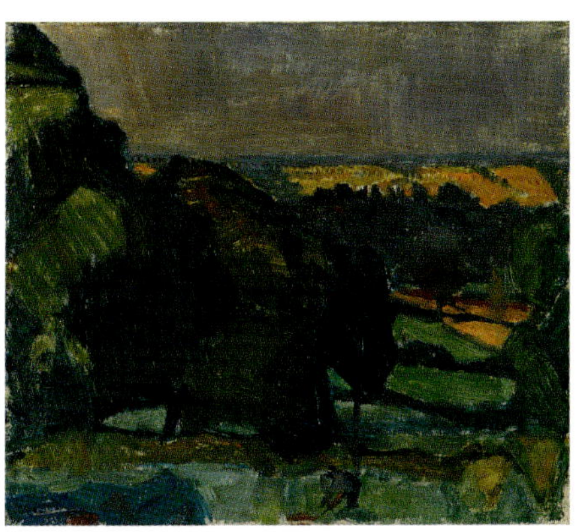

Matthews, Philip 1916–1984
Landscape, Cookham Dean 1957
oil on canvas 31.1 x 35.6
AC 641

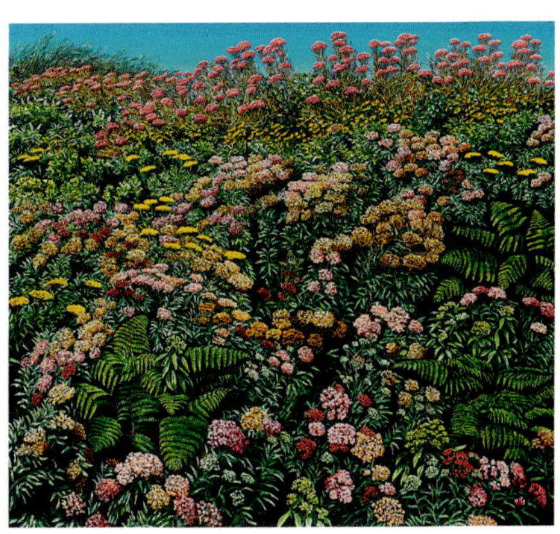

Maughan, Karl b.1964
Aro Valley 1999
oil on canvas 228.5 x 259
ACC25/1999

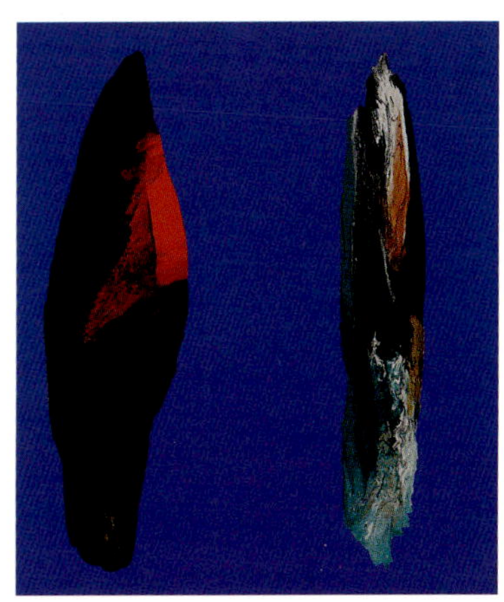

May, Nicholas b.1962
Guardians of Acheron 1992
oil, resin & metallic powder on canvas
274 x 244
ACC13/1992

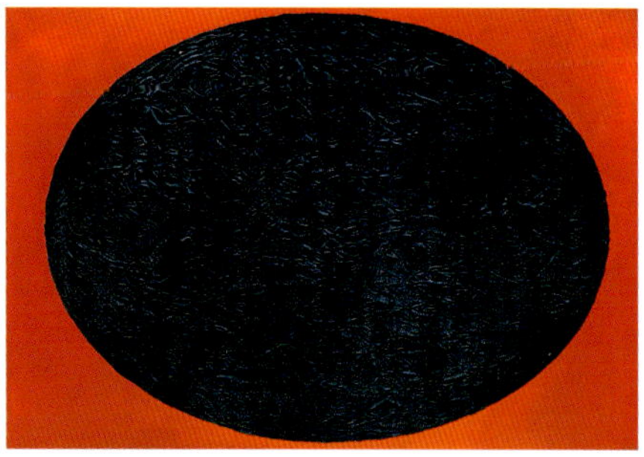

May, Nicholas b.1962
Liminal Ellipse (Orange) 1996
acrylic silicone & metallic powder on canvas
213.5 x 320
ACC209/1998

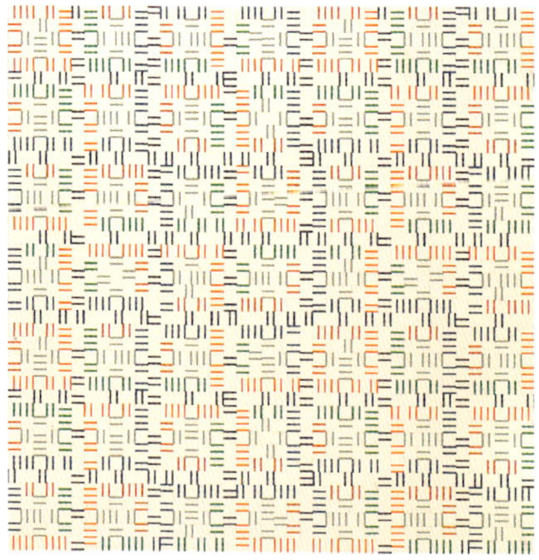

Mayer, Michael John b.1932
Telegraph 1978
acrylic on canvas 152.2 x 152.2
AC 1948

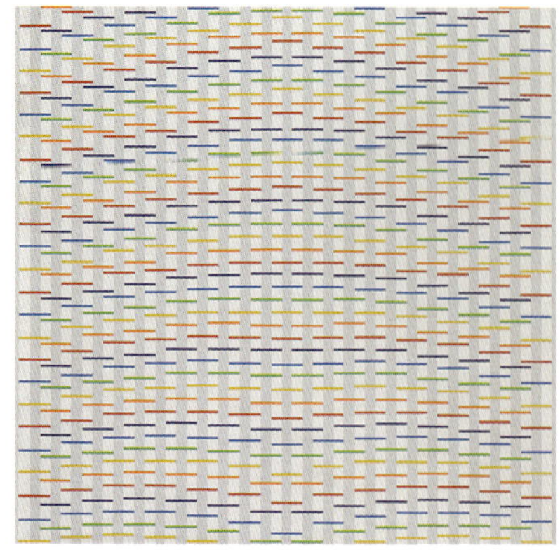

Mayer, Michael John b.1932
The Aura of Joseph 'Cornbread' Thomas 1979
acrylic on canvas 152 x 152.2
AC 3048

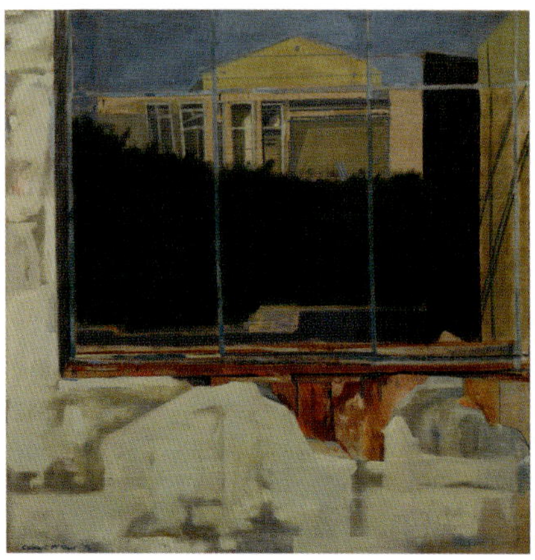

McAleer, Clement b.1949
Dark Hedge 1978
oil on canvas 100.5 x 99
AC 2028

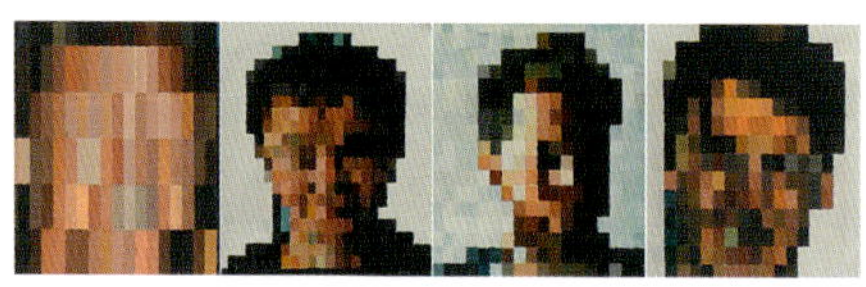

McCann, Paddy b.1963
Cryptbrick 1991
oil on canvas 41.5 x 35.5; 41.5 x 35.5;
41.5 x 35.5; 41.5 x 35.5
ACC85/1991

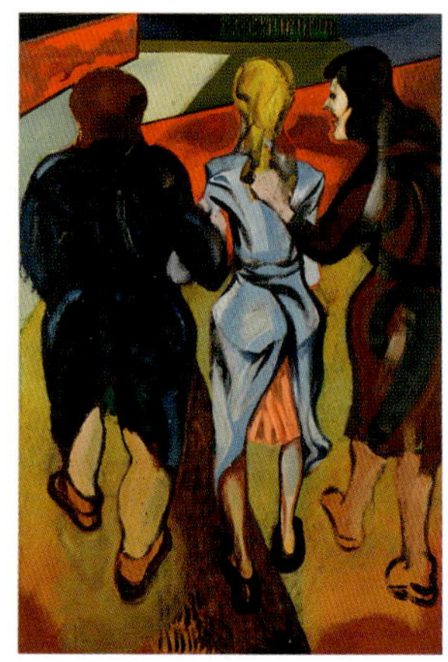

McCracken, John Wilson 1936–1982
Saturday Night 1977
oil on hardboard 183.5 x 122
AC 1840

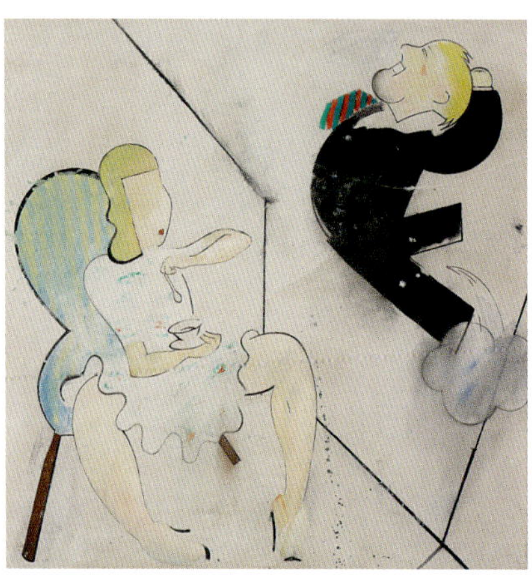

McFadyen, Jock b.1950
Those heady days seemed to last forever, Siegfried jumping around like the big idiot he was 1978
oil on canvas 122.8 x 121.8
AC 2068

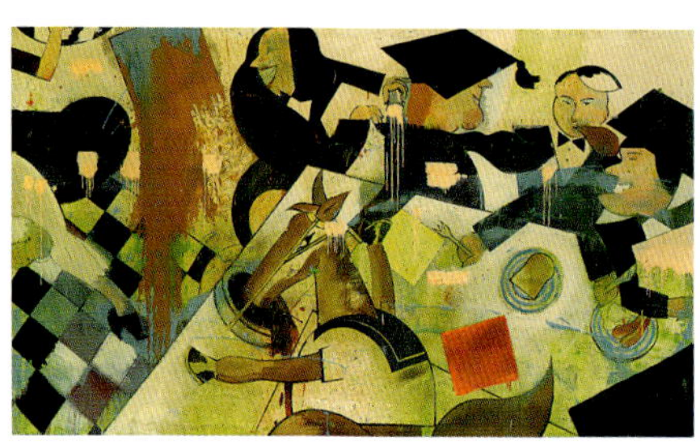

McFadyen, Jock b.1950
The distinguished professors (who couldn't suppress a giggle) and the injustice of ergonomics 1979
oil on canvas 182.9 x 314
AC 2099

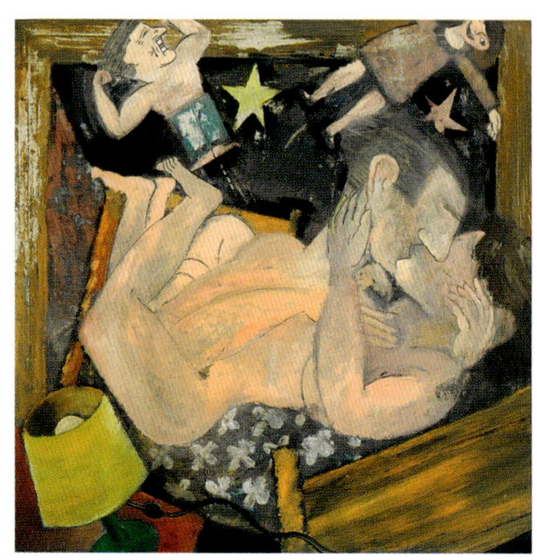

McFadyen, Jock b.1950
In the Bedroom 1981
oil on canvas 123.1 x 124
AC 5058

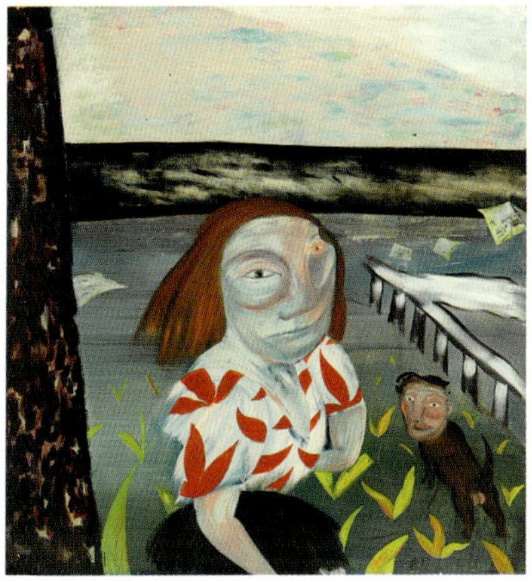

McFadyen, Jock b.1950
Mile End Park 1985
oil on canvas 155 x 147
AC 5422

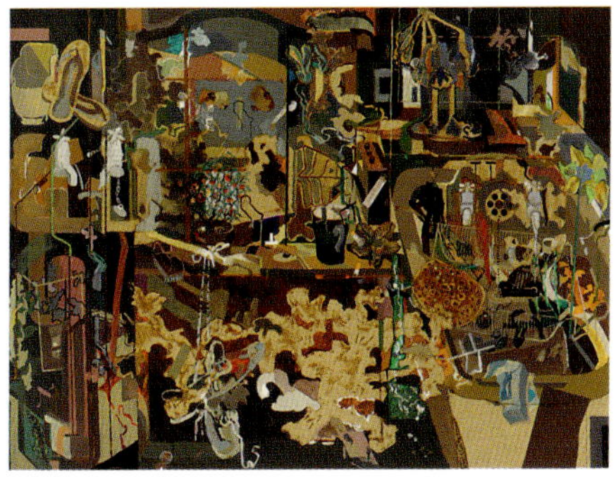

McGrath, Alan b.1948
Bathroom Interior No.6 1976–1978
acrylic & canvas collage on hardboard
91.4 x 122.5
AC 1912

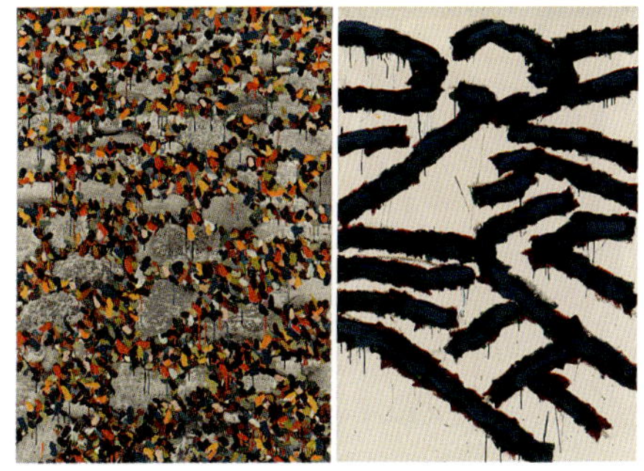

McKeever, Ian b.1946
Islands 8a & 8b 1981 1981
photograph, charcoal & acrylic on paper
151.3 x 104.4; 151.3 x 104.4
AC 4066

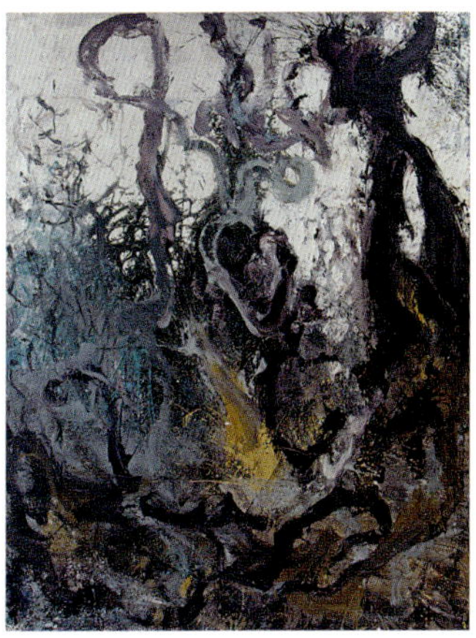

McKeever, Ian b.1946
Caspar's Tree 1986
oil & photograph on canvas 220 x 170
AC 5444

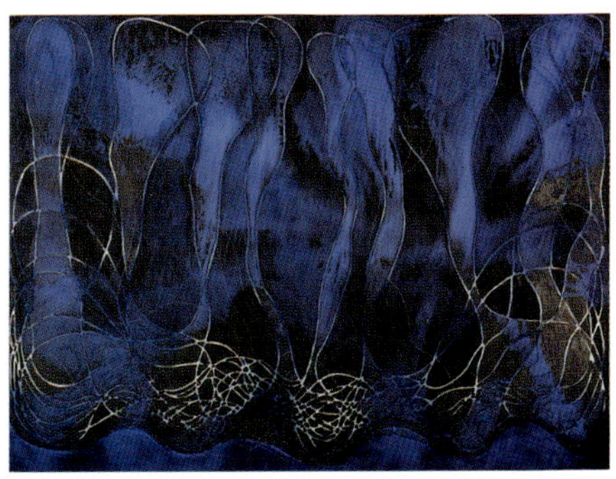

McKeever, Ian b.1946
Assumptio (Murmur) 1998–1999
oil & acrylic on cotton duck 245 x 330
ACC67/1999

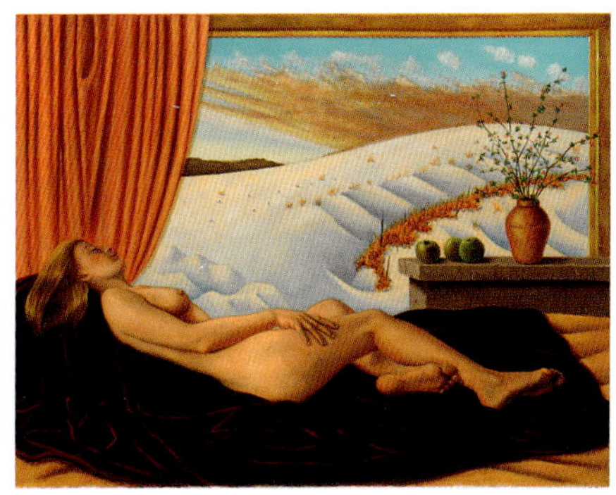

McKenna, Stephen b.1939
Winter 1978–1979
oil on canvas 74.2 x 97.1
AC 2040

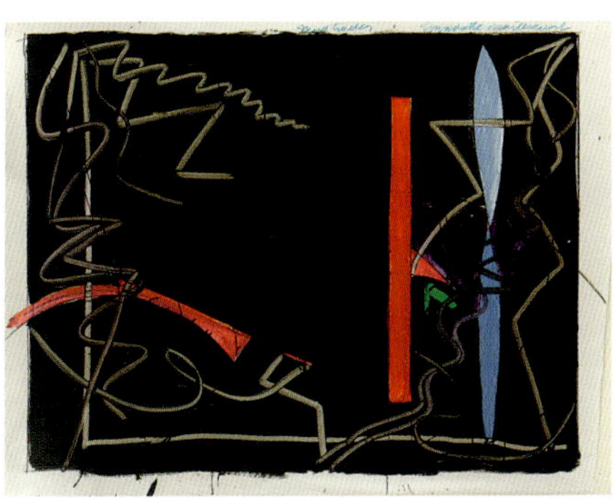

McLean, Bruce b.1944
Sound Tracking towards the Masterwork 1979
acrylic & oil pastel on paper 136 x 179.5
AC 2064

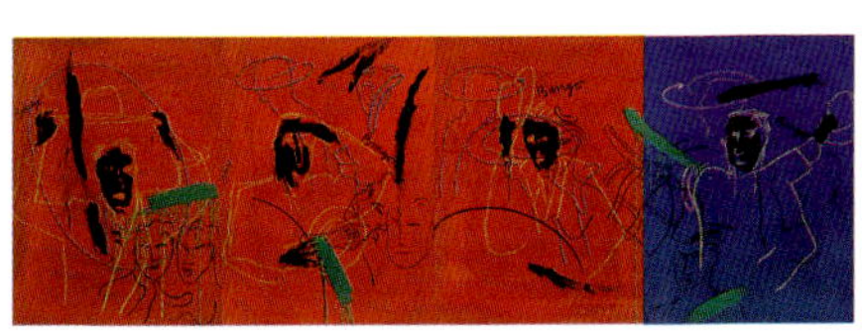

McLean, Bruce b.1944
Bingo Bingo Bango Bongo 1982
wax & acrylic on canvas 200 x 601.4
AC 5280

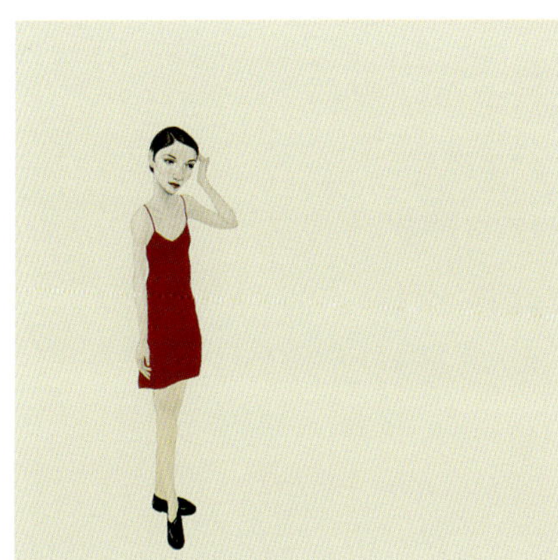

McLean, Ian 1973–2000
Armour jamais 1996
oil on canvas 218 x 218
ACC211/1998

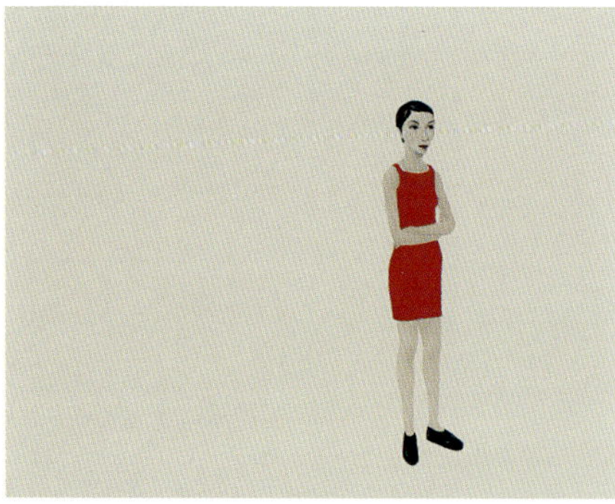

McLean, Ian 1973–2000
Armour rien 1996
oil on canvas 218 x 279
ACC210/1998

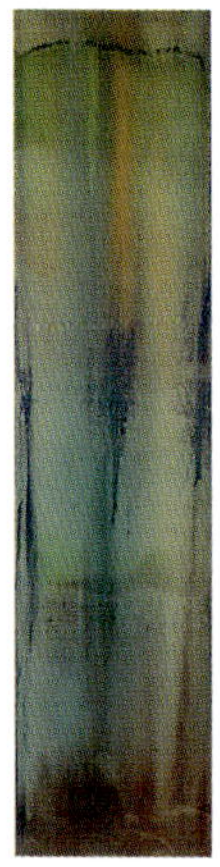

McLean, John b.1939
1969 1969
acrylic on canvas 162.9 x 40.3
AC 1102

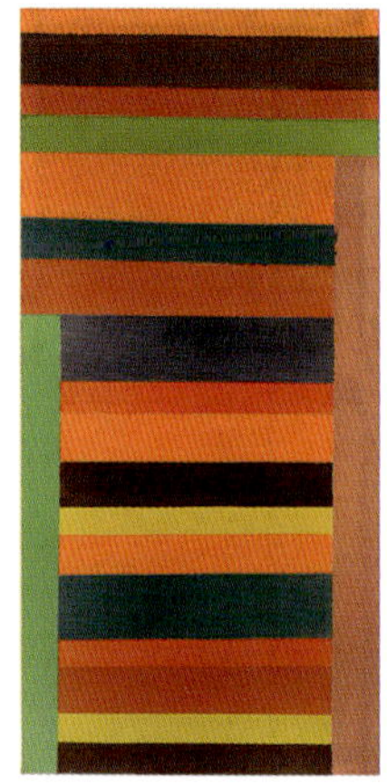

McLean, John b.1939
Pagoda I 1975
acrylic on canvas 186 x 97
AC 1514

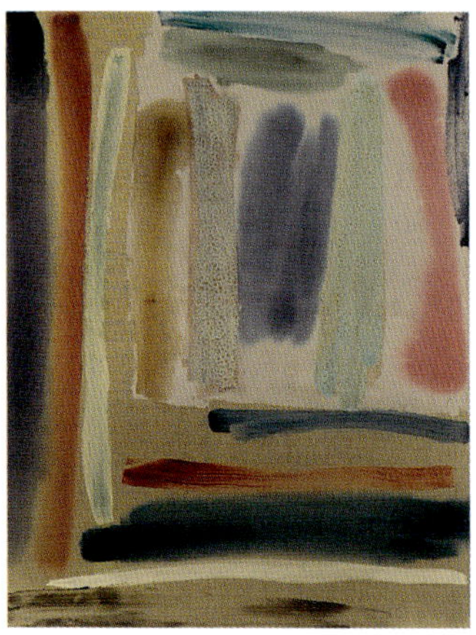

McLean, John b.1939
Grey Granite 1978
acrylic on canvas 203.5 x 158.5
AC 1924

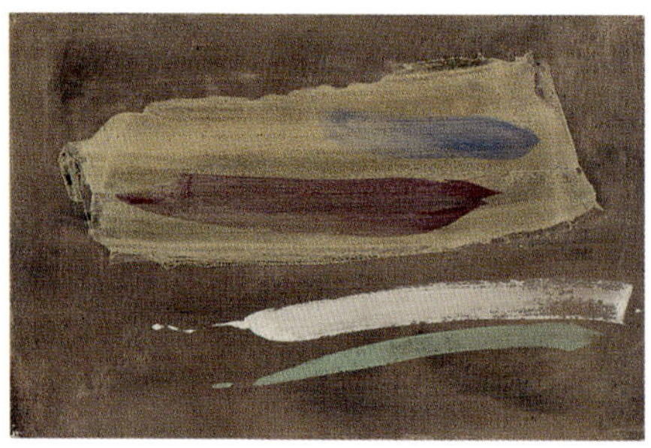

McLean, John b.1939
Breakwater 1981
acrylic on canvas 74.3 x 114.8
AC 5079

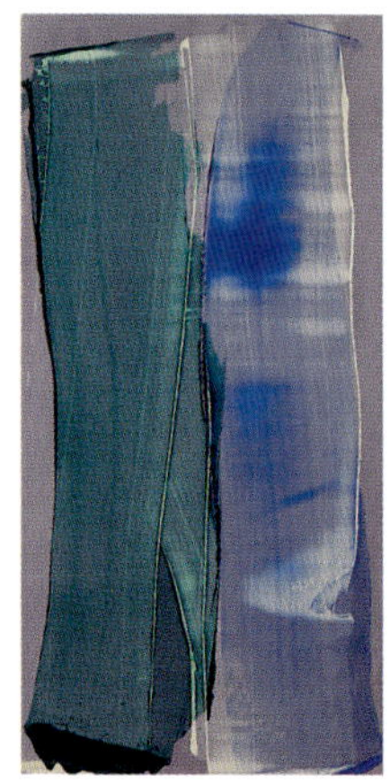

McLean, John b.1939
Neiss Beach II 1981
acrylic on canvas 228.4 x 111.7
AC 5080

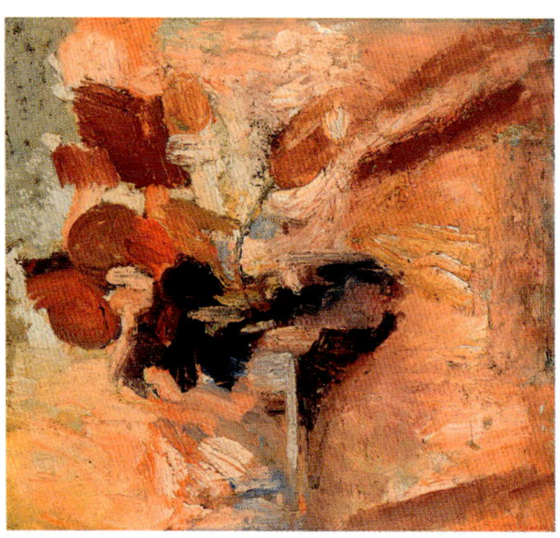

Mead, Dorothy 1928–1975
Flowers 1961
oil on canvas 91.4 x 101.6
AC 616

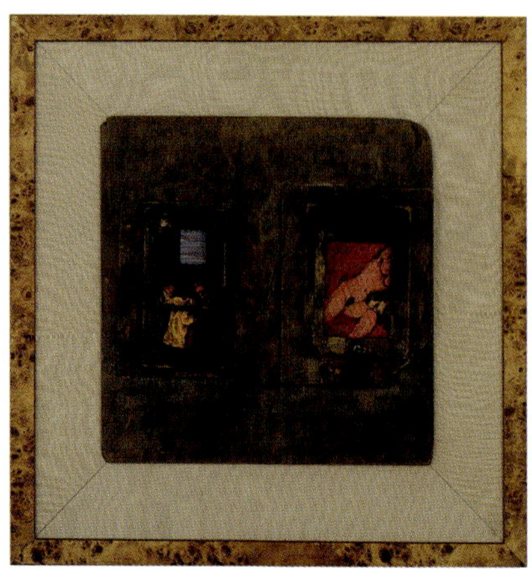

Medalla, David b.1938
Rhapsody of the Dagger and Ammonia Boy (Interior Scene) 1979
acrylic on wood 66.5 x 65.2
AC 4084

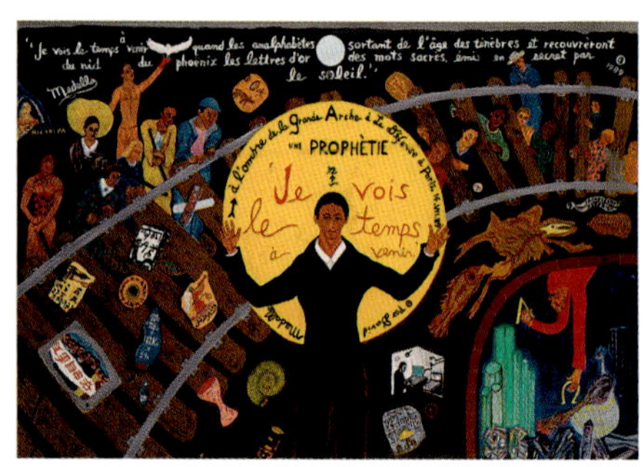

Medalla, David b.1938
A Prophecy 1989
oil on canvas 210 x 310
ACC10/1990

Facing page: Dragicevic, Milena, b.1965, *Opet* (detail), 2002, (p. 43)

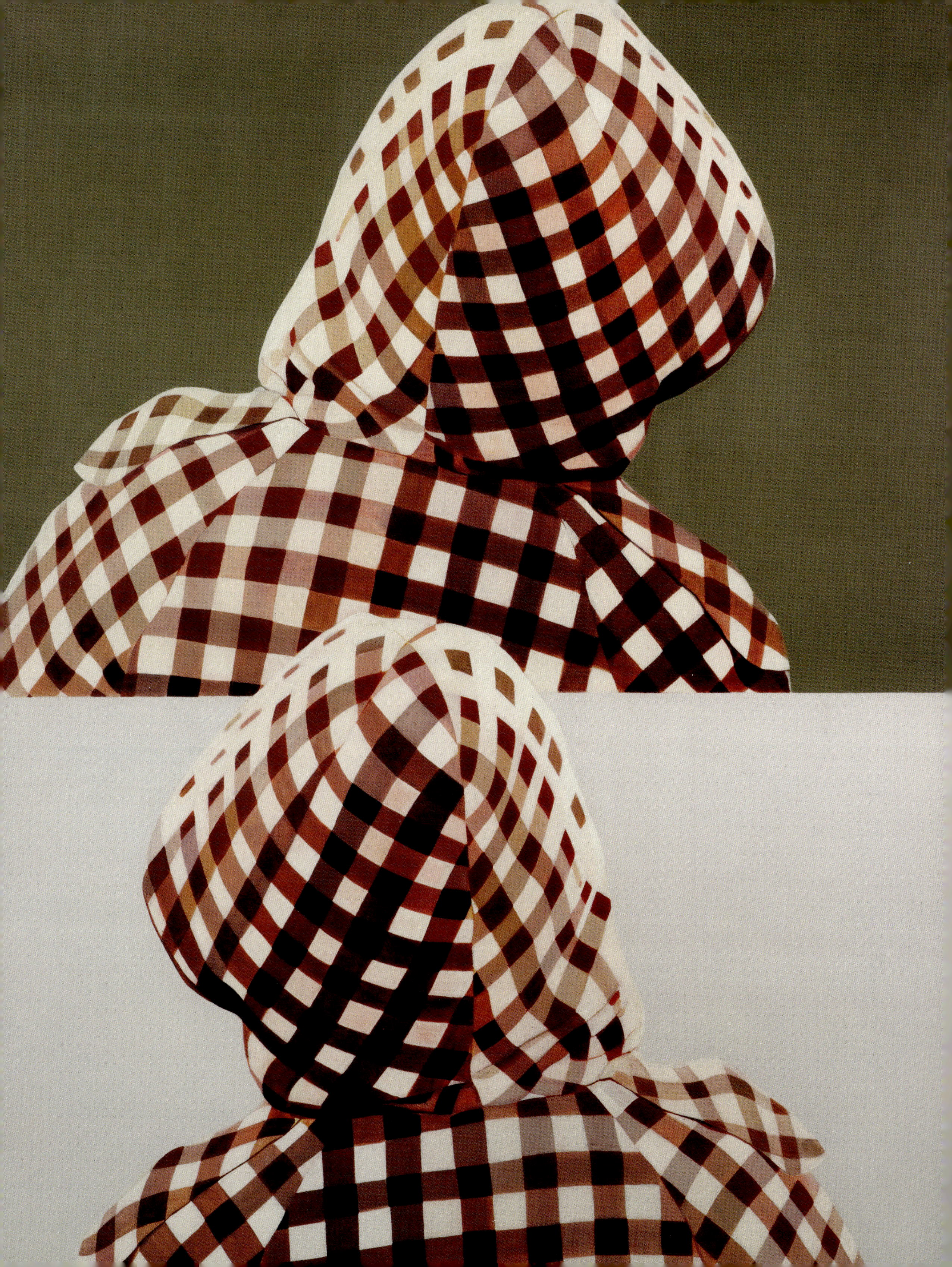

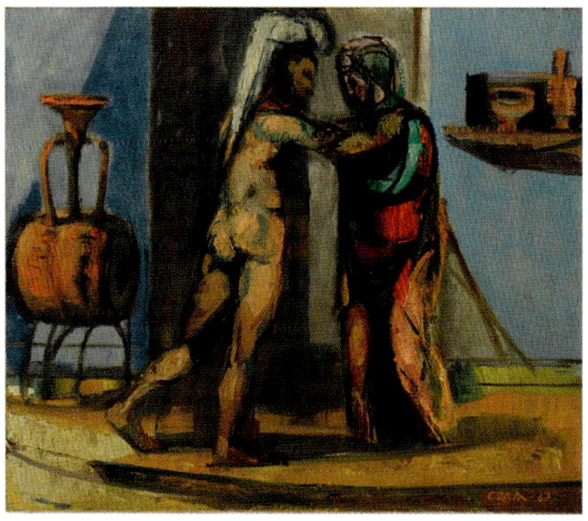

Medley, Robert 1905–1994
Ulysses and Penelope 1947
oil on canvas 48.3 x 60.3
AC 21

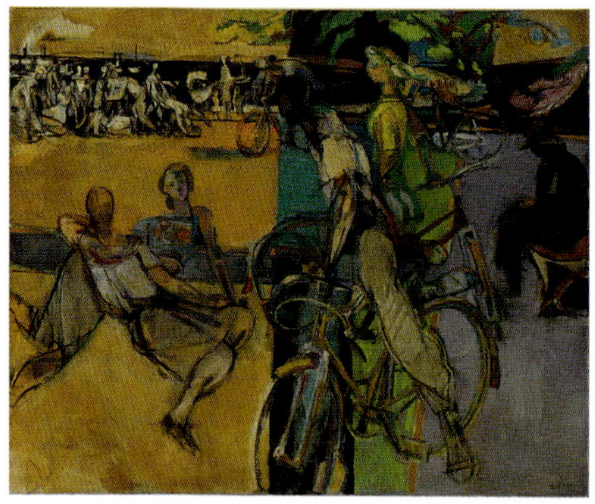

Medley, Robert 1905–1994
Summer Eclogue 1951
oil on canvas 128.5 x 160
AC 285

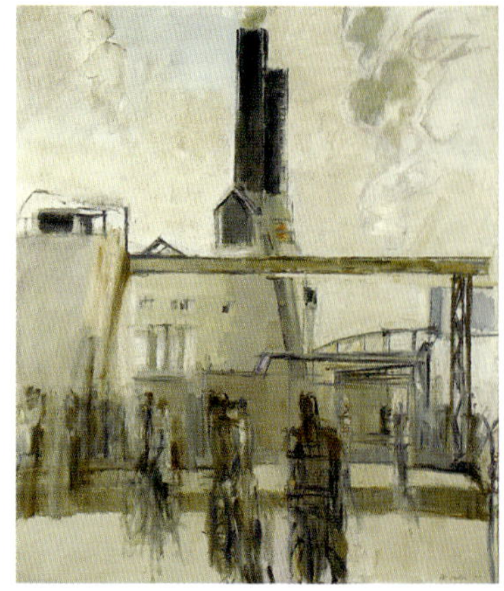

Medley, Robert 1905–1994
Bowaters Paper Works, Gravesend, Kent 1955
oil on canvas 126 x 106
AC 401

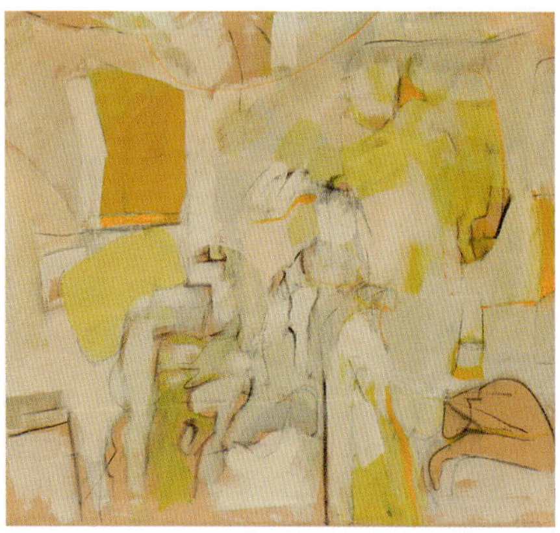

Medley, Robert 1905–1994
Yellow and White Figuration 1965
oil on canvas 99 x 109
ACA 72

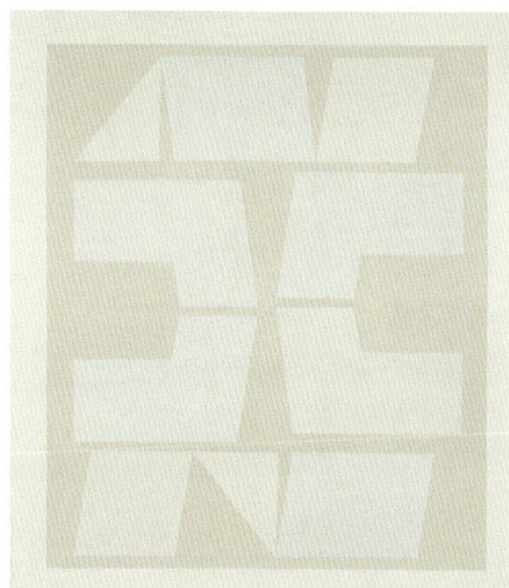

Medley, Robert 1905–1994
China 1973
acrylic on canvas 182.9 x 162.6
AC 1370

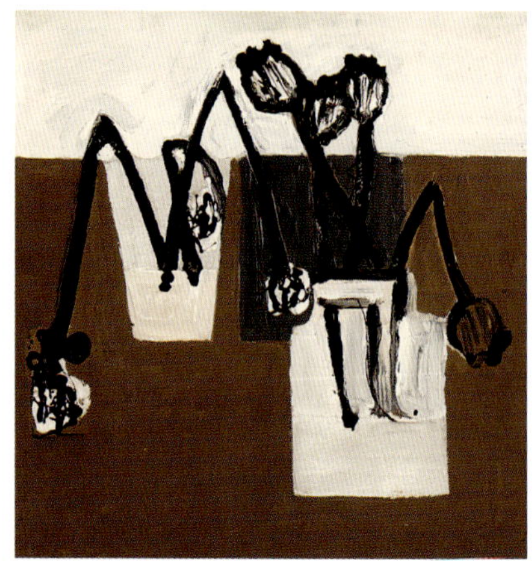

Mellis, Margaret 1914–2009
Seeding Flowers 1957
oil on board 52.7 x 49.8
AC 5022

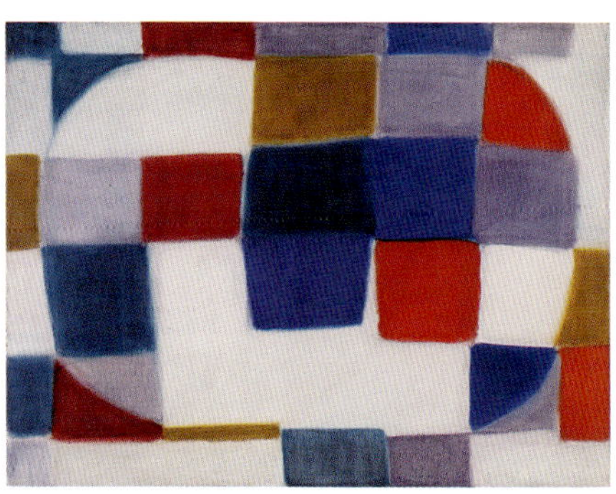

Mellis, Margaret 1914–2009
Two Circles (Red, Blue, Yellow, Violet and White) 1964
oil on board 91.4 x 121.9
AC 733

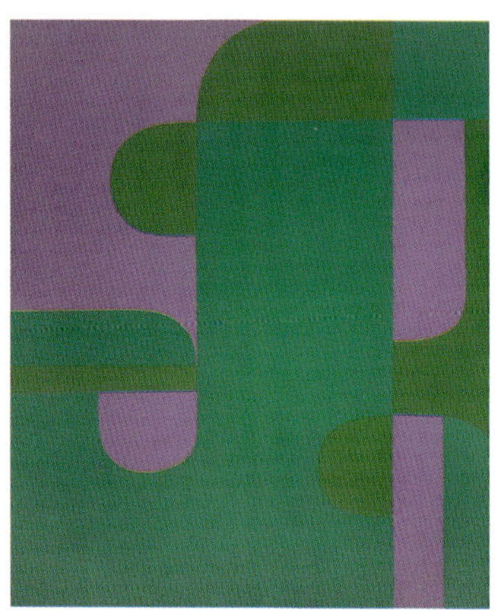

Mellis, Margaret 1914–2009
Green and Violet 1967
oil on cotton duck 152 x 122
AC 1075

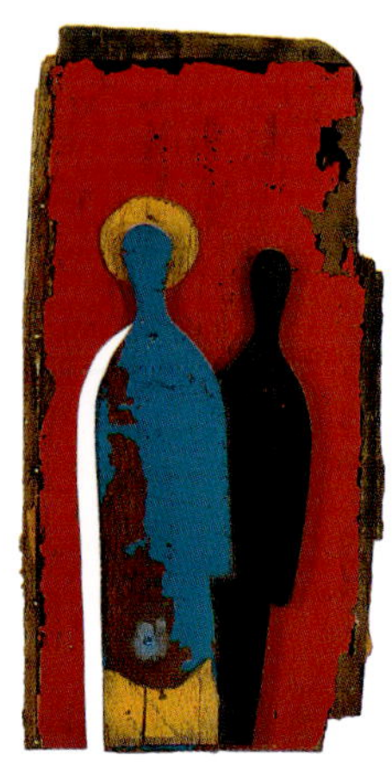

Mellis, Margaret 1914–2009
Temptation 1986
paint on wood relief 59.1 x 30.1
AC 5469

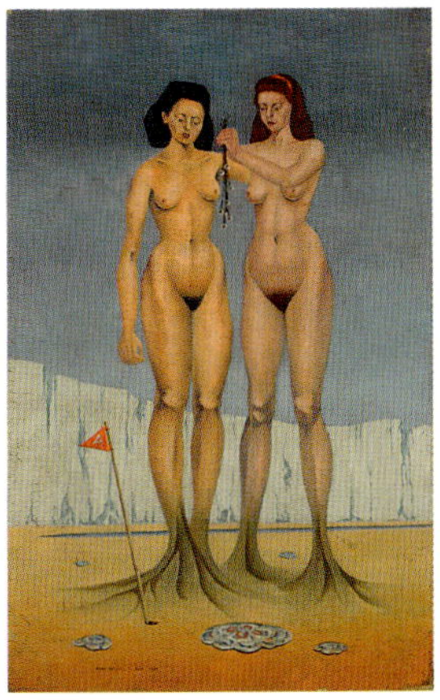

Mellor, Oscar 1921–2005
A Small Bunch of Eyes 1948
oil on canvas 57 x 36.5
AC 4027

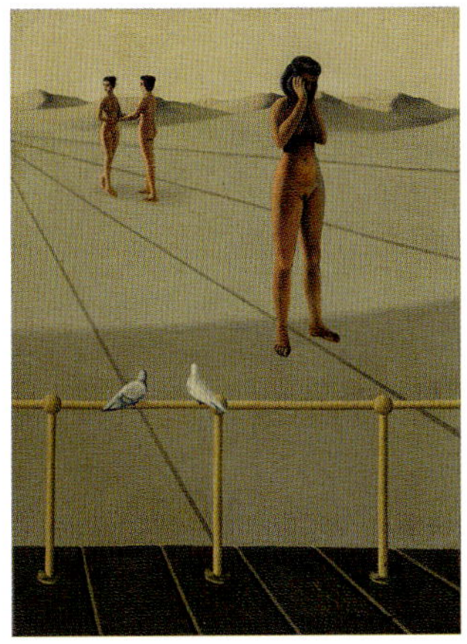

Mellor, Oscar 1921–2005
The Inquisitors 1955
oil on canvas 40.5 x 30
AC 4029

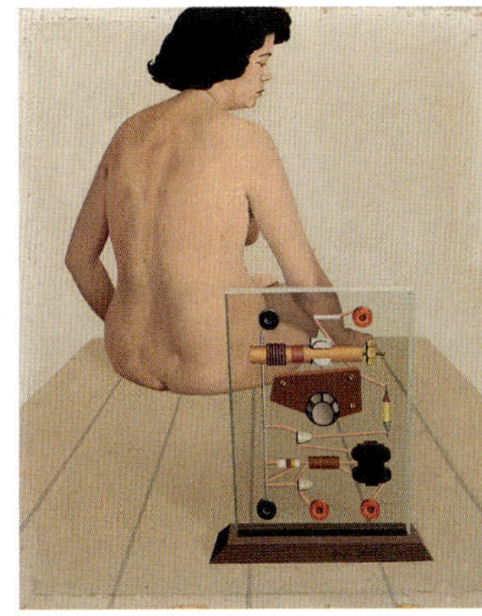

Mellor, Oscar 1921–2005
The Prototype 1957
oil on board 29.5 x 25
AC 4031

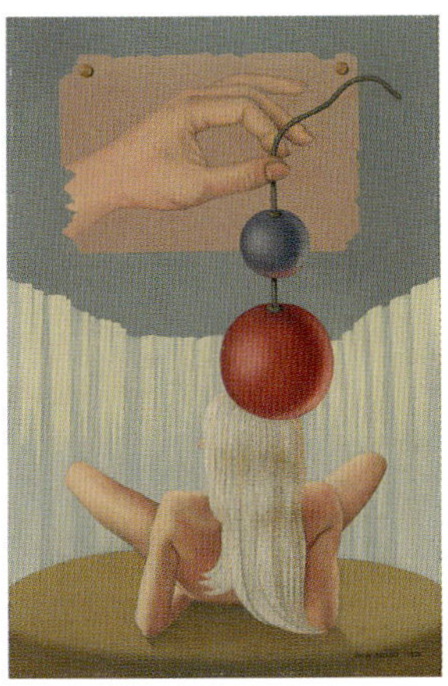

Mellor, Oscar 1921–2005
The Pursuit of Pleasure 1972
oil on board 63 x 40
AC 4026

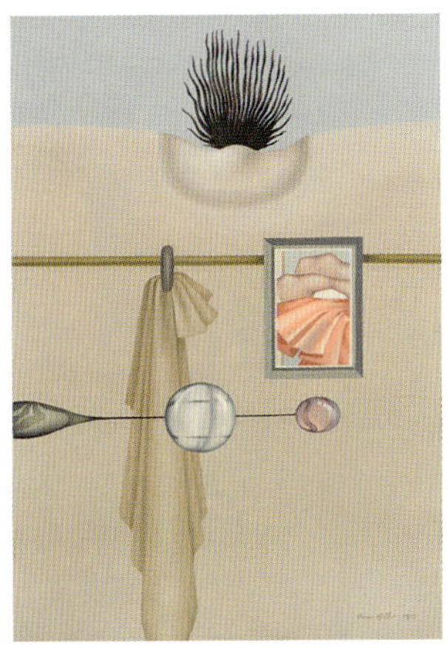

Mellor, Oscar 1921–2005
When the Leaves Fall 1972
oil on canvas 66 x 45.5
AC 4025

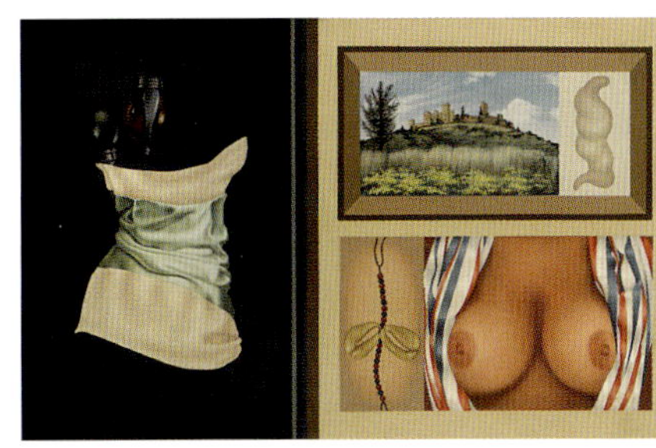

Mellor, Oscar 1921–2005
La Bastide 1973
oil on canvas 51 x 81.5
AC 4024

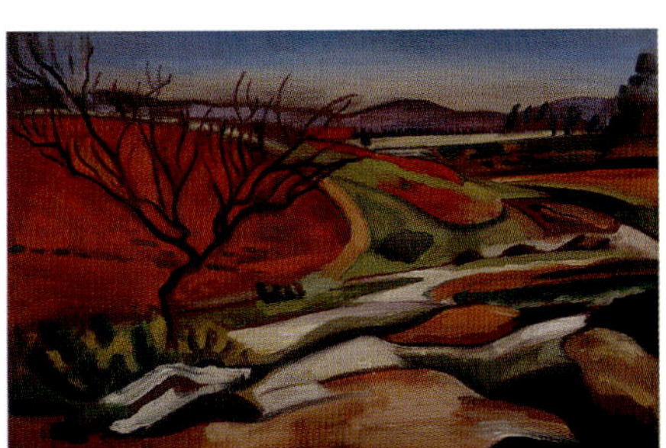

Meninsky, Bernard 1891–1950
Andalusian Landscape c.1937
oil on canvas 40.6 x 61
AC 474

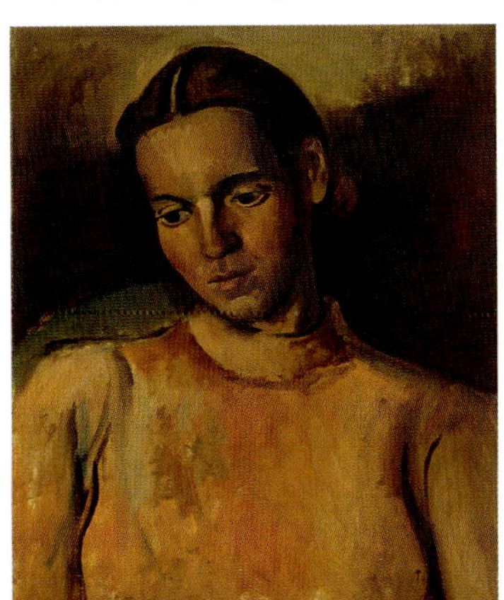

Meninsky, Bernard 1891–1950
Portrait of a Girl 1942
oil on canvas 61 x 50.8
AC 75

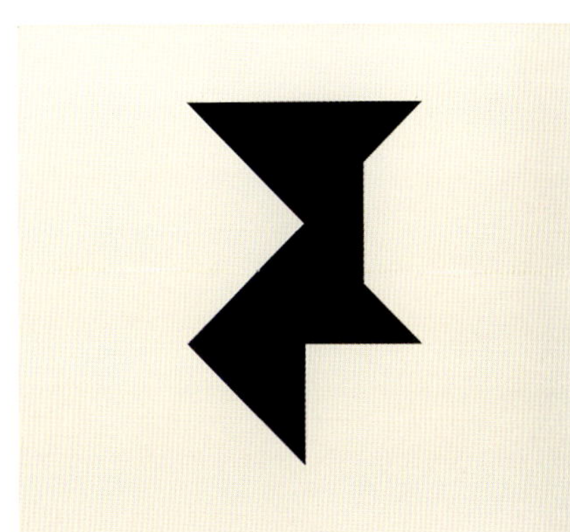

Meyrick, George b.1953
Drawing 1982 1982
ink, acrylic & gouache on paper 66.9 x 74.6
AC 5128

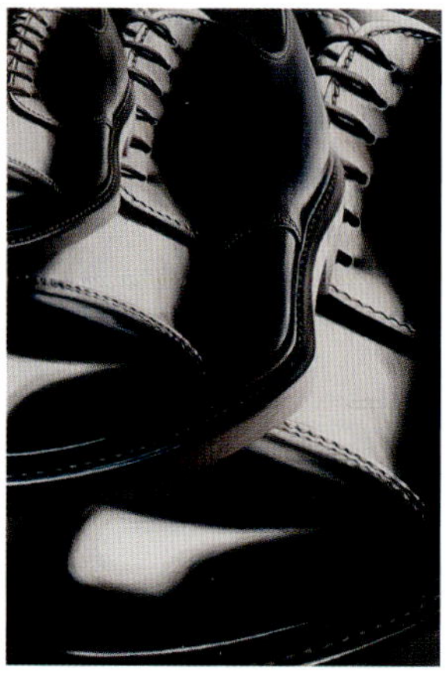

Michael, Alan b.1967
Untitled 2006
oil on canvas 82 x 57
ACC28/2006

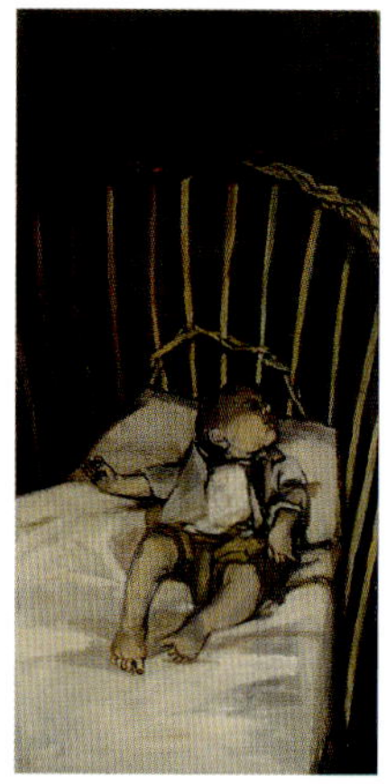

Middleditch, Edward 1923–1987
Baby 1952
oil on board 121.5 x 60.2
AC 320

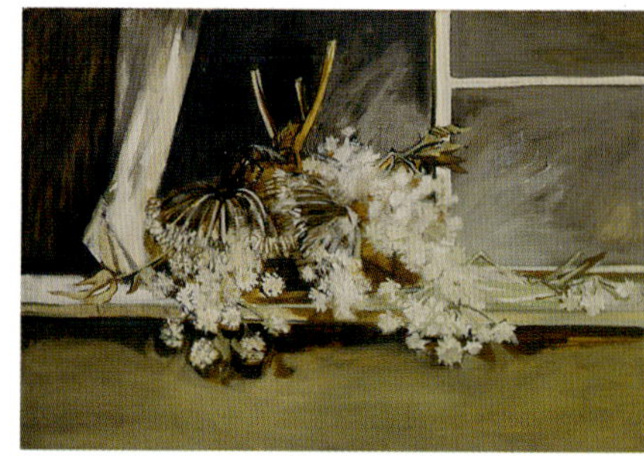

Middleditch, Edward 1923–1987
Cow Parsley 1955
oil on canvas 91.4 x 137.2
AC 392

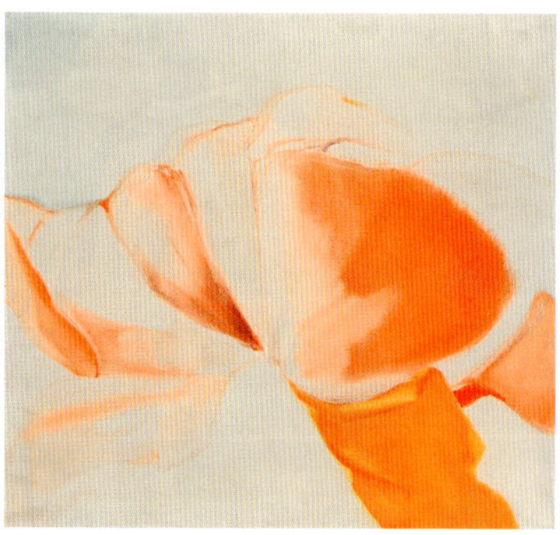

Middleditch, Edward 1923–1987
Rose, Pink 1965
oil on canvas 91.4 x 101.6
ACA 30

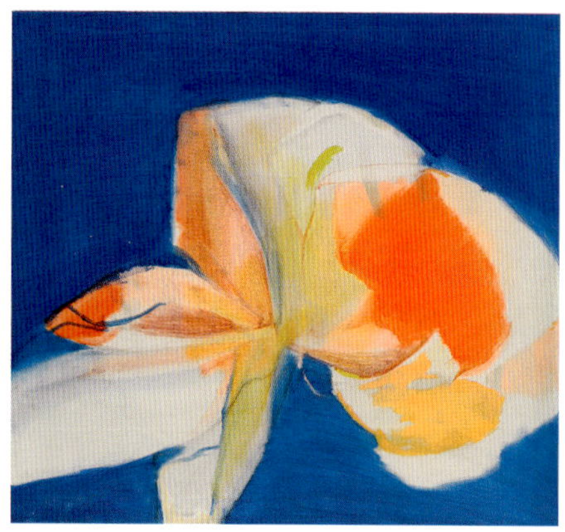

Middleditch, Edward 1923–1987
Rose, Red and Blue 1965
oil on canvas 91.4 x 101.6
ACA 31

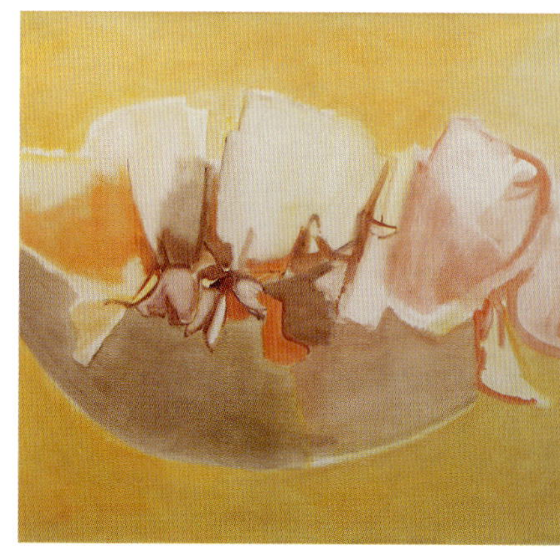

Middleditch, Edward 1923–1987
Still Life 1965
oil on canvas 142.2 x 152.4
AC 868/ACA 12

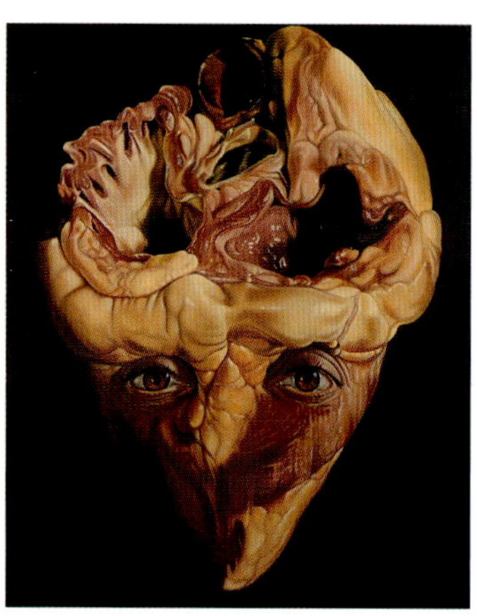

Miller, Alain b.1963
On My Way to Paradise 1997
oil on canvas 235 x 195
ACC76/1997

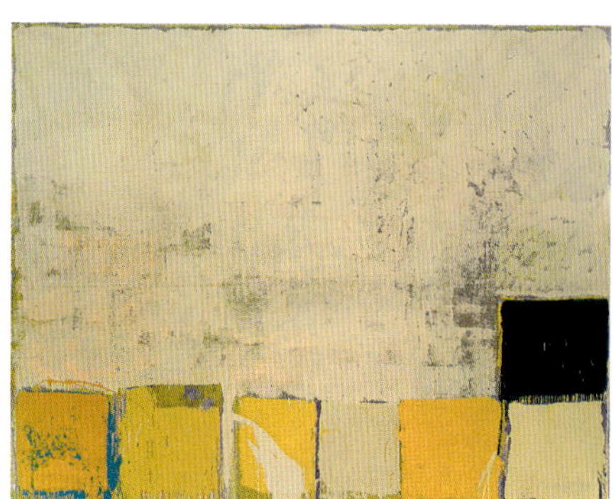

Miller, Alan 1941–2009
Untitled 1971–72 1971–1972
acrylic on canvas 261 x 339
AC 1186

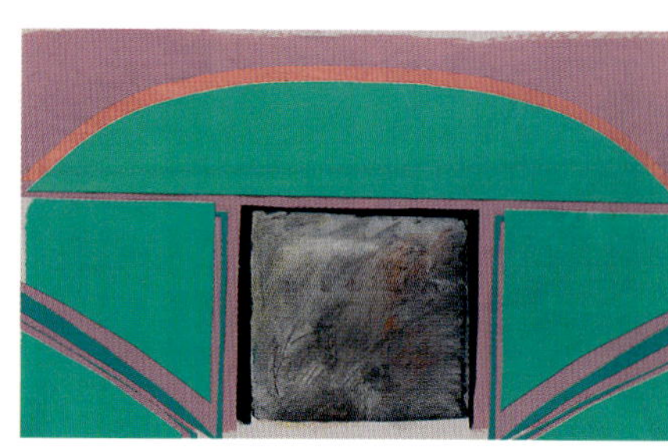

Miller, Alan 1941–2009
Collage I (Untitled) 1973
acrylic on paper collage 83.8 x 141.6
AC 1372

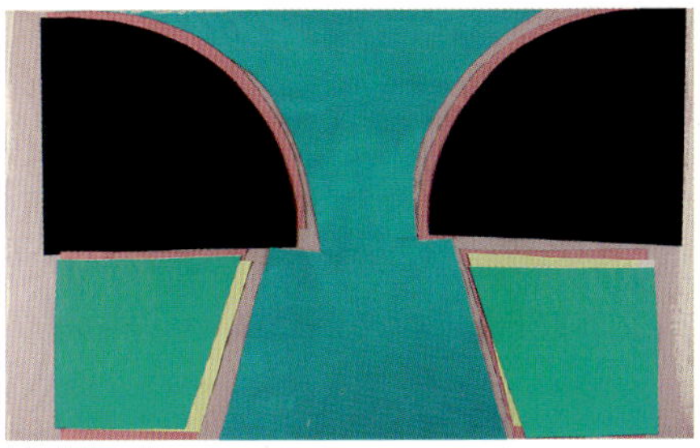

Miller, Alan 1941–2009
Collage II (Untitled) 1973
acrylic on paper collage 90.8 x 151.8
AC 1373

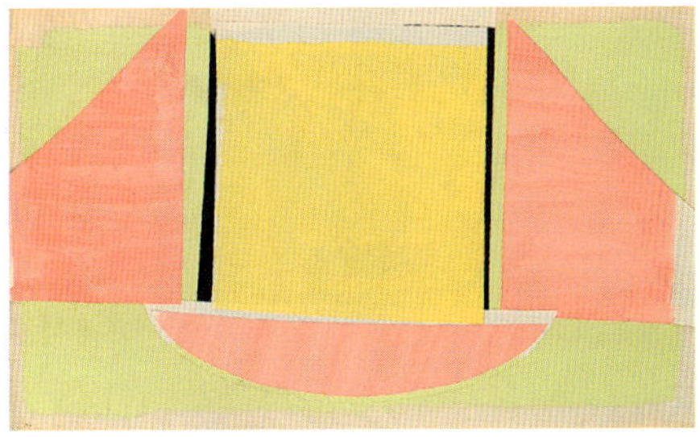

Miller, Alan 1941–2009
Collage III (Untitled) 1973
acrylic on paper collage 90.5 x 152
AC 1374

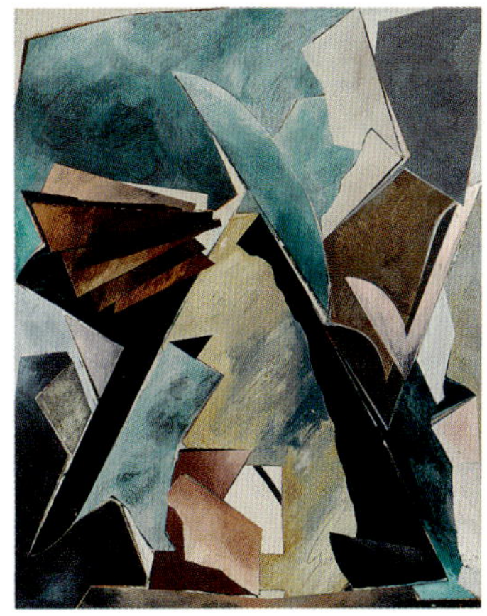

Miller, Alan 1941–2009
For P. S. 1975–1976
acrylic on canvas 303 x 242.3
AC 1675

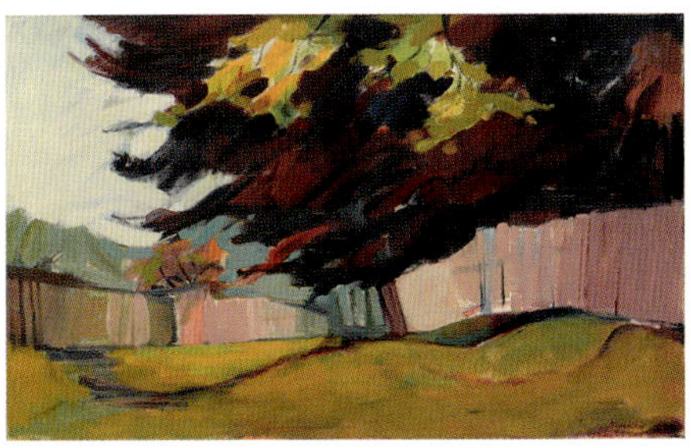

Millichip, Paul b.1929
Oving Footpath 1977
oil on canvas 70 x 101.6
AC 2025

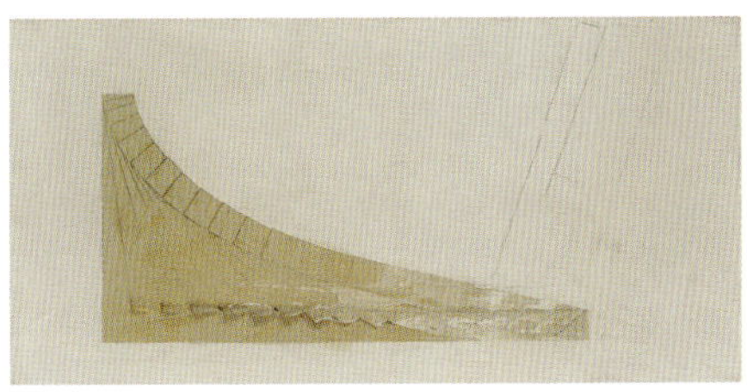

Milow, Keith b.1945
1 2 3 4 5 6 … A 1970
acrylic on canvas 121.5 x 243.5
AC 1104

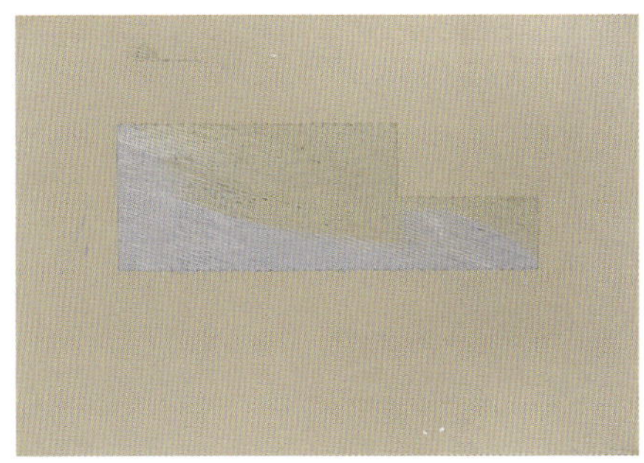

Milow, Keith b.1945
Grey 1 1971
acrylic on card 53.3 x 82.5
AC 1174

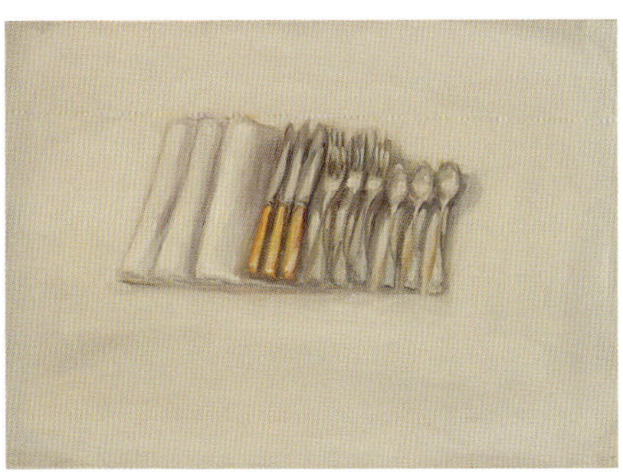

Milroy, Lisa b.1959
Silverware 1983
oil on canvas 65.5 x 90.5
AC 5342

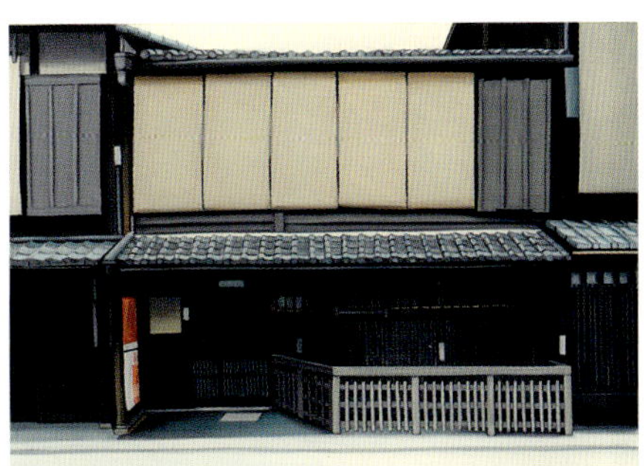

Milroy, Lisa b.1959
Kyoto House 1994
oil on canvas 71.5 x 99.2
ACC55/1995

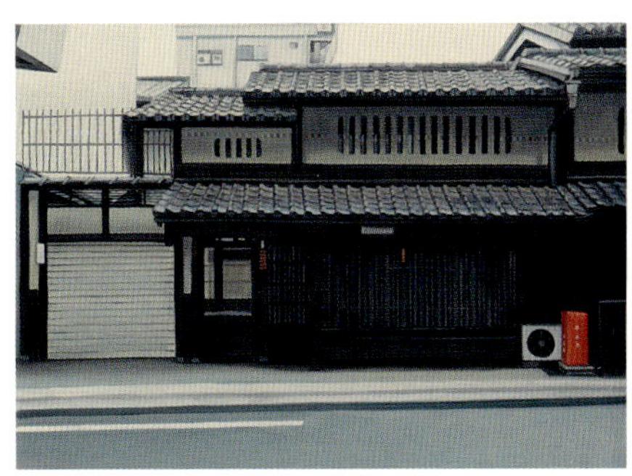

Milroy, Lisa b.1959
Kyoto House 1994
oil on canvas 71.5 x 99.2
ACC56/1995

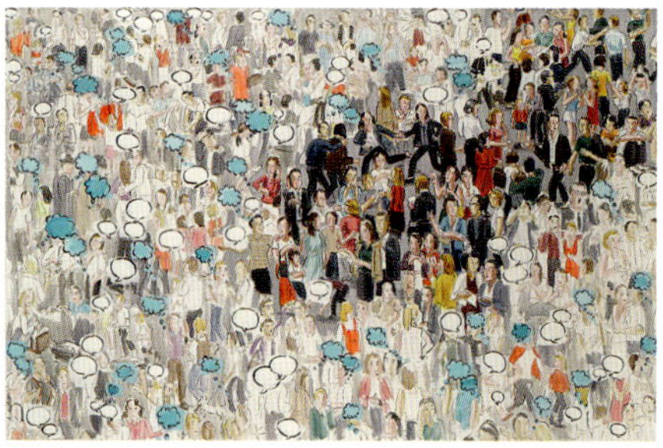

Milroy, Lisa b.1959
Doing, Thinking, Speaking 2000
oil & acrylic on canvas 193 x 305
ACC47/2000

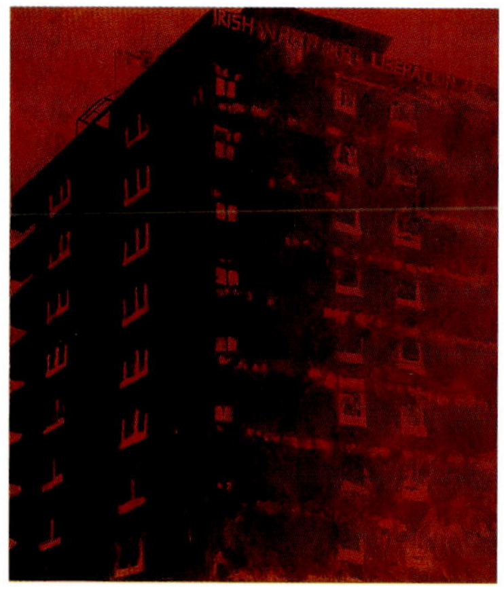

Minnis, Michael b.1964
Irish Liberation in Shades of Red 1989
oil on canvas 266.7 x 233.5
ACC3/1991

Minnis, Michael b.1964
Untitled 1989
oil on canvas 274.3 x 228.6
ACC21/1990

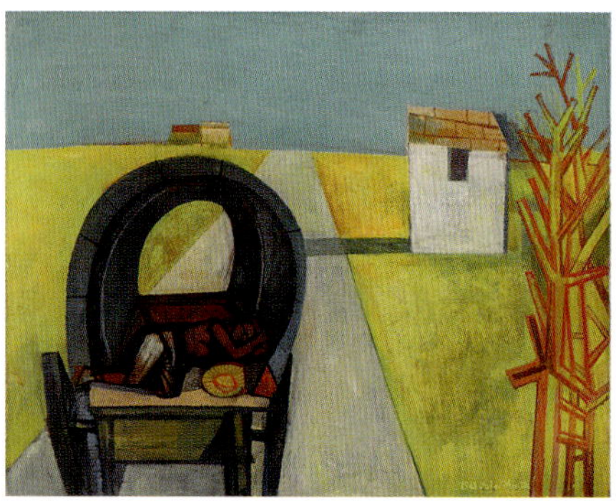

Minton, John 1917–1957
The Road to Valencia 1949
oil on canvas 71.1 x 91.4
AC 153

Mitchell, John b.1942
'Gate' 1976
charcoal & tempera on paper 78 x 153.4
AC 1810

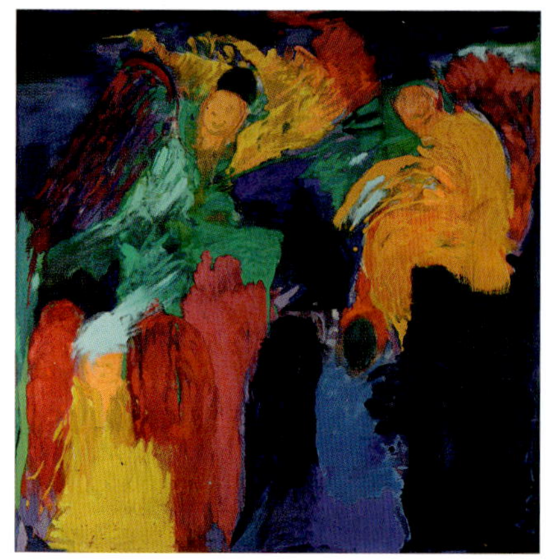

Mitha, Alnoor b.1961
Ascension 1983
oil on canvas 121.5 x 121.5
ACC51/1995

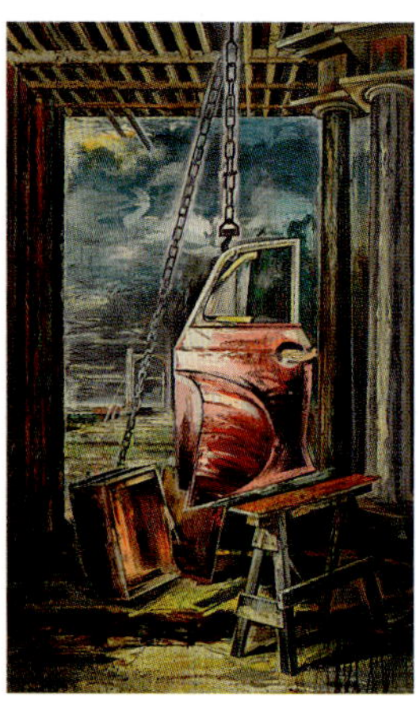

Monks, John Christopher b.1954
Car Door in a Landscape 1989–1990
oil on canvas 228.6 x 152.4
ACC1/1990

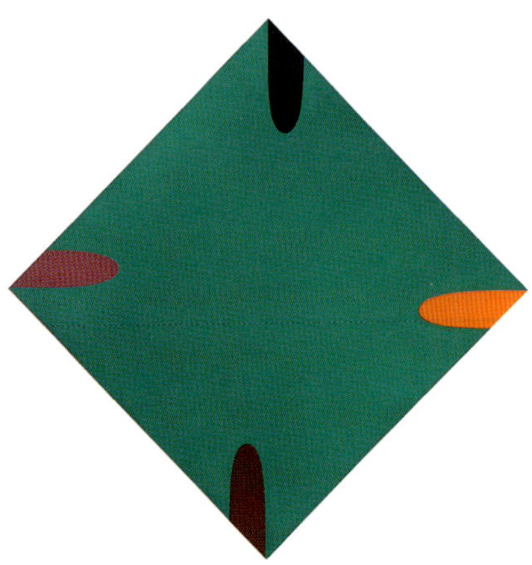

Moon, Jeremy 1934–1973
Green Chariot 1965
acrylic on canvas 142.2 x 142.2
AC 879

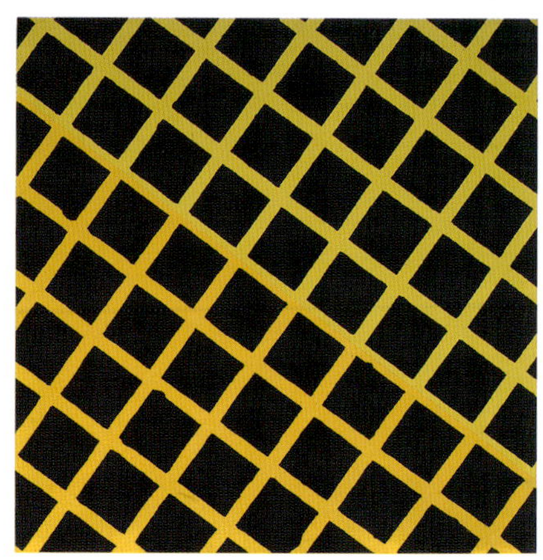

Moon, Jeremy 1934–1973
No.11/68 1968
acrylic on canvas 91.4 x 91.4
AC 1379

Moon, Mick b.1937
Untitled (1968) 1968
acrylic on board 140.1 x 350
AC 991

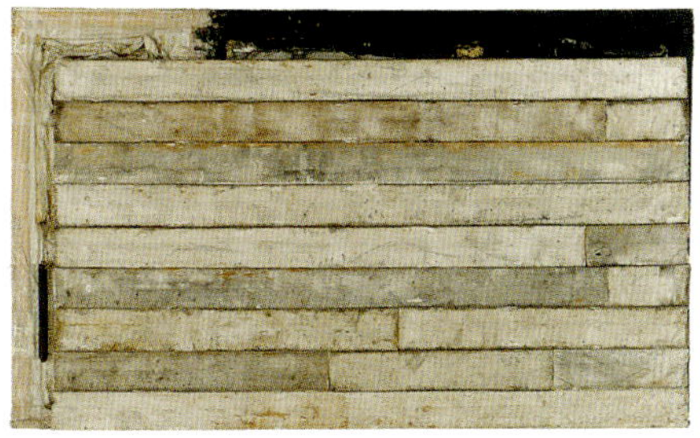

Moon, Mick b.1937
Low Light 1978
acrylic on unbleached calico 174 x 292.5
AC 1963

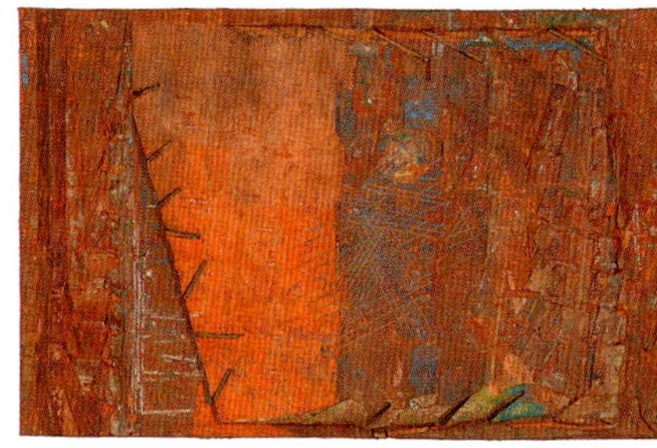

Moon, Mick b.1937
First Floor 1980
acrylic & calico with wood 228.6 x 363.2
AC 4044

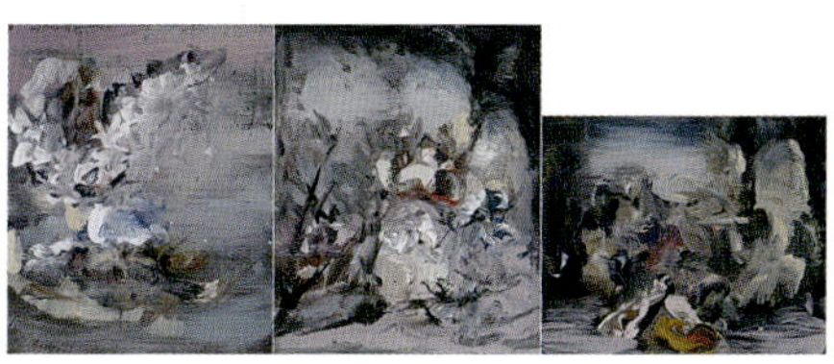

Moran, Katy b.1975
Freddy's Friends 2006
acrylic on canvas 117.2 x 46; 117.2 x 46; 46 x 117.2
ACC25/2006

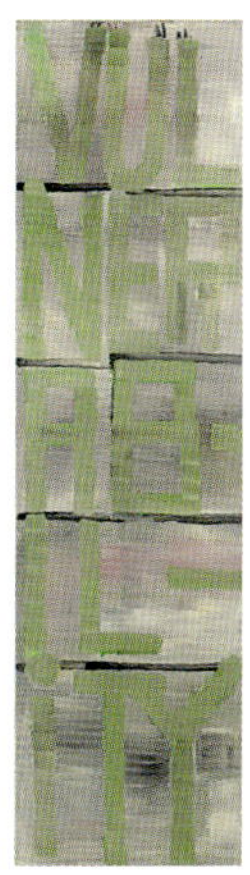

Morgan, Tony 1938–2005
Vulnerability 1996
oil & acrylic on canvas 220 x 61
ACC28/1999

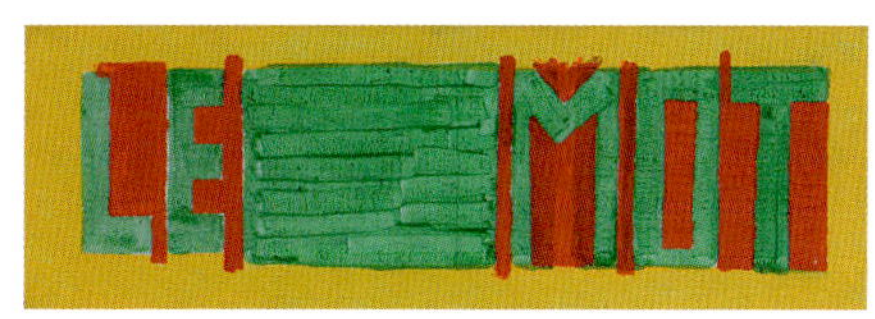

Morgan, Tony 1938–2005
Le mot 1997
oil & acrylic on canvas 24.5 x 75
ACC46/1999

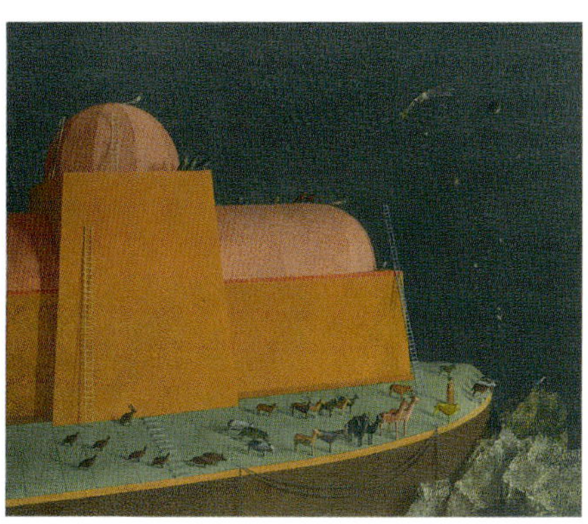

Morley, John b.1942
Noah's Ark 1977
oil on canvas 50.5 x 61
AC 3076

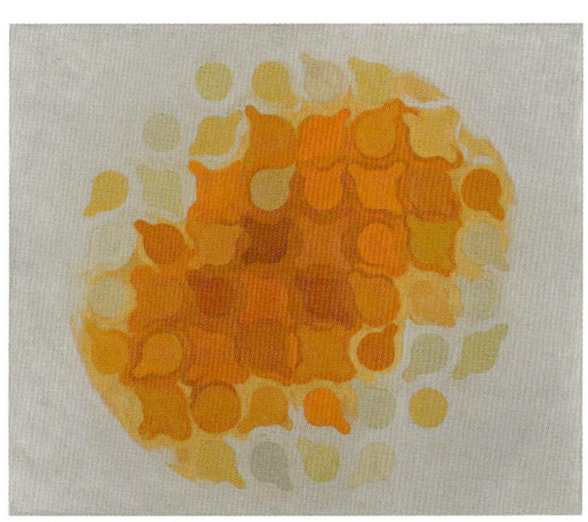

Morrell, Peter John b.1931
Spot 1964
oil on canvas 63.5 x 76.2
AC 754

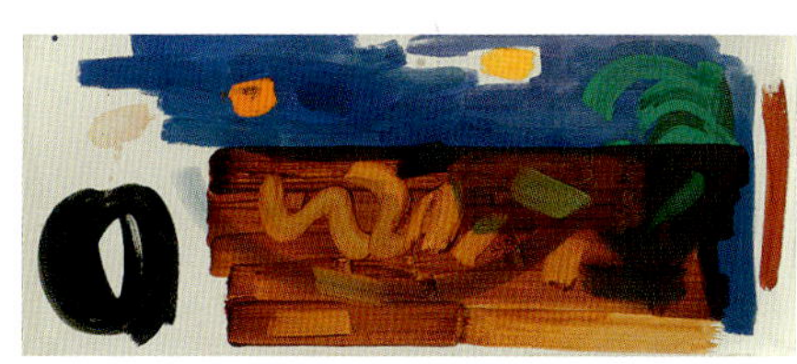

Morris, Mali b.1945
A Vision of the Mermaids 1983
acrylic on canvas 61 x 152.5
AC 5230

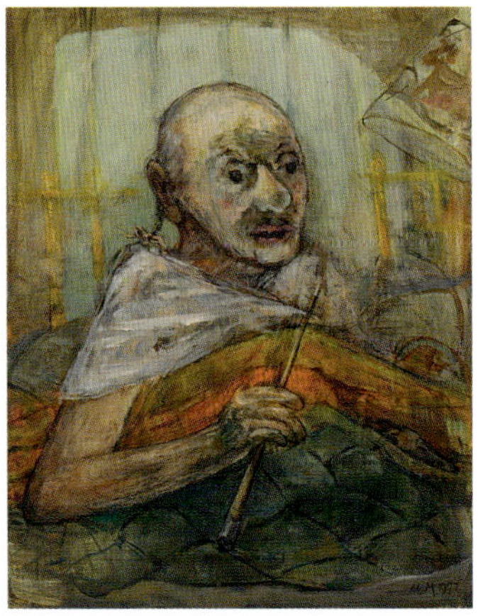

Motesiczky, Marie Louise von 1906–1996
Old Lady with a Baton 1977
oil on canvas 76.4 x 60.7
AC 5108

Moyes, James b.1937
SA5/2 1967
oil on canvas 76.2 x 76.2
AC 1100

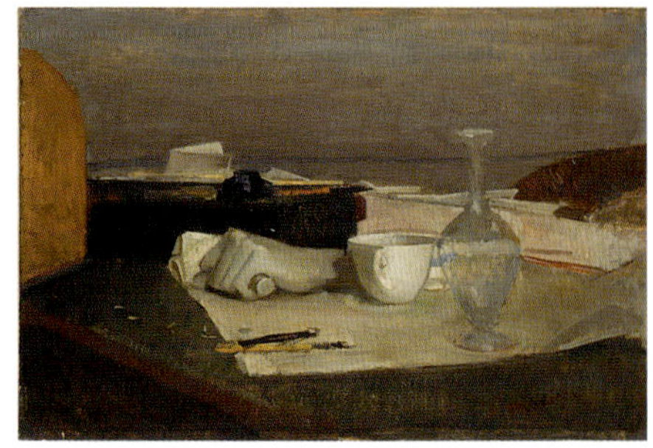

Moynihan, Rodrigo 1910–1990
The Office Desk 1951
oil on canvas 40.6 x 61
AC 210

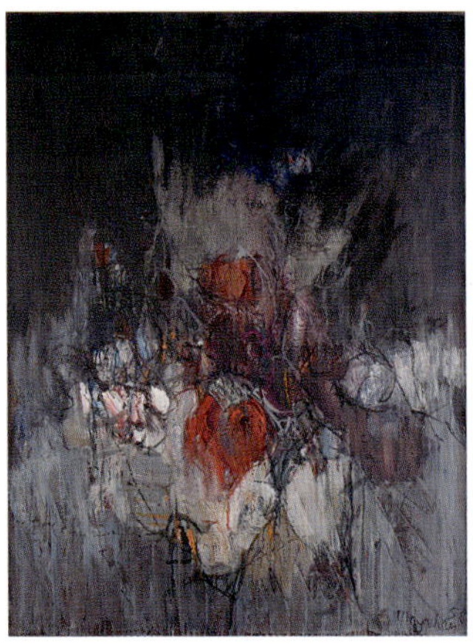

Moynihan, Rodrigo 1910–1990
Dark on White and Pink 1958
oil on canvas 115.5 x 89
AC 454

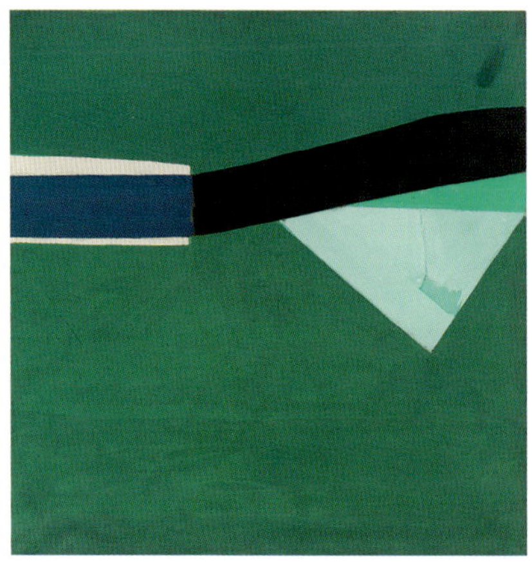

Moynihan, Rodrigo 1910–1990
Painting 12 1966
oil on canvas 100.5 x 100.2
AC 897

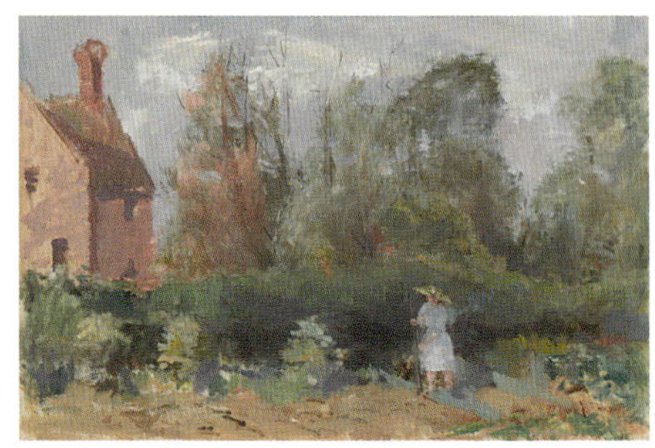

Moynihan, Rodrigo 1910–1990
The Garden
oil on canvas 49 x 74.5
AC 98

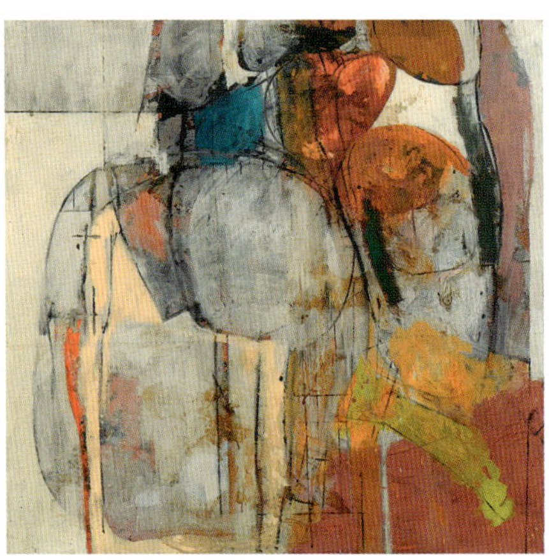

Mundy, Henry b.1919
Weathered 1959
oil on board 152 x 159
AC 534

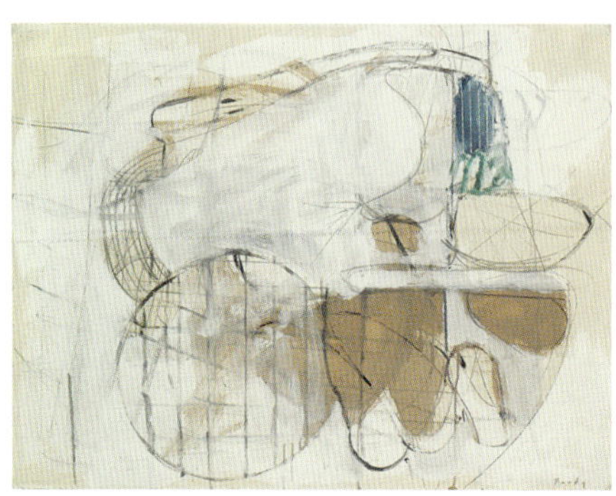

Mundy, Henry b.1919
Composition 1962
oil on paper 55.8 x 75.5
AC 627

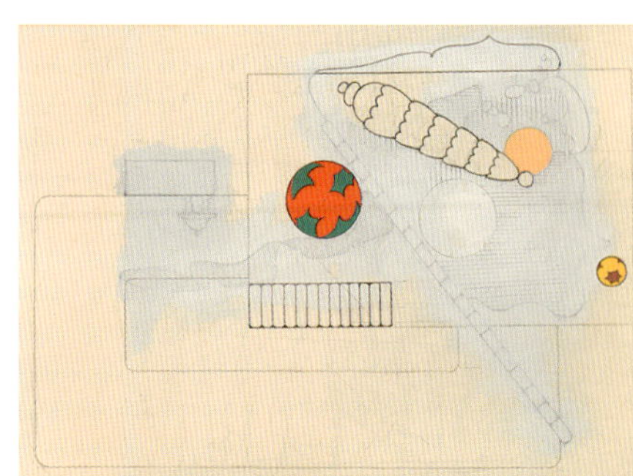

Mundy, Henry b.1919
Jumna 1966
tempera, pencil, watercolour & collage on paper 102.9 x 139.7
ACA 73

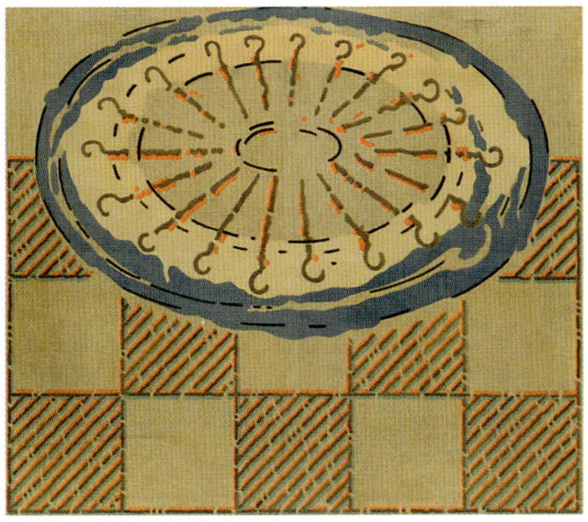

Mundy, Henry b.1919
Wizzer 1969
acrylic on canvas 182.9 x 213.4
AC 943

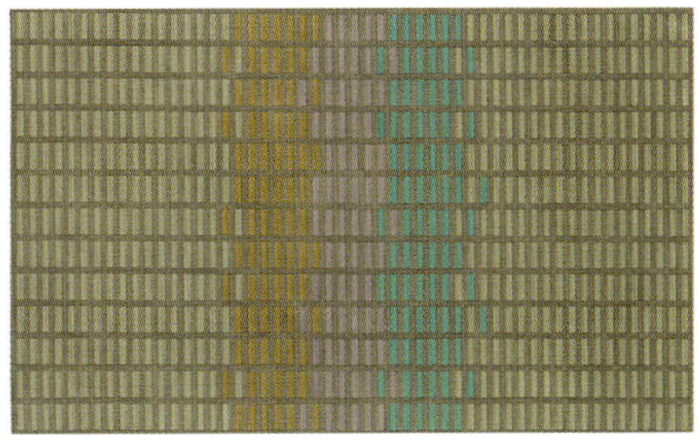

Mundy, Henry b.1919
Untitled 1980
acrylic on canvas 83.8 x 136.7
AC 5725

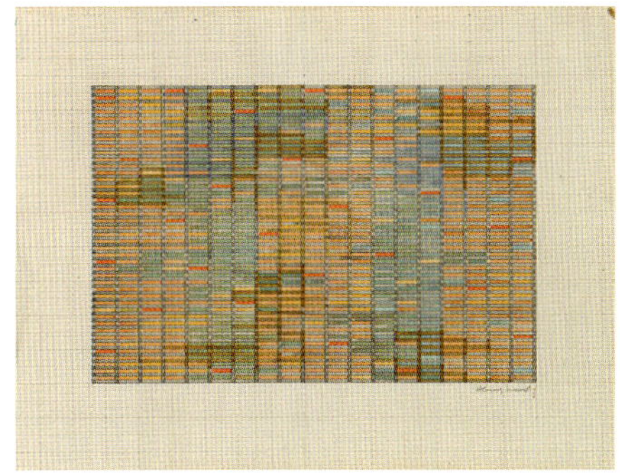

Mundy, Henry b.1919
Untitled Drawing 1982
acrylic on paper 55.8 x 75.9
AC 5073

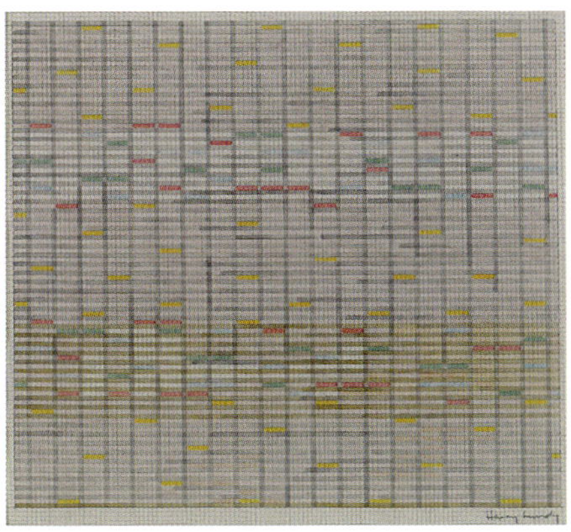

Mundy, Henry b.1919
Untitled Drawing 1982
acrylic on paper 34.4 x 46.1
AC 5074

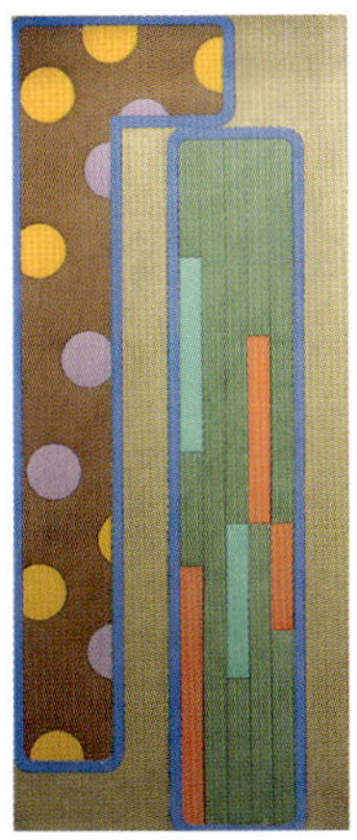

Mundy, Henry b.1919
Untitled 1990
acrylic on canvas 180 x 76.5
ACC39/1991

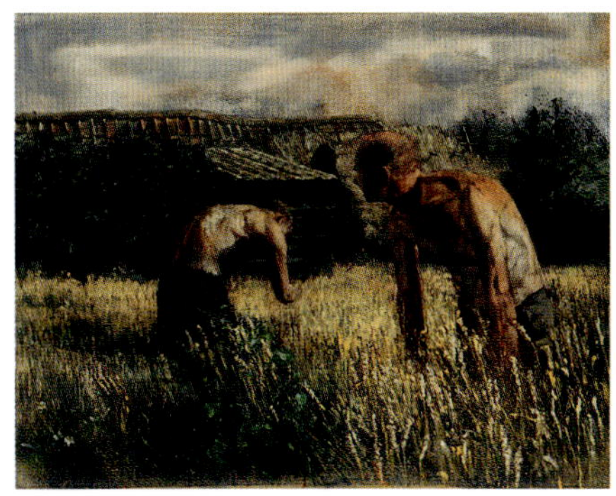

Murfin, Michael b.1954
Hot Day 1980
oil on canvas 107 x 152
AC 5003

Murphy, John b.1945
12.8.69 1969
acrylic on canvas 182.9 x 731.5
AC 1089

Murphy, John b.1945
Petals of Lust (Epidendrum nocturnum) 1984
oil on linen 198 x 167.7
AC 5355

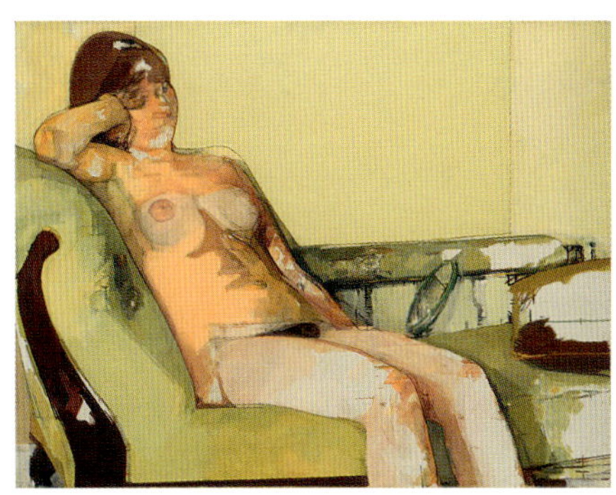

Murphy, Myles F. b.1927
Yellow Nude 1963
oil on canvas 59 x 81.5
AC 734

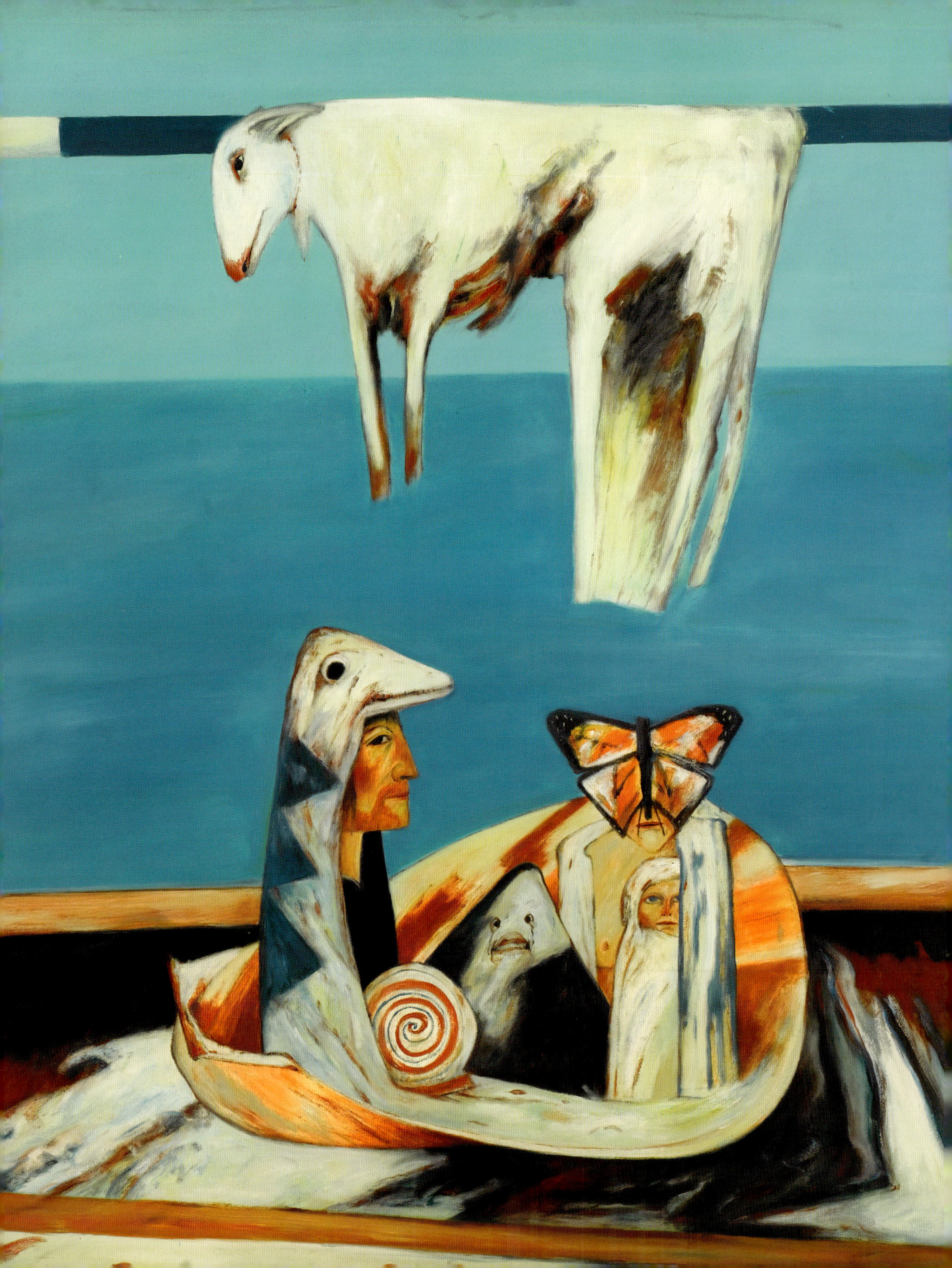

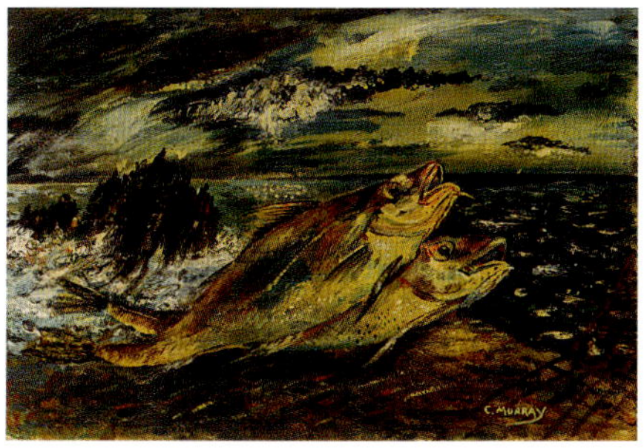

Murray, Charles 1894–1954
Sea and Fish 1940
oil on wood 41 x 61.3
AC 76

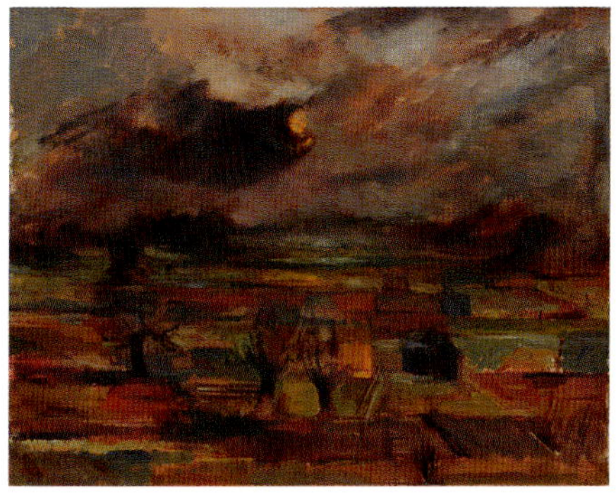

Myers, Bernard 1925–2007
View of Allotment Gardens, Eton - Sun Behind Cloud 1951–1954
oil on canvas 70 x 91
AC 657

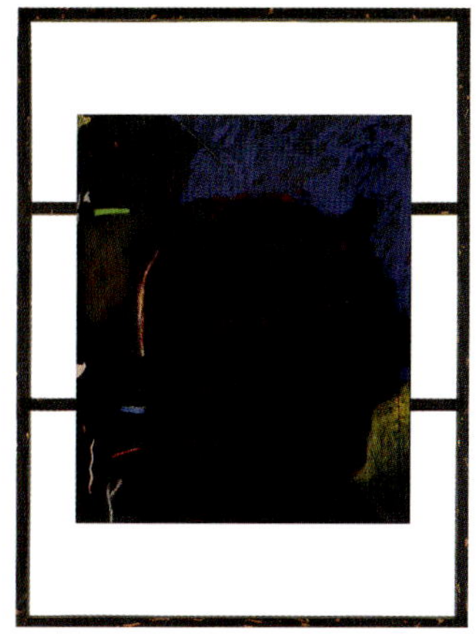

Naylor, Martin b.1944
Villain 1980–1981
oil & gesso on board 151 x 126
AC 5014

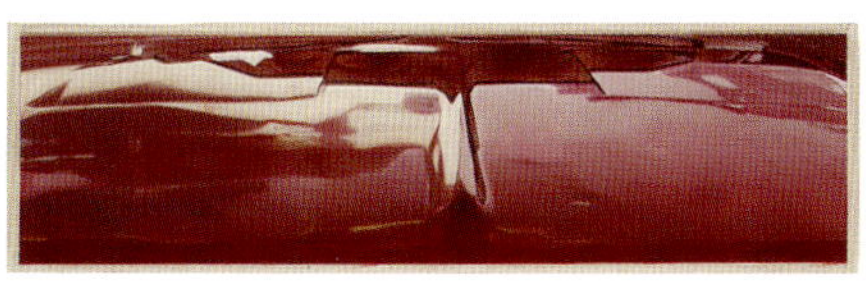

Neiland, Brendan b.1941
Sunset Bonnet 1969
acrylic on canvas 243.8 x 914.4
AC 1090

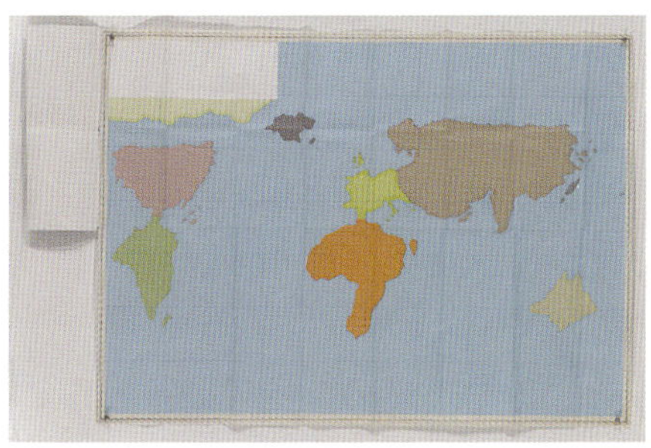

Neudecker, Mariele b.1965
Never Eat Shredded Wheat (Memory Maps), English, Male, 32 1996
acrylic & felt pen on paper 87.5 x 131
ACC64/1996

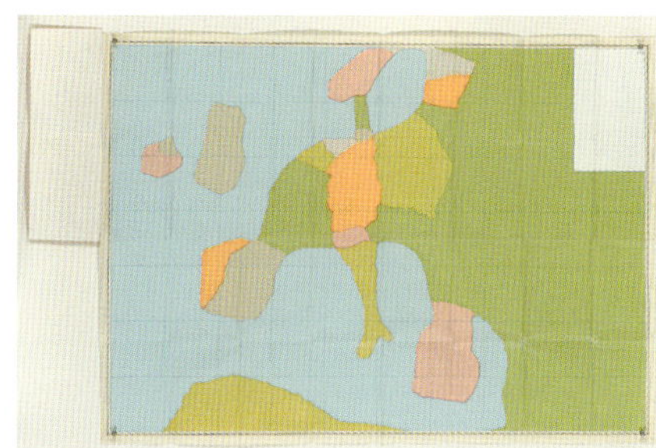

Neudecker, Mariele b.1965
Never Eat Shredded Wheat (Memory Maps), German, Female, 31 1996
acrylic & felt pen on paper 87.5 x 131
ACC65/1996

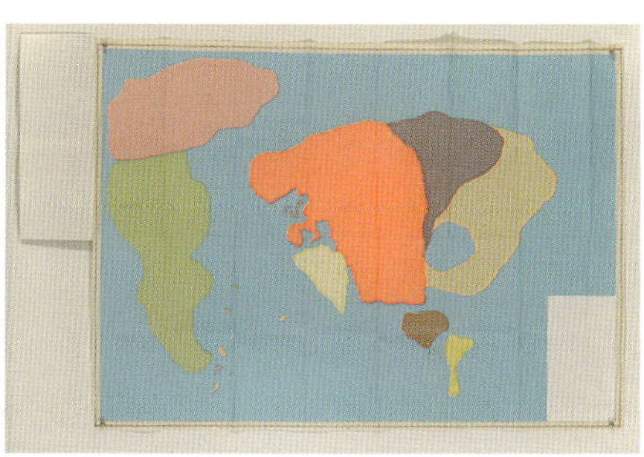

Neudecker, Mariele b.1965
Never Eat Shredded Wheat (Memory Maps), Italian, Female, 32 1996
acrylic & felt pen on paper 87.5 x 131
ACC66/1996

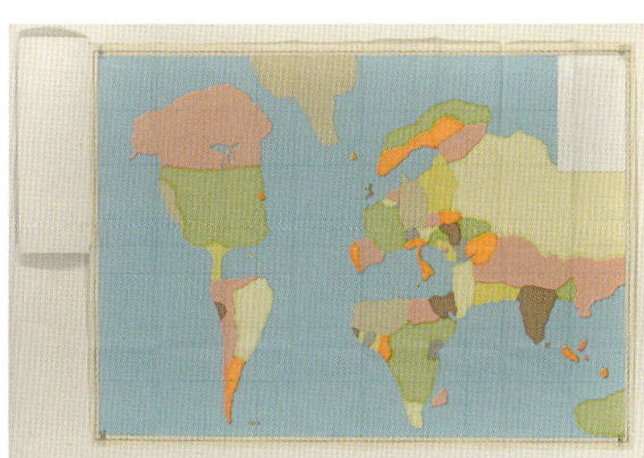

Neudecker, Mariele b.1965
Never Eat Shredded Wheat (Memory Maps), English, Male, 32 1996
acrylic & felt pen on paper 82 x 112
ACC67/1996

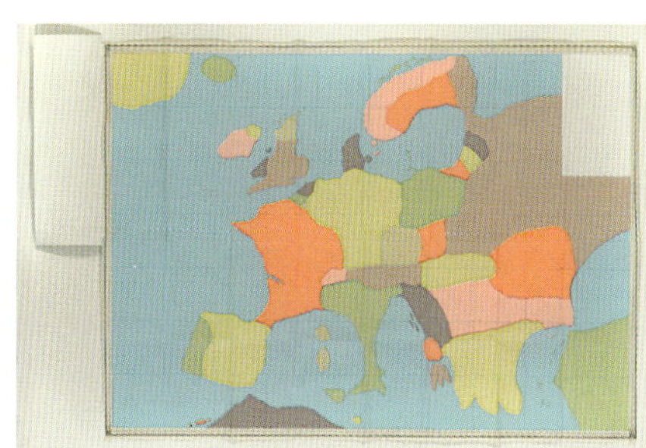

Neudecker, Mariele b.1965
Never Eat Shredded Wheat (Memory Maps), German, Male, 33 1996
acrylic & felt pen on paper 82 x 112
ACC68/1996

Facing page: Bellany, John, b.1942, *The Voyage* (detail), 1973, (p. 17)

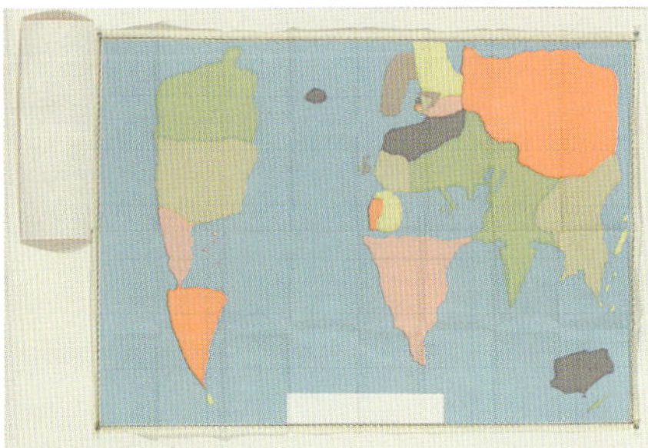

Neudecker, Mariele b.1965
Never Eat Shredded Wheat (Memory Maps), French, Male, 29 1996
acrylic & felt pen on paper 82 x 112
ACC69/1996

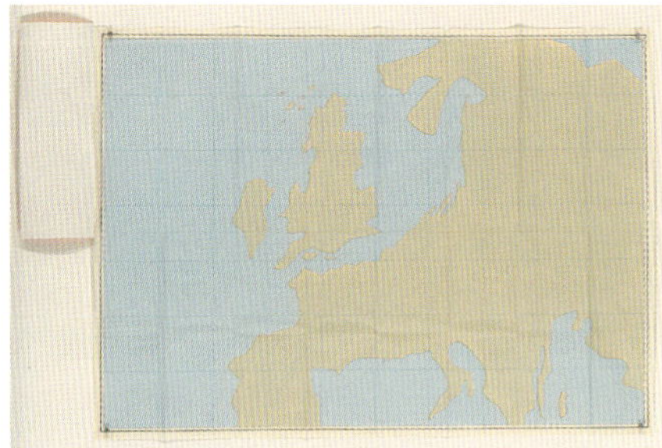

Neudecker, Mariele b.1965
Never Eat Shredded Wheat (Memory Maps), English, Female, 35 1996
acrylic & felt pen on paper 82 x 112
ACC70/1996

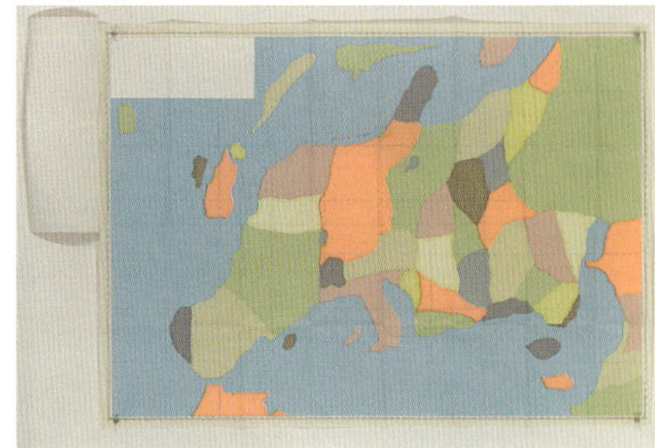

Neudecker, Mariele b.1965
Never Eat Shredded Wheat (Memory Maps), German, Male, 67 1996
acrylic & felt pen on paper 82 x 112
ACC71/1996

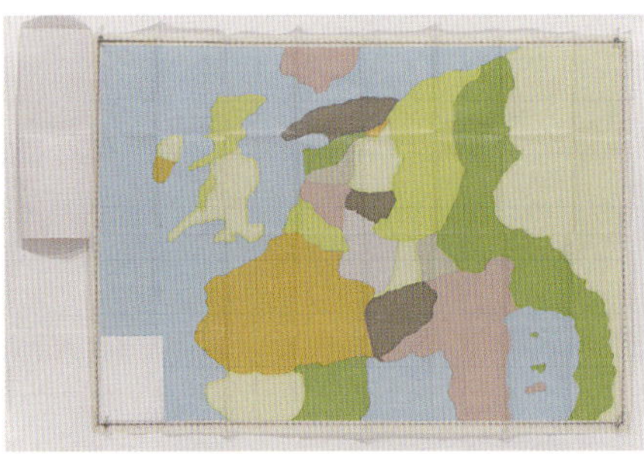

Neudecker, Mariele b.1965
Never Eat Shredded Wheat (Memory Maps), English, Female, 32 1996
acrylic & felt pen on paper 82 x 112
ACC72/1996

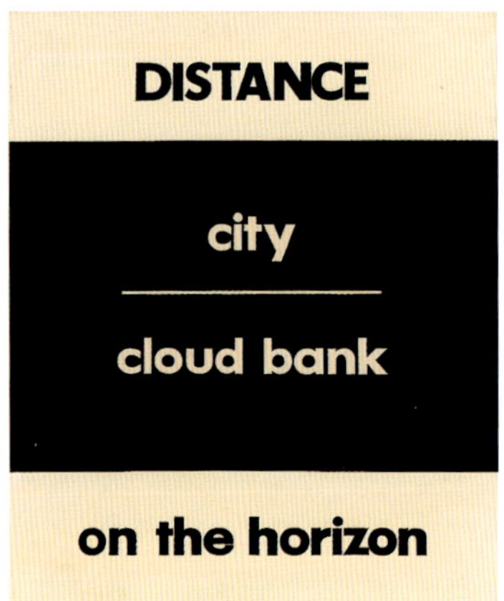

Newman, Gerald b.1945
No.54/Orders V, on the Horizon 1975
oil on panel & tape recording, running time: 6 minutes 2 seconds 104 x 86.2
AC 1837

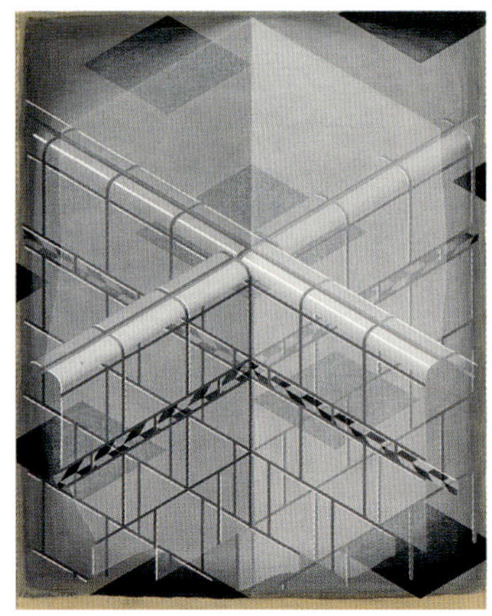

Newsome, Victor b.1935
Corner of a Bathroom 1975
acrylic on wood 62 x 51
AC 1527

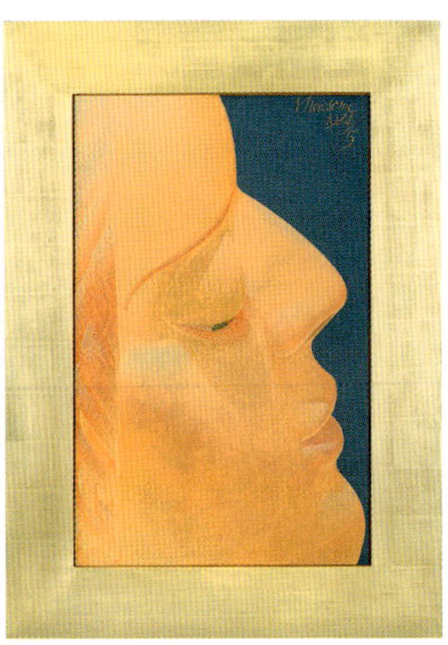

Newsome, Victor b.1935
Profile 1984–1985
tempera on panel 76.8 x 50.2
AC 5373

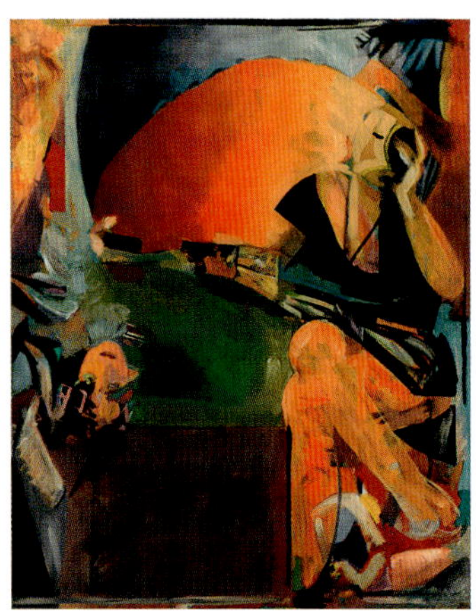

Newton, Duncan b.1945
Academic Study 'Seated Figure A' 1978–1979
oil on canvas 151.9 x 121.6
AC 3034

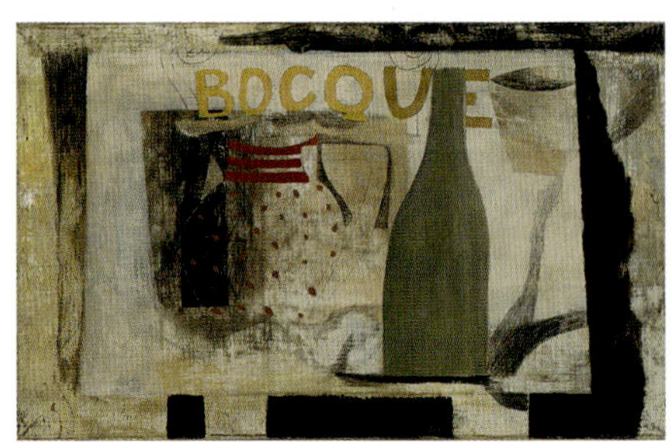

Nicholson, Ben 1894–1982
1932 (Bocque) 1932
oil & pencil on board 48 x 78.5
AC 168

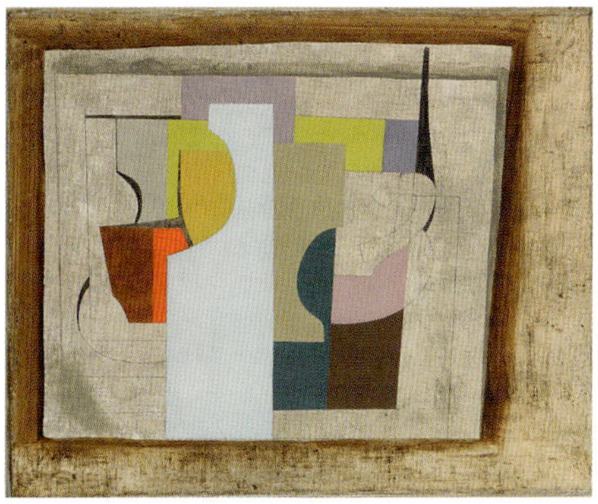

Nicholson, Ben 1894–1982
1946 (still life) 1946
oil & pencil on canvas 40.6 x 50.8
AC 28

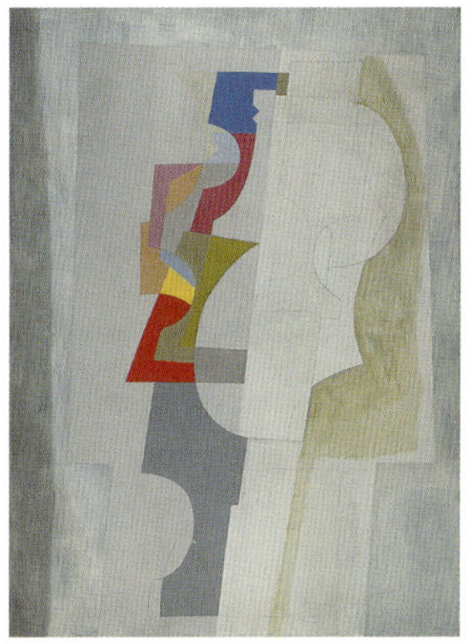

Nicholson, Ben 1894–1982
February 1953 (contrapuntal) 1953
oil & pencil on board 167.6 x 121.9
AC 286

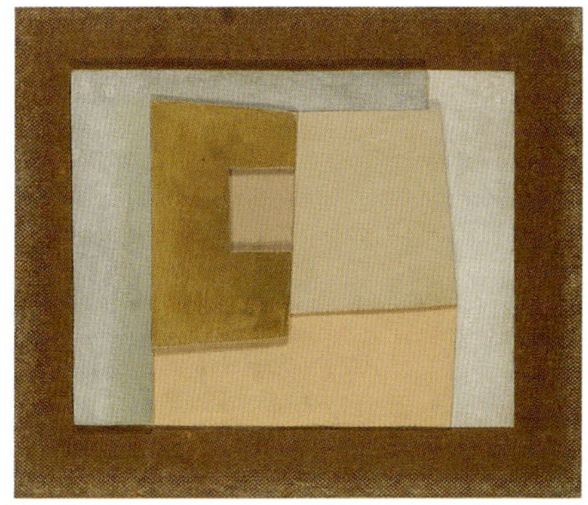

Nicholson, Ben 1894–1982
May 1956 (hendrifter) 1956
oil on board 36 x 43
AC 435

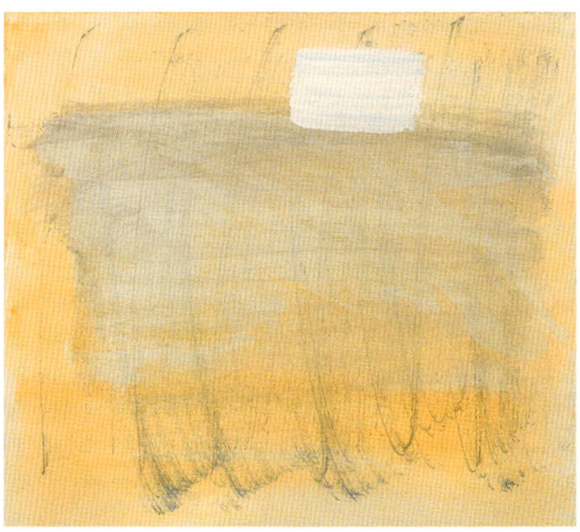

Nicholson, Kate b.1929
Dendra 1962
oil on card 24.2 x 27
AC 640

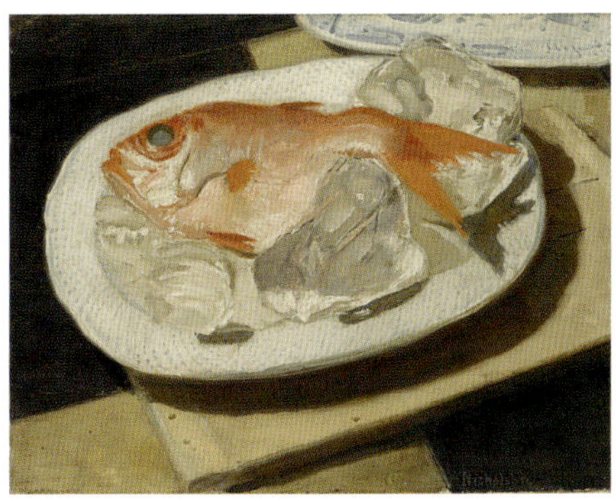

Nicholson, William 1872–1949
Sun Fish 1935
oil on canvas 50.8 x 63.5
AC 29

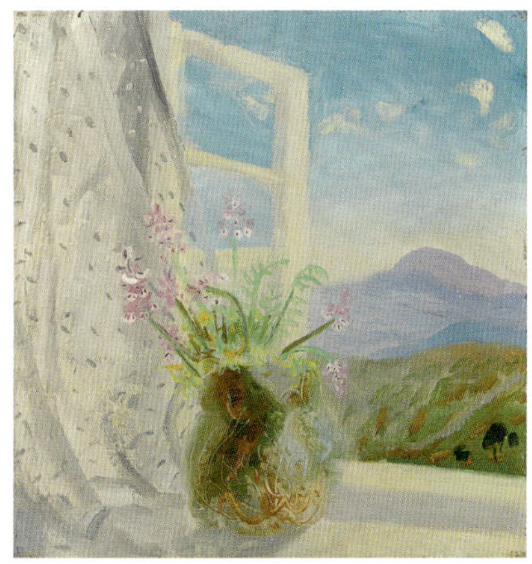

Nicholson, Winifred 1893–1981
Cumberland Hills 1948
oil on wood 47 x 45.6
AC 137

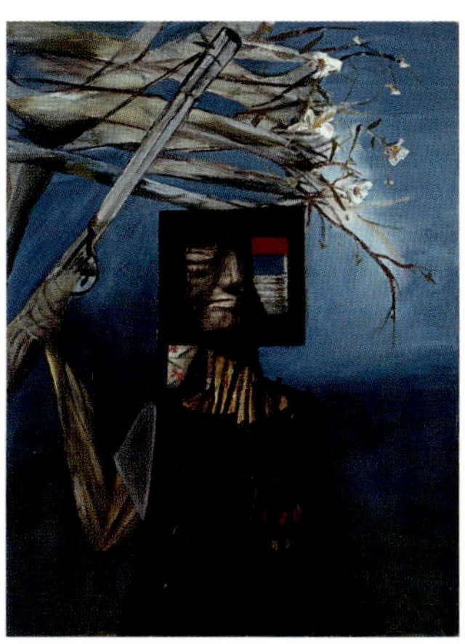

Nolan, Sidney 1917–1992
Kelly, Spring 1956 1956
ripolin on board 121.9 x 91.4
AC 431

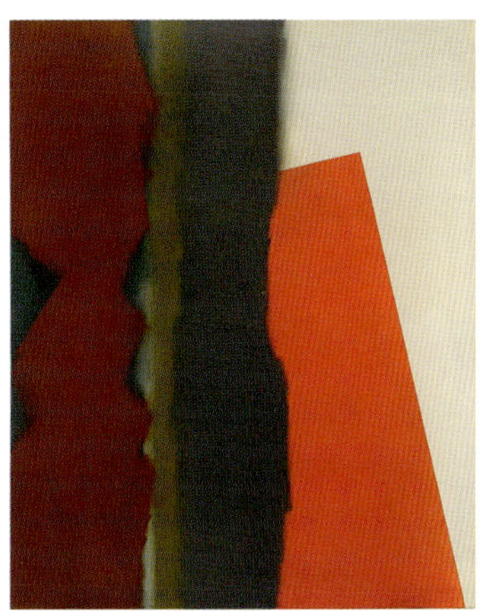

Norwich, Anne b.1929
Painting Untitled 1968
acrylic on canvas 153 x 122.5
AC 1031

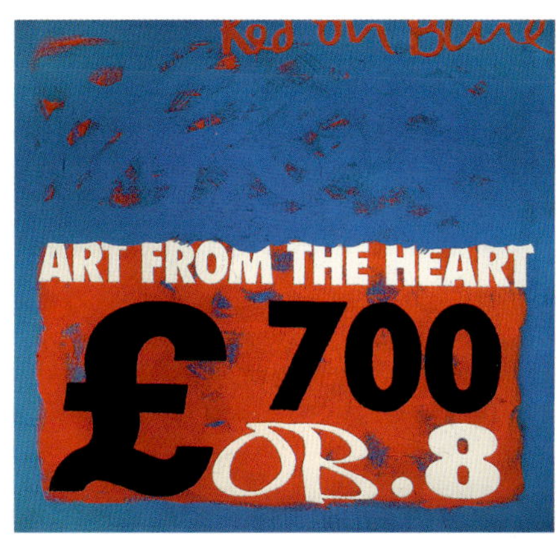

Obuabang, Henry b.1969
Obuabang SRS: B Painting No.8 (Art from the Heart) 1991
acrylic on canvas 110 x 110
ACC89/1991

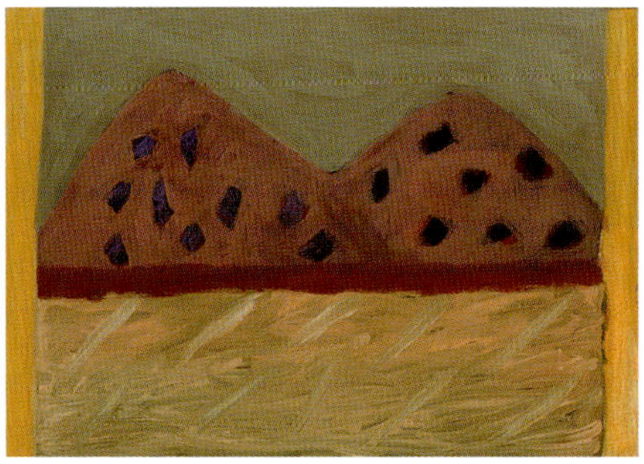

O'Casey, Breon 1928–2011
Mountains 1980–1981
acrylic on canvas 65.7 x 97
AC 4086

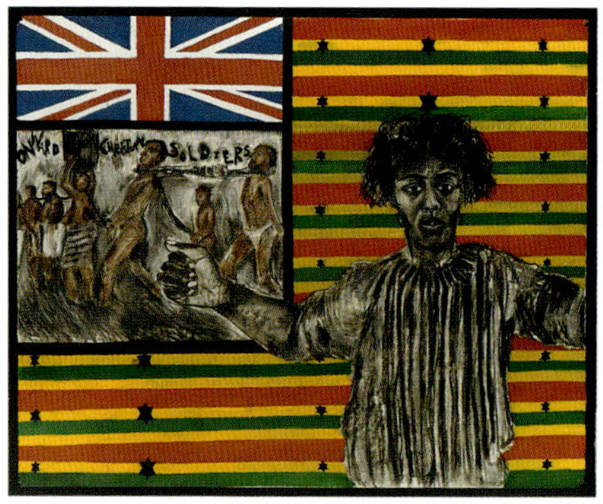

Odonkor, Mowbray b.1962
Onward Christian Soldiers 1987
acrylic on paper 152 x 182
AC 5565

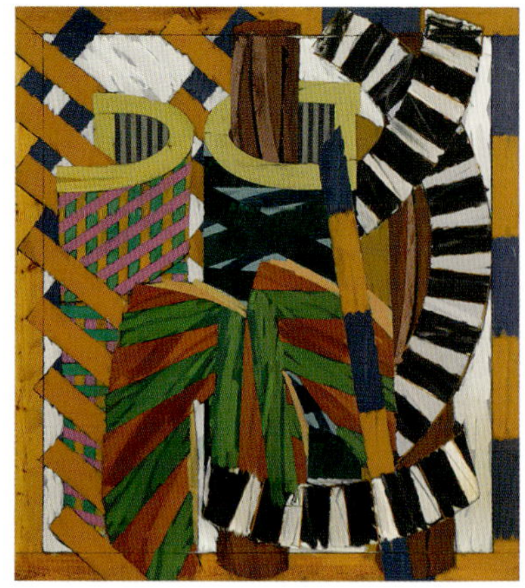

O'Donnell, Hugh b.1950
Bacarole 1978
oil on canvas & wood 203.4 x 183
AC 2085

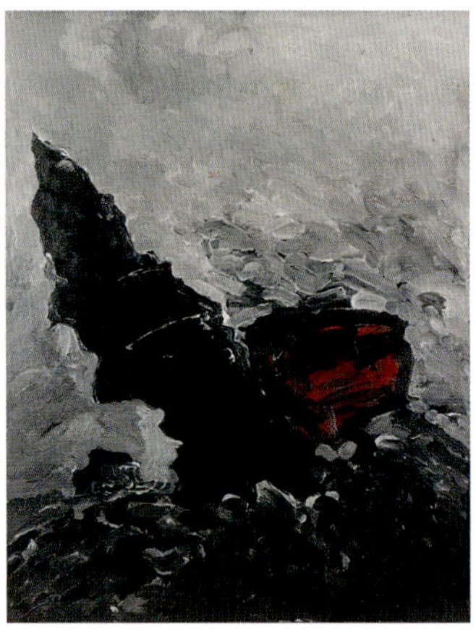

O'Donoghue, Hughie b.1953
Dolmen 1982
acrylic & wax on paper on plywood
152.4 x 122
AC 5339

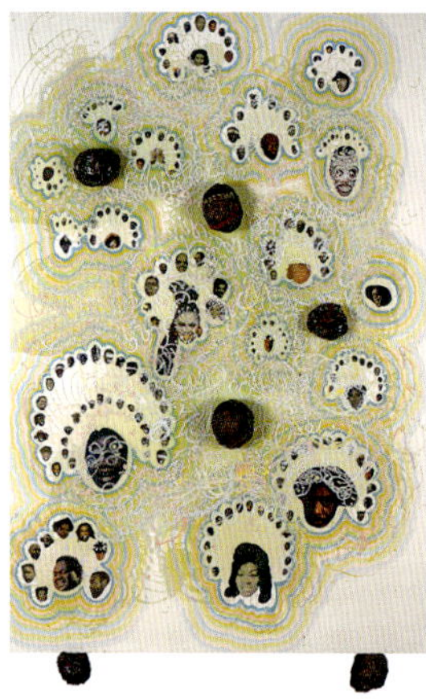

Ofili, Chris b.1968
Popcorn Shells 1995
paper collage, oil, polyester resin, map-pins & elephant dung on linen & two elephant dung props 182.9 x 121.9
ACC58/1995

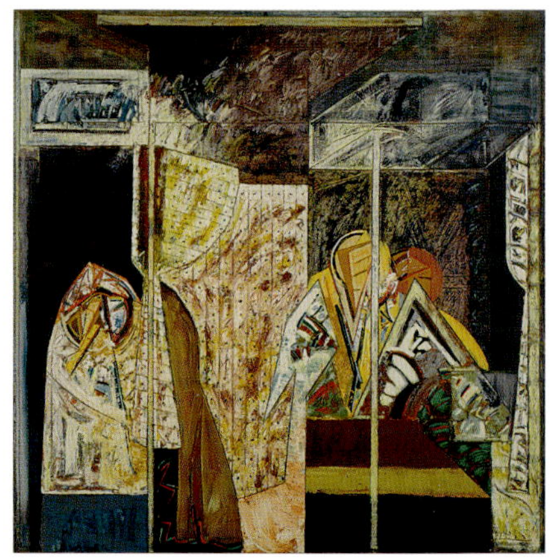

Oliver, Ken b.1948
Interior 1981
acrylic, wax & collage on canvas
240.5 x 243.5
AC 5037

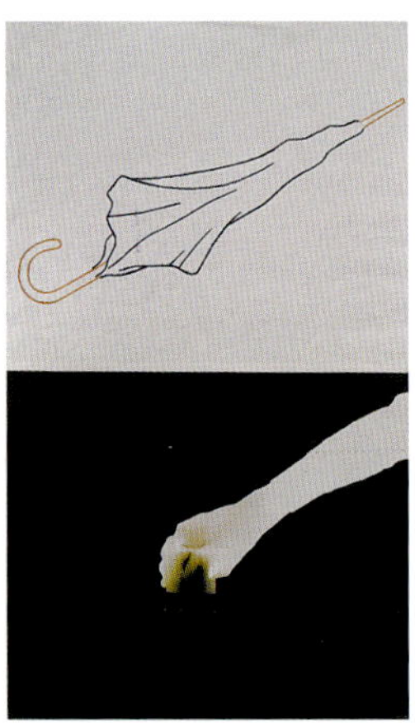

Ormerod, Susan b.1955
Photogram/Drawing with Umbrella 1982
acrylic on canvas, paper & photographic paper 102.2 x 61
AC 5054

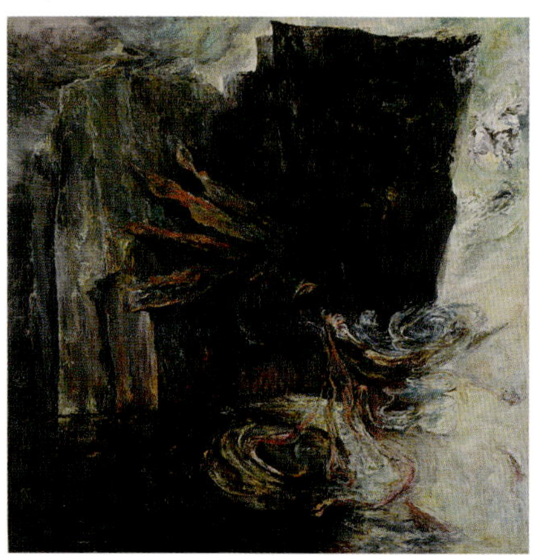

Oulton, Thérèse b.1953
Dispossessed 1983
oil on canvas 259.5 x 261
AC 5241

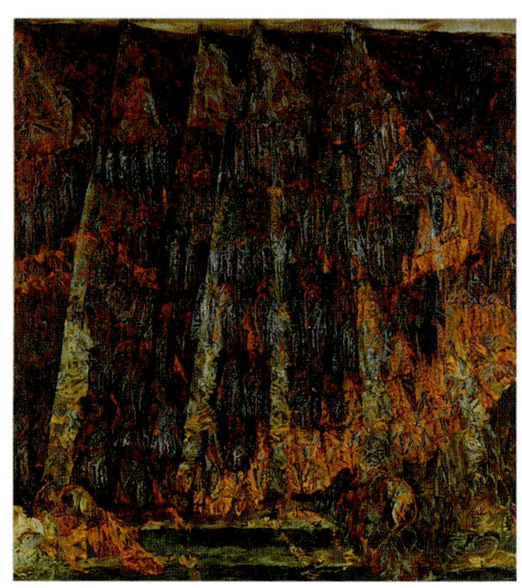

Oulton, Thérèse b.1953
Counterfoil 1987
oil on canvas 233.6 x 213.2
AC 5503

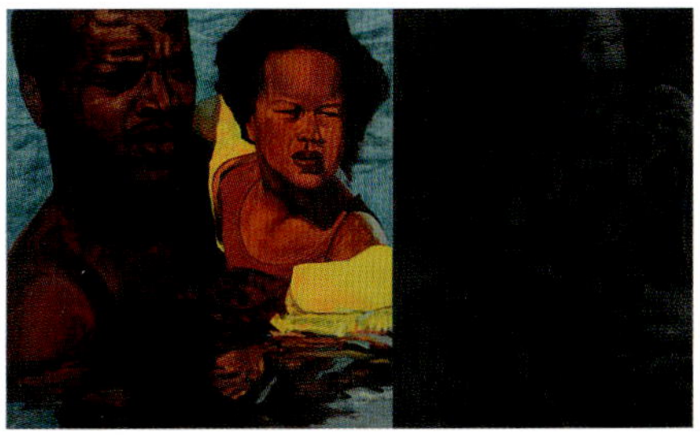

Palmer, Eugene b.1955
The Laughing Christ 1991
oil on canvas 137.1 x 221.3
ACC4/1993

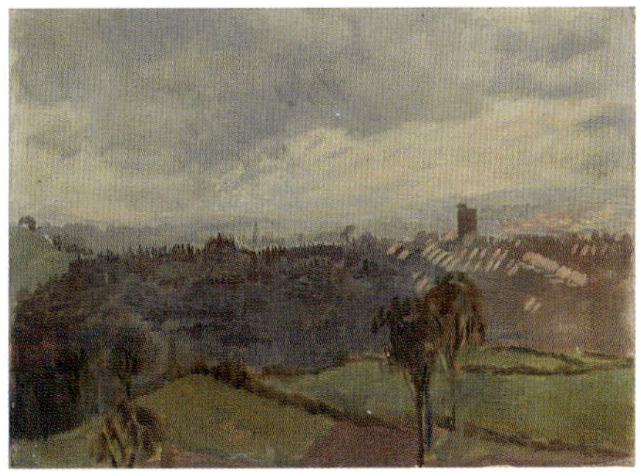

Palmer, Susan 1912–2000
Yeovil 1936
oil on canvas 41 x 56
AC 99

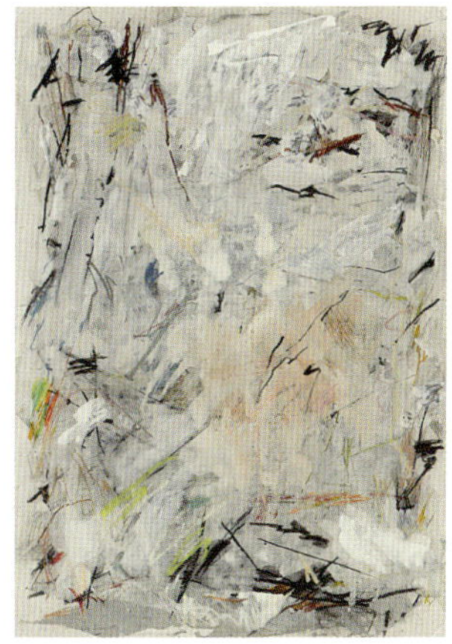

Pannett, Elizabeth Jane b.1947
14.1.79 – 8.80 1980
acrylic, chalk & charcoal on paper
88.6 x 63.7
AC 4008

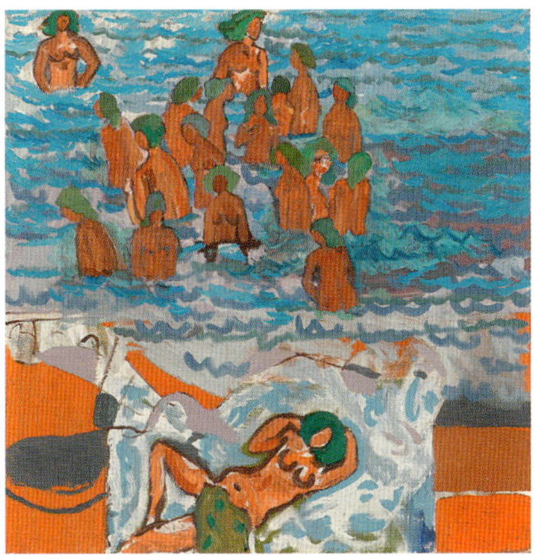

Paraskos, Stass b.1933
Bathing 1968
oil on hardboard 61 x 61
AC 1088

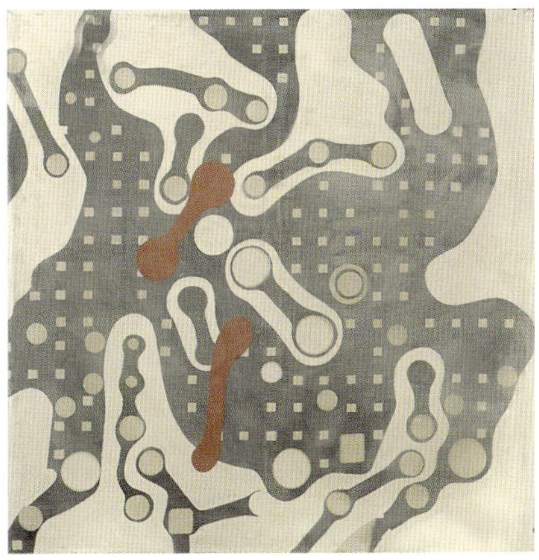

Parsons, David b.1943
Painting I 1964
acrylic on canvas 153.5 x 153.5
AC 775

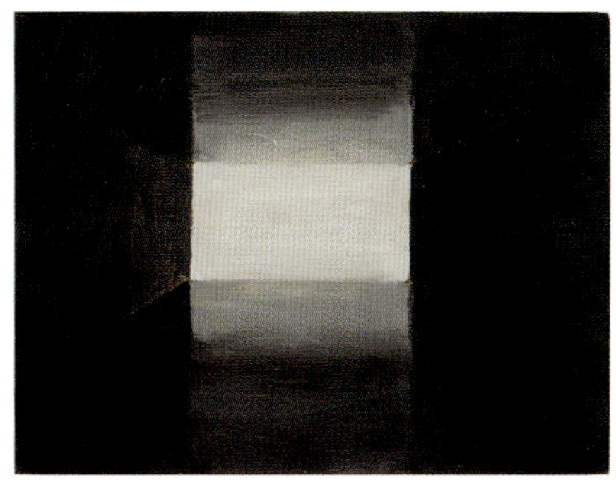

Parsons, Vicken b.1957
Untitled 2000
oil on birch plywood panel 15 x 20
ACC5/2002

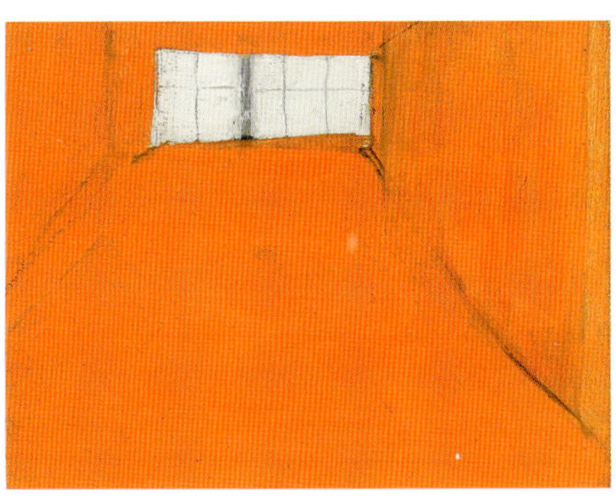

Parsons, Vicken b.1957
Untitled 2001
oil & charcoal on birch plywood panel
15 x 20
ACC6/2002

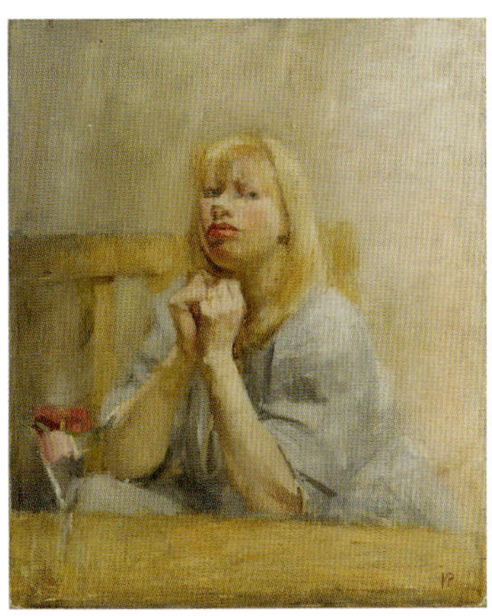

Pasmore, Victor 1908–1998
Portrait of a Girl 1941
oil on canvas 61 x 50.8
AC 100

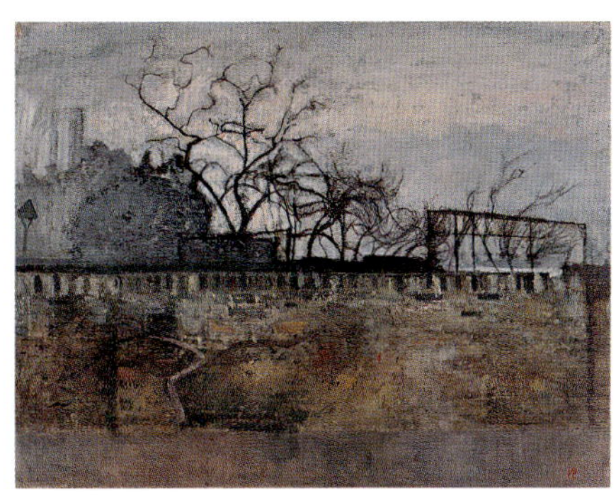

Pasmore, Victor 1908–1998
Riverside Gardens, Hammersmith c.1944
oil on canvas 45.7 x 61
ACC2/1957

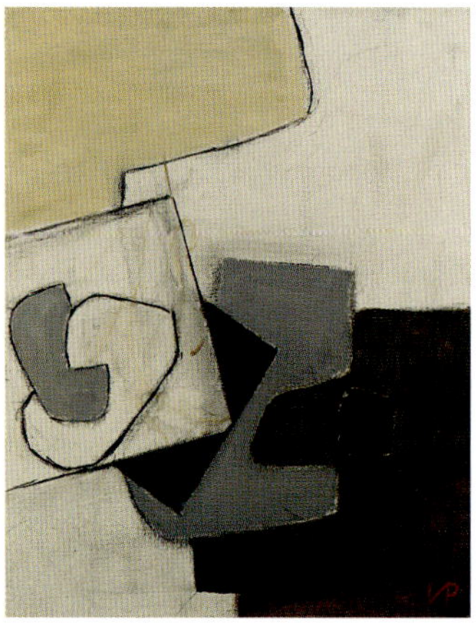

Pasmore, Victor 1908–1998
Rectangular Motif, Black and Olive 1950
oil on canvas 45.7 x 35.6
AC 176

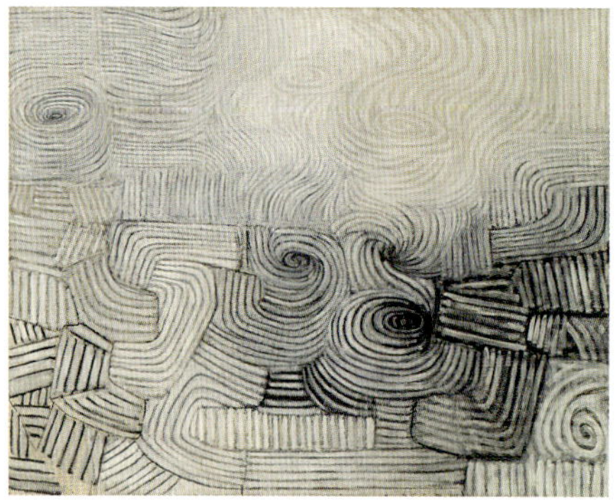

Pasmore, Victor 1908–1998
The Snowstorm: Spiral Motif in Black and White 1950–1951
oil on canvas 119.4 x 152.4
ACC3/1951

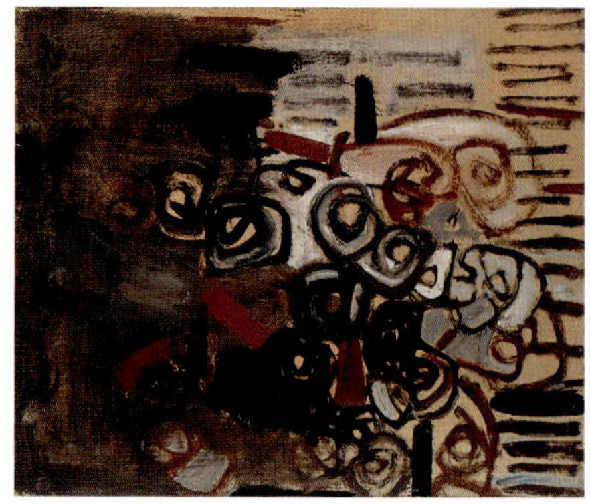

Pasmore, Wendy b.1915
Abstract in Maroon 1959
oil on board 43.2 x 52
AC 515

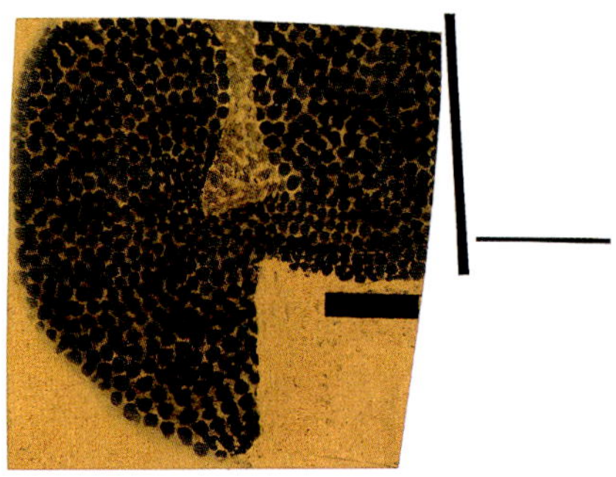

Pasmore, Victor 1908–1998
Black Abstract 1963
oil on panel 91.4 x 91.4
AC 712

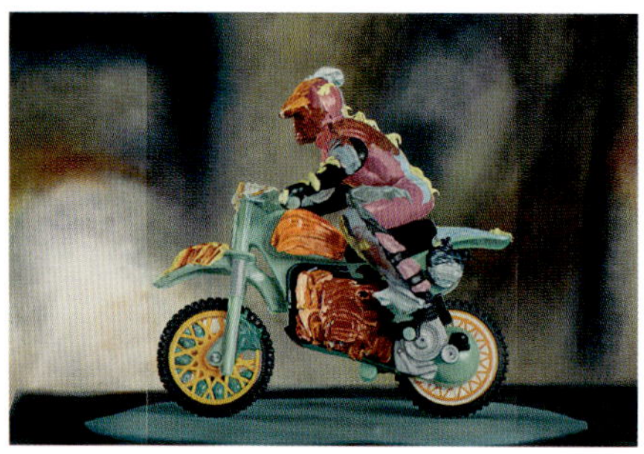

Patterson, Richard b.1963
Motocrosser 1995
oil & acrylic spray paint on canvas
208.3 x 315
ACC6/1995

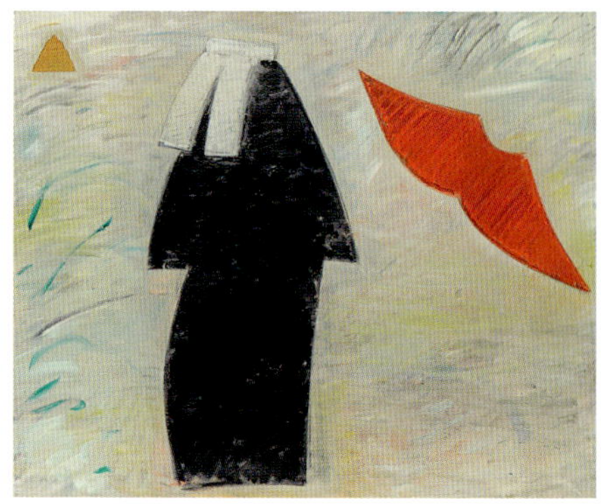

Peake, Fabian b.1942
The Red Moustache 1987
oil on canvas 190.5 x 231
AC 5483

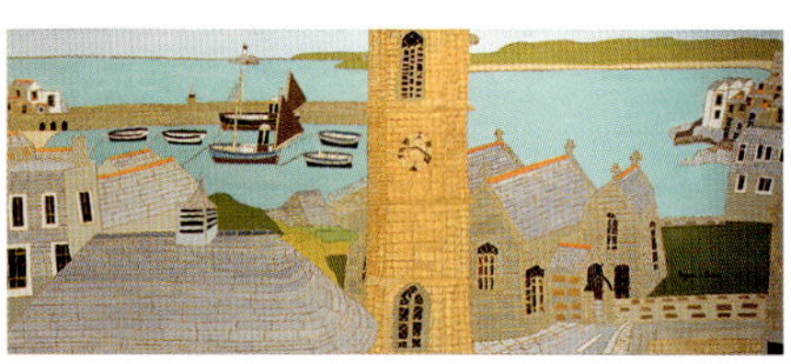

Pearce, Bryan 1929–2007
The Harbour and St Ia's Church, St Ives 1967
oil on board 60.5 x 151
AC 944

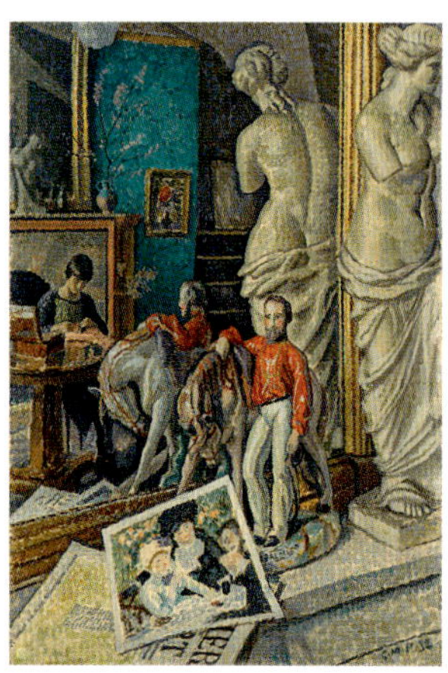

Pearce, Charles Maresco 1874–1964
Garibaldi 1932
oil on canvas 74.3 x 51.4
AC 77

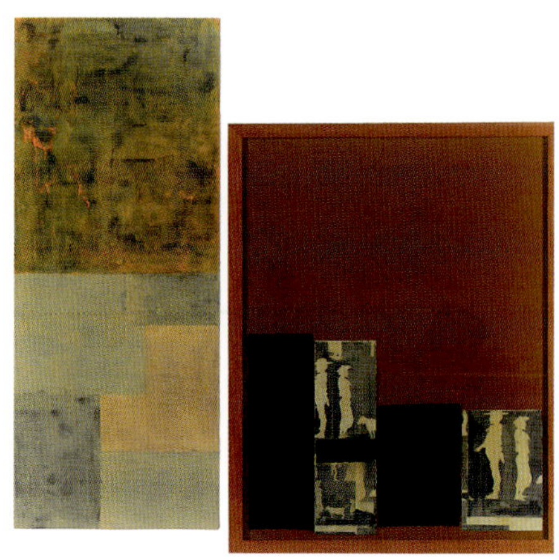

Penalva, João b.1949
Huckleberry 1992
tempera, oil, encaustic wax, paper, velvet, glass, wood & canvas 161 x 178.4
ACC7/1992

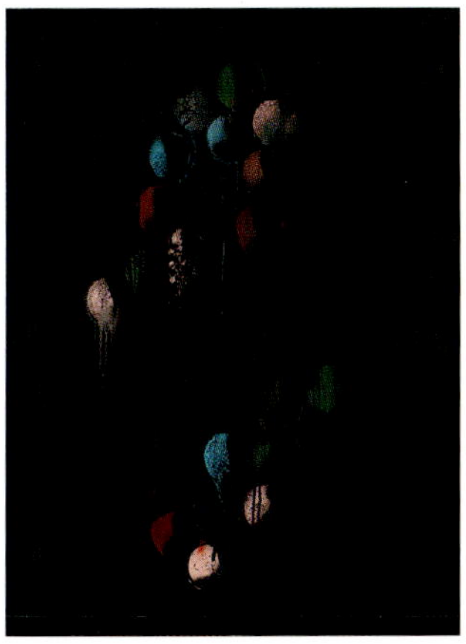

Peri, Peter b.1971
Pageant 2005
mixed media on canvas 102 x 76.5
ACC4/2005

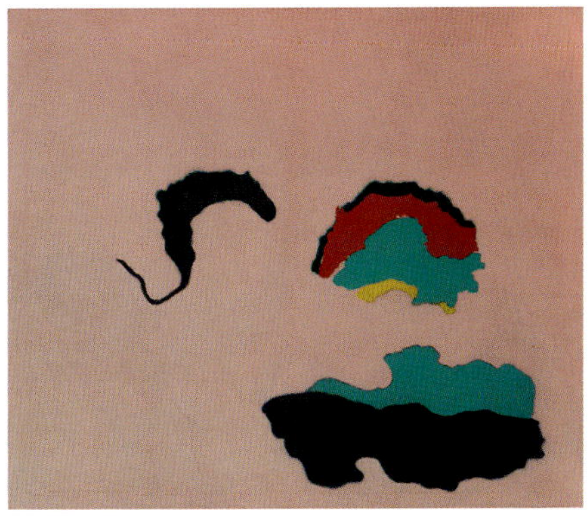

Perryman, Margot b.1938
Untitled No.25 1964
oil on canvas 147.3 x 172.7
AC 809

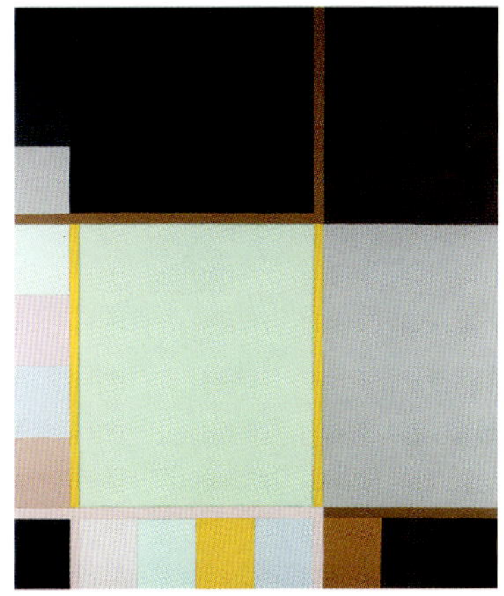

Perryman, Margot b.1938
Octave No.3 1969
acrylic on canvas 147 x 127
AC 1151

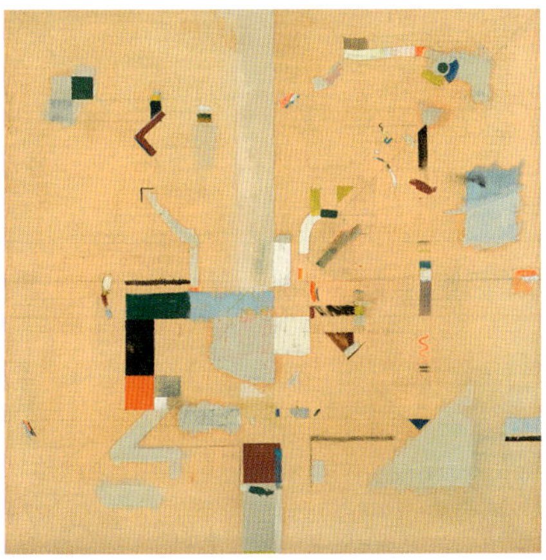

Perton, Michael 1935–1996
Free Composition (Item 13) 1970
oil & pencil on canvas 80 x 80
AC 1269

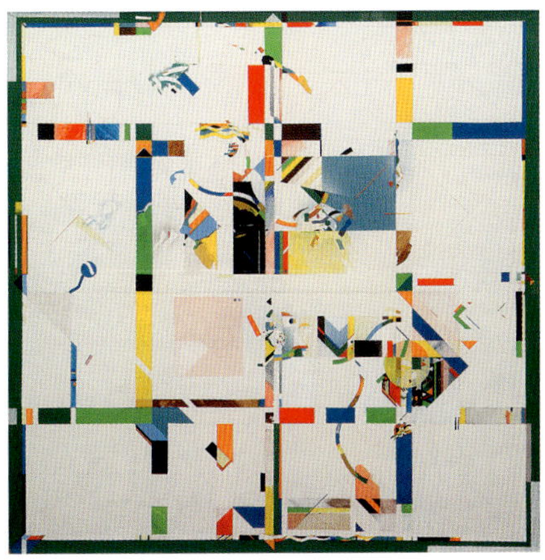

Perton, Michael 1935–1996
Activities on a White Window Grid 1976
oil on canvas 122.1 x 121.3
AC 1846

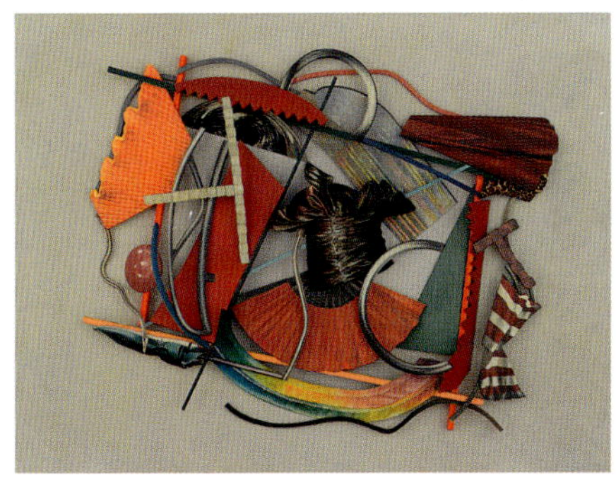

Phillips, Peter b.1939
Entanglement Series: Perpetual Flux
1981–1982
oil, acrylic & wax on canvas on wood
200 x 267
AC 5163

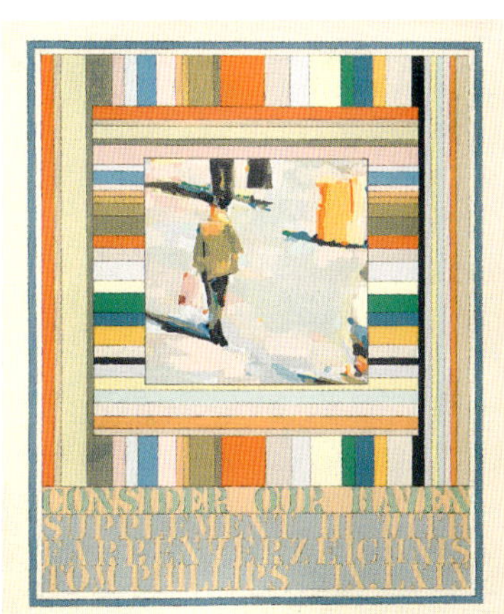

Phillips, Tom b.1937
Consider Our Haven: Supplement III 1968
1968–1969
acrylic & pencil on canvas 30.5 x 25.4
AC 1101

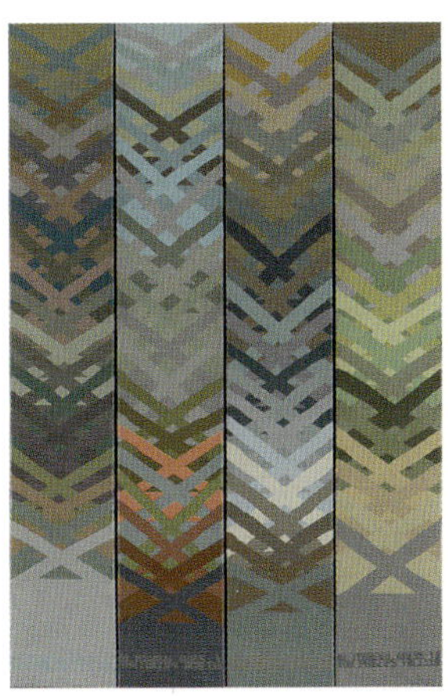

Phillips, Tom b.1937
Terminal Greys IV–VII 1971–1973
acrylic on canvas 122 x 101.6
AC 1321

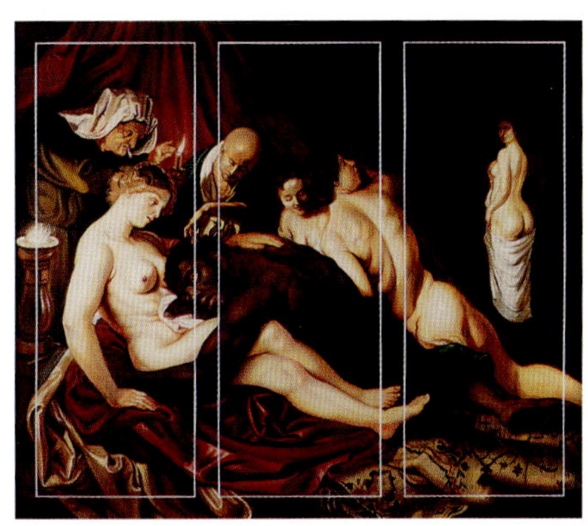

Phokela, Johannes b.1966
Candle Bathing 1997
oil on board 102 x 121.7
ACC2/1998

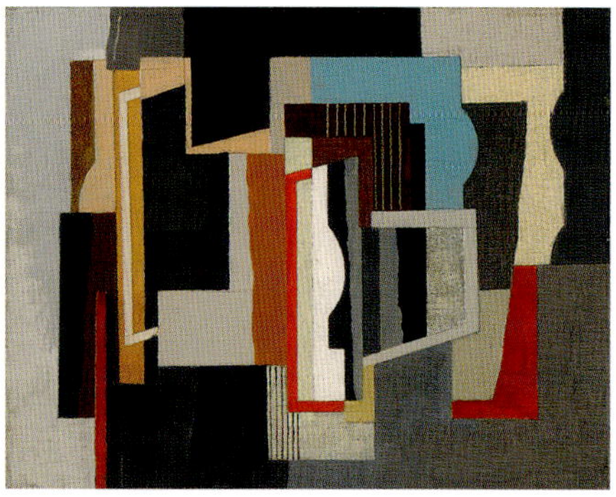

Piper, John 1903–1992
Abstract II 1935
oil on canvas on panel 29.5 x 39.7
AC 348

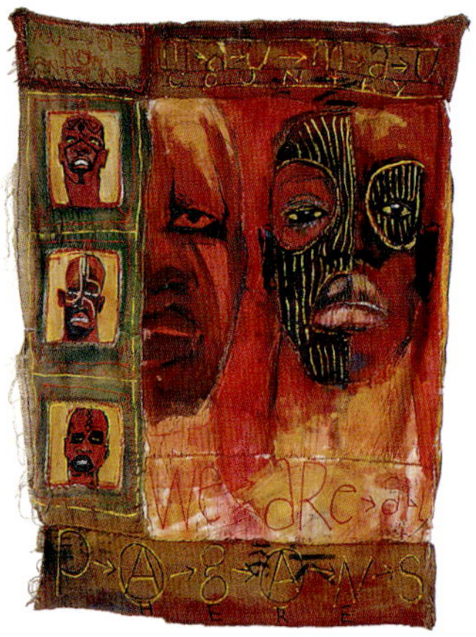

Piper, Keith b.1960
(You are now entering) Mau Mau Country 1983
acrylic on hessian & canvas 246.5 x 192
AC 5346

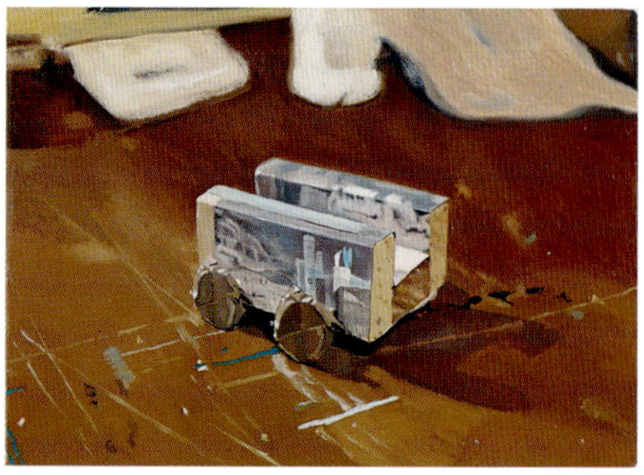

Pollard, Alex b.1977
Brontë Truck 2003
oil on board 21 x 29.5
ACC2/2003

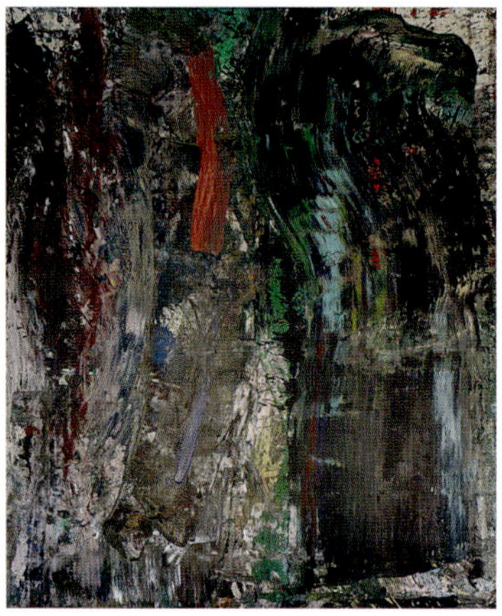

Pollock, Fred b.1937
Untitled No.III 1978
oil & acrylic on canvas 199.4 x 168.7
AC 5123

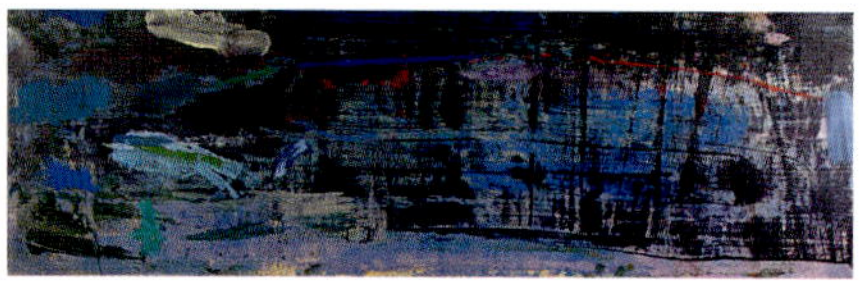

Pollock, Fred b.1937
Lunar Thrust 1982
acrylic on canvas 79 x 257.4
AC 5124

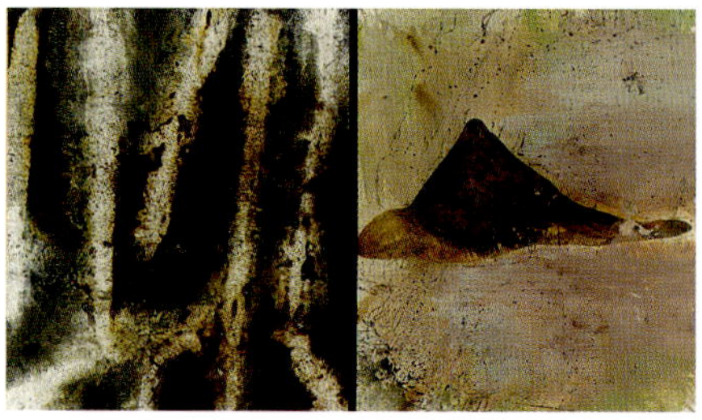

Porter, Michael b.1948
Fungus and Silver Birch 1989–1990
mixed media on canvas 200 x 171.5; 200 x 171.5
ACC13/1990

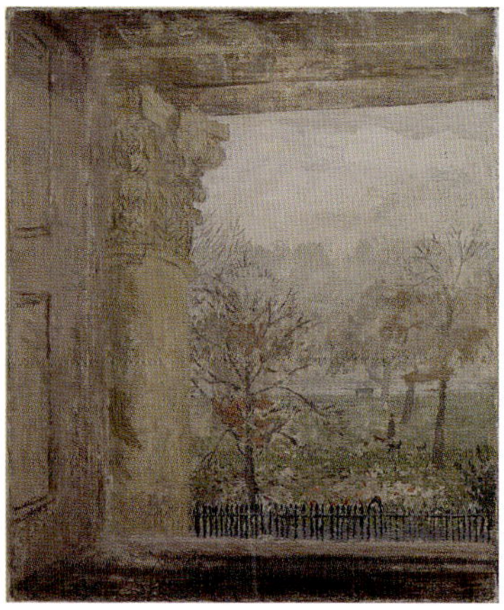

Potter, Mary 1900–1981
Regent's Park, Autumn 1949
oil on canvas 69.9 x 59.7
AC 170

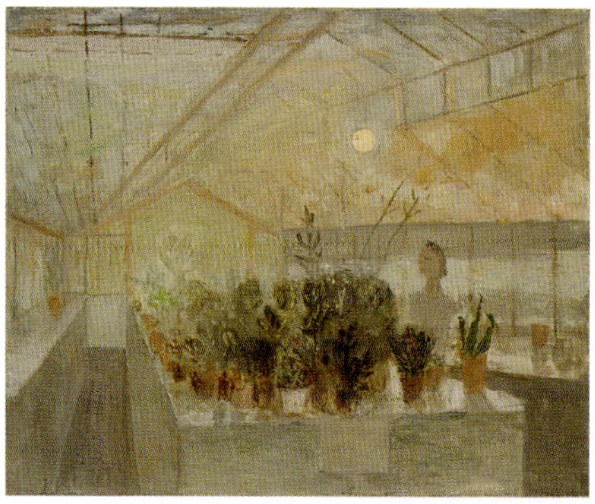

Potter, Mary 1900–1981
The Erica House, Kew 1951
oil on canvas 59.5 x 75
AC 215

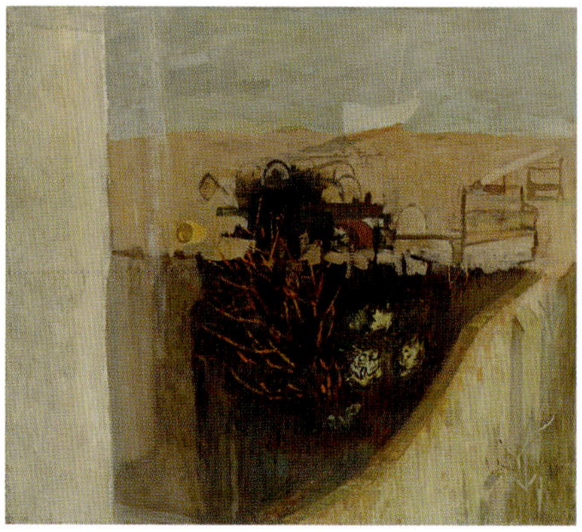

Potter, Mary 1900–1981
Sun on the Beach 1961
oil on canvas 82.5 x 92.7
AC 562

Facing page: Rae, Fiona, b.1963, *Untitled (Pale Green I)* (detail), 1990, (p. 129)

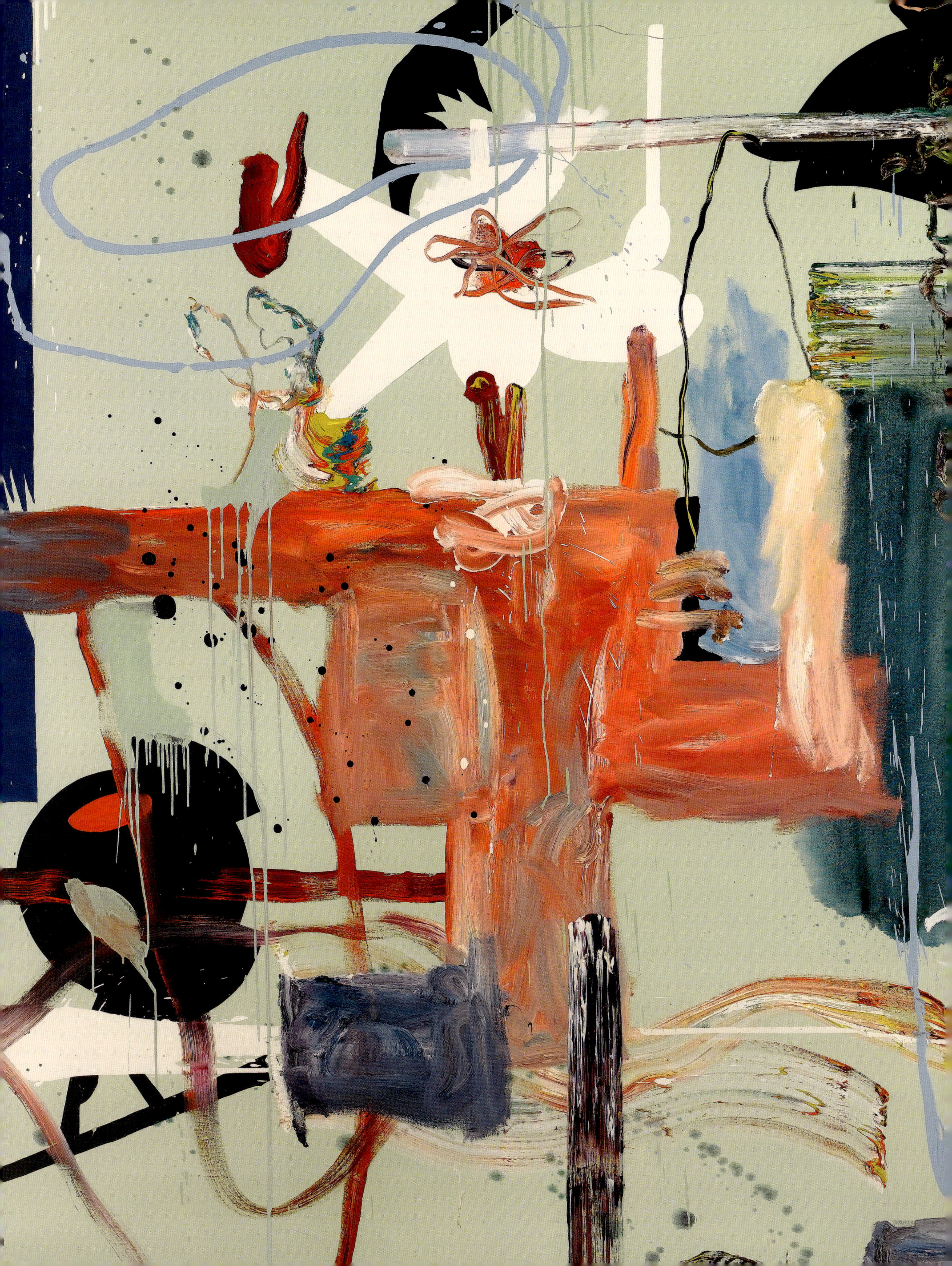

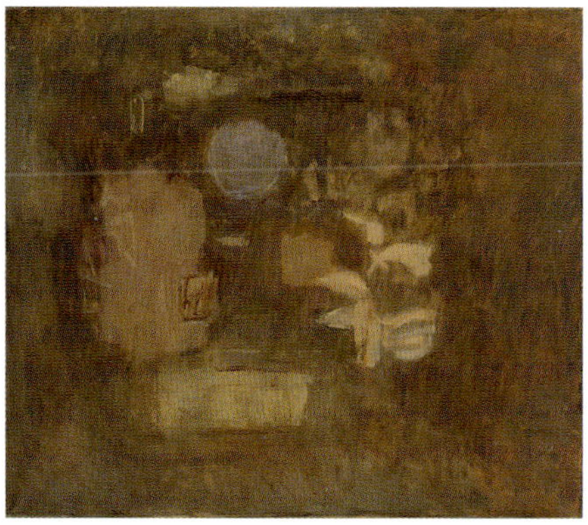

Potter, Mary 1900–1981
Dark Painting 1977
oil on canvas 86.3 x 101.6
AC 1899

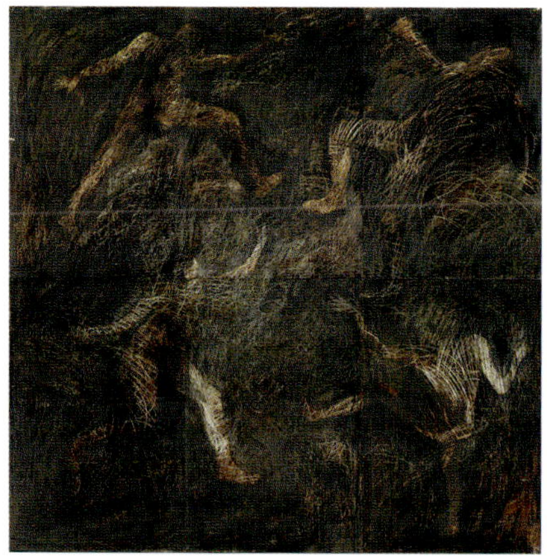

Power, Gary b.1958
My Addaura 1983
paint, wax, charcoal & acquaseal on paper
202 x 205.5
AC 5259

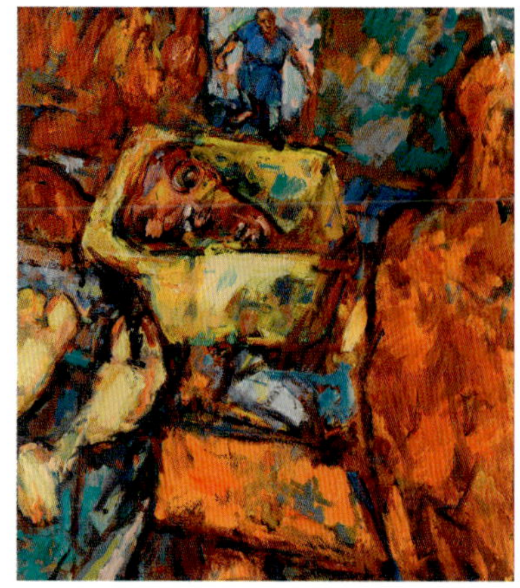

Praag, Arnold van b.1926
Butcher, Sheep's Head and Trotters 1982
oil on canvas 137 x 122
AC 5356

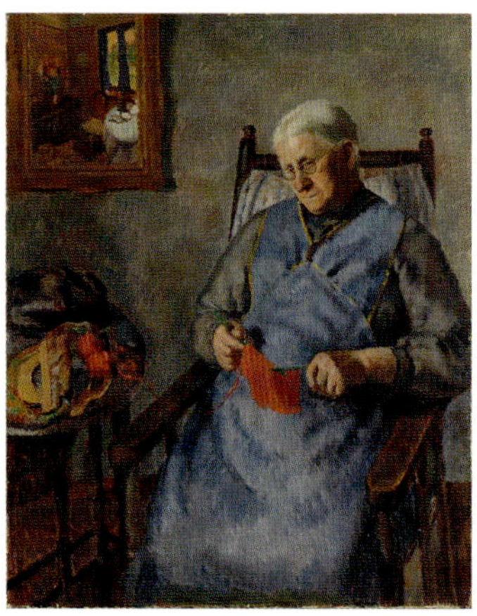

Preece, Patricia 1894–1966
Old Woman Knitting 1937
oil on canvas 76.8 x 61.6
AC 101

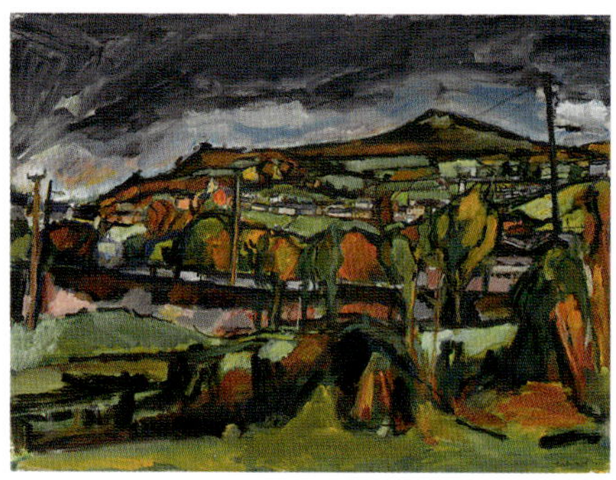

Prendergast, Peter 1946–2007
Road to Bethesda from Garden 1979
PVA on paper 54.5 x 74.6
AC 3060

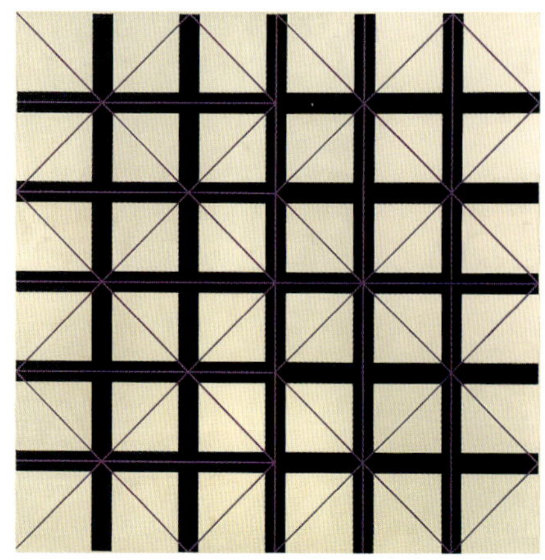

Prentice, David b.1936
Field Grid – Pleiades 1968
oil & polyurethane on canvas 167.6 x 167.6
AC 907

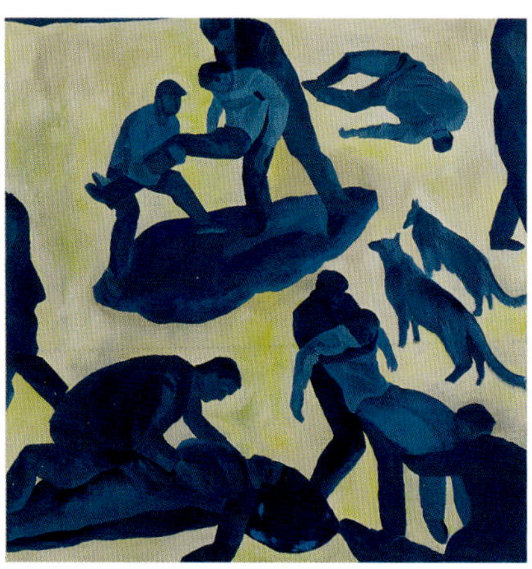

Price, Joanna b.1956
Blue Pietà 1992
oil on canvas 183 x 183
ACC234/1998

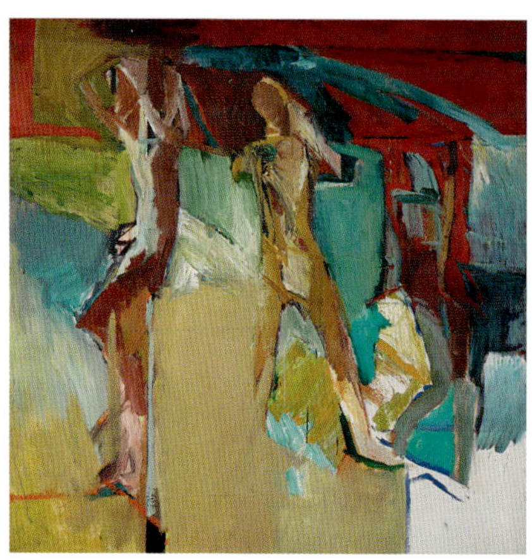

Procktor, Patrick 1936–2003
Three Figures in Landscape 1962
oil on canvas 122 x 122.2
AC 690

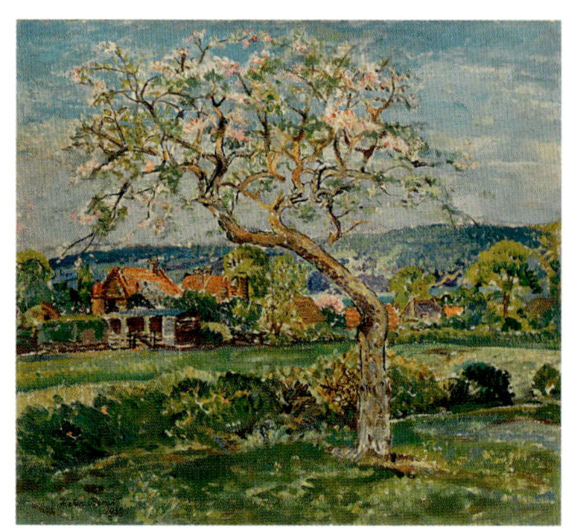

Prout, Margaret Fisher 1875–1963
Near Betchworth 1939
oil on canvas 55.2 x 62
AC 93

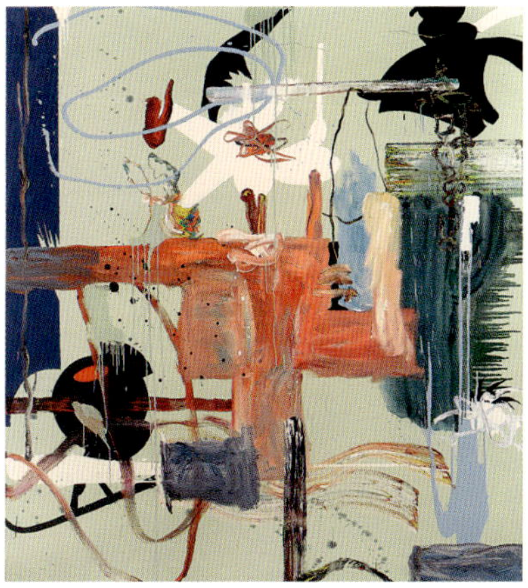

Rae, Fiona b.1963
Untitled (Pale Green I) 1990
oil on canvas 213.5 x 198.2
ACC40/1991

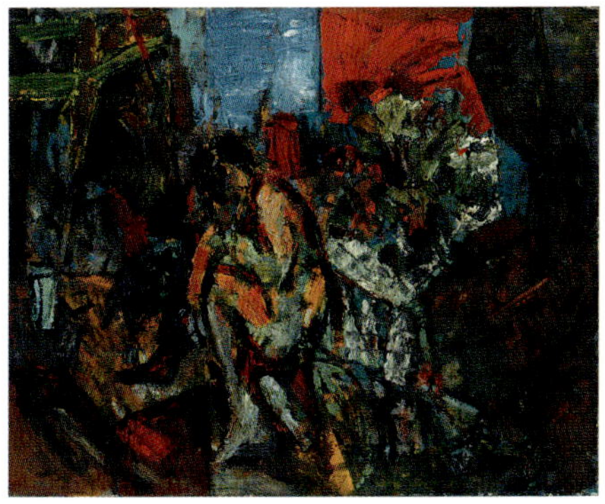

Reason, Cyril b.1931
Odalisque 1960
oil on board 121.9 x 152.4
AC 543

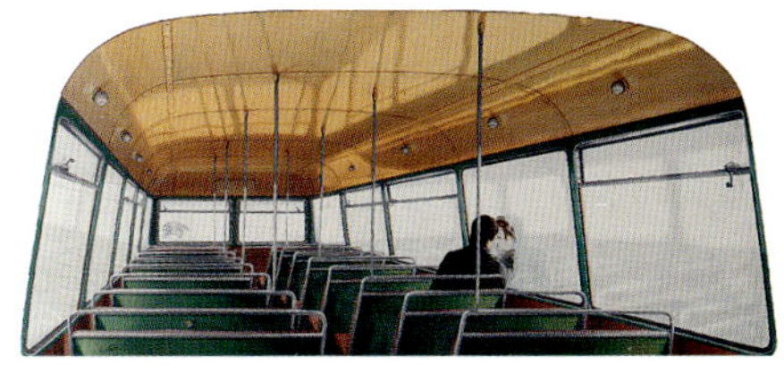

Redfern, David b.1947
No.9 1973
oil on canvas 53 x 120
AC 1651

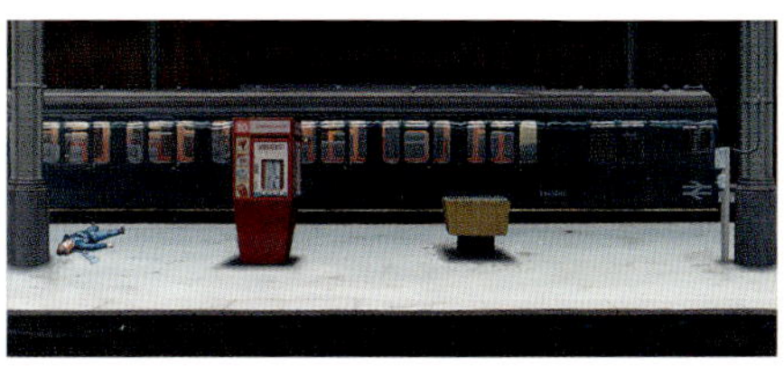

Redfern, David b.1947
Incident at Charing Cross 1978
oil on canvas 68.3 x 159.7
AC 1938

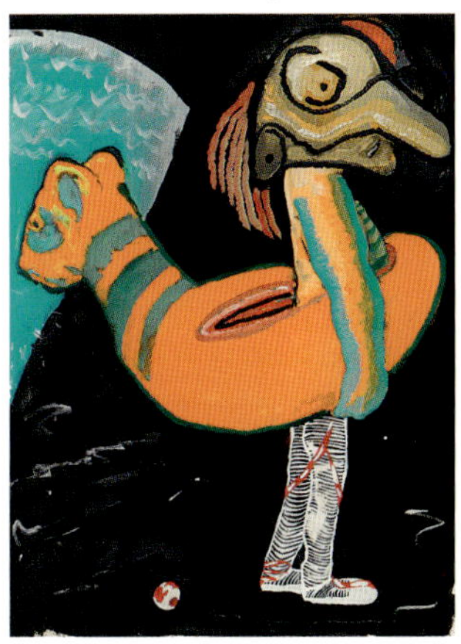

Rego, Paula Figueiroa b.1935
Girl by Swimming Pool 1981
acrylic on paper 76.4 x 56.5
AC 4068

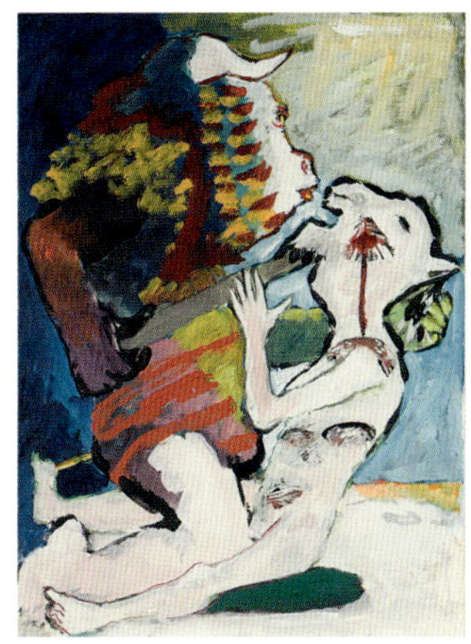

Rego, Paula Figueiroa b.1935
Minotaur Slicing Goat 1981
acrylic on paper 76.5 x 56.8
AC 5021

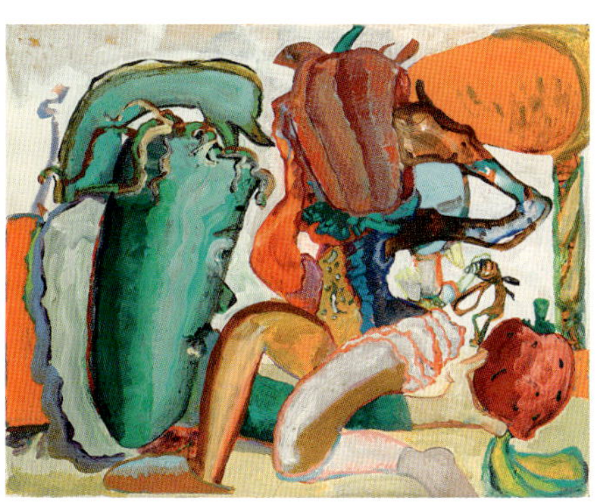

Rego, Paula Figueiroa b.1935
The Family 1982
acrylic on paper 121.4 x 151.5
AC 5166

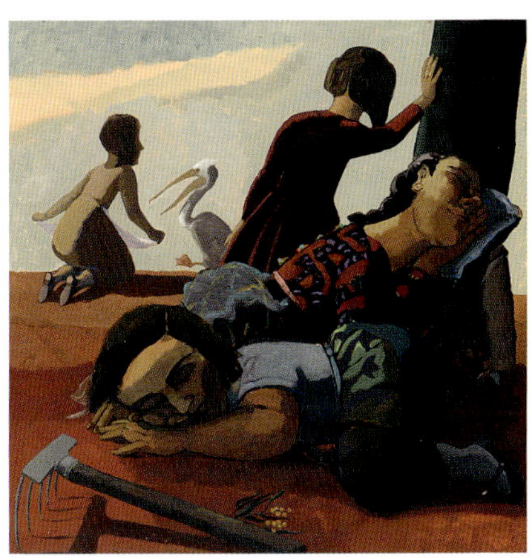

Rego, Paula Figueiroa b.1935
Sleeping 1986
acrylic on canvas 149.8 x 149.5
AC 5465

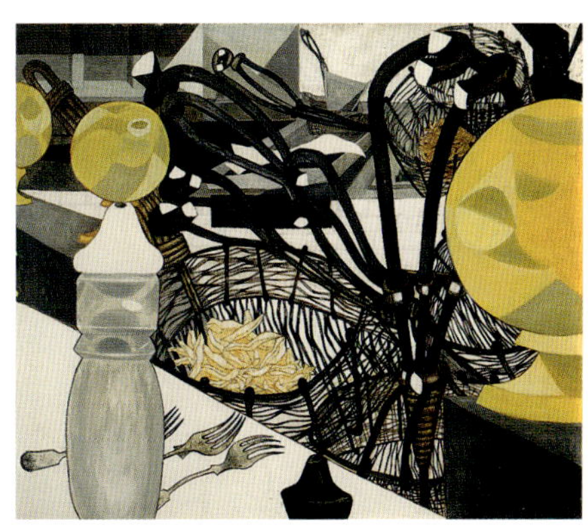

Reid, Nan 1905–1981
Fish and Chip Shop in Chelsea 1952
tempera on board 63 x 75.6
AC 242

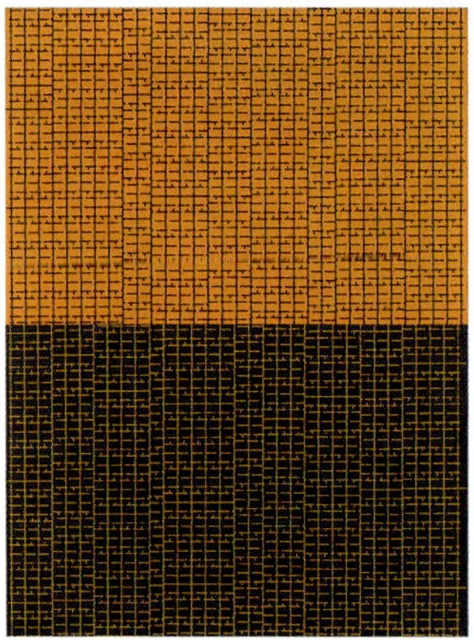

Renshaw, Tim b.1964
Returning 1994
oil on canvas 244 x 183
ACC62/1997

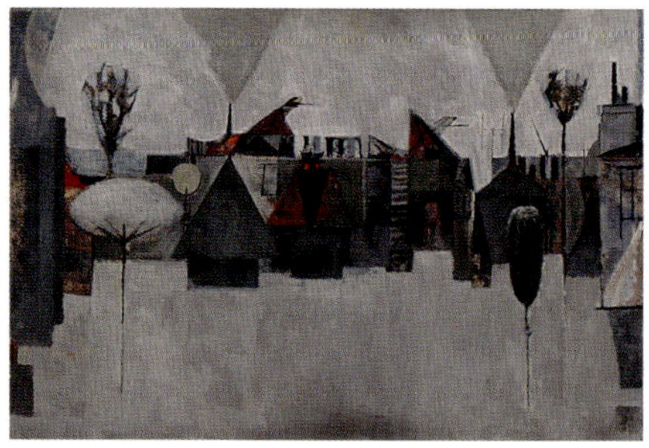

Reynolds, Alan b.1926
The Village – Winter 1952
oil on board 61 x 91.8
AC 247

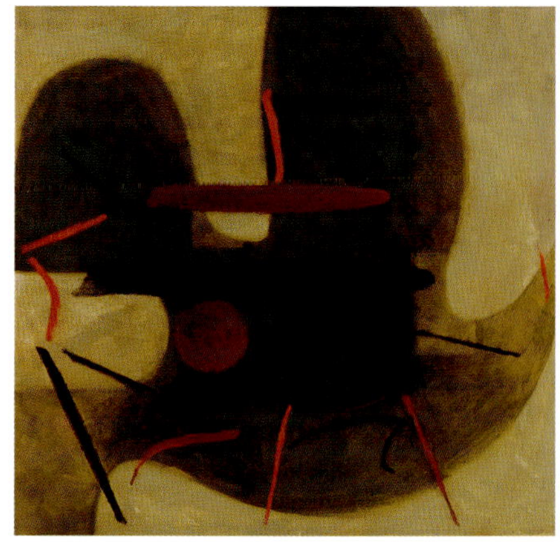

Reynolds, Alan b.1926
Legend – Red and Green 1967
oil on canvas 112 x 117
ACA 75

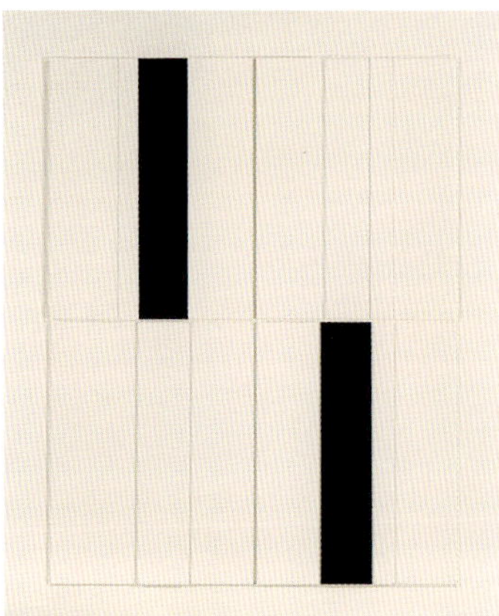

Reynolds, Alan b.1926
Vertical Structure III 1977
emulsion on card on wood 79 x 63
AC 1879

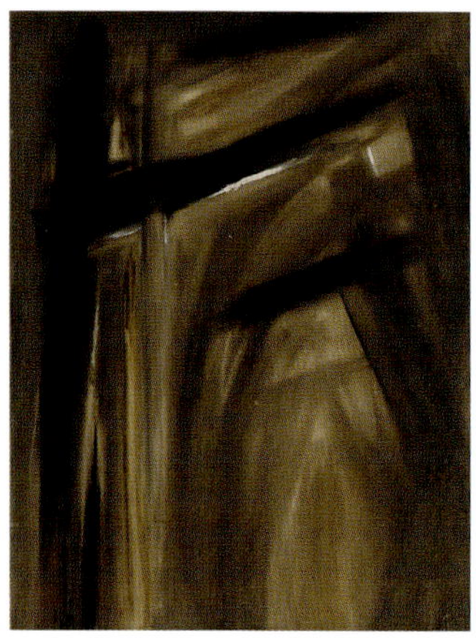

Reynolds, Daphne 1918–2002
Spectral Cross 1961
oil on canvas 118 x 86.4
AC 584

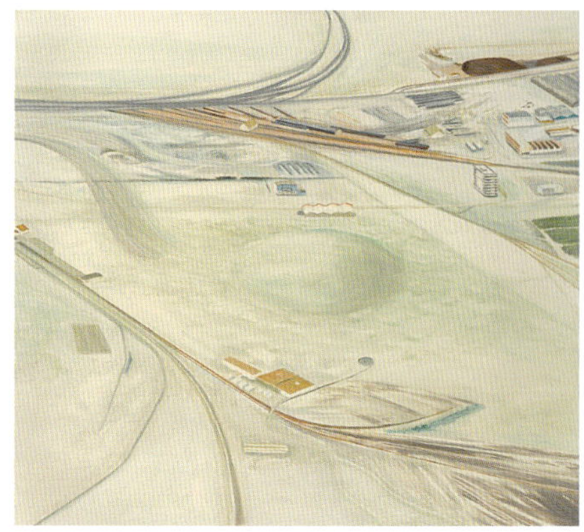

Rhodes, Carol b.1959
Industrial Landscape 1997
oil on board 42.5 x 47.5
ACC56/1997

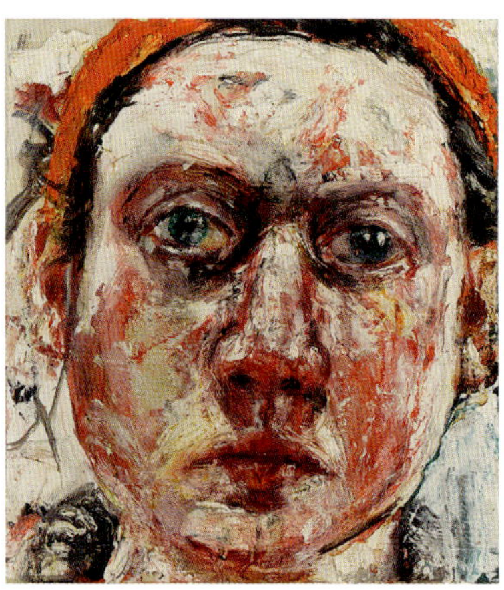

Rhys-James, Shani b.1953
Stare 1997
oil on gesso on board 30 x 27.6
ACC50/1997

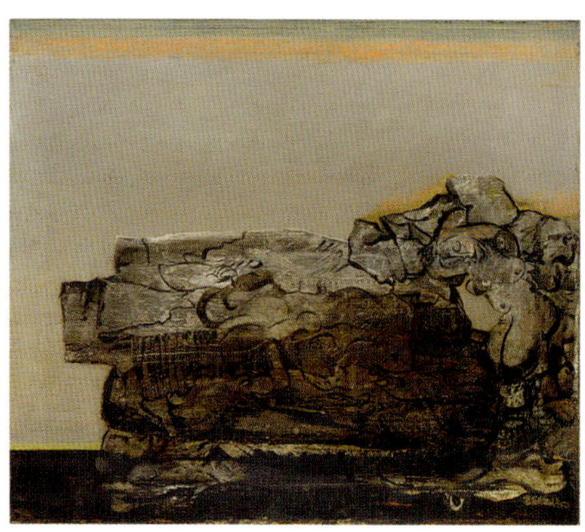

Richards, Ceri Geraldus 1903–1971
Rocks 1942
oil on canvas 62 x 74
AC 78

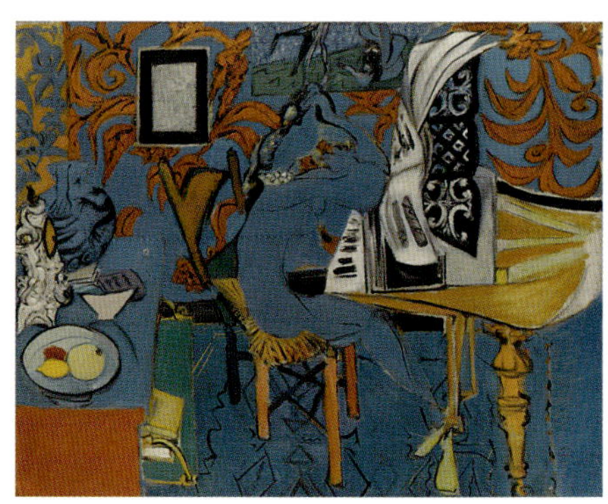

Richards, Ceri Geraldus 1903–1971
Blue Interior with Dice 1950
oil on canvas 89.5 x 110.6
AC 164

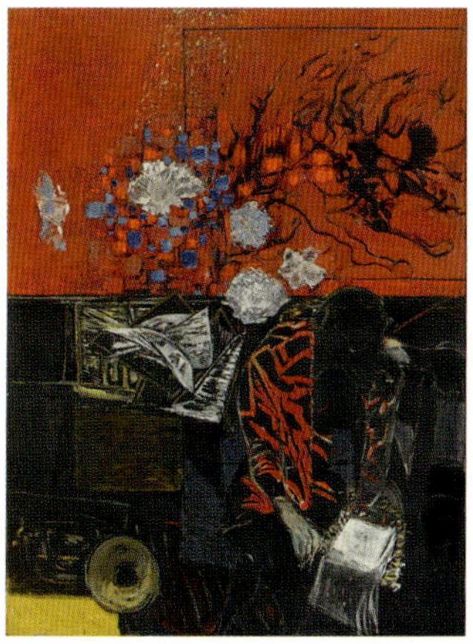

Richards, Ceri Geraldus 1903–1971
Homage to Beethoven II 1953
oil on canvas 152.4 x 114.9
AC 366

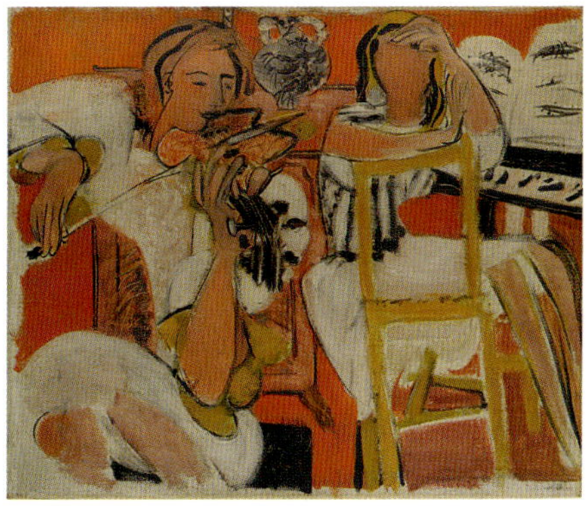

Richards, Ceri Geraldus 1903–1971
Two Musicians c.1954
oil on canvas 51 x 61
ACC4/1983

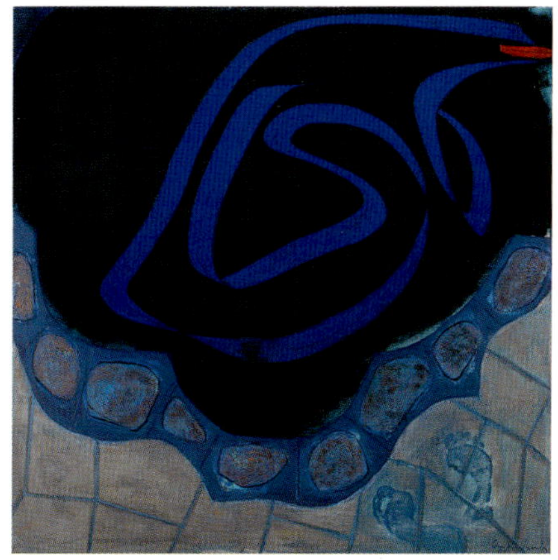

Richards, Ceri Geraldus 1903–1971
Poissons d'or 1963
oil on canvas 127 x 127
AC 692

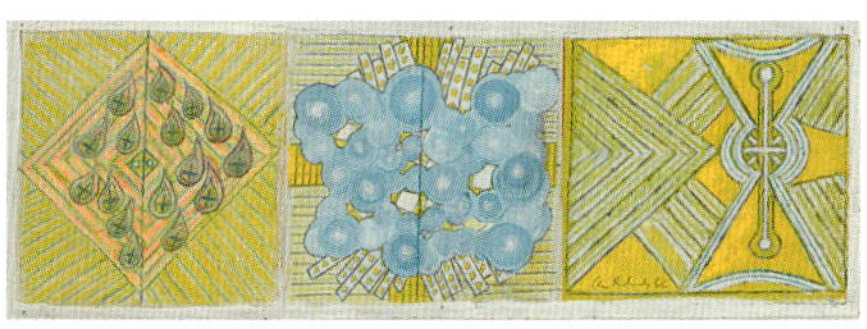

Richards, Ceri Geraldus 1903–1971
Study for Tabernacle of the Blessed Sacrament Chapel, Liverpool Metropolitan Cathedral of Christ the King 1966
acrylic & chalk on board 23.5 x 72.3
AC 901

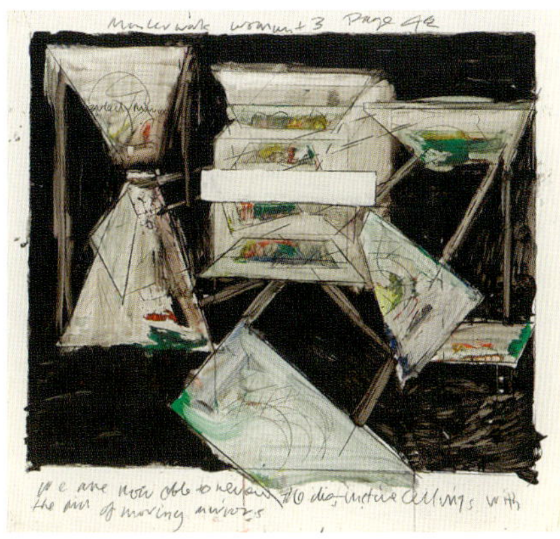

Richards, Paul b.1949
Masterwork: Scene Page 43 1979–1980
acrylic on paper 137.2 x 153.8
AC 5004

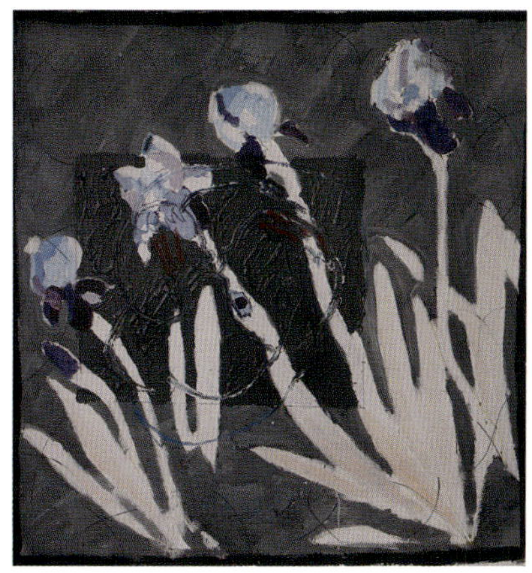

Richards, Paul b.1949
The Kiss (No.1) 1982
acrylic on canvas 122.2 x 121.7
AC 5100

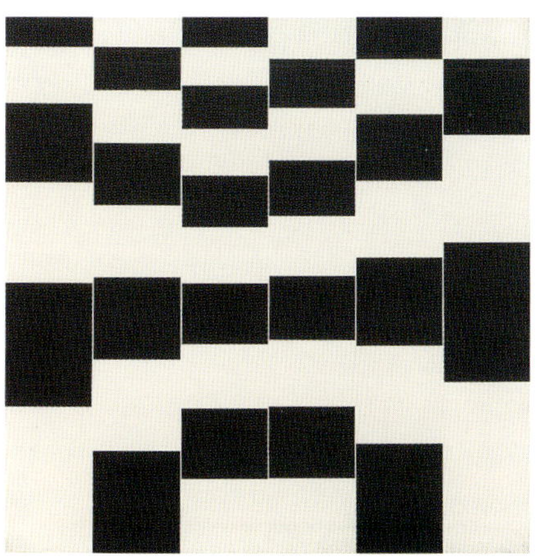

Richardson-Jones, Keith 1925–2005
Series 288 24/18 (i) 6/8/10/9/7/5 1975
acrylic on canvas 80 x 80
AC 1821a

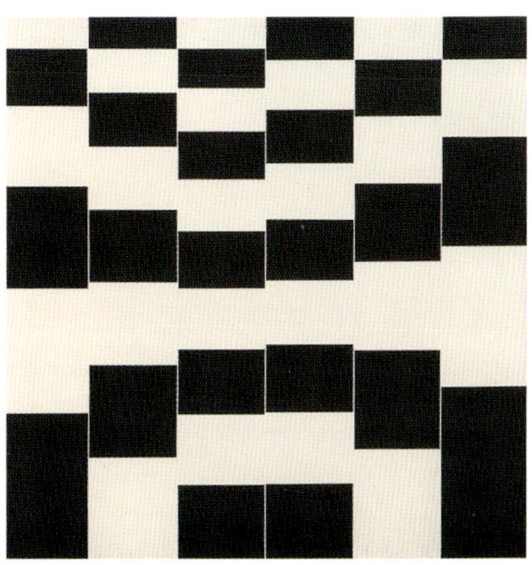

Richardson-Jones, Keith 1925–2005
Series 288 24/18 (ii) 6/8/10/9/7/5 1975
acrylic on canvas 80 x 80
AC 1821b

Richardson-Jones, Keith 1925–2005
Series 288: Log/Thirds 1980
routed, painted plywood 60 x 60
AC 5217

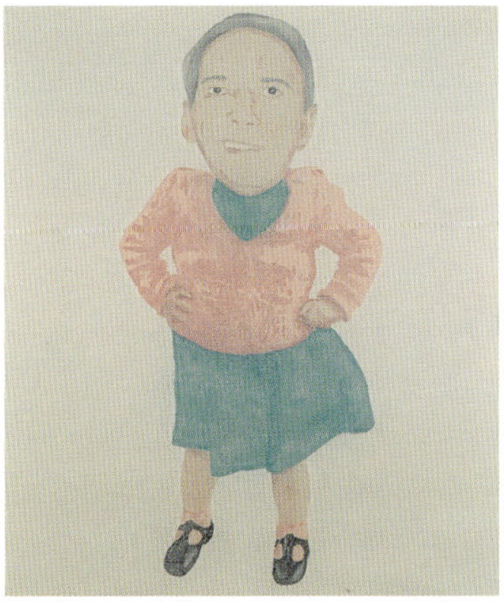

Rielly, James Malcolm b.1956
Object of Fun 1995
oil on canvas 213.1 x 183
ACC235/1998

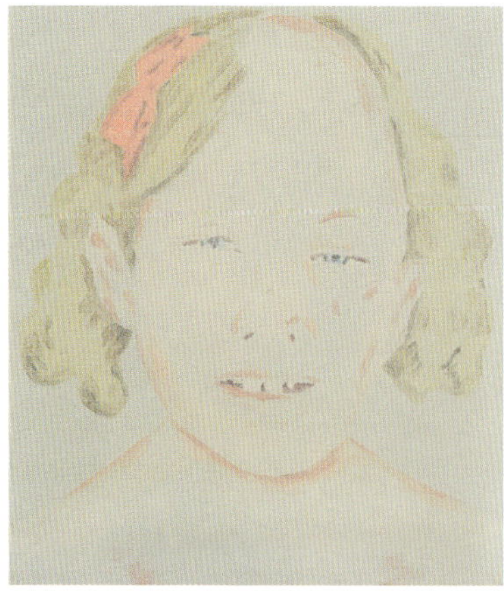

Rielly, James Malcolm b.1956
Daddy, I Love You 1996
oil on canvas 81.2 x 71.1
ACC6/1996

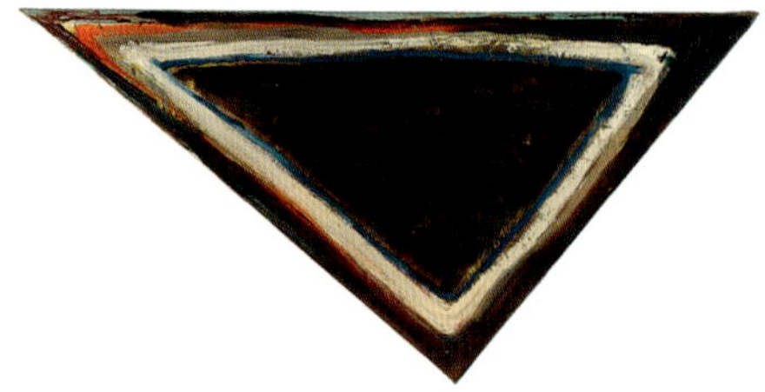

Rigden, Geoff b.1943
Paphos 1978–1979
watercolour on board & acrylic & oil on canvas 106.7 x 139
AC 2007

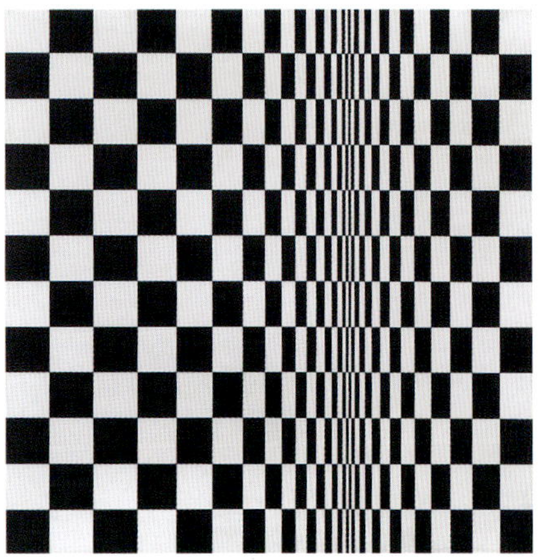

Riley, Bridget b.1931
Movement in Squares 1961
tempera on hardboard 123.2 x 121.2
ACC6/1962

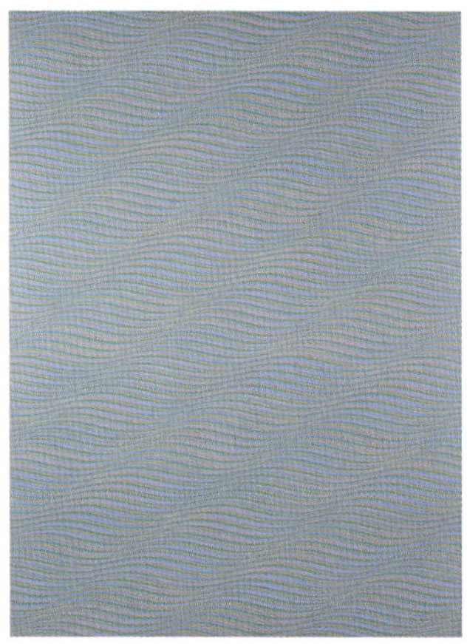

Riley, Bridget b.1931
Song of Orpheus IV 1978
acrylic on canvas 195.6 x 259.7
AC 1882

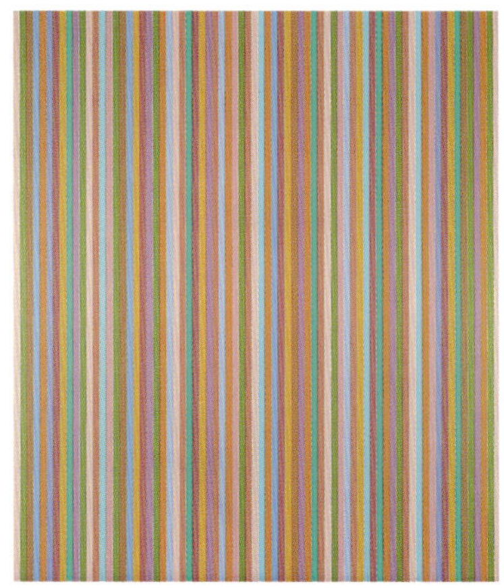

Riley, Bridget b.1931
Ecclesia 1985
oil on canvas 161.5 x 140
AC 5406

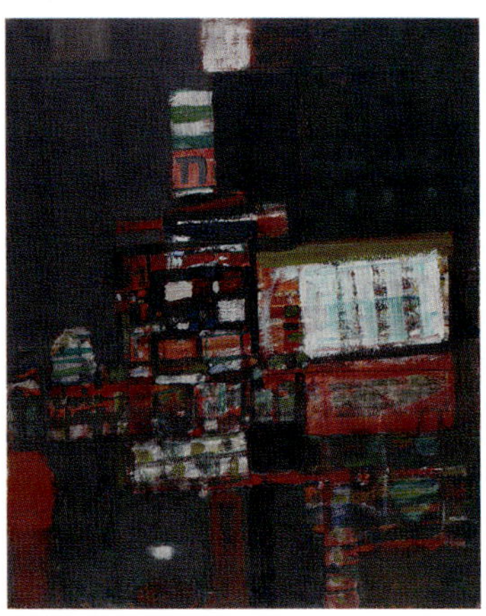

Robb, Brian 1913–1979
Townscape 1959
oil on canvas 76.8 x 63.8
AC 545

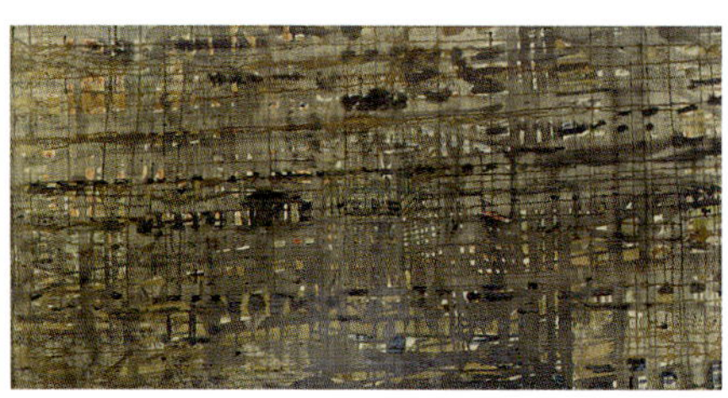

Robb, Brian 1913–1979
Lagoon c.1964
oil on canvas 45.7 x 91.4
AC 787

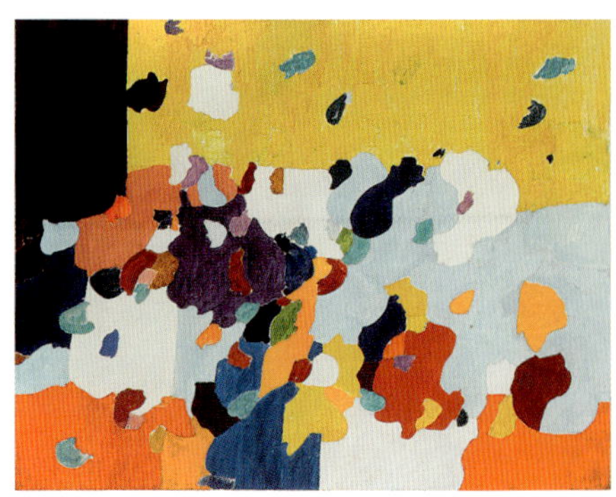

Roberts, Derek b.1947
Painting No.2 August/December 1980 1980
oil & wax on canvas 129.3 x 168.4
AC 5130

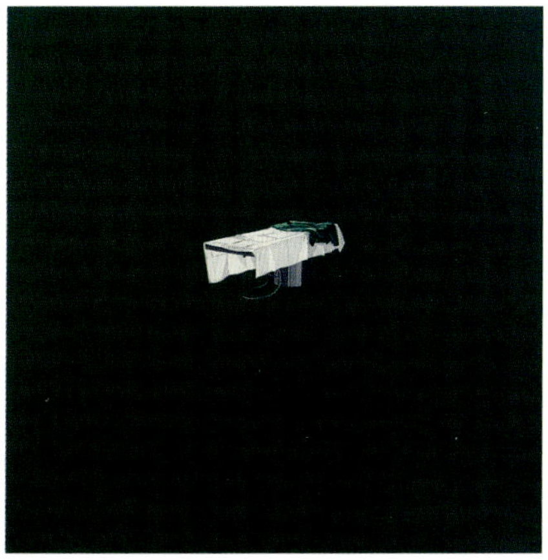

Roberts, Julie b.1963
Mortuary Table (green) 1994
oil & acrylic on canvas 150 x 150
ACC110/1995

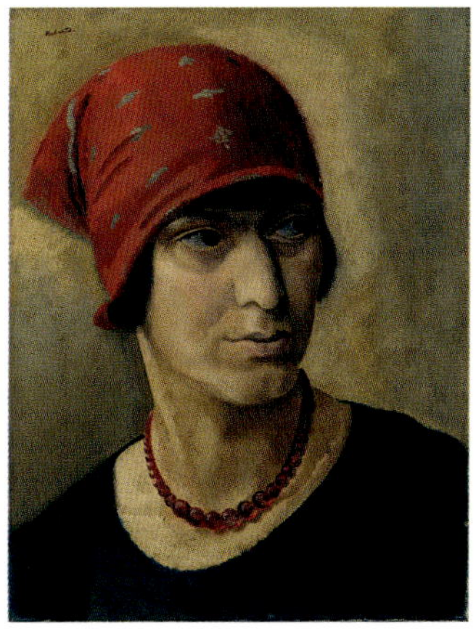

Roberts, William Patrick 1895–1980
A Gipsy Girl 1925–1926
oil on canvas 41.5 x 31.2
AC 171

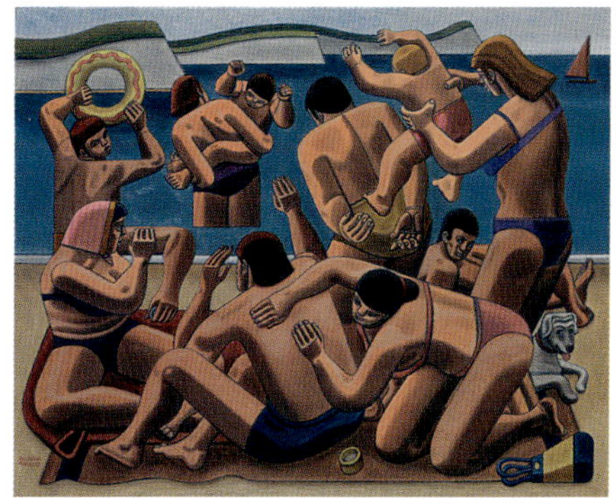

Roberts, William Patrick 1895–1980
The Seaside c.1966
oil on canvas 61 x 76.2
AC 863

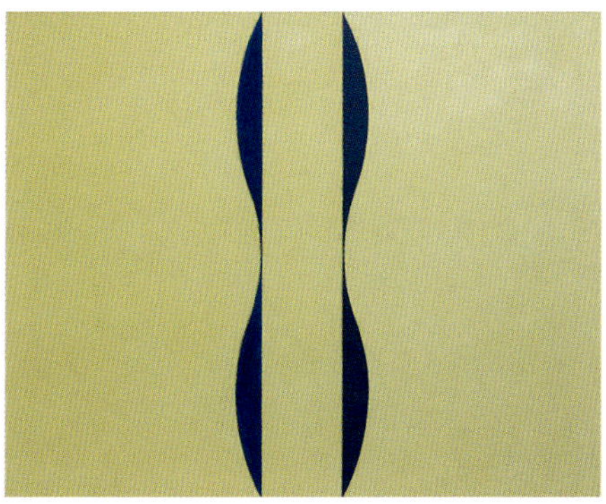

Robertson, Carol b.1955
Over and Under 1990
oil & wax on canvas 122 x 153
ACC34/1991

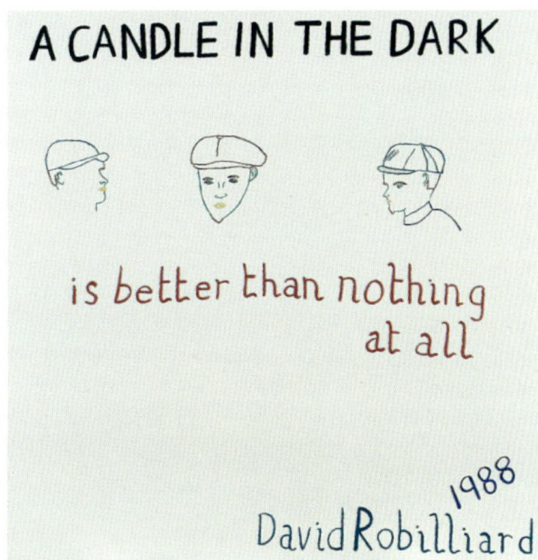

Robilliard, David 1952–1988
A candle in the dark is better than nothing at all 1988
acrylic on canvas 182.5 x 182.5
ACC16/1988

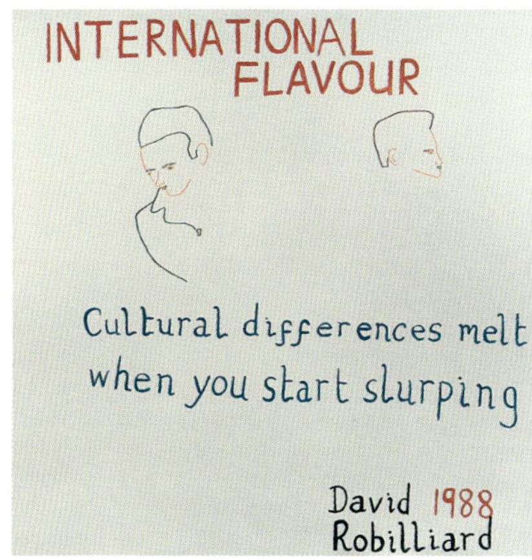

Robilliard, David 1952–1988
International flavour: cultural differences melt when you start slurping 1988
acrylic on canvas 182.5 x 182.5
ACC17/1988

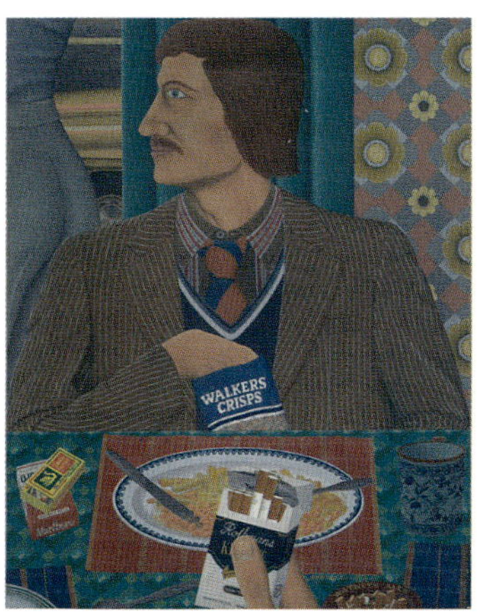

Robinson, Bob b.1951
A Preference for Crisps 1979
acrylic on canvas 76 x 61
AC 3070

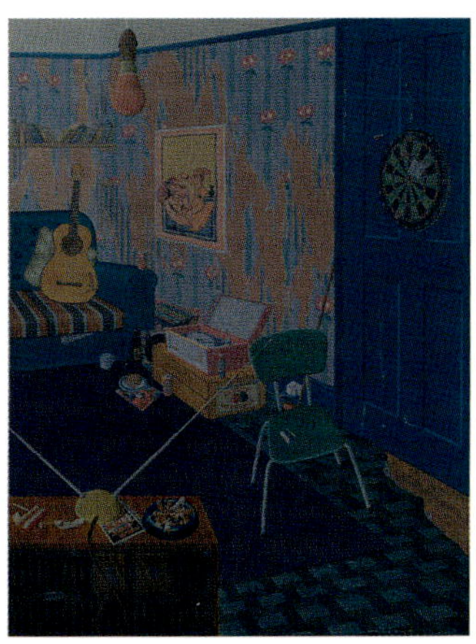

Robinson, Bob b.1951
Van Gogh: waits for Gauguin and is now living in Nottingham.' 1980
acrylic on canvas 84 x 64
AC 3071

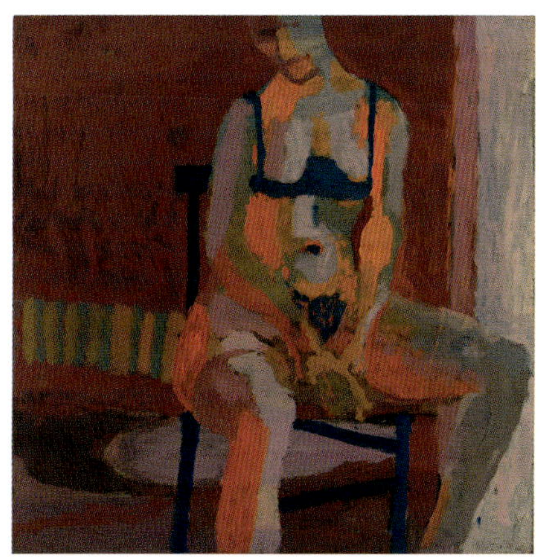

Robinson, Peter
Seated Figure 1962
oil on board 121.9 x 121.9
AC 776

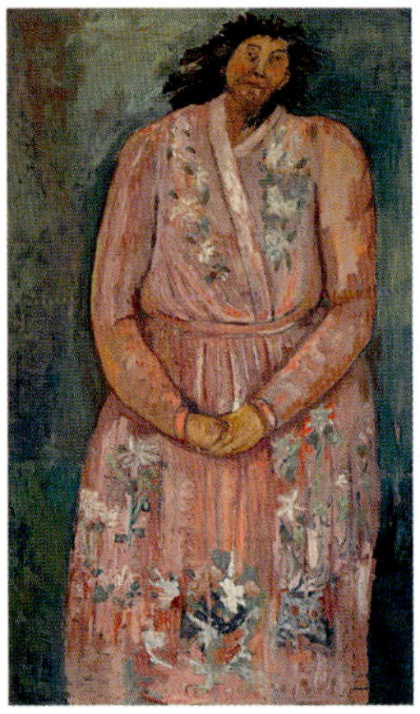

Robinson, Val b.1944
Big Mother 1987
oil on canvas 254.2 x 152.5
AC 5489

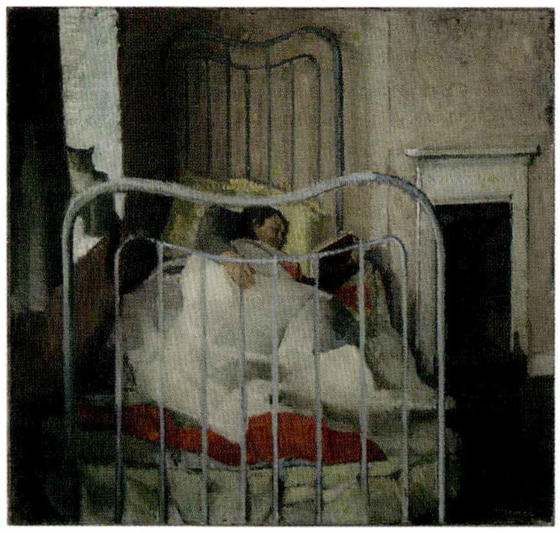

Rogers, Claude 1907–1979
The Cottage Bedroom 1944
oil on canvas 63.5 x 76
AC 39

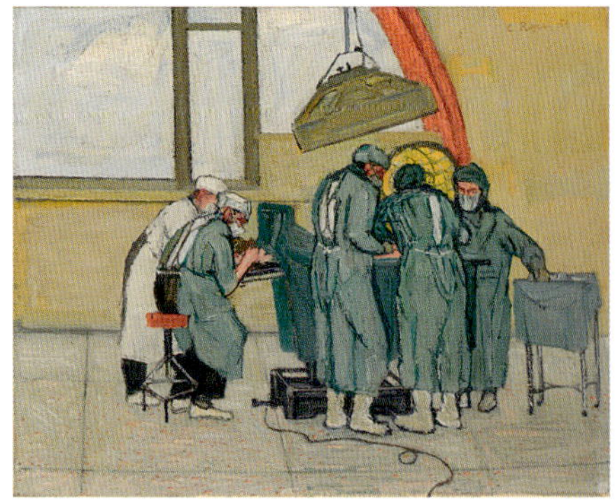

Rogers, Claude 1907–1979
Operation in Progress 1954
oil on canvas 40 x 50
AC 322

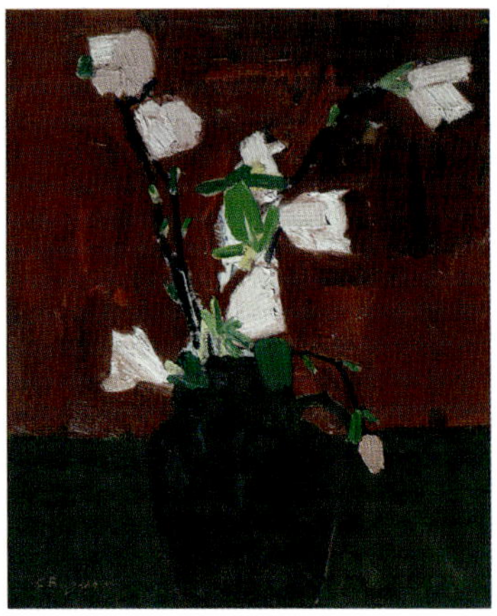

Rogers, Claude 1907–1979
Magnolias in a Brown Jug 1957
oil on canvas 78 x 63.5
AC 451

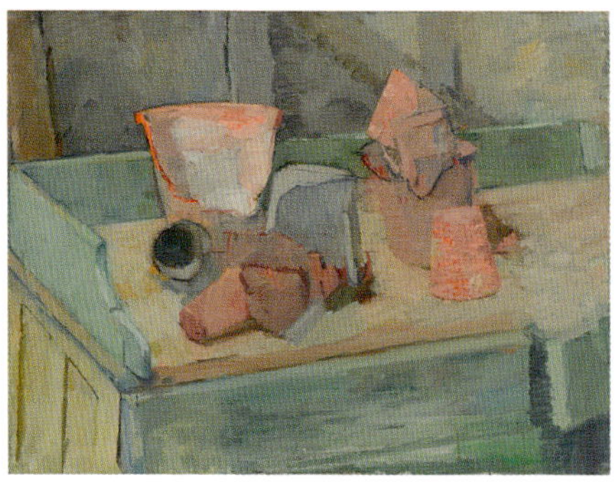

Rogers, Claude 1907–1979
Still Life 1961
oil on canvas 75.6 x 101
AC 615

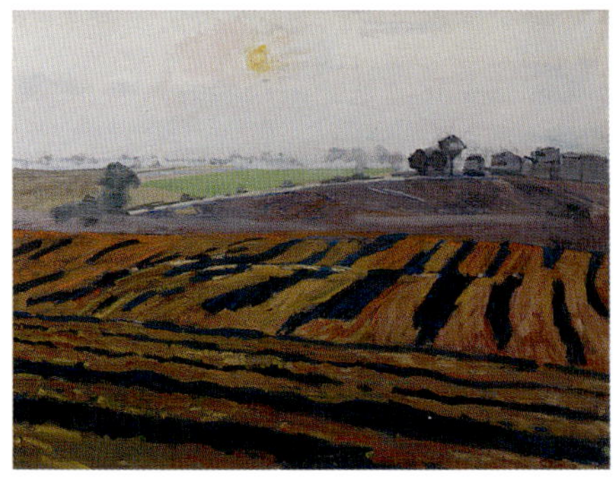

Rogers, Claude 1907–1979
Sunrise over Burnt Field 1977
oil on canvas 76.5 x 102.5
AC 1878

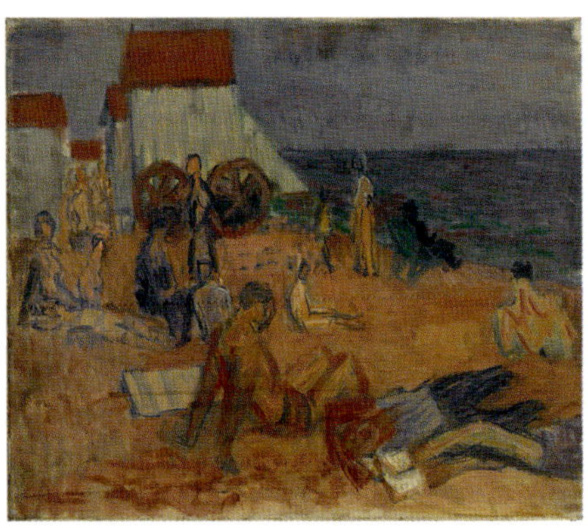

Rogers, Claude 1907–1979
Aldeburgh Beach 1937
oil on canvas 50.8 x 61
AC 79

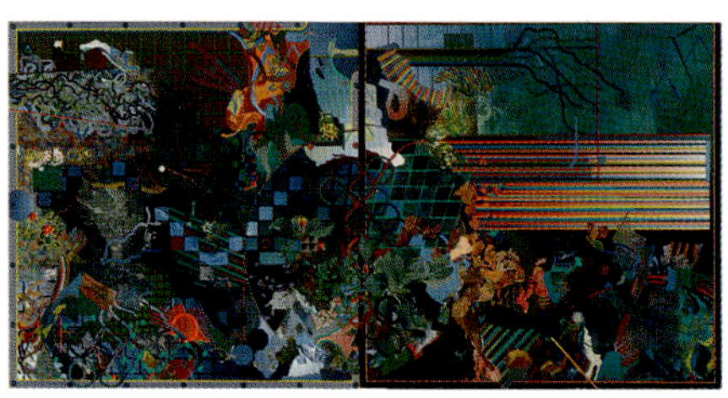

Rose, Colin b.1950
Amongst Drifting Tides – Verse and Refrain 1980
acrylic on board 121.3 x 120.4; 121.3 x 120.4
AC 5111

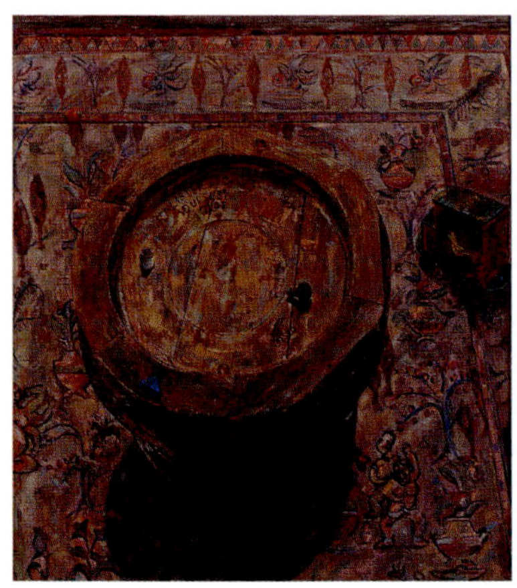

Rose, Kate b.1948
Pattern on a Persian Carpet 1981
oil & acrylic on canvas 101.6 x 91.1
AC 5035

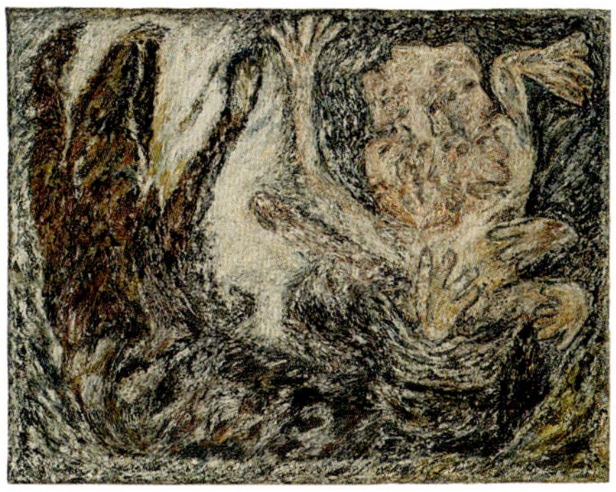

Rose, Rose b.1946
Passage Four: Binary Fission 1987
oil on canvas 164 x 214
AC 5470

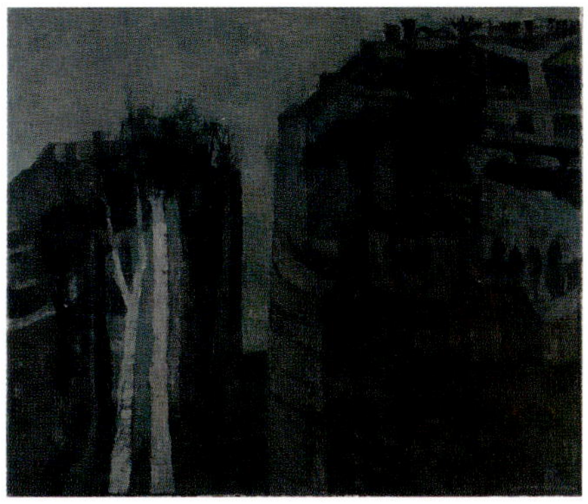

Rosoman, Leonard Henry 1913–2012
Gardens on Different Levels 1955
oil on canvas 62 x 75
AC 377

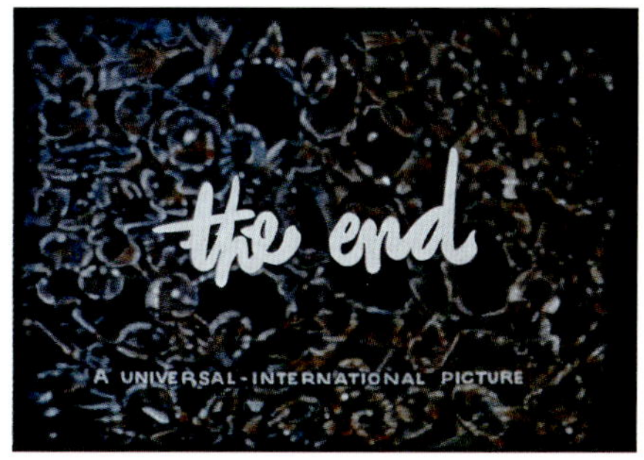

Rossi, Mario b.1958
The End/Untitled, Series 1996–2000
acrylic on canvas 61 x 86.5
ACC24/2001

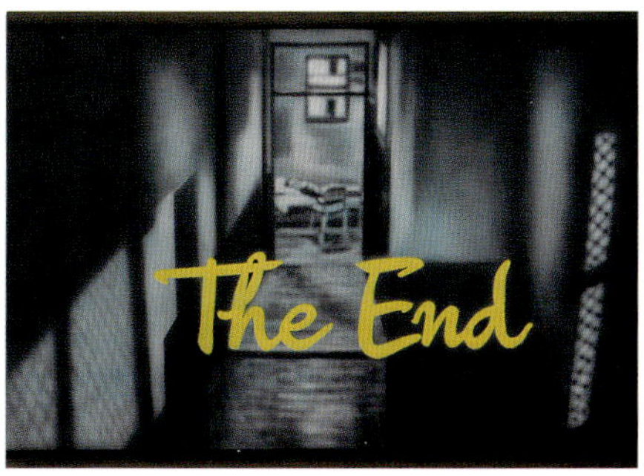

Rossi, Mario b.1958
The End/Untitled, Series 1996–2000
acrylic on canvas 61 x 86.5
ACC25/2001

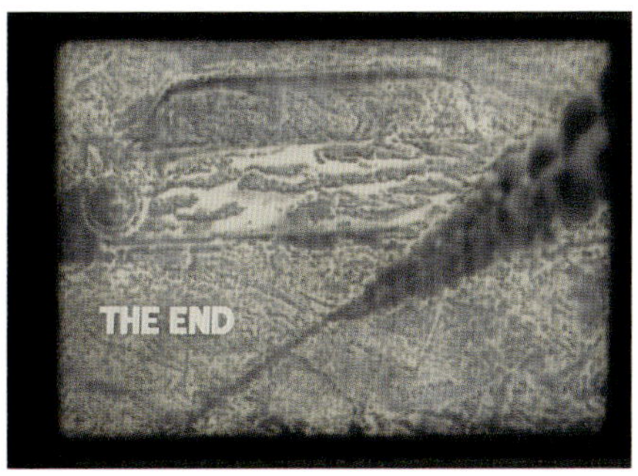

Rossi, Mario b.1958
The End/Untitled, Series 1996–2000
acrylic on canvas 61 x 86.5
ACC26/2001

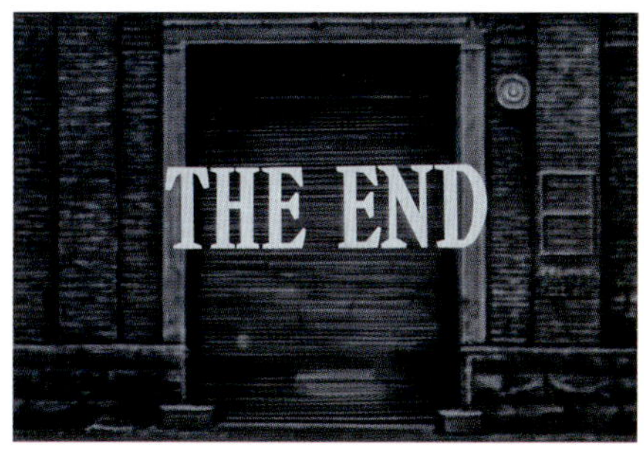

Rossi, Mario b.1958
The End/Untitled, Series 1996–2000
acrylic on canvas 61 x 86.5
ACC27/2001

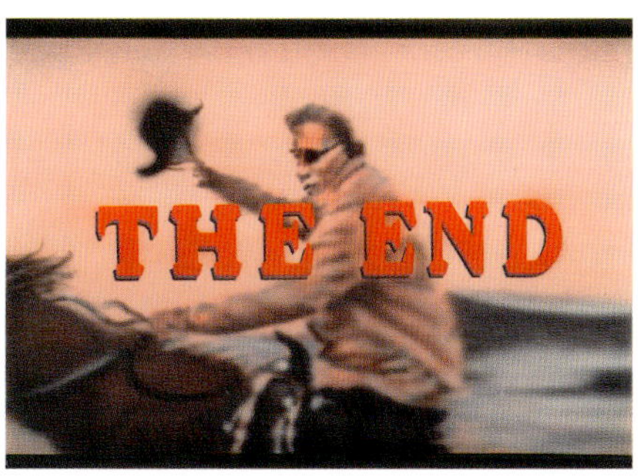

Rossi, Mario b.1958
The End/Untitled, Series 1996–2000
acrylic on canvas 61 x 86.5
ACC28/2001

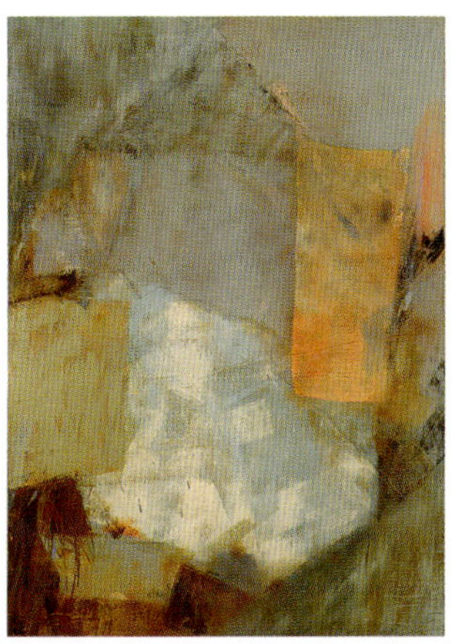

Rothwell, Vivien b.1945
Bank Holiday 1978
canvas, muslin, acrylic, paint & chalk on canvas 213 x 152.3
AC 2078

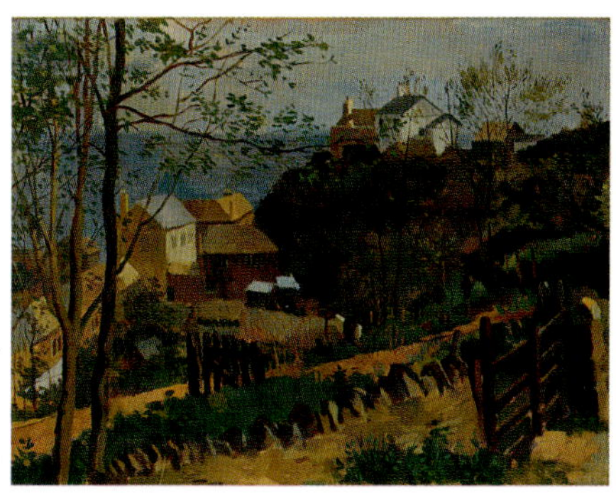

Rowntree, Kenneth 1915–1997
The White House, Torcross 1938
oil on canvas 37.5 x 50.8
AC 102

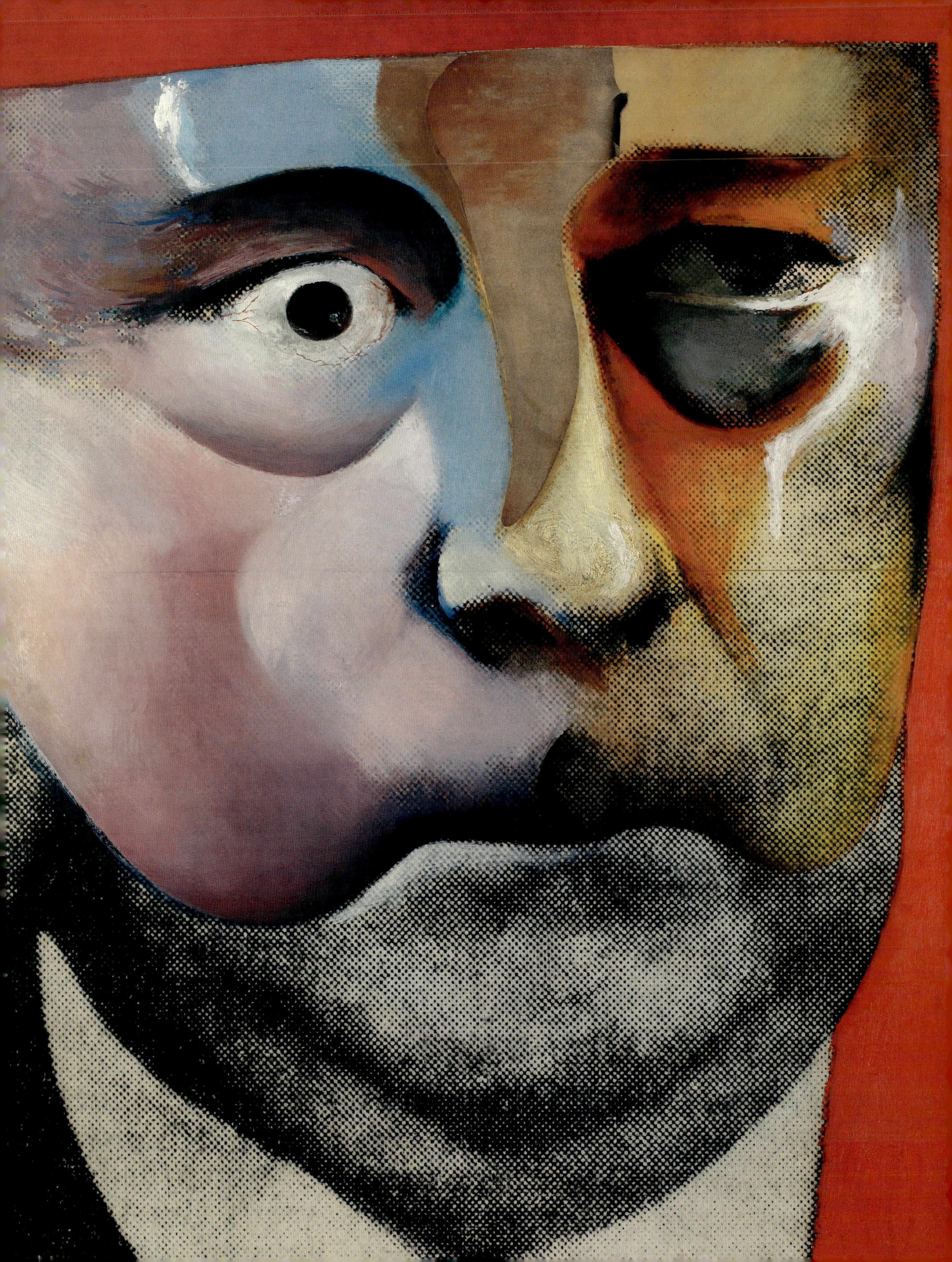

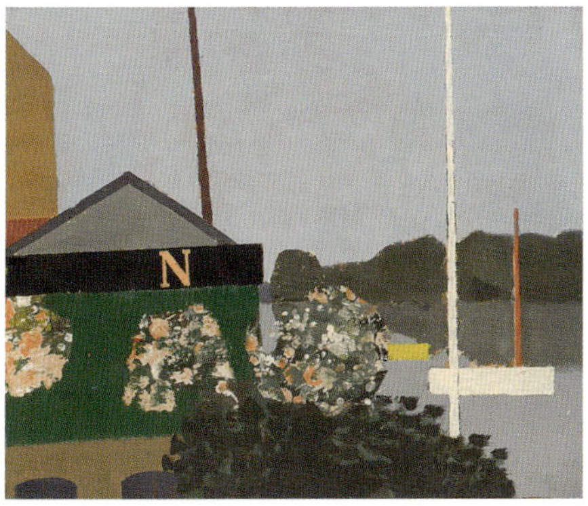

Rowntree, Kenneth 1915–1997
Putney Landscape 1961
oil on board 63.5 x 76.2
AC 618

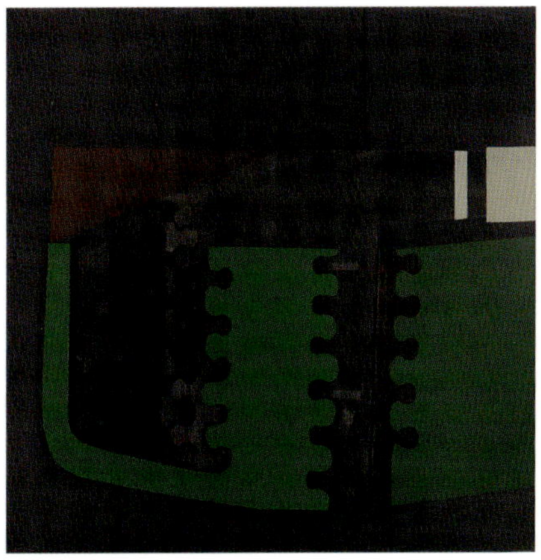

Rugg, Matt b.1935
Relief Painting 1964
paint on wood 154.5 x 154
AC 755

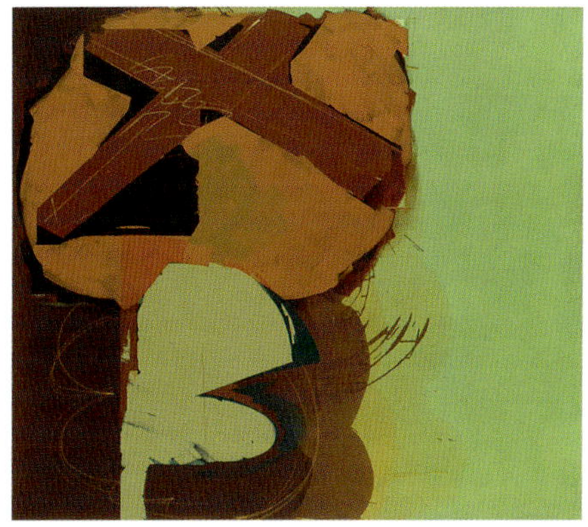

Russell, Bruce John b.1946
Untitled No.8 1975
acrylic, ink & emulsion on canvas 150 x 210
AC 1623

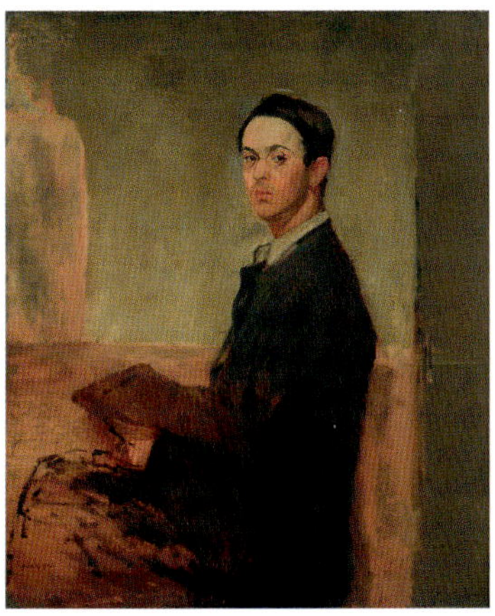

Rutherston, Albert 1881–1953
Self Portrait 1902
oil on canvas 55.9 x 48.3
AC 264

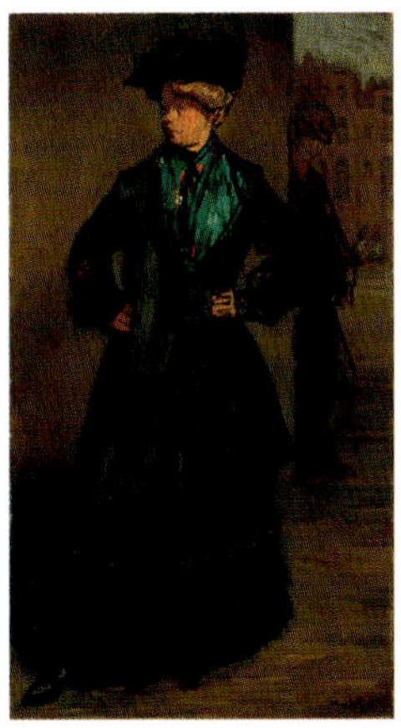

Rutherston, Albert 1881–1953
Coster Girl 1907
oil on canvas 81.3 x 44.5
AC 103

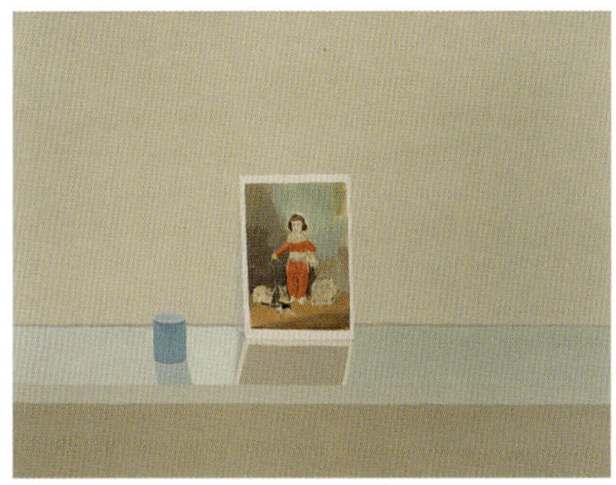

Rüthi, Andreas b.1956
Goya (Toy) 1997
oil on MDF 30 x 40
ACC63/1997

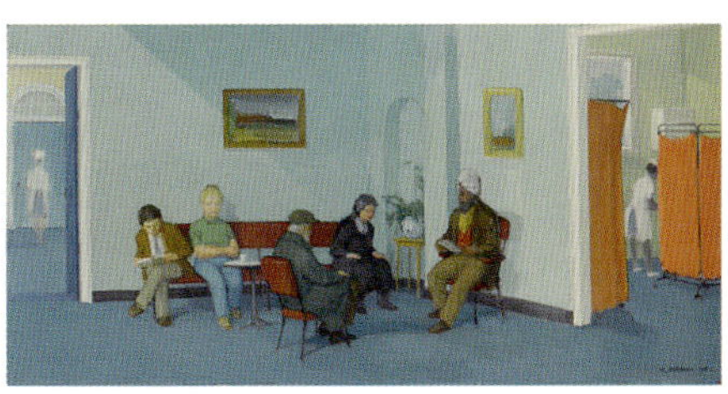

Salaman, Michael 1911–1987
Hospital Waiting Room 1982
oil on board 60 x 120.5
AC 5177

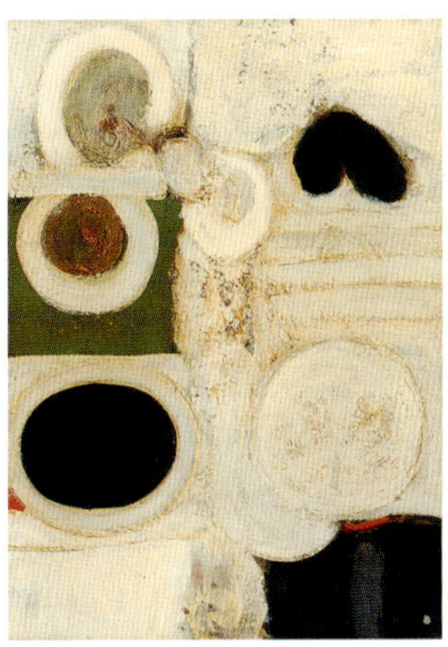

Sandle, Michael b.1936
Sunset 1960–1961
oil on canvas 73 x 54.6
AC 664

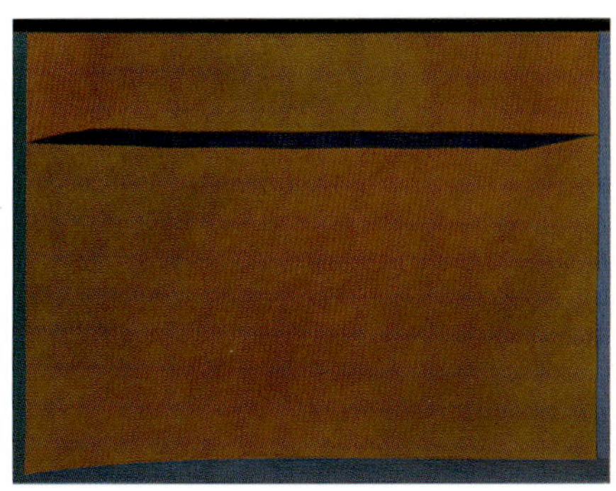

Saunders, David b.1936
Milan c.1967
acrylic on canvas 125.7 x 174
AC 932

Facing page: Hamilton, Richard, b.1922, *Hugh Gaitskell as a Famous Monster of Filmland* (detail), 1964, (p. 66)

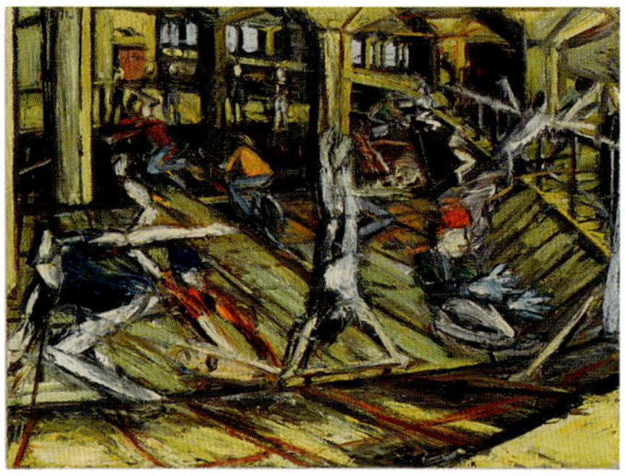

Saunders, Peter 1940–2011
Skateboarding, South Bank 1980
oil on canvas 145.5 x 198.3
AC 5278

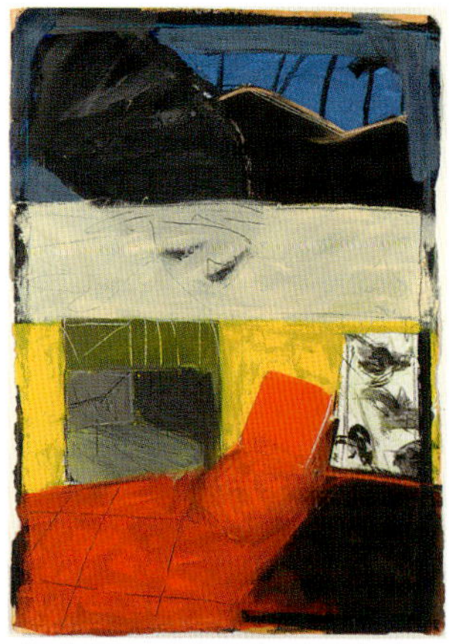

Scheihing, Vivian b.1947
Ashes on the South 1979
oil on paper 151 x 108
AC 2039

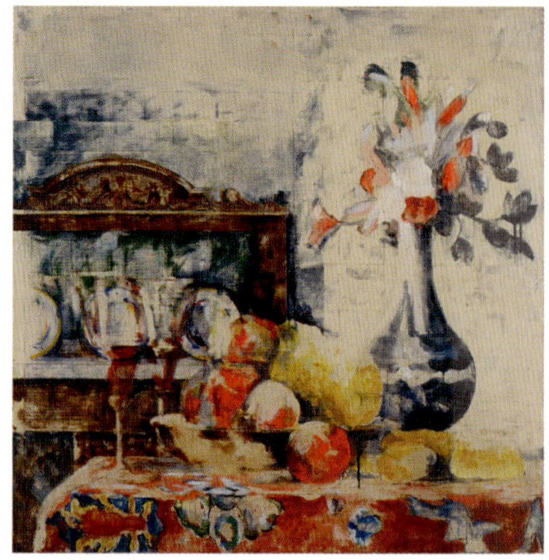

Scherman, Tony b.1950
The Kitchen 1975
encaustic & oil on canvas 89.5 x 90.5
AC 1579

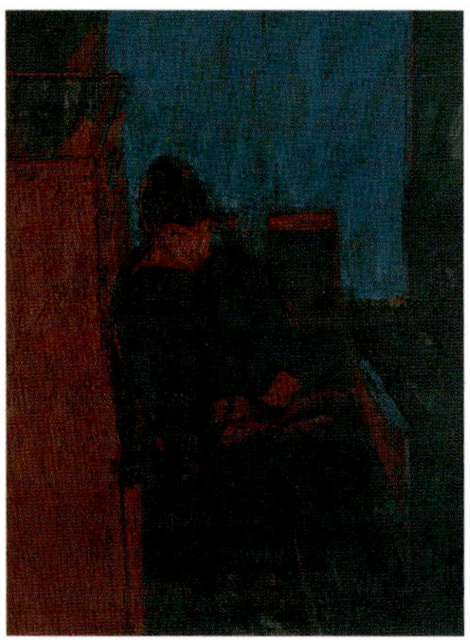

Schmidt, Peter 1931–1980
Ruth Reading 1961
oil on canvas 167 x 126.4
AC 590

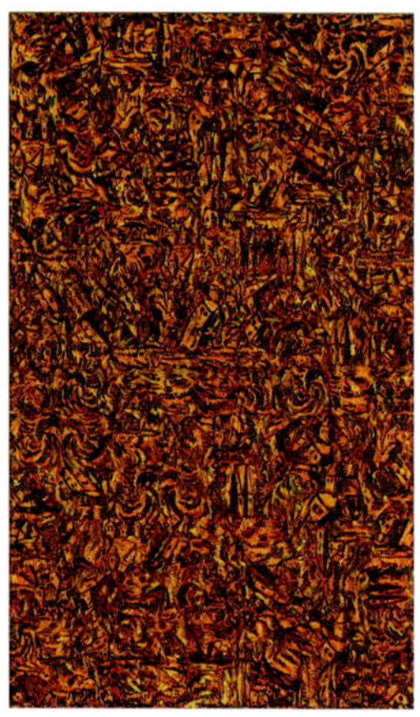

Scott, Michael b.1954
Earthquake of Lisbon, All Saints' Day 1755 1986
oil on canvas 230.2 x 140.3
AC 5454

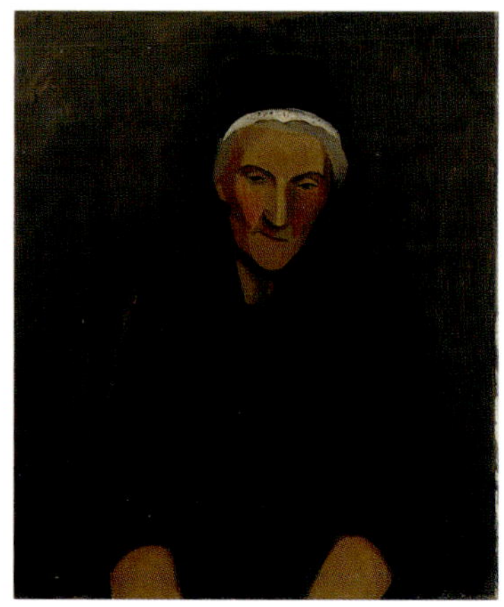

Scott, William George 1913–1989
Breton Woman 1946
oil on canvas 61.1 x 50.3
ACC2/1950

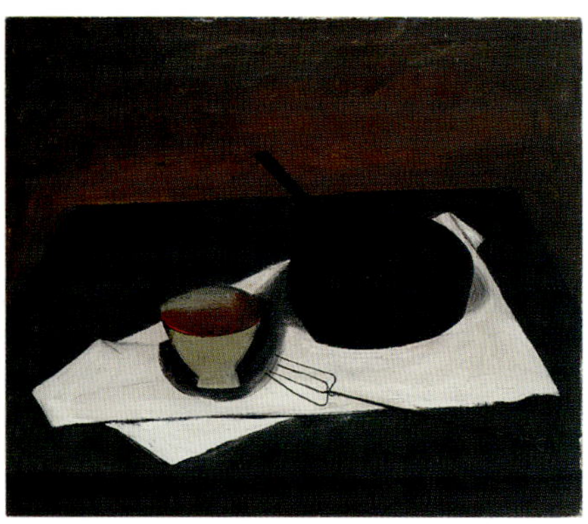

Scott, William George 1913–1989
The Frying Pan 1946
oil on canvas 54.5 x 65.1.
AC 50

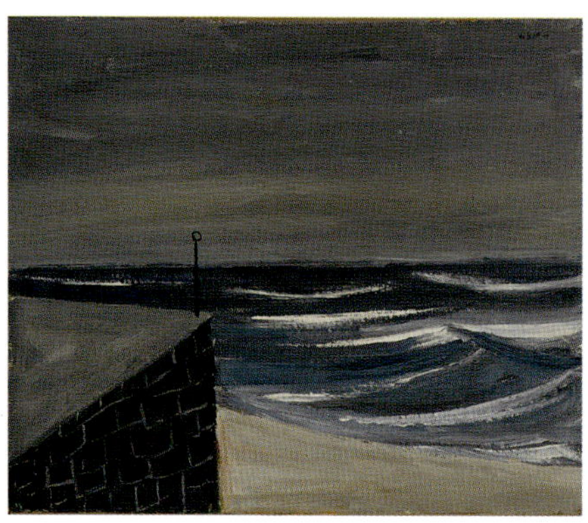

Scott, William George 1913–1989
Sennen 1950
oil on board 45.8 x 56.1
AC 5261

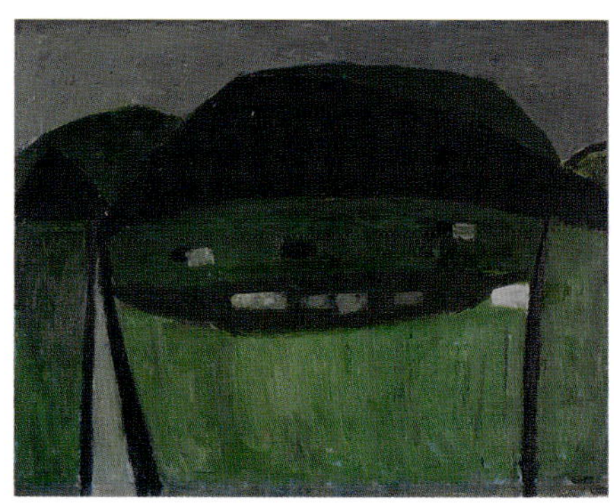

Scott, William George 1913–1989
Slagheap Landscape 1952
oil on canvas 72.9 x 91.6
ACC5/1953

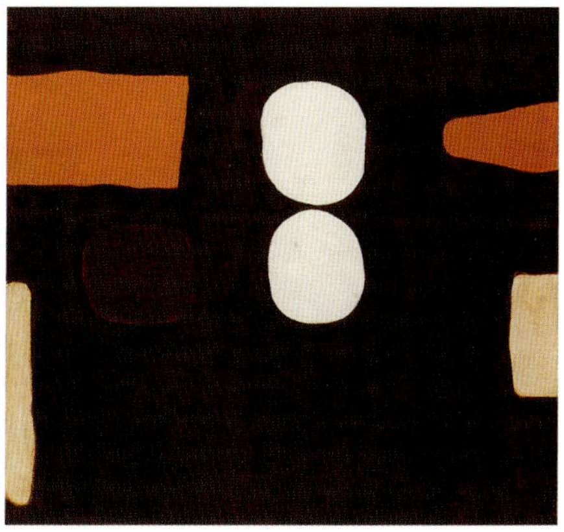

Scott, William George 1913–1989
Dark Brown, Orange and White 1963
oil on canvas 160.5 x 173.1
AC 691

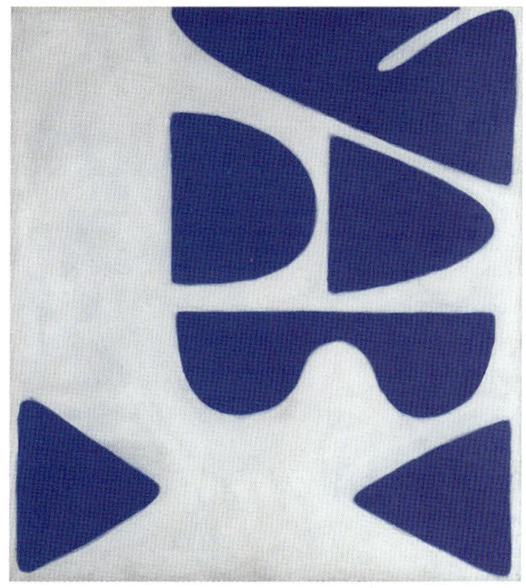

Scott, William George 1913–1989
Berlin Blues 6 1966
oil on canvas 183 x 167
AC 933

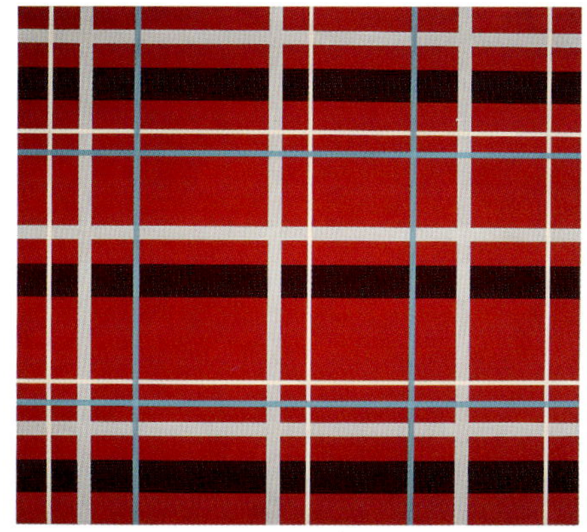

Scully, Sean b.1945
Red 1972
acrylic on canvas 243.8 x 274.3
AC 1180

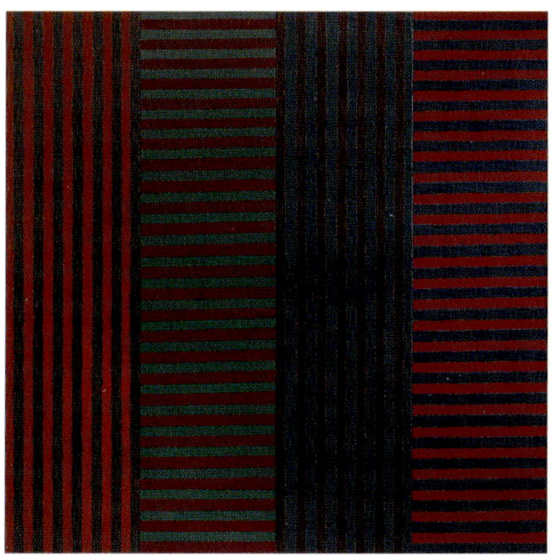

Scully, Sean b.1945
How it is 1981
oil on canvas 104.2 x 107.2
AC 5146

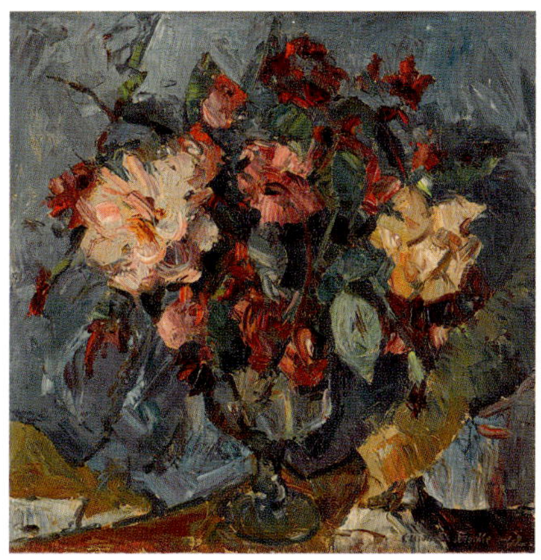

Seabrooke, Elliott 1886–1950
Roses 1942
oil on canvas 61 x 61
AC 180

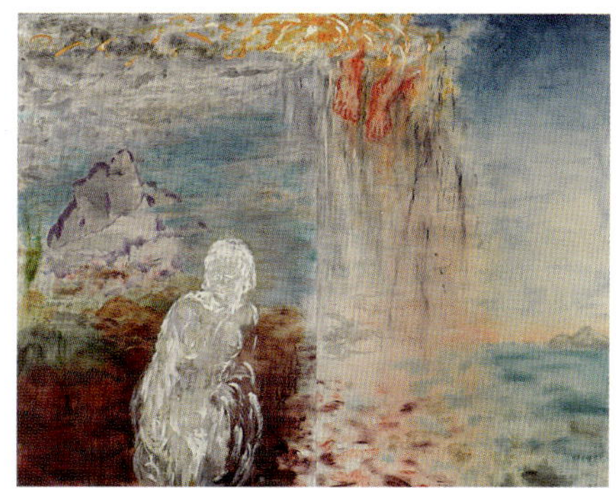

Searle, Adrian b.1953
Hubris 1984
oil on canvas 193.2 x 126.3; 193.2 x 126.3
AC 5352

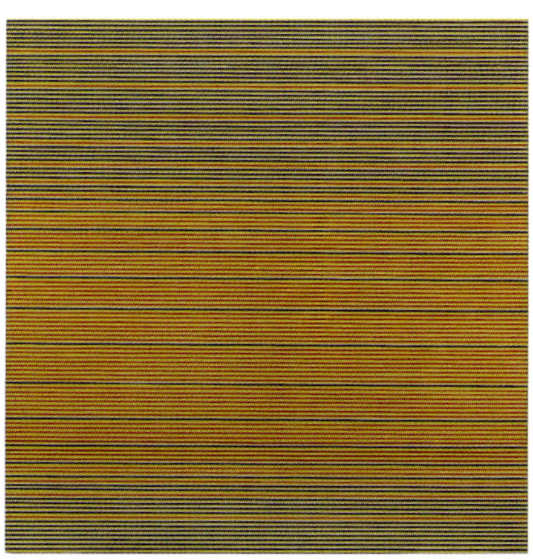

Sedgley, Peter b.1930
Red Shift 1965
emulsion on board 122.7 x 121.8
AC 786

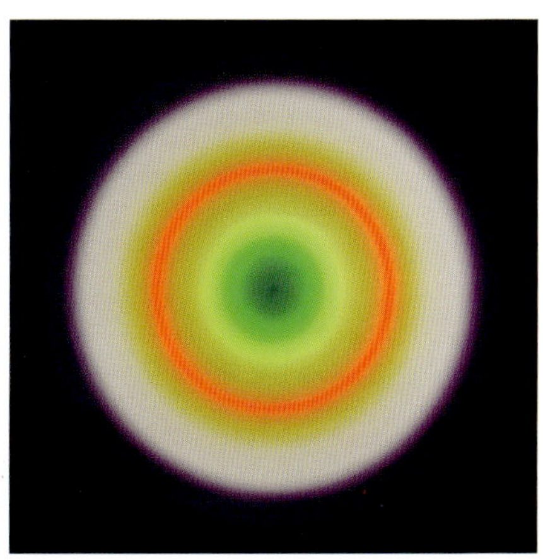

Sedgley, Peter b.1930
Corona 1970
PVA & pigment on canvas with optional kinetic lights 200 x 200
ACC69/2000

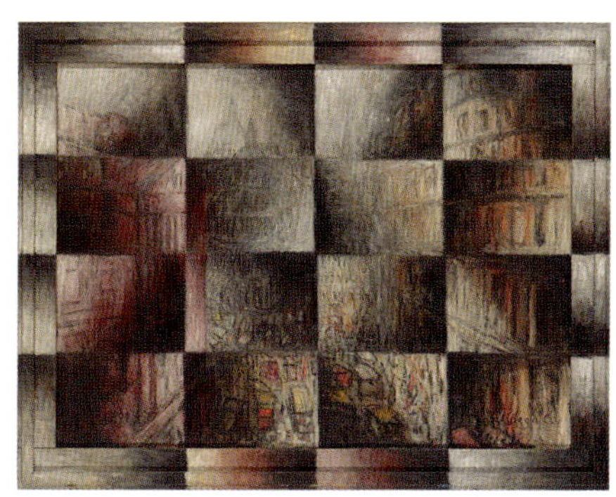

Segal, Arthur 1875–1944
City of London 1927
oil on canvas 91.4 x 121.9
AC 946

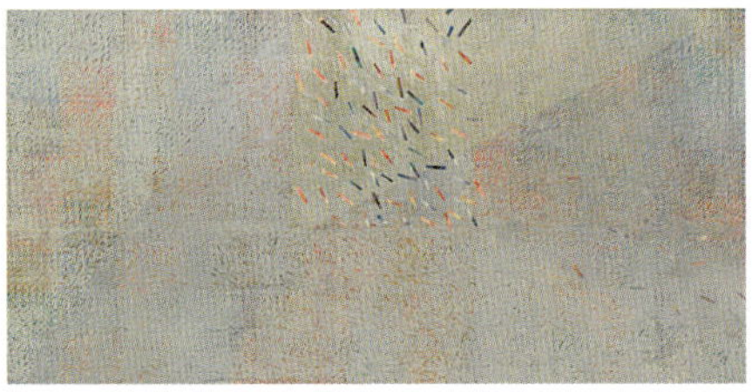

Serra, Paolo b.1946
Horizon 1977–1978
oil & gold leaf screenprint with acrylic on canvas 162.7 x 332.4
AC 3057

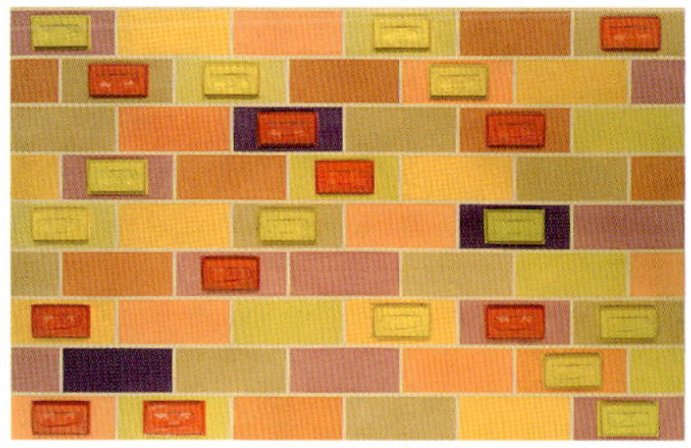

Setch, Terry b.1936
SGB Wallscape 1968
acrylic & plastic on canvas 152.4 x 244.8
AC 970

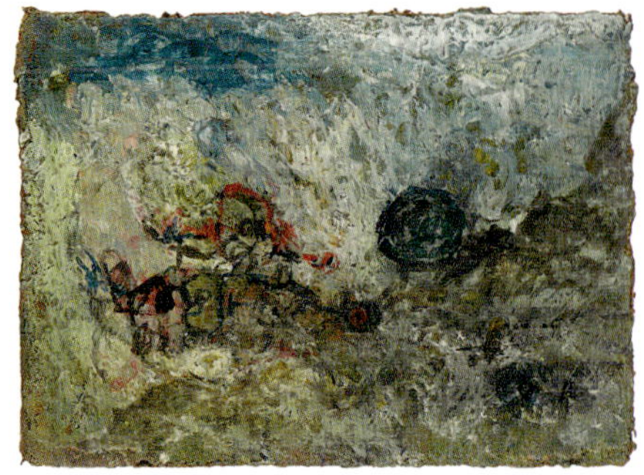

Setch, Terry b.1936
Car Wreck Penarth Beach VI 1978
oil & encaustic on carpet 33.6 x 47.9
AC 5143

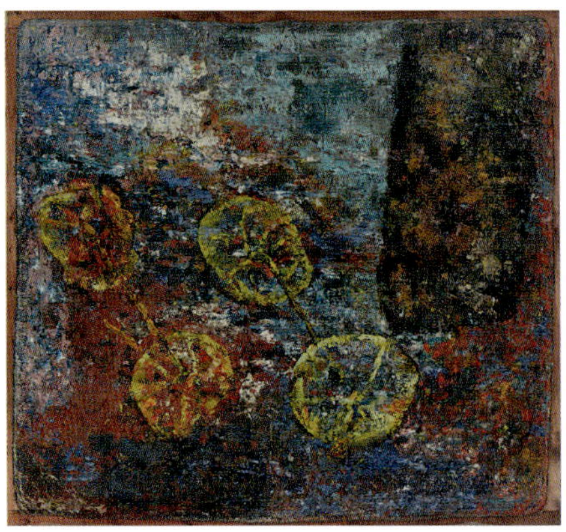

Setch, Terry b.1936
Waterwheel 1980
oil & wax on canvas 265.5 x 296.6
AC 4052

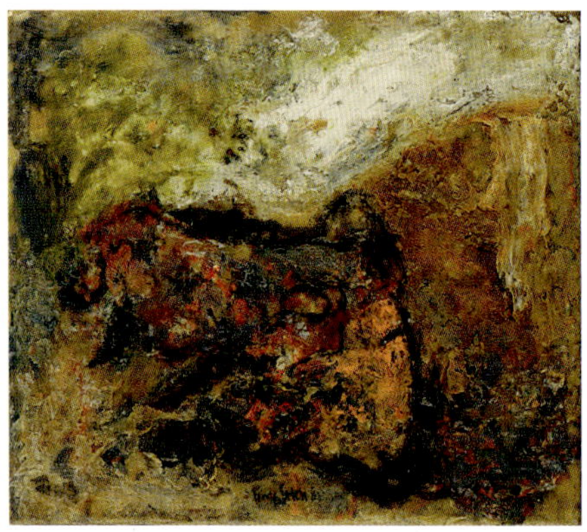

Setch, Terry b.1936
Penarth III 1981
oil & encaustic on canvas 35 x 40.5
AC 5144

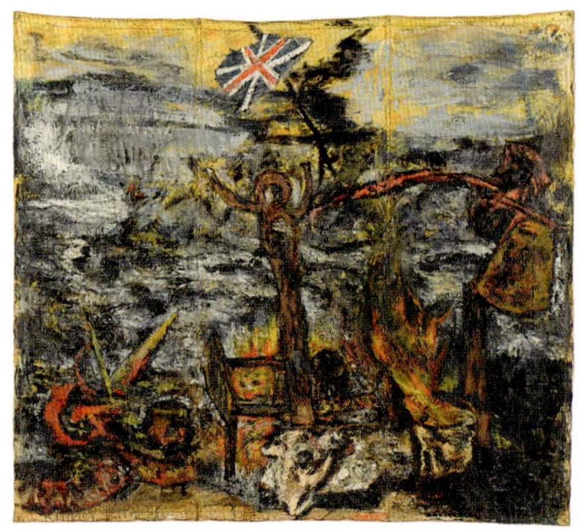

Setch, Terry b.1936
The Moon Falls as the Flags Wave Panel 1 Flag 1982
oil & encaustic on canvas 242.3 x 267
AC 5142

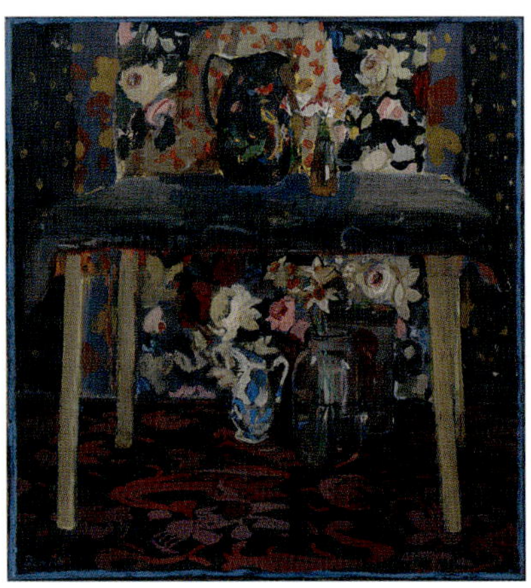

Shanks, Duncan b.1937
Flowers All-Over 1976–1979
pastel & oil on canvas 101 x 96.4
AC 2065

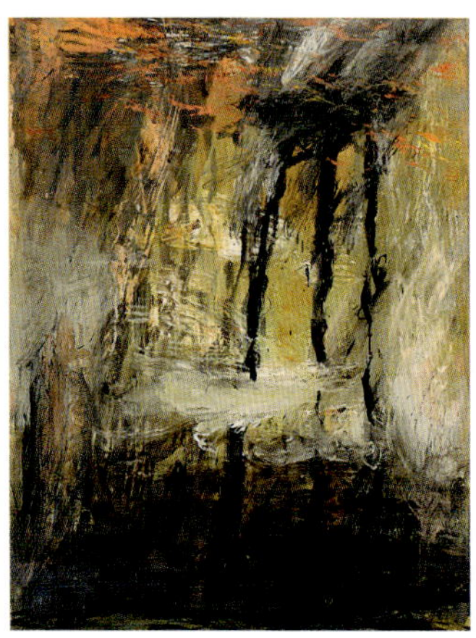

Shave, Terry b.1952
Inferno Storms 1986
oil on canvas 304.5 x 229
AC 5455

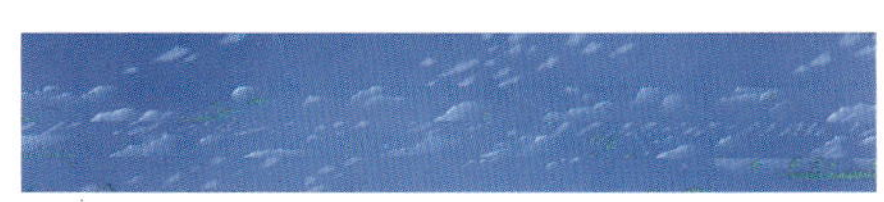

Shaw, David Carson b.1942
Reflections, Summer 1982
acrylic on card 18 x 98
AC 5129

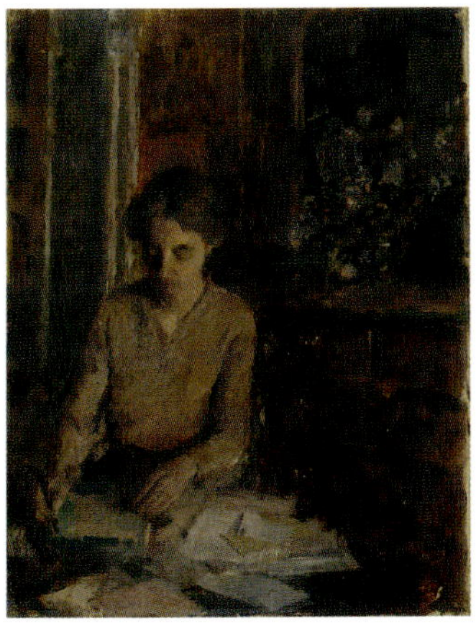

Shephard, Rupert 1909–1992
Woman Writing a Letter 1939
oil on canvas 45.9 x 35.7
AC 104

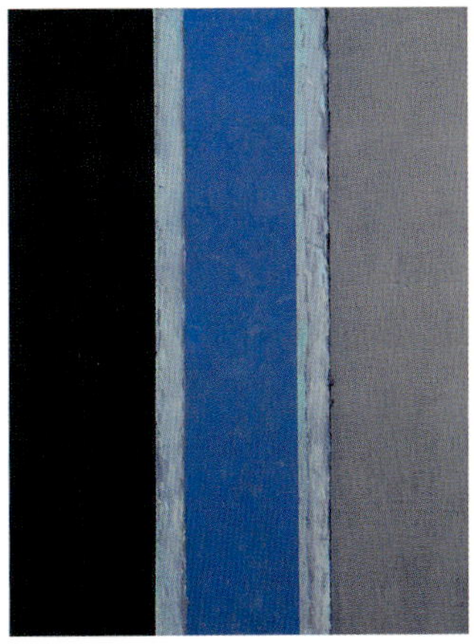

Shiraishi, Yuko b.1956
Dewfall 1990
oil on canvas 244 x 183
ACC23/1990

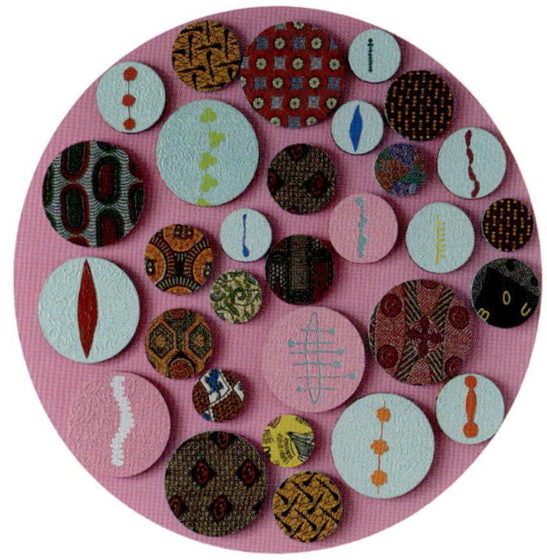

Shonibare, Yinka b.1962
Line Painting 2003
emulsion & acrylic on textile 312
ACC49/2003

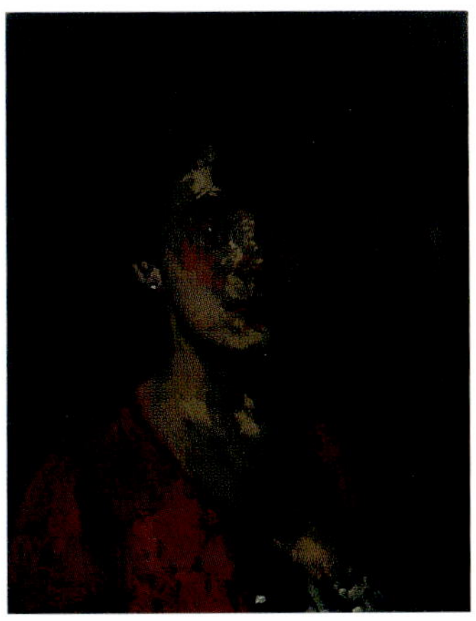

Sickert, Walter Richard 1860–1942
Head of a Woman (The Belgian Cocotte) 1906
oil on canvas 49.3 x 39.3
AC 261

Sickert, Walter Richard 1860–1942
Woman Seated on a Bed, Dieppe 1907
oil on canvas 66 x 78.7
AC 371

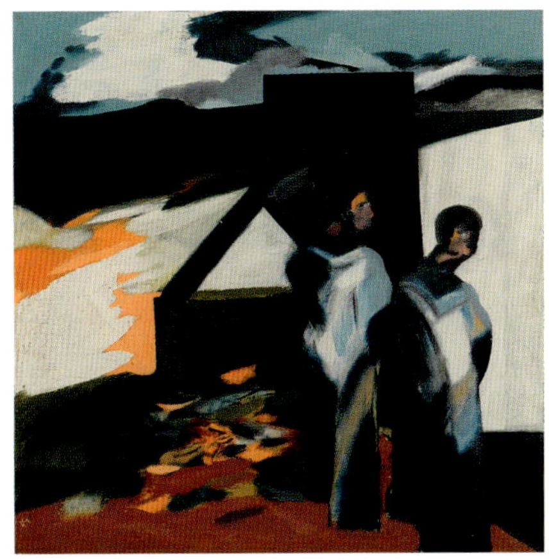

Simpson, Michael b.1940
Two Sailors in Summer 1964
oil on canvas 60.5 x 61
AC 749

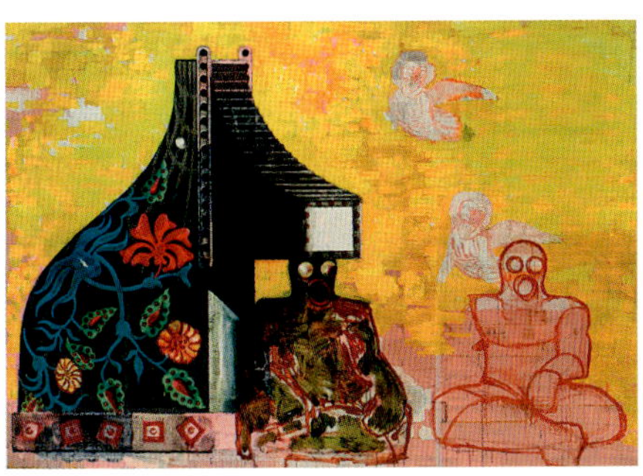

Simpson, Michael b.1940
The Survival Kit 1981–1983
oil on canvas 228.4 x 335.6
AC 5215

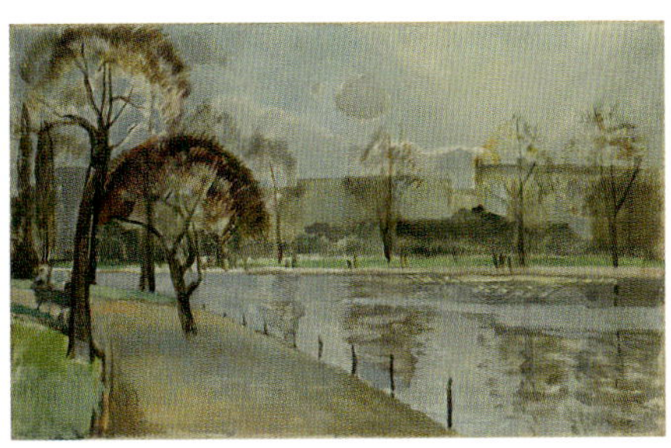

Sinclair, Beryl 1901–1967
Regent's Park, London 1939
oil on canvas 30.5 x 50.6
AC 105

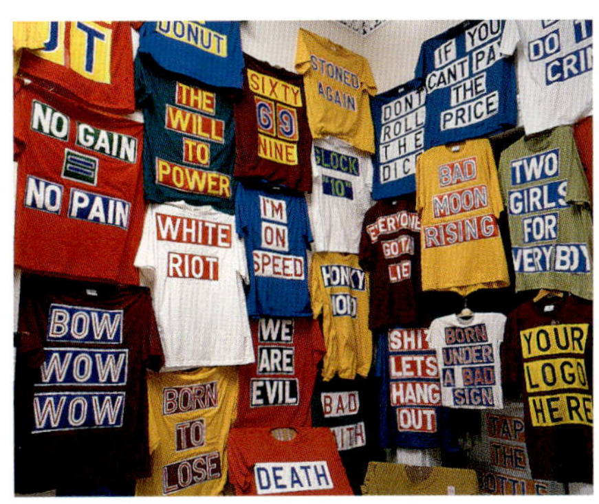

Sinclair, Ross b.1966
T-Shirt Paintings 1–80 (detail) 1993–1998
gesso & acrylic on cotton (61 x 61) x 80
ACC43/1998–ACC122/1998

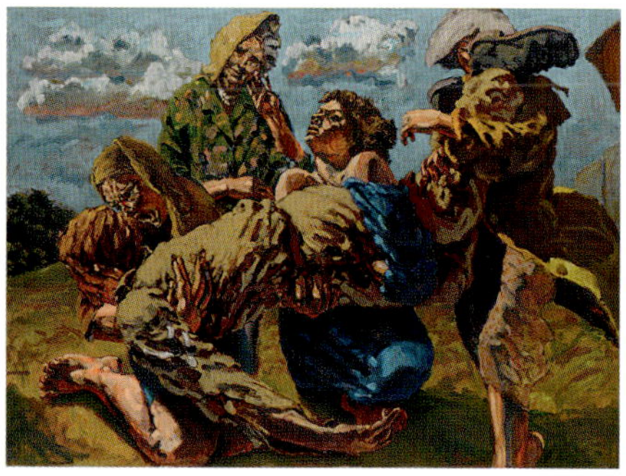

Sinnott, Kevin b.1947
In Greenham Common Did the Peacemakers 1983
oil on canvas 183.5 x 251.5
AC 5267

Skiöld, Birgit 1923–1982
Water's Edge 1979
acrylic & pencil on handmade paper 38.8 x 54.6
AC 2098

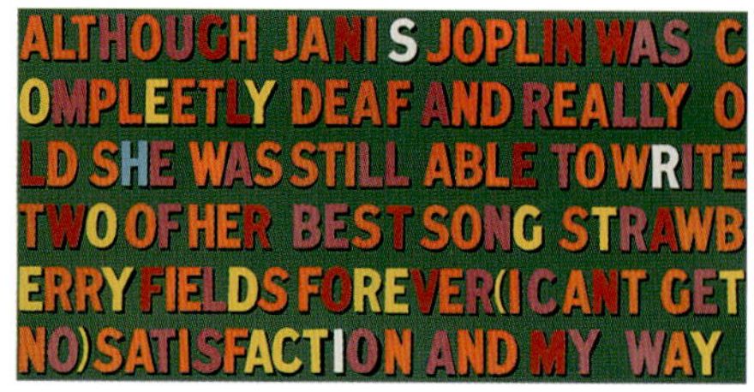

Smith, Bob and Roberta b.1963
Although Janis Joplin… (Idiot Board) 1997
paint on board 243.8 x 487.7
ACC69/1997

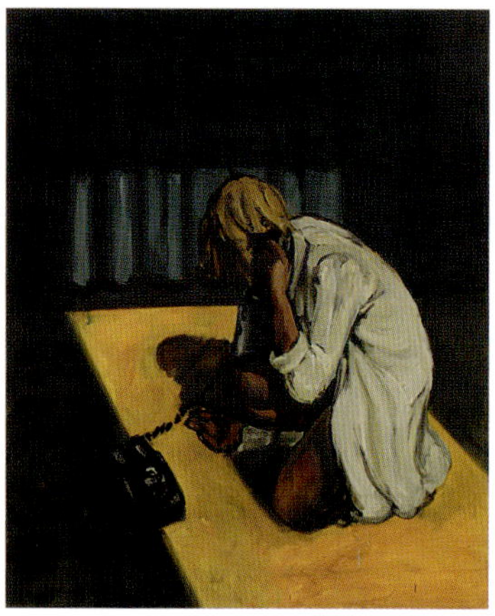

Smith, Colin b.1953
2am 1984
oil on canvas 183.1 x 152.6
AC 5364

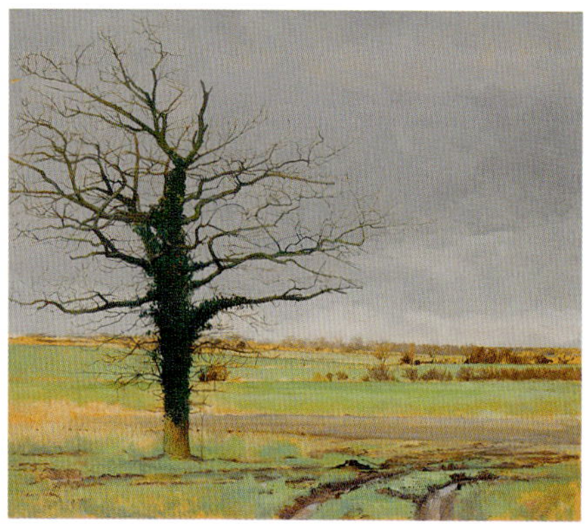

Smith, David Henry b.1947
When Winter Had Gone Spring Came Back 1983
oil on board 32.4 x 37.9
AC 5283

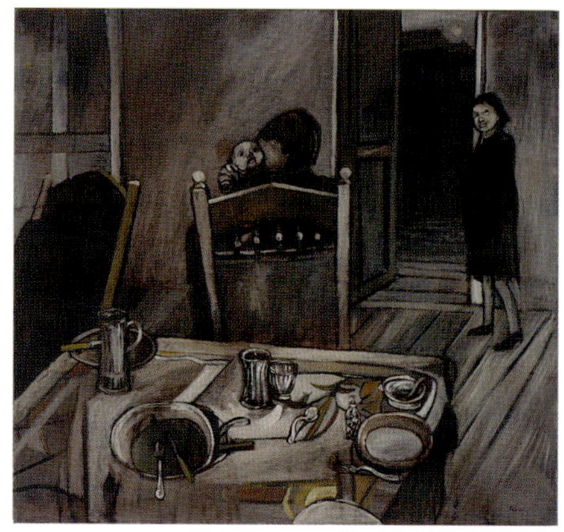

Smith, Jack 1928–2011
After the Meal 1952
oil on canvas 112 x 121
AC 260

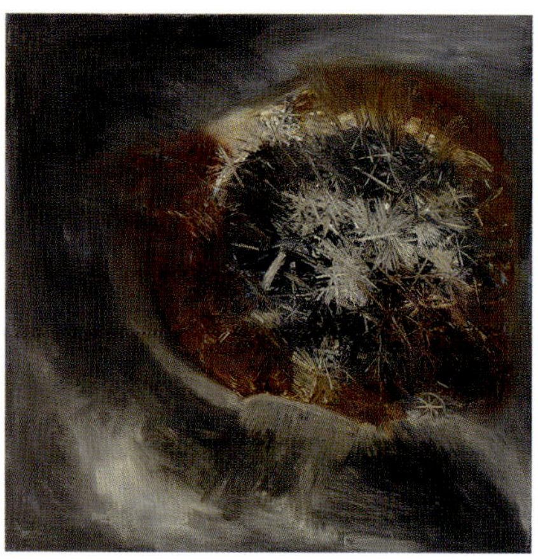

Smith, Jack 1928–2011
Night Sky with Stars 1957
oil on board 121.9 x 121.6
AC 444

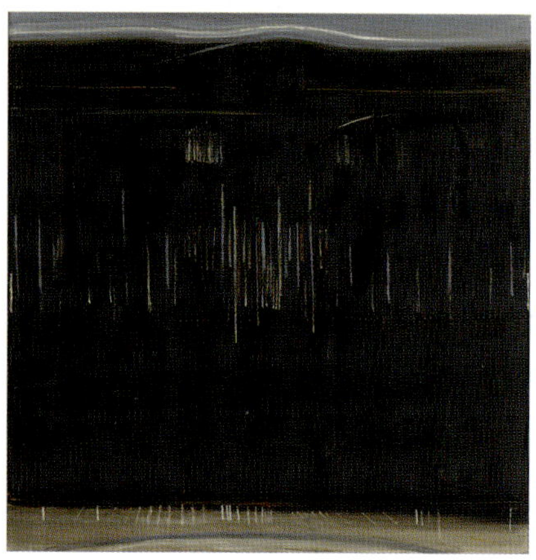

Smith, Jack 1928–2011
Dark Wave 1959
oil on canvas 90 x 91
AC 498

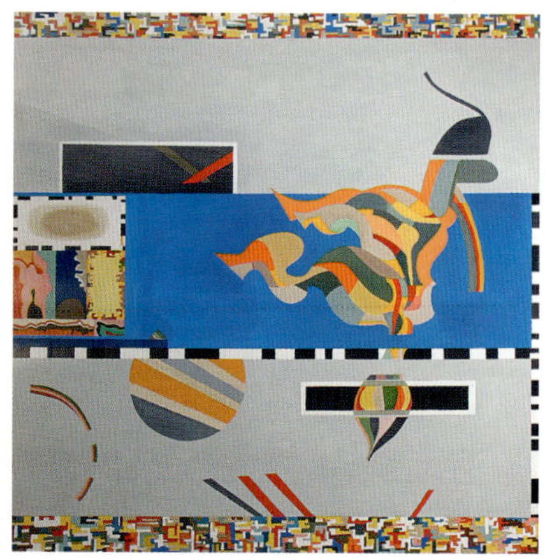

Smith, Jack 1928–2011
Floating I 1963
oil on canvas 149 x 149
AC 869/ACA 14

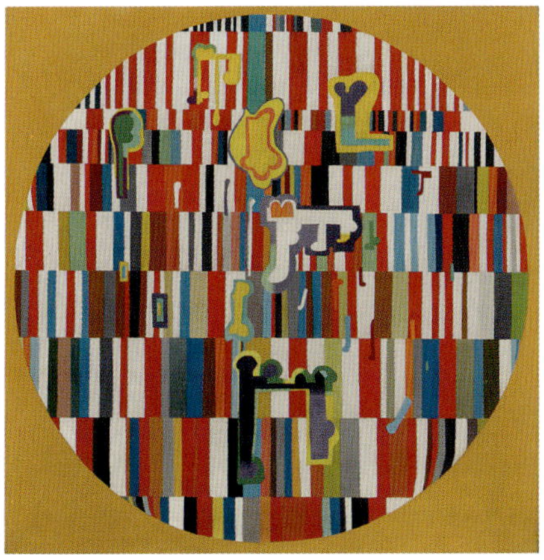

Smith, Jack 1928–2011
Musical Painting 1964
oil on canvas 106.7 x 106.7
AC 804

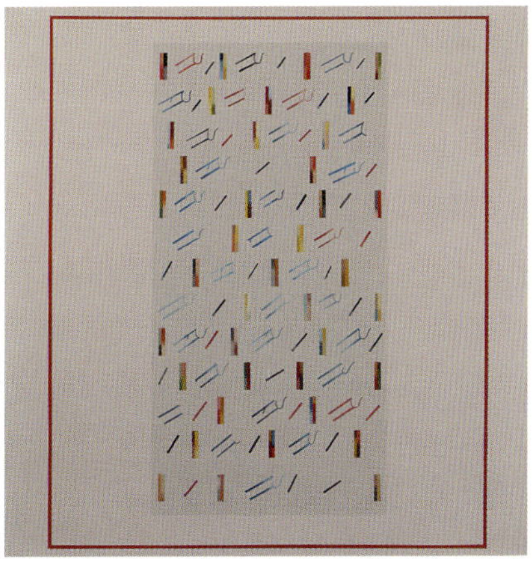

Smith, Jack 1928–2011
Active Intervals (Sound) 1970
oil on canvas 106 x 102.9
AC 1239

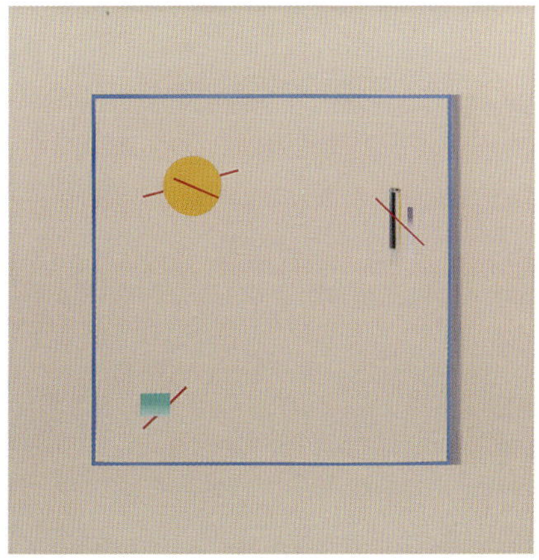

Smith, Jack 1928–2011
Ten Elements 1975
oil on board 91.4 x 91.4
AC 1613

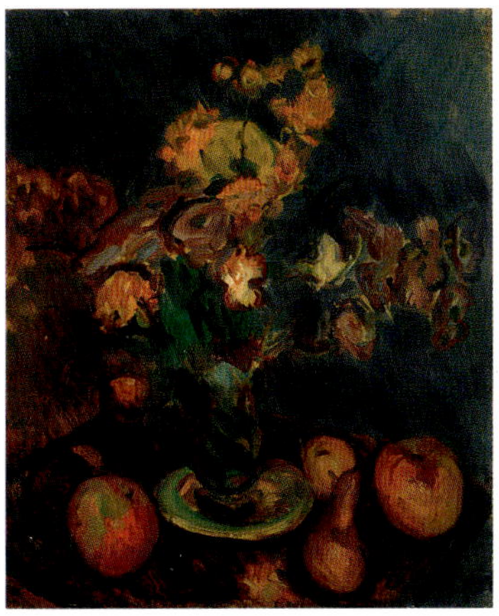

Smith, Matthew Arnold Bracey 1879–1959
Flowers and Fruit 1928
oil on canvas 76 x 64
AC 227

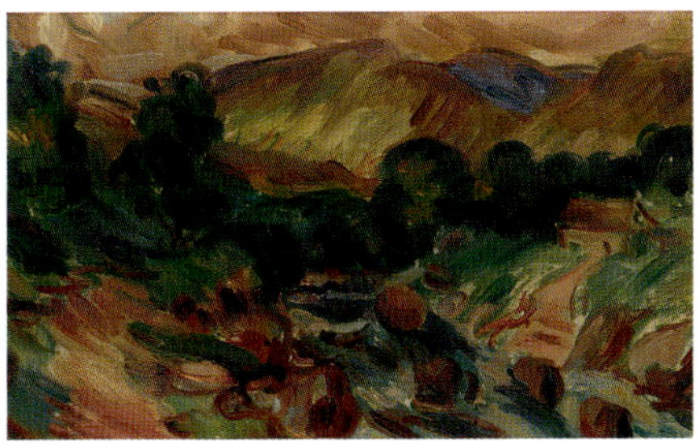

Smith, Matthew Arnold Bracey 1879–1959
Provençal Landscape c.1935
oil on canvas 25 x 41
AC 372

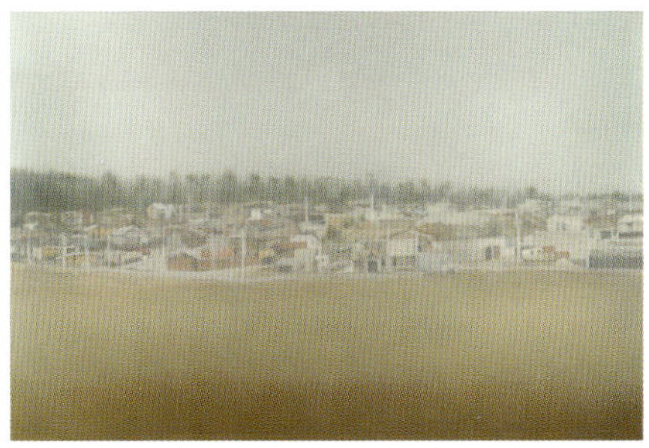

Smith, Melanie b.1965
Parres (No.2) 2005
acrylic enamel on acrylic sheet, mounted on aluminium 130.5 x 200
ACC18/2005

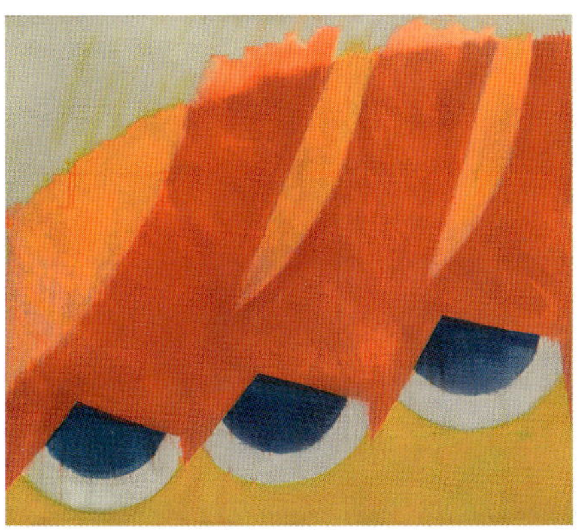

Smith, Richard b.1931
Trio 1963
oil on canvas 152.4 x 172.7
AC 694

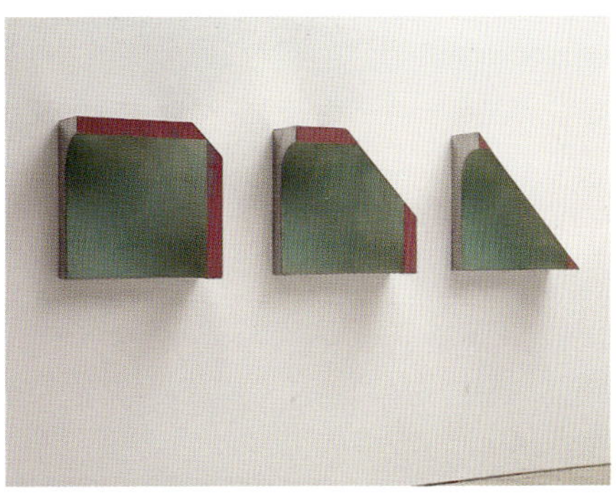

Smith, Richard b.1931
Brief Alphabet, Triptych 1966
acrylic on canvas 66 x 66; 66 x 66; 66 x 66
AC 966

Smith, Richard b.1931
Corner A (Nursery Slope) 1966
acrylic on canvas 213.4 x 213.4
AC 853

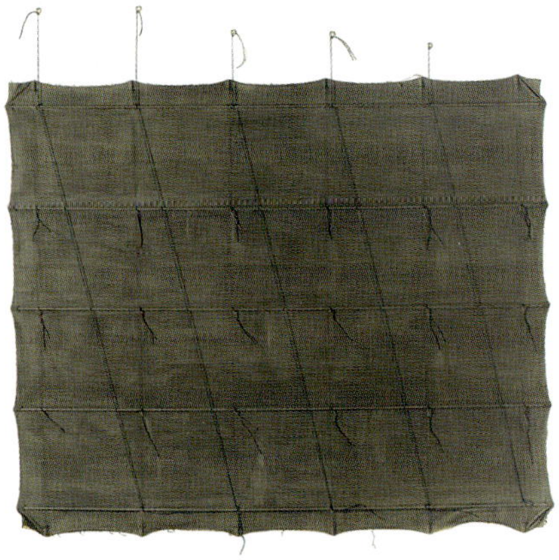

Smith, Richard b.1931
Livorno 1972
acrylic, canvas & string 198 x 214
AC 1245

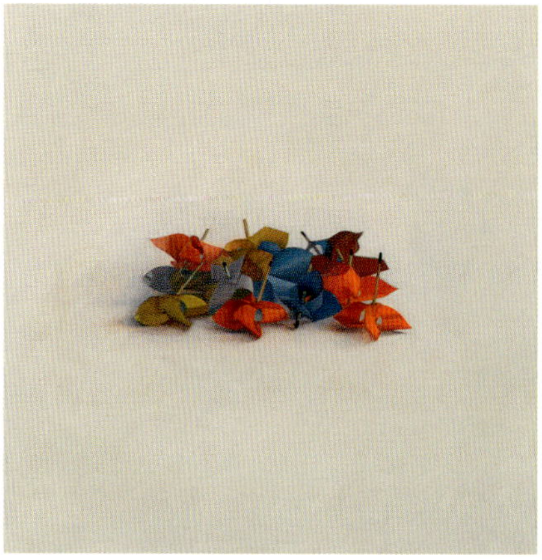

Smith, Sue b.1925
Cluster No.3 1976–1977
oil on board 44.4 x 44.4
AC 2020

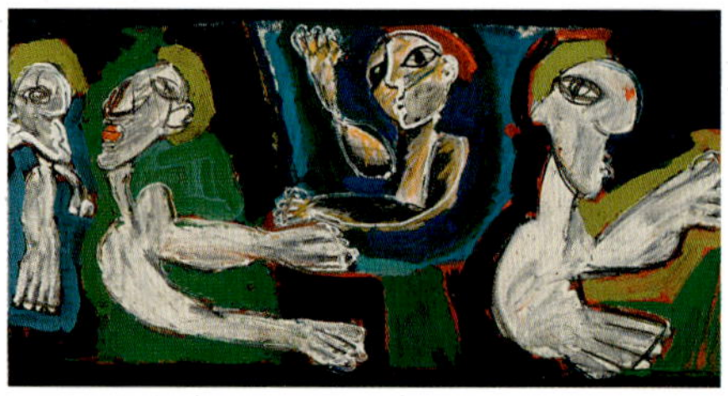

Smith, Tony b.1953
An Angel, the Knight, Death and the Devil 1980
oil on paper 20 x 38.6
AC 4000

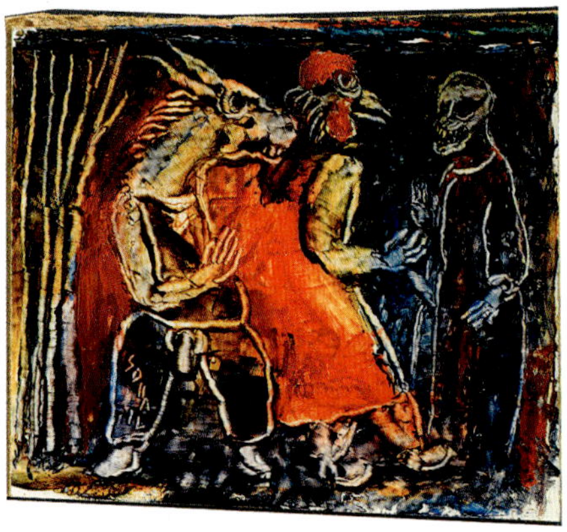

Sohail, Tassadaq b.1930
Untitled 1983
oil on paper 10.3 x 12.4
AC 5474

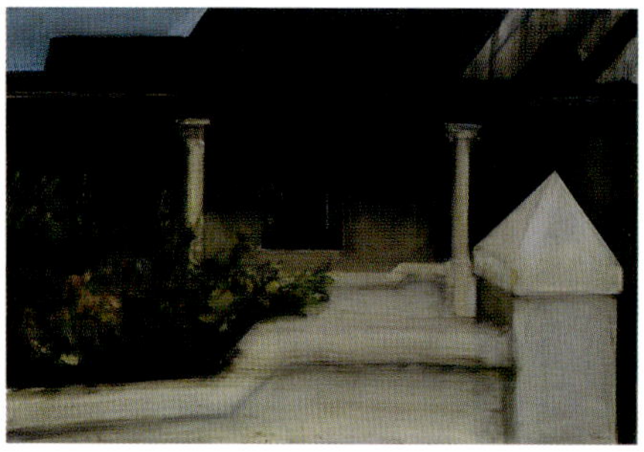

Sonnabend, Yolanda b.1935
Lobengula Street (Bulawayo) 1979
oil on canvas 101.2 x 152
AC 5216

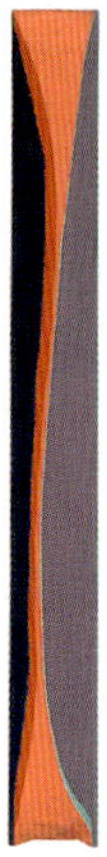

Southall, Derek b.1930
Marcus Curtius 1965
acrylic on canvas 182.9 x 20.3
AC 829

Southall, Derek b.1930
Black U 1969
acrylic on canvas 184.8 x 123.2
AC 1071

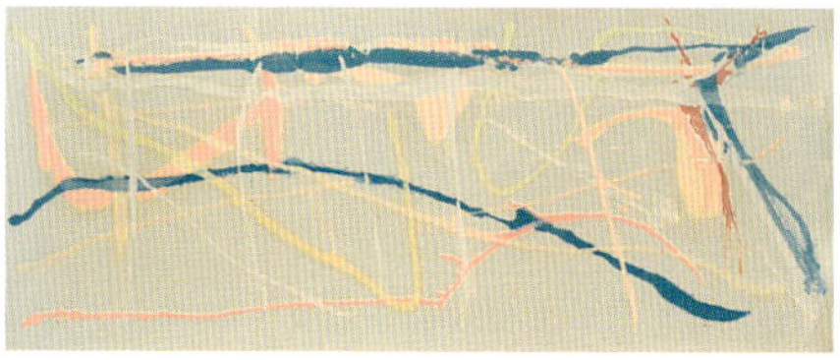

Southall, Derek b.1930
Untitled 1976
oil on canvas 122.3 x 304.3
AC 1722

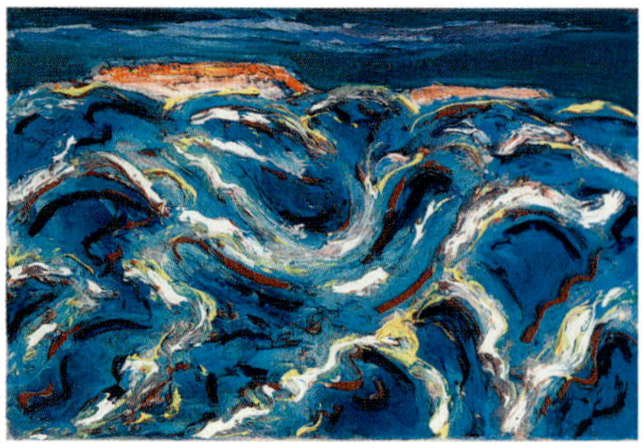

Southall, Derek b.1930
Two Islands 1983
acrylic & alkyd on canvas 30.2 x 44.6
AC 5291

Facing page: Woods,Clare, b.1972, *Daddy Witch* (detail), 2008, (p. 170)

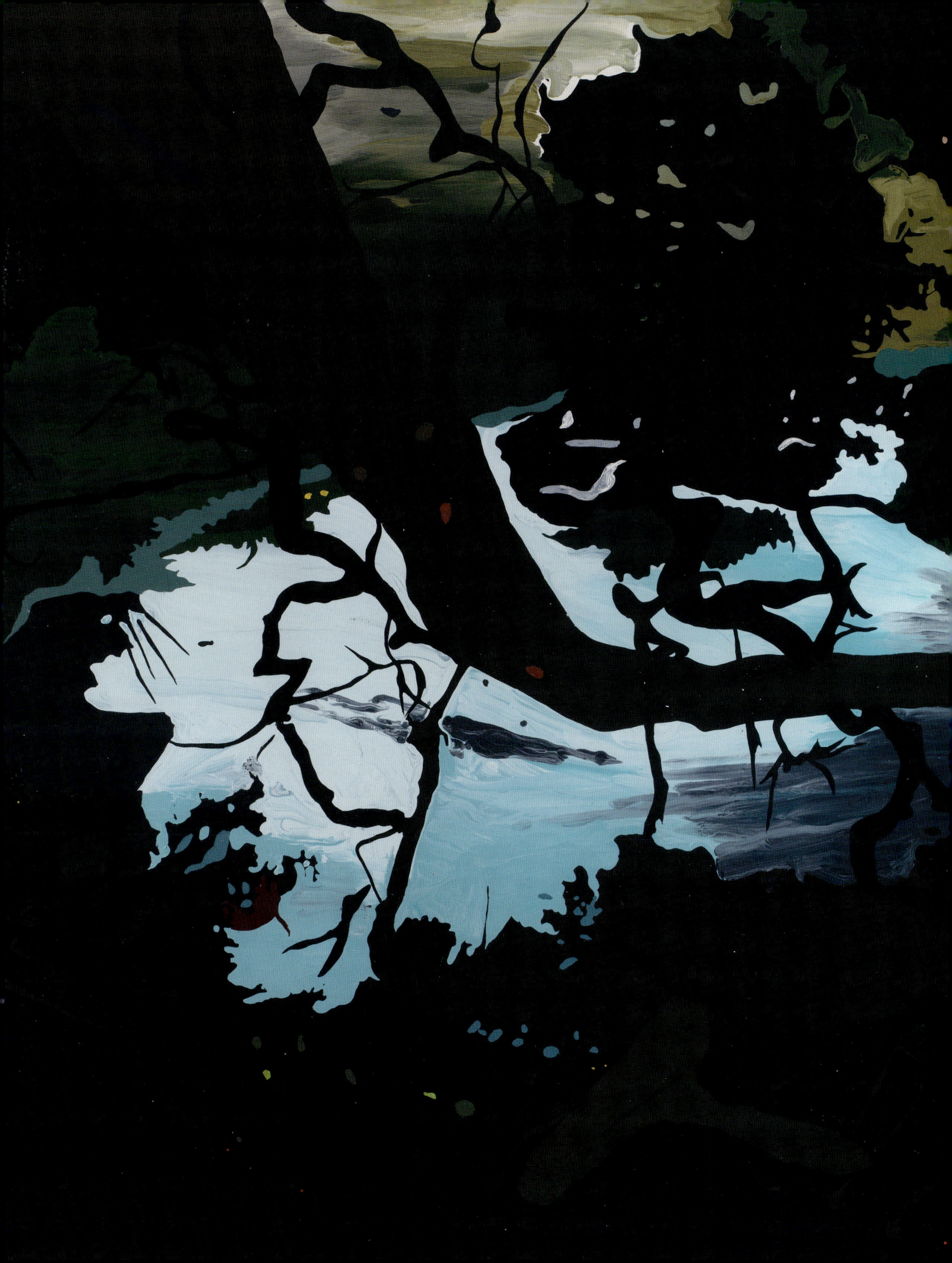

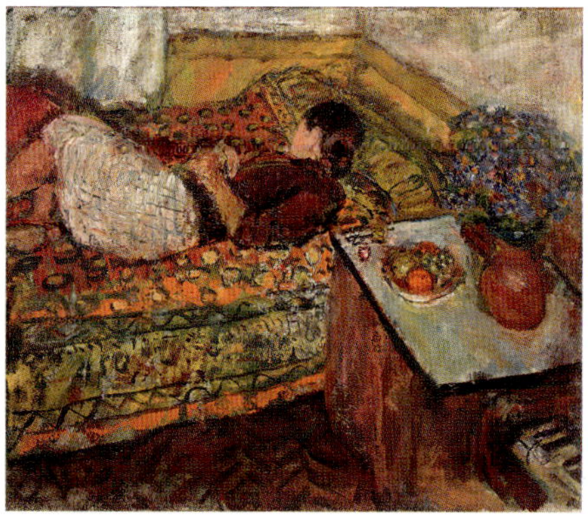

Spear, Ruskin 1911–1990
Siesta 1938
oil on canvas 63 x 75
AC 80

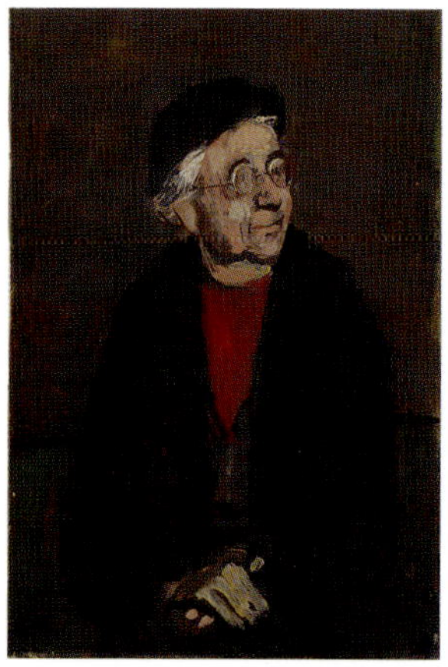

Spear, Ruskin 1911–1990
Woman in a Red Jumper 1948
oil on canvas 55.9 x 38.1
AC 42

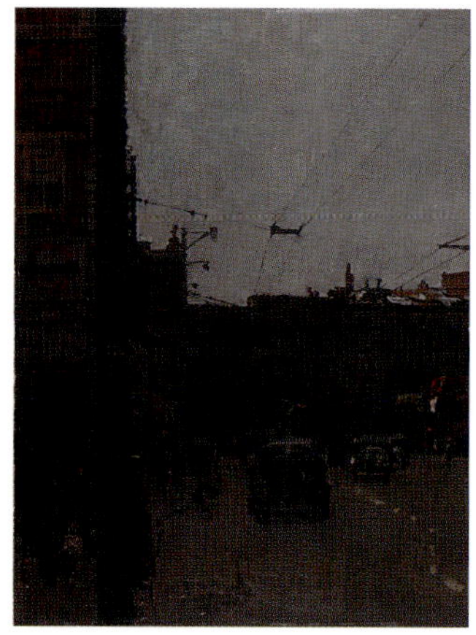

Spear, Ruskin 1911–1990
Hammersmith Broadway 1950
oil on board 45 x 34
AC 183

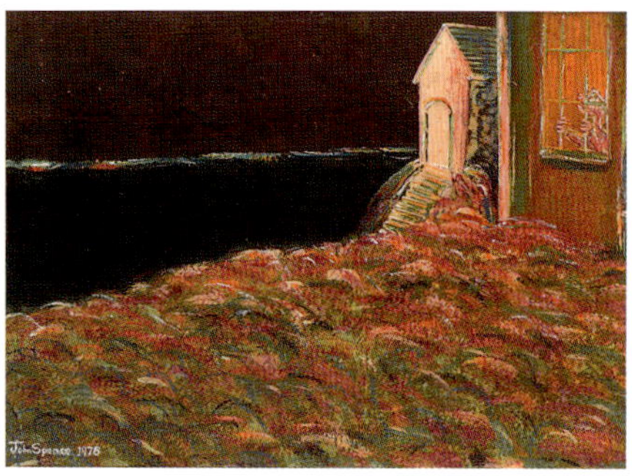

Spence, John b.1944
Fruits of Love 1978
oil, pastel & varnish on paper 15.6 x 21.3
AC 2050

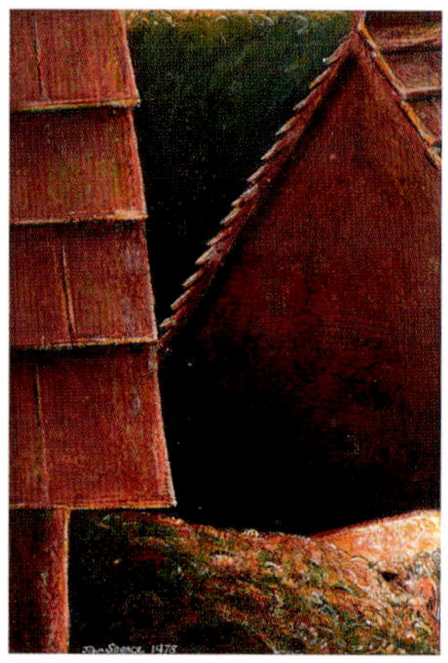

Spence, John b.1944
Isn't it Romantic 1978
oil, pastel & varnish on paper 21.5 x 16.1
AC 2046

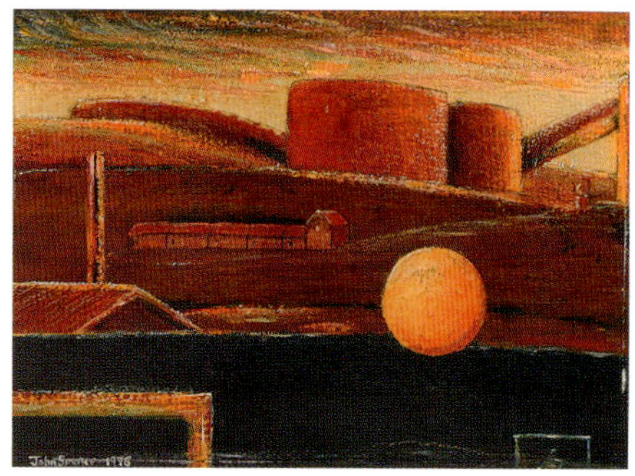

Spence, John b.1944
Rules of the Game 1978
oil, pastel & varnish on paper 16 x 21.5
AC 2048

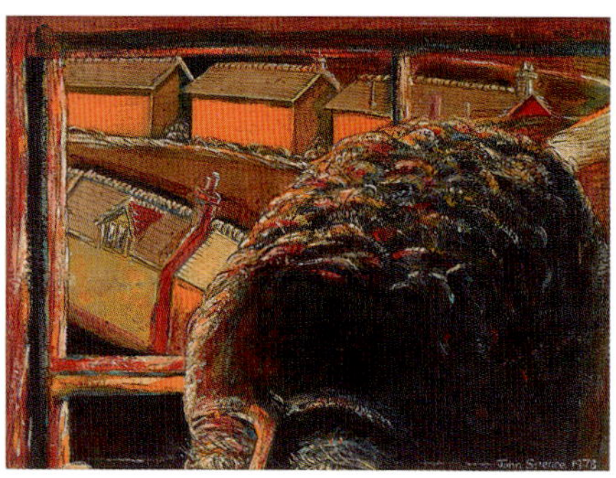

Spence, John b.1944
The Haunting 1978
oil, pastel & varnish on paper 16.1 x 21.3
AC 2049

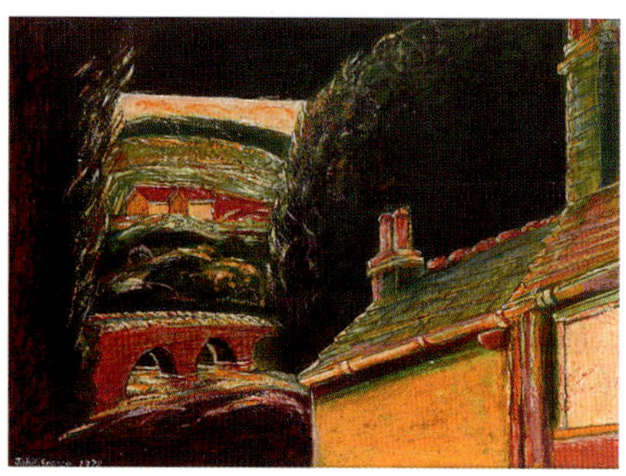

Spence, John b.1944
The Secret Hour 1978
oil, pastel & varnish on paper 16.1 x 21.5
AC 2051

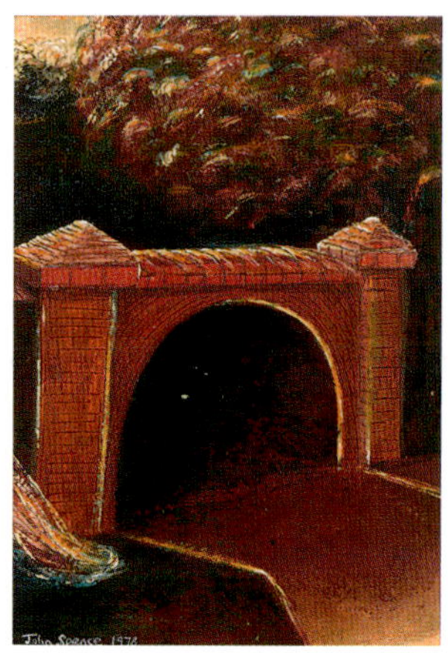

Spence, John b.1944
Zero Take Off 1978
oil, pastel & varnish on paper 17.8 x 12.7
AC 2047

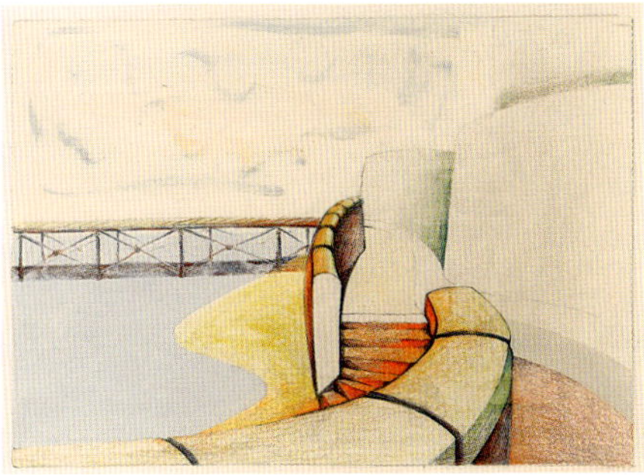

Spence, John b.1944
Cromer Drawing (No.3) 1981–1986
pencil, crayon, oil & varnish on paper
17.2 x 36.1
ACC4/1986

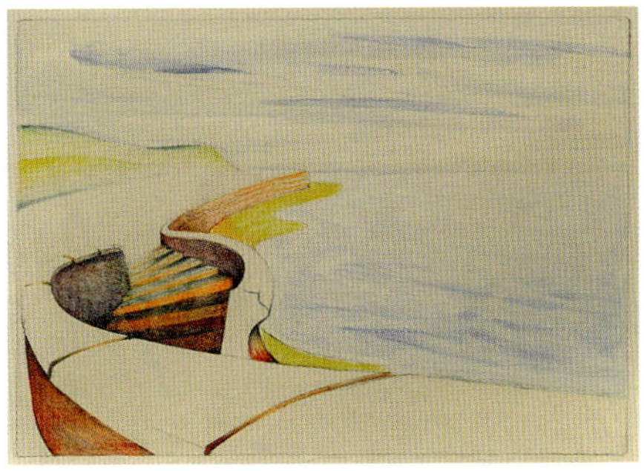

Spence, John b.1944
Cromer Drawing (No.5) 1981–1986
pencil, crayon, oil & varnish on paper
17.2 x 36.1
ACC2/1986

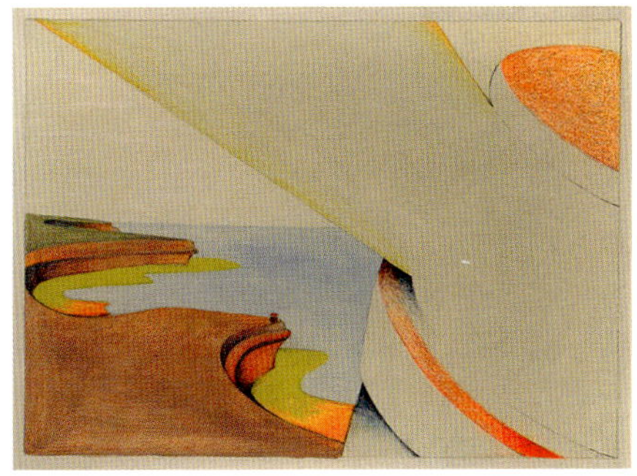

Spence, John b.1944
Cromer Drawing (No.11) 1981–1986
pencil, crayon, oil & varnish on paper
17.2 x 36.1
ACC5/1986

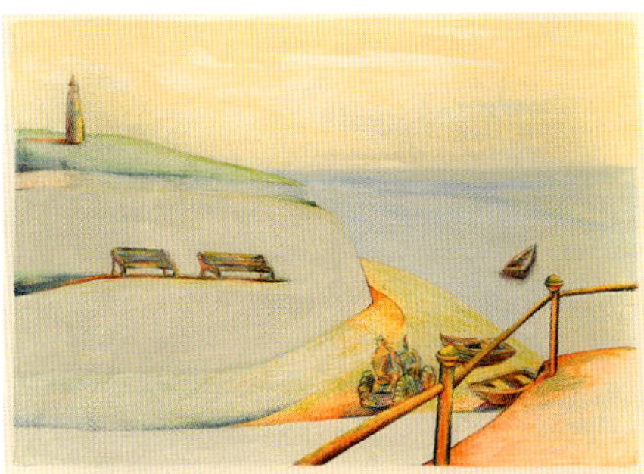

Spence, John b.1944
Cromer Drawing (No.15) 1981–1986
pencil, crayon, oil & varnish on paper
17.2 x 36.1
ACC3/1986

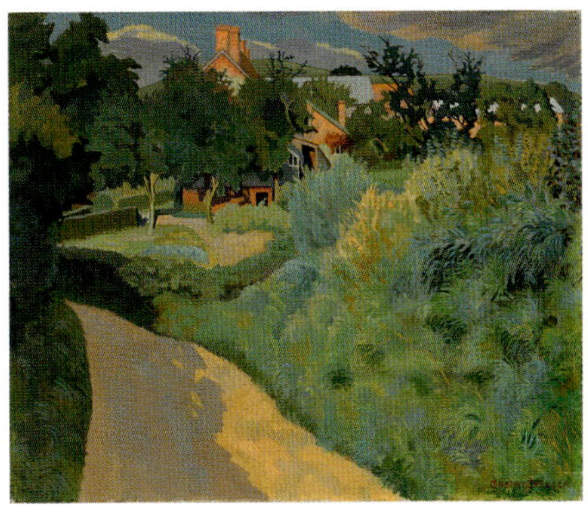

Spencer, Gilbert 1892–1979
Budden's Lane 1939
oil on canvas 50.8 x 61
AC 106

Spencer, Jean 1942–1998
Relief (4 units) 1971
emulsion on board & wood 61 x 61; 61 x 61; 61 x 61; 61 x 61
AC000

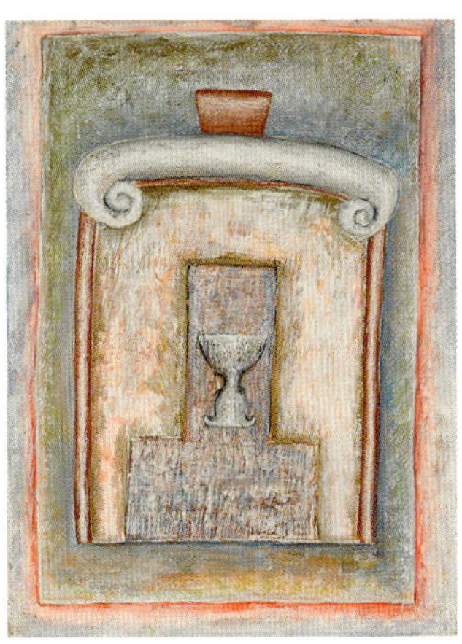

Stahl, Andrew b.1954
Chalice 1981
acrylic on paper 32.1 x 23.8
AC 5204

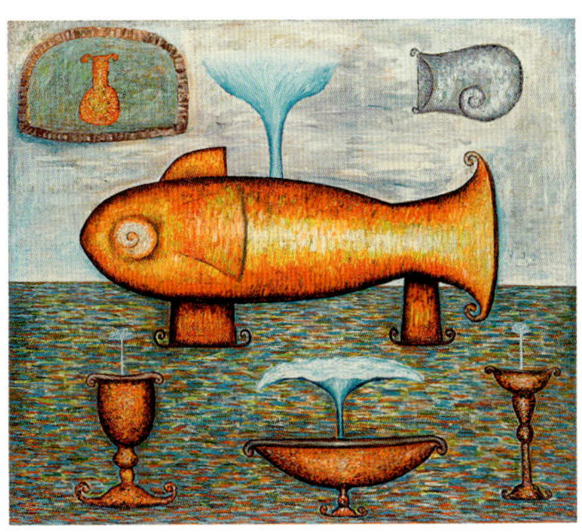

Stahl, Andrew b.1954
Spring Rites 1982
acrylic on canvas 182.8 x 213.4
AC 5203

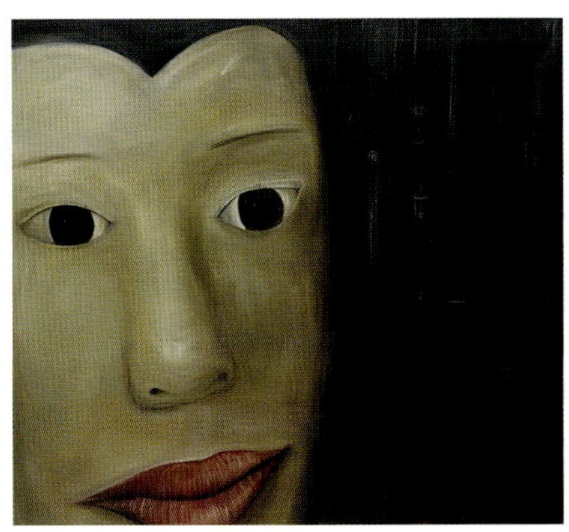

Stahl, Andrew b.1954
Close 1998
oil on canvas 198 x 229
ACC9/1998

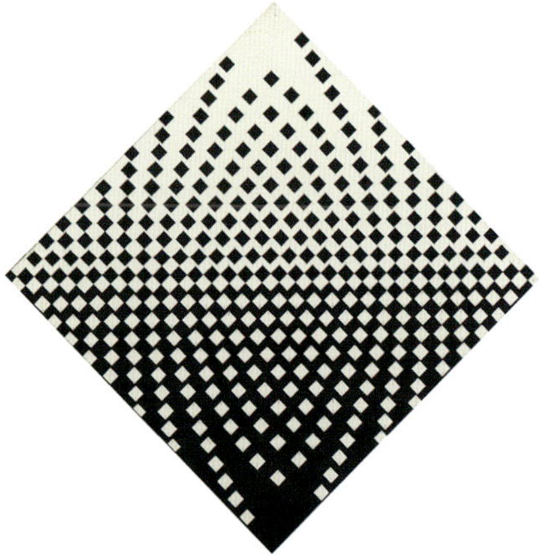

Steele, Jeffrey b.1931
Wasserfläsche 1964
oil on canvas 40.8 x 40.8
AC 746

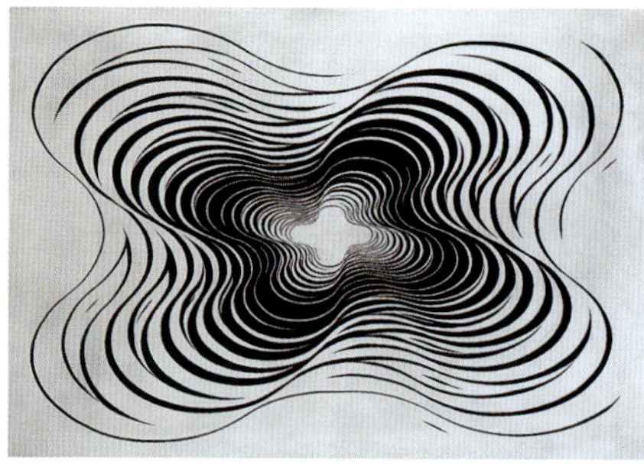

Steele, Jeffrey b.1931
Ilmatar 1966–1967
oil on canvas 91.4 x 137.2
AC 911

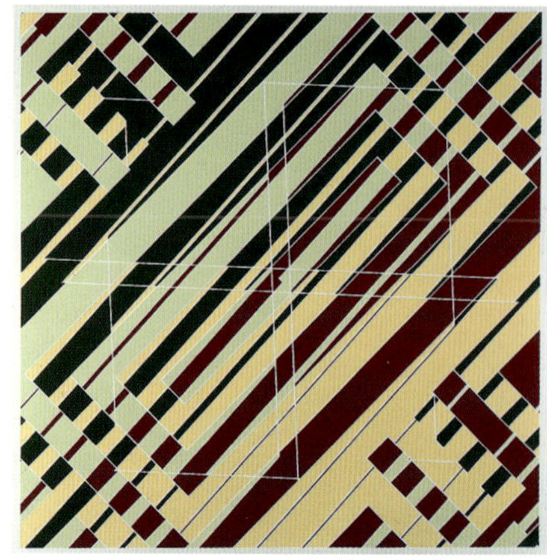

Steele, Jeffrey b.1931
SG I 62 1972–1977
oil on canvas 152.5 x 152.5
AC 1851

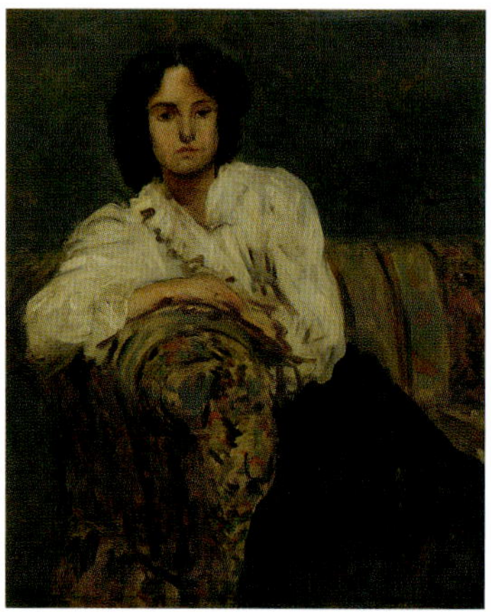

Steer, Philip Wilson 1860–1942
Girl in a White Blouse on a Sofa 1892
oil on canvas 61 x 50.8
AC 488

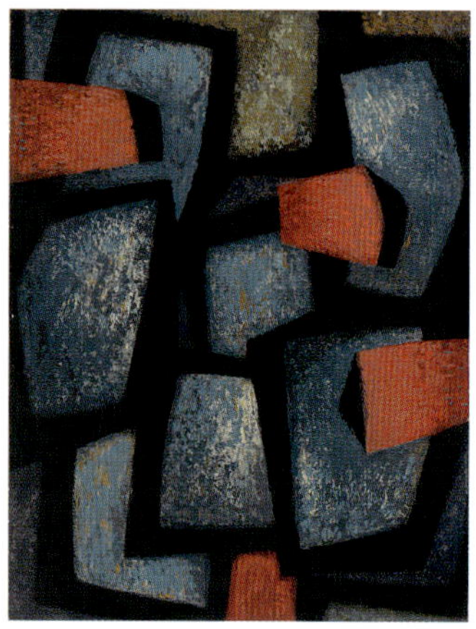

Stephenson, Cecil 1889–1965
Canon (2) 1958
oil on board 90 x 69.6
AC 493

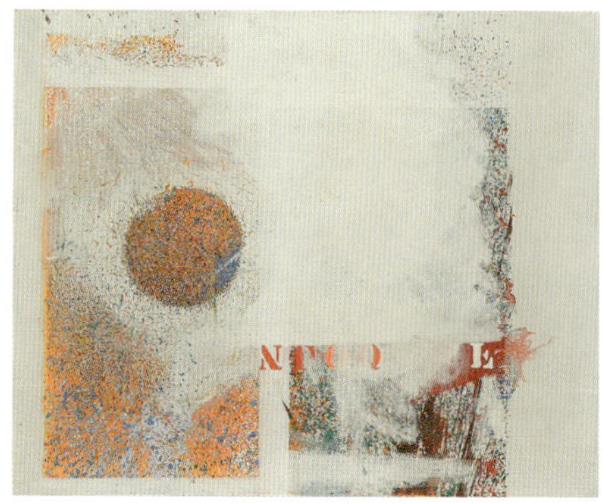

Stephenson, Ian 1934–2000
Shhh 1960
oil on canvas 101.6 x 127
AC 588

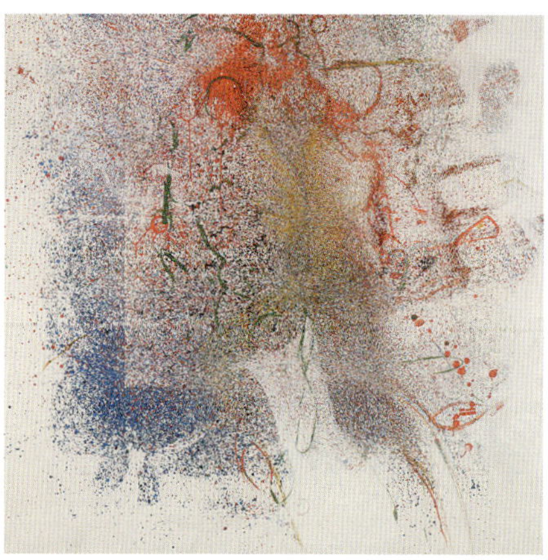

Stephenson, Ian 1934–2000
Red Adumbration 1961
oil on canvas 126 x 127
AC 626

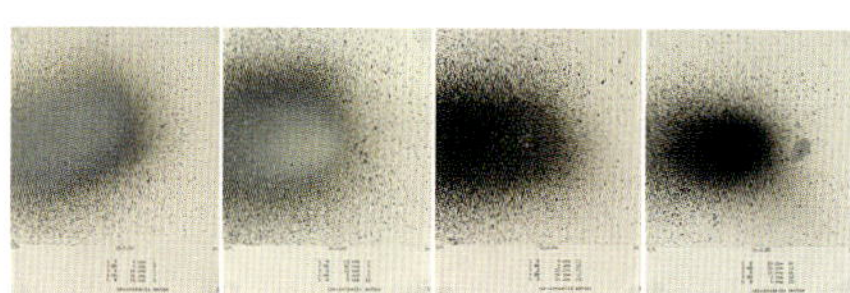

Stephenson, Ian 1934–2000
Small Spray Studies 1–4 1962
enamel on paper 25.3 x 20.3; 25.3 x 20.3; 25.3 x 20.3; 25.3 x 20.3
AC 1033

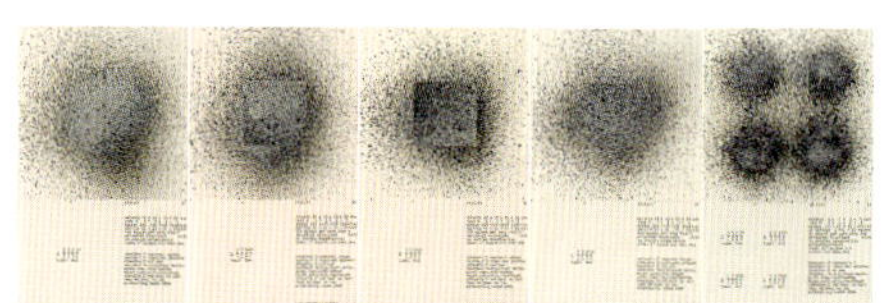

Stephenson, Ian 1934–2000
Small Spray Studies 1–5 1962
enamel on paper 33 x 20.3; 33 x 20.3; 33 x 20.3; 33 x 20.3; 33 x 20.3
AC 1034

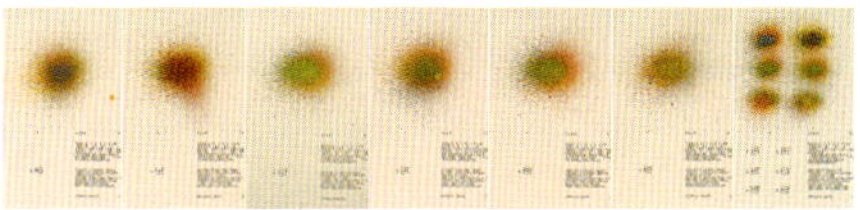

Stephenson, Ian 1934–2000
Small Spray Studies 1–7 1962
enamel on paper 36.8 x 24.1; 36.8 x 24.1; 36.8 x 24.1; 36.8 x 24.1; 36.8 x 24.1; 36.8 x 24.1; 36.8 x 24.1
AC 1083

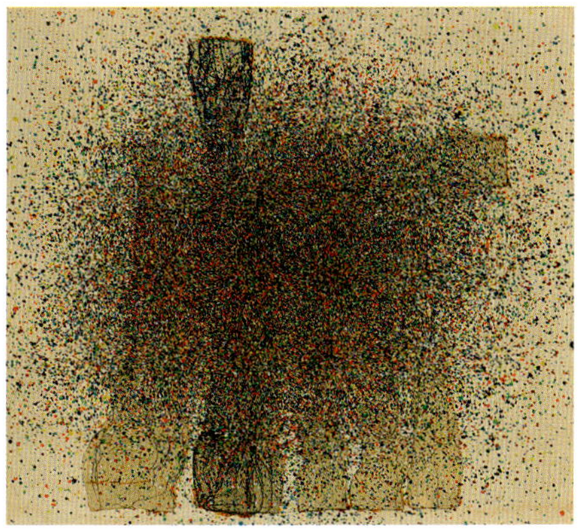

Stephenson, Ian 1934–2000
Retrospect 4 Spray Study 1963
oil & collage on paper 56.5 x 64
AC 764

Stephenson, Ian 1934–2000
Diorama SS.5.67 1967
oil & enamel on canvas 167.4 x 334.8
AC 971

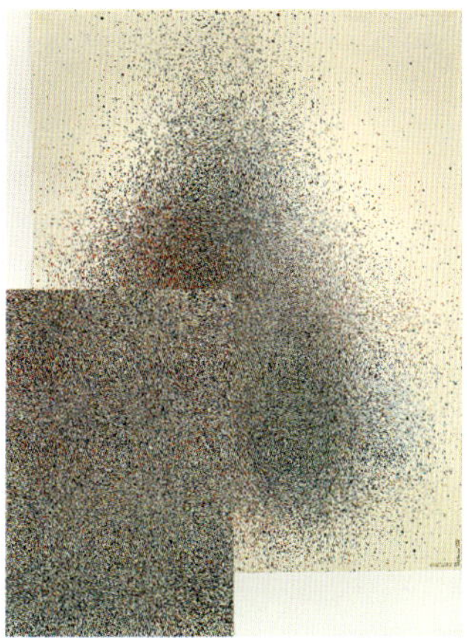

Stephenson, Ian 1934–2000
Border Series: Easement I 1975
oil & enamel on paper collage 101.8 x 76.3
AC 1664

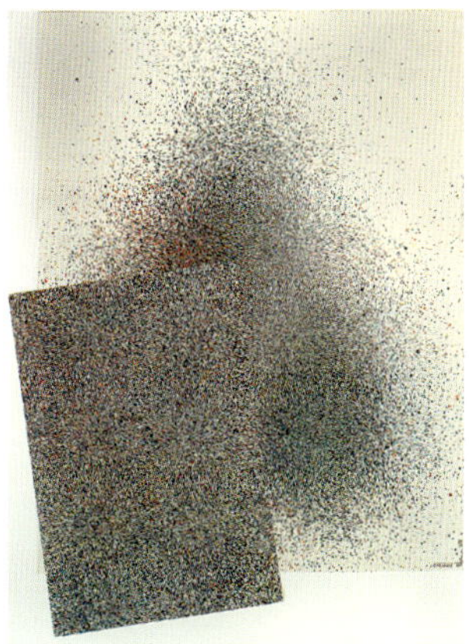

Stephenson, Ian 1934–2000
Border Series: Easement II 1975
oil & enamel on paper collage 101.8 x 76.3
AC 1665

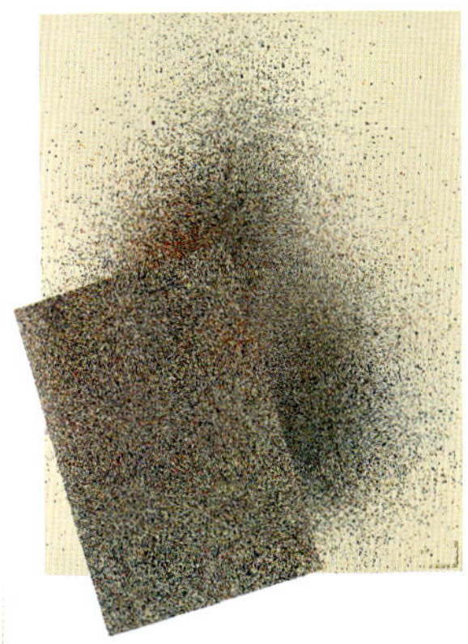

Stephenson, Ian 1934–2000
Border Series: Easement III 1975
oil & enamel on paper collage 101.8 x 76.3
AC 1666

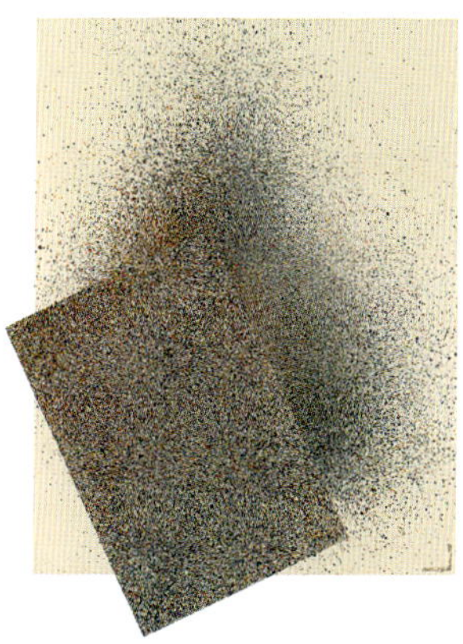

Stephenson, Ian 1934–2000
Border Series: Easement IV 1975
oil & enamel on paper collage 101.8 x 76.3
AC 1667

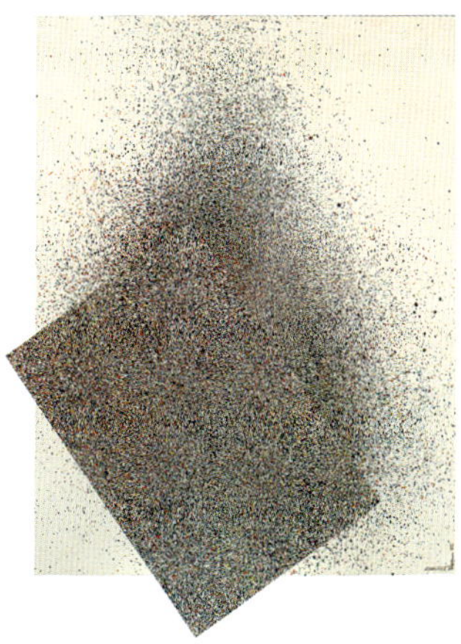

Stephenson, Ian 1934–2000
Border Series: Easement V 1975
oil & enamel on paper collage 101.8 x 76.3
AC 1668

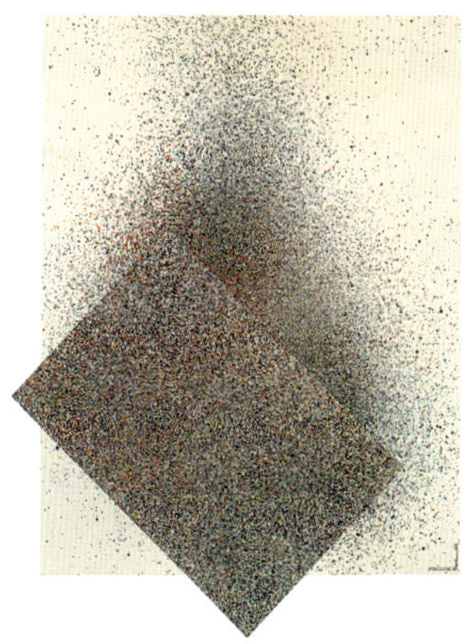

Stephenson, Ian 1934–2000
Border Series: Easement VI 1975
oil & enamel on paper collage 101.8 x 76.3
AC 1669

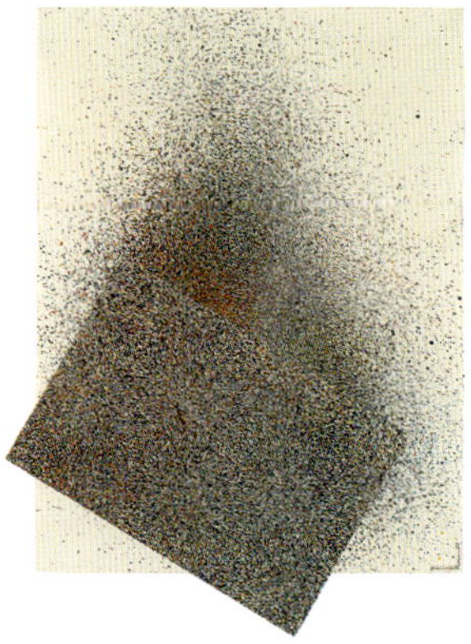

Stephenson, Ian 1934–2000
Border Series: Easement VII 1975
oil & enamel on paper collage 101.8 x 76.3
AC 1670

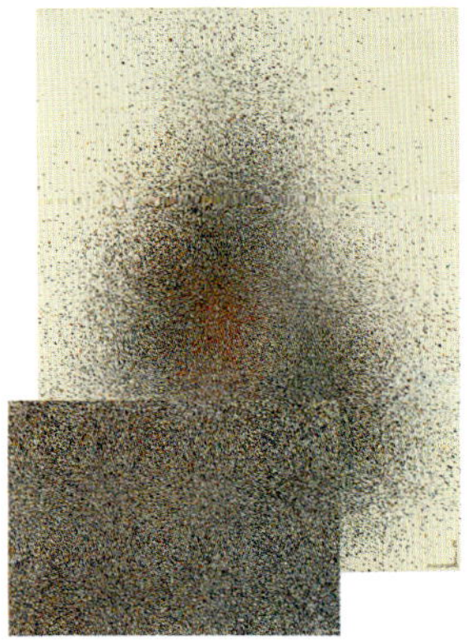

Stephenson, Ian 1934–2000
Border Series: Easement VIII 1975
oil & enamel on paper collage 101.8 x 76.3
AC 1671

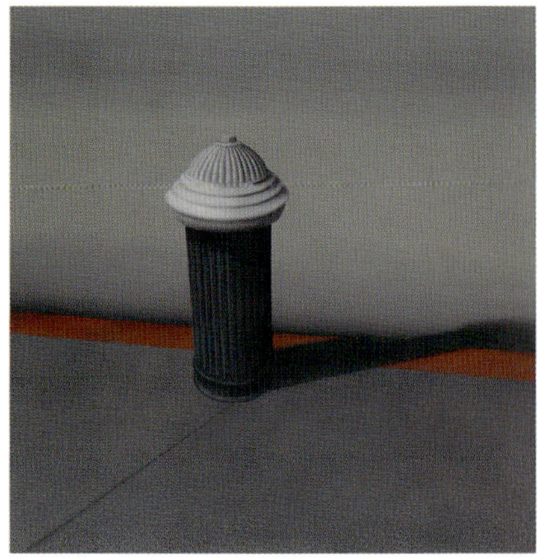

Stevens, Norman 1937–1988
Fire Hydrant, N. Y. 1968
acrylic on canvas 152.5 x 152.5
AC 969

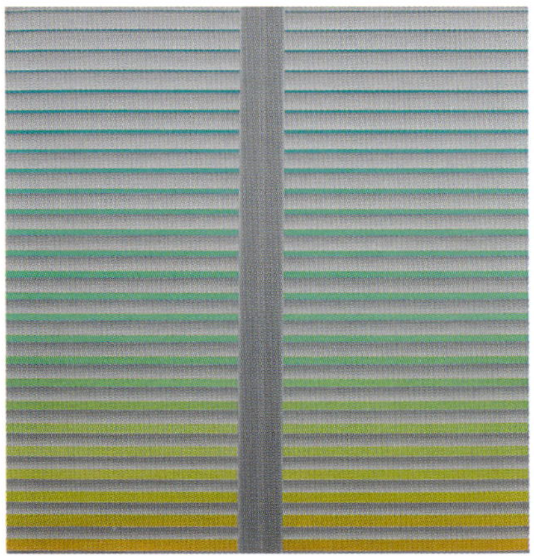

Stevens, Norman 1937–1988
Louvered Shutter (Morning) 1972
acrylic on canvas 151 x 150
AC 1242

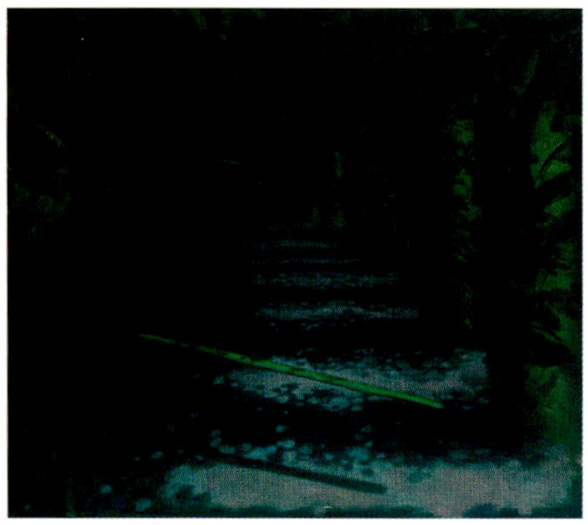

Stevens, Norman 1937–1988
Aaron's Rod 1975
oil on canvas 182.9 x 213.4
AC 1736

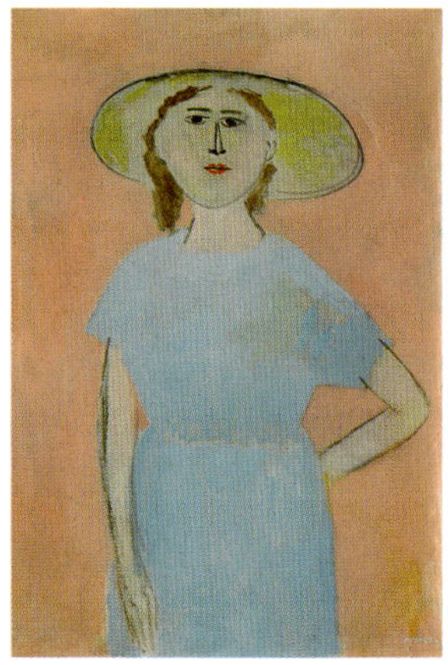

Steyn, Stella 1907–1987
Girl in a Blue Dress 1951
oil on canvas 90.2 x 59.7
AC 241

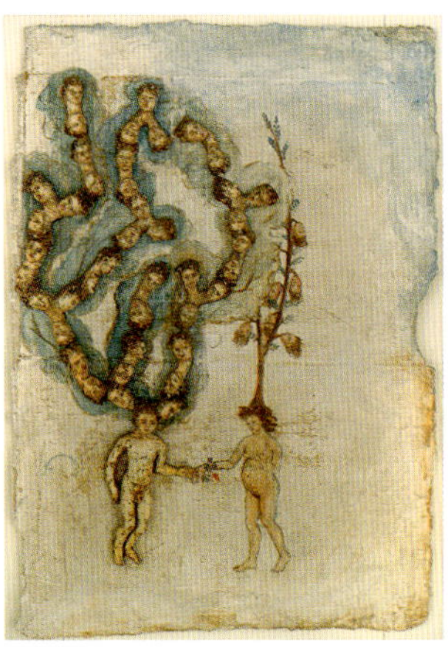

Stimson, Myra b.1961
The Will to Live 1987
paint & plaster on board 135 x 94
AC 5559

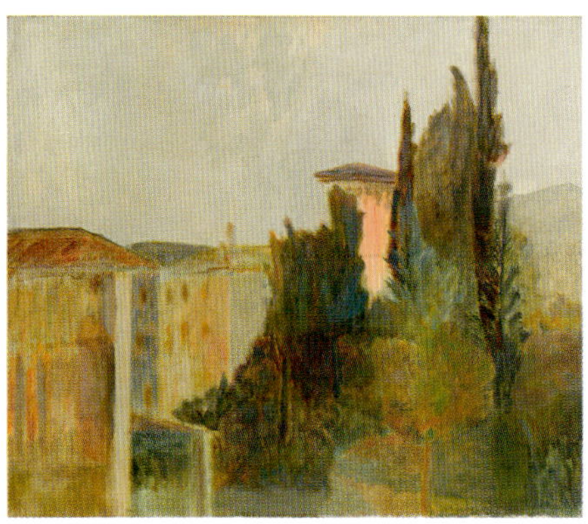

Stokes, Adrian Durham 1902–1972
San Materno, Ascona 1949
oil on canvas 53 x 63.5
AC 181

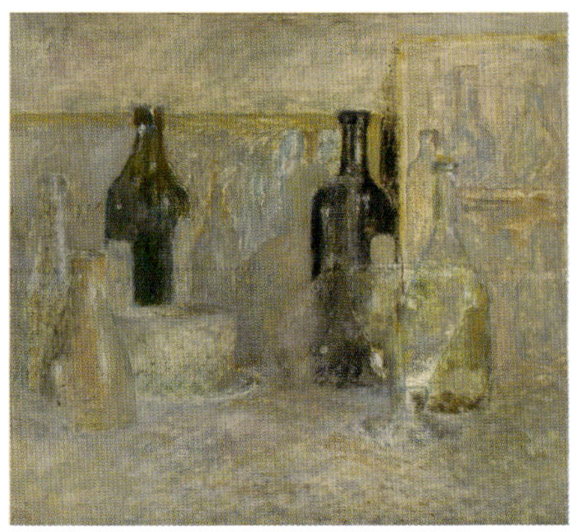

Stokes, Adrian Durham 1902–1972
Still Life XIX 1963
oil on canvas 50.8 x 53.3
AC 770

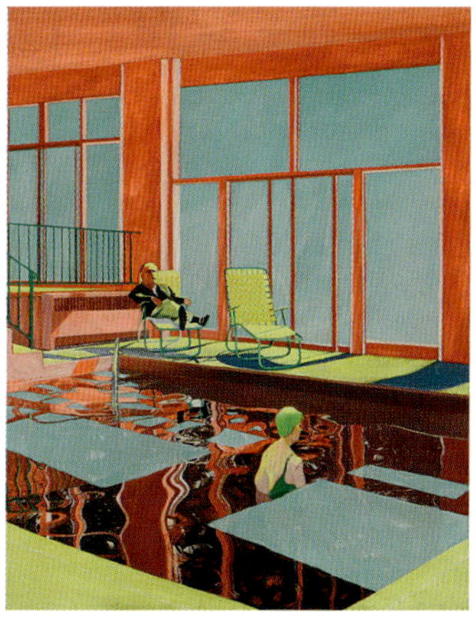

Stokoe, Neil b.1935
Man and Woman with Swimming Pool 1967
oil on canvas 218.4 x 173
AC 1144

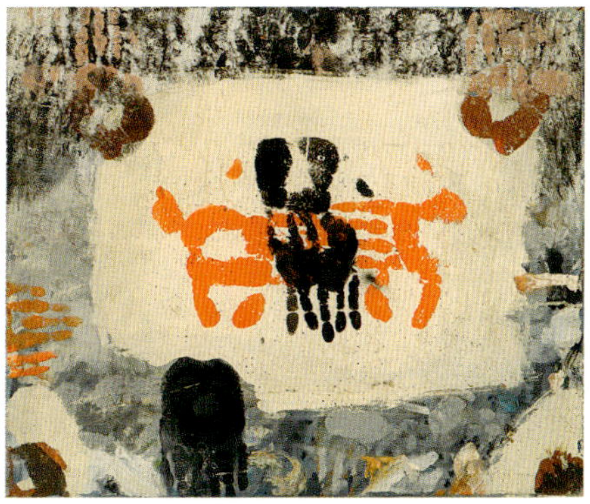

Stubbing, Newton Haydn (Tony)
1921–1983
Untitled 1958
oil on canvas 60 x 72.5
ACC88/1991

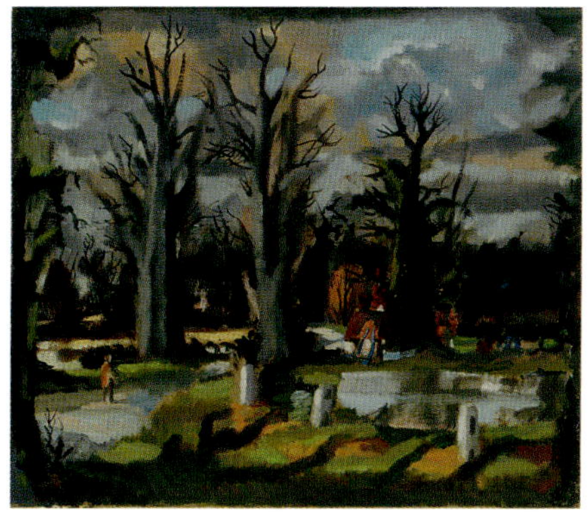

Suddaby, Rowland 1912–1972
Winter Landscape, near Lavenham 1942
oil on canvas 63.5 x 76.2
AC 81

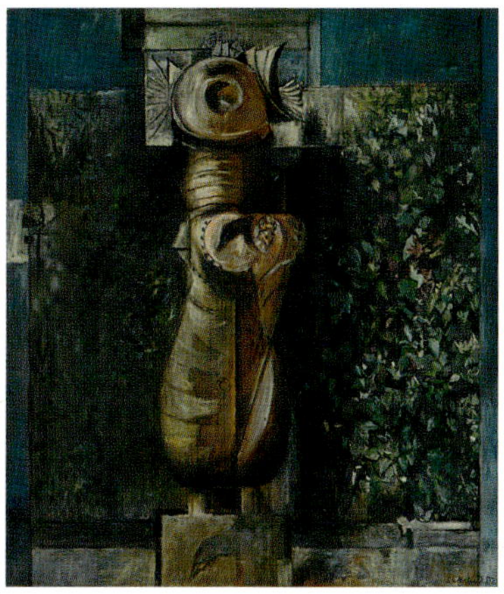

Sutherland, Graham Vivian 1903–1980
Standing Form Against a Hedge 1950
oil on canvas 134.6 x 116.8
AC 188

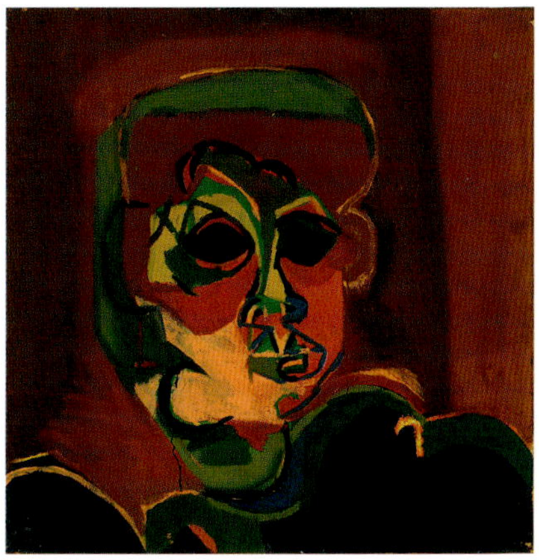

Sutton, Philip b.1928
Orange Head 1953–1954
oil on canvas 74.5 x 74.5
AC 345

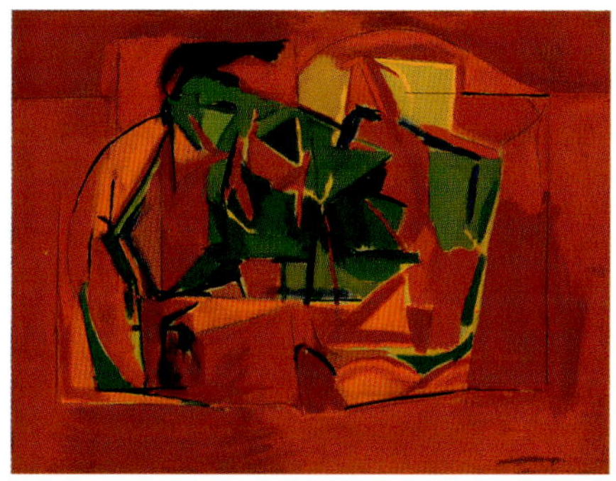

Sutton, Philip b.1928
Flower Still Life 1955
oil on canvas 75 x 100.5
AC 378

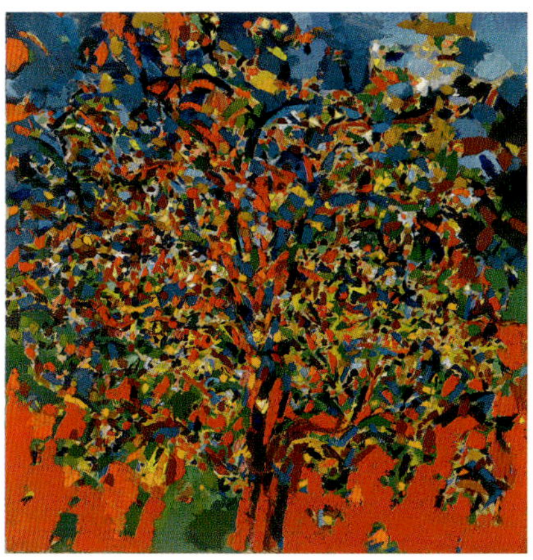

Sutton, Philip b.1928
Fruit Tree 1956
oil on canvas 85.1 x 86.4
AC 540

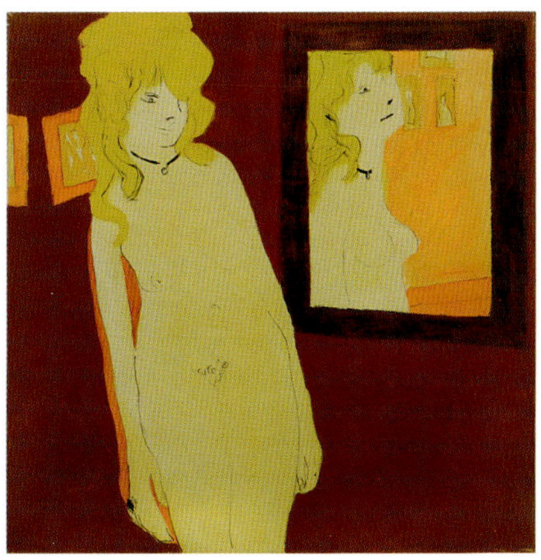

Sutton, Philip b.1928
Sonya 1967
oil on canvas 127 x 127
ACA 77

Sutton, Trevor b.1948
A. B. B. 1976
acrylic on canvas 152 x 152
AC 1723

Sutton, Trevor b.1948
Portrait of a Woman 1981
acrylic on plywood 28.5 x 169.2
AC 4090

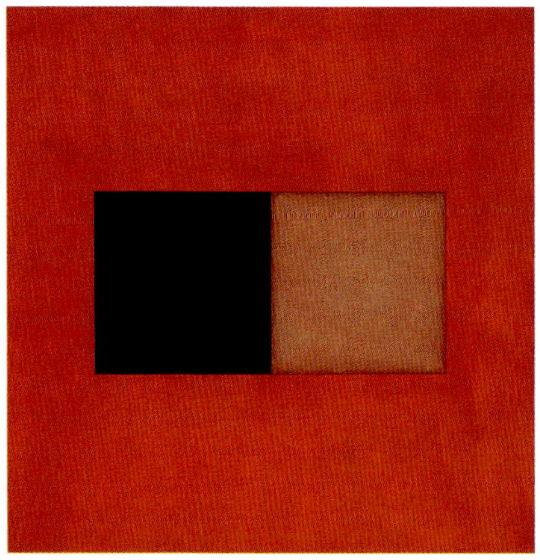

Sutton, Trevor b.1948
Friendship 1990
oil on board 61.8 x 61.8
ACC47/1991

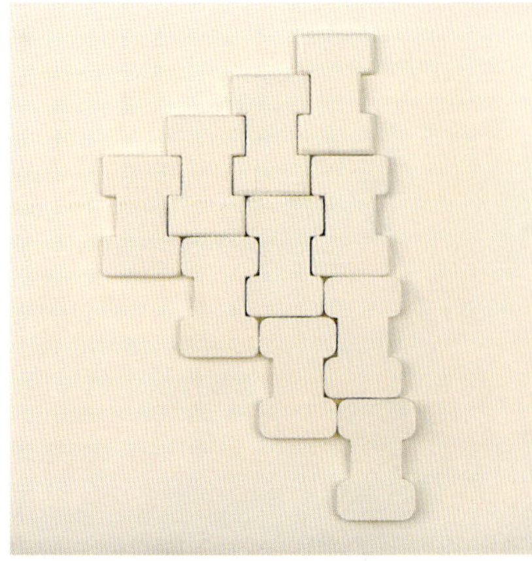

Tebby, Susan b.1944
Relief No.VIII: Re-entrant White 1967
acrylic on wood 98 x 97
AC 935

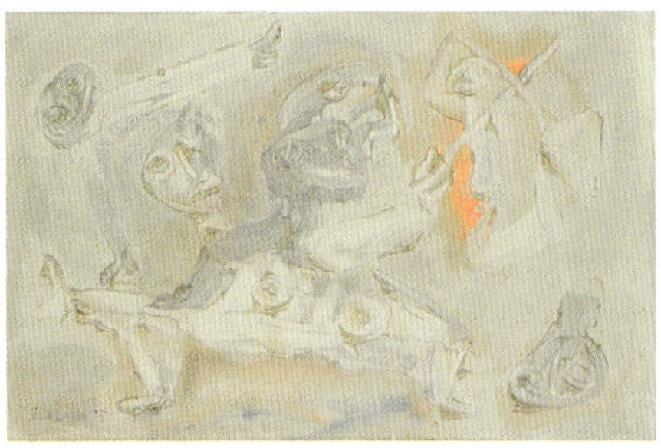

Themerson, Franciszka 1907–1988
People are generally kind 1975
oil on canvas 87.7 x 139
AC 5333

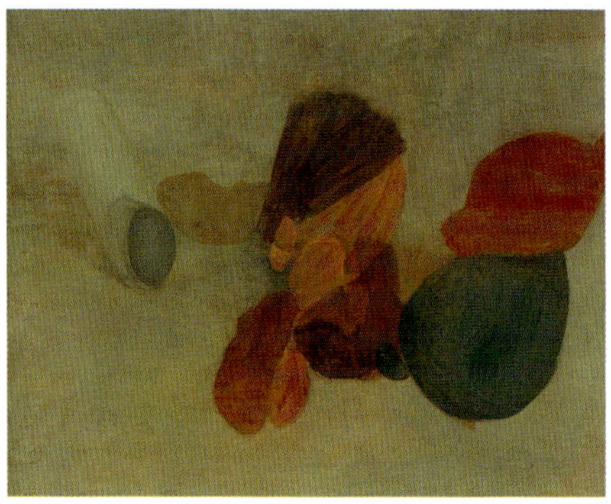

Thesiger, Amanda b.1964
Arrangement 1994
oil on canvas 84 x 107
ACC37/1995

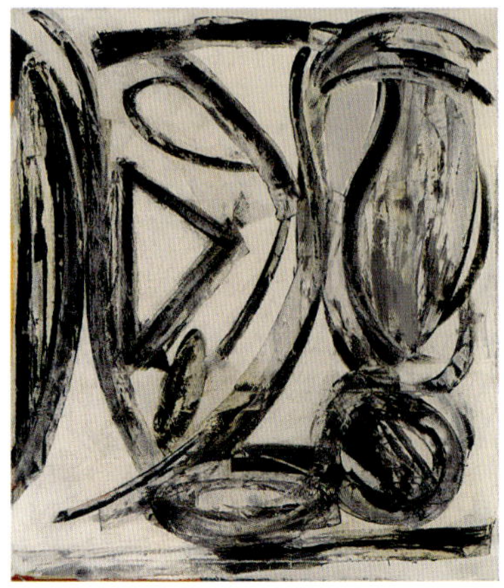

Thomas, Keith b.1946
Snake 1977
acrylic on canvas 220.1 x 184.2
AC 3032

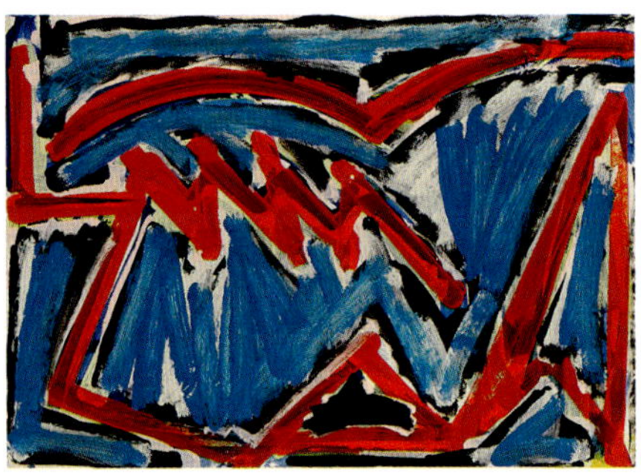

Thomas, Keith b.1946
Crawler 1978
acrylic on paper 52 x 76.9
AC 1957

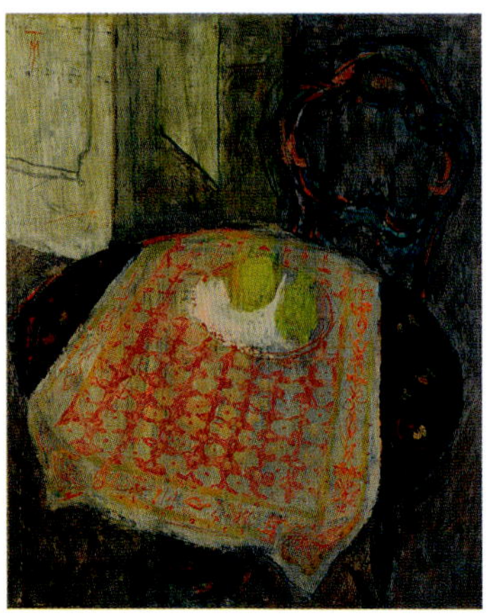

Thomas, Margaret b.1916
The Chintz Tablecloth 1948
oil on canvas 61.3 x 51.1
AC 144

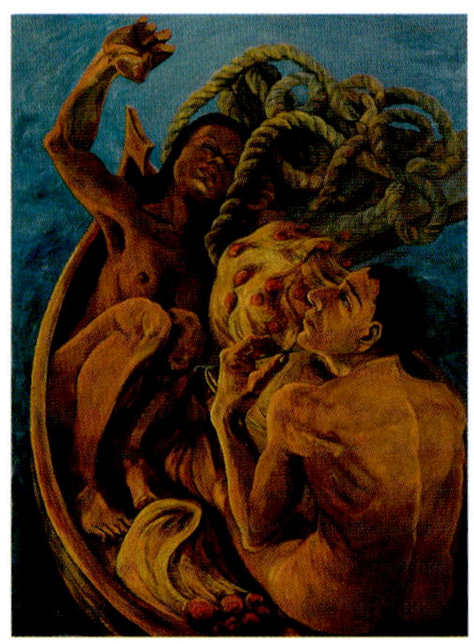

Thomas, Shanti b.1949
The Voyagers 1984
acrylic on paper 120.8 x 90
AC 5471

Thompson, Estelle b.1960
Virgin Ground 1988
oil on canvas 152 x 152.5
ACC14/1990

Thompson, Estelle b.1960
Whiteishwhiteishness 2003
oil on board 50 x 40
ACC47/2003

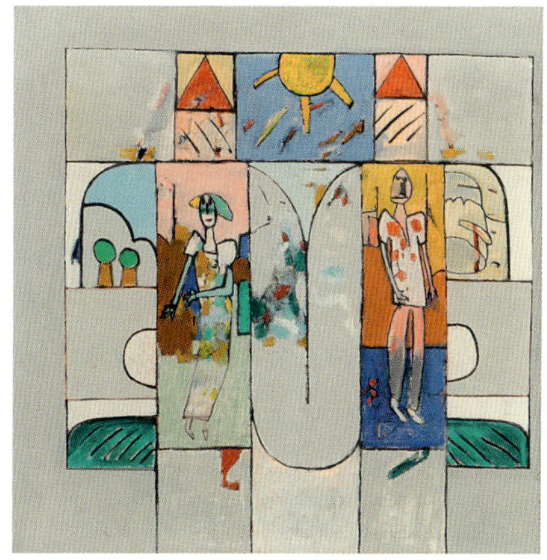

Thompson, Philip 1928–2007
Bonnie and Clyde 1968
oil on canvas 121.9 x 121.9
AC 960

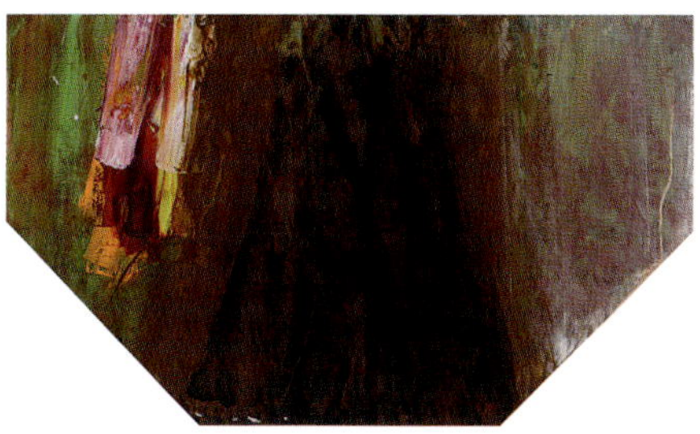

Thomson, Alexander b.1942
Untitled Drawing I 1974
acrylic on paper 46 x 77.8
ACC44/1974

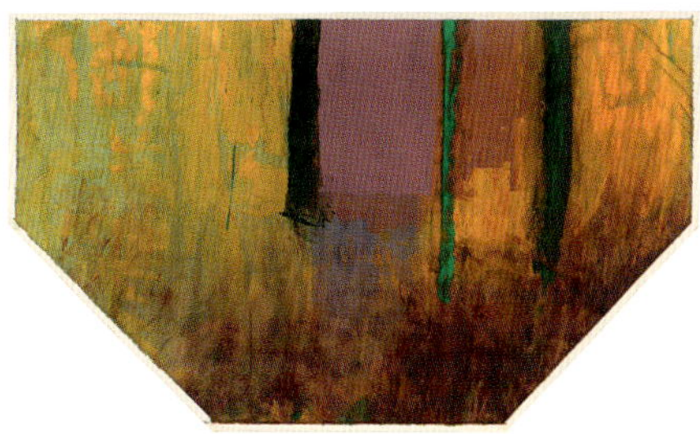

Thomson, Alexander b.1942
Untitled Drawing II 1974
acrylic on paper 83.3 x 142.3
ACC45/1974

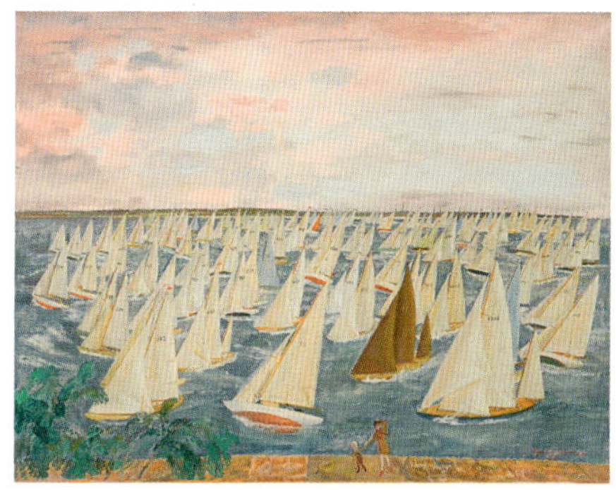

Thomson, Alfred Reginald 1894–1979
Round the Island Races 1966
oil on canvas 76.2 x 101.6
AC 866

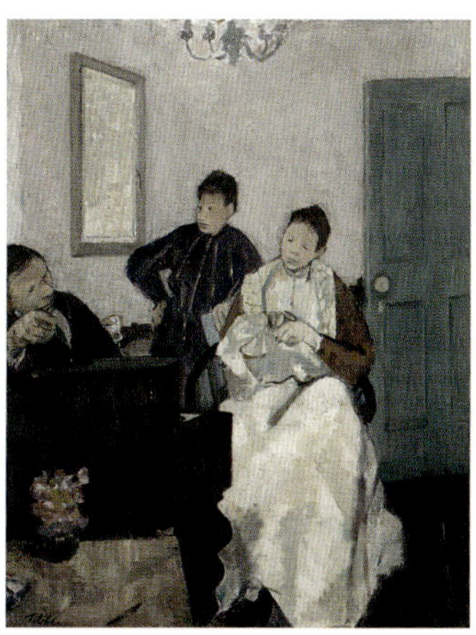

Tibble, Geoffrey Arthur 1909–1952
Music Room 1948
oil on canvas 133.4 x 107.3
AC 146

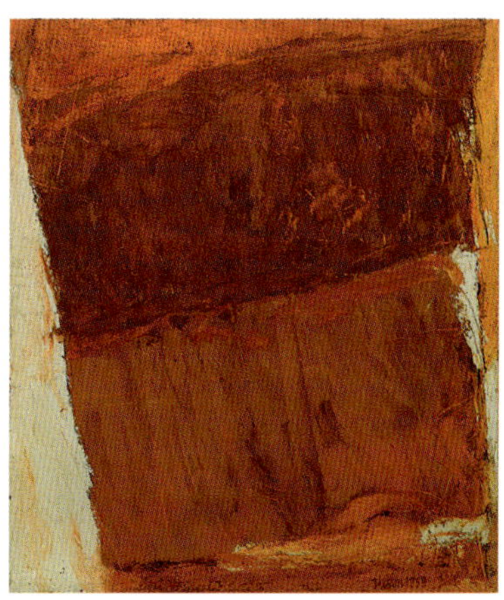

Tilson, Joe b.1928
Summer 1959
oil on canvas 120.5 x 107
AC 539

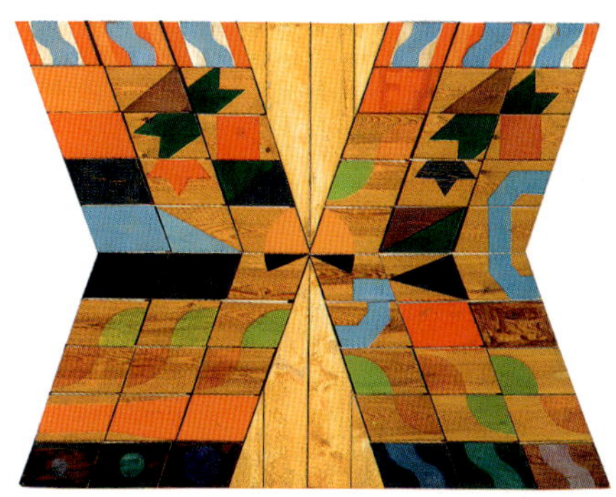

Tilson, Joe b.1928
Space Trophy 1961–1962
paint on wood 95.9 x 127
AC 719

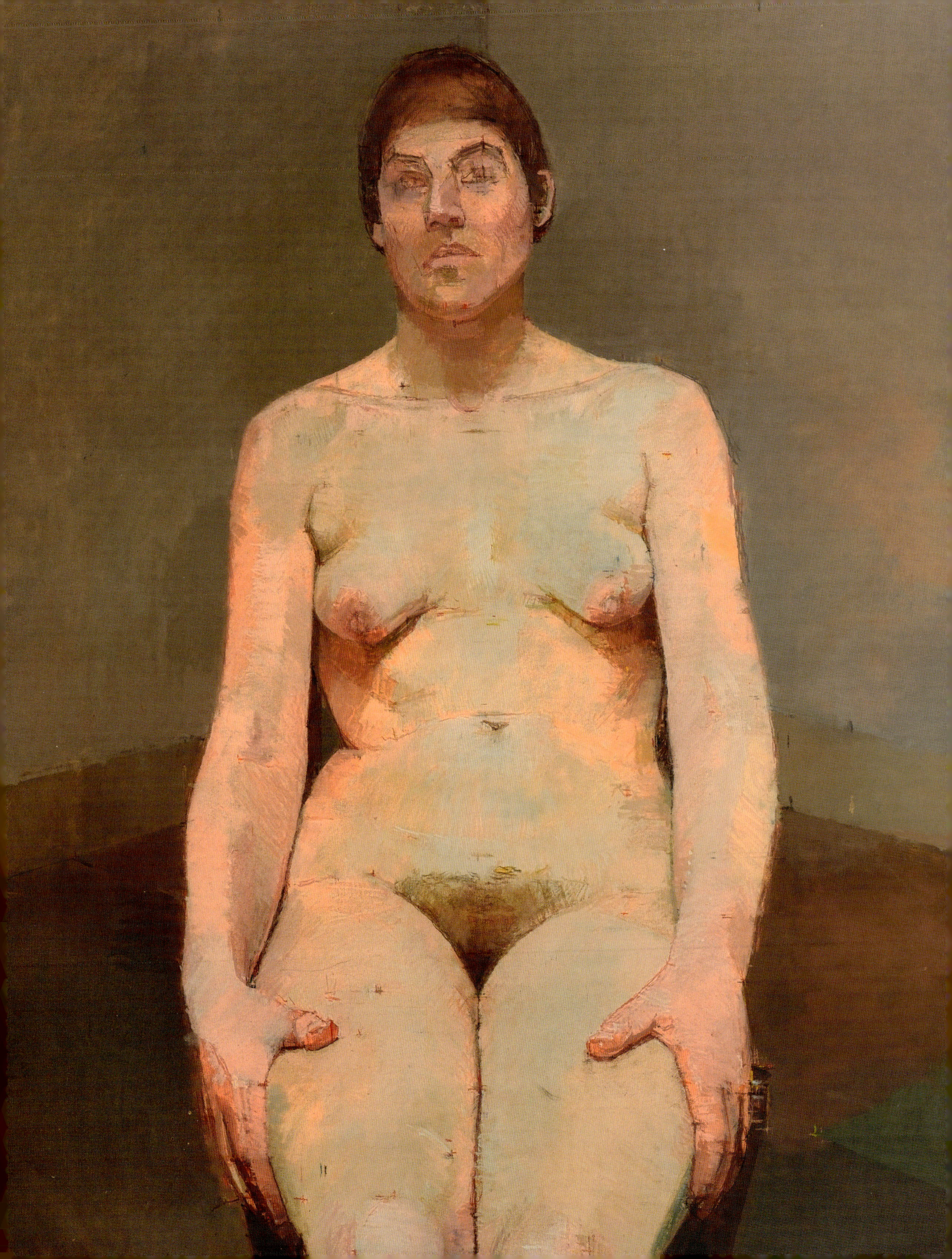

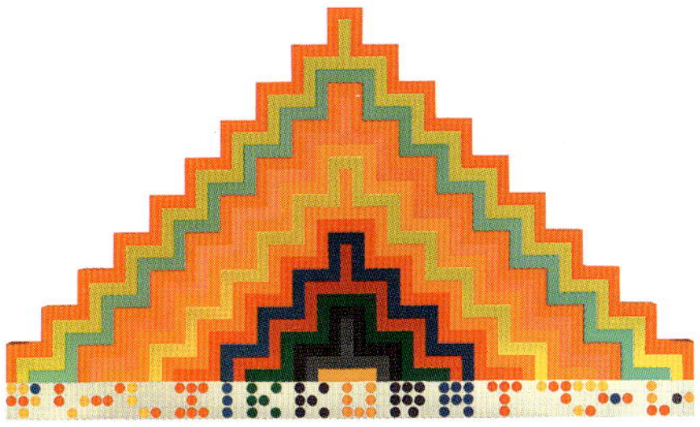

Tilson, Joe b.1928
Zikkurat 7 1967
oil & acrylic on wood 187 x 295
AC 913

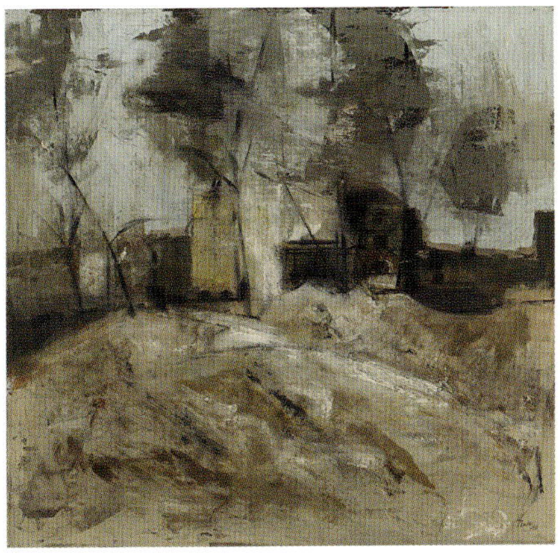

Tindle, David b.1932
Delamere Terrace 1960
oil on board 120 x 130
AC 528

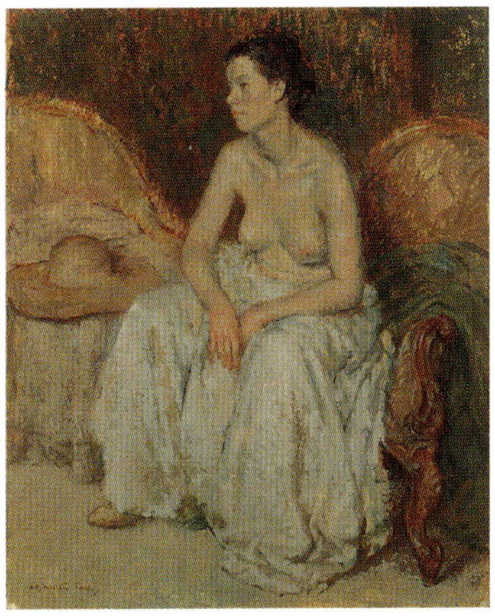

Todd, Arthur Ralph Middleton 1891–1966
Draped Nude
oil on board 66 x 61
AC 107

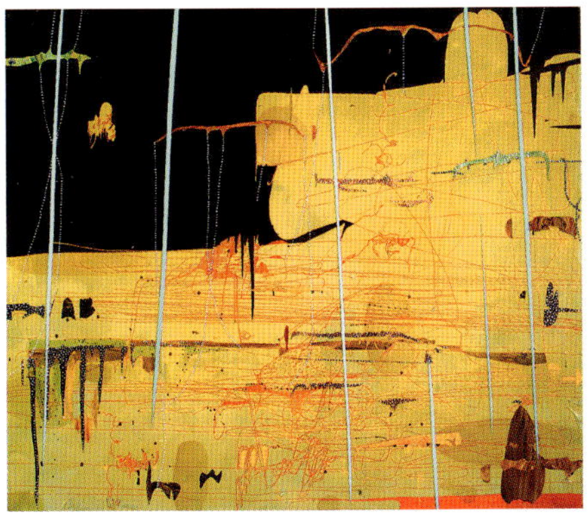

Todd, Graeme b.1962
Mushroom 2003
paint, ink & varnish on MDF 105 x 122
ACC39/2003

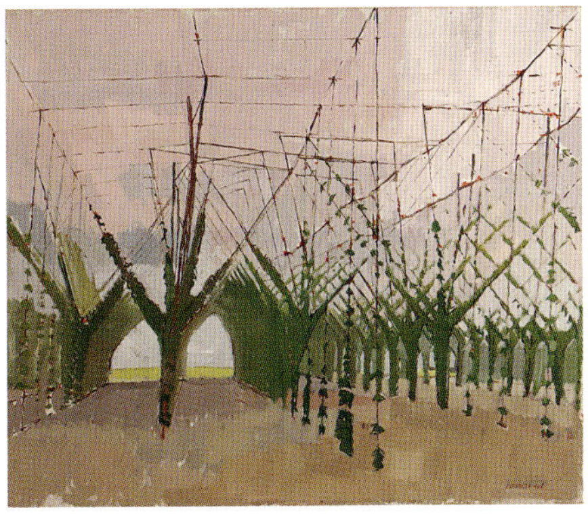

Townsend, William 1909–1973
The Hop Garden 1950
oil on canvas 63.5 x 76.2
AC 177

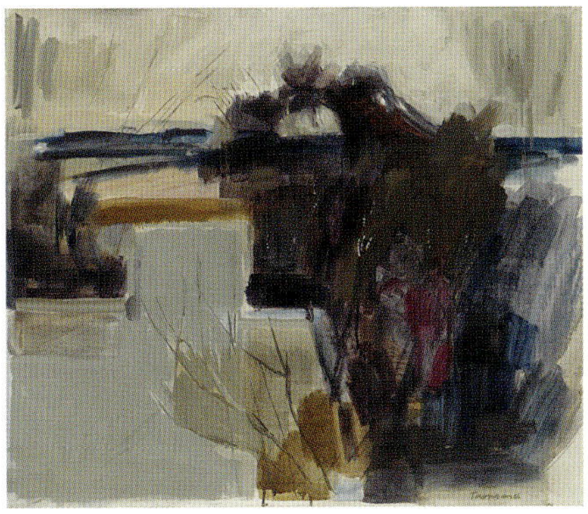

Townsend, William 1909–1973
Landscape with Pond 1958
oil on canvas 63 x 76.2
AC 509

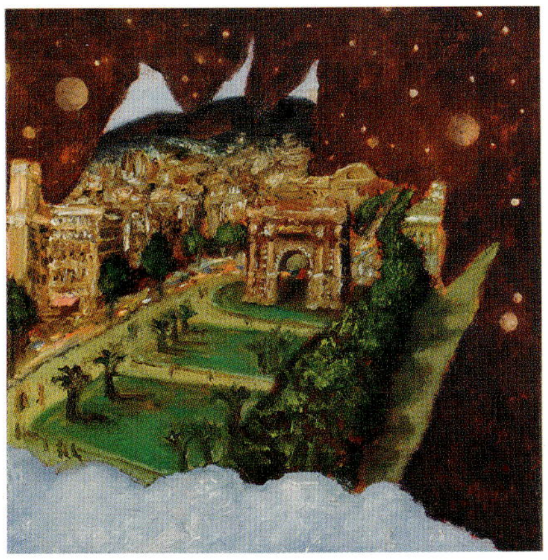

Treister, Suzanne b.1958
Barcelona in Outer Space 1986
oil on canvas 25.4 x 25.5
AC 5447

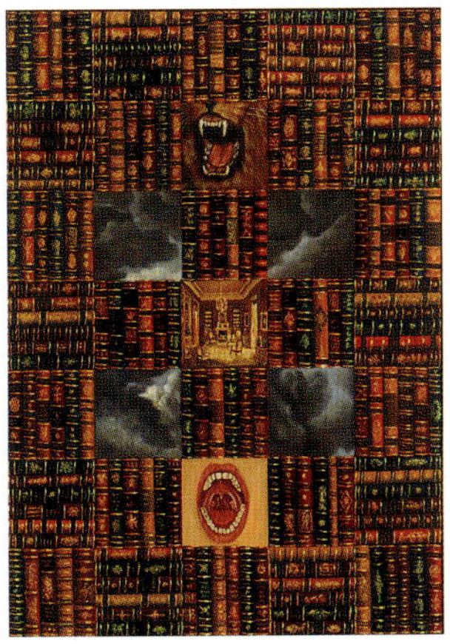

Treister, Suzanne b.1958
Black Hole 1987
oil on canvas 213.5 x 152.4
AC 5502

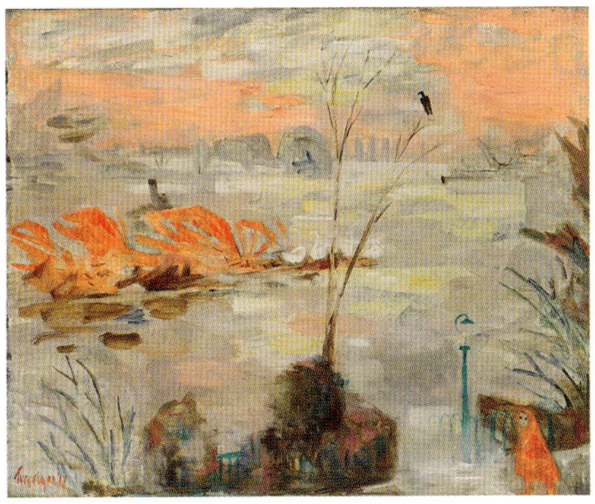

Trevelyan, Julian 1910–1988
High Tide, Chiswick Reach 1947
oil on canvas 63.5 x 80
AC 44

Facing page: Uglow, Euan, 1932–2000, *The German Girl* (detail), 1961–1962, (p. 157)

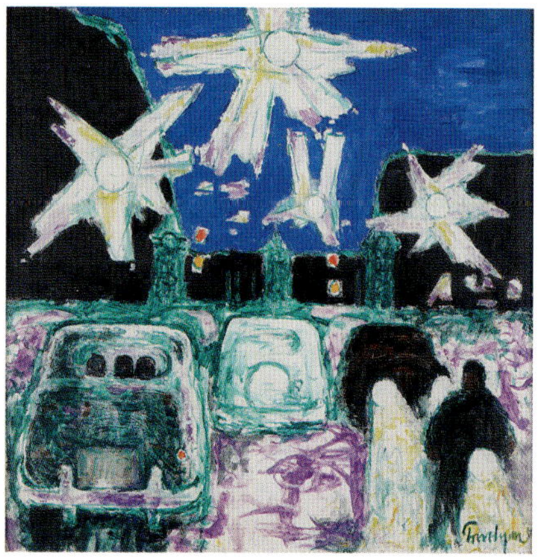

Trevelyan, Julian 1910–1988
Hyde Park 1956
oil on canvas 75 x 75
AC 403

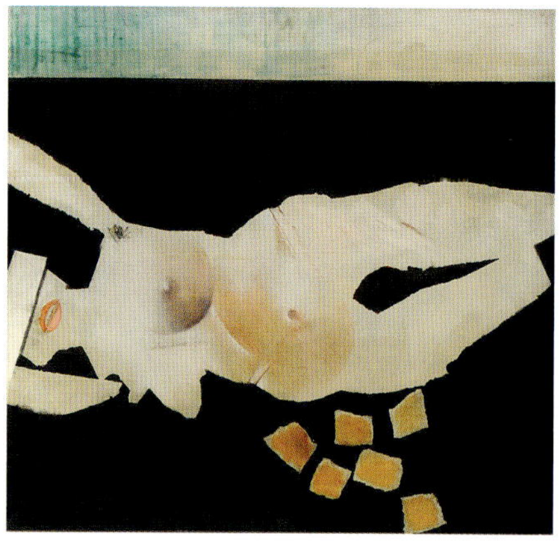

Trollope, Roy b.1933
Reclining Woman 1962
oil on canvas 91.4 x 91.4
AC 659

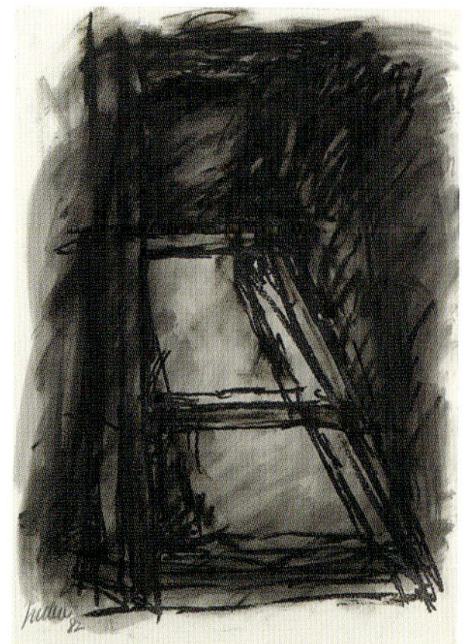

Tucker, William b.1935
Untitled Study for Sculpture 1982
paint on paper 105.1 x 75.4
AC 5125

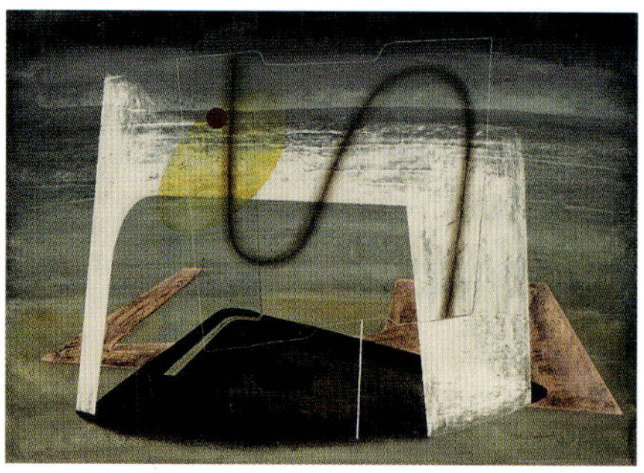

Tunnard, John 1900–1971
Cornwall 1942
oil on board 45.2 x 65.9
AC 82

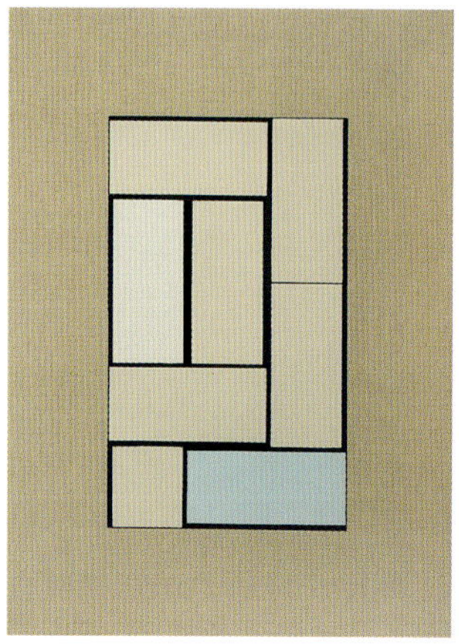

Turnbull, Alison b.1956
Hagi (from the 'Little Japanese Paintings' series) 2000
oil & acrylic on canvas 43.2 x 58.4
ACC17/2000

Turnbull, William b.1922
Untitled 13 1966
acrylic on canvas 152.4 x 203.2
AC 902

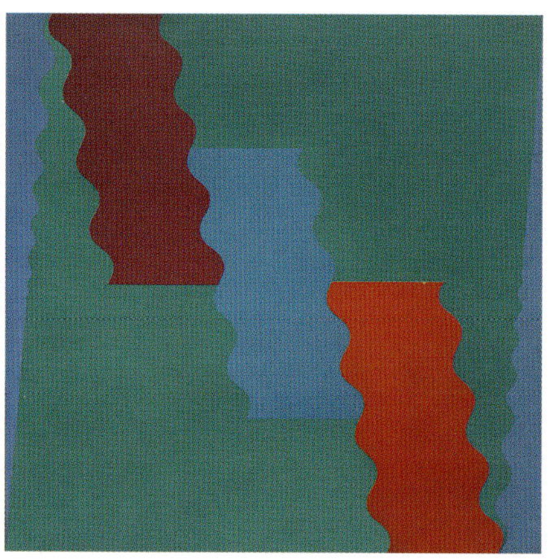

Tyzack, Michael 1933–2007
Praetorius 1966
acrylic on canvas 182.9 x 182.9
AC 847

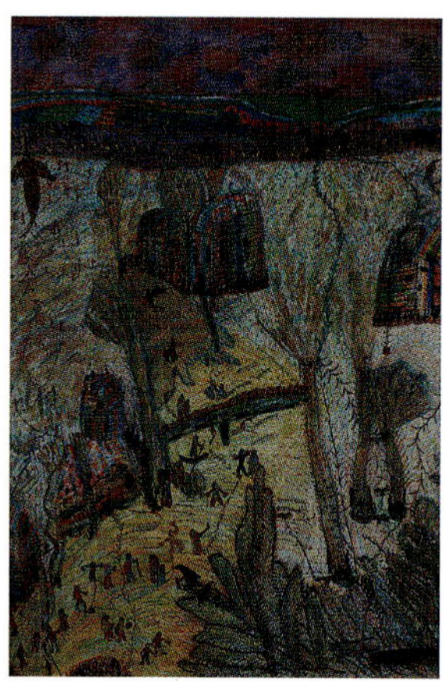

Uddin, Shafique b.1962
Untitled 1986
acrylic & pastel on paper 167.5 x 119.4
AC 5416

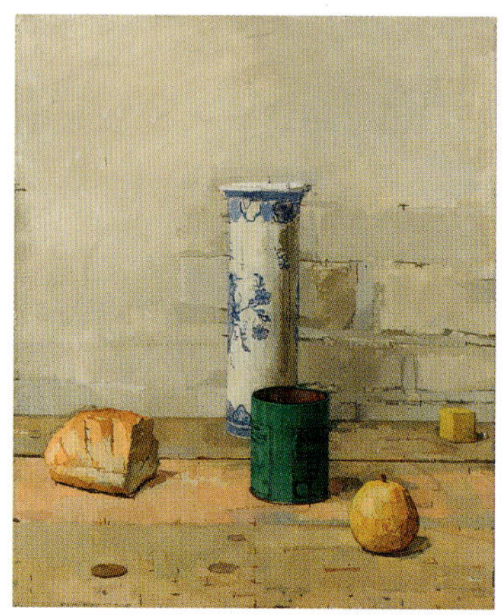

Uglow, Euan 1932–2000
Still Life with Delft Jar 1958
oil on canvas 61 x 51
AC 564

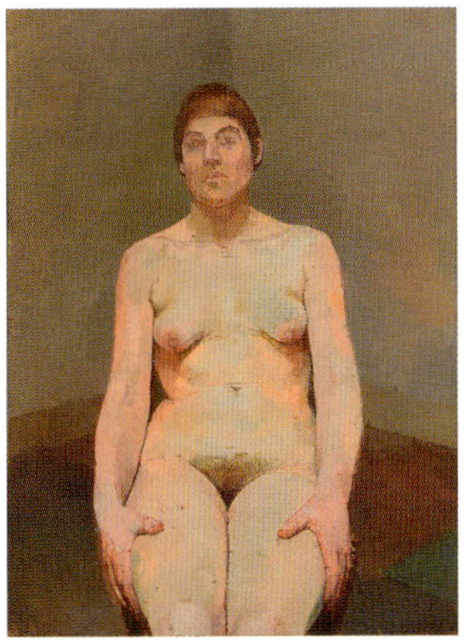

Uglow, Euan 1932–2000
The German Girl 1961–1962
oil on canvas 102.9 x 77.5
AC 868

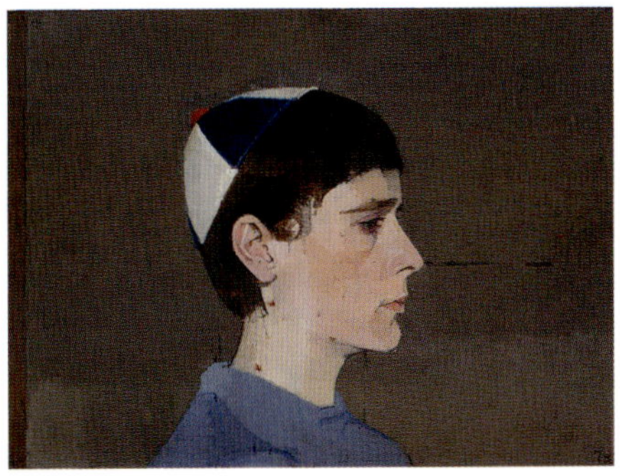

Uglow, Euan 1932–2000
Girl's Head in Profile with Cap on 1963–1964
oil on board 40 x 55.9
AC 735

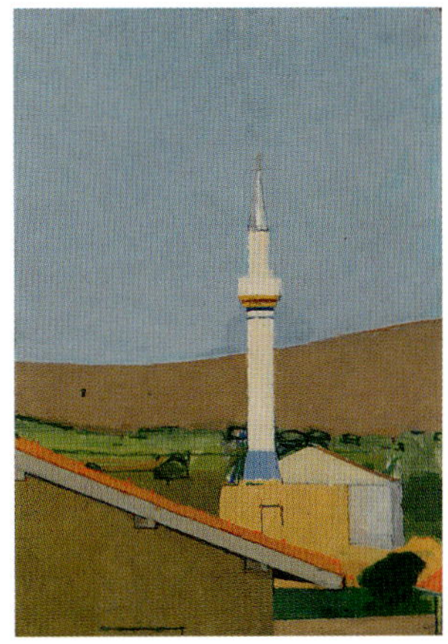

Uglow, Euan 1932–2000
The Mosque at Çiftlik Köyü 1965
oil on board 43.2 x 30.5
AC 894

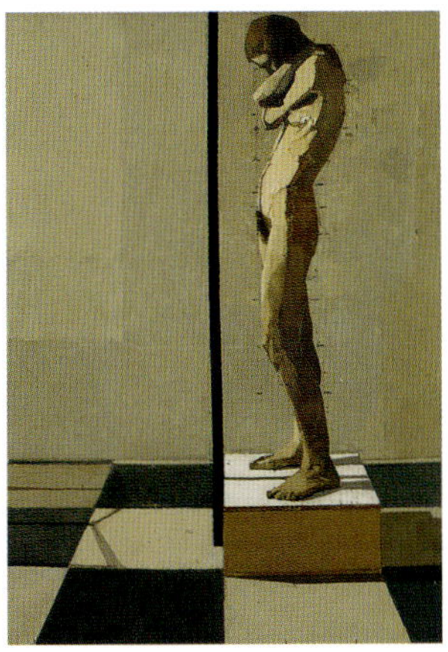

Uglow, Euan 1932–2000
Snake 1976
oil on canvas 49.5 x 35
AC 1586

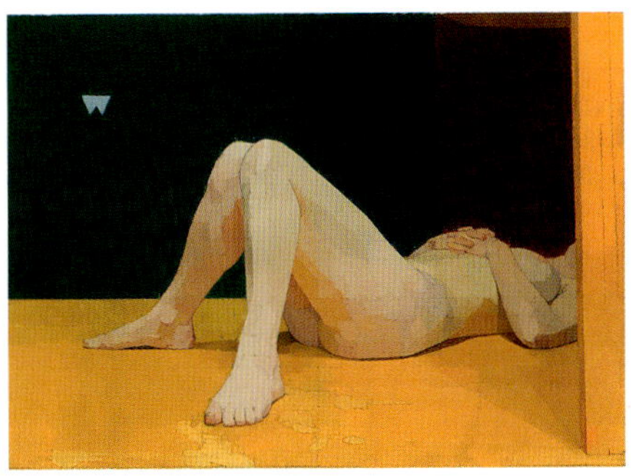

Uglow, Euan 1932–2000
The Quarry Pignano 1979–1980
oil on canvas 80 x 113.1
ACC12/1980

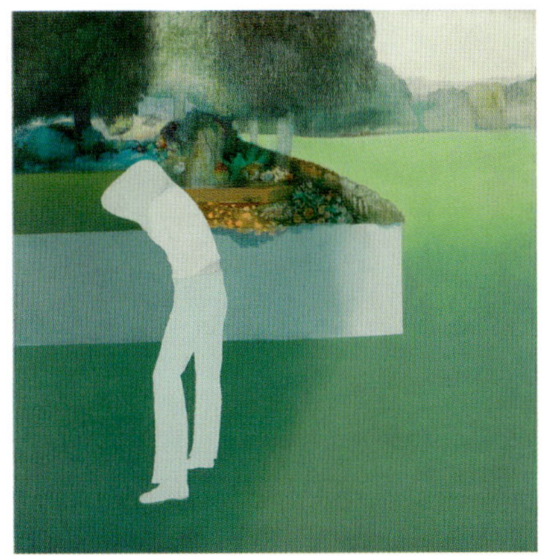

Unsworth, Peter b.1937
Still Garden 1965
oil on canvas 76.2 x 76.2
AC 819

Upton, Michael 1938–2002
The Portrait 1976
oil on panel 43.7 x 42
AC 1791

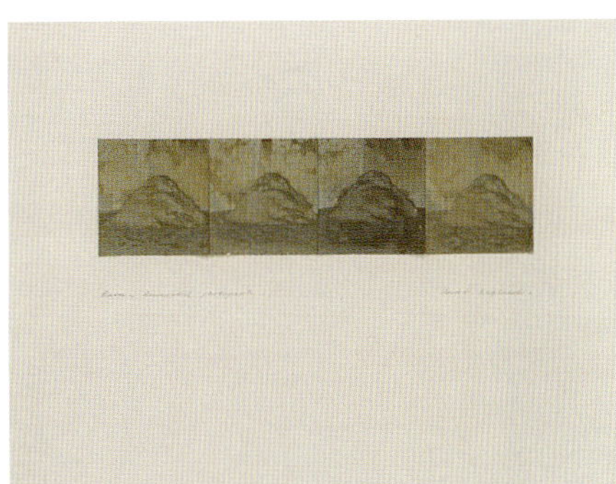

Upton, Michael 1938–2002
Barn, Dorset, England 1978
oil & photographs on card 38.1 x 55.9
AC 1970

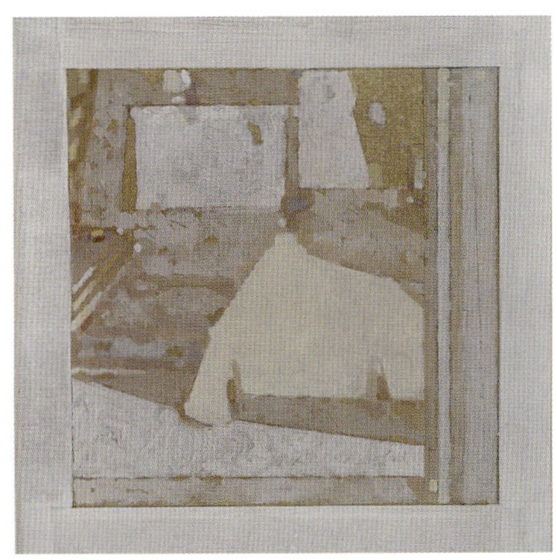

Upton, Michael 1938–2002
The Bed I 1978
oil on card 19.3 x 19.3
AC 1967

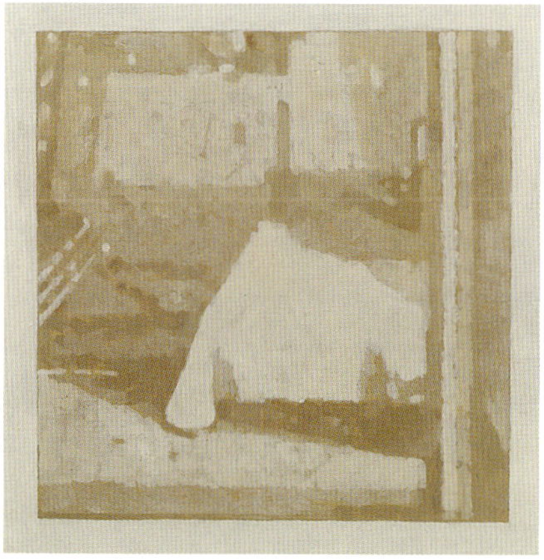

Upton, Michael 1938–2002
The Bed II 1978
oil on card 19.3 x 19.3
AC 1968

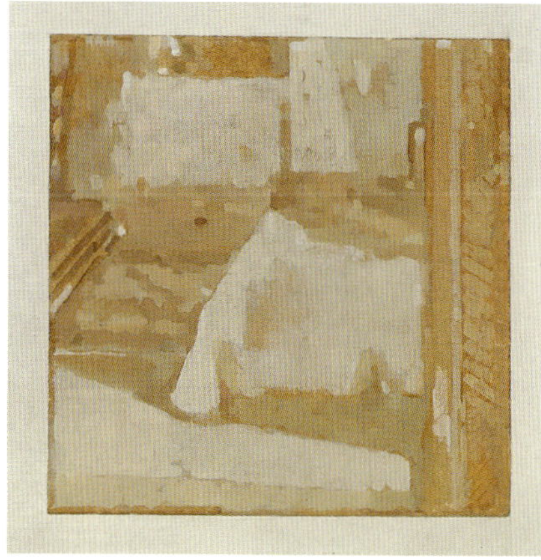

Upton, Michael 1938–2002
The Bed III 1978
oil on card 19.3 x 19.3
AC 1969

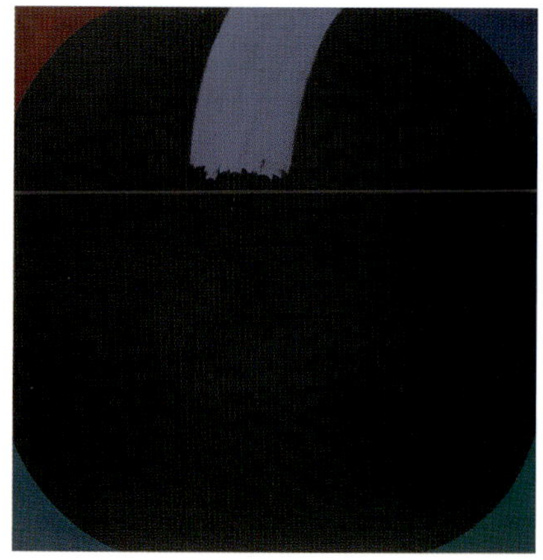

Urkom, Gera b.1940
Apple painting with hyacinth blue brush stroke
1986
acrylic on canvas 164 x 165.2
ACC76/1991

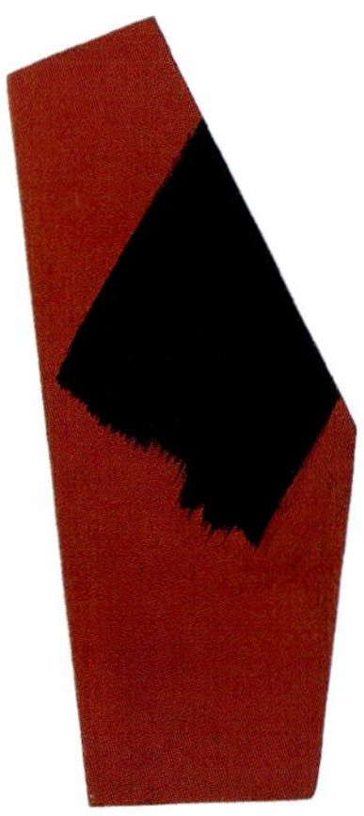

Urkom, Gera b.1940
Small segment, red with black brush stroke
(from the 'Defamiliarisation of the Apple' series) 1988
acrylic on canvas, wood & plaster 40.1 x 15.8
ACC79/1991

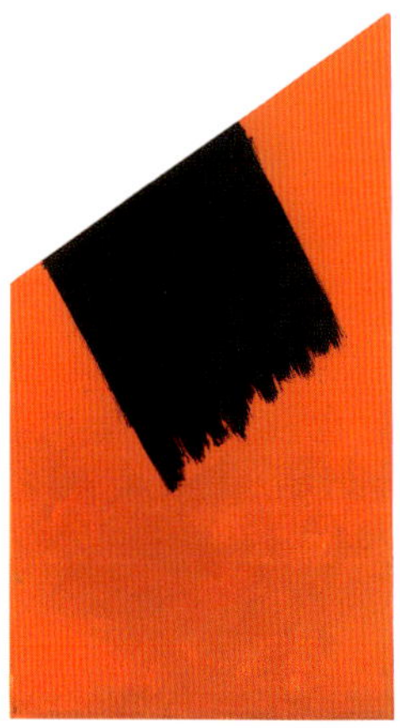

Urkom, Gera b.1940
Medium segment, red with black brush stroke
(from the 'Defamiliarisation of the Apple' series) 1990
acrylic on canvas, wood & plaster 105 x 59.3
ACC78/1991

Urkom, Gera b.1940
Red segment with in-the-centre brush stroke
(from the 'Defamiliarisation of the *(...)* 1991
acrylic on canvas, wood & plaster
121.9 x 121.9
ACC77/1991

Valdivia, Marco b.1947
Untitled 1989–1992
acrylic on wood & canvas 21.2 x 28.5
ACC253/1998

Valdivia, Marco b.1947
Oda a los Mapuches 1994
acrylic & wood on canvas 21.2 x 28.5
ACC35/1998

Valdivia, Marco b.1947
Oda a Tehuiriche 1994
acrylic on wood & canvas 21.2 x 28.5
ACC36/1998

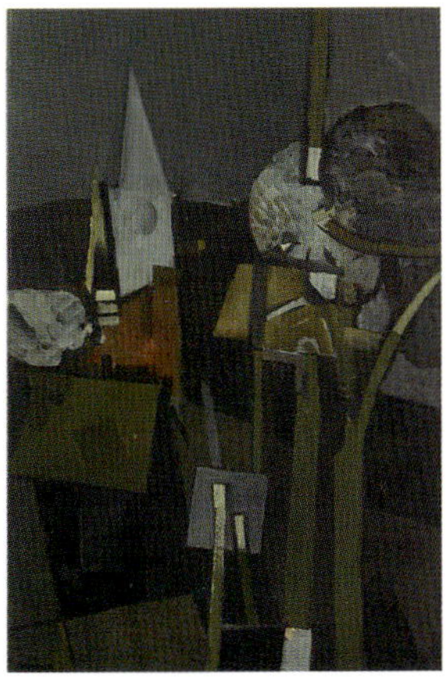

Vaughan, John Keith 1912–1977
The Village 1953
oil on canvas 76 x 51
AC 290

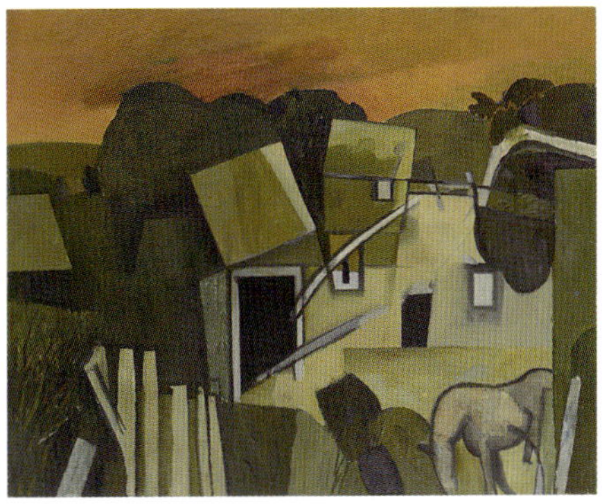

Vaughan, John Keith 1912–1977
September 1956
oil on board 121.3 x 152.4
AC 399

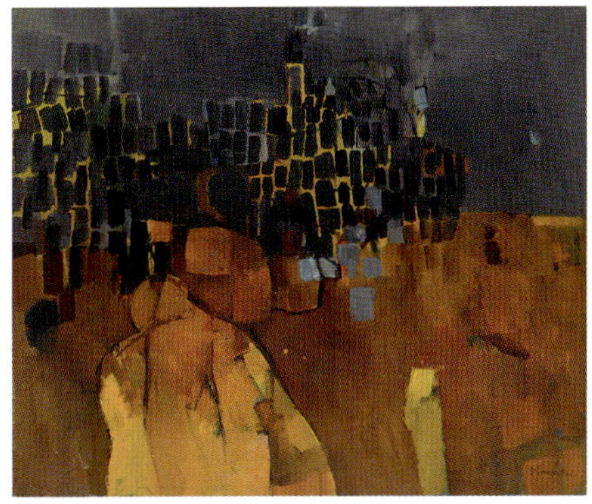

Vaughan, John Keith 1912–1977
Landscape with Figure 1958
oil on canvas 63 x 75.5
AC 457

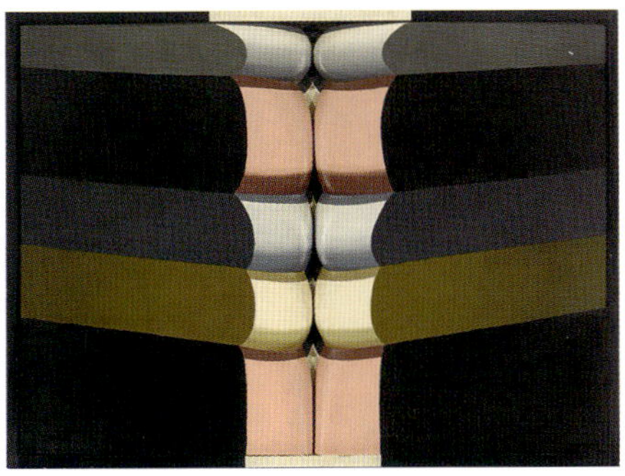

Vaughan, Michael b.1938
Corner Piece: Cake Series 1967
oil & cellulose on board 85.2 x 110.5
AC 1118

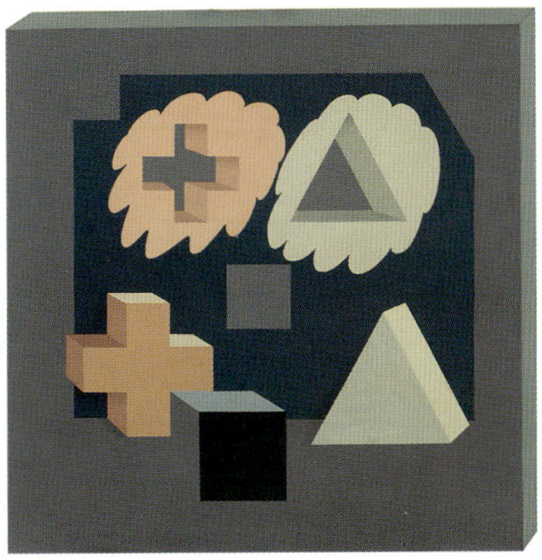

Vaughan, Michael b.1938
Still Life: Square, Cross, Triangle 1970
oil on wood 127 x 127
AC 1116

Vaux, Marc b.1932
PY 70 1970
acrylic on canvas 259 x 213.4
AC 1138

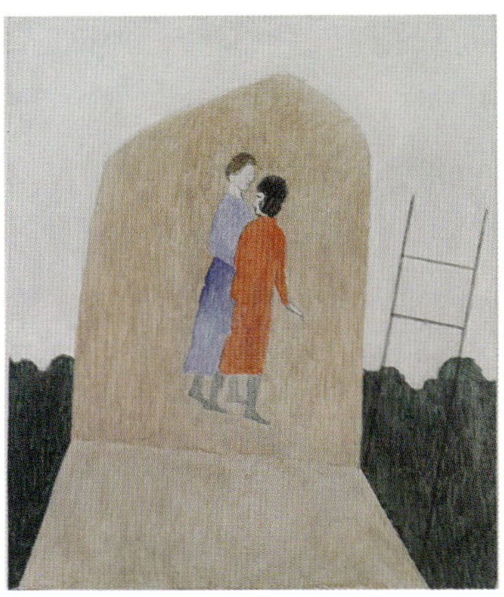

Vellacott, Elisabeth 1905–2002
Vestigial Room 1963
oil on board 65.5 x 56.5
AC 1107

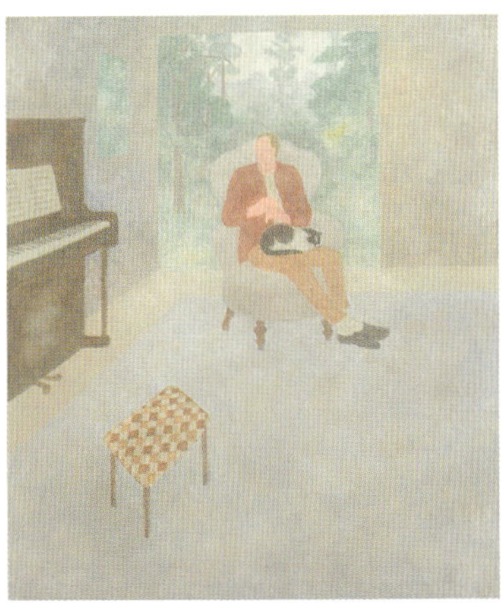

Vellacott, Elisabeth 1905–2002
Man, Cat and Piano 1982
oil on wood 80.5 x 70.2
AC 5254

Verran, Virginia b.1961
Pink Painting No.1 1995
oil on canvas 228 x 198
ACC60/1995

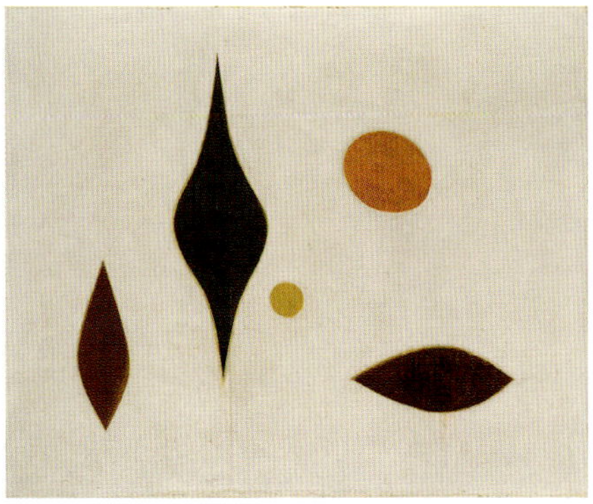

Vézelay, Paule 1893–1984
Yellow Circle 1956
oil on canvas 63 x 73
AC 591

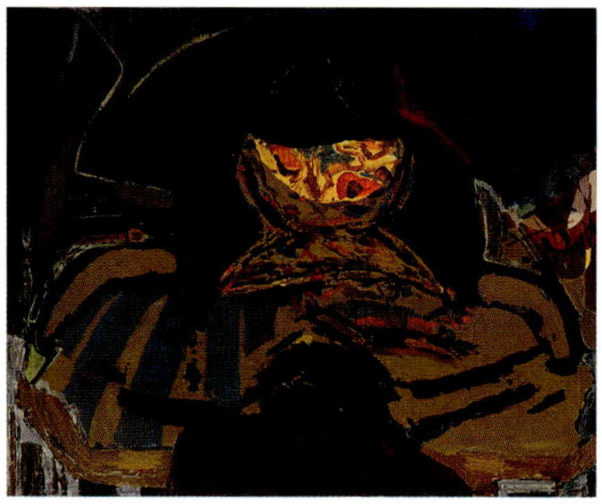

Vilaincour, Leon Julius b.1923
The Chalice 1962
oil on canvas 121.9 x 152.4
ACA 15

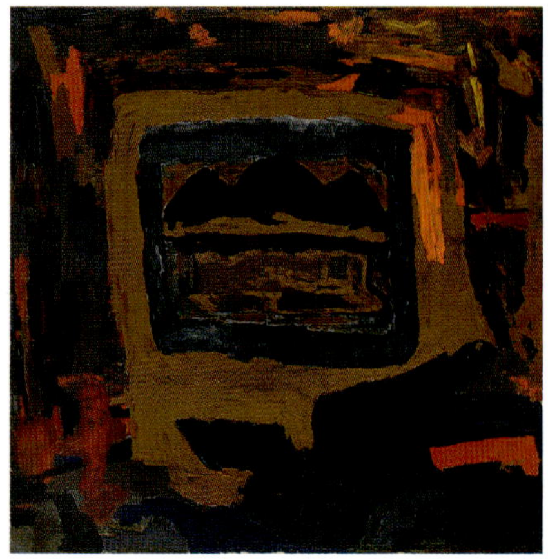

Vilaincour, Leon Julius b.1923
Pietà 1964
oil on canvas 152.4 x 152.4
ACA 33

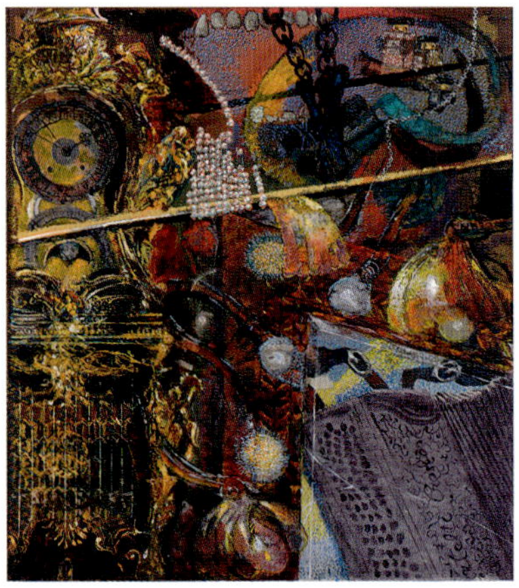

Vilaincour, Leon Julius b.1923
Jean Pierre Latz/Jeanne Lanvin 1993–1994
oil on canvas 121.9 x 111.8
ACC59/1996

Virtue, John b.1947
Landscape 301 1966
acrylic, ink, shellac emulsion & earth on canvas 275 x 330
ACC67/2000

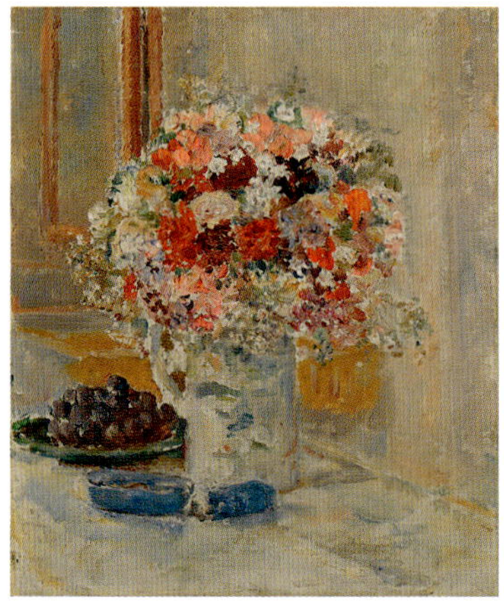

Walker, Ethel 1861–1951
Flowers and Grapes
oil on canvas 61 x 50.8
AC 108

Walker, John b.1939
Tense 1967
acrylic on canvas 304.8 x 213.4
AC 953

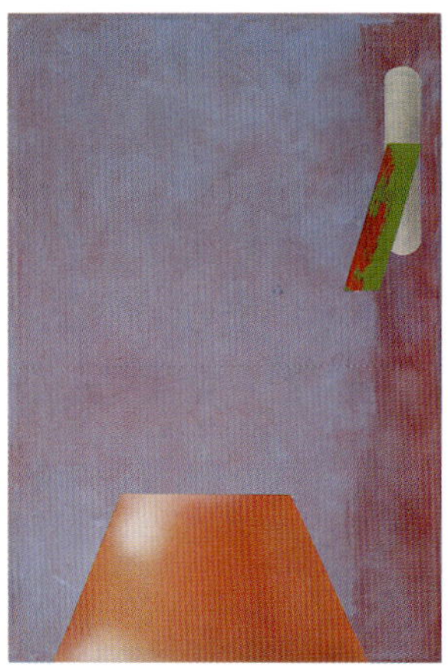

Walker, John b.1939
Seven 1969
acrylic on canvas 304.8 x 213.4
AC 1003

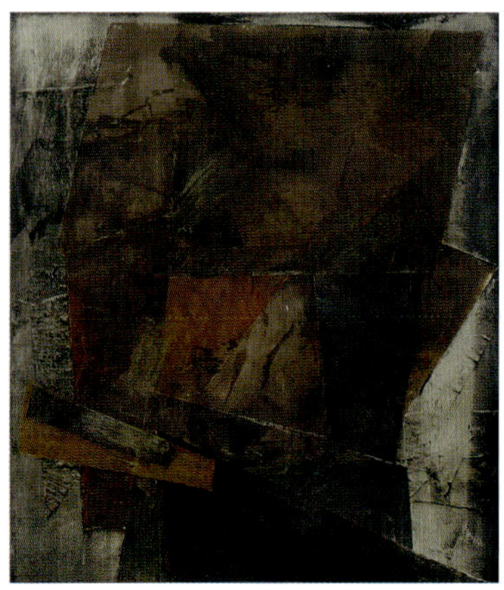

Walker, John b.1939
Untitled 1975 1975
acrylic & chalk on canvas 243.8 x 214
AC 1539

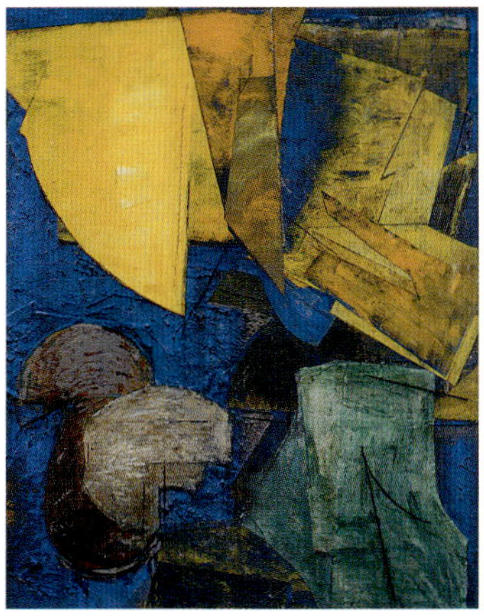

Walker, John b.1939
Ostraca V 1975–1978
acrylic & oil on canvas 302 x 245.7
AC 1944

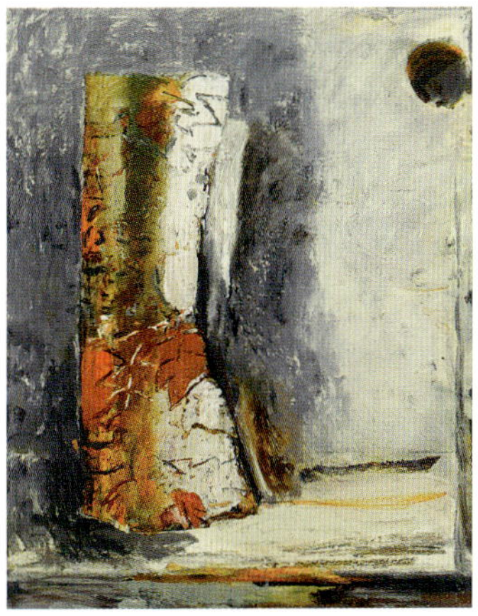

Walker, John b.1939
Conversation 1984
oil on canvas 214 x 169.4
ACC17/1985

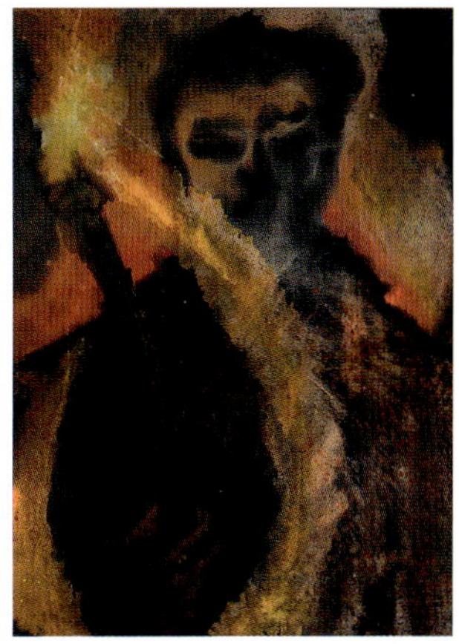

Walker, Richard b.1955
The Power of Fire 1986
acrylic on canvas 231 x 172.8
AC 5467

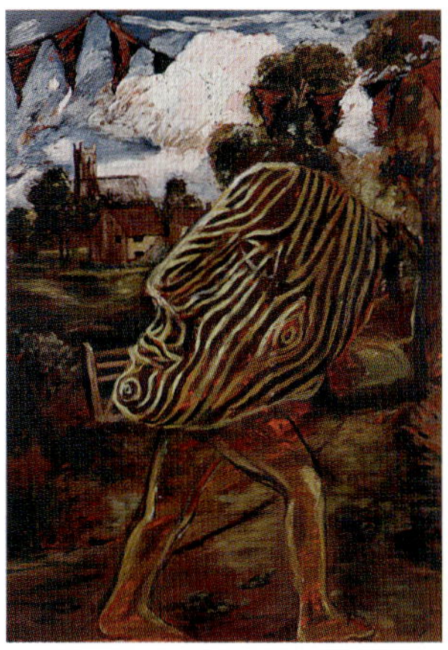

Wallinger, Mark b.1959
John Barleycorn 1984
oil on canvas 213 x 152
AC 5427

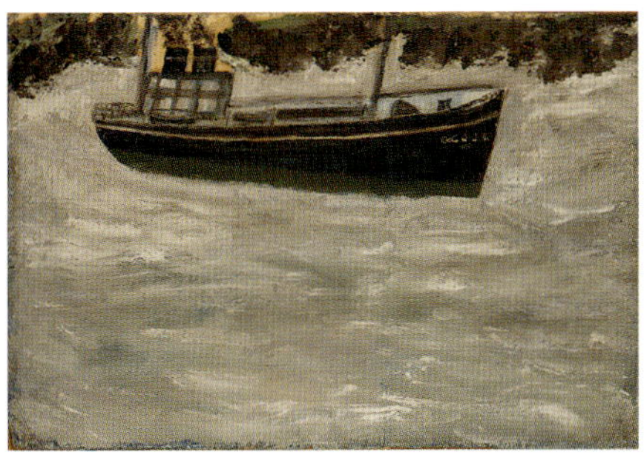

Wallis, Alfred 1855–1942
Trawler c.1925
oil on board 31.8 x 48.9
AC 630

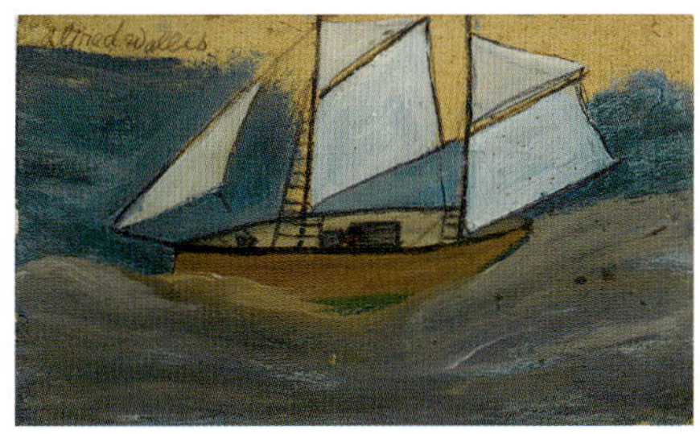

Wallis, Alfred 1855–1942
Ship in Rough Sea
oil on card 11.5 x 19.2
AC 888

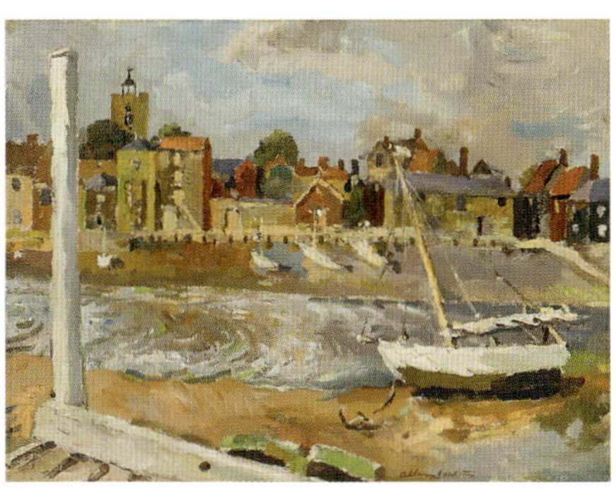

Walton, Allan 1891–1948
Wyvenhoe, Essex
oil on canvas 48 x 63.5
ACC1/1946

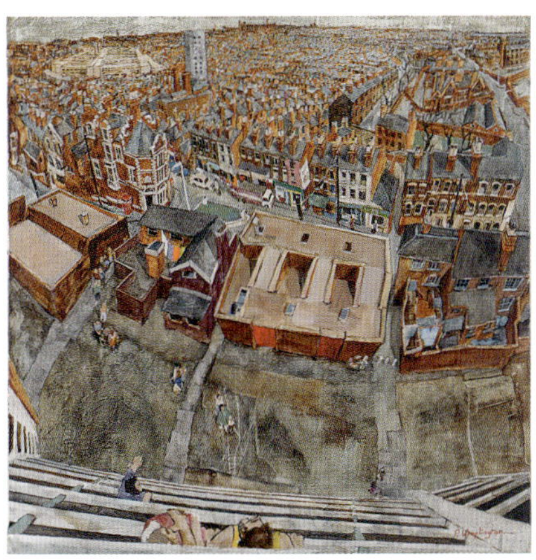

Waplington, Paul Anthony b.1938
Alfreton Road 1979 1979
acrylic on canvas 119.6 x 120
AC 2041

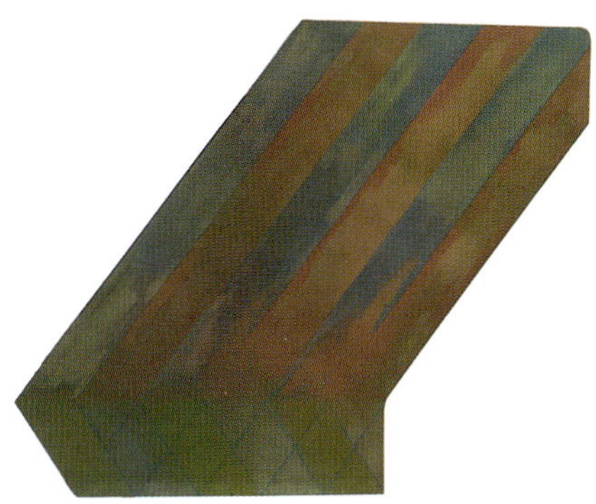

Ward, Richard b.1937
Painting 1968
acrylic on canvas 219 x 113.7
AC 959

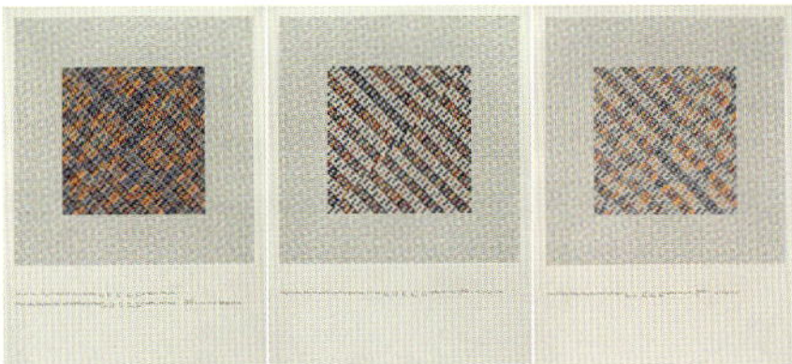

Watts, Chris b.1947
Two Stages and the Composite 2A, 2B & 2C, a Set of Three Drawings 1981
acrylic, ink & letraset on paper 76.1 x 57; 76.1 x 57; 76.1 x 57
AC 5121

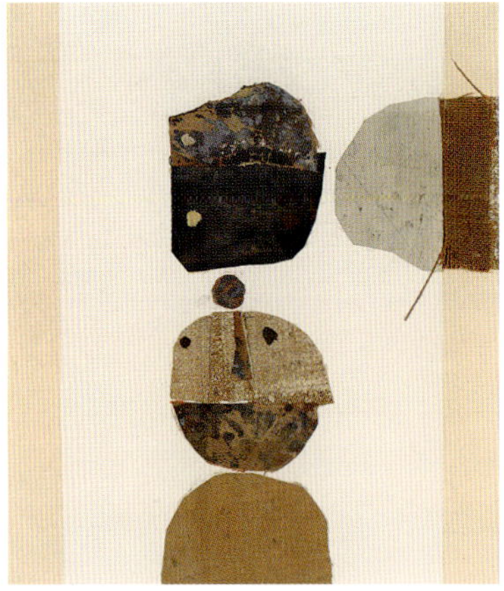

Weatherson, Alexander b.1930
Vis-à-vis 1961
canvas, paper & oil on card 42.7 x 37.4
AC 582

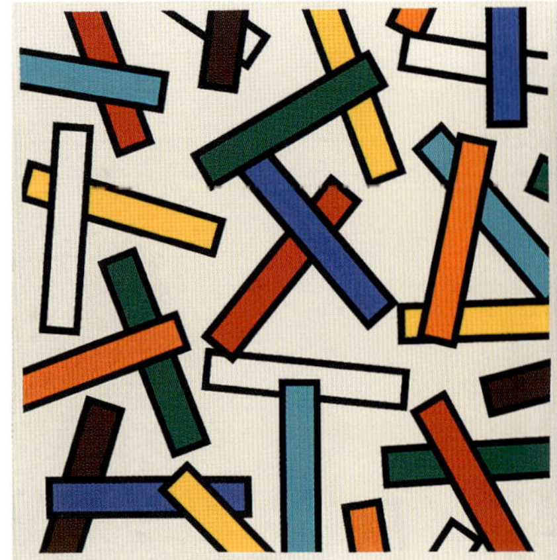

Webb, Mary b.1939
Spring Colour Study No.19 1995
oil on canvas 112 x 112
ACC7/1997

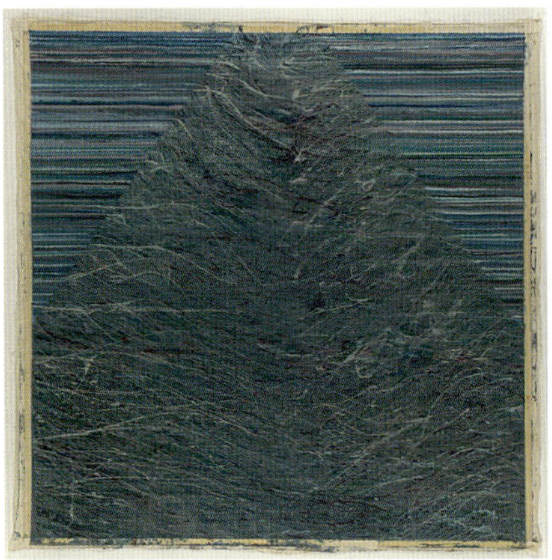

Webster, Catrin b.1966
Level Playing Fields 1995–1996
oil on canvas 259.1 x 259.1
ACC51/1997

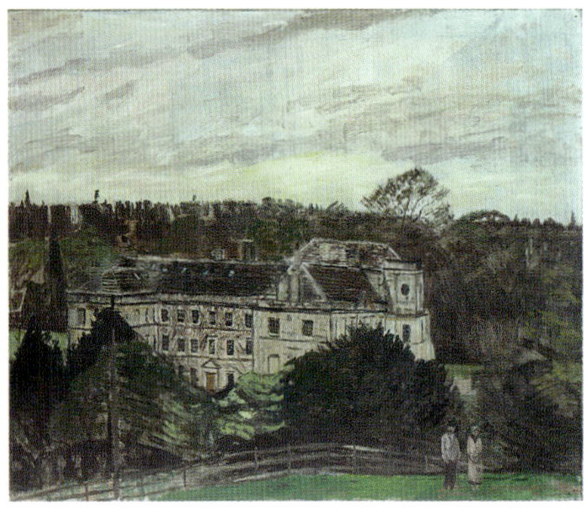

Weight, Carel Victor Morlais 1908–1997
Dans le vieux parc 1951
oil on canvas 60 x 73
AC 190

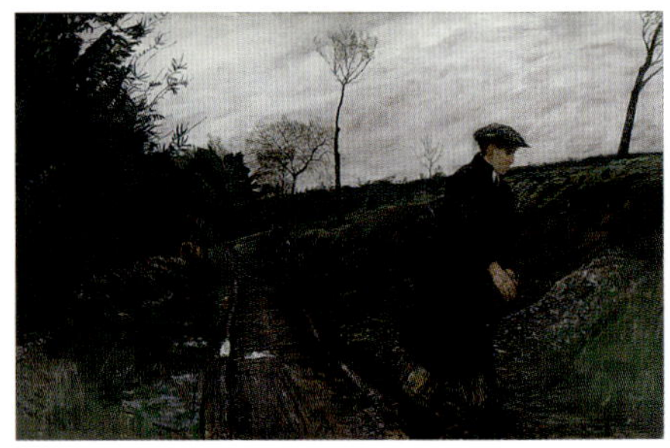

Weight, Carel Victor Morlais 1908–1997
The Good Samaritan 1958
oil on canvas 104.1 x 157.5
AC 508

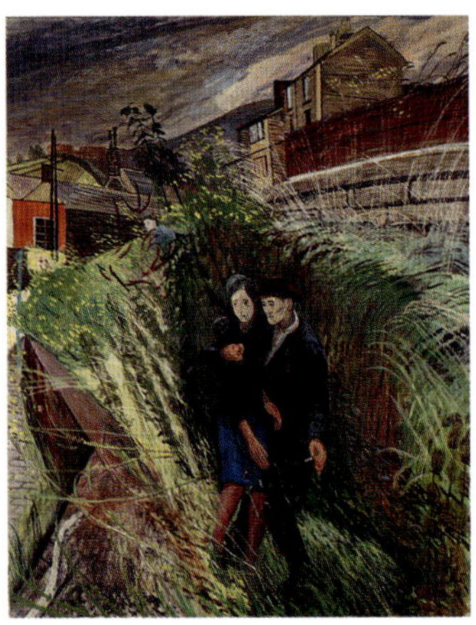

Weight, Carel Victor Morlais 1908–1997
The Snake 1966
oil on canvas 127 x 101.6
AC 865

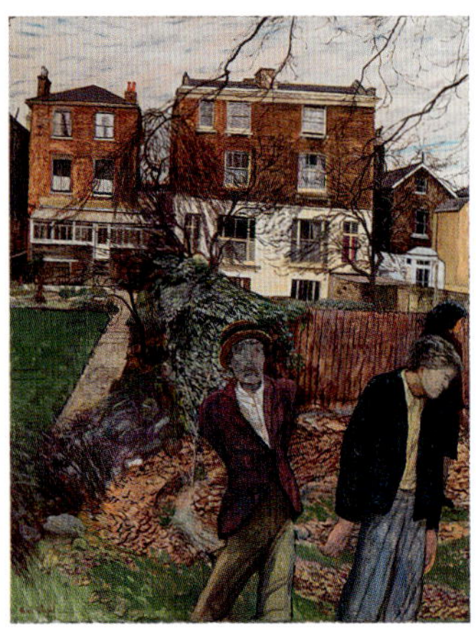

Weight, Carel Victor Morlais 1908–1997
The World We Live In 1970–1973
oil on board 120.5 x 94.5
AC 1549

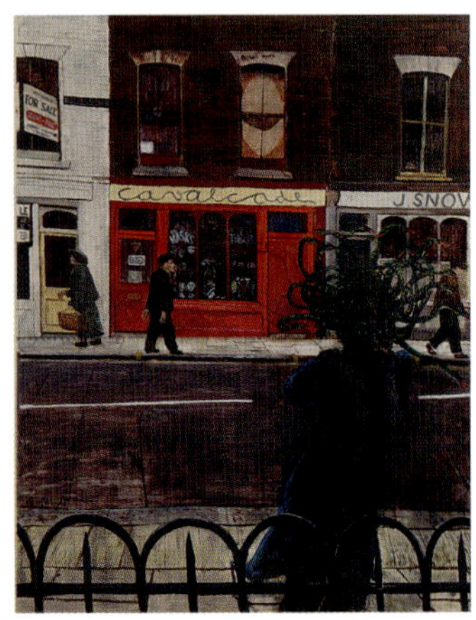

Weight, Carel Victor Morlais 1908–1997
Battersea Medusa 1974–1975
oil on board 91 x 70
AC 1550

Facing page: Hodgkin, Howard, b.1932, *Foy Nissen's Bombay* (detail), 1975–1977, (p. 75)

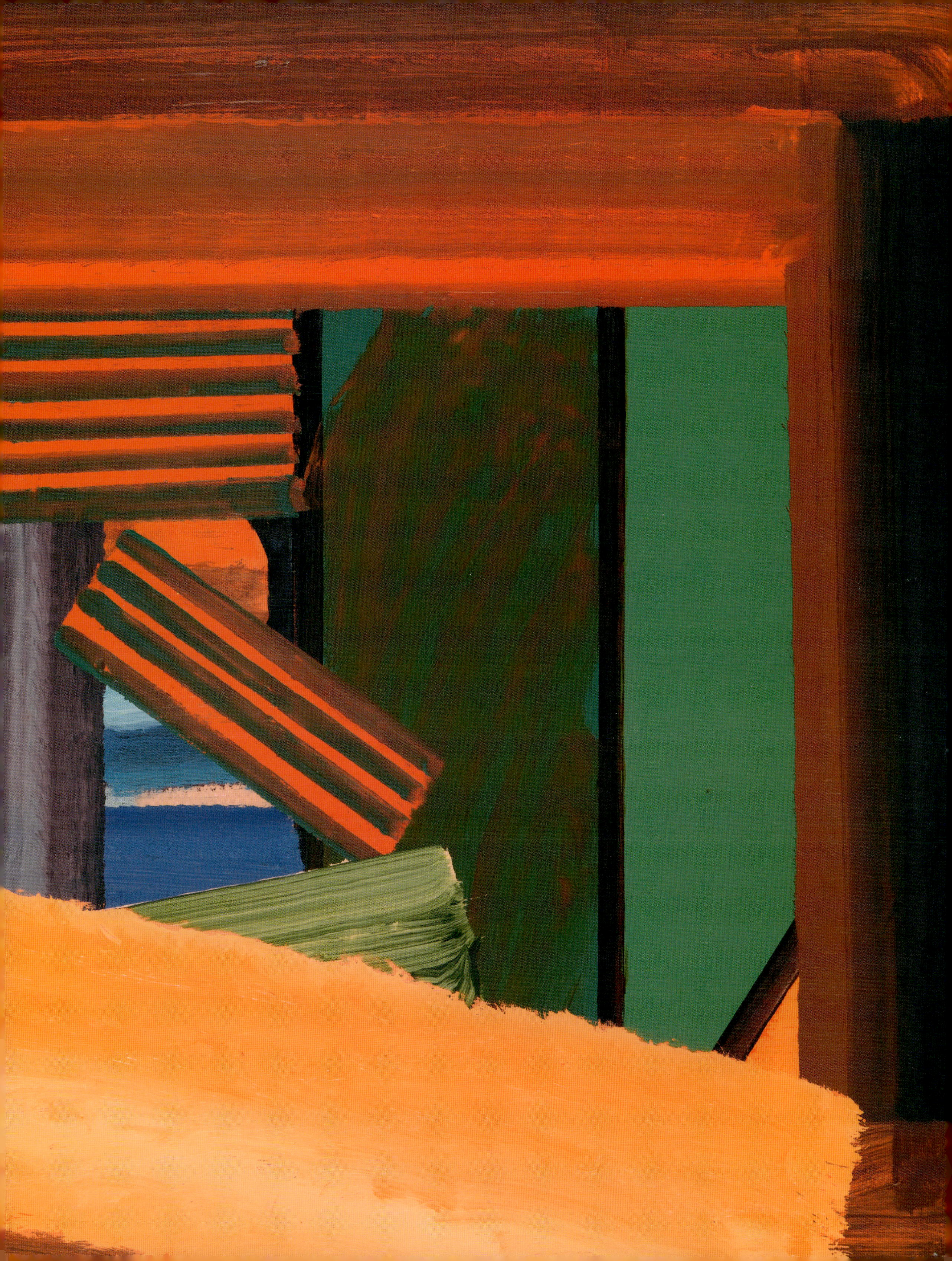

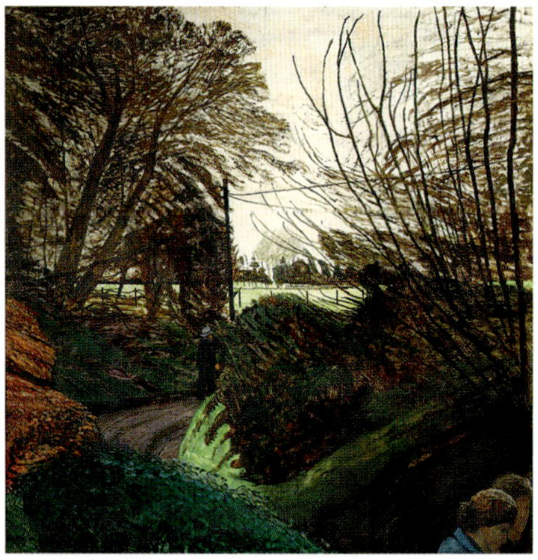

Weight, Carel Victor Morlais 1908–1997
Deep Lane 1974–1978
oil on board 121.9 x 121.9
AC 1950

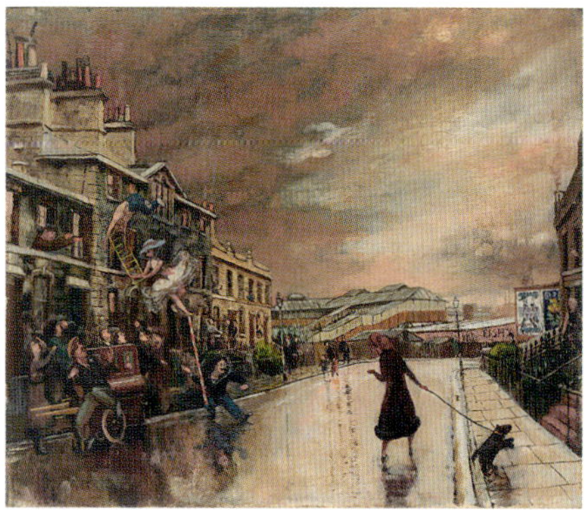

Weight, Carel Victor Morlais 1908–1997
Love at First Sight
oil on canvas 63.5 x 76.2
AC 83

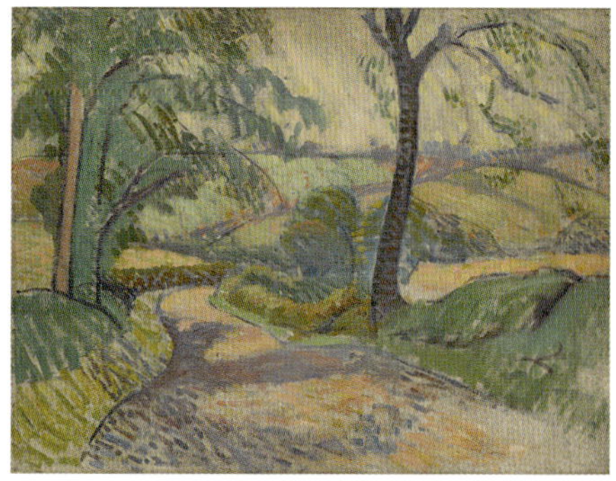

Wellington, Hubert Lindsay 1879–1967
Lane to Walton, Staffordshire 1914
oil on canvas 45.7 x 61
AC 600

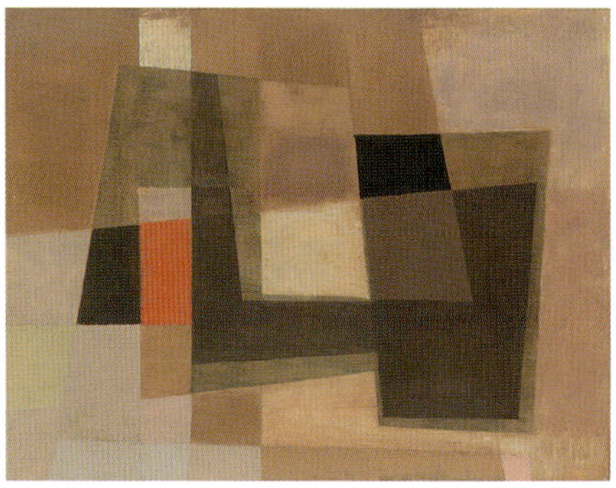

Wells, John 1907–2000
Variation II 1960
oil on board 45.7 x 58.4
AC 537

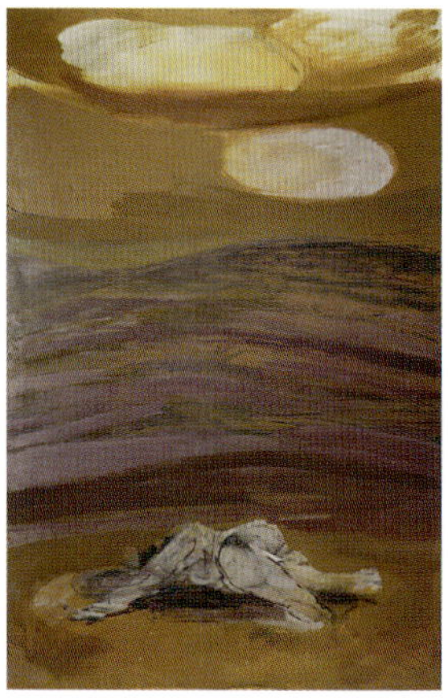

Weschke, Karl 1925–2005
Figure in a Landscape 1972
oil on board 182.2 x 123.8
ACC23/1972

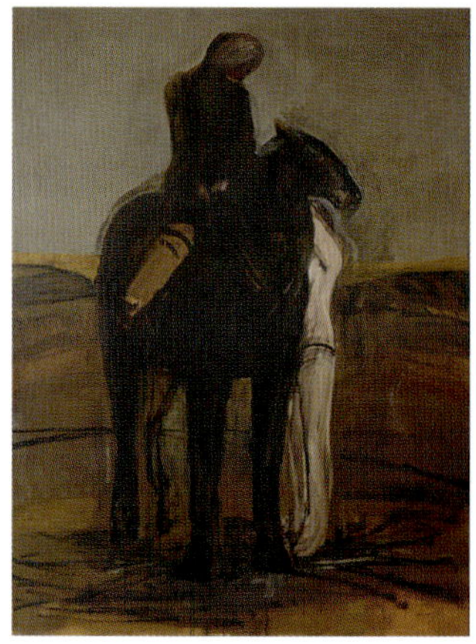

Weschke, Karl 1925–2005
The Meeting 1974
oil on canvas 181.6 x 136.9
AC 4004

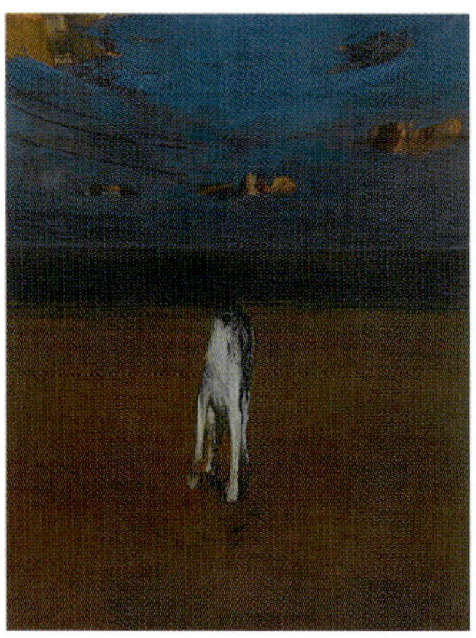

Weschke, Karl 1925–2005
Portrait of a Dog 1975–1978
oil on canvas 213.6 x 167.5
AC 5223

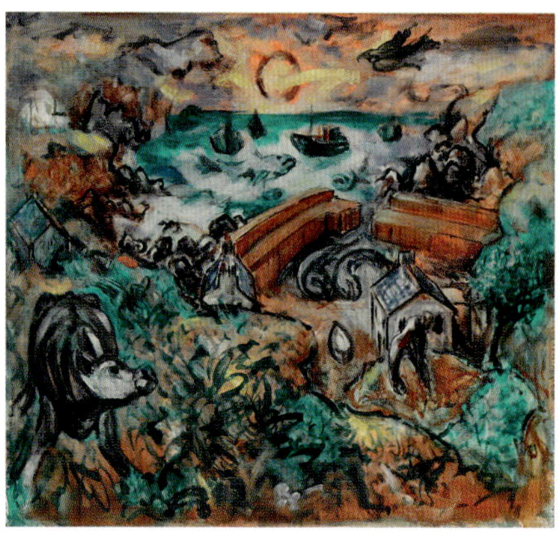

West, Francis b.1936
As I walked out one evening 1984
oil on wood 120.7 x 134
AC 5394

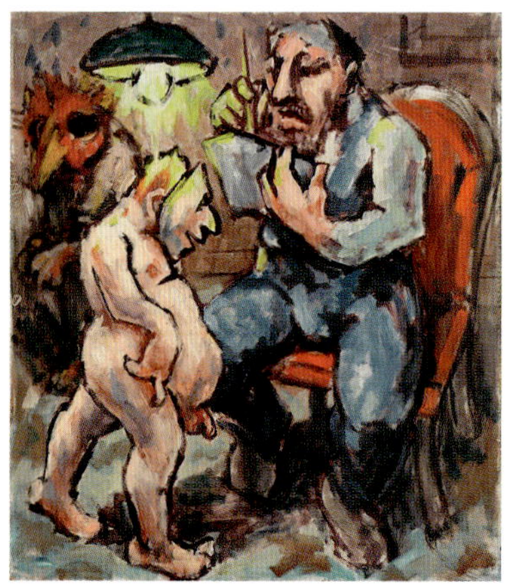

West, Francis b.1936
The Artist in Search of a Persona 1984
oil on wood 122.5 x 108.4
AC 5395

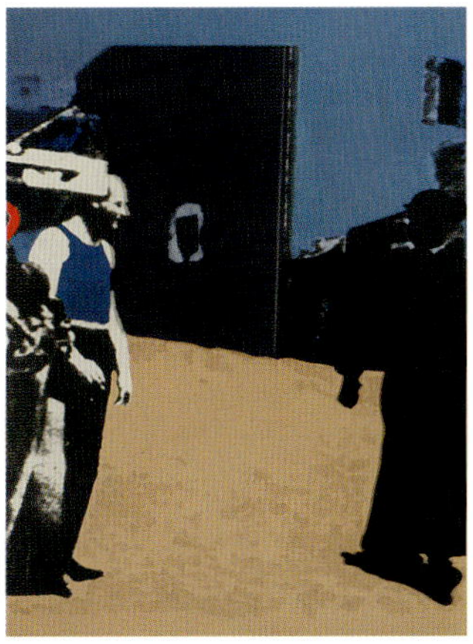

Westwood, Roger b.1936
Peret Insulting the Priest 1971–1972
oil, photograph & varnish on wood
152 x 111
AC 1789

Whamond, Andrew b.1947
Second drawing for 'White Monument' 1975
acrylic & pigment on paper 48 x 78
AC 1540

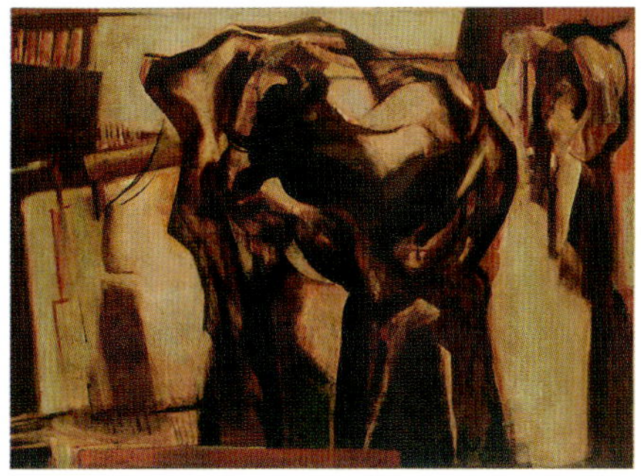

Whishaw, Anthony b.1930
Two Cows 1961
oil on board 152.4 x 213.4
AC 592

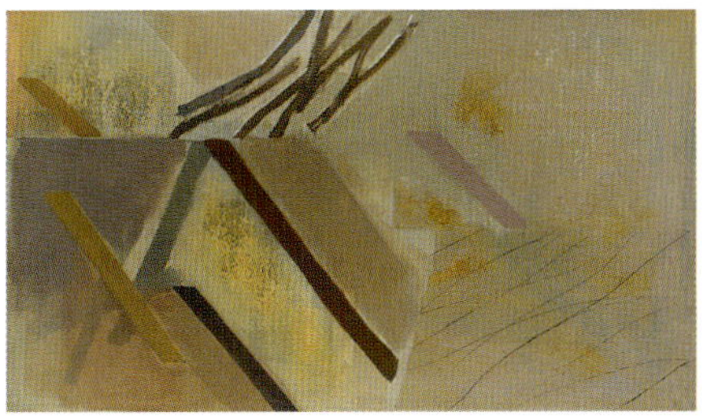

Whishaw, Anthony b.1930
Monks Horton 1976–1977
acrylic on canvas 175 x 305
AC 1774

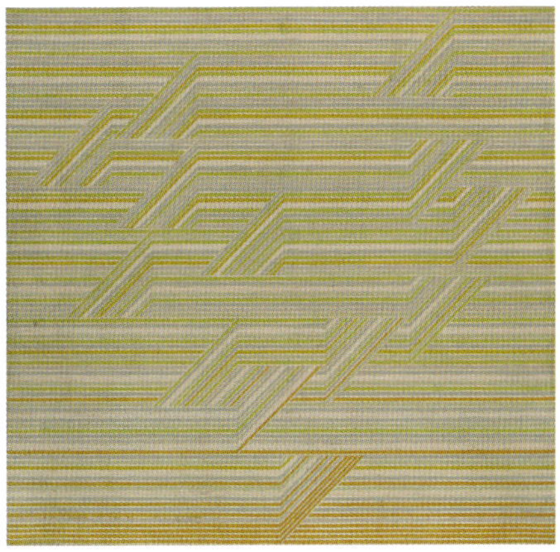

Whitaker, David 1938–2007
Triscape 1969
oil on canvas 196.9 x 210.8
AC 1106

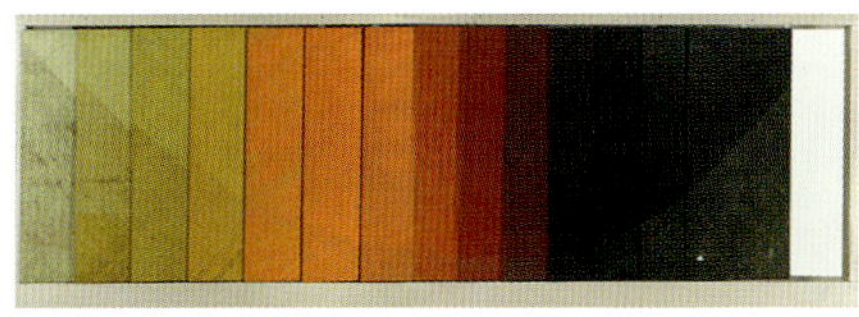

Whitaker, David 1938–2007
Orbit (recto) 1972
acrylic, emulsion, canvas & wood 232 x 776
AC 1267

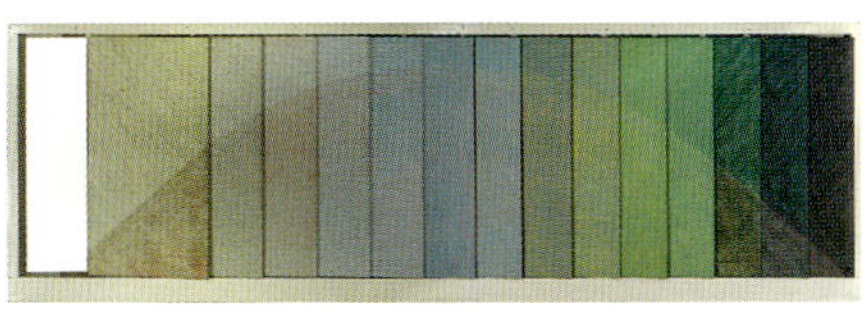

Whitaker, David 1938–2007
Orbit (verso) 1972
acrylic, emulsion, canvas & wood 232 x 776
AC 1267

Whitaker, David 1938–2007
The Estuary 'Four Ages' 1975
string, acrylic & oil on canvas 207 x 260
AC 1812

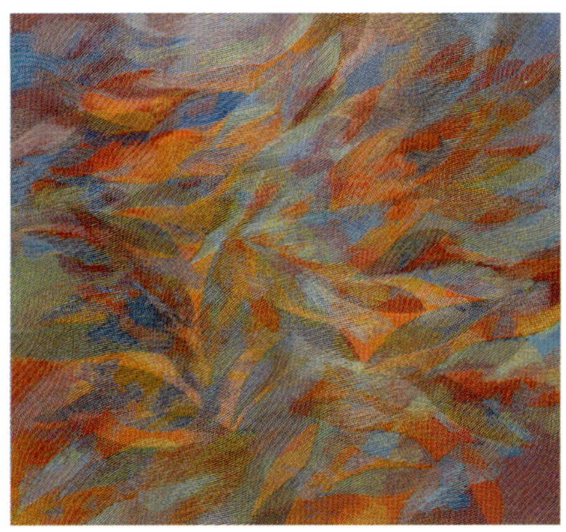

Whitaker, David 1938–2007
Untitled No.2 1978–1979
acrylic, oil & string on canvas 236 x 263.4
AC 2018

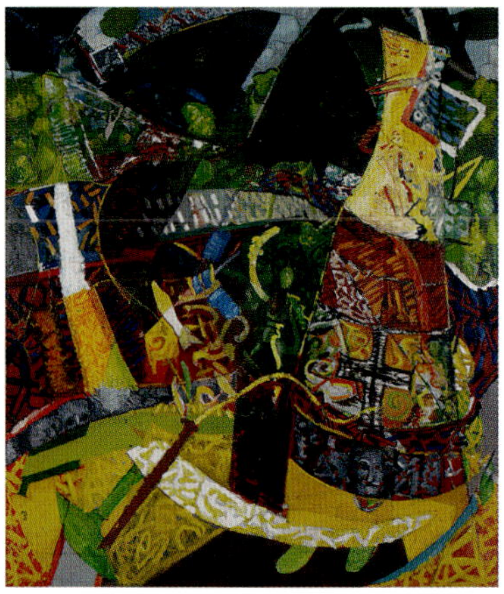

Whitaker, Jon b.1943
Memory of Trogir 1983
oil & oleopasto on canvas 213 x 177.6
AC 5307

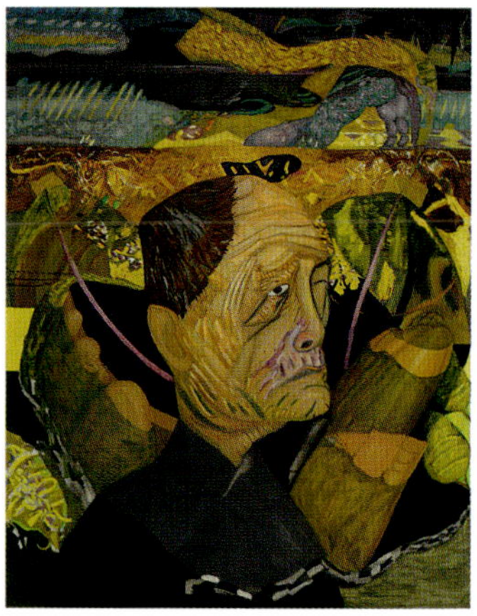

Whitaker, Jon b.1943
The Wanderer II 1984
oil & tempera on canvas 194 x 152
AC 5402

Whiteford, Kate b.1952
Beaker Burial 1983
acrylic, pigment & sand on wood
121.6 x 243.9
AC 5248

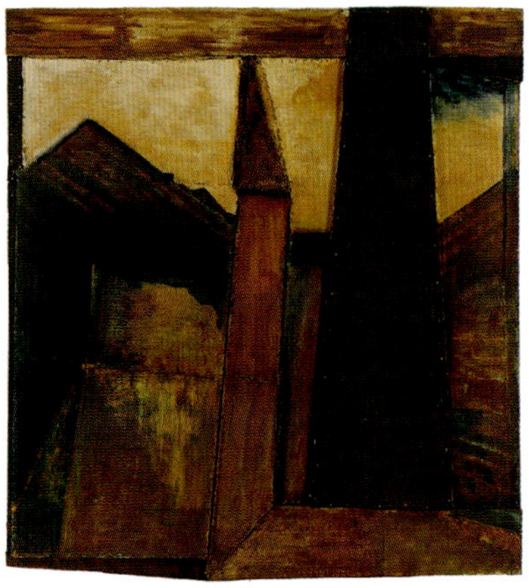

Whittaker, Edward b.1948
Untitled 1980–1981
oil on hessian & roofing felt 198 x 187.5
ACC1/1983

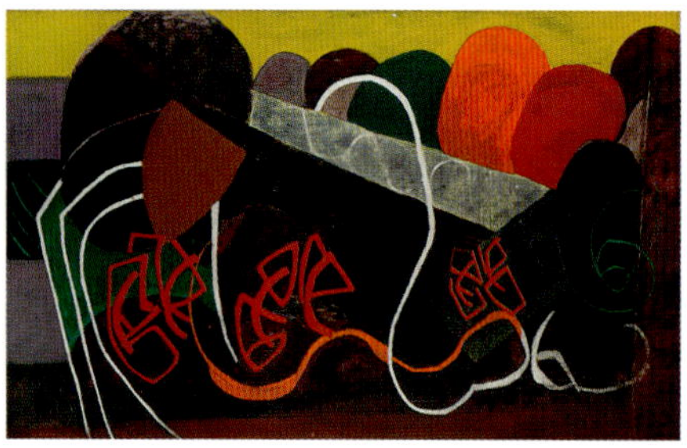

Wilde, Gerald 1905–1986
Untitled Painting c.1973
acrylic on canvas 249 x 413
AC 1685

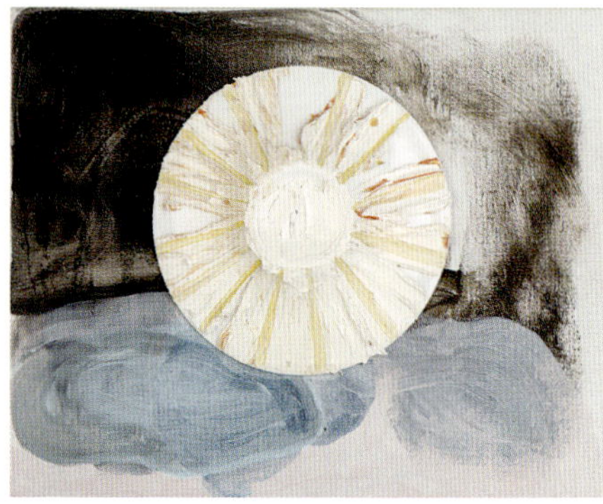

Wilkes, Cathy b.1966
Untitled 2005
oil & mixed media on canvas 20 x 25
ACC20/2005

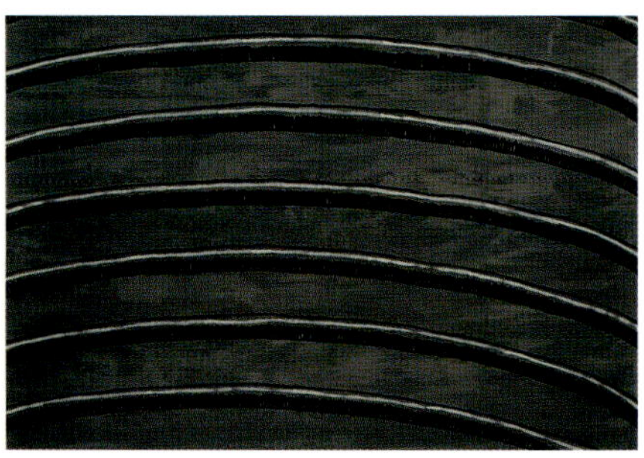

Wilkins, John b.1951
Dancing in the Dark 1993
acrylic on canvas 244 x 366
ACC245/1998

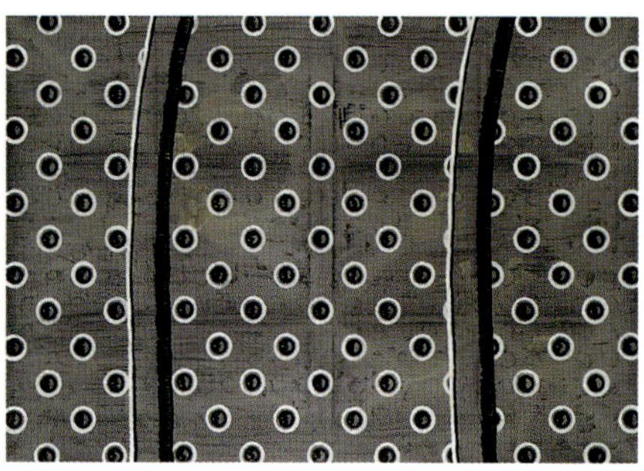

Wilkins, John b.1951
Winterwonderland 1993
acrylic on canvas 244 x 366
ACC244/1998

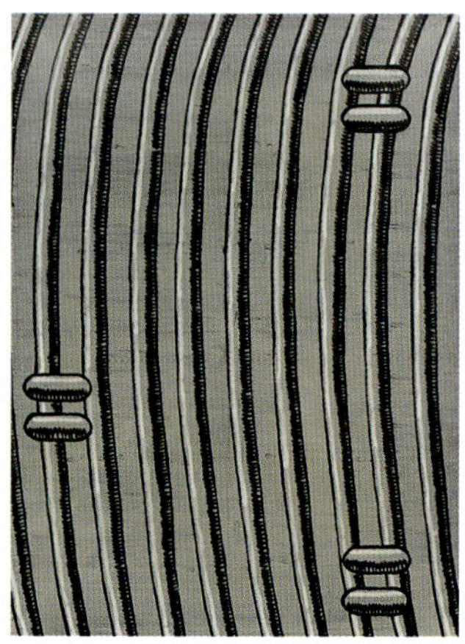

Wilkins, John b.1951
Was Wondering 1995
acrylic on canvas 244 x 183
ACC47/1995

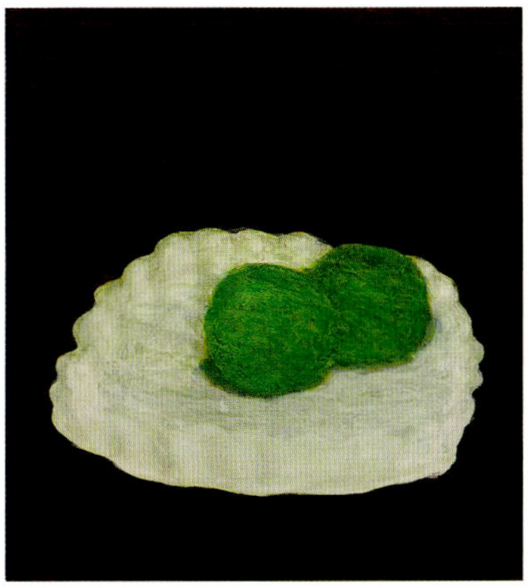

Willetts, David b.1939
Apples 1973
acrylic on board 28.9 x 26.4
AC 3091

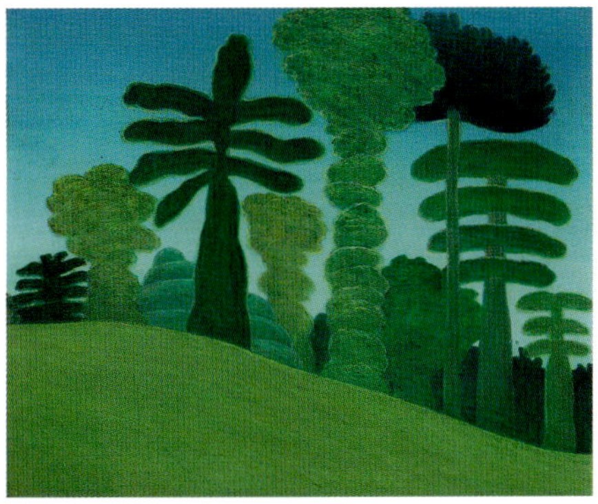

Willetts, David b.1939
On the Return Journey 1973
acrylic on board 27.8 x 36
AC 3090

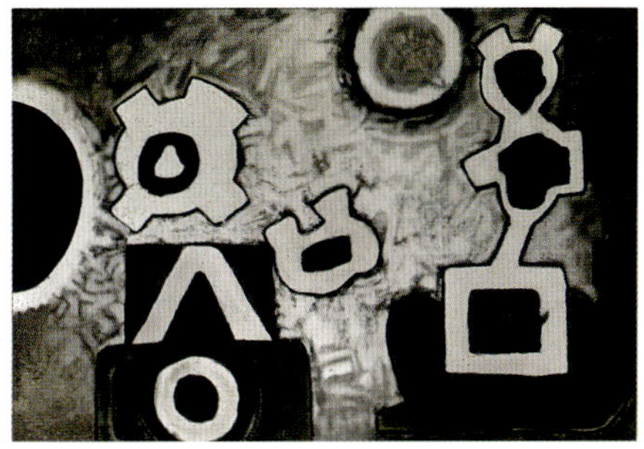

Williams, Aubrey 1926–1990
Olmec Stasis 1984–1985
oil on canvas 119 x 177.5
AC 5499

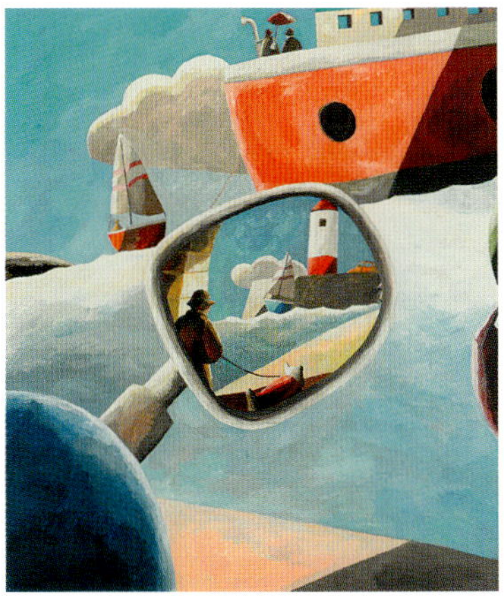

Williams, Emrys b.1958
To the Lighthouse No.13, December/January
1994–1995
acrylic on paper 127 x 109
ACC46/1996

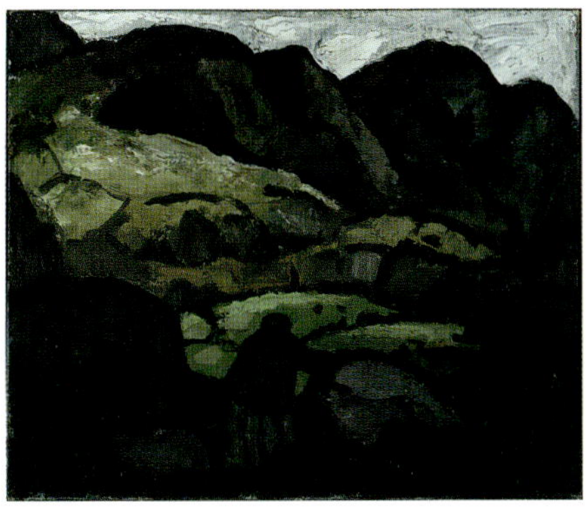

Williams, Kyffin 1918–2006
Landscape at Llanaelhaearn 1947
oil on canvas 51.1 x 61
AC 48

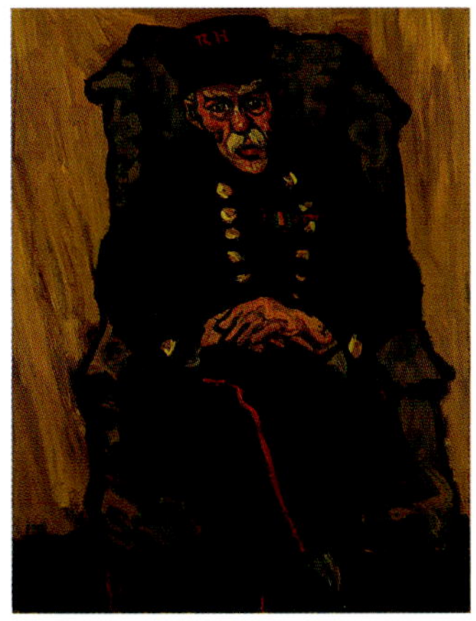

Williams, Kyffin 1918–2006
The Old Soldier 1951
oil on canvas 91.4 x 70.5
AC 229

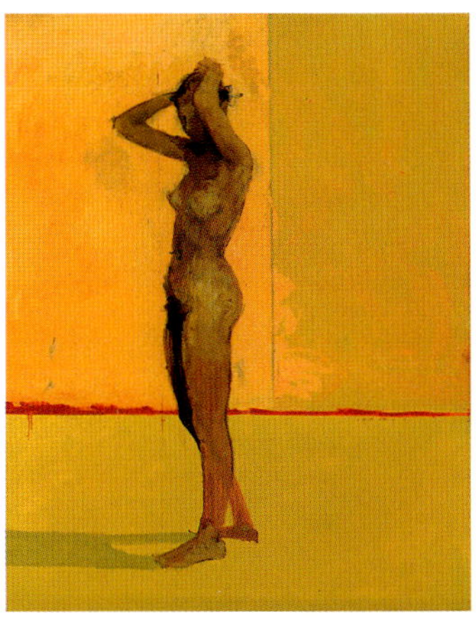

Willing, Victor 1928–1988
Standing Nude 1955
oil on canvas 127 x 101.6
AC 374

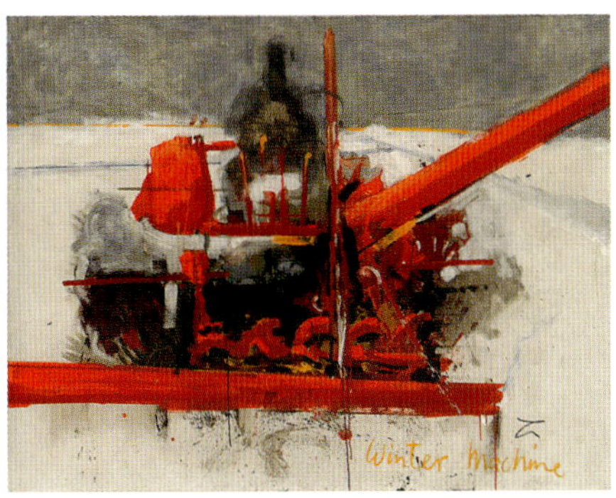

Willing, Victor 1928–1988
Winter Machine 1956
oil on canvas 116.8 x 152.4
AC 397

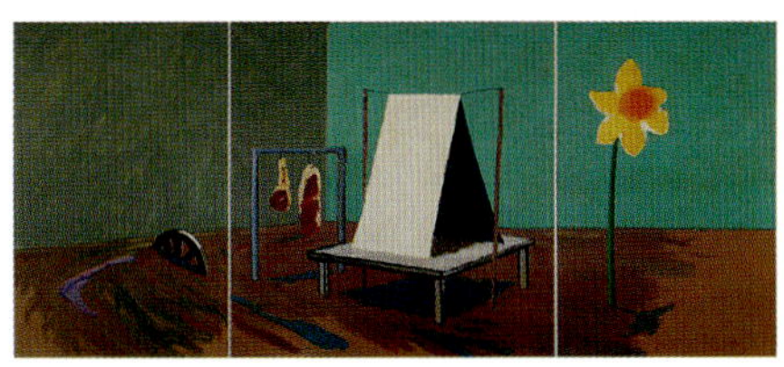

Willing, Victor 1928–1988
Mud 1979–1980
oil on canvas 183.2 x 426.1
AC 4058

Wilson, Chris b.1959
Some Day You Will Be One Of Those Who Lived Long Ago 1987
mixed media on board 101.8 x 68.7
ACC15/1990

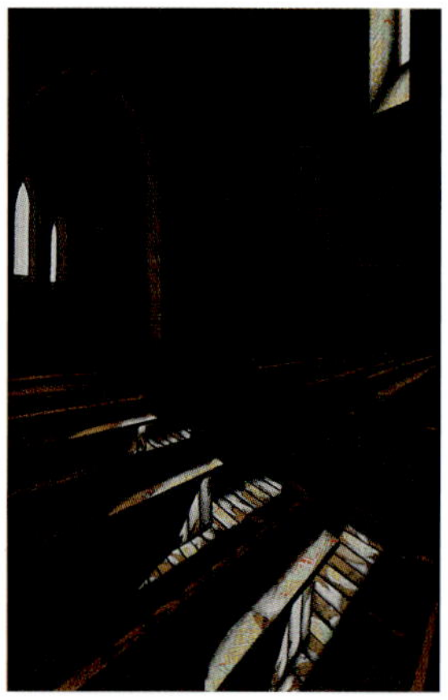

Wilson, Chris b.1959
All Will Be Forgotten 1987
mixed media on board 101.5 x 68.6
ACC17/1990

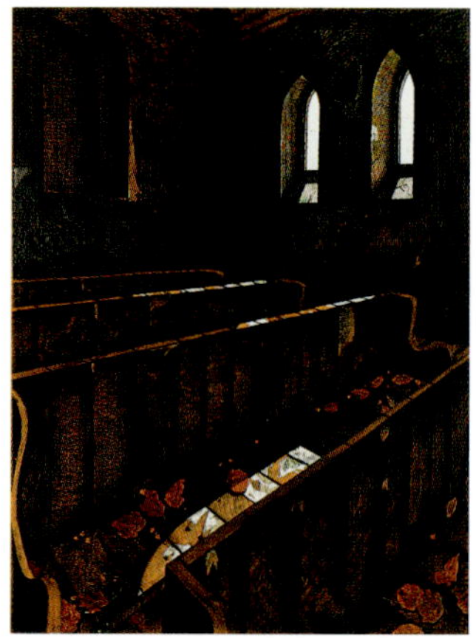

Wilson, Chris b.1959
In October Light 1987
mixed media on board 101.8 x 76.2
ACC16/1990

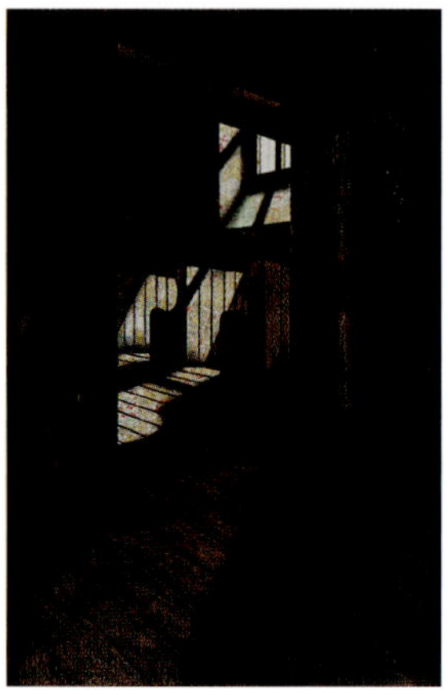

Wilson, Chris b.1959
Interior World 1987
mixed media on board 101.7 x 68.6
ACC18/1990

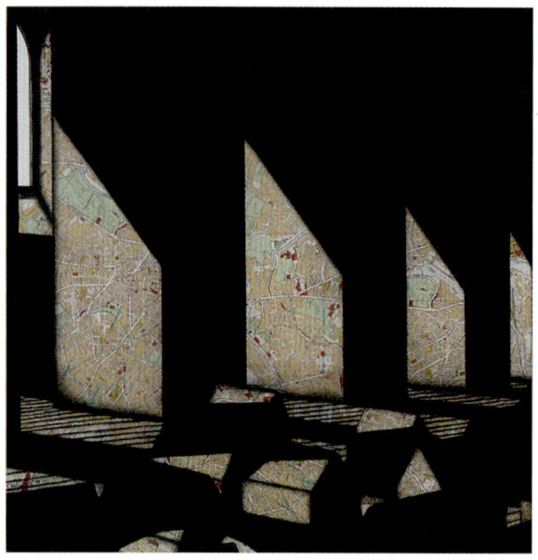

Wilson, Chris b.1959
North 1989–1990
mixed media on board 71 x 71
ACC19/1990

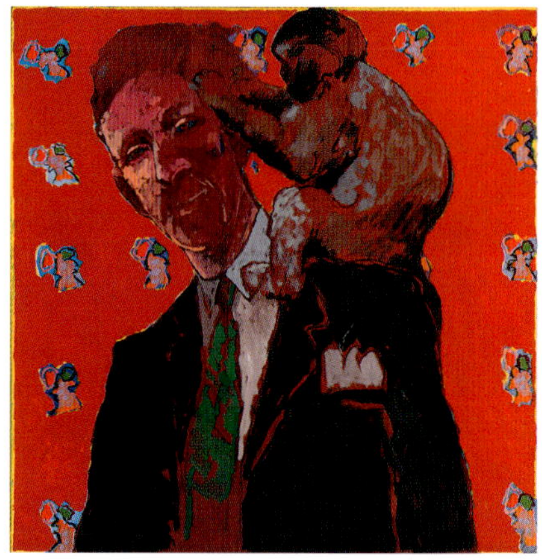

Wilson, Peter b.1940
Well Groomed 1979–1981
oil on canvas 128.5 x 126.5
AC 4071

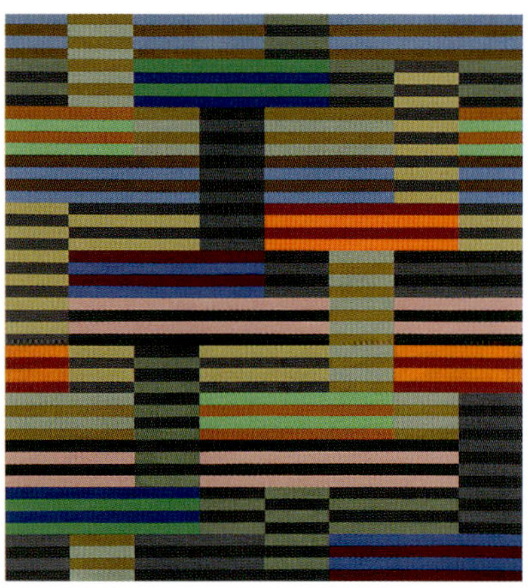

Winstanley, Paul b.1954
City Flats 1982
oil on canvas 167.3 x 158
AC 5180

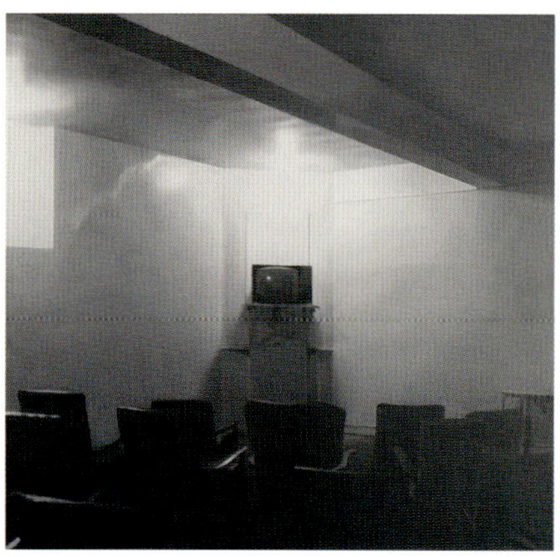

Winstanley, Paul b.1954
TV Room 1991
oil on canvas 160.1 x 170
ACC67/1991

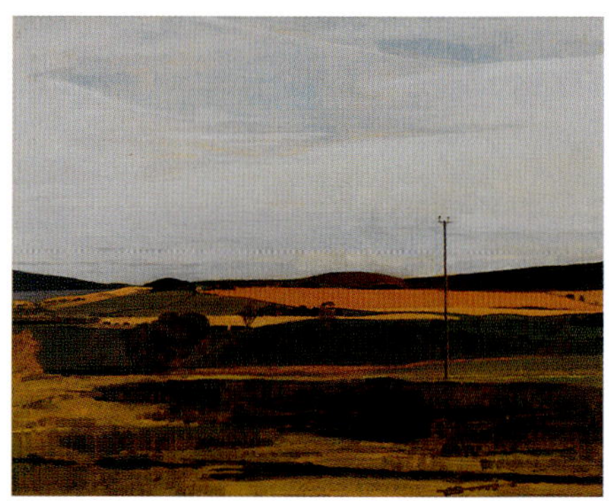

Wise, Derwent 1933–2003
Northumbrian Landscape 1975
acrylic on board 26.9 x 36.6
AC 1869

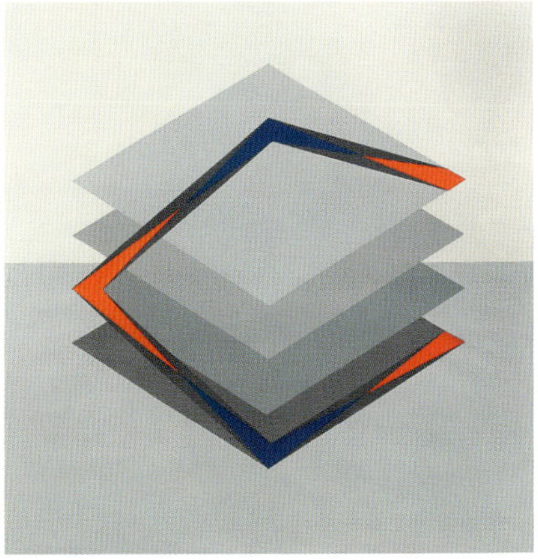

Wise, Gillian b.1936
Opening Movement 1976
acrylic on paper 60 x 60
AC 1728

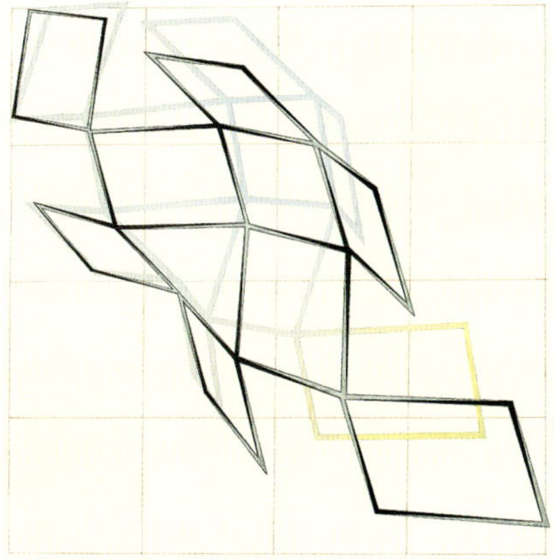

Wise, Gillian b.1936
Winged Net, Shadow Trace, Yellow and Blue 1976
acrylic & ink on paper 60 x 60
AC 1729

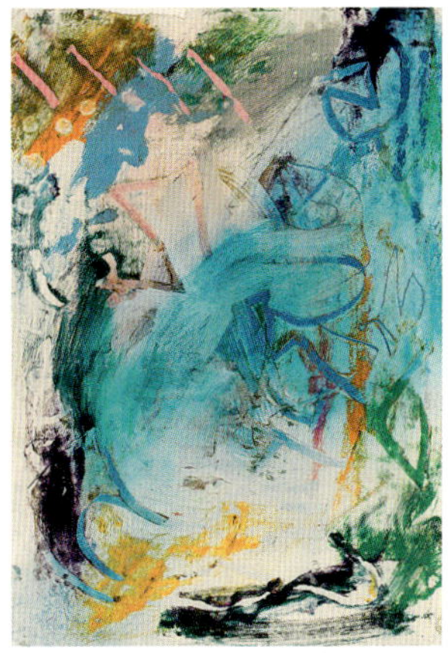

Wiseman, David b.1949
Morning 1979
acrylic on paper 41.6 x 29.4
AC 3042

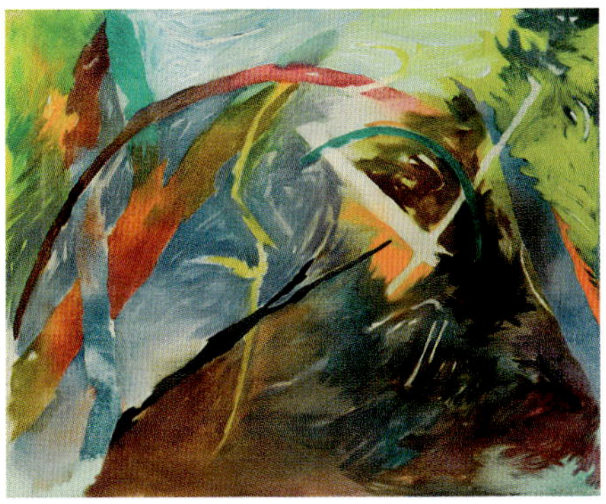

Wiseman, David b.1949
Winter – Ivythorn Wood 1980
oil on canvas 40 x 50.2
AC 3041

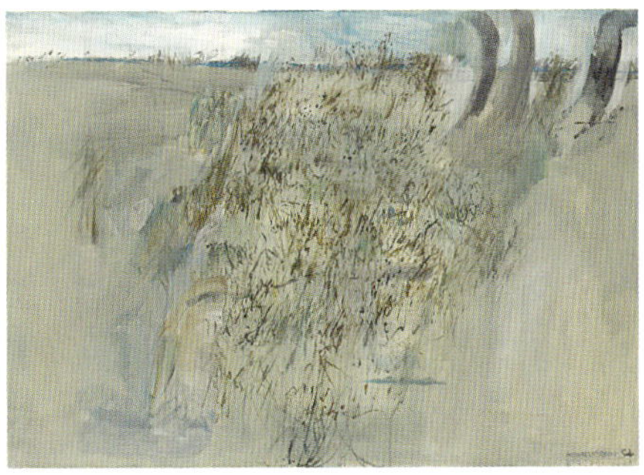

Wishart, John Michael 1928–1996
Camarguais Landscape II 1954
oil on canvas 81.3 x 115.6
AC 390

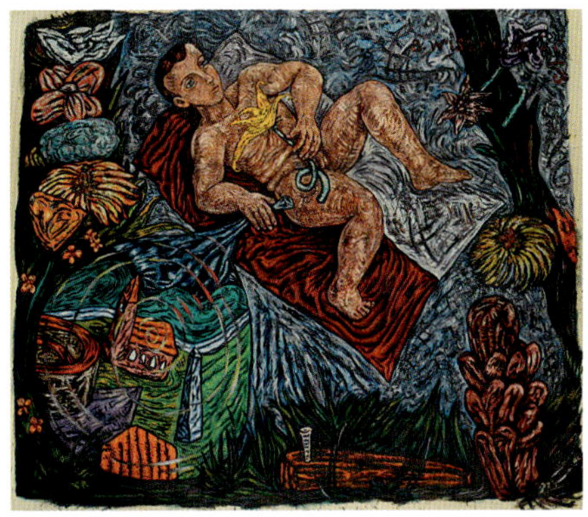

Wiszniewski, Adrian b.1958
Moses on a Polish Flag 1984
oil on canvas 239 x 278.5
AC 5365

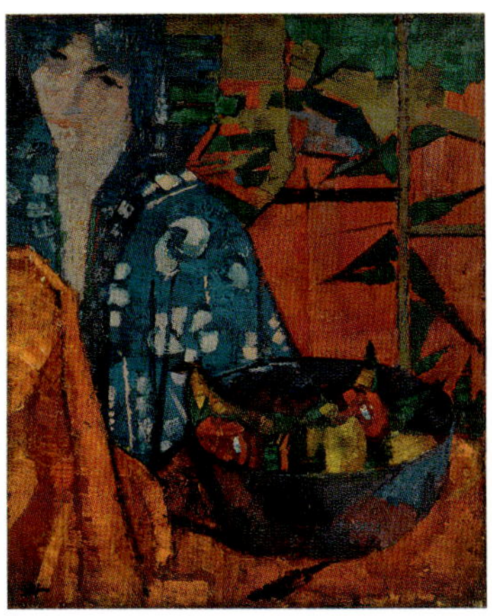

Wolmark, Alfred Aaron 1877–1961
Woman with a Bowl of Fruit 1913
oil on canvas 61 x 50.8
AC 482

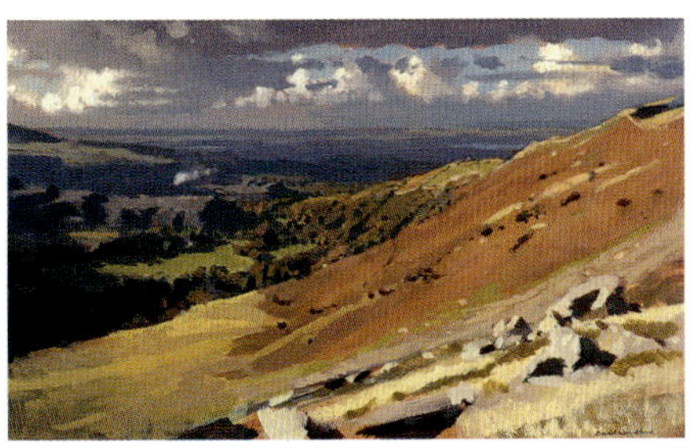

Woodford, David James b.1938
Sketch for 'The Kestrel' 1975
oil & paper on board 19 x 31.7
AC 3066

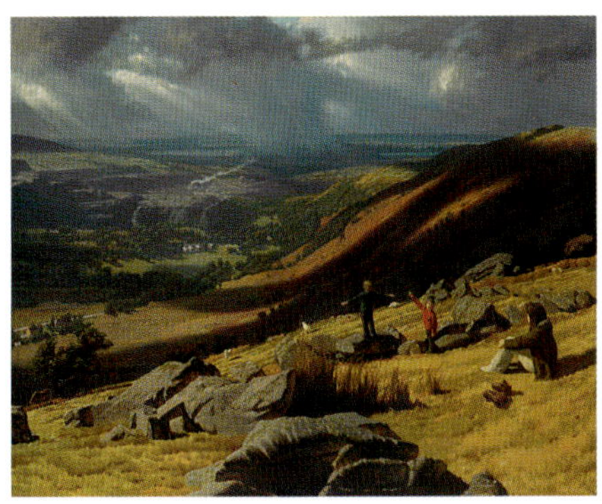

Woodford, David James b.1938
The Kestrel 1974–1980
oil on canvas 120 x 153
AC 3067

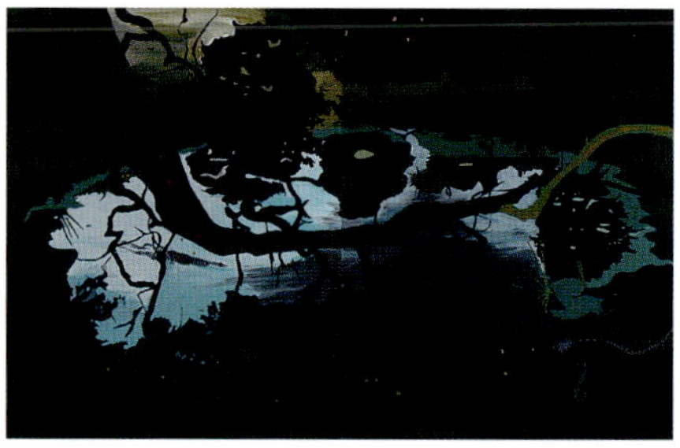

Woods, Clare b.1972
Daddy Witch 2008
enamel & oil on aluminium 218.5 x 350.5
ACC1/2008

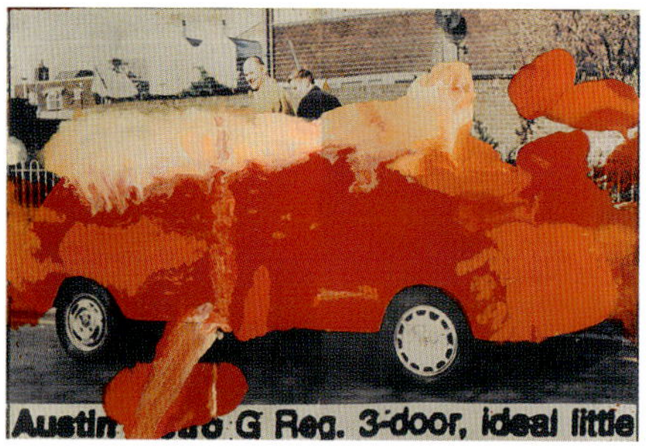

Woods, Richard b.1966
Austin Metro (Red), Deptford 1996
enamel on printed canvas 245 x 366
ACC248/1998

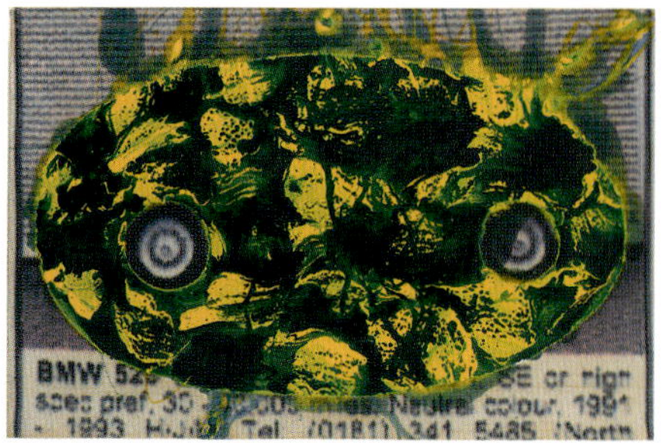

Woods, Richard b.1966
BMW 525 as Biological Experiment (Green)
1996
enamel on printed canvas 25.4 x 39.4
ACC249/1998

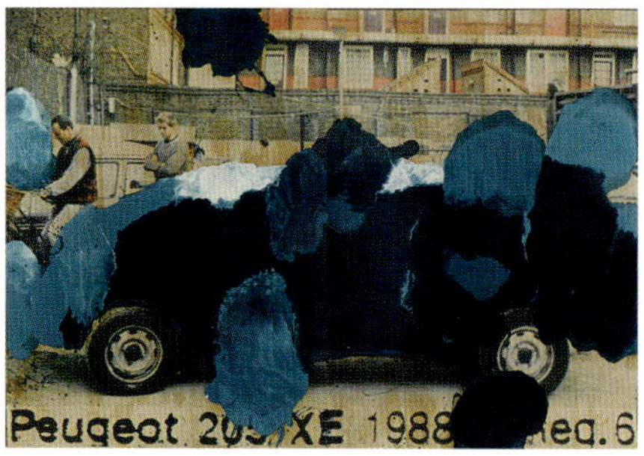

Woods, Richard b.1966
Peugeot 205 (Blue) Bermondsey 1996
enamel on printed canvas 243.8 x 365.7
ACC251/1998

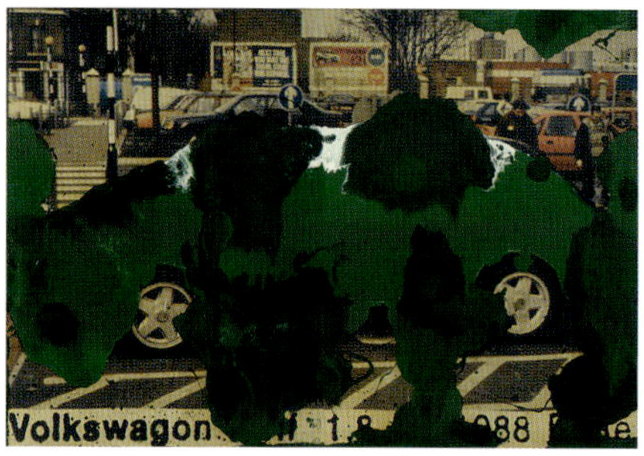

Woods, Richard b.1966
Volkswagen Golf (Green), Old Kent Road
1996
enamel on printed canvas 245 x 366
ACC250/1998

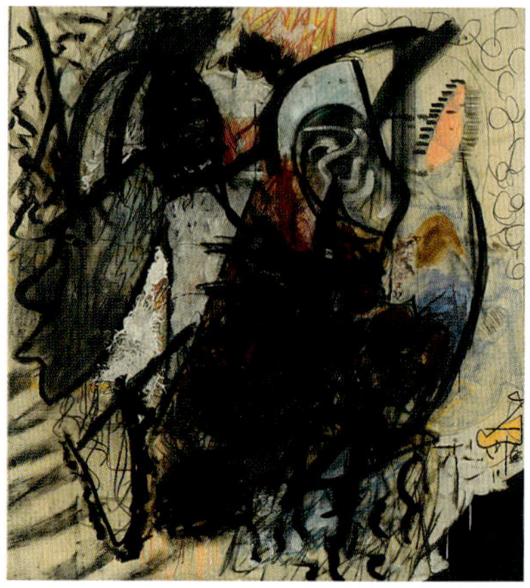

Wragg, Gary b.1946
Big Ear 1976
charcoal, pastel, acrylic & Rohplex on canvas
182.5 x 167.2
AC 1854

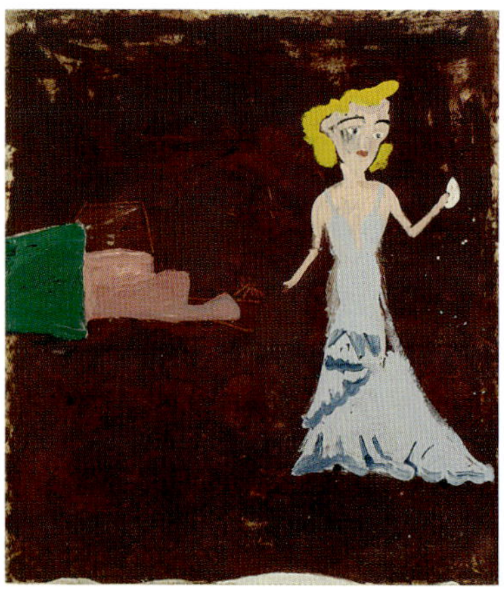

Wylie, Rose b.1934
Girl on Liner 1996
oil on canvas 183 x 163
ACC71/1997

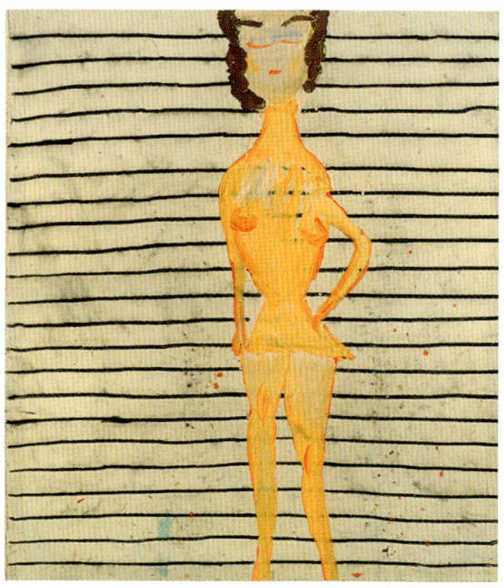

Wylie, Rose b.1934
Size 8: Orange 1996
oil & charcoal on canvas 183 x 165
ACC70/1997

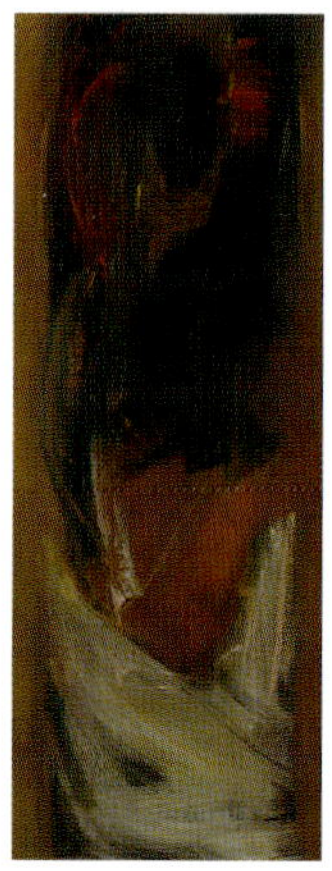

Wynne-Jones, Nancy 1922–2006
Lazarus 1961
oil on board 122.2 x 47
AC 614

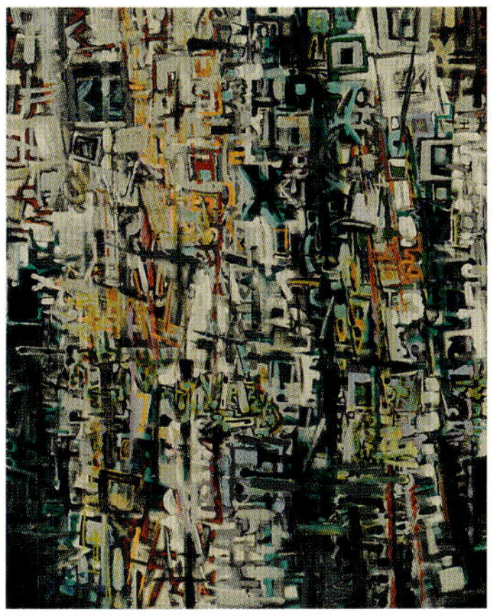

Wynter, Bryan 1915–1975
Mineral World 1957
oil on canvas 137.2 x 111.8
AC 422

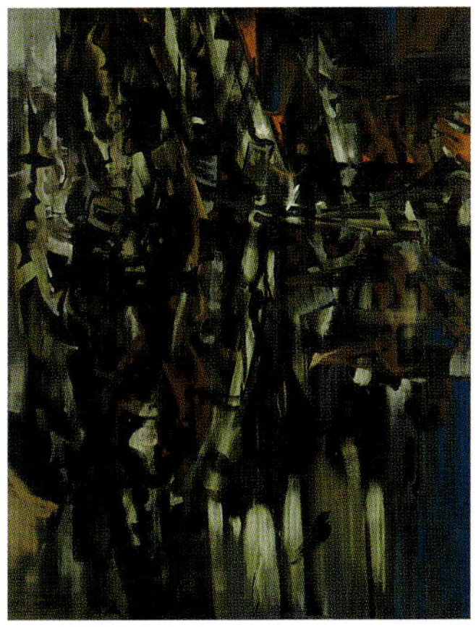

Wynter, Bryan 1915–1975
Dark Threshold 1960
oil on canvas 183 x 142
AC 526

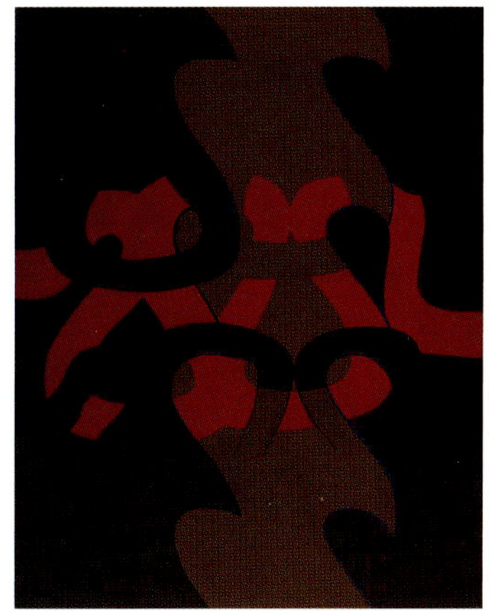

Wynter, Bryan 1915–1975
Meander 3 1967
oil on canvas 152.5 x 122
AC 921

Yale, Brian 1936–2009
Solitary Spaces 1973–1974
acrylic on canvas 122 x 213.3
AC 1542

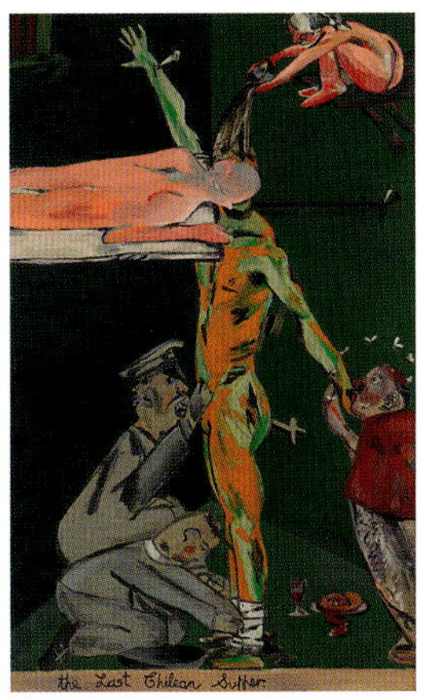

Yeadon, John David b.1948
The Last Chilean Supper 1982
acrylic on canvas 203 x 127
AC 5174

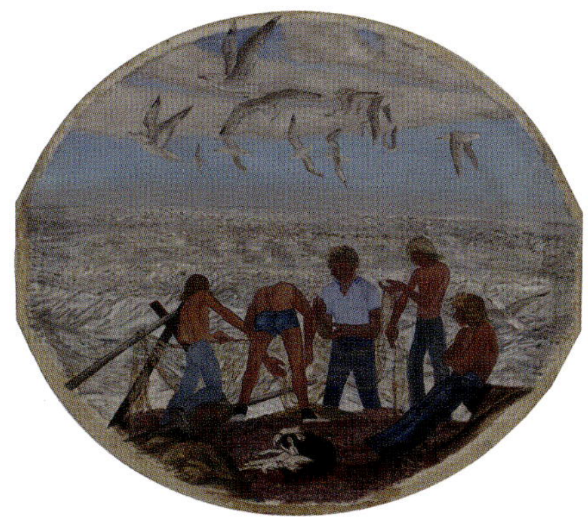

Yhap, Laetitia b.1941
Paul, Michael, Stephen and Tim in Summer
1977–1979
oil & sand on board 122.4 x 143
AC 3043

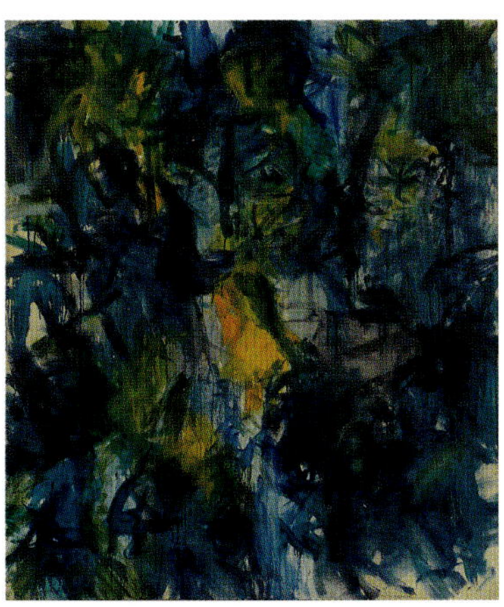

Young, Brian b.1934
Extension I 1958
oil on canvas 172.7 x 147.3
AC 471

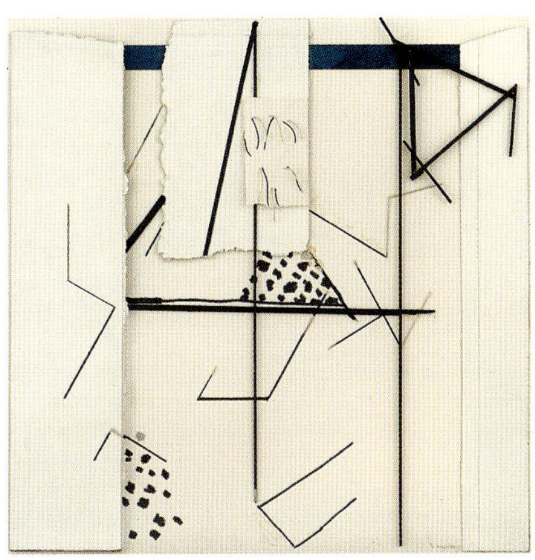

Yule, Ainslie b.1941
White Space with Blue Strip 1981
wood, board, acrylic, string, paint & card on board 93.2 x 93.5
AC 5019

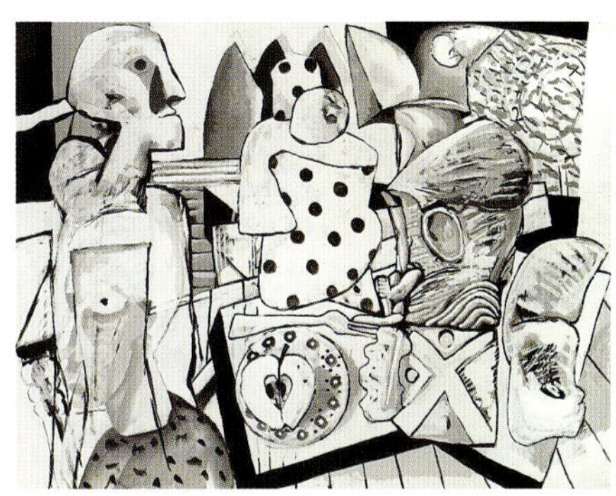

Zehnder, Benno b.1941
On the Way to the Room Beyond 1977–1978
plaka on paper 70 x 93
AC 2061

Ziegler, Toby b.1972
Je t'adore, baby 2003–2004
acrylic on Scotchbrite 215 x 252
ACC38/2006

Facing page: Lloyd-Jones, Peter, 1940–2001, *Laughter (9 conditions)* (detail), 1979–1980, (p. 98)

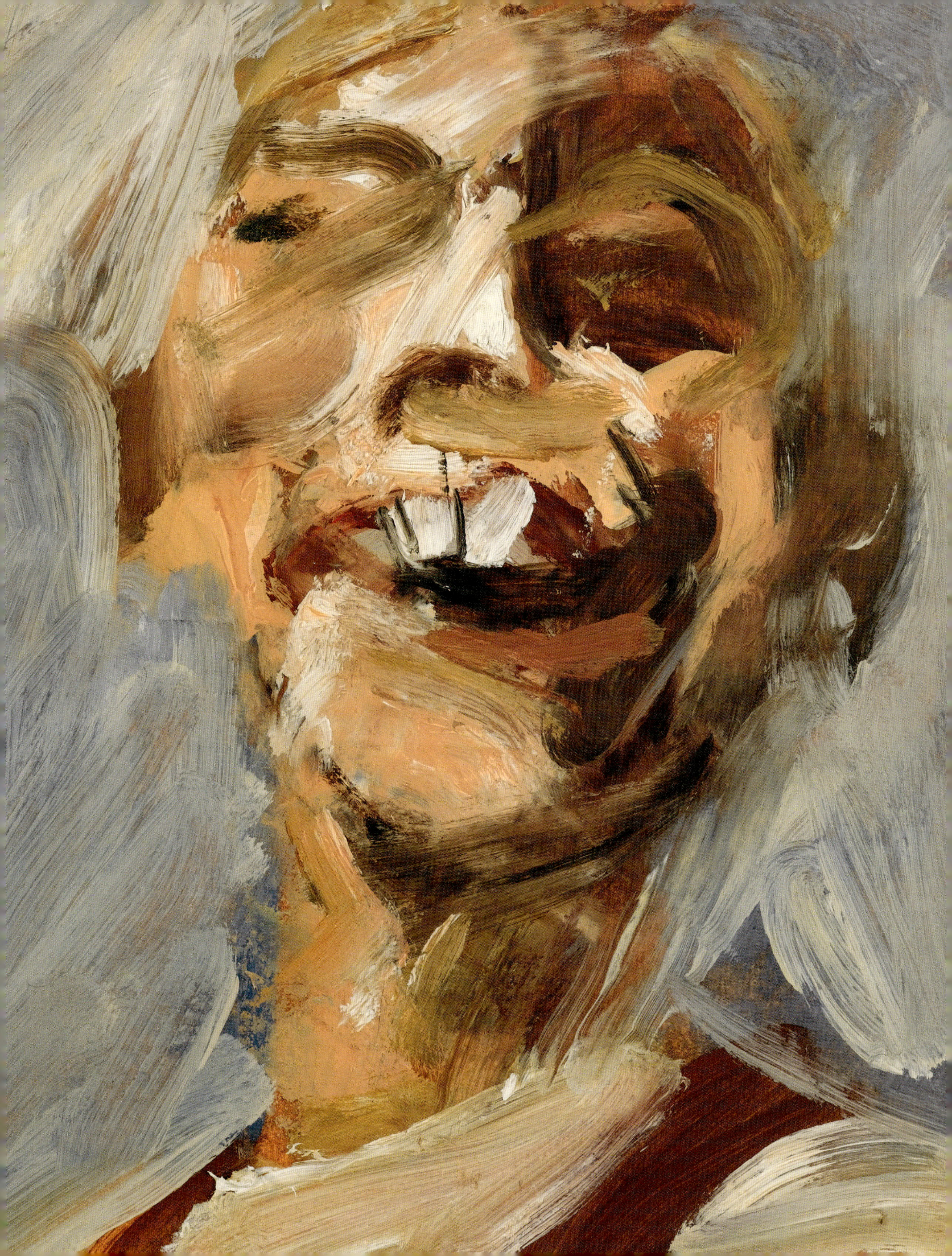

Paintings Without Reproductions

This section lists all the paintings that have not been included in the main pages of the catalogue. They were excluded as it was not possible to photograph them for this project. Additional information relating to acquisition credit lines or loan details is also included. For this reason the information below is not repeated in the Further Information section.

Coe, Sue b.1951, *Apocalypse*, 1984, 181 x 211, oil & mixed media on canvas, AC 5351, purchased from the Gimpel Fils Gallery, 1984, copyright fee sought for reproduction

Further Information

The paintings listed in this section have additional information relating to one or more of the five categories outlined below. This extra information is only provided where it is applicable and where it exists. Paintings listed in this section follow the same order as in the illustrated pages of the catalogue.

I	The full name of the artist if this was too long to display in the illustrated pages of the catalogue. Such cases are marked in the catalogue with a (...).
II	The full title of the painting if this was too long to display in the illustrated pages of the catalogue. Such cases are marked in the catalogue with a (...).
III	Acquisition information or acquisition credit lines as well as information about loans, copied from the records of the owner collection.
IV	Artist copyright credit lines where the copyright owner has been traced. Exhaustive efforts have been made to locate the copyright owners of all the images included within this catalogue and to meet their requirements. Any omissions or mistakes brought to our attention will be duly attended to and corrected in future publications.
V	The credit line of the lender of the transparency if the transparency has been borrowed. Bridgeman images are available subject to any relevant copyright approvals from the Bridgeman Art Library at www.bridgemanart.com

Arts Council Collection

Abrahams, Ivor b.1935, *Drawing for Cut-Out Wall*, purchased from the artist, 1974, © the artist
Adams, Norman 1927–2005, *The Holy Trees*, purchased from the Contemporary Art Society, 1958, © the artist's estate
Adams, Norman 1927–2005, *The Shore*, purchased from the artist, 1966, © the artist's estate
Adams, Norman 1927–2005, *Our Mother Who Art in Heaven*, purchased from the artist, 1969, © the artist's estate
Agar, Eileen 1899–1991, *Poet and His Muse*, purchased from the London Group, 1959, © the artist's estate/Bridgeman Art Library
Ainsworth, Mark b.1954, *Crag*, purchased from the John Moores Liverpool Exhibition XI, 1978, © the artist
Aitchison, Craigie Ronald John 1926–2009, *Crucifixion*, purchased from the Beaux Arts Gallery, 1959, © the artist's estate/Bridgeman Art Library, photo credit: ACC
Aitchison, Craigie Ronald John 1926–2009, *Female Nude*, purchased from the artist, 1966, © the artist's estate/Bridgeman Art Library
Aitchison, Craigie Ronald John 1926–2009, *Grey Vase: Still Life*, purchased from the Hampstead Arts Centre, 1966, © the artist's estate/Bridgeman Art Library
Aitchison, Craigie Ronald John 1926–2009, *Daphne Against a Black Background*, purchased from Marlborough Fine Art, 1969, © the artist's estate/Bridgeman Art Library
Aitchison, Craigie Ronald John 1926–2009, *Crucifixion No.2*, purchased from Knoedler and Co. Ltd, 1977, © the artist's estate/Bridgeman Art Library, photo credit: ACC
Aldridge, John Arthur Malcolm 1905–1983, *The Pink Farm*, purchased from the artist, 1942
Aldridge, John Arthur Malcolm 1905–1983, *Autumn*, purchased from the Leicester Galleries, 1947, photo credit: ACC
Allen, Tim b.1950, *In the Future*, purchased from the artist, 1993, © the artist
Anderson, Michael b.1952, *The Labyrinth*, purchased from the artist, 1985
Andrews, Michael 1928–1995, *Four People Sunbathing*, purchased from the Institute of Contemporary Arts, 1955, © June & Melanie Andrews
Andrews, Michael 1928–1995, *Flats*, purchased from the artist, 1965, © June & Melanie Andrews
Andrews, Michael 1928–1995, *Digswell Man II*, purchased from the Beaux Arts Gallery, 1963, © June & Melanie Andrews
Andrews, Michael 1928–1995, *Study for 'All Night Long'*, purchased from the artist, 1965, © June & Melanie Andrews, photo credit: ACC
Andrews, Michael 1928–1995, *Study of a Head for a Group of Figures No.6*, purchased from Marlborough Fine Art, 1976, © June & Melanie Andrews
Andrews, Michael 1928–1995, *Study of a Head for a Group of Figures No.10*, purchased from Marlborough Fine Art, 1976, © June & Melanie Andrews
Andrews, Michael 1928–1995, *Study of a Head for 'Lights' No.2*, purchased from Marlborough Fine Art, 1976, © June & Melanie Andrews
Andrews, Michael 1928–1995, *Lights II: The Ship Engulfed*, purchased from the Anthony d'Offay Gallery, 1977, © June & Melanie Andrews, photo credit: ACC
Appelbee, Leonard 1914–2000, *Barns in a Field*, purchased from the artist, 1942
Appelbee, Leonard 1914–2000, *Peaches*, purchased from the Leicester Galleries, 1948
Archer, Peter b.1946, *Turning Track*, purchased from the Edward Totah Gallery, 1986, © the artist
Arif Quadri, Saleem b.1949, *Pressed Against Good and Evil*, purchased from Anderson O'Day Fine Art, 1988, © the artist
Armstrong, John 1893–1973, *The Villa*, purchased from the artist, 1942, © the artist's estate/Bridgeman Art Library
Armstrong, John 1893–1973, *Tocsin*, purchased from the Royal Academy, 1967, © the artist's estate/Bridgeman Art Library
Arnold, Liz 1964–2001, *Uncovered*, gift from Charles Saatchi, 1999, © estate Liz Arnold
Arnold, Liz 1964–2001, *Felicity*, gift from Charles Saatchi, 1999, © estate Liz Arnold
Arrowsmith, Sue b.1968, *Pickett*, purchased from the Entwistle Gallery, 1997, © the artist
Atkins, Ray b.1937, *Cornwall County Council Refuse Tip, Carharrack II*, purchased from the artist, 1984, © the artist
Atkinson, Lawrence 1873–1931, *Abstract*, purchased from the Leicester Galleries, 1959, photo credit: ACC
Auerbach, Frank Helmuth b.1931, *Head of E. O. W. VIII*, purchased from the Beaux Arts Gallery, 1956, © the artist
Auerbach, Frank Helmuth b.1931, *Primrose Hill*, purchased from the Beaux Arts Gallery, 1959, © the artist, photo credit: ACC
Auerbach, Frank Helmuth b.1931, *Jym in the Studio*, purchased from the Hampstead Arts Centre, 1966, © the artist, photo credit: ACC
Auerbach, Frank Helmuth b.1931, *Primrose Hill, Summer Sunshine*, purchased from Marlborough Fine Art, 1965, © the artist, photo credit: ACC
Auerbach, Frank Helmuth b.1931, *Seated Figure with Arms Raised*, purchased from Marlborough Fine Art, 1975, © the artist, photo credit: ACC
Auerbach, Frank Helmuth b.1931, *Reclining Head of J. Y. M.*, purchased from Marlborough Fine Art, 1976, © the artist, photo credit: ACC
Auerbach, Frank Helmuth b.1931, *Euston Steps (study)*, purchased from Marlborough Fine Art, 1982, © the artist
Austen, David b.1960, *Mia's Dream*, purchased from the Anthony Reynolds Gallery, 1985, © the artist
Austen, David b.1960, *The King, The Church, The Judge, The Knight*, purchased from the Anthony Reynolds Gallery, 1985, © the artist
Austen, David b.1960, *Men Kill Sleeping Women*, purchased from the Anthony Reynolds Gallery, 1991, © the artist
Austen, David b.1960, *On the Edge of Night*, purchased from the Anthony Reynolds Gallery, 1991, © the artist
Austen, David b.1960, *City*, purchased from the Anthony Reynolds Gallery, 2000, © the artist, photo credit: ACC
Ayres, Gillian b.1930, *Lure*, purchased from the Hamilton Gallery, 1963, © the artist
Ayres, Gillian b.1930, *Shiraz*, purchased from the Kasmin Gallery Ltd, 1965, © the artist
Ayres, Gillian b.1930, *Umbria*, purchased from the artist, 1967, © the artist
Ayres, Gillian b.1930, *Untitled*, purchased from the Kasmin Gallery Ltd, 1967, © the artist
Ayres, Gillian b.1930, *Bellona*, purchased from Kettle's Yard Gallery, Cambridge, 1978, © the artist, photo credit: ACC
Ayres, Gillian b.1930, *Orlando Furioso*, purchase award, 1979, © the artist
Ayres, Gillian b.1930, *Ultima Thule*, purchase award via Knoedler and Co. Ltd, 1980, © the artist

Ayres, Gillian b.1930, *Spica*, purchased from Fischer Fine Art, 1991, © the artist
Ayrton, Michael 1921–1975, *Entrance to a Wood*, purchased from The Redfern Gallery, 1947, © the artist's estate
Ayrton, Michael 1921–1975, *Still Life at Christmas*, purchased from the Whitechapel Art Gallery, 1955, © the artist's estate
Ayrton, Michael 1921–1975, *Icarus in Flight*, purchased from the Matthiesen Gallery, 1961, © the artist's estate
Bacon, Francis 1909–1992, *Head VI*, purchased from the Hanover Gallery, 1952, © estate of Francis Bacon. All rights reserved. DACS 2012
Bacon, Francis 1909–1992, *Study for a Portrait of Van Gogh VI*, purchased from the Hanover Gallery, 1957, © estate of Francis Bacon. All rights reserved. DACS 2012
Baer, Jo b.1929 **& Robbins, Bruce** b.1946 *Pike*, purchased from the Lisson Gallery, 1982, Jo Baer: © the artist
Baker, Chris b.1944, *Vent*, purchased from the artist, 1983
Ball, Alan b.1962, *Stress Fracture*, gift from Charles Saatchi, 1999, photo credit: ACC
Barclay, Colville 1913–2010, *Landscape*, purchased from the London Group, 1959, © the artist's estate
Barker, David Walker b.1947, *Six Small Drawings in One Frame*, purchased from the artist, 1982, © the artist
Barker, Kit 1916–1988, *Lincolnshire Waterway and Distant Wash*, purchased from the artist, 1983, © the artist's estate
Barns-Graham, Wilhelmina 1912–2004, *Grindelwald Glacier*, purchased from the artist, 1950, © by courtesy of the Barns-Graham Charitable Trust
Barns-Graham, Wilhelmina 1912–2004, *Purple Painting*, purchased from the artist, 1970, © by courtesy of the Barns-Graham Charitable Trust
Bassingthwaighte, Lewin 1928–1983, *The Front Door*, purchased from the Piccadilly Gallery, 1964, © estate of Lewin Bassingthwaighte, 2012. All rights reserved, DACS
Batty, Joyce 1919–2005, *Neilotikos*, purchased from the A. I. A. Gallery, 1964
Bayes, Walter 1869–1956, *Wine and Fruit*, purchased from the Leicester Galleries, 1952, © the artist's estate
Bayes, Walter 1869–1956, *Box at the Lyceum Theatre*, purchased from the artist, 1942, © the artist's estate
Baynes, Keith 1887–1977, *Flowers*, purchased from the artist, 1942
Baynes, Keith 1887–1977, *Place des Esplanades, Perpignan, France*, purchased from the Lefevre Gallery, 1955
Beattie, Basil b.1935, *Orange No.1*, purchased from the artist, 1970, © the artist
Beattie, Basil b.1935, *Cause and Effect IV*, purchased from the artist, 1974, © the artist
Beattie, Basil b.1935, *Cause and Effect V*, purchased from the artist, 1974, © the artist
Beattie, Basil b.1935, *Reds*, purchased from the artist, 1975, © the artist
Beattie, Basil b.1935, *Imagine If*, purchased from the Maak Gallery, 1994, © the artist
Beddington, Sarah b.1964, *Forty Nights 1*, purchased from the Hales Gallery, 2001, © the artist
Beddington, Sarah b.1964, *Forty Nights 2*, purchased from the Hales Gallery, 2001, © the artist
Beddington, Sarah b.1964, *Forty Nights 3*, purchased from the Hales Gallery, 2001, © the artist
Beddington, Sarah b.1964, *Forty Nights 4*, purchased from the Hales Gallery, 2001, © the artist
Beddington, Sarah b.1964, *Forty Nights 5*, purchased from the Hales Gallery, 2001, © the artist
Beddington, Sarah b.1964, *Forty Nights 6*, purchased from the Hales Gallery, 2001, © the artist
Beddington, Sarah b.1964, *Forty Nights 7*, purchased from the Hales Gallery, 2001, © the artist
Behrens, Timothy b.1937, *A Lunch Party*, purchased from the Beaux Arts Gallery, 1962
Bell, Richard b.1955, *Four Colour Sets Mapped Deictically Presented Twice in Logical Form*, purchased from the artist, 1983
Bell, Trevor b.1930, *Yorkshire, January 1960*, purchased from the Waddington Galleries, 1960, © the artist
Bell, Vanessa 1879–1961, *Snow at Tilton*, purchased from the artist, 1942, © 1961 estate of Vanessa Bell courtesy Henrietta Garnett
Bell, Vanessa 1879–1961, *The Cook*, purchased from Thomas Agnew and Sons Ltd, 1949, © 1961 estate of Vanessa Bell courtesy Henrietta Garnett
Bellany, John b.1942, *The Voyage*, purchased from the Drian, 1973, © the artist/Bridgeman Art Library
Bellany, John b.1942, *The Sea People*, purchased from the Acme Gallery, 1978, © the artist/ Bridgeman Art Library
Bellany, John b.1942, *The Gambler*, purchase award, 1983, © the artist/Bridgeman Art Library
Bellany, John b.1942, *The Capercaillie Sings His Lovesong*, purchased from the artist, 1986, © the artist/Bridgeman Art Library
Bellingham, David b.1966, *Ruler Painting (blue)*, purchased from the artist, 1997, © the artist
Bellingham-Smith, Elinor 1906–1988, *The Island*, purchased from the artist, 1951, © the artist's estate
Bellingham-Smith, Elinor 1906–1988, *Winter Afternoon*, purchased from the Leicester Galleries, 1952, © the artist's estate
Bellingham-Smith, Elinor 1906–1988, *The Fenn, Boxford*, purchased from the Leicester Galleries, 1962, © the artist's estate
Bellingham-Smith, Elinor 1906–1988, *Sunset*, purchased from the artist, 1966, © the artist's estate, photo credit: ACC
Bellingham-Smith, Elinor 1906–1988, *The Sky over Wattisham*, purchased from the artist, 1966, © the artist's estate
Benjamin, Anthony 1931–2002, *On the Edge*, purchased from the Institute of Contemporary Arts, 1966, © the artist's estate and The Benjamin Trust
Bennett, Michael b.1948, *Crimson Lake*, purchased from the Felicity Samuel Gallery Ltd, 1979, © the artist
Bennett, Michael b.1948, *Midnight Sonata*, purchase award, 1980, © the artist
Benois, Nadia 1896–1975, *Derrycornerry, Bantry Bay*, purchased from the artist, 1942 © the artist's estate
Berg, Adrian 1929–2011, *Regent's Park*, purchased from Arthur Tooth & Sons Ltd, 1969, © estate of Adrian Berg
Berg, Adrian 1929–2011, *Gloucester Lodge, Regent's Park, Late June 1974*, purchased from Arthur Tooth & Sons Ltd, 1975, © estate of Adrian Berg
Berg, Adrian 1929–2011, *Gloucester Gate, Regent's Park, June 1982*, purchased from the Waddington Galleries Ltd, 1983, © estate of Adrian Berg
Berger, John b.1926, *Scaffolding – Festival of Britain*, purchased from the artist, 1950, © the artist, photo credit: ACC
Bergman, Stephenie b.1946, *Blind Venetian*, purchased from the Garage Gallery, 1976, © the artist
Bergman, Stephenie b.1946, *Thunderthighs*, purchased from the Crafts Council Gallery, 1984, © the artist
Bevan, Graham 1935–2006, *Interior for Figure*, purchased from the artist, 1960, © the artist's estate
Bevan, Tony b.1951, *Head Horizon*, purchased from Theo Waddington Fine Art Ltd, 1996, © the artist
Bicât, André 1909–1996, *Fugue*, purchased from the Leicester Galleries, 1960, © the artist's estate
Binder, Douglas b.1941, *Ruins*, purchased from the artist, 1970, © the artist
Blacker, Kate b.1955, *Khumbu Himal*, purchased from the artist, 1982, © the artist
Blacklock, George b.1952, *Composition*, purchased from the artist, 1980, © the artist/ courtesy Flowers Gallery, London
Blake, Peter b.1932, *Boy Eating a Hot Dog*, purchased from the Robert Fraser Gallery, 1965, © Peter Blake. All rights reserved, DACS 2012
Blake, Peter b.1932, *Baron Adolf Kaiser*, purchased from Arthur Tooth & Sons Ltd, 1963, © Peter Blake. All rights reserved, DACS 2012
Bloch, Martin 1883–1954, *Down from the Welsh Quarries*, purchased from Mrs Martin Bloch, 1956, © Martin Bloch Trust
Blomfield, Richard C. b.1930, *Strolling Figures, Statue and Trees*, purchased from the A. I. A. Gallery, 1969
Blow, Sandra 1925–2006, *Painting (57)*, purchased from the Gimpel Fils Gallery, 1958, © the artist's estate
Blow, Sandra 1925–2006, *Painting*, purchased from the artist, 1966, © the artist's estate
Blow, Sandra 1925–2006, *Untitled*, purchased from the artist, 1966, © the artist's estate
Blow, Sandra 1925–2006, *White No.1*, purchased from the New Art Centre, 1969, © the artist's estate
Bomberg, David 1890–1957, *Self Portrait (David)*, purchased from Mrs Lilian Bomberg, 1963, © the estate of David Bomberg. All rights reserved, DACS 2012, photo credit: ACC
Bomberg, David 1890–1957, *Diana*, purchased from Mrs Lilian Bomberg, 1963, © the estate of David Bomberg. All rights reserved, DACS 2012
Bomberg, David 1890–1957, *Trendrine, Cornwall*, purchased from Mrs Lilian Bomberg, 1957, © the estate of David Bomberg. All rights reserved, DACS 2012
Bonvin, Susan b.1948, *Adrift*, purchased from the artist, 1991, © the artist
Boston, Allan b.1951, *Untitled*, purchased from the artist, 1983, © the artist
Bourne, Bob b.1931, *Lover's Leap*, purchased from Miss Bourne, 1980, © the artist
Bourne, Bob b.1931, *Self Portrait*, purchased from the artist, 1980, © the artist
Bowling, Frank b.1936, *Birthday*, purchased from the Grabowski Gallery, © Frank Bowling. All rights reserved, DACS 2012
Bowling, Frank b.1936, *Great Thames IV*, purchased from the artist, 1991, © Frank Bowling. All rights reserved, DACS 2012
Bowstead, John b.1940, *The Language of Love*, purchased from the Institute of Contemporary Arts, 1962 © the artist
Box, Eden 1919–1988, *Holy City*, purchased from the New Art Centre, 1982
Boyce, Sonia b.1962, *So Amazing*, gift from the artist, 2002 © Sonia Boyce. All rights reserved, DACS 2012
Boyd, Arthur 1920–1999, *Nude Floating over a Dark Pond II*, purchased from the Whitechapel Art Gallery, 1962
Boyd, Fionnuala b.1944 **& Evans, Leslie** b.1945 *Views 1 and 2*, purchased from the Angela Flowers Gallery, 1976, © the artists/ courtesy Flowers Gallery, London
Branch, Winston b.1947, *First Light 'For Polly'*, purchased from the artist, 1980, © the artist
Bratby, John Randall 1928–1992, *Jean Reading*, purchased from the Beaux Arts Gallery, 1954, © the artist's estate/Bridgeman Art Library
Bratby, John Randall 1928–1992, *Jean and Susan*, purchased from the Beaux Arts Gallery, 1956, © the artist's estate/Bridgeman Art Library
Bratby, John Randall 1928–1992, *Coach House Door*, purchased from the Zwemmer Gallery, 1959, © the artist's estate/Bridgeman Art Library
Breakwell, Ian 1943–2005, *Gathering Storm*, purchased from the Anthony Reynolds Gallery, 1987, © the artist's estate, courtesy Anthony Reynolds Gallery
Brick, Michael b.1946, *Sous-Bois III*, purchased from the John Moores Liverpool Exhibition XI, 1978, © the artist
Brooker, William 1918–1983, *Ikaria*, purchased from Arthur Tooth & Sons Ltd, 1969, © the artist's estate
Brown, Cleveland b.1943, *St James's Park*, purchased from the artist, 1978
Brown, Glenn b.1966, *Decline and Fall*, purchased from Karsten Schubert Ltd, 1995, © the artist, photo credit: ACC
Buckland Wright, John 1897–1954, *Interior*, purchased from the London Group, 1954
Buckley, Stephen b.1944, *Rannoch*, purchased from Thomas Gibson, 1971, © the artist
Buckley, Stephen b.1944, *Head of a Young Girl No.2*, purchased from the Museum of Modern Art, Oxford, 1975, © the artist
Buhler, Michael 1940–2009, *Figure and Cars*, purchased from the New Art Centre, 1966, © the artist's estate/Bridgeman Art Library
Buhler, Robert A. 1916–1989, *Kale Field, Beaumont Quay*, purchased from the Royal Academy, 1950, © the artist's estate/Bridgeman Art Library
Burn, Rodney Joseph 1899–1984, *White House, Chiswick*, purchased from the artist, 1961, © the artist's estate
Callery, Simon b.1960, *Borough and Trinity*, gift from Charles Saatchi, 1999, © the artist

Camp, Jeffery b.1923, *Blue Sea*, purchased from the Beaux Arts Gallery, 1959, © the artist
Camp, Jeffery b.1923, *Laetitia Picking Blackcurrants*, purchased from the New Art Centre, 1968, © the artist
Camp, Jeffery b.1923, *Beachy Head: Lighthouse by Night*, purchased from the artist, 1973, © the artist
Camp, Jeffery b.1923, *Sleeper with Passing Liner*, purchased from the artist, 1978, © the artist
Camp, Jeffery b.1923, *Venice*, purchased from Nigel Greenwood Inc., 1986, © the artist
Campbell, Steven 1953–2007, *Napoleonic Silhouettist Cutting the Progress of the War*, purchased from Marlborough Fine Art, 1987, © the artist's estate
Carnegie, Gillian b.1971, *Mono*, purchased from the Cabinet Gallery, 2005, © the artist
Carr, Thomas James 1909–1999, *High Tide*, purchased from the artist, 1942, © the artist's estate
Carter, Bernard Arthur Ruston (Sam) 1909–2006, *Roofs at Swiss Cottage*, purchased from the artist, 1965
Carter, John b.1942, *Squares I*, purchased from Tolly Cobbold Eastern Arts, Second National Exhibition, 1979, © the artist
Carter, John b.1942, *Two Frames: Greys*, purchase award, 1983, © the artist
Cartwright, Peter b.1939, *Three*, purchased from Camden Borough Survey Exhibition, 1967, © the artist, photo credit: ACC
Caughlin, Ian b.1948, *View from a Roof, Rostrevor Road, Fulham*, purchased from the House Gallery, 1979, © the artist
Caulfield, Patrick 1936–2005, *Artist's Studio*, purchased from the Robert Fraser Gallery, 1965, © the estate of Patrick Caulfield. All rights reserved, DACS 2012
Caulfield, Patrick 1936–2005, *Sculpture in a Landscape*, purchased from the Robert Fraser Gallery, 1967, © the estate of Patrick Caulfield. All rights reserved, DACS 2012
Caulfield, Patrick 1936–2005, *Dining Recess*, purchased from the Waddington Galleries Ltd, 1974, © the estate of Patrick Caulfield. All rights reserved, DACS 2012
Caulfield, Patrick 1936–2005, *Registry Office*, purchased from the Waddington Galleries Ltd, 1997, © the estate of Patrick Caulfield. All rights reserved, DACS 2012
Chalkley, Brian b.1948, *Stratford Landscape*, purchased from the artist, 1987, © the artist
Chambers, Stephen b.1960, *Sicily*, purchased from the artist, 1986, © the artist/ courtesy Flowers Gallery, London
Chambers, Stephen b.1960, *This is a Woman You Know Well*, purchased from Flowers East, 1996, © the artist/ courtesy Flowers Gallery, London
Chaplin, Stephen b.1934, *Painting 1967: 1*, purchased from the artist, 1971, © the artist
Charlett, Nicole b.1957, *4 Colour Elements, 2 Directions*, purchased from the artist, 1983
Charlton, Alan b.1948, *Channel, 1972*, purchased from Nigel Greenwood Inc., 1973, © the artist
Charlton, Alan b.1948, *Sixteen Part Line Painting*, purchased from the artist, 1986, © the artist
Chevska, Maria b.1948, *Convulsive Cloak*, purchased from the Anderson O'Day Gallery, 1990, © the artist
Christopherson, John 1921–1996, *Endgame*, purchased from the artist, 1979
Christophorou, Christopher b.1957, *Remnants*, purchased from the Whitechapel Art Gallery, 1988, © the artist
Chubb, Shirley b.1959, *Change*, purchased from the artist, 1991, © the artist
Chuhan, J. b.1955, *Self Portrait*, purchased from the artist, 1996, © J. Chuhan
Cina, Colin b.1943, *Running Deep*, purchased from the artist, 1967, © the artist
Cina, Colin b.1943, *MH/8*, purchased from the Arnolfini Gallery, Bristol, 1970, © the artist
Cina, Colin b.1943, *Untitled Drawing V*, purchased from the artist, 1974, © the artist
Clarke, Pete b.1951, *Municipal Modernism: The Cloth Cap and the Red Glove*, purchased from the artist, 1987, © the artist
Clarke, Trevor b.1949, *Rotated Variations in Relation to a Constant, Series 2, T. C. O. Variations III B4*, purchased from the artist, 1983
Clough, Prunella 1919–1999, *Lowestoft Harbour*, purchased from the artist, 1951, © estate of Prunella Clough 2012. All rights reserved, DACS
Clough, Prunella 1919–1999, *Industrial Plant II*, purchased from the artist, 1958, © estate of Prunella Clough 2012. All rights reserved, DACS
Clough, Prunella 1919–1999, *Industrial Interior V*, purchased from the Whitechapel Art Gallery, 1960, © estate of Prunella Clough 2012. All rights reserved, DACS
Clough, Prunella 1919–1999, *Landscape with Sections*, purchased from the Grosvenor Gallery, 1964, © estate of Prunella Clough 2012. All rights reserved, DACS
Clough, Prunella 1919–1999, *Garden Hedge*, purchased from the artist, 1974, © estate of Prunella Clough 2012. All rights reserved, DACS
Clough, Prunella 1919–1999, *Untitled*, purchased from the Grosvenor Gallery, 1968, © estate of Prunella Clough 2012. All rights reserved, DACS
Clough, Prunella 1919–1999, *Edge*, purchased from the artist, 1967, © estate of Prunella Clough 2012. All rights reserved, DACS
Clough, Prunella 1919–1999, *South-West Nocturne*, purchased from the artist, 1970, © estate of Prunella Clough 2012. All rights reserved, DACS
Clough, Prunella 1919–1999, *Waterford Yard*, purchased from the artist, 1971, © estate of Prunella Clough 2012. All rights reserved, DACS
Clough, Prunella 1919–1999, *Inside and Outside*, purchased from Monika Kinley, 1976, © estate of Prunella Clough 2012. All rights reserved, DACS
Clough, Prunella 1919–1999, *Study for 'Perforated Fragment'*, gift from the artist, 1986, © estate of Prunella Clough 2012. All rights reserved DACS
Clough, Prunella 1919–1999, *Study for 'Perforated Fragment'*, gift from the artist, 1986, © estate of Prunella Clough 2012. All rights reserved DACS
Clough, Prunella 1919–1999, *Perforated Fragment*, purchased from the artist, 1986, © estate of Prunella Clough 2012. All rights reserved DACS
Clough, Prunella 1919–1999, *Samples*, purchased from Annely Juda Fine Art, 1999, © estate of Prunella Clough 2012. All rights reserved, DACS
Clutton-Brock, Alan Francis 1904–1976, *Early Tulips*, purchased from the artist, 1953, © the artist's estate
Cockrill, Maurice b.1936, *Night*, purchased from the Edward Totah Gallery, 1985, © the artist
Cohen, Bernard b.1933, *Petersburg*, purchased from the Molton Gallery, 1962, © the artist/ courtesy Flowers Gallery, London
Cohen, Bernard b.1933, *Glow*, purchased from the artist, 1965, © the artist/ courtesy Flowers Gallery, London
Cohen, Bernard b.1933, *Mask*, purchased from the Waddington Galleries Ltd, 1976, © the artist/ courtesy Flowers Gallery, London
Cohen, Harold b.1928, *Standing Figure*, purchased from the Gimpel Fils Gallery, 1955, © the artist
Cohen, Harold b.1928, *Beta Orionis*, purchased from the artist, 1961, © the artist
Cohen, Harold b.1928, *Untitled*, purchased from the Robert Fraser Gallery, 1966, © the artist
Coker, Peter 1926–2004, *Dead Hare on Table*, purchased from the Zwemmer Gallery, 1956, © Peter Coker, RA
Coldstream, William Menzies 1908–1987, *Cripplegate*, purchased from the Leicester Galleries, 1949, © the artist's estate/Bridgeman Art Library
Coldstream, William Menzies 1908–1987, *Reclining Nude*, purchased from Arthur Tooth & Sons Ltd, 1958, © the artist's estate/Bridgeman Art Library
Coldstream, William Menzies 1908–1987, *Westminster Abbey*, purchased from the Anthony d'Offay Gallery, 1976, © the artist's estate/Bridgeman Art Library
Collinge, Robert Anthony b.1934, *Grey and Brown III*, purchased from the New Art Centre, 1965, © the artist
Colquhoun, Robert 1914–1962, *Church Lench*, purchased from the artist, 1942, © the artist's estate/ Bridgeman Art Library
Colquhoun, Robert 1914–1962, *Seated Woman and Cat*, purchased from Reid Lefevre, 1947, © the artist's estate/Bridgeman Art Library
Colquhoun, Robert 1914–1962, *The Gardener*, purchased from the Whitechapel Art Gallery, 1958, © the artist's estate/Bridgeman Art Library
Constable, Martin b.1961, *Untitled*, purchased from Long and Ryle, 1992, © the artist
Cook, Barrie b.1929, *Coleshill*, purchased from the artist, 1970, © the artist
Cook, Barrie b.1929, *Continuum*, purchased from the artist, 1981, © the artist
Cook, Ben b.1967, *Aerial View of the Harbour, Marseilles* (from the 'Found Paintings' series), purchased from the artist, 1999, © the artist
Cook, Richard Vernon Francis b.1947, *Summer Morning, Lelant*, purchased from the artist, 2001, © the artist
Cook, Roger b.1940, *Untitled R.11*, purchased from the Rowan Gallery, 1964, © the artist
Coombs, Daniel b.1971, *Night Bungalow I*, gift from Charles Saatchi, 1999
Coombs, Daniel b.1971, *Night Bungalow II*, gift from Charles Saatchi, 1999
Coombs, Daniel b.1971, *The Creation of the World*, gift from Charles Saatchi, 1999
Cooper, Eileen b.1953, *Going Ape*, purchased from Blond Fine Art Ltd, 1983, © Eileen Cooper 2012. All rights reserved, DACS
Cooper, Eileen b.1953, *Putting Down Roots*, purchased from Blond Fine Art Ltd, 1985, © Eileen Cooper 2012. All rights reserved, DACS
Cooper, Julian b.1947, *Piece of Ground near Vence*, purchased from the artist, 1979, © the artist
Cooper, Julian b.1947, *Bella Vista Hotel (Under the Volcano)*, purchased from the artist, 1983, © the artist, photo credit: ACC
Copnall, John 1928–2007, *Diagonals No.1*, purchased from the artist, 1977, © the artist's estate
Core, Philip 1951–1989, *The Chance Meeting on an Operating Table of a Sewing Machine and an Umbrella: Andy Warhol and Marcel Duchamp*, purchased from the Francis Kyle Gallery, 1979
Couch, Christopher b.1946, *Saturday*, purchased from House, 1980, © the artist
Coventry, Keith b.1958, *White Suprematist Painting*, purchased from Karsten Schubert Ltd, 1993, © Keith Coventry. DACS 2012
Coventry, Keith b.1958, *White Abstract (Ullein Reviesky, the Last Deb)*, gift from Charles Saatchi, 1999, © Keith Coventry. DACS 2012
Coventry, Keith b.1958, *Black Crack Pipes*, purchased from the Haunch of Venison with the assistance of the Art Fund, 2009, © Keith Coventry. DACS 2012
Coventry, Keith b.1958, *Crack Pipes*, purchased from the Haunch of Venison with the assistance of the Art Fund, 2009, © Keith Coventry. DACS 2012
Coventry, Keith b.1958, *Crack Pipes 3*, purchased from the Haunch of Venison with the assistance of the Art Fund, 2009, © Keith Coventry. DACS 2012
Coviello, Peter b.1930, *Hanuman*, purchased from the artist, 1967
Craig-Martin, Michael b.1941, *Painting and Picturing*, purchased from the Rowan Gallery, 1979 © Michael Craig-Martin
Craig-Martin, Michael b.1941, *History Painting*, purchased from the Waddington Galleries Ltd, 1995 © Michael Craig-Martin
Craxton, John 1922–2009, *Study for 'Sleeping Fisherman'*, purchased from the Mayor Gallery, 1950, © John Craxton 2012. All rights reserved, DACS
Craxton, John 1922–2009, *Landscape, Hydra, Greece*, purchased from the Leicester Galleries, 1961, © John Craxton 2012. All rights reserved, DACS
Creffield, Dennis b.1931, *Chessmen*, purchased from the Hampstead Arts Centre, 1966, © the artist
Creffield, Dennis b.1931, *The Resource of Loneliness*, purchased from Monika Kinley, 1977, © the artist
Crone, David b.1937, *Summer Music*, purchased from the Fenderesky Gallery at Queen's, 1991, © the artist
Crowley, Graham b.1950, *Tug*, purchased from the artist, 1976, © courtesy of Beaux Arts
Crowley, Graham b.1950, *Spider with Mushroom Soup*, purchased from the Museum of Modern Art, Oxford, 1983, © courtesy of Beaux Arts
Crowther, Michael b.1946, *Salvo II*, purchased from the artist, 1981, © the artist

Croxon, Jeanne b.1932, *Untitled (Green)*, purchased from the artist, 1979, © the artist
Croxon, Jeanne b.1932, *Untitled (Pink)*, purchased from the artist, 1979, © the artist
Crozier, William 1930–2011, *Landscape, Wivenhoe*, purchased from the Drian Gallery, 1960, © the estate of William Crozier/ courtesy Flowers Gallery, London
Crozier, William 1930–2011, *North London Garden*, purchased from the artist, 1980, © the estate of William Crozier/ courtesy Flowers Gallery, London
Crozier, William 1930–2011, *Still Life*, purchased from the London Borough of Camden, 1980, © the estate of William Crozier/ courtesy Flowers Gallery, London
Crozier, William 1930–2011, *Still Life*, purchased from the London Borough of Camden, 1980, © the estate of William Crozier/ courtesy Flowers Gallery, London
Crumplin, Colin b.1946, *Coincidence VII*, purchased from Anthony Stokes, 1980, © the artist
Cuddihy, Mikey b.1952, *Iron Gates of Life: Strength and Sweetness*, purchased from Flowers East, 1991, © the artist
Culbert, Bill b.1935, *St Paul's*, purchased from the artist, 1961, © the artist
Cumming, Diana b.1929, *The Flood*, purchased from the artist, 1954, © the artist
Dalwood, Dexter b.1960, *The Room*, purchased from the artist, 1985
Darach, Peter b.1940, *The Swing*, purchased from the artist, 1985, © the artist
Davenport, Ian b.1966, *Poured Lines: Light Orange, Blue, Yellow, Dark Green and Orange*, purchased from the Waddington Galleries Ltd, 1995, © the artist
Davie, Alan b.1920, *Ghost Creation*, purchased from the Whitechapel Art Gallery, 1958, © the artist
Davie, Alan b.1920, *Target*, purchased from the Gimpel Fils Gallery, 1960, © the artist
Davies, Ivor b.1935, *At the Photographer's*, purchased from the artist, 1983 © Ivor Davies
Davies, Peter b.1970, *Striped Painting*, purchased from The Approach, 1998, © the artist
Davis, Peter b.1972, *Untitled 3mm Blue – November 1995*, gift from Charles Saatchi, 1999, © the artist
de Francia, Peter 1921–2012, *Monsieur et Madame Beylac*, purchased from the Arkwright Arts Trust, 1977, © estate of Peter de Francia, courtesy James Hyman Fine Art, London
de Grey, Roger 1918–1995, *Contre-jour II*, purchased from the Royal Academy of Arts, 1967, © the artist's estate
de Grey, Roger 1918–1995, *Orchard, Meopham*, purchased from the Leicester Galleries, 1966, © the artist's estate
de Maistre, Leroy Leveson Laurent Joseph 1894–1968, *Third Station of the Cross*, purchased from the artist, 1958, © the artist's estate
de Maistre, Leroy Leveson Laurent Joseph 1894–1968, *The Green Shade*, purchased from Adams Brothers, 1950, © the artist's estate
de Thame, Gerard b.1958, *Tall and Old*, purchased from the Air Gallery, 1983, © the artist
Delargy, Diarmuid b.1958, *Breda*, purchased from the Fenderesky Gallery, 1991, © the artist
Dellow, Jeffrey b.1949, *Marsyas*, purchased from the artist, 1982, © the artist
Dennis, Jeffrey b.1958, *Echo*, purchased from the artist, 1982, © Jeffrey Dennis
Dennis, Jeffrey b.1958, *A Spy in the House of Frank*, gift from Charles Saatchi, 1999, © Jeffrey Dennis, photo credit: ACC
Dennis, Jeffrey b.1958, *Strange Fruit*, gift from Charles Saatchi, 1999, © Jeffrey Dennis
Dennis, Jeffrey b.1958, *The Lost City*, gift from Charles Saatchi, 1999, © Jeffrey Dennis
Denny, Robyn b.1930, *Bland*, purchased from the Kasmin Gallery, 1964, © the artist
Denny, Robyn b.1930, *Over Reach*, purchased from the Kasmin Gallery, 1967, © the artist
Denny, Robyn b.1930, *Gently*, purchased from the Kasmin Gallery, 1969, © the artist
Denny, Robyn b.1930, *Landscape Painting No.5*, purchased from the artist, 1981, © the artist
Derges, Susan b.1955, *Spiral Construction*, purchased from the artist, 1979, © the artist
Devas, Anthony 1911–1958, *Six O'Clock News*, purchased from the artist, 1942, © the artist's estate/ Bridgeman Art Library
Dickinson, Rod b.1965, *Egg Bag*, gift from Charles Saatchi, 1999
Dickinson, Rod b.1965, *Venereal Daze*, gift from Charles Saatchi, 1999
Dismorr, Jessica 1885–1939, *Related Forms*, purchased from the Mayor Gallery, 1965, © the artist's estate
Dodgson, John Arthur 1890–1969, *Death of a Child*, purchased from the Beaux Arts Gallery, 1959, © the artist's estate
Doig, Peter b.1959, *Red Deer*, purchased from the artist, 1992, © Peter Doig
Donagh, Rita b.1939, *'Taking the trouble to sound it'*, purchased from Nigel Greenwood Inc., 1972
Donaldson, Antony b.1939, *Starr-Queen' – for Jenny Davis*, purchased from the Rowan Gallery, 1962, © Antony Donaldson
Donaldson, Antony b.1939, *Untitled 'I'*, purchased from the Rowan Gallery, 1969, © Antony Donaldson
Donnelly, Micky b.1952, *Olive*, purchased from the Anderson O'Day Gallery, 1991, © the artist
Donnelly, Micky b.1952, *Landscape Painting No.5* (after Paul Henry), purchased from the Anderson O'Day Gallery, 1991, © the artist
Dower, Natalie b.1931, *Working Drawing, Double Square 1980*, purchased from Hayward Annual, 1982, © the artist
Dower, Natalie b.1931, *Sortie*, purchased from the Crane Kalman Gallery, 2001, © the artist, photo credit: ACC
Dragicevic, Milena b.1965, *Opet*, purchased from the artist, 2002, © the artist
Draper, Kenneth b.1944, *Enclosures*, purchased from the artist, 1980, © the artist
Drever, Timothy b.1935, *Negatron*, purchased from the Lisson Gallery, 1968, © the artist
Drummond, Malcolm 1880–1945, *Brompton Oratory*, purchased from Mrs Malcolm Drummond, 1964, © the artist's estate
Du Plessis, Enslin 1894–1978, *Cotswold Landscape*, purchased from the artist, 1942
Du Plessis, Enslin 1894–1978, *The Mantelpiece*, purchased from Thomas Agnew and Sons Ltd, 1959
Dubsky, Mario 1939–1985, *Svodebka*, purchased from the artist, 1969, © the artist's estate
Dunbar, Evelyn Mary 1906–1960, *Rochester from Strood*, purchased from the artist, 1942, © the artist's estate
Dunlop, Ronald Ossory 1894–1973, *Snow at Stratford-on-Avon*, purchased from the artist, 1942
Dunn, Anne b.1929, *Watercourse*, purchased from the Leicester Galleries, 1964, © the artist
Dunstan, Bernard b.1920, *The Campo, Siena*, purchased from Roland Browse and Delbanco, 1967, © the artist/Bridgeman Art Library
Durrant, Jennifer b.1942, *Slide*, purchased from the Camden Borough Survey Exhibition, 1967, © the artist
Durrant, Jennifer b.1942, *Birthday I*, purchased from the artist, 1974, © the artist
Durrant, Jennifer b.1942, *Lone*, purchased from the artist, 1974, © the artist
Durrant, Jennifer b.1942, *Scar Series Number Eleven, June 1974*, purchased from the artist, 1974, © the artist
Durrant, Jennifer b.1942, *Jean Blue Painting*, purchased from the artist, 1976, © the artist
Durrant, Jennifer b.1942, *Early On*, purchased from the Nicola Jacobs Gallery, 1982, © the artist
Duxbury, Leslie 1921–2001, *Tenement Dwellers*, purchased from the Art Exhibitions Bureau, 1956, © the artist's estate
Dyer, Alan b.1944, *Desert Painting No.3*, purchased from the Sandford Gallery, 1979, © the artist
Eardley, Joan Kathleen Harding 1921–1963, *A Field of Oats*, purchased from Roland Browse and Delbanco, 1963, © DACS 2012
Easydorchik, Edwin b.1949, *Girone della Mano – One Criminal Passion*, purchase award, 1979
Edgcumbe, Ursula 1900–1985, *Drainpipes*, purchased from the Annexe Gallery, 1982
Edmond, Terry b.1947, *Sekela Khuluma*, purchased from the artist, 1982, © the artist
Edmondson, Simon b.1955, *Second Night*, purchased from the Nicola Jacobs Gallery, 1984, © the artist
Edwards, John 1938–2009, *Interiors*, purchased from the Juda Rowan Gallery, 1984, © John Edwards 2012. All Rights Reserved, DACS
Egonu, Uzo 1928 (?)–1996, *A New Lease of Life*, purchased from the artist, 1988, © Uzo Egonu estate
Elliott, Ashley b.1974, *A100-100 (Uniform White, Red, Ultramarine Blue)*, purchased from Jason and Rhodes, 1997
Elliott, John b.1953, *Phaeax*, purchased from the Anne Berthoud Gallery, 1981
Ellis, Peter b.1951, *Blank Firing*, purchased from the Anthony Wilkinson Gallery, 1998, © the artist
English, Michael 1941–2009, *Man Machine Side of British Rail Parcels Van*, purchased from the artist, 1980, © the artist's estate
English, Simon b.1959, *Box II (Large)*, gift from Charles Saatchi, 1999
Evans, Merlyn Oliver 1910–1973, *Nocturnal Drama (Fantasy)*, bequeathed by Enid Morse, 1962, © the artist's estate, photo credit: ACC
Evans, Merlyn Oliver 1910–1973, *Metropolitan Crowd Forming a Procession*, purchased from the artist, 1970, © the artist's estate
Evans, Merlyn Oliver 1910–1973, *Relief*, purchased from McRoberts and Tunnard, 1963, © the artist's estate, photo credit: ACC
Evans, Merlyn Oliver 1910–1973, *Composition*, purchased from the artist, 1966, © the artist's estate
Evans, Merlyn Oliver 1910–1973, *Building – Morning*, purchased from the Leicester Galleries, 1953, © the artist's estate
Evans, Nicholas 1907–2004, *Collapse of the Roof*, purchased from Browse and Darby, 1978, © the artist's estate
Eyton, Anthony John Plowden b.1923, *Newcastle*, purchased from the St George's Gallery, 1955, © the artist/Bridgeman Art Library
Eyton, Anthony John Plowden b.1923, *Standing Nude*, purchased from the New Art Centre, 1962, © the artist/Bridgeman Art Library
Eyton, Anthony John Plowden b.1923, *Bathers*, purchased from the artist, 1976, © the artist/ Bridgeman Art Library
Fairnington, Mark b.1957, *The Greek Madonna*, gift from Charles Saatchi, 1999, © the artist, photo credit: ACC
Faithfull, Leila 1896–1994, *Evacuees*, purchased from the artist, 1942, © Leila E. Evans
Farmer, Bernard 1919–2002, *Pelagic II*, purchased from the artist, 1968
Farmer, Bernard 1919–2002, *Helios II*, purchased from the Angela Flowers Gallery, 1982
Farrell, Anthony b.1945, *Winter, Leigh Beach*, purchased from the artist, 1986, © the artist
Farthing, Stephen b.1950, *Mrs G's Chair*, purchased from the artist, 1983, © the artist
Farthing, Stephen b.1950, *Florence*, gift from the artist, 1989, © the artist
Feeney, Jacinta b.1954, *This Brief Transit*, purchased from the artist, 1991, © the artist
Feiler, Paul b.1918, *Large Welsh Bay*, purchased from The Redfern Gallery, 1953, © the artist/ Bridgeman Art Library
Fell, Sheila Mary 1931–1979, *Woman in the Snow*, purchased from the artist, 1967
Fell, Sheila Mary 1931–1979, *Snowscape with Clouds*, purchased from the Beaux Arts Gallery, 1958
Fell, Sheila Mary 1931–1979, *Potato Pickers I*, purchased from the Beaux Arts Gallery, 1960
Fell, Sheila Mary 1931–1979, *Silage Heap and Cows, Drumburgh*, purchased from the artist, 1967
Fergusson, John Duncan 1874–1961, *'Hillhead', Eileen*, purchased from the artist, 1959, © The Fergusson Gallery, Perth and Kinross Council, Scotland
Fergusson, John Duncan 1874–1961, *Self Portrait*, purchased from the London Group, 1956, © The Fergusson Gallery, Perth and Kinross Council, Scotland
Fernández, Erasmo b.1924, *Untitled (Abstract: Fish and Nets)*, bequeathed by Enid Morse, 1962, © the artist
Fernández, Erasmo b.1924, *Untitled Still Life (Jug, Basket and Fruit)*, bequeathed by Miss Enid Morse, 1962, © the artist
Ferris, Dee b.1973, *Ideal Homes (this is the beginning of forever)*, purchased from Corvi-Mora, 2005, © courtesy: Corvi Mora, London, photo credit: ACC
Few, Elsie Evelyn 1909–1980, *The Iron Maiden*, purchased from the

Annexe Gallery, 1979, © the artist's estate
Few, Elsie Evelyn 1909–1980, *The Pond at Hawkshall*, purchased from the London Group, 1954, © the artist's estate
Fielding, Brian 1933–1987, *Mandala 39*, purchased from the Camden Borough Survey Exhibition, 1967, © the artist's estate
Fielding, Brian 1933–1987, *Painting No.323*, purchased from the artist, 1975, © the artist's estate
Fielding, Brian 1933–1987, *Milk Bar*, purchased from the Ikon Gallery, 1987, © the artist's estate
Fields, Duggie b.1945, *Stumped*, purchased from the artist, 1979, © the artist
Finer, Stephen b.1949, *Seated Nude*, purchased from the Anthony Reynolds Gallery, 1983, © Stephen Finer
Finer, Stephen b.1949, *Sandra Fisher*, purchased from the artist, 1979, © Stephen Finer
Finer, Stephen b.1949, *Woman Handling Her Left Breast*, purchased from the Anthony Reynolds Gallery, 1986, © Stephen Finer
Fitton, James 1899–1982, *The Breakwater*, purchased from the artist, 1942, © the artist's estate
Flannigan, Moyna b.1963, *The Last Minister*, purchased from Doggerfisher, Edinburgh, 2002, © the artist
Flannigan, Moyna b.1963, *Toujours la même chose*, purchased from Doggerfisher, Edinburgh, 2002, © the artist
Folkes, Peter L. b.1923, *The Hayfield*, purchased from the London Group, 1952, © the artist
Forbes, Richard b.1953, *Two Lexical Groups for L1, Two Morphemic Groups for L1*, purchased from the artist, 1982
Forge, Andrew 1923–2002, *Landscape, Ericeira*, purchased from the A. I. A. Gallery, 1961, © the estate of Andrew Forge, courtesy Betty Cunningham Gallery, New York
Forge, Andrew 1923–2002, *Summertime*, purchased from R. I. Galleries, 1967, © the estate of Andrew Forge, courtesy Betty Cunningham Gallery, New York
Forrester, Denzil b.1956, *Witchdoctor*, purchased from the Riverside Studios, 1983
Forrester, John 1922–2002, *Two of a Kind*, purchased from McRoberts and Tunnard, 1962, © the artist's estate
Forster, Noel 1932–2007, *Two Units, One in Grey*, purchased from the artist, 1977, © the artist's estate/ courtesy Flowers Gallery, London
Forster, Noel 1932–2007, *Untitled*, purchased from the artist, 1982, © the artist's estate/ courtesy Flowers Gallery, London
Forster, Noel 1932–2007, *Untitled*, purchased from the artist, 1998, © the artist's estate/ courtesy Flowers Gallery, London
Foster, Dilys *Pink Head*, purchased from Brighton Museum and Art Gallery, 1978
Foster, Graham b.1950, *Untitled*, purchased from the artist, 1981
Francis, Mark b.1962, *Positive*, gift from Charles Saatchi, 1999, © Mark Francis
Francis, Mark b.1962, *Untitled (Negative 2)*, gift from Charles Saatchi, 1999, © Mark Francis
Fraser, Donald Hamilton 1929–2009, *Beachscape II*, purchased from Arthur Tooth & Sons Ltd, 1955, © estate of Donald Hamilton Fraser
Fraser, Donald Hamilton 1929–2009, *Mont Saint-Geneviève*, purchased from the Gimpel Fils Gallery, 1965, © estate of Donald Hamilton Fraser
Fredman, Nick b.1955, *In My Back Yard*, purchased from the artist, 1986
Freud, Lucian 1922–2011, *Dead Cock's Head*, purchased from the Hanover Gallery, 1952, © estate of Lucian Freud
Freud, Lucian 1922–2011, *Girl in a Green Dress*, purchased from the Daily Express Exhibition, 1955, © estate of Lucian Freud
Freud, Lucian 1922–2011, *Small Head*, purchased from the Anthony d'Offay Gallery, 1981, © estate of Lucian Freud
Frost, Terry 1915–2003, *Movement, Green and Black*, purchased from the Leicester Galleries, 1952, © the estate of Terry Frost. All rights reserved, DACS 2012
Frost, Terry 1915–2003, *Red, Black, White (1955)*, purchased from the Leicester Galleries, 1956, © the estate of Terry Frost. All rights reserved, DACS 2012
Frost, Terry 1915–2003, *Red, Yellow and Blue*, purchased from the Waddington Galleries Ltd, 1963, © the estate of Terry Frost. All rights reserved, DACS 2012
Frost, Terry 1915–2003, *Red, Black, White (1965)*, purchased from the artist, 1967, © the estate of Terry Frost. All rights reserved, DACS 2012
Frost, Terry 1915–2003, *Ginger and Purple 'Chirpy'*, purchased from the artist, 1967, © the estate of Terry Frost. All rights reserved, DACS 2012
Frost, Terry 1915–2003, *Black and White Sept. 78*, purchased from the artist, 1980, © the estate of Terry Frost. All rights reserved, DACS 2012
Froy, Martin b.1926, *Seated Girl*, purchased from the Hanover Gallery, 1952, © the artist
Froy, Martin b.1926, *Landscape with Figures*, purchased from the artist, 1967, © the artist
Froy, Martin b.1926, *Colham*, purchased from the Hanover Gallery, 1969, © the artist
Fry, Anthony b.1927, *Nude*, purchased from the London Group, 1954, © the artist
Fry, Anthony b.1927, *Landscape*, purchased from the Institute of Contemporary Arts, 1956, © the artist
Fry, Anthony b.1927, *Dance White*, purchased from the Leicester Galleries, 1961, © the artist
Fussell, Michael 1927–1974, *Garlic*, purchased from the Beaux Arts Gallery, 1956
Fussell, Michael 1927–1974, *Sharp Division*, purchased from the Hanover Gallery, 1962
Gear, William 1915–1997, *Christmas Tree*, purchased from the Gimpel Fils Gallery, 1951, © the artist's estate
Gear, William 1915–1997, *Black Armature with Yellow*, purchased from the R. I. Galleries, 1967, © the artist's estate
Geoffrey, Iqbal b.1939, *In Search of the Ideal Landscape*, purchased from the Drian Gallery, 1966, © Paris Biennial (1965) Laureate Iqbal Geoffrey
George, Patrick b.1923, *Nicholas Browne*, purchased from the London Group, 1958, © the artist
George, Patrick b.1923, *June in Bed*, purchased from the London Group, 1956, © the artist
George, Patrick b.1923, *Nigerian Landscape: View of Kuffena*, purchased from the artist, 1966, © the artist
George, Patrick b.1923, *Joanna Drew (1929–2003)*, gift from the sitter, 1992, © the artist, photo credit: ACC
George, Patrick b.1923, *Seated Girl*, purchased from the artist, 1966, © the artist
George, Patrick b.1923, *View Towards Henny Church from Little Hickbush*, purchased from the artist, 1980, © the artist
George, Patrick b.1923, *Interior: Nude on a Bed*, purchased from the artist, 1976, © the artist
Gertler, Mark 1891–1939, *Self Portrait*, purchased from Mrs W. Hannay, 1954, © by permission of Luke Gertler
Ghosh, Amal b.1933, *Allegory III*, purchased from the artist, 1989, © the artist
Gibbs, Evelyn 1905–1991, *Cliff Projection*, purchased from the Drian Gallery, 1970, © the artist's estate
Gilbert, Dick 1935–2008, *Approaching Wave*, purchased from the New Vision Gallery, 1965, © the artist's estate
Gillies, William George 1898–1973, *Eildon*, purchased from the artist, 1951, © Royal Scottish Academy
Gillies, William George 1898–1973, *Still Life*, purchased from Aitken Dott and Son, 1955, © Royal Scottish Academy
Gilman, Harold 1876–1919, *The Model*, purchased from the Leicester Galleries, 1958
Ginner, Charles 1878–1952, *The Rib, Standon, 1939*, purchased from the artist, 1942
Ginner, Charles 1878–1952, *Spring Day at Boscastle*, purchased, 1949
Ginsborg, Michael b.1943, *Untitled*, purchased from the Lisson Gallery, 1970, © the artist
Ginsborg, Michael b.1943, *Echoes*, purchased from the Warehouse Gallery, 1976, © the artist
Gladwell, Rodney 1928–1979, *Pumpkin and Pears*, purchased from the Lisson Gallery, 1970
Goede, Jules de 1937–2007, *SS7 No.1*, purchased from House Gallery, 1977, © the artist's estate courtesy of Broadbent
Golden, Pamela b.1959, *Mrs Watson, Signor Treci and Traldi at the Hospital* (from the 'Mrs Watson Pours the Coffee' series), purchased from the Gimpel Fils Gallery, 1997, © the artist
Golden, Pamela b.1959, *Three Men, Three Women* (from the 'Mrs Watson Pours the Coffee' series), purchased from the Gimpel Fils Gallery, 1997, © the artist
Golding, John b.1929, *Phaestos – Green*, purchased from the Axiom Gallery, 1966, © the artist
Golding, John b.1929, *D (C. S.) VI*, purchased from the Rowan Gallery, 1975, © the artist
Gordon, Douglas b.1966, *Painting No.19: Mark Rothko/Betty Parsons*, purchased from the artist, 1992, © Douglas Gordon
Gore, Spencer 1878–1914, *Landscape, Somerset*, purchased from The Redfern Gallery, 1962
Gore, Spencer 1878–1914, *Chisholm Road, Richmond*, purchased from the Leicester Galleries, 1955
Gormley, Antony b.1950, *Art*, purchased from the artist, 1982, © courtesy of the artist and Jay Jopling/White Cube
Gotlib, Henryk 1890–1966, *The Boat*, purchased from the Crane Kalman Gallery, 1961, © the artist's estate
Gouk, Alan b.1939, *Painting No.7*, purchased from the artist, 1969, © the artist, photo credit: ACC
Gowing, Lawrence 1918–1991, *Julia Strachey (1901–1979)*, purchased from the artist, 1942, © estate of Sir Lawrence Gowing
Gowing, Lawrence 1918–1991, *Miss Baker*, purchased from the Leicester Galleries, 1948, © estate of Sir Lawrence Gowing
Gowing, Lawrence 1918–1991, *Cherry Copse at Stock Close, near Aldbourne*, purchased from the artist, 1952, © estate of Sir Lawrence Gowing
Gowing, Lawrence 1918–1991, *Gifford's Copse*, purchased from the London Group exhibition, 1962, © estate of Sir Lawrence Gowing
Gowing, Lawrence 1918–1991, *Wood: Yellow and Blue II*, purchased from Marlborough Fine Art, 1965, © estate of Sir Lawrence Gowing
Gowing, Lawrence 1918–1991, *Sir William Rees-Mogg (b.1928)*, commissioned by the Arts Council, 1986, © estate of Sir Lawrence Gowing
Graham Bell, Frank 1910–1943, *Baylham Mill*, purchased from the artist, 1943, © the artist's estate
Grandjean, Lee b.1949, *Dancer*, purchased from the artist, 1976, © the artist
Grant, Duncan 1885–1978, *The Doorway*, purchased from the Leicester Galleries, 1951, © estate of Duncan Grant. All rights reserved, DACS 2012
Grant, Duncan 1885–1978, *Artificial Flowers*, purchased from the artist, 1951, © estate of Duncan Grant. All rights reserved, DACS 2012
Grant, Duncan 1885–1978, *Cow Stalls*, purchased from the artist, 1942, © estate of Duncan Grant. All rights reserved, DACS 2012
Grant, Duncan 1885–1978, *Flowers Against Chintz*, purchased from the Leicester Galleries, 1957, © estate of Duncan Grant. All rights reserved, DACS 2012, photo credit: ACC
Grant, Keith b.1930, *Skroven from Svolvær*, purchased from Browse and Darby, 1979, © the artist
Grassie, Andrew b.1966, *Edward Airforce Base 1, 2, 3*, purchased from Mobile Home, 2000, © courtesy of the artist
Grayson, Roy b.1936, *The Blind Poet in Pursuit of the Muse of Fashion*, purchased from the artist, 1984
Greaves, Derrick b.1927, *Dog*, purchased from the Beaux Arts Gallery, 1955, © the artist, photo credit: ACC
Greaves, Derrick b.1927, *A Pair of Green Shoes*, purchased from the artist, 1967, © the artist
Greaves, Derrick b.1927, *Three Leaves (Second Day of Spring)*, purchased from the artist, 1967, © the artist
Greaves, Derrick b.1927, *Chimney and Iris*, purchased from Monika Kinley, 1969, © the artist
Green, Alan 1932–2003, *Sugar Ice*, purchased from the artist, 1968, © the artist's estate
Green, Alan 1932–2003, *Exit*, purchased from Annely Juda Fine Art, 1975, © the artist's estate
Green, Alan 1932–2003, *Red over Crimson*, purchased from Annely Juda Fine Art, 1981, © the artist's estate
Green, Anthony b.1939, *Mary in Her Bra and Corset*, purchased from the Rowan Gallery, 1966, © Anthony Green RA

Green, Anthony b.1939, *Victory in Europe/The Greens 1945*, purchased from the Rowan Gallery, 1981, © Anthony Green RA
Green, Paul Henry b.1951, *Graig Yr Hesg*, purchased from the artist, 1988, © the artist
Greenham, Peter 1909–1992, *Study*, purchased from the artist, 1981, © the artist's estate/ Bridgeman Art Library
Greenwood, John b.1959, *Enjoy Yourself*, gift from Charles Saatchi, 1999
Greenwood, John b.1959, *How Many Doughnuts Have You Collected?*, gift from Charles Saatchi, 1999
Groom, Jon b.1953, *Untitled II*, purchased from the Nicola Jacobs Gallery, 1980, © DACS 2012
Groom, Jon b.1953, *Clay*, purchased from the Nicola Jacobs Gallery, 1982, © DACS 2012
Gross, Anthony 1905–1984, *Yellow Valley*, purchased from the Leicester Galleries, 1957, © Anthony Gross, RA, CBE – painter/etcher
Gross, Anthony 1905–1984, *Saplings*, purchased from the Leicester Galleries, 1962, © Anthony Gross, RA, CBE – painter/etcher, photo credit: ACC
Gross, Anthony 1905–1984, *Landscape with Stones*, purchased from the artist, 1966, © Anthony Gross, RA, CBE – painter/etcher
Guerrier, Barrero *Untitled (Still Life: Lamp, Jug of Thistles)*, bequeathed by Miss Enid Morse, 1962
Gwynne-Jones, Allan 1892–1982, *Roses*, purchased from the artist, 1942, © the artist's estate/ Bridgeman Art Library
Haig, George Douglas 1918–2009, *Red-Haired Nude*, purchased from The Redfern Gallery, 1955, © the artist's estate
Hall, Clifford 1904–1973, *The Girl with a Cat*, purchased from the artist, 1970
Hall, Colin b.1952, *Man on a Couch*, purchased from the Ikon Gallery, Birmingham, 1980 © the artist
Hall, Colin b.1952, *Sunbather*, purchased from the Ikon Gallery, Birmingham © the artist
Halliday, Trevor b.1939, *Tardibigge*, purchased from Nigel Greenwood, 1971
Hambling, Maggi b.1945, *Frances Rose (3)*, purchased from the artist, 1977, © the artist/Bridgeman Art Library
Hambling, Maggi b.1945, *Frances Rose (4)*, purchased from the artist, 1977, © the artist/Bridgeman Art Library
Hambling, Maggi b.1945, *Lett, Evening*, purchased from the artist, 1979, © the artist/Bridgeman Art Library
Hamilton, Richard 1922–2011, *Hugh Gaitskell as a Famous Monster of Filmland*, purchased from the Hanover Gallery, 1964, © estate of Richard Hamilton 2012. All rights reserved DACS
Hampson, Derek b.1952, *From Cairo to the Gulf of Mexico*, purchased from the artist, 1985, © the artist
Hampson, Derek b.1952, *Liverpool '64*, purchased from the artist, 1985, © the artist
Harding, Alexis b.1973, *Untitled (study)*, purchased from Martin Maloney, 1996, © the artist
Harris, Jane b.1937, *Sea*, purchased from the New Art Centre, 1963
Harris, Jane b.1956, *Aureole*, purchased from Anderson O'Day Fine Art, 1995, © the artist
Harris, Jeffrey b.1932, *Black, Grey and White*, purchased from the artist, 1960, © the artist
Harrison, Jon b.1961, *Hors-d'oeuvre*, purchased from the artist, 1987
Harrison, Margaret b.1940, *Women of the World Unite, You have Nothing to Lose but Cheese Cake*, gift from the artist, 2008, © the artist
Harrison, Margaret b.1940, *Rape*, purchased from the artist, 1978, © the artist
Harvey, William b.1957, *Mirror*, purchased from the artist, 1988
Haselden, Ron b.1944, *Mexican Desert*, purchased from the artist, 1980, © the artist
Haselden, Ron b.1944, *Plant*, purchased from the artist, 1980, © the artist
Haselden, Ron b.1944, *Red Engine*, purchased from the artist, 1980, © the artist
Hatt, Christine b.1954, *Painting No.5iii*, purchased from the artist, 1983, © the artist
Hatt, Christine b.1954, *Painting No.6iii*, purchased from the artist, 1983, © the artist, photo credit: ACC
Haugas, Maret *Dark Landscape*, purchased from the artist, 1960
Haughton, David 1924–1991, *Yellow Grid*, purchased from the artist, 1975
Haughton, David 1924–1991, *Rooftops St Just*, purchased from the artist, 1984
Hayes, Colin Graham Frederick 1919–2003, *Oxford Roofs, January 1947*, purchased, 1949, © the artist's estate
Hayman, Patrick 1915 1988, *King Lear and Cordelia*, purchased from the Grosvenor Gallery, 1962, © Patrick Hayman. All rights reserved, DACS 2012
Hayman, Patrick 1915–1988, *The Fall of Byzantium*, purchased from the artist, 1968, © Patrick Hayman. All rights reserved, DACS 2012
Hayman, Patrick 1915–1988, *Night-Sea Crossing*, purchased from the artist, 1968, © Patrick Hayman. All rights reserved, DACS 2012
Hayman, Patrick 1915–1988, *Lady with a Friend on Wheels*, purchased from the artist, 1985, © Patrick Hayman. All rights reserved, DACS 2012
Hays, Dan b.1966, *Guinea Pig*, purchased from Studio and Education Access, 1995, © the artist
Hays, Dan b.1966, *Guinea Pig*, purchased from Studio and Education Access, 1995, © the artist
Hays, Dan b.1966, *Guinea Pig*, purchased from Studio and Education Access, 1995, © the artist
Hays, Dan b.1966, *Guinea Pig*, purchased from Studio and Education Access, 1995, © the artist
Hays, Dan b.1966, *Guinea Pig*, gift from the artist, 1995, © the artist
Hayter, Stanley William 1901–1988, *Island Labyrinth*, purchased from the London Group, 1956, © ADAGP, Paris and DACS, London 2012
Heath, Adrian 1920–1992, *Curved Form, Black and White*, purchased from The Redfern Gallery, 1955, © the estate of Adrian Heath
Heath, Adrian 1920–1992, *Composition, Black and Grey*, purchased from the Hanover Gallery, 1959, © the estate of Adrian Heath
Heath, Adrian 1920–1992, *Debdou*, purchased from The Redfern Gallery, 1966, © the estate of Adrian Heath
Heath, Claude b.1964, *Tender Ground No.1*, gift from Charles Saatchi, 1999, © the artist
Heath, Claude b.1964, *Tender Ground No.2*, gift from Charles Saatchi, 1999, © the artist
Heath, Claude b.1964, *Tender Ground No.3*, gift from Charles Saatchi, 1999, © the artist
Heath, Claude b.1964, *Tender Ground No.4*, gift from Charles Saatchi, 1999, © the artist
Heindorff, Michael b.1949, *I.1*, purchased from the Bernard Jacobson Gallery, 1978, © the artist
Hempton, Paul b.1946, *Marker V – Hill, Rod and Stone*, purchased from the Ikon Gallery, Birmingham, 1979, © the artist
Hemsworth, Gerard b.1945, *Scenario*, purchase award, 1981, © the artist
Hemsworth, Gerard b.1945, *Table Manners*, purchased from the Anthony Reynolds Gallery, 1984, © the artist
Hemsworth, Gerard b.1945, *Kiss My Arse*, purchased from the Anthony Reynolds Gallery, 1995, © the artist
Henderson, William b.1941, *Gjalla*, purchased from the Ian Birkstead Gallery, 1979, © the artist
Henri, Adrian 1932–2000, *Edge of a Wood, Early Summer*, purchased from the artist, 1978, © the artist's estate
Hepher, David b.1935, *Arrangement in Turquoise and Cream*, purchased from the Angela Flowers Gallery, 1981, © the artist/ courtesy Flowers Gallery, London
Hepher, David b.1935, *Study for 'Arrangement in Turquoise and Cream'*, purchased from the Angela Flowers Gallery, 1981, © the artist/ courtesy Flowers Gallery, London
Hepworth, Barbara 1903–1975, *Reconstruction*, purchased, 1947, © Bowness, Hepworth estate
Hepworth, Barbara 1903–1975, *Two Girls with Teacups*, purchased from the Lefevre Gallery, 1950, © Bowness, Hepworth estate
Herman, Josef 1911–2000, *The Welsh Miner*, purchased, 1949, © estate of Josef Herman. All rights reserved, DACS 2012
Heron, Patrick 1920–1999, *The Round Table: 1950*, purchased from The Redfern Gallery, 1950, © Susanna Heron. All rights reserved, DACS 2012, photo credit: Glynn Vivian Art Gallery, Swansea
Heron, Patrick 1920–1999, *Ultramarine, Cinnamon and Dull Yellow: August 1960*, purchased from the Waddington Galleries, 1960, © Susanna Heron. All rights reserved, DACS 2012
Heron, Patrick 1920–1999, *Green Painting with White Disc: 1964*, purchased from the Waddington Galleries, 1964, © Susanna Heron. All rights reserved, DACS 2012, photo credit: ACC
Hetherington, Iain b.1978, *Composite Picture 3 (Diversified Cultural Worker)*, purchased from the Mary Mary Gallery, Glasgow, 2009, © the artist, photo credit: ACC
Hetherington, Iain b.1978, *Diversified Cultural Worker 3*, purchased from the Mary Mary Gallery, Glasgow, 2009, © the artist, photo credit: ACC
Hetherington, Iain b.1978, *Diversified Cultural Worker 4*, purchased from the Mary Mary Gallery, Glasgow, 2009, © the artist, photo credit: ACC
Hill, Anthony b.1930, *Parity Study No.2 First Version*, purchased from the artist, 1976, © Anthony Hill.
All rights reserved, DACS 2012
Hill, Derek 1916–2000, *Mrs Aubrey Waterfield*, purchased from the Leicester Galleries, 1950, © the artist's estate
Hill, Derek 1916–2000, *Corbignano*, purchased from the Leicester Galleries, 1951, © the artist's estate
Hill, Derek 1916–2000, *Cliff Face, Tory Island*, purchased from the artist, 1958, © the artist's estate, photo credit: ACC
Hilton, Roger 1911–1975, *February – March 1954*, purchased from the artist, 1958, © estate of Roger Hilton. All rights reserved, DACS 2012
Hilton, Roger 1911–1975, *Dark Continent*, purchased from the Waddington Galleries, 1960, © estate of Roger Hilton. All rights reserved, DACS 2012
Hilton, Roger 1911–1975, *January 1964, Red*, purchased from Lilian Somerville, 1974, © estate of Roger Hilton. All rights reserved, DACS 2012
Hilton, Roger 1911–1975, *Shell*, purchased from the Arnolfini Gallery, Bristol, 1968, © estate of Roger Hilton. All rights reserved, DACS 2012, photo credit: ACC
Hilton, Roger 1911–1975, *Untitled*, purchased from Monika Kinley, 1977, © estate of Roger Hilton. All rights reserved, DACS 2012
Hirst, Derek 1930–2006, *Perdido*, purchased from Arthur Tooth & Sons Ltd, 1962, © the artist's estate/ courtesy Flowers Gallery, London
Hirst, Derek 1930–2006, *Second Visit: Second Variation*, purchased from the Angela Flowers Gallery, 1980, © the artist's estate/ courtesy Flowers Gallery, London
Hirst, Derek 1930–2006, *Odeon: Red/Blue*, purchased from the Angela Flowers Gallery, 1974, © the artist's estate/ courtesy Flowers Gallery, London
Hitchens, Ivon 1893–1979, *Flowers*, purchased from the artist, 1942, © Ivon Hitchens' estate/ Jonathan Clark & Co.
Hitchens, Ivon 1893–1979, *Lilies and Purple Poppy*, purchased from the Leicester Galleries, 1949, © Ivon Hitchens' estate/Jonathan Clark & Co.
Hitchens, Ivon 1893–1979, *Garden Cove*, purchased from The Redfern Gallery, 1948–1950, © Ivon Hitchens' estate/Jonathan Clark & Co.
Hockney, David b.1937, *We Two Boys Together Clinging*, purchased from the artist, 1961, © David Hockney, photo credit: John Webb
Hockney, David b.1937, *Portrait Surrounded by Artistic Devices*, purchased from the Kasmin Gallery, 1966, © David Hockney, photo credit: Richard Schmidt
Hockney, David b.1937, *Sur la terrace*, purchased from the artist, 1972, © David Hockney
Hodgkin, Howard b.1932, *Luxembourg Gardens*, purchased from Arthur Tooth & Sons Ltd, 1963, © Howard Hodgkin
Hodgkin, Howard b.1932, *Widcombe Crescent*, purchased from the artist, 1967, © Howard Hodgkin, photo credit: ACC
Hodgkin, Howard b.1932, *Mrs K*, purchased from the artist, 1967, © Howard Hodgkin
Hodgkin, Howard b.1932, *Foy Nissen's Bombay*, purchased from the Kasmin Gallery, 1977, © Howard Hodgkin

Hodgson, Clive b.1953, *Angela Asleep*, purchased from the artist, 1982, © the artist
Hodgson, Clive b.1953, *Intimate Scene*, purchased from the artist, 1982, © the artist
Hodgson, Clive b.1953, *A Little Conversation*, purchased from the artist, 1987, © the artist
Hodgson, Clive b.1953, *Blossom and blue sky*, purchased from the artist, 1987, © the artist
Hodgson, Clive b.1953, *People and Water*, purchased from the artist, 1987, © the artist
Holden, Cliff b.1919, *Seated Figure*, purchased from the R. I. Galleries, 1966, © the artist
Hopkins, Clyde D. F. b.1946, *Untitled/Sturm*, purchased from the artist, 1980, © the artist
Hopkins, Louise b.1965, *Aurora 13*, gift from Charles Saatchi, 1999, © the artist
Horsfield, Nicholas 1917–2005, *Le Pollet Noir, Dieppe*, purchased from the Walker Art Gallery, 1959, © the artist's estate
Horsfield, Nicholas 1917–2005, *Vétheuil Street Scene*, purchased from the artist, 1962, © the artist's estate
Horsfield, Nicholas 1917–2005, *'River Epte' (Oil)*, purchased from the Liverpool Academy of Arts, 1978, © the artist's estate, photo credit: ACC
Horsfield, Nicholas 1917–2005, *'River Epte' (2) (Oil)*, purchased from the Liverpool Academy of Arts, 1978, © the artist's estate
Horsley, Michael Leonard b.1941, *Untitled 77–78*, purchased from the New Art Centre, 1980, © the artist
Hosking, Knighton Stephen b.1944, *Earth Band*, purchased from Monika Kinley, 1975, © the artist
House, Gordon 1932–2004, *Double Green Dropped Initial*, purchased from the artist, 1973, © the artist's estate
Howard, Ian b.1952, *Summa Theologiae*, purchased from the Third Eye Centre, 1988 © the artist
Howlin, John b.1941, *Brandenburg*, purchased from the artist, 1970
Hoyland, Francis b.1930, *Crucifixion*, purchased from the Beaux Arts Gallery, 1962, © the artist
Hoyland, John 1934–2011, *19.12.66*, purchased from the artist, 1967, © estate of John Hoyland. All rights reserved, DACS 2012
Hoyland, John 1934–2011, *20.5.68*, purchased from the Waddington Galleries, 1969, © estate of John Hoyland. All rights reserved, DACS 2012
Hoyland, John 1934–2011, *Red Over Yellow, 18.9.73*, purchased from the artist, 1974, © estate of John Hoyland. All rights reserved, DACS 2012
Hoyland, John 1934–2011, *Wotan*, purchased from the Waddington and Tooth Gallery, 1977, © estate of John Hoyland. All rights reserved, DACS 2012
Hoyland, John 1934–2011, *Untitled Drawing (Blue)*, purchase award, 1980, © estate of John Hoyland. All rights reserved, DACS 2012
Hoyland, John 1934–2011, *Untitled Drawing (Yellow)*, purchase award, 1980, © estate of John Hoyland. All rights reserved, DACS 2012
Hubbard, John b.1931, *Wood with Filtered Light*, purchased from the New Art Centre, 1965, © the artist
Hubbard, John b.1931, *In the High Atlas*, purchased from the New Art Centre, 1970, © the artist
Hubbard, John b.1931, *Quarry*, purchased from the New Art Centre, 1976, © the artist, photo credit: ACC
Hughes, Malcolm Edward 1920–1997, *Three Unit Relief/ Painting*, purchased from the artist, 1976, © the artist's estate
Hughes, Patrick 1939–2004, *The Differentiation of Nothing*, purchased from the Portal Gallery, 1962, © the artist/ courtesy Flowers Gallery, London
Hughes, Patrick 1939–2004, *The Revolting Bottle*, purchased from the Hanover Gallery, 1966, © the artist/ courtesy Flowers Gallery, London
Hughes, Patrick 1939–2004, *Next Door*, purchased from the Angela Flowers Gallery, 1971, © the artist/ courtesy Flowers Gallery, London
Hughes, Patrick 1939–2004, *Leaning on a Landscape*, purchased from the Angela Flowers Gallery, 1978, © the artist/ courtesy Flowers Gallery, London
Hugonin, James b.1950, *White Drawing, Light Grey Intervals V*, purchased from the artist, 1978, © the artist
Hugonin, James b.1950, *White Drawing, Light Grey Intervals VIII*, purchased from the artist, 1978, © the artist
Hugonin, James b.1950, *Untitled*, purchased from the artist, 1989, © the artist
Hulbert, Thelma 1913–1995, *The Cellar, Ischia*, purchased from the Leicester Galleries, 1958
Hulbert, Thelma 1913–1995, *The Studio I*, purchased from the artist, 1970
Hulbert, Thelma 1913–1995, *Rocks under Water*, purchased from the artist, 1970
Hume, Gary b.1962, *Moonbeam Rising*, purchased from the artist, 1994, © the artist, courtesy White Cube
Hume, Gary b.1962, *Four Feet in the Garden*, purchased from White Cube, 1995, © the artist, courtesy White Cube
Huxley, Paul b.1938, *Drawing Related to 'Untitled No.28' (1963)*, purchased from the Rowan Gallery, 1972, © Paul Huxley
Huxley, Paul b.1938, *Untitled No.32*, purchased from the Rowan Gallery, 1965, © Paul Huxley
Huxley, Paul b.1938, *Untitled No.57*, purchased from the Rowan Gallery, 1969, © Paul Huxley
Huxley, Paul b.1938, *Untitled No.146*, purchased from the Rowan Gallery, 1974, © Paul Huxley
Huxley, Paul b.1938, *Neither Dead nor Alive*, purchased from the Rowan Gallery, 1978, © Paul Huxley
Huxley, Paul b.1938, *Herald*, purchased from the Juda Rowan Gallery, 1983, © Paul Huxley
Hyman, Timothy b.1946, *Judith in Hospital*, purchased from the artist, 1988, © the artist
Hyman, Timothy b.1946, *Reading on the Bus*, purchased from the artist, 1988, © the artist
Ingham, Bryan 1936–1997, *Table Top*, purchased from the Lords Gallery, 1964
Ingham, Gillian b.1951, *Grey Spirit*, purchased from the artist, 1979
Inlander, Henry 1925–1983, *Italian Landscape*, purchased from the artist, 1955, © the artist's estate
Inlander, Henry 1925–1983, *Eucalyptus 3*, purchased from the Leicester Galleries, 1956, © the artist's estate
Inlander, Henry 1925–1983, *Water Reflection*, purchased from the Leicester Galleries, 1961, © the artist's estate
Inlander, Henry 1925–1983, *Orang-Outang II*, purchased from the artist, 1967, © the artist's estate
Inlander, Henry 1925–1983, *Open Window (Mirror Image)*, purchased from Roland, Browse and Delbanco, 1969, © the artist's estate
Inlander, Henry 1925–1983, *Night Landscape*, purchased from the artist, 1978, © the artist's estate
Innes, Callum b.1962, *Two Identified Forms*, purchased from the Frith Street Gallery, 1992, © the artist
Inshaw, David b.1943, *Window*, purchased from the artist, 1970, © the artist/Bridgeman Art Library
Irvin, Albert b.1922, *Evening*, purchased from the New Art Centre, 1961, © Albert Irvin. All rights reserved, DACS 2012
Irvin, Albert b.1922, *Musbury*, purchased from the New Art Centre, 1976, © Albert Irvin. All rights reserved, DACS 2012
Irvin, Albert b.1922, *Admiral*, purchase award, 1981, © Albert Irvin. All rights reserved, DACS 2012
Irwin, Gwyther 1931–2008, *Medium Straight*, purchased from the Gimpel Fils Gallery, 1963, © the artist's estate
Jacklin, Bill b.1943, *Erebus*, purchased from Nigel Greenwood, 1972, © the artist
Jacklin, Bill b.1943, *Double Buddha*, purchased from the Hester van Royen Gallery, 1977, © the artist
Jackowski, Andrzej b.1947, *The Tower of Copernicus*, purchased from the artist, 1981, © the artist
Jackowski, Andrzej b.1947, *Settlement*, purchased from Marlborough Fine Art, 1986, © the artist, photo credit: ACC
Jamieson, Robert Kirkland 1881–1950, *London Garden*, purchased from the artist, 1942, photo credit: ACC
Jantjes, Gavin b.1948, *Untitled*, purchased from the Edward Totah Gallery, 1991, © the artist, photo credit: ACC
Jaray, Tess b.1937, *St Stephen's Way*, purchased from the Hamilton Gallery, 1965, © the artist, photo credit: ACC
Jaray, Tess b.1937, *Mistral*, purchased from the Axiom Gallery, 1969, © the artist
Jaray, Tess b.1937, *Follies*, purchased from the artist, 1978, © the artist
Jaray, Tess b.1937, *Always Now*, purchased from the artist, 1982, © the artist
Jardine, George Wallace 1920–2002, *The Coming of Spring*, purchased from the artist, 1979, © the artist's estate
Jarman, Derek 1942–1994, *Landscape with a Blue Pool*, purchased from the Camden Arts Centre, 1968, © the estate of Derek Jarman
Jarman, Derek 1942–1994, *Morphine*, purchased from Karsten Schubert, 1993, © the estate of Derek Jarman
Jeffs, Roger b.1942, *Vittis*, purchased from the Young Contemporaries exhibition, 1963, © the artist
Joffe, Chantal b.1969, *Untitled (No.1)*, gift from Charles Saatchi, 1999, © the artist, photo credit: ACC
Joffe, Chantal b.1969, *Untitled (No.2)*, gift from Charles Saatchi, 1999, © the artist, photo credit: ACC
Joffe, Chantal b.1969, *Untitled (No.3)*, gift from Charles Saatchi, 1999, © the artist, photo credit: ACC
Joffe, Chantal b.1969, *Untitled (No.4)*, gift from Charles Saatchi, 1999, © the artist, photo credit: ACC
Joffe, Chantal b.1969, *Untitled (No.5)*, gift from Charles Saatchi, 1999, © the artist, photo credit: ACC
Joffe, Chantal b.1969, *Untitled (No.6)*, gift from Charles Saatchi, 1999, © the artist, photo credit: ACC
John, Gwen 1876–1939, *Bust of a Girl with a Bow Before a Pink Background*, purchased from the Matthiesen Gallery, 1957
Johnstone, John 1937–2001, *Entering an Innocent Room*, purchased from the Mercury Gallery, 1970
Jones, Allen b.1937, *Reflected Man*, purchased from Arthur Tooth & Sons Ltd, 1964, © Allen Jones, photo credit: ACC
Jones, Lucy b.1955, *Admiralty Arch*, purchased from the artist, 1986, © the artist
Jones, Wynn b.1939, *Getting Ready*, purchased from the House Gallery, 1978
Jones, Zebedee b.1970, *Blue/Green*, purchased from the artist, 1994, © the artist
Jonzen, Basil 1913–1967, *Still Life (Dead Birds and Lemons)*, purchased from the artist, 1942
Joseph, Peter b.1929, *Untitled*, purchased from the Camden Borough Survey exhibition, 1967, © the artist, photo credit: ACC
Joseph, Peter b.1929, *Yellow Painting*, purchased from the Lisson Gallery, 1969, © the artist
Joseph, Peter b.1929, *Drawing 1971 (Untitled, Blue/Green)*, purchased from the Lisson Gallery, 1971, © the artist
Joseph, Peter b.1929, *Drawing 1971 (Untitled, Cream/Black)*, purchased from the Lisson Gallery, 1971, © the artist
Joseph, Peter b.1929, *Dark Ochre with Black Border*, purchased from the artist, 1973, © the artist
Joseph, Peter b.1929, *Brown Colour with Grey/Black Border*, purchased from the Lisson Gallery, 1981, © the artist
Joseph, Peter b.1929, *Bright Orange with Green*, purchased from the Lisson Gallery, 1993, © the artist
Joseph, Tam b.1947, *Monkey dey Chop, Baboon dey Cry*, purchased from the artist, 1988, © the artist
Joseph, Tam b.1947, *Learning to Walk*, purchased from the artist, 1988, © the artist
Joy, Clair b.1958, *Untitled*, purchased from Interim Art, 1987, © the artist
Kalkhof, Peter b.1933, *Centrepoint Colour and Space Series*, purchased from the artist, 1976, © the artist
Kent, Sarah b.1941, *Orthian 1*, purchased from the Camden Borough Survey exhibition, 1967
Kerma, Ingrid b.1942, *Brutum fulmen*, purchased from the artist, 1976, © the artist
Kerma, Ingrid b.1942, *The Fugitives*, purchased from the artist, 1984, © the artist
Kerr, Bernadette b.1958, *Red Curtain*, purchased from the Winchester Gallery, 1988
Kestelman, Morris 1905–1998, *Still Life with Vegetables*, purchased from the Upper Grosvenor Galleries, 1961, © by permission of Sara Kestleman

Kevill Davies, Benita b.1954, *Two Bushes*, purchased from the artist, 1987 © the artist
Key, Joan b.1948, *BOO (II)*, purchased from the Richard Salmon Gallery, 1996
Khanna, Balraj b.1940, *Splash*, purchased from the artist, 1978, © the artist
Khanna, Balraj b.1940, *Coming from Rajasthan*, purchased from the artist, 1989, © the artist
Khanna, Balraj b.1940, *Apple Green* (detail), purchased from the artist, 1991, © the artist
Kidd, Richard 1952–2008, *Soul Patter*, purchased from the artist, 1976, © the artist's estate
Kidner, Michael 1917–2009, *Mars, Violet and White*, purchased from the Grabowski Gallery, 1962, © the artist's estate/ courtesy Flowers Gallery, London
Kidner, Michael 1917–2009, *Orange, Blue, Pink and Green No.2*, purchased from the Axiom Gallery, 1967, © the artist's estate/ courtesy Flowers Gallery, London
Kidner, Michael 1917–2009, *Yellow, Violet, Light Red and Blue*, purchased from the artist, 1968, © the artist's estate/ courtesy Flowers Gallery, London
Kidner, Michael 1917–2009, *Red, Green, Violet and White*, purchased from the artist, 1968, © the artist's estate/ courtesy Flowers Gallery, London
Kidner, Michael 1917–2009, *Analysis of a Wave Pattern*, purchased from the artist, 1976, © the artist's estate/ courtesy Flowers Gallery, London
Kidner, Michael 1917–2009, *Mosquito Larvae II*, purchased from Flowers East, 2003, © the artist's estate/ courtesy Flowers Gallery, London
Kiff, Ken 1935–2001, *Man Greeting Woman*, purchased from the artist, 1969, © the artist's estate
Kiff, Ken 1935–2001, *Echo and Narcissus, Sequence 81*, purchased from the Nicola Jacobs Gallery, 1984, © the artist's estate
Kiff, Ken 1935–2001, *Portrait from Memory*, purchased from the Nicola Jacobs Gallery, 1986, © the artist's estate
Kilbourn, Oliver 1904–1993, *Changing the Chummin, Giving the Final Twist before Rounding the Turn*, purchased from the Midland Group, 1977, © the artist's estate
Kilbourn, Oliver 1904–1993, *Shoving the Chummin in by Hand and Changing the Points*, purchased from the Midland Group, 1977, © the artist's estate
Kilbourn, Oliver 1904–1993, *Shoving the Chummin in from Behind after Rounding the Turn*, purchased from the Midland Group, 1977, © the artist's estate
Kinley, Peter 1926–1988, *Seascape*, purchased from the Gimpel Fils Gallery, 1954, © the artist's estate
Kinley, Peter 1926–1988, *Standing Figure No.1*, purchased from the Gimpel Fils Gallery, 1957, © the artist's estate
Kinley, Peter 1926–1988, *Interior*, purchased from the artist, 1967, © the artist's estate
Kinley, Peter 1926–1988, *Still Life*, purchased from the artist, 1967, © the artist's estate
Kinley, Peter 1926–1988, *Aeroplane*, purchased from Anthony Stokes, 1983, © the artist's estate
Kinley, Peter 1926–1988, *Red Monkey*, purchase award, 1980, © the artist's estate
Kirk, Eve 1900–1969, *Demolition near St Paul's*, purchased from the artist, 1942
Kitaj, R. B. 1932–2007, *Screenplay*, purchased from Marlborough Fine Art, 1967, © the estate of R. B. Kitaj
Kite, Roger b.1947, *Diagonal I*, purchased from the Acme Gallery, 1977, © the artist
Knox, Jack b.1936, *Oysters in a Basket*, purchased from the Royal Scottish Academy, Edinburgh, 1979, © the artist
Koenig, Robert b.1951, *Rustic Umbrellas*, purchased from Tolly Cobbold Eastern Arts 4th National Exhibition, 1983, © the artist
Kondracki, Henry b.1953, *Gifts*, purchased from the artist, 1986, © the artist
Koppel, Heinz 1919–1980, *Head*, purchased from the Beaux Arts Gallery, 1958, © the artist's estate
Kossoff, Leon b.1926, *Building Site, Victoria Street*, purchased from the Beaux Arts Gallery, 1962, © the artist, photo credit: ACC
Kossoff, Leon b.1926, *Seated Nude*, purchased from the artist, 1966, © the artist, photo credit: ACC
Kossoff, Leon b.1926, *York Way Railway Bridge from Caledonian Road, Stormy Day*, purchased from Marlborough Fine Art, 1967, © the artist
Kossoff, Leon b.1926, *Children's Swimming Pool, Autumn 1972*, purchased from Fischer Fine Art, 1978, © the artist, photo credit: ACC
Kossoff, Leon b.1926, *George Thompson*, purchased from Fischer Fine Art, 1976, © the artist, photo credit: ACC
Lake, John Gascoyne 1903–1975, *Feeding Birds*, purchased from the Mayor Gallery, 1963
Lalić, Maria b.1952, *Lead Fall – Chrome Yellow*, purchased from the Todd Gallery, 1991
Lamb, Henry 1883–1960, *Manon*, purchased, 1947, © estate of Henry Lamb
Lamb, Lynton Harold 1907–1977, *Sandon Place*, purchased, 1950, © the artist's estate
Lancaster, Mark b.1938, *First Spread*, purchased from the Whitechapel Art Gallery, 1966, © the artist
Lancaster, Mark b.1938, *Cambridge Violet*, purchased from the Rowan Gallery, 1969, © the artist
Lancaster, Mark b.1938, *Henry VI Black and White*, purchased from the Rowan Gallery, 1974, © the artist
Lanyon, Peter 1918–1964, *Bicyclist in Penwith*, purchased from the Gimpel Fils Gallery, 1952, © Sheila Lanyon. All Rights Reserved, DACS 2012
Lanyon, Peter 1918–1964, *Moor Cliffe, Kynance*, purchased from the Gimpel Fils Gallery, 1954, © Sheila Lanyon. All Rights Reserved, DACS 2012
Lanyon, Peter 1918–1964, *Soaring Flight*, purchased from the Gimpel Fils Gallery, 1960, © Sheila Lanyon. All Rights Reserved, DACS 2012
Lanyon, Peter 1918–1964, *Mexico*, gift from Mrs Sheila Lanyon, 1969, © Sheila Lanyon. All Rights Reserved, DACS 2012
Law, Bob 1934–2004, *Bordeaux Black Blue Black*, purchased from the Lisson Gallery, 1979, © the artist's estate
Law, Bob 1934–2004, *Red, White + Blue Castle CCLIX PZ 22.01.99*, purchased from the Marlene Eleini Gallery, 1999, © the artist's estate
Lawson, Sonia b.1934, *Exercising Dogs on Watling Street*, purchased from the Royal Academy of Arts Summer Exhibition, 1980, © the artist
Lawson, Thomas b.1951, *Christminster*, purchased from the Anthony Reynolds Gallery, 1991
Lawtey, Brian b.1945, *Summation Series sy.B.Op. III (A.I.B + Y = O) Set 1.0.*, purchased from the Quay Art Centre, Newport, Isle of Wight, 1983, © the artist
Le Bas, Edward 1904–1966, *Girl with Violin*, purchased from the artist, 1942
Le Bas, Edward 1904–1966, *Angelica Garnett (b.1918)*, purchased from the artist, 1951
le Brocquy, Louis b.1916, *Head*, purchased from the Gimpel Fils Gallery, 1959, © the artist
Le Brun, Christopher b.1951, *Painting on a Red Ground*, purchased from Nigel Greenwood, 1980, © the artist/Bridgeman Art Library
Le Brun, Christopher b.1951, *Painting on a Dark Ground*, purchased from Nigel Greenwood, 1980, © the artist/Bridgeman Art Library
Leapman, David b.1959, *Past Behaviour*, purchased from the Todd Gallery, 1990, © the artist
Leapman, David b.1959, *Pilot Schemer*, gift from Charles Saatchi, 1999, © the artist, photo credit: ACC
Leapman, David b.1959, *Slowburn Escort*, gift from Charles Saatchi, 1999, © the artist, photo credit: ACC
Leapman, Edwina b.1931, *Untitled '77 No.6*, purchased from Annely Juda Fine Art, 1977, © the artist
Leapman, Edwina b.1931, *Untitled No.5*, purchase award, 1980, © the artist
Leapman, Edwina b.1931, *Tall, Very Dark Blue*, purchased from Annely Juda Fine Art, 1991, © the artist
Lee, Dick 1923–2001, *Summer*, purchased from Sarn, 1958, © the artist's estate
Lee, Dick 1923–2001, *Laetitia*, purchased from the artist, 1965, © the artist's estate
Lee, Terry b.1932, *The Spider's Debris*, purchased from the New Art Centre, 1963, © the artist
Lessore, Helen 1907–1994, *Self Portrait II*, purchased from the artist, 1968, © the artist's estate
Lessore, John b.1939, *La Gardie*, purchased from the Beaux Arts Gallery, 1965, © the artist
Lessore, John b.1939, *Writing a Letter*, purchased from the artist, 1967, © the artist
Lessore, John b.1939, *The Articulation of the Knee*, purchased from Stoppenbach & Delestre, 1987, © the artist
Leverett, David b.1938, *Centre Point Shift*, purchased from The Redfern Gallery, 1970, © the artist
Levine, Paula b.1948, *The Artist's Studio*, purchased from the artist, 1978
Lewis, Greg b.1950, *'Red Dress'*, purchased from the artist, 1977
Lewis, Kit 1911–1998, *Amphytrion*, purchased from the London Group Exhibition, 1951
Lewis, Wyndham 1882–1957, *Inca with Birds*, purchased from the Leicester Galleries, 1959, © by kind permission of the Wyndham Lewis Memorial Trust
Lewty, Simon b.1941, *The Return*, purchased from the Ikon Gallery, Birmingham, 1984, © the artist
Lin, Richard b.1933, *Painting Relief 1961*, purchased from the Gimpel Fils Gallery, 1964, © the artist
Lin, Richard b.1933, *Painting Relief 1965*, purchased from Marlborough Fine Art, 1967, © the artist
Linke, Simon b.1958, *Untitled*, purchased from the Lisson Gallery, 1994, © the artist
Linke, Simon b.1958, *Lost*, purchased from the Lisson Gallery, 1997, © the artist
Linley, David b.1954, *Tree/Dark Rain/Red Pool*, purchased from the artist, 1987
Lloyd, Pamela b.1932, *Pigeon Lofts, Whitby*, purchased from the London Group, 1956
Lloyd-Jones, Peter 1940–2001, *Laughter (9 conditions)*, purchased from the artist, 1980, © the artist's estate
Lloyd-Jones, Peter 1940–2001, *Laughter (9 conditions)*, purchased from the artist, 1980, © the artist's estate
Lloyd-Jones, Peter 1940–2001, *Laughter (9 conditions)*, purchased from the artist, 1980, © the artist's estate
Lloyd-Jones, Peter 1940–2001, *Laughter (9 conditions)*, purchased from the artist, 1980, © the artist's estate
Lloyd-Jones, Peter 1940–2001, *Laughter (9 conditions)*, purchased from the artist, 1980, © the artist's estate
Lloyd-Jones, Peter 1940–2001, *Laughter (9 conditions)*, purchased from the artist, 1980, © the artist's estate
Lloyd-Jones, Peter 1940–2001, *Laughter (9 conditions)*, purchased from the artist, 1980, © the artist's estate
Lloyd-Jones, Peter 1940–2001, *Laughter (9 conditions)*, purchased from the artist, 1980, © the artist's estate
Lloyd-Jones, Peter 1940–2001, *Laughter (9 conditions)*, purchased from the artist, 1980, © the artist's estate
Lochore, Brad b.1960, *Shadow No.52*, gift from Charles Saatchi, 1999, © the artist, photo credit: ACC
Loker, John b.1938, *Dorset Horizon I Series 2*, purchased from the Angela Flowers Gallery, 1973, © the artist/ courtesy Flowers Gallery, London
Loker, John b.1938, *Dorset Horizon II Series 2*, purchased from the Angela Flowers Gallery, 1973, © the artist/ courtesy Flowers Gallery, London
Loker, John b.1938, *Four Extracts II*, purchased from the artist, 1976, © the artist/ courtesy Flowers Gallery, London
Lowndes, Alan 1921–1978, *Stockport*, purchased from the artist, 1967, © the artist's estate, photo credit: ACC
Lowndes, Alan 1921–1978, *Entering the Circus (1)*, purchased from the artist, 1967, © the artist's estate
Lowndes, Alan 1921–1978, *Telling the Tale*, purchased from the artist, 1967, © the artist's estate
Lowndes, Alan 1921–1978, *The Park: Panorama of Stockport*, purchased from the Crane Kalman Gallery, 1965, © the artist's estate
Lowry, Laurence Stephen 1887–1976, *July, the Seaside*, purchased from the artist, 1943, © courtesy of the estate of L. S. Lowry. All rights reserved, DACS 2012, photo credit: ACC
Lowry, Laurence Stephen 1887–1976, *The Park*, purchased from the London Group exhibition, 1951, © courtesy of the estate of L. S. Lowry. All rights reserved, DACS 2012, photo credit: ACC

Lowry, Laurence Stephen 1887–1976, *Woman Riding on a Tractor*, acquired through the Sir William Emrys and Lady Williams Bequest, 1983, © courtesy of the estate of L. S. Lowry. All rights reserved, DACS 2012
Lowry, Laurence Stephen 1887–1976, *Seascape*, purchased from the Lefevre Gallery, 1967, © courtesy of the estate of L. S. Lowry. All rights reserved, DACS 2012, photo credit: ACC
Lydiat, Anne b.1947, *The Craft of Art/The Art of Craft*, purchased from the artist, 1987
Lyon, Robert 1894–1978, *K. F. M. Prescott, Author*, purchased from the artist, 1942, © the artist's estate
Lyons, John C. M. b.1933, *Victim of Papa Bois*, purchased from the artist, 1996, © the artist
Mabbutt, Mary b.1951, *Study for 'Self Portrait with Poussin'*, purchased from The New Grafton Gallery, 1980, © the artist
MacBryde, Robert 1913–1966, *Table in a Red Room*, purchased from The Redfern Gallery, 1950
MacBryde, Robert 1913–1966, *Figure and Still Life*, purchased, 1951
Macdonald, Frances 1914–2002, *Backs of Houses, Keats Grove, Hampstead*, purchased from the artist, 1942
Machin, Geoffrey b.1937, *Untitled*, purchased from the Midland Group Gallery, Nottingham, 1973
Machin, Geoffrey b.1937, *Italic Towers*, purchased from the Midland Group Gallery, Nottingham, 1973
MacKenzie, Alexander 1923–2001, *White Painting*, purchased from the Waddington Galleries, 1961, © the artist's estate
MacKenzie, Alexander 1923–2001, *Granite, Brown, Black on White*, purchased from the Waddington Galleries, 1963, © the artist's estate
MacKinnon, Hugh b.1925, *Girl's Head*, purchased from the Gimpel Fils Gallery, 1954, © the artist
MacTaggart, William 1903–1981, *Winter Sunset, the Red Soil*, purchased from the Royal Scottish Academy, Edinburgh, 1957, © by permission of the artist's family
Madden, Anne b.1932, *Atlantic Suite*, purchased from the New Art Centre, 1978, © the artist
Magill, Elizabeth b.1959, *Without*, purchased from the Anthony Wilkinson Gallery, 2002, © the artist, photo credit: ACC
Mak, Kum-Siew b.1940, *Singapore I*, purchased from the artist, 1969, © the artist
Mak, Kum-Siew b.1940, *Singapore II*, purchased from the artist, 1969, © the artist
Mak, Kum-Siew b.1940, *Buddhist Television I*, purchased from the artist, 1976, © the artist
Makhoul, Bashir b.1963, *Zigzag*, purchased from the Huddersfield Art Gallery, 1994, © the artist
Malinowski, Antoni b.1955, *Not titled*, purchased from the artist, 1990, © the artist
Mann, Sargy b.1937, *River Box, Evening Sun*, purchased from the artist, 1985, © the artist
Mansfield, Andrew b.1953, *Nature morte*, purchased from the Anthony Reynolds Gallery, 1985, © the artist
Mansfield, Andrew b.1953, *Untitled No.130*, purchased from the Anthony Reynolds Gallery, 1996, © the artist
Marks, Gerald b.1921, *Untitled*, purchase award, 1983, © the artist
Martin, Kenneth 1905–1984, *Abstract, Orange and Red*, purchased from the artist, 1958, © the artist's estate
Martin, Kenneth 1905–1984, *Endless Configuration*, purchased from the artist, 1964, © the artist's estate
Martin, Kenneth 1905–1984, *Chance and Order 5 (Red)*, purchased from the Waddington Galleries, 1971, © the artist's estate
Martin, Kenneth 1905–1984, *Chance, Order, Change 2 (Ultramarine Blue)*, purchased from the Waddington and Tooth Galleries, 1976, © the artist's estate
Martin, Michael b.1955, *Young Miner*, purchased from the artist, 1980
Masoero, Jeanne b.1937, *At an Instant*, purchased from the artist, 1972, © the artist
Mason, Robert b.1946, *From Tougourt*, purchased from Monika Kinley, 1978, © the artist
Mason, Robert b.1946, *From the Oulad III*, purchase award, 1980, © the artist
Mason, Robert b.1946, *The Bowl (of Shadows)*, purchased from the Anne Berthoud Gallery, 1985, © the artist
Matthews, Philip 1916–1984, *Landscape, Cookham Dean*, purchased from the Leicester Galleries, 1962
Maughan, Karl b.1964, *Aro Valley*, purchased from The Approach, 1999
May, Nicholas b.1962, *Guardians of Acheron*, purchased from the artist, 1993, © the artist
May, Nicholas b.1962, *Liminal Ellipse (Orange)*, gift from Charles Saatchi, 1999, © the artist
Mayer, Michael John b.1932, *Telegraph*, purchased from the Gimpel Fils Gallery, 1978, © the artist
Mayer, Michael John b.1932, *The Aura of Joseph 'Cornbread' Thomas*, purchase award, 1980, © the artist
McAleer, Clement b.1949, *Dark Hedge*, purchased from the Bluecoat Arts Centre, 1979, © the artist
McCann, Paddy b.1963, *Cryptbrick*, purchased from the artist, 1992, © the artist
McCracken, John Wilson 1936–1982, *Saturday Night*, purchased from the Durham Light Infantry Museum and Durham Art Gallery, 1977, © the artist's estate
McFadyen, Jock b.1950, *Those heady days seemed to last forever, Siegfried jumping around like the big idiot he was*, purchased from the Acme Gallery, 1979, © the artist
McFadyen, Jock b.1950, *The distinguished professors (who couldn't suppress a giggle) and the injustice of ergonomics*, purchase award, 1980, © the artist
McFadyen, Jock b.1950, *In the Bedroom*, purchase award, 1982, © the artist
McFadyen, Jock b.1950, *Mile End Park*, purchased from Blond Fine Art, 1986, © the artist
McGrath, Alan b.1948, *Bathroom Interior No.6*, purchased from the House Gallery, 1978, © the artist
McKeever, Ian b.1946, *Islands 8a & 8b 1981*, purchased from Nigel Greenwood, 1981, © Ian McKeever. All rights reserved, DACS 2012
McKeever, Ian b.1946, *Caspar's Tree*, purchased from Nigel Greenwood, 1986, © Ian McKeever. All rights reserved, DACS 2012
McKeever, Ian b.1946, *Assumptio (Murmur)*, purchased from the Alan Cristea Gallery, 2000, © Ian McKeever. All rights reserved, DACS 2012
McKenna, Stephen b.1939, *Winter*, purchased from the Barry Barker Gallery, 1979, © the artist
McLean, Bruce b.1944, *Sound Tracking towards the Masterwork*, purchased from the artist, 1979, © the artist
McLean, Bruce b.1944, *Bingo Bingo Bango Bongo*, purchased from the Anthony d'Offay Gallery, 1983, © the artist
McLean, Ian 1973–2000, *Armour jamais*, gift from Charles Saatchi, 1999, © the artist's estate
McLean, Ian 1973–2000, *Armour rien*, gift from Charles Saatchi, 1999, © the artist's estate
McLean, John b.1939, *1969*, purchased from the artist, 1970, © the artist
McLean, John b.1939, *Pagoda I*, purchased from the artist, 1975, © the artist
McLean, John b.1939, *Grey Granite*, purchased from the House Gallery, 1978, © the artist
McLean, John b.1939, *Breakwater*, purchase award, 1982, © the artist
McLean, John b.1939, *Neiss Beach II*, purchase award, 1982, © the artist
Mead, Dorothy 1928–1975, *Flowers*, purchased from the London Group exhibition, 1962, © Val Long
Medalla, David b.1938, *Rhapsody of the Dagger and Ammonia Boy (Interior Scene)*, purchased from the artist, 1981, © David Medalla
Medalla, David b.1938, *A Prophecy*, purchased from the artist, 1991, © David Medalla
Medley, Robert 1905–1994, *Ulysses and Penelope*, purchased from the Lefevre Gallery, 1948, © the estate of Robert Medley, courtesy of James Hyman Gallery, London
Medley, Robert 1905–1994, *Summer Eclogue*, purchased from the artist, 1953, © the estate of Robert Medley, courtesy of James Hyman Gallery, London
Medley, Robert 1905–1994, *Bowaters Paper Works, Gravesend, Kent*, purchased from the London Group, 1956, © the estate of Robert Medley, courtesy of James Hyman Gallery, London
Medley, Robert 1905–1994, *Yellow and White Figuration*, purchased from the artist, 1967, © the estate of Robert Medley, courtesy of James Hyman Gallery, London
Medley, Robert 1905–1994, *China*, purchased from the artist, 1973, © the estate of Robert Medley, courtesy of James Hyman Gallery, London
Mellis, Margaret 1914–2009, *Seeding Flowers*, purchased from the artist, 1982, © the estate of Margaret Mellis
Mellis, Margaret 1914–2009, *Two Circles (Red, Blue, Yellow, Violet and White)*, purchased from the London Group, 1964, © the estate of Margaret Mellis
Mellis, Margaret 1914–2009, *Green and Violet*, purchased from the Grabowski Gallery, 1969, © the estate of Margaret Mellis
Mellis, Margaret 1914–2009, *Temptation*, purchased from The Redfern Gallery, 1987, © the estate of Margaret Mellis
Mellor, Oscar 1921–2005, *A Small Bunch of Eyes*, purchased from the artist, 1980
Mellor, Oscar 1921–2005, *The Inquisitors*, purchased from the artist, 1980
Mellor, Oscar 1921–2005, *The Prototype*, purchased from the artist, 1980
Mellor, Oscar 1921–2005, *The Pursuit of Pleasure*, purchased from the artist, 1980
Mellor, Oscar 1921–2005, *When the Leaves Fall*, purchased from the artist, 1980
Mellor, Oscar 1921–2005, *La Bastide*, purchased from the artist, 1980
Meninsky, Bernard 1891–1950, *Andalusian Landscape*, purchased from the Adams Gallery, 1958, © the artist's estate/Bridgeman Art Library
Meninsky, Bernard 1891–1950, *Portrait of a Girl*, purchased from the artist, 1942, © the artist's estate/Bridgeman Art Library
Meyrick, George b.1953, *Drawing 1982*, purchased from the artist, 1982
Michael, Alan b.1967, *Untitled*, purchased from Stuart Shave Modern Art, 2006, © courtesy Sorcha Dallas, Stuart Shave/Modern Art & Hotel, photo credit: ACC
Middleditch, Edward 1923–1987, *Baby*, purchased from the Institute of Contemporary Arts, 1952, © the estate of Edward Middleditch, courtesy James Hyman Gallery, London
Middleditch, Edward 1923–1987, *Cow Parsley*, purchased from the Beaux Arts Gallery, 1956, © the estate of Edward Middleditch, courtesy James Hyman Gallery, London
Middleditch, Edward 1923–1987, *Rose, Pink*, purchased from the artist, 1966, © the estate of Edward Middleditch, courtesy James Hyman Gallery, London
Middleditch, Edward 1923–1987, *Rose, Red and Blue*, purchased from the artist, 1966, © the estate of Edward Middleditch, courtesy James Hyman Gallery, London
Middleditch, Edward 1923–1987, *Still Life*, purchased from the artist, 1966, © the estate of Edward Middleditch, courtesy James Hyman Gallery, London
Miller, Alain b.1963, *On My Way to Paradise*, purchased from the Anthony Reynolds Gallery, 1998, © the artist, courtesy Anthony Reynolds Gallery
Miller, Alan 1941–2009, *Untitled 1971–72*, purchased from the artist, 1972, © the artist's estate
Miller, Alan 1941–2009, *Collage I (Untitled)*, purchased from the artist, 1973, © the artist's estate
Miller, Alan 1941–2009, *Collage II (Untitled)*, purchased from the artist, 1973, © the artist's estate
Miller, Alan 1941–2009, *Collage III (Untitled)*, purchased from the artist, 1973, © the artist's estate
Miller, Alan 1941–2009, *For P. S.*, purchased from the artist, 1976, © the artist's estate
Millichip, Paul b.1929, *Oving Footpath*, purchased from the artist, 1979, © the artist
Milow, Keith b.1945, *1 2 3 4 5 6 … A*, purchased from Nigel Greenwood, 1970, © the artist
Milow, Keith b.1945, *Grey 1*, purchased from Nigel Greenwood, 1971, © the artist
Milroy, Lisa b.1959, *Silverware*, purchased from the Nicola Jacobs Gallery, 1984, © Lisa Milroy
Milroy, Lisa b.1959, *Kyoto House*, purchased from the artist, 1996, © Lisa Milroy
Milroy, Lisa b.1959, *Kyoto House*, purchased from the artist, 1996, © Lisa Milroy
Milroy, Lisa b.1959, *Doing, Thinking, Speaking*, purchased from the Waddington Galleries, 2001, © Lisa Milroy
Minnis, Michael b.1964, *Irish Liberation in Shades of Red*,

purchased from the artist, 1991, © the artist
Minnis, Michael b.1964, *Untitled*, purchased from the artist, 1991, © the artist
Minton, John 1917–1957, *The Road to Valencia*, purchased from the Lefevre Gallery, 1950, © Royal College of Art
Mitchell, John b.1942, *'Gate'*, purchased from the artist, 1977, © the artist
Mitha, Alnoor b.1961, *Ascension*, purchased from the artist, 1996, © the artist
Monks, John Christopher b.1954, *Car Door in a Landscape*, anonymous gift, 1990, © the artist
Moon, Jeremy 1934–1973, *Green Chariot*, purchased from the Rowan Gallery, 1966, © the estate of Jeremy Moon
Moon, Jeremy 1934–1973, *No.11/68*, purchased from the Rowan Gallery, 1974, © the estate of Jeremy Moon, photo credit: ACC
Moon, Mick b.1937, *Untitled (1968)*, purchased from the Waddington Galleries, 1969, © the artist
Moon, Mick b.1937, *Low Light*, purchased from the Waddington Galleries, 1978, © the artist
Moon, Mick b.1937, *First Floor*, purchase award, acquired through the Waddington Galleries, 1981, © the artist
Moran, Katy b.1975, *Freddy's Friends*, purchased from Stuart Shave Modern Art, 2006, © courtesy of Stuart Shave/Modern Art London, photo credit: ACC
Morgan, Tony 1938–2005, *Vulnerability*, purchased from the artist, 1999
Morgan, Tony 1938–2005, *Le mot*, purchased from the artist, 2000, photo credit: ACC
Morley, John b.1942, *Noah's Ark*, purchased from the artist, 1980, © the artist
Morrell, Peter John b.1931, *Spot*, purchased from the New Art Centre, 1964, © the artist
Morris, Mali b.1945, *A Vision of the Mermaids*, purchased from the Nicola Jacobs Gallery, 1983, © Mali Morris
Motesiczky, Marie Louise von 1906–1996, *Old Lady with a Baton*, purchased from the artist, 1982, © Marie Louise von Motesiczky Trust
Moyes, James b.1937, *SA5/2*, purchased from Arthur Tooth & Sons Ltd, 1970
Moynihan, Rodrigo 1910–1990, *The Office Desk*, purchased from the artist, 1951, © the artist's estate
Moynihan, Rodrigo 1910–1990, *Dark on White and Pink*, purchased from The Redfern Gallery, 1958, © the artist's estate
Moynihan, Rodrigo 1910–1990, *Painting 12*, purchased from the Hanover Gallery, 1967, © the artist's estate
Moynihan, Rodrigo 1910–1990, *The Garden*, purchased from the artist, 1942, © the artist's estate
Mundy, Henry b.1919, *Weathered*, purchased from the Hanover Gallery, 1960, © the artist
Mundy, Henry b.1919, *Composition*, purchased from the Hanover Gallery, 1962, © the artist
Mundy, Henry b.1919, *Jumna*, purchased, 1967, © the artist
Mundy, Henry b.1919, *Wizzer*, purchased from the artist, 1968, © the artist
Mundy, Henry b.1919, *Untitled*, purchased from the artist, 1982, © the artist
Mundy, Henry b.1919, *Untitled Drawing*, purchased from the artist, 1982, © the artist
Mundy, Henry b.1919, *Untitled Drawing*, purchased from the artist, 1982, © the artist
Mundy, Henry b.1919, *Untitled*, purchased from Nigel Greenwood Gallery, 1991, © the artist
Murfin, Michael b.1954, *Hot Day*, purchased from the artist, 1981, on long-term loan to Milton Keynes Hospital until 2016 © the artist
Murphy, John b.1945, *12.8.69*, purchased from the artist, 1969
Murphy, John b.1945, *Petals of Lust (Epidendrum nocturnum)*, purchased from the Lisson Gallery, 1985
Murphy, Myles F. b.1927, *Yellow Nude*, purchased from the London Group, 1964, © the artist's estate
Murray, Charles 1894–1954, *Sea and Fish*, purchased from the artist, 1942
Myers, Bernard 1925–2007, *View of Allotment Gardens, Eton - Sun Behind Cloud*, purchased from the Royal College of Art, 1962, © the artist's estate
Naylor, Martin b.1944, *Villain*, purchase award, acquired through the Juda Rowan Gallery, 1981
Neiland, Brendan b.1941, *Sunset Bonnet*, purchased from the artist, 1969, © the artist
Neudecker, Mariele G. A. b.1965, *Never Eat Shredded Wheat (Memory Maps), English, Male, 32*, purchased from the Whitechapel Art Gallery, 1996, © the artist
Neudecker, Mariele G. A. b.1965, *Never Eat Shredded Wheat (Memory Maps), German, Female, 31*, purchased from the Whitechapel Art Gallery, 1996, © the artist
Neudecker, Mariele G. A. b.1965, *Never Eat Shredded Wheat (Memory Maps), Italian, Female, 32*, purchased from the Whitechapel Art Gallery, 1996, © the artist
Neudecker, Mariele G. A. b.1965, *Never Eat Shredded Wheat (Memory Maps), English, Male, 32*, purchased from the Whitechapel Art Gallery, 1996, © the artist
Neudecker, Mariele G. A. b.1965, *Never Eat Shredded Wheat (Memory Maps), German, Male, 33*, purchased from the Whitechapel Art Gallery, 1996, © the artist
Neudecker, Mariele G. A. b.1965, *Never Eat Shredded Wheat (Memory Maps), French, Male, 29*, purchased from the Whitechapel Art Gallery, 1996, © the artist
Neudecker, Mariele G. A. b.1965, *Never Eat Shredded Wheat (Memory Maps), English, Female, 35*, purchased from the Whitechapel Art Gallery, 1996, © the artist
Neudecker, Mariele G. A. b.1965, *Never Eat Shredded Wheat (Memory Maps), German, Male, 67*, purchased from the Whitechapel Art Gallery, 1996, © the artist
Neudecker, Mariele G. A. b.1965, *Never Eat Shredded Wheat (Memory Maps), English, Female, 32*, purchased from the Whitechapel Art Gallery, 1996, © the artist
Newman, Gerald b.1945, *No.54/ Orders V, on the Horizon*, purchased from the Robert Self Gallery, 1977
Newsome, Victor b.1935, *Corner of a Bathroom*, purchased from the Anthony d'Offay Gallery, 1975, © the artist
Newsome, Victor b.1935, *Profile*, purchased from Marlborough Fine Art, 1985, © the artist
Newton, Duncan b.1945, *Academic Study 'Seated Figure A'*, purchased from the artist, 1980, © the artist
Nicholson, Ben 1894–1982, *1932 (Bocque)*, purchased from the Leicester Galleries, 1950, © Angela Verren Taunt 2012. All rights reserved, DACS
Nicholson, Ben 1894–1982, *1946 (still life)*, purchased from the Lefevre Gallery, 1947, © Angela Verren Taunt 2012. All rights reserved, DACS
Nicholson, Ben 1894–1982, *February 1953 (contrapuntal)*, purchased from the Penwith Gallery, St Ives, 1953, © Angela Verren Taunt 2012. All rights reserved, DACS, photo credit: ACC
Nicholson, Ben 1894–1982, *May 1956 (hendrifter)*, purchased from the Gimpel Fils Gallery, 1957, © Angela Verren Taunt 2012. All rights reserved, DACS
Nicholson, Kate b.1929, *Dendra*, purchased from the Waddington Galleries, 1962
Nicholson, William 1872–1949, *Sun Fish*, gift from the Contemporary Art Society, 1948, © Elizabeth Banks
Nicholson, Winifred 1893–1981, *Cumberland Hills*, purchased from Thomas Agnew and Sons, 1949, © trustees of Winifred Nicholson
Nolan, Sidney 1917–1992, *Kelly, Spring 1956*, purchased from the Whitechapel Art Gallery, 1957, © the artist's estate/Bridgeman Art Library, photo credit: ACC
Norwich, Anne b.1929, *Painting Untitled*, purchased from the Bear Lane Gallery, Oxford, 1969, © the artist
Obuabang, Henry b.1969, *Obuabang SRS: B Painting No.8 (Art from the Heart)*, purchased from the artist, 1992, © the artist
O'Casey, Breon 1928–2011, *Mountains*, purchased from the artist, 1981, © the artist's estate
Odonkor, Mowbray b.1962, *Onward Christian Soldiers*, purchased from the artist, 1988
O'Donnell, Hugh b.1950, *Bacarole*, purchased from the Ikon Gallery, Birmingham, 1979, © the artist
O'Donoghue, Hughie b.1953, *Dolmen*, purchased from the Air Gallery, 1984, © the artist
Ofili, Chris b.1968, *Popcorn Shells*, purchased from the Victoria Miro Gallery, 1996, © Chris Ofili
Oliver, Ken b.1948, *Interior*, purchased from Moira Kelly Fine Art Ltd, 1982
Ormerod, Susan b.1955, *Photogram/Drawing with Umbrella*, purchased from the artist, 1982
Oulton, Thérèse b.1953, *Dispossessed*, purchased from the Gimpel Fils Gallery, 1983, © the artist
Oulton, Thérèse b.1953, *Counterfoil*, purchased from Marlborough Fine Art with the assistance of English Estates, 1988, © the artist
Palmer, Eugene b.1955, *The Laughing Christ*, purchased from the artist, 1993, © the artist
Palmer, Susan 1912–2000, *Yeovil*, purchased from the artist, 1942
Pannett, Elizabeth Jane b.1947, *14.1.79 – 8.80*, purchased from the Air Gallery, 1980, © the artist
Paraskos, Stass b.1933, *Bathing*, purchased from the Walton Gallery, 1969, © the artist
Parsons, David b.1943, *Painting I*, purchased from the F. B. A. Galleries, 1965 © David Parsons. All rights reserved, DACS 2012
Parsons, Vicken b.1957, *Untitled*, purchased from the artist, 2002, © the artist
Parsons, Vicken b.1957, *Untitled*, purchased from the artist, 2002, © the artist
Pasmore, Victor 1908–1998, *Portrait of a Girl*, purchased from the artist, 1942, © Victor Pasmore estate
Pasmore, Victor 1908–1998, *Riverside Gardens, Hammersmith*, purchased from the Leicester Galleries, 1957, © Victor Pasmore estate, photo credit: ACC
Pasmore, Victor 1908–1998, *Rectangular Motif, Black and Olive*, purchased from The Redfern Gallery, 1951, © Victor Pasmore estate
Pasmore, Victor 1908–1998, *The Snowstorm: Spiral Motif in Black and White*, purchased from the artist, 1951, © Victor Pasmore estate
Pasmore, Wendy b.1915, *Abstract in Maroon*, purchased from the London Group, 1960
Pasmore, Victor 1908–1998, *Black Abstract*, purchased from the New London Gallery, 1964, © Victor Pasmore estate
Patterson, Richard b.1963, *Motocrosser*, purchased from the Anthony d'Offay Gallery, 1995, © the artist, courtesy Timothy Taylor Gallery, London
Peake, Fabian b.1942, *The Red Moustache*, purchased from the artist, 1987, © the artist
Pearce, Bryan 1929–2007, *The Harbour and St Ia's Church, St Ives*, purchased from the New Art Centre, 1968, © the estate of Bryan Pearce. All rights reserved, DACS 2012
Pearce, Charles Maresco 1874–1964, *Garibaldi*, purchased from the artist, 1942
Penalva, João b.1949, *Huckleberry*, purchased from the artist, 1993, © the artist
Peri, Peter b.1971, *Pageant*, purchased from the Carl Freedman Gallery, 2005, © the artist
Perryman, Margot b.1938, *Untitled No.25*, purchased from the New Art Centre, 1965, © the artist
Perryman, Margot b.1938, *Octave No.3*, purchased from the New Art Centre, 1970, © the artist
Perton, Michael 1935–1996, *Free Composition (Item 13)*, purchased from the artist, 1973, © the artist's estate
Perton, Michael 1935–1996, *Activities on a White Window Grid*, purchased from the House Gallery, 1977, © the artist's estate
Phillips, Peter b.1939, *Entanglement Series: Perpetual Flux*, purchased from the artist, 1982, © Peter and Zoe Phillips
Phillips, Tom b.1937, *Consider Our Haven: Supplement III 1968*, purchased from Tooth's Gallery, 1970, © Tom Phillips. All rights reserved, DACS 2012
Phillips, Tom b.1937, *Terminal Greys IV–VII*, purchased from Marlborough Fine Art, 1974, © Tom Phillips. All rights reserved, DACS 2012
Phokela, Johannes b.1966, *Candle Bathing*, purchased from the Rack Gallery, 1998, © the artist
Piper, John 1903–1992, *Abstract II*, purchased from the Gimpel Fils Gallery, 1954, © the artist's estate
Piper, Keith b.1960, *(You are now entering) Mau Mau Country*, purchased from the Mappin Art Gallery, Sheffield, 1984, © the artist
Pollard, Alex b.1977, *Brontë Truck*, purchased from the Andrew Mummery Gallery, 2003, © the artist, photo credit: ACC
Pollock, Fred b.1937, *Untitled No.III*, purchase award, 1980, © the artist
Pollock, Fred b.1937, *Lunar Thrust*, purchase award, 1982, © the artist

Porter, Michael b.1948, *Fungus and Silver Birch*, purchased from the Pomeroy Purdy Gallery, 1991, © the artist
Potter, Mary 1900–1981, *Regent's Park, Autumn*, purchased from the Leicester Galleries, 1950, © estate of Mary Potter. All rights reserved, DACS 2012
Potter, Mary 1900–1981, *The Erica House, Kew*, purchased from the Leicester Galleries, 1951, © estate of Mary Potter. All rights reserved, DACS 2012
Potter, Mary 1900–1981, *Sun on the Beach*, purchased from the Leicester Galleries, 1961, © estate of Mary Potter. All rights reserved, DACS 2012
Potter, Mary 1900–1981, *Dark Painting*, purchased from the New Art Centre, 1978, © estate of Mary Potter. All rights reserved, DACS 2012
Power, Gary b.1958, *My Addaura*, purchased from the artist, 1983
Praag, Arnold van b.1926, *Butcher, Sheep's Head and Trotters*, purchased from the artist, 1985, © the artist
Preece, Patricia 1894–1966, *Old Woman Knitting*, purchased from the artist, 1942, © Dorothy Hepworth. All rights reserved, DACS 2012
Prendergast, Peter 1946–2007, *Road to Bethesda from Garden*, purchased from the artist, 1980, © estate of Peter Prendergast. All rights reserved, DACS 2012
Prentice, David b.1936, *Field Grid – Pleiades*, purchased from the artist, 1969, © the artist
Price, Joanna b.1956, *Blue Pietà*, gift from Charles Saatchi, 1999, © the artist
Procktor, Patrick 1936–2003, *Three Figures in Landscape*, purchased from The Redfern Gallery, 1963, © the artist's estate
Prout, Margaret Fisher 1875–1963, *Near Betchworth*, purchased from the artist, 1942
Rae, Fiona b.1963, *Untitled (Pale Green I)*, purchased from the Waddington Galleries, 1991, © the artist, courtesy of the Timothy Taylor Gallery, London
Reason, Cyril b.1931, *Odalisque*, purchased from the Beaux Arts Gallery, 1960
Redfern, David b.1947, *No.9*, purchased from the artist, 1976, © the artist
Redfern, David b.1947, *Incident at Charing Cross*, purchased from the artist, 1978, © the artist
Rego, Paula Figueiroa b.1935, *Girl by Swimming Pool*, purchased from the Air Gallery, 1981, © the artist
Rego, Paula Figueiroa b.1935, *Minotaur Slicing Goat*, purchased from the Edward Totah Gallery, 1982, © the artist
Rego, Paula Figueiroa b.1935, *The Family*, purchased from the artist, 1982, © the artist
Rego, Paula Figueiroa b.1935, *Sleeping*, purchased from the Edward Totah Gallery with the assistance of English Estates, 1987, © the artist
Reid, Nan 1905–1981, *Fish and Chip Shop in Chelsea*, purchased from the artist, 1952
Renshaw, Tim b.1964, *Returning*, purchased from the artist, 1998, © the artist
Reynolds, Alan b.1926, *The Village – Winter*, purchased from The Redfern Gallery, 1952, © the artist
Reynolds, Alan b.1926, *Legend – Red and Green*, purchased from the artist, 1967, © the artist
Reynolds, Alan b.1926, *Vertical Structure III*, purchased from Annely Juda Fine Art, 1978, © the artist
Reynolds, Daphne 1918–2002, *Spectral Cross*, purchased from the Drian Gallery, 1961, © the artist's estate
Rhodes, Carol b.1959, *Industrial Landscape*, purchased from the Andrew Mummery Gallery, 1997, © the artist
Rhys-James, Shani b.1953, *Stare*, purchased from the artist, 1997, © the artist
Richards, Ceri Geraldus 1903–1971, *Rocks*, purchased from the artist, 1942, © estate of Ceri Richards. All rights reserved, DACS 2012
Richards, Ceri Geraldus 1903–1971, *Blue Interior with Dice*, purchased from The Redfern Gallery, 1950, © estate of Ceri Richards. All rights reserved, DACS 2012
Richards, Ceri Geraldus 1903–1971, *Homage to Beethoven II*, purchased from The Redfern Gallery, 1955, © estate of Ceri Richards. All rights reserved, DACS 2012
Richards, Ceri Geraldus 1903–1971, *Two Musicians*, acquired through the Sir William Emrys and Lady Williams Bequest, 1983, © estate of Ceri Richards. All rights reserved, DACS 2012
Richards, Ceri Geraldus 1903–1971, *Poissons d'or*, purchased from the New London Gallery, 1963, © estate of Ceri Richards. All rights reserved, DACS 2012
Richards, Ceri Geraldus 1903–1971, *Study for Tabernacle of the Blessed Sacrament Chapel, Liverpool Metropolitan Cathedral of Christ the King*, purchased from Marlborough Fine Art, 1967, © estate of Ceri Richards. All rights reserved, DACS 2012
Richards, Paul b.1949, *Masterwork: Scene Page 43*, purchased from the Lewis Johnstone Gallery, 1981, © the artist
Richards, Paul b.1949, *The Kiss (No.1)*, purchased from the Lewis Johnstone Gallery, 1982, © the artist
Richardson-Jones, Keith 1925–2005, *Series 288 24/18 (i) 6/8/10/9/7/5*, purchased from the artist, 1977, © the artist's estate
Richardson-Jones, Keith 1925–2005, *Series 288 24/18 (ii) 6/8/10/9/7/5*, purchased from the artist, 1977, © the artist's estate
Richardson-Jones, Keith 1925–2005, *Series 288: Log/Thirds*, purchased from the artist, 1983, © the artist's estate
Rielly, James Malcolm b.1956, *Object of Fun*, gift from Charles Saatchi, 1999, © the artist
Rielly, James Malcolm b.1956, *Daddy, I Love You*, purchased from the Laurent Delaye Gallery, 1996, © the artist
Rigden, Geoff b.1943, *Paphos*, purchased from Tolly Cobbold Eastern Arts 2nd National Exhibition, 1979, © the artist
Riley, Bridget b.1931, *Movement in Squares*, purchased from Gallery One, 1962, © the artist
Riley, Bridget b.1931, *Song of Orpheus IV*, purchased from the Rowan Gallery, 1978, © the artist, photo credit: ACC
Riley, Bridget b.1931, *Ecclesia*, purchased from the Juda Rowan Gallery, 1986, © the artist, photo credit: ACC
Robb, Brian 1913–1979, *Townscape*, purchased from the artist, 1960, © the artist's estate
Robb, Brian 1913–1979, *Lagoon*, purchased from the London Group, 1965, © the artist's estate
Roberts, Derek b.1947, *Painting No.2 August/December 1980*, purchased from the Fruitmarket Gallery, Edinburgh, 1982, © the artist
Roberts, Julie b.1963, *Mortuary Table (green)*, purchased from Interim Art, 1995, © the artist
Roberts, William Patrick 1895–1980, *A Gipsy Girl*, purchased from the Leicester Galleries, 1950, © estate of John David Roberts. By courtesy of The William Roberts Society
Roberts, William Patrick 1895–1980, *The Seaside*, purchased from the Royal Academy of Arts, 1967, © estate of John David Roberts. By courtesy of The William Roberts Society
Robertson, Carol b.1955, *Over and Under*, purchased from the artist, 1991, © the artist/ courtesy Flowers Gallery, London
Robilliard, David 1952–1988, *A candle in the dark is better than nothing at all*, purchased from the artist, 1988
Robilliard, David 1952–1988, *International flavour: cultural differences melt when you start slurping*, purchased from the artist, 1988
Robinson, Bob b.1951, *A Preference for Crisps*, purchased from the artist, 1980, © the artist
Robinson, Bob b.1951, *Van Gogh: waits for Gauguin and is now living in Nottingham.'*, purchased from the artist, 1980, © the artist
Robinson, Peter *Seated Figure*, purchased from the artist, 1965
Robinson, Val b.1944, *Big Mother*, purchased from the artist, 1987
Rogers, Claude 1907–1979, *The Cottage Bedroom*, purchased from the Leicester Galleries, 1947, © Crispin Rogers
Rogers, Claude 1907–1979, *Operation in Progress*, purchased from the Leicester Galleries, 1954, © Crispin Rogers
Rogers, Claude 1907–1979, *Magnolias in a Brown Jug*, purchased from the artist, 1958, © Crispin Rogers
Rogers, Claude 1907–1979, *Still Life*, purchased from the London Group Exhibition, 1962, © Crispin Rogers
Rogers, Claude 1907–1979, *Sunrise over Burnt Field*, purchased from Fischer Fine Art, 1978, © Crispin Rogers
Rogers, Claude 1907–1979, *Aldeburgh Beach*, purchased from the artist, 1942, © Crispin Rogers
Rose, Colin b.1950, *Amongst Drifting Tides – Verse and Refrain*, purchased from the artist, 1982, © the artist, photo credit: ACC
Rose, Kate b.1948, *Pattern on a Persian Carpet*, purchased from the artist, 1982, © the artist
Rose, Rose b.1946, *Passage Four: Binary Fission*, purchased from the artist, 1987, © the artist
Rosoman, Leonard Henry 1913–2012, *Gardens on Different Levels*, purchased from Arthur Tooth & Sons Ltd, 1955, © the artist
Rossi, Mario b.1958, *The End/ Untitled, Series*, purchased from the artist, 2001, © the artist, photo credit: ACC
Rossi, Mario b.1958, *The End/ Untitled, Series*, purchased from the artist, 2001, © the artist, photo credit: ACC
Rossi, Mario b.1958, *The End/ Untitled, Series*, purchased from the artist, 2001, © the artist
Rossi, Mario b.1958, *The End/ Untitled, Series*, purchased from the artist, 2001, © the artist, photo credit: ACC
Rossi, Mario b.1958, *The End/ Untitled, Series*, purchased from the artist, 2001, © the artist
Rothwell, Vivien b.1945, *Bank Holiday*, purchased from the artist, 1979, © Vivien Rothwell 2012. All Rights Reserved, DACS
Rowntree, Kenneth 1915–1997, *The White House, Torcross*, purchased from the artist, 1942, © the artist's estate
Rowntree, Kenneth 1915–1997, *Putney Landscape*, purchased from the Zwemmer Gallery, 1962, © the artist's estate
Rugg, Matt b.1935, *Relief Painting*, purchased from the New Art Centre, 1964
Russell, Bruce John b.1946, *Untitled No.8*, purchased from the artist, 1976, © the artist
Rutherston, Albert 1881–1953, *Self Portrait*, purchased from the Leicester Galleries, 1953, © the grandchildren of the artist, Max, Selina and Jane Rutherston
Rutherston, Albert 1881–1953, *Coster Girl*, purchased from the artist, 1942, © the grandchildren of the artist, Max, Selina and Jane Rutherston
Rüthi, Andreas b.1956, *Goya (Toy)*, purchased from the artist, 1998, © the artist
Salaman, Michael 1911–1987, *Hospital Waiting Room*, purchased from Browse and Darby, 1983, © the artist's estate
Sandle, Michael b.1936, *Sunset*, purchased from the Drian Gallery, 1963, © the artist/ courtesy Flowers Gallery, London
Saunders, David b.1936, *Milan*, purchased from the Camden Borough Survey Exhibition, 1967, © the artist
Saunders, Peter 1940–2011, *Skateboarding, South Bank*, purchased from the artist, 1983, © the artist
Scheihing, Vivian b.1947, *Ashes on the South*, purchased from the artist, 1979, © the artist
Scherman, Tony b.1950, *The Kitchen*, purchased from the artist, 1976
Schmidt, Peter 1931–1980, *Ruth Reading*, purchased from the Beaux Arts Gallery, 1961, © DACS 2012
Scott, Michael b.1954, *Earthquake of Lisbon, All Saints' Day 1755*, purchased from the artist, 1987
Scott, William George 1913–1989, *Old Breton Woman*, purchased from Howard Bliss, 1950, © estate of William Scott, 2012
Scott, William George 1913–1989, *The Frying Pan*, purchased, 1948, © estate of William Scott, 2012
Scott, William George 1913–1989, *Sennen*, acquired through the Sir William Emrys and Lady Williams Bequest, 1983, © estate of William Scott, 2012
Scott, William George 1913–1989, *Slagheap Landscape*, purchased from the Hanover Gallery, 1953, © estate of William Scott, 2012
Scott, William George 1913–1989, *Dark Brown, Orange and White*, purchased from the Hanover Gallery, 1963, © estate of William Scott, 2012
Scott, William George 1913–1989, *Berlin Blues 6*, purchased from the Hanover Gallery, 1967, © estate of William Scott, 2012
Scully, Sean b.1945, *Red*, purchased from the Rowan Gallery, 1973, photo credit: ACC
Scully, Sean b.1945, *How it is*, purchased from the Juda Rowan Gallery, 1982
Seabrooke, Elliott 1886–1950, *Roses*, purchased from the

Leicester Galleries, 1951

Searle, Adrian b.1953, *Hubris*, purchased from the artist, 1984

Sedgley, Peter b.1930, *Red Shift*, purchased from McRoberts and Tunnard, 1965, © the artist

Sedgley, Peter b.1930, *Corona*, gift from the Arnolfini Collection Trust, Bristol, 2001, © the artist

Segal, Arthur 1875–1944, *City of London*, gift from Mrs Arthur Segal, 1968, © the artist's estate

Serra, Paolo b.1946, *Horizon*, purchased from the artist, 1980, © the artist

Setch, Terry b.1936, *SGB Wallscape*, purchased from the Grabowski Gallery, 1969, © the artist

Setch, Terry b.1936, *Car Wreck Penarth Beach VI*, purchased from Nigel Greenwood, 1982, © the artist

Setch, Terry b.1936, *Waterwheel*, purchased from Nigel Greenwood, 1981, © the artist

Setch, Terry b.1936, *Penarth III*, purchased from Nigel Greenwood, 1982, © the artist

Setch, Terry b.1936, *The Moon Falls as the Flags Wave Panel 1 Flag*, purchased from Nigel Greenwood, 1982, © the artist

Shanks, Duncan b.1937, *Flowers All-Over*, purchased from the Royal Scottish Academy, Edinburgh, 1979, © the artist

Shave, Terry b.1952, *Inferno Storms*, purchased from the artist, 1987, © the artist

Shaw, David Carson b.1942, *Reflections, Summer*, purchased from the artist, 1982

Shephard, Rupert 1909–1992, *Woman Writing a Letter*, purchased from the artist, 1942, © the artist's estate

Shiraishi, Yuko b.1956, *Dewfall*, purchased from the Edward Totah Gallery, 1991, © the artist

Shonibare, Yinka b.1962, *Line Painting*, purchased from Stephen Friedman, 2004, © Courtesy the artist and Stephen Friedman Gallery, London

Sickert, Walter Richard 1860–1942, *Head of a Woman (The Belgian Cocotte)*, purchased from Roland Browse and Delbanco, 1953, © estate of Walter R. Sickert. All rights reserved, DACS 2012, photo credit: ACC

Sickert, Walter Richard 1860–1942, *Woman Seated on a Bed, Dieppe*, purchased from the Leicester Galleries, 1955, © estate of Walter R. Sickert. All rights reserved, DACS 2012, photo credit: ACC

Simpson, Michael b.1940, *Two Sailors in Summer*, purchased from the Piccadilly Gallery, 1964, © the artist

Simpson, Michael b.1940, *The Survival Kit*, purchased from the artist, 1983, © the artist

Sinclair, Beryl 1901–1967, *Regent's Park, London*, purchased from the artist, 1942

Sinclair, Ross b.1966, *T-Shirt Paintings 1–80 (detail)*, purchased from the artist, 1999, photo credit: ACC

Sinnott, Kevin b.1947, *In Greenham Common Did the Peacemakers*, purchased from Blond Fine Art, 1983, © the artist

Skiöld, Birgit 1923–1982, *Water's Edge*, purchased from Jonathan Phipps, 1980, © the artist's estate

Smith, Bob and Roberta b.1963, *Although Janis Joplin… (Idiot Board)*, purchased from the artists, 1998, © the artists

Smith, Colin b.1953, *2am*, purchased from the Nicola Jacobs Gallery, 1985, © the artist

Smith, David Henry b.1947, *When Winter Had Gone Spring Came Back*, purchased from Fischer Fine Art, 1983

Smith, Jack 1928–2011, *After the Meal*, purchased from the Beaux Arts Gallery, 1953, © the artist's estate/ courtesy Flowers Gallery, London

Smith, Jack 1928–2011, *Night Sky with Stars*, purchased from the Beaux Arts Gallery, 1957, © the artist's estate/ courtesy Flowers Gallery, London

Smith, Jack 1928–2011, *Dark Wave*, purchased from the Whitechapel Art Gallery, 1959, © the artist's estate/ courtesy Flowers Gallery, London

Smith, Jack 1928–2011, *Floating I*, purchased from the artist, 1966, © the artist's estate/ courtesy Flowers Gallery, London

Smith, Jack 1928–2011, *Musical Painting*, purchased from the Grosvenor Gallery, 1965, © the artist's estate/ courtesy Flowers Gallery, London

Smith, Jack 1928–2011, *Active Intervals (Sound)*, purchased from the artist, 1972, © the artist's estate/ courtesy Flowers Gallery, London

Smith, Jack 1928–2011, *Ten Elements*, purchased from Monika Kinley, 1976, © the artist's estate/ courtesy Flowers Gallery, London

Smith, Matthew Arnold Bracey 1879–1959, *Flowers and Fruit*, purchased from Arthur Tooth & Sons Ltd, 1952, © by permission of the copyright holder

Smith, Matthew Arnold Bracey 1879–1959, *Provençal Landscape*, purchased from the Leicester Galleries, 1955, © by permission of the copyright holder

Smith, Melanie b.1965, *Parres (No.2)*, purchased from the Peter Kilchmann Gallery, 2005

Smith, Richard b.1931, *Trio*, purchased from the Kasmin Gallery, 1963, © the artist/ courtesy Flowers Gallery, London

Smith, Richard b.1931, *Brief Alphabet, Triptych*, purchased from the Kasmin Gallery, 1968, © the artist/ courtesy Flowers Gallery, London

Smith, Richard b.1931, *Corner A (Nursery Slope)*, purchased from the Kasmin Gallery, 1966, © the artist/ courtesy Flowers Gallery, London

Smith, Richard b.1931, *Livorno*, purchased from the Kasmin Gallery, 1972, © the artist/ courtesy Flowers Gallery, London

Smith, Sue b.1925, *Cluster No.3*, purchased from the House Gallery, 1979

Smith, Tony b.1953, *An Angel, the Knight, Death and the Devil*, purchased from Moira Kelly Fine Art, 1980 © ARS, NY and DACS, London 2012

Sohail, Tassadaq b.1930, *Untitled*, purchased from the Horizon Gallery, 1987

Sonnabend, Yolanda b.1935, *Lobengula Street (Bulawayo)*, purchased from the artist, 1983, © the artist

Southall, Derek b.1930, *Marcus Curtius*, purchased from the Rowan Gallery, 1966

Southall, Derek b.1930, *Black U*, purchased from the artist, 1969

Southall, Derek b.1930, *Untitled*, purchased from the artist, 1976

Southall, Derek b.1930, *Two Islands*, purchased from the artist, 1983

Spear, Ruskin 1911–1990, *Siesta*, purchased from the artist, 1942, © the artist's estate/Bridgeman Art Library

Spear, Ruskin 1911–1990, *Woman in a Red Jumper*, purchased, 1948, © the artist's estate/Bridgeman Art Library

Spear, Ruskin 1911–1990, *Hammersmith Broadway*, purchased from the Leicester Galleries, 1951, © the artist's estate/Bridgeman Art Library

Spence, John b.1944, *Fruits of Love*, purchased from the artist, 1979

Spence, John b.1944, *Isn't it Romantic*, purchased from the artist, 1979

Spence, John b.1944, *Rules of the Game*, purchased from the artist, 1979

Spence, John b.1944, *The Haunting*, purchased from the artist, 1979

Spence, John b.1944, *The Secret Hour*, purchased from the artist, 1979

Spence, John b.1944, *Zero Take Off*, purchased from the artist, 1979

Spence, John b.1944, *Cromer Drawing (No.3)*, purchased from the artist, 1986

Spence, John b.1944, *Cromer Drawing (No.5)*, purchased from the artist, 1986

Spence, John b.1944, *Cromer Drawing (No.11)*, purchased from the artist, 1986

Spence, John b.1944, *Cromer Drawing (No.15)*, purchased from the artist, 1986

Spencer, Gilbert 1892–1979, *Budden's Lane*, purchased from the artist, 1942, © the artist's estate/ Bridgeman Art Library

Spencer, Jean 1942–1998, *Relief (4 units)*, purchased from the artist, 1973, © the artist's estate

Stahl, Andrew b.1954, *Chalice*, purchased from the artist, 1983, © the artist

Stahl, Andrew b.1954, *Spring Rites*, purchased from the artist, 1983, © the artist

Stahl, Andrew b.1954, *Close*, purchased from the Angela Flowers Gallery, 1998, © the artist

Steele, Jeffrey b.1931, *Wasserfläsche*, purchased from the Grabowski Gallery, 1964, © the artist

Steele, Jeffrey b.1931, *Ilmatar*, purchased from McRoberts and Tunnard, 1967, © the artist, photo credit: ACC

Steele, Jeffrey b.1931, *SG I 62*, purchased from Annely Juda Fine Art, 1977, © the artist, photo credit: ACC

Steer, Philip Wilson 1860–1942, *Girl in a White Blouse on a Sofa*, purchased from the Leicester Galleries, 1959, © Tate, London 2012

Stephenson, Cecil 1889–1965, *Canon (2)*, purchased from the London Group, 1959, © the artist's estate

Stephenson, Ian 1934–2000, *Shhh*, purchased from the New Art Centre, 1961, © the artist's estate

Stephenson, Ian 1934–2000, *Red Adumbration*, purchased from the New Art Centre, 1962, © the artist's estate

Stephenson, Ian 1934–2000, *Small Spray Studies 1–4*, purchased from the New Art Centre, 1969, © the artist's estate

Stephenson, Ian 1934–2000, *Small Spray Studies 1–5*, purchased from the New Art Centre, 1969, © the artist's estate

Stephenson, Ian 1934–2000, *Small Spray Studies 1–7*, purchased from the New Art Centre, 1969, © the artist's estate

Stephenson, Ian 1934–2000, *Retrospect 4 Spray Study*, purchased from the New Art Centre, 1964, © the artist's estate

Stephenson, Ian 1934–2000, *Diorama SS.5.67*, purchased from the New Art Centre, 1968, © the artist's estate

Stephenson, Ian 1934–2000, *Border Series: Easement I*, purchased from the artist, 1976, © the artist's estate

Stephenson, Ian 1934–2000, *Border Series: Easement II*, purchased from the artist, 1976, © the artist's estate

Stephenson, Ian 1934–2000, *Border Series: Easement III*, purchased from the artist, 1976, © the artist's estate

Stephenson, Ian 1934–2000, *Border Series: Easement IV*, purchased from the artist, 1976, © the artist's estate

Stephenson, Ian 1934–2000, *Border Series: Easement V*, purchased from the artist, 1976, © the artist's estate

Stephenson, Ian 1934–2000, *Border Series: Easement VI*, purchased from the artist, 1976, © the artist's estate

Stephenson, Ian 1934–2000, *Border Series: Easement VII*, purchased from the artist, 1976, © the artist's estate

Stephenson, Ian 1934–2000, *Border Series: Easement VIII*, purchased from the artist, 1976, © the artist's estate

Stevens, Norman 1937–1988, *Fire Hydrant, N. Y.*, purchased from the Hanover Gallery, 1968, © the artist's estate

Stevens, Norman 1937–1988, *Louvered Shutter (Morning)*, purchased from the artist, 1972, © the artist's estate

Stevens, Norman 1937–1988, *Aaron's Rod*, purchased from the artist, 1976, © the artist's estate

Steyn, Stella 1907–1987, *Girl in a Blue Dress*, purchased from the Leicester Galleries, 1951

Stimson, Myra b.1961, *The Will to Live*, purchased from the Whitechapel Art Gallery, 1988, © the artist

Stokes, Adrian Durham 1902–1972, *San Materno, Ascona*, purchased from the Leger Galleries, 1951, © the artist's estate

Stokes, Adrian Durham 1902–1972, *Still Life XIX*, purchased from the Marlborough Galleries, 1965, © the artist's estate

Stokoe, Neil b.1935, *Man and Woman with Swimming Pool*, purchased from the Clytie Jessop Gallery, 1970, © the artist

Stubbing, Newton Haydn (Tony) 1921–1983, *Untitled*, purchased from England and Co., 1992, © the estate of N. H. Stubbing

Suddaby, Rowland 1912–1972, *Winter Landscape, near Lavenham*, purchased from the artist, 1942, © the artist's estate

Sutherland, Graham Vivian 1903–1980, *Standing Form Against a Hedge*, purchased from the Hanover Gallery, 1951, © estate of Graham Sutherland

Sutton, Philip b.1928, *Orange Head*, purchased from the London Group, 1954, © Philip Sutton. All rights reserved, DACS 2012

Sutton, Philip b.1928, *Flower Still Life*, purchased from Arthur Tooth & Sons Ltd, 1955, © Philip Sutton. All rights reserved, DACS 2012

Sutton, Philip b.1928, *Fruit Tree*, purchased from the artist, 1960, © Philip Sutton. All rights reserved, DACS 2012

Sutton, Philip b.1928, *Sonya*, purchased from the artist, 1967, © Philip Sutton. All rights reserved,

DACS 2012
Sutton, Trevor b.1948, *A. B. B.*, purchased from the artist, 1976, © the artist/ courtesy Flowers Gallery, London
Sutton, Trevor b.1948, *Portrait of a Woman*, purchased from the Lisson Gallery, 1981, © the artist/ courtesy Flowers Gallery, London
Sutton, Trevor b.1948, *Friendship*, purchased from the artist, 1991, © the artist/ courtesy Flowers Gallery, London
Tebby, Susan b.1944, *Relief No. VIII: Re-entrant White*, purchased from the artist, 1967
Themerson, Franciszka 1907–1988, *People are generally kind*, purchased from the artist, 1984, © Themerson estate
Thesiger, Amanda b.1964, *Arrangement*, purchased from the Francis Graham-Dixon Gallery, 1995, © the artist
Thomas, Keith b.1946, *Snake*, purchased from the artist, 1980
Thomas, Keith b.1946, *Crawler*, purchased from the artist, 1978
Thomas, Margaret b.1916, *The Chintz Tablecloth*, purchased from the Leicester Galleries, 1949, © the artist
Thomas, Shanti b.1949, *The Voyagers*, purchased from the artist, 1987
Thompson, Estelle b.1960, *Virgin Ground*, purchased from Pomeroy Purdy, 1991, © the artist
Thompson, Estelle b.1960, *Whiteishwhiteishness*, purchased from the Purdy Hicks Gallery, 2003, © the artist, photo credit: ACC
Thompson, Philip 1928–2007, *Bonnie and Clyde*, purchased from the A. I. A. Galleries, 1968
Thomson, Alexander b.1942, *Untitled Drawing I*, purchased from the artist, 1974
Thomson, Alexander b.1942, *Untitled Drawing II*, purchased from the artist, 1974
Thomson, Alfred Reginald 1894–1979, *Round the Island Races*, purchased from the Royal Academy of Arts, 1967
Tibble, Geoffrey Arthur 1909–1952, *Music Room*, purchased from Arthur Tooth & Sons Ltd, 1949
Tilson, Joe b.1928, *Summer*, purchased from the artist, 1960, © Joe Tilson 2012. All rights reserved, DACS
Tilson, Joe b.1928, *Space Trophy*, purchased, 1964, © Joe Tilson 2012. All rights reserved, DACS
Tilson, Joe b.1928, *Zikkurat 7*, purchased from Marlborough Fine Art, 1967, © Joe Tilson 2012. All rights reserved, DACS
Tindle, David b.1932, *Delamere Terrace*, purchased from the Piccadilly Gallery, 1960, © the artist
Todd, Arthur Ralph Middleton 1891–1966, *Draped Nude*, purchased from the artist, 1942, © the artist's estate
Todd, Graeme b.1962, *Mushroom*, purchased from the Andrew Mummery Gallery, 2003, © the artist
Townsend, William 1909–1973, *The Hop Garden*, purchased from the Leicester Galleries, 1951, © the artist's estate
Townsend, William 1909–1973, *Landscape with Pond*, purchased from the artist, 1959, © the artist's estate
Treister, Suzanne b.1958, *Barcelona in Outer Space*, purchased from the artist, 1986, © the artist
Treister, Suzanne b.1958, *Black Hole*, purchased from the Edward Totah Gallery, 1988, © the artist
Trevelyan, Julian 1910–1988, *High Tide, Chiswick Reach*, purchased, 1947, © the artist's estate
Trevelyan, Julian 1910–1988, *Hyde Park*, purchased from the London Group, 1956, © the artist's estate
Trollope, Roy b.1933, *Reclining Woman*, purchased from the Portal Gallery, 1963, © the artist
Tucker, William b.1935, *Untitled Study for Sculpture*, purchased from the Bernard Jacobson Gallery, 1982, © the artist
Tunnard, John 1900–1971, *Cornwall*, purchased from the artist, 1942
Turnbull, Alison b.1956, *Hagi (from the 'Little Japanese Paintings' series)*, purchased from Mobile Home, 2000, © the artist
Turnbull, William b.1922, *Untitled 13*, purchased from the Waddington Galleries, 1967, © William Turnbull. All rights reserved, DACS 2012, photo credit: ACC
Tyzack, Michael 1933–2007, *Praetorius*, purchased from the Axiom Gallery, 1966, © the artist's estate
Uddin, Shafique b.1962, *Untitled*, purchased from Monika Kinley, 1986
Uglow, Euan 1932–2000, *Still Life with Delft Jar*, purchased from the Beaux Arts Gallery, 1961, © the estate of Euan Uglow
Uglow, Euan 1932–2000, *The German Girl*, purchased from the Hampstead Arts Centre, 1966, © the estate of Euan Uglow
Uglow, Euan 1932–2000, *Girl's Head in Profile with Cap on*, purchased from the London Group, 1964, © the estate of Euan Uglow, photo credit: ACC
Uglow, Euan 1932–2000, *The Mosque at Çiftlik Köyü*, purchased from the London Group, 1967, © the estate of Euan Uglow
Uglow, Euan 1932–2000, *Snake*, purchased from the artist, 1976, © the estate of Euan Uglow, photo credit: ACC
Uglow, Euan 1932–2000, *The Quarry Pignano*, purchased from Browse and Darby, 1980, © the estate of Euan Uglow
Unsworth, Peter b.1937, *Still Garden*, purchased from the Piccadilly Gallery, 1965, © the artist
Upton, Michael 1938–2002, *The Portrait*, purchased from the artist, 1977, © the artist's estate
Upton, Michael 1938–2002, *Barn, Dorset, England*, purchased from the Hester van Roijen Gallery, 1978, © the artist's estate
Upton, Michael 1938–2002, *The Bed I*, purchased from the Hester van Roijen Gallery, 1978, © the artist's estate
Upton, Michael 1938–2002, *The Bed II*, purchased from the Hester van Roijen Gallery, 1978, © the artist's estate
Upton, Michael 1938–2002, *The Bed III*, purchased from the Hester van Roijen Gallery, 1978, © the artist's estate
Urkom, Gera b.1940, *Apple painting with hyacinth blue brush stroke*, purchased from the artist, 1991, © the artist
Urkom, Gera b.1940, *Small segment, red with black brush stroke* (from the 'Defamiliarisation of the Apple' series), purchased from the artist, 1991, © the artist
Urkom, Gera b.1940, *Medium segment, red with black brush stroke* (from the 'Defamiliarisation of the Apple' series), purchased from the artist, 1991, © the artist
Urkom, Gera b.1940, *Red segment with in-the-centre brush stroke* (from the 'Defamiliarisation of the Apple' series), purchased from the artist, 1991, © the artist
Valdivia, Marco b.1947, *Untitled*, gift from the artist, 1998, photo credit: ACC
Valdivia, Marco b.1947, *Oda a los Mapuches*, purchased from the artist, 1999
Valdivia, Marco b.1947, *Oda a Tehuiriche*, purchased from the artist, 1999, photo credit: ACC
Vaughan, John Keith 1912–1977, *The Village*, purchased from the Leicester Galleries, 1953, © the estate of Keith Vaughan. All rights reserved, DACS 2012
Vaughan, John Keith 1912–1977, *September*, purchased from the Contemporary Art Society, 1956, © © the estate of Keith Vaughan. All rights reserved, DACS 2012
Vaughan, John Keith 1912–1977, *Landscape with Figure*, purchased from the Leicester Galleries, 1958, © the estate of Keith Vaughan. All rights reserved, DACS 2012
Vaughan, Michael b.1938, *Corner Piece: Cake Series*, purchased from the artist, 1970, © the artist
Vaughan, Michael b.1938, *Still Life: Square, Cross, Triangle*, purchased from the artist, 1970, © the artist
Vaux, Marc b.1932, *PY 70*, purchased from the Axiom Gallery, 1970, © the artist
Vellacott, Elisabeth 1905–2002, *Vestigial Room*, purchased from the artist, 1970, © the artist's estate
Vellacott, Elisabeth 1905–2002, *Man, Cat and Piano*, purchased from the New Art Centre, 1983, © the artist's estate
Verran, Virginia b.1961, *Pink Painting No.1*, purchased from the Francis Graham-Dixon Gallery, 1996, © the artist
Vézelay, Paule 1893–1984, *Yellow Circle*, purchased from the artist, 1961, © the artist's estate
Vilaincour, Leon Julius b.1923, *The Chalice*, purchased from the artist, 1966, © the artist
Vilaincour, Leon Julius b.1923, *Pietà*, purchased from the artist, 1966, © the artist
Vilaincour, Leon Julius b.1923, *Jean Pierre Latz/Jeanne Lanvin*, purchased from the artist, 1997, © the artist
Virtue, John b.1947, *Landscape 301*, gift from the Arnolfini Collection Trust, Bristol, 2001, © John Virtue. All rights reserved, DACS 2012
Walker, Ethel 1861–1951, *Flowers and Grapes*, purchased from the artist, 1942, © the artist's estate/ Bridgeman Art Library
Walker, John b.1939, *Tense*, purchased from the Axiom Gallery, 1968, © the artist
Walker, John b.1939, *Seven*, purchased from the Axiom Gallery, 1969, © the artist
Walker, John b.1939, *Untitled 1975*, purchased from Nigel Greenwood, 1975, © the artist
Walker, John b.1939, *Ostraca V*, purchased from Nigel Greenwood, 1978, © the artist
Walker, John b.1939, *Conversation*, gift from the artist, 1985, © the artist
Walker, Richard b.1955, *The Power of Fire*, purchased from the artist, 1987, © the artist
Wallinger, Mark b.1959, *John Barleycorn*, purchased from the Anthony Reynolds Gallery, 1986, © the artist, courtesy Anthony Reynolds Gallery
Wallis, Alfred 1855–1942, *Trawler*, purchased from the Piccadilly Gallery, 1962
Wallis, Alfred 1855–1942, *Ship in Rough Sea*, purchased from the Crane Kalman Gallery, 1967
Walton, Allan 1891–1948, *Wyvenhoe, Essex*
Waplington, Paul Anthony b.1938, *Alfreton Road 1979*, purchased from the artist, 1979, © the artist
Ward, Richard b.1937, *Painting*, purchased from the artist, 1968
Watts, Chris b.1947, *Two Stages and the Composite 2A, 2B & 2C, a Set of Three Drawings*, purchased from the artist, 1982
Weatherson, Alexander b.1930, *Vis-à-vis*, purchased from Gallery One, 1961, © the artist
Webb, Mary b.1939, *Spring Colour Study No.19*, purchased from the artist, 1997, © the artist
Webster, Catrin b.1966, *Level Playing Fields*, purchased from the artist, 1997
Weight, Carel Victor Morlais 1908–1997, *Dans le vieux parc*, purchased from the Leicester Galleries, 1951, © the artist's estate/Bridgeman Art Library
Weight, Carel Victor Morlais 1908–1997, *The Good Samaritan*, purchased from Thomas Agnew and Sons, 1959, © the artist's estate/Bridgeman Art Library
Weight, Carel Victor Morlais 1908–1997, *The Snake*, purchased from the Royal Academy of Arts, 1967, © the artist's estate/ Bridgeman Art Library, photo credit: ACC
Weight, Carel Victor Morlais 1908–1997, *The World We Live In*, purchased from the artist, 1975, © the artist's estate/Bridgeman Art Library
Weight, Carel Victor Morlais 1908–1997, *Battersea Medusa*, purchased from the artist, 1975, © the artist's estate/Bridgeman Art Library
Weight, Carel Victor Morlais 1908–1997, *Deep Lane*, purchased from the artist, 1978, © the artist's estate/Bridgeman Art Library
Weight, Carel Victor Morlais 1908–1997, *Love at First Sight*, purchased from the artist, 1942, © the artist's estate/Bridgeman Art Library
Wellington, Hubert Lindsay 1879–1967, *Lane to Walton, Staffordshire*, purchased from the artist, 1962, © the artist's estate
Wells, John 1907–2000, *Variation II*, purchased from the Waddington Galleries, 1960, © the estate of John Wells
Weschke, Karl 1925–2005, *Figure in a Landscape*, purchased from the artist, 1974, © the estate of Karl Weschke. All rights reserved, DACS 2012
Weschke, Karl 1925–2005, *The Meeting*, purchased from the artist, 1980, © the estate of Karl Weschke. All rights reserved, DACS 2012
Weschke, Karl 1925–2005, *Portrait of a Dog*, purchase award, 1983, © the estate of Karl Weschke. All rights reserved, DACS 2012
West, Francis b.1936, *As I walked out one evening*, purchased from the Edward Totah Gallery, 1985, © the artist
West, Francis b.1936, *The Artist in Search of a Persona*, purchased from the Edward Totah Gallery, 1985, © the artist
Westwood, Roger b.1936, *Peret Insulting the Priest*, purchased from the Ikon Gallery, Birmingham, 1977
Whamond, Andrew b.1947, *Second drawing for 'White Monument'*, purchased from the

artist, 1975, © the artist
Whishaw, Anthony b.1930, *Two Cows*, purchased from Roland Browse and Delbanco, 1961, © the artist, www.anthonywhishaw.com
Whishaw, Anthony b.1930, *Monks Horton*, purchased from the artist, 1977, © the artist, www.anthonywhishaw.com
Whitaker, David 1938–2007, *Triscape*, purchased from the artist, 1970, © Rebecca Hossack Art Gallery
Whitaker, David 1938–2007, *Orbit* (recto), purchased from the artist, 1973, © Rebecca Hossack Art Gallery
Whitaker, David 1938–2007, *Orbit* (verso), purchased from the artist, 1973, © Rebecca Hossack Art Gallery
Whitaker, David 1938–2007, *The Estuary 'Four Ages'*, purchased from the artist, 1977, © Rebecca Hossack Art Gallery
Whitaker, David 1938–2007, *Untitled No.2*, purchased from the artist, 1979, © Rebecca Hossack Art Gallery
Whitaker, Jon b.1943, *Memory of Trogir*, purchased award, 1984, © the artist
Whitaker, Jon b.1943, *The Wanderer II*, purchased from the artist, 1986, © the artist
Whiteford, Kate b.1952, *Beaker Burial*, purchased from the Riverside Studios, 1983, © the artist
Whittaker, Edward b.1948, *Untitled*, purchased from the Ikon Gallery, Birmingham, 1983, © the artist
Wilde, Gerald 1905–1986, *Untitled Painting*, purchased from the artist, 1976, © courtesy October Gallery
Wilkes, Cathy b.1966, *Untitled*, purchased from the Modern Institute, Glasgow, 2005, photo credit: ACC
Wilkins, John b.1951, *Dancing in the Dark*, gift from Charles Saatchi, 1999
Wilkins, John b.1951, *Winterwonderland*, gift from Charles Saatchi, 1999
Wilkins, John b.1951, *Was Wondering*, purchased from the Anthony Reynolds Gallery, 1996
Willetts, David b.1939, *Apples*, purchased from the Coracle Press Gallery, 1980, © the artist
Willetts, David b.1939, *On the Return Journey*, purchased from the Coracle Press Gallery, 1980, © the artist
Williams, Aubrey 1926–1990, *Olmec Stasis*, purchased from the Commonwealth Institute, 1988, © estate of Aubrey Williams. All rights reserved, DACS 2012
Williams, Emrys b.1958, *To the Lighthouse No.13, December/January*, purchased from the artist, 1997, © the artist
Williams, Kyffin 1918–2006, *Landscape at Llanaelhaearn*, purchased, 1948, © estate of Kyffin Williams. All rights reserved, DACS 2012
Williams, Kyffin 1918–2006, *The Old Soldier*, purchased from the Leicester Galleries, 1952, © estate of Kyffin Williams. All rights reserved, DACS 2012
Willing, Victor 1928–1988, *Standing Nude*, purchased from the Hanover Gallery, 1955, © the artist's estate
Willing, Victor 1928–1988, *Winter Machine*, purchased from the Contemporary Art Society, 1956, © the artist's estate
Willing, Victor 1928–1988, *Mud*, purchased from the artist, 1981, © the artist's estate, photo credit: ACC
Wilson, Chris b.1959, *Some Day You Will Be One Of Those Who Lived Long Ago*, purchased from the artist, 1991, © the artist
Wilson, Chris b.1959, *All Will Be Forgotten*, purchased from the artist, 1991, © the artist
Wilson, Chris b.1959, *In October Light*, purchased from the artist, 1991, © the artist
Wilson, Chris b.1959, *Interior World*, purchased from the artist, 1991, © the artist
Wilson, Chris b.1959, *North*, purchased from the artist, 1991, © the artist
Wilson, Peter b.1940, *Well Groomed*, purchased from the New Style Gallery, 1981, © Peter Wilson, photo credit: ACC
Winstanley, Paul b.1954, *City Flats*, purchased from the artist, 1983, © the artist
Winstanley, Paul b.1954, *TV Room*, purchased from Interim Art, 1991, © the artist
Wise, Derwent 1933–2003, *Northumbrian Landscape*, purchased from the artist, 1978, © the artist's estate
Wise, Gillian b.1936, *Opening Movement*, purchased from the artist, 1976, © the artist
Wise, Gillian b.1936, *Winged Net, Shadow Trace, Yellow and Blue*, purchased from the artist, 1976, © the artist
Wiseman, David b.1949, *Morning*, purchased from the artist, 1980, © the artist
Wiseman, David b.1949, *Winter – Ivythorn Wood*, purchased from the artist, 1980, © the artist
Wishart, John Michael 1928–1996, *Camarguais Landscape II*, purchased from The Redfern Gallery, 1956, © the artist's estate
Wiszniewski, Adrian b.1958, *Moses on a Polish Flag*, purchased from the Air Gallery, 1985, © the artist
Wolmark, Alfred Aaron 1877–1961, *Woman with a Bowl of Fruit*, purchased from the Woodstock Gallery, 1959, © permission of Mrs Diana S. Hall
Woodford, David James b.1938, *Sketch for 'The Kestrel'*, purchased from the artist, 1980, © the artist
Woodford, David James b.1938, *The Kestrel*, purchased from the artist, 1980, © the artist
Woods, Clare b.1972, *Daddy Witch*, purchased from Stuart Shave, 2008, © courtesy of Stuart Shave/Modern Art, photo credit: ACC
Woods, Richard b.1966, *Austin Metro (Red), Deptford*, gift from Charles Saatchi, 1999
Woods, Richard b.1966, *BMW 525 as Biological Experiment (Green)*, gift from Charles Saatchi, 1999
Woods, Richard b.1966, *Peugeot 205 (Blue) Bermondsey*, gift from Charles Saatchi, 1999
Woods, Richard b.1966, *Volkswagen Golf (Green), Old Kent Road*, gift from Charles Saatchi, 1999
Wragg, Gary b.1946, *Big Ear*, purchased from the artist, 1977, © the artist
Wylie, Rose b.1934, *Girl on Liner*, purchased from the artist, 1998, © the artist
Wylie, Rose b.1934, *Size 8: Orange*, purchased from the artist, 1998, © the artist
Wynne-Jones, Nancy 1922–2006, *Lazarus*, purchased from the New Vision Gallery, 1962, © the estate of Nancy Wynne-Jones
Wynter, Bryan 1915–1975, *Mineral World*, purchased from The Redfern Gallery, 1957, © estate of Bryan Winter. All rights reserved, DACS 2012
Wynter, Bryan 1915–1975, *Dark Threshold*, purchased from the Waddington Galleries, 1960, © estate of Bryan Winter. All rights reserved, DACS 2012
Wynter, Bryan 1915–1975, *Meander 3*, purchased from the artist, 1967, © estate of Bryan Winter. All rights reserved, DACS 2012, photo credit: ACC
Yale, Brian 1936–2009, *Solitary Spaces*, purchased from the artist, 1975, © the artist/Bridgeman Art Library
Yeadon, John David b.1948, *The Last Chilean Supper*, purchased, 1983, © the artist
Yhap, Laetitia b.1941, *Paul, Michael, Stephen and Tim in Summer*, purchased from the artist, 1980, © the artist
Young, Brian b.1934, *Extension I*, purchased from the Gimpel Fils Gallery, 1958, © the artist
Yule, Ainslie b.1941, *White Space with Blue Strip*, purchased from the artist, 1982, © the artist
Zehnder, Benno b.1941, *On the Way to the Room Beyond*, purchased from the artist, 1979
Ziegler, Toby b.1972, *Je t'adore, baby*, purchased from the Simon Lee Gallery, 2006, © courtesy of the artist and Simon Lee, photo credit: ACC

Facing page: Reid, Nan, 1905–1981, *Fish and Chip Shop in Chelsea* (detail), 1952, (p. 129)

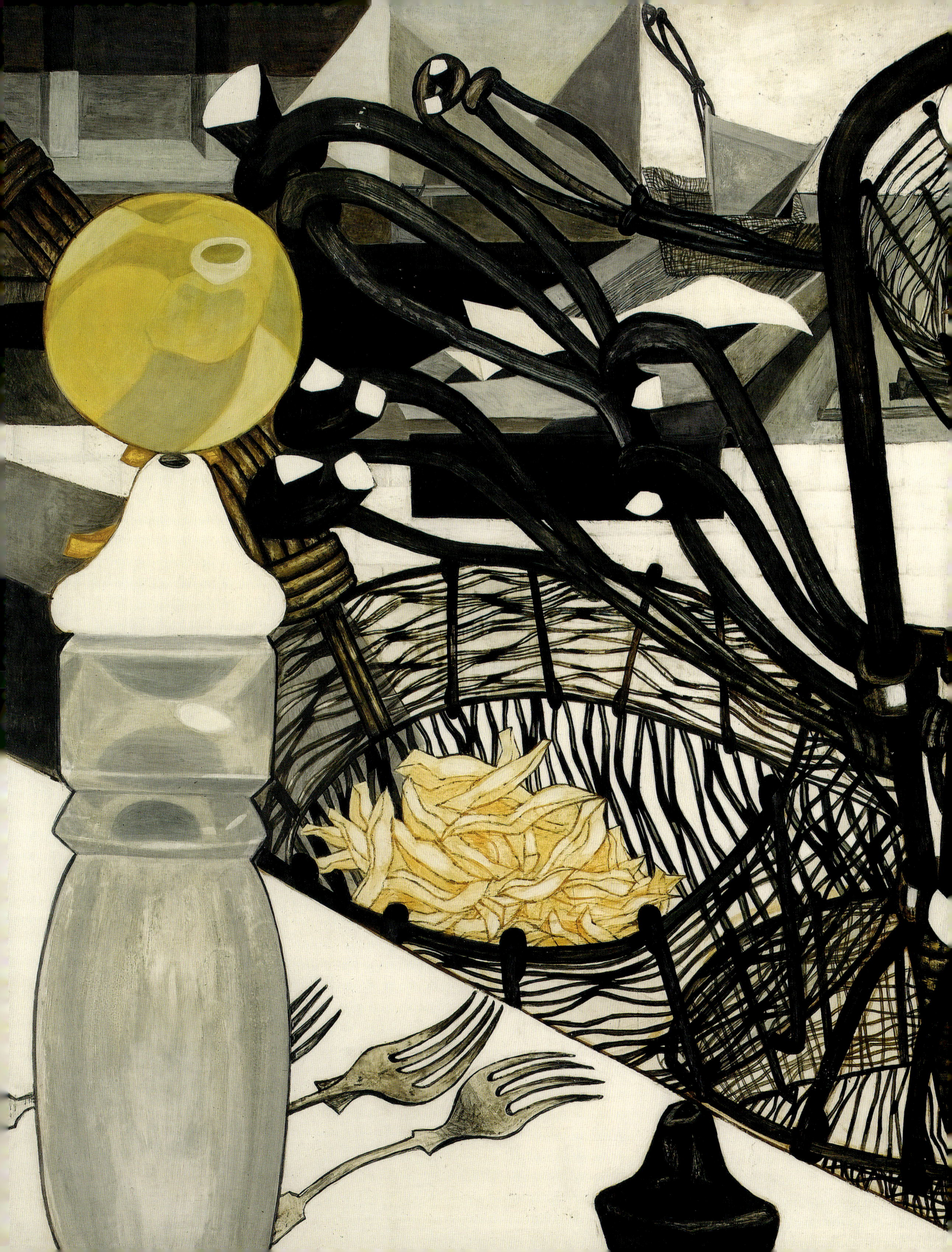

Collection Address

Arts Council Collection

Southbank Centre, Belvedere Road, London SE1 8XX
Telephone 020 7921 7521
www.artscouncilcollection.org.uk

Index of Artists

In this catalogue, artists' names and the spelling of their names follow the preferred presentation of the name in the Getty Union List of Artist Names (ULAN) as of February 2004, if the artist is listed in ULAN.

The page numbers next to each artist's name below direct readers to paintings that are by the artist; are attributed to the artist; or, in a few cases, are more loosely related to the artist being, for example, 'after', 'the circle of' or copies of a painting by the artist. The precise relationship between the artist and the painting is listed in the catalogue.

Acknowledgements

The Public Catalogue Foundation would like to thank the individual artists and copyright holders for their permission to reproduce for free the paintings in this catalogue. Exhaustive efforts have been made to locate the copyright owners of all the images included within this catalogue and to meet their requirements. Copyright credit lines for copyright owners who have been traced are listed in the Further Information section.

As a small team, almost every member of The Arts Council Collection staff has contributed to the immense effort involved in photographing more than a thousand paintings. The contributions of the following members of staff should be highlighted in particular: Jill Constantine, Senior Collection Curator, Monika McConnell, Loans Coordinator, Ann Jones, Curator, and Rachel Arndt, Acquisitions Coordinator, as well as the interns Marthe Fjellestad and Sarah Campbell, all of whom have worked tirelessly on the considerable administrative and curatorial aspects of the project. The meticulous work of Sussana Chan, Andy Craig, Jonny Aldous, Alex Flinn, Richard Morrow and Clive Caswell, who managed the physical process of conservation, and handling involved in the photography itself must also be mentioned.

The Public Catalogue Foundation would like to express its great appreciation to the following organisations for their kind assistance in the preparation of this catalogue:

Bridgeman Art Library
Flowers East
Marlborough Fine Art
National Association of Decorative & Fine Arts Societies (NADFAS)
National Gallery, London
National Portrait Gallery, London
Royal Academy of Arts, London
Tate

The Public Catalogue Foundation

The Public Catalogue Foundation is a registered charity. It was launched in 2003 to create a photographic record of the entire national collection of oil, tempera and acrylic paintings in public ownership in the United Kingdom.

Whilst our public galleries and civic buildings hold arguably the greatest collection of oil paintings in the world, over 80 per cent of these are not on view. Few collections have a complete photographic record of their paintings let alone a comprehensive illustrated catalogue. What is publicly owned is not publicly accessible.

The Foundation is publishing a series of fully illustrated, county-by-county catalogues that will cover, eventually, the entire national UK collection. To date, it has published over 30 volumes, presenting over 72,000 paintings.

In partnership with the BBC, the Foundation will make its database of the entire UK collection of 200,000 oil paintings available online through a new website called *Your Paintings*. The website was launched in the summer of 2011.

Your Paintings (*www.bbc.co.uk/arts/yourpaintings*) offers a variety of ways of searching for paintings as well as further information about the paintings and artists, including links to the participating collections' websites. For those interested in paintings and the subjects they portray *Your Paintings* is an unparalleled learning resource.

Collections benefit substantially from the work of the Foundation, not least from the digital images that are given to them for free following photography, and from the increased recognition that the project brings. These substantial benefits come at no financial cost to the collections.

The Foundation is funded by a combination of support from individuals, charitable trusts, companies and the public sector although the latter provides less than 20 per cent of the Foundation's financial support.

Supporters

Master Patrons

The Public Catalogue Foundation is greatly indebted to the following Master Patrons who have helped it in the past or are currently working with it to raise funds for the publication of their county catalogues. All of them have given freely of their time and have made an enormous contribution to the work of the Foundation.

Peter Andreae *(Hampshire)*
Sir Henry Aubrey-Fletcher, Bt, Lord Lieutenant of Buckinghamshire *(Buckinghamshire)*
Sir Nicholas Bacon, DL, High Sheriff of Norfolk *(Norfolk)*
Sir John Bather, Lord Lieutenant of Derbyshire *(Derbyshire)*
The Hon. Mrs Bayliss, JP, Lord Lieutenant of Berkshire *(Berkshire)*
Ian Bonas *(County Durham)*
Peter Bretherton *(West Yorkshire: Leeds)*
Michael Brinton, Lord Lieutenant of Worcestershire *(Worcestershire)*
Sir Hugo Brunner, KCVO, JP *(Oxfordshire)*
Mr John Bush, OBE, Lord-Lieutenant of Wiltshire *(Wiltshire)*
Lady Butler *(Warwickshire)*
Richard Compton *(North Yorkshire)*
George Courtauld, DL, Vice Lord Lieutenant of Essex *(Essex)*

The Countess of Darnley, Lord Lieutenant of Herefordshire *(Herefordshire)*
The Marquess of Downshire *(North Yorkshire)*
Martin Dunne, Lord Lieutenant of Warwickshire *(Warwickshire)*
Sir Henry Elwes, KCVO, Lord-Lieutenant of Gloucestershire *(Gloucestershire)*
Jenny Farr, MBE, DL *(Nottinghamshire)*
John Fenwick *(Tyne & Wear Museums)*
Mark Fisher, MP *(Staffordshire)*
Patricia Grayburn, MBE, DL *(Surrey)*
The Earl of Halifax, KStJ, JP, DL *(East Riding of Yorkshire)*
Lord Roy Hattersley, PC *(South Yorkshire: Sheffield*
Algy Heber-Percy, Lord Lieutenant of Shropshire *(Shropshire)*
The Lady Mary Holborow, Lord Lieutenant of Cornwall *(Cornwall)*
Sarah Holman *(Warwickshire)*
Tommy Jowitt *(West Yorkshire)*
Alderman Sir David Lewis, The Rt Hon. The Lord Mayor of London, 2007–2008 *(The City of London)*
Sir Michael Lickiss *(Cornwall)*
Magnus Linklater *(Scotland)*
Lord Marlesford, DL *(Suffolk)*
Dr Bridget McConnell *(Glasgow)*
Lady Sarah Nicholson *(County Durham)*
Malcolm V. L. Pearce, MP *(Somerset)*
Sir John Riddell, Lord Lieutenant of Northumberland *(Northumberland)*
Venetia Ross Skinner *(Dorset)*
The Most Hon. The Marquess of Salisbury, PC, DL *(Hertfordshire)*
Julia Somerville *(Government Art Collection)*
Tim Stevenson, OBE, Lord Lieutenant of Oxfordshire *(Oxfordshire)*
Phyllida Stewart-Roberts, OBE *(East Sussex)*
Lady Juliet Townsend, Lord Lieutenant of Northamptonshire *(Northamptonshire)*
Leslie Weller, DL *(West Sussex)*
Sir Samuel C. Whitbread, KCVO, Lord Lieutenant of Bedfordshire *(Bedfordshire)*

Financial support

The Public Catalogue Foundation is particularly grateful to the following organisations and individuals who have given it generous financial support since the project started in 2003.

National Sponsor

Christie's

Benefactors (£10,000–£50,000)

The 29th May 1961 Charitable Trust
Arts Council England
The Barbour Trust
Binks Trust
City of Bradford Metropolitan District Council
Deborah Loeb Brice Foundation
The Bulldog Trust
A. & S. Burton 1960 Charitable Trust
Christie's
City of London Corporation
The John S. Cohen Foundation
Covent Garden London
Creative Scotland
Department for Culture, Media and Sport
Sir Harry Djanogly, CBE
Mr Lloyd Dorfman
Dunard Fund
The Elmley Foundation
Fenwick Ltd
Fidelity UK Foundation
Marc Fitch Fund
The Foyle Foundation
J. Paul Getty Jr Trust
Hampshire County Council
The Charles Hayward Foundation
Peter Harrison Foundation
Mr Robert Hiscox
Hiscox plc
David Hockney, CH, RA
ICAP plc

The Jordan Charitable Foundation
Kent County Council
The Linbury Trust
The Manifold Trust
Paul Mellon Centre for Studies in British Art
The Mercers' Company
Robert Warren Miller
Mr & Mrs A. Mittal
The Monument Trust
Miles Morland
Allan and Carol Murray
National Gallery Trust
Stavros Niarchos Foundation
Norfolk County Council
Northern Rock Foundation
Nottingham City Council
Malcolm V. L. Pearce, MP
P. F. Charitable Trust
The Pilgrim Trust
Provident Financial
RAB Capital plc
The Radcliffe Trust
Renaissance East Midlands
Renaissance West Midlands
Renaissance Yorkshire
Saga Group Ltd
Scottish Government
The Bernard Sunley Charitable Foundation
Townsend Family Trust
University College, London
University of Leeds
The Walker Trust
The Wolfson Foundation
Sir Siegmund Warburg's Voluntary Settlement
Garfield Weston Foundation
Mr & Mrs A. H. Wilkinson
The Wixamtree Trust

Series Patrons
(Minimum donation of £2,500)

James & Lindsay Adam
Sir John Bather
Harry Bott
Janey Buchan
Mrs Rhona Callander
Dr Peter Cannon-Brookes
The John S. Cohen Foundation
Bushey Museum in memory of Lavender Watson
Mr Lloyd Dorfman
Lord Douro
Jenny Farr, MBE, DL
Mrs Greta Fenston
The FIRS Trust
Glasgow Museums
Patricia Grayburn, MBE, DL
G. Laurence Harbottle
R. K. Harrison Insurance Services Limited
Paul & Fiona Hart
Paul & Kathrine Haworth
Lord & Lady Heseltine
Patrik Holden & Lin Hinds
Neil Honebon
Michael Jacobson
Grace Jenkins
Dr David Johnson, DL
The Keatley Trust
John Kendall, Esq.
Michael A. Lambert, CBE
David & Amanda Leathers
Miles Morland
Allan & Carol Murray
North East Regional Museums Hub
The University of Northampton
Nottingham Civic Society
Richard & Amika Oldfield
The Roper Family Charitable Trust
Adam Sedgwick
Sir Harry & Lady Soloman
Stuart M. Southall
Simon Still
Chloe Teacher
University of Surrey
David & Cissy Walker
Tony Wilkinson
Mr & Mrs Jo Windsor
Mr & Mrs Charles Wyvill

Catalogue Patrons
(£1,000–£10,000)

The 29th May 1961 Charitable Trust
ACE Study Tours
Adams & Remers
Marcus & Kate Agius
The AIM Foundation
D. C. R. Allen
John Alston, CBE
Amberley Castle
The Astor Foundation
The Aylesford Family Charitable Trust
Chairman of Cornwall County Council, Mrs Doris Anson, OBE, JP
Archant Ltd

G. F. Armitage Family Charitable Trust
Mr Ian Askew
Aurelius Charitable Trust
The Bacon Charitable Trust
Lawrence Banks, CBE, DL
Barlow Robbins LLP
Mr James & Lady Emma Barnard
Basingstoke and Deane Borough Council
Bath & North East Somerset District Council Heritage Services
Robert Baxter, DL
Birmingham Common Good Trust
Sir Christopher Bland
Johnnie Boden
The Charlotte Bonham-Carter Charitable Trust
H. R. Pratt Boorman Family Foundation
A. J. H. du Boulay Charitable Trust
The Bowerman Charitable Trust
Viscountess Boyd Charitable Trust
Lord & Lady Bradbury
Bramdean Asset Management LLP
Peter Bretherton
Brewin Dolphin
J. & M. Britton Charitable Trust
Mrs T. Brotherton-Ratcliffe
Janey Buchan
Mr & Mrs Patrick Burgess
Mr & Mrs Mark Burrell
Arnold J. Burton Charitable Trust
Bushey Museum in Memory of Lavender Watson
Mrs Anne Cadbury, OBE, JP, DL
Roger Cadbury
C. J. R. & Mrs C. L. Calderwood
Sir Ralph Carr-Ellison
Mr & Mrs J. Chambers
Chichester District Council
His Honour Richard Cole, DL & Mrs Sheila Cole
The Timothy Colman Charitable Trust
Mr & Mrs Derek Coombs
The Helen Jean Cope Trust
Mr & Mrs Ian Copesteak
Cornwall County Council
Mr S. J. D. Corsan
Graeme Cottam & Gloriana Marks de Chabris
Coutts Charitable Trust
David Crane Trust
Elaine Craven, Earl Street Employment Consultants Ltd
Harriett Cullen
Culture North East
Rt Hon. Viscount Daventry
N. Davie-Thornhill
Brigadier Mike Dauncey, DSO, DL
De La Rue Charitable Trust
Mr Robert Dean
Deborah Gage (Works of Art) Ltd
Derek Johns Ltd, London
Derby City Council
Derby High School Trust Ltd
Derbyshire Building Society
Derbyshire Community Foundation (The Ashby Fund)
J. N. Derbyshire Trust
The Duke of Devonshire's Charitable Trust
S. Dewhirst Charitable Trust
Sir Harry Djanogly, CBE
Dorset County Council
Lord Douro
Professor Patrick & Dr Grace Dowling
Dunn Family Charitable Trust
East Sussex County Council
Eastbourne Borough Council
EEMLAC, through the Association for Suffolk Museums
Lord & Lady Egremont
Sir John & Lady Elliott
Andrew & Lucy Ellis
Peter & Judy Ellwood
Essex County Council
John & Felicity Fairbairn
Fairfield Charitable Trust
Jenny Farr, MBE, DL
John Feeney Charitable Trust
The Trustees of the Finnis Scott Foundation
The Fishmongers' Company
David & Ann FitzWilliam-Lay
Elizabeth & Val Fleming
The Follett Trust
Richard & Elizabeth Fothergill

Christopher & Catherine Foyle
Freemasons of Derbyshire
The Friends of Historic Essex
The Friends of the Laing Art Gallery
The Friends of the Royal Pavilion, Art Gallery & Museums, Brighton
The Friends of Southampton's Museums, Archives and Galleries
The Friends of Sunderland Museums
The Friends of York Art Gallery (E. J. Swift Bequest)
Philip Gibbs
The Hon. H. M. T. Gibson's Charity Trust
Lewis & Jacqueline Golden
The Goldsmiths' Company
Gorringes
Charles Gregson
The Grocers' Company
The Gulland Family
David Gurney
Philip Gwyn
Sir Ernest Hall
The Earl of Halifax, KStJ, JP, DL
The W. A. Handley Charity Trust
The Hartnett Charitable Trust
Hazlitt, Gooden & Fox Ltd
Heartwood Wealth Management Ltd
The Trustees of the King Henry VIII Endowed Trust, Warwick
The Rt Hon. the Lord Heseltine, CH, PC & Lady Heseltine
The Lady Hind Trust
Hobart Charitable Trust
Edward and Anna Hocknell
David Hockney CH, RA
Patrick Holden & Lin Hinds
Mrs Michael Hollingbery
The Holman Family
Mr & Mrs A. Holman-West
The Honourable Company of Gloucestershire
The Hope Scott Trust
David & Prue Hopkinson
Major & Mrs Bill Hutchinson
His Honour Gabriel Hutton
Isle of Wight Council
The J. and S. B. Charitable Trust
Alan & Penny Jerome
James & Lucilla Joll Charitable Trust
Mr & Mrs Peter Jones
Tommy Jowitt
The Keatley Trust
Kent Messenger Group
Garrett Kirk, Jr
Mr John Kirkland, OBE & Mrs Sheila Kirkland
Robert Kirkland
Kirklees Council
The David Laing Foundation
Landau Foundation
Lord Lea of Crondall, OBE
The Leche Trust
Leeds Art Collections Fund
Leeds City Council
Leeds Philosophical and Literary Society
The Hon. David Legh, DL
Lord Leverhulme's Charitable Trust
Mr & Mrs John Lewis
Mark & Sophie Lewisohn
Tom Lugg & the Lane Family
The Orr Mackintosh Foundation
The MacRobert Trust
Maidstone Borough Council
John Manser
Mr & Mrs Derek Mapp
Walter & Barbara Marais
The Marlay Group
Marshall Charitable Trust
Stephen & Carolyn Martin
Tom & Anne Martin
The Medlock Charitable Trust
The Piet Mendels Foundation
MLA East of England
MLA North East of England
Museums Galleries Scotland
Mr Paul Myners
Rupert Nabarro
Nancie Massey Charitable Trust
Newcastle City Council
Bryan Norman
Lord & Lady Northampton
The University of Northampton
NP Aerospace Ltd
Oakmoor Trust
Jasper & Virginia Olivier
The Orr Mackintosh Foundation
Mr Christopher Oughtred
The Owen Family Trust

Sir Idris Pearce
Roger Neville Russ Peers
The Pennycress Trust
Perkins Family
The Lord & Lady Phillimore
Mrs Margaret Pollett
Simon & Ursula Pomeroy
The Portland Family
Portsmouth City Council
George Pragnell Ltd
The Prince Philip Trust Fund for the Royal Borough of Windsor and Maidenhead
Provident Financial plc
Mr John Rank
Rathbone Investment Management Ltd
The Hans and Märit Rausing Charitable Trust
Roger & Jane Reed
Renaissance North East
Renaissance South East
Renaissance South West
Michael Renshall, CBE, MA, FCA
Sir John Riddell
Sir Miles & Lady Rivett-Carnac
Rockley Charitable Trust
Rolls-Royce plc
The Roper Family Charitable Trust
Rothschild Foundation
Royal Cornwall Museum
Graham & Ann Rudd
Sir Nigel Rudd
Russell New
The J. S. & E. C. Rymer Charitable Trust
The Earl St Aldwyn
The Sammermar Trust
Scarfe Charitable Trust
Andrew & Belinda Scott
The Trustees of the Finnis Scott Foundation
Shaftesbury PLC
Mr W. Sharpe
The Shears Foundation
Robert Shields, DL
Smith & Williamson
South West of England Regional Development Agency
Caroline M. Southall
Stuart M. Southall
Southampton City Council
The Jessie Spencer Trust
Hugh & Catherine Stevenson
Mrs Andrew Stewart-Roberts, OBE
Mr Michael Stone
Mr Peter Stormonth Darling
The Stratford-upon-Avon Town Trust
Strutt and Parker
Suffolk County Council, through the Association for Suffolk Museums
Surrey County Council
The John Swire 1989 Charitable Trust
The Tanner Trust
Tennants Auctioneers
Tesco Charity Trust
The Thistle Trust
Prof. Caroline Tisdall
Trusthouse Charitable Foundation
Gladwyn Turbutt
TWM Business Partners
Tyne & Wear Museums
University College Falmouth
University of Derby
University of Essex
David & Grizelda Vermont
Wakefield Metropolitan District Council
Robert & Felicity Waley-Cohen
The Peggy Walker Charitable Trust
The Walland Trust Fund
John Wates Charitable Trust
Leslie Weller, DL
The Welton Foundation
West Sussex County Council
Mr & Mrs David Wigglesworth
Wilkin & Sons Ltd
Mr & Mrs Jo Windsor
Peter Wolton Charitable Trust
Michael J. Woodhall, FRICS
Sir Philip Wroughton
Mrs Angela Yeoman

First published in 2012 by The Public Catalogue Foundation, Printed Catalogue Division, 8 Frederick's Place, London, EC2R 8AB

The responsibility for the accuracy of the information presented in this catalogue lies solely with the holding collections. Suggestions that might improve the accuracy of the information contained in this catalogue should be sent to the relevant collection and emailed to info@thepcf.org.uk.

ISBN 978-1-904931-55-3

Arts Council Collection photography:
Andy Johnson, Anna Arca, Stephen White & Daniel Brown

Designed by Sally Jeffery

Printed in Hong Kong by Paramount Printing Company Limited

Cover image:

Caulfield, Patrick 1936–2005
Dining Recess (detail), 1972
(p. 27)

Back cover images (from top to bottom):

Rego, Paula Figueiroa b.1935
Sleeping, 1986 (detail)
(see p. 129)

Riley, Bridget b.1931
Movement in Squares, 1961 (detail)
(see p. 132)

Ayres, Gillian b.1930
Spica, 1989–1990 (detail)
(see p. 13)